New Age in Latin America

Religion in the Americas Series

General Editors

VOLUME 16

The titles published in this series are listed at *brill.com/ream*

New Age in Latin America

Popular Variations and Ethnic Appropriations

Edited by

Renée de la Torre
Cristina Gutiérrez Zúñiga
Nahayeilli B. Juárez Huet

Translated from the Spanish by

Nicholas Barrett

BRILL

LEIDEN | BOSTON

Originally published as *Variaciones y apropiaciones del new age en Latinoamérica*, Renée de la Torre, Cristina Gutiérrez Zúñiga, and Nahayeilli Juárez Huet eds., CIESAS, El Colegio de Jalisco México (2013). ISBN 978-607-486-218-8

Cover illustration: *Olpamitzin*, 'sowing the name' and celebrating the Equinox. Cerro de la Reina, Tonalá, Jalisco, Mexico, March 2006 (photo: Renée de la Torre).

Library of Congress Cataloging-in-Publication Data

Names: Torre, Renée de la, editor. | Gutiérrez Zúñiga, Cristina, editor. | Juárez Huet, Nahayeilli, editor.
Title: New age in Latin America : popular variations and ethnic appropriations /
edited by Renee de la Torre, Cristina Gutierrez Zuniga, Nahayeilli Juárez Huet ;
translated from the Spanish original by Nicholas Barrett.
Other titles: Variaciones y apropiaciones latinoamericanas del new age. English
Description: Boston : Brill, 2016. | Series: Religion in the Americas series,
ISSN 1542-1279 ; VOLUME 16 | Includes bibliographical references and index.
Identifiers: LCCN 2016013907 (print) | LCCN 2016014616 (ebook) | ISBN
9789004316331 (hardback : alk. paper) | ISBN 9789004316485 (E-book)
Subjects: LCSH: New Age movement--Latin America. | Spiritual life--New Age movement. |
Christianity and other religions--New Age movement. | Latin America--Religion.
Classification: LCC BP605.N48 V3613 2016 (print) | LCC BP605.N48 (ebook) | DDC 299/.93098--dc23
LC record available at http://lccn.loc.gov/2016013907

Typeface for the Latin, Greek, and Cyrillic scripts: "Brill". See and download: brill.com/brill-typeface.

ISSN 1542-1279
ISBN 978-90-04-31633-1 (hardback)
ISBN 978-90-04-31648-5 (e-book)

This book is printed on acid-free paper and produced in a sustainable manner.

Contents

Preface

Renée de la Torre and Cristina Gutiérrez Zúñiga

The subject of this book is the dynamics of hybridization set in motion by the circuation and exchange of symbolic goods between the New Age spiritual movement and the different traditions that comprise the syncretic folk religiosity in Latin America. Classic anthropologists, who tend to write papers on the ethnic groups and traditional practices considered the cultural heritage of different peoples (such as Shamanisms, faith healing, African-American devotions, folk Catholicism, spiritualism and indigenous rituals), have almost entirely overlooked this topic. Scholarly interest in revealing the mechanisms for the transmission and preservation of ancient, indigenous and traditional culture often leads researchers to ignore or even overlook the presence of meanings that stem from New Age spirituality. On the other hand, there are studies that seek to emphasize the most novel aspects of the New Age in contemporary culture, focusing on the displacements and transformations of new religious movements. These movements—fluid (or liquid, as Bauman, 1999 would say), individualized and deinstitutionalized—are viewed then as symptoms of postmodern culture. This book offers a rich selection of new hibrid expressions of popular religiosity in Latin America that have received little attention to date. Two distinct academic perspectives are included in this volume. The first is that of classic ethnologists who, over the course of their studies on traditional cultures, have come across cultural transformations and innovations that are influenced by New Age trends, though they may not be recognized as such. Instead, such innovations are described as de-institutionalized, secular, mobile, transnationalized, commercialized, etc.

The first group of scholars, focusing on the study of native tribes in the present, were most interested in their survival strategies,[1] but soon detected the presence of a new cultural framework which some recognized as New Age spirituality. These scholars noted that this was having an effect on the

1 Some scholars who focus on the native spiritualties of North America are indicative of this trend. For example, in the book by Lee Irwin (2000) various authors explain that their initial aim was to reconstruct the roots of an authentically indigenous spirituality as a fundamental element for the original inhabitants of North America to be able to gain political recognition. The New Age elements, then, could pose a threat to the sacred traditions as to some extent, the accompanying commercialization and secularization can be thought of as a new version of the various forms of exploitation that indigenous peoples have been victims ever since their initial contact with Western culture.

construction of ethnic identities (Báez and Lupo, 2010) in one of two ways. In some cases, New Age spirituality inspired the communities to have a voice and reclaim their rights on the basis of either ancestry or a reinvented imperial lineage (Galinier, 2008). In other cases, new urban agents, known as Neo-shamans (Sarrazin, 2008) or urban-shamans were reappropriating the group's hybridized and decontextualized wisdom and identity. From this perspective, what matters is not New Age in and of itself but its effects on the construction of ethnicities today. A note of protest can even be found in these writings, as if the New Age hybridization were a contemporary version of colonial forms of exploitation (see Molinié in this volume).

According to the sociology on new religious forms, the New Age movement originated in urban centers of the West as the manifestation of a countercultural spirituality, an alternative to Western materialism and consumerism. At the same time, it is emblematic of postmodernity and global cosmopolitanism (Melton 1990; Heelas, 1996; Hanegraaff, 2001; Champion, 1995). Researchers who have studied the New Age worldwide emphasize its character as globalizing, individualizing, de-institutionalized, eclectic and dynamic. Scholars in Latin America have also observed the same innovative features.[2]

In the literature on New Age and religion, common topics have included orientalist variations based on a quest for perfection of the individual through body techniques; alternative health techniques; the appropriations of quantum mechanics; UFO movements; Zen Buddhism promoted by New Agers; and a large variety of self-realisation workshops; much self-help literature, including best sellers by Paulo Coelho. Other frequent New Age trends include seminars on spiritual and material prosperity and the abundantly merchandised New Age products (that include relaxing music and television channels like *Infinito*, which also organizes New Age events in Latin America). Two final topics common in the literature include the presence of the New Age in the spas of luxury hotels and even its use in advertising by Coca Cola, which has promoted its dark brown drink as '*buena vibra líquida*' (good liquid vibrations) or '*buen karma con burbujas*' (good karma with bubbles) in Mexico. While such topics can be explored in other studies,[3] we have deliberately focused on popular variations and ethnic appropriations of the New Age in Latin America as the subject of this book.

Although the reader may be surprised to find many of these topics missing, this book does not intend to serve as an encyclopedia of all the different New

2 See the pioneering works of Carozzi, 1999; Amaral, 1999; Gutiérrez Zúñiga, 1996.

3 For Brazil, see Amaral, 2000; D'Andrea, 2000; for Argentina, Carozzi 2000; and for Mexico, De la Torre 2012c.

Age hybrids that have formed along the way. We shall not focus on how the New Age is transformed in different types of individual beliefs, as the central argument of this book is the New Ages's impact on popular syncretic religions, traditions, ethnic rituals and world views such as those found in shamanisms and in the field of popular health.

New Agers in Latin America: Transversal Spiritualities

It is hard to obtain an exact figure for the number of New Agers in Latin America, as this spiritual movement is not limited to a single religion, church or sect and does not oblige followers to abandon other religious affiliations. In his work on Brazil, using the Gallup survey, D'Andrea has estimated that as in the United States, England and France:

> A similar process is occurring within elite or upper-middle classes of Western developing countries, such as Brazil. Therefore, if one assumes a reasonable rate of 1 to 3% of a population is involved with the NAM (Roland Robertson sets it at 2.5%), then there are more than 15 million New Agers in the 'first world', and 2 million in Brazil.
>
> D'ANDREA, 2000

New Age spirituality has grown as part of a type of religion described as 'believing without belonging' by Davie (1996) in countries like England, where only 14.4% acknowledged any religious affiliation. This is not the case in Latin American countries, which generally show low figures for 'no religion'; according to the Pew Research Center (2014), only 8% of Latin Americans have no religious affiliation.[4] Catholicism has been the predominant religion in the region historically and nowadays New Age spirituality is practiced by people who are 'Catholics in their own particular way' (Parker, 2008). Surveys conducted in different countries of Latin America take into account the processes of individualizing and deinstitutionalizing religion in various countries, where the model of 'Do it yourself' religiosity translates into this particular form of being Catholic.[5] Hervieu-Léger saw the various expressions of religious beliefs as a kind of patchwork with pieces taken from other traditions combined with the basics of the official teachings of the world's most well-known religions.

4 Available for consultation at: http://www.pewresearch.org/topics/latin-america/.

5 See Parker, 2008 in Santiago de Chile, Malimacci, 2011 in Argentina, and De la Torre et al., 2015 in Mexico.

As a result, she referred to such believers as 'Christians in their way' (Hervieu-Léger, 2004). Because of this transversal feature, New Age spirituality is not does not appear in censuses that track religious affiliation, and in this sense can be described as invisible (Luckmann, 1967), fluid, and without an institutional framework (Champion and Hervieu-Léger, 1990).

However, there is another type of research focused on capturing the dynamics of identification among believers, that has abandoned the one-sided idea of exclusive religious identities. This makes it possible to appreciate the subjective reconfigurations of contemporary religious practices and beliefs, enabling us to pinpoint the New Age's presence in Latin American societies.

Christian Parker defined 'Catholics in their own particular way' as people who keep their Catholic affiliation but with a markedly subjective approach that incorporates popular beliefs. The sociologist noted that the shift towards a postmodern culture has brought a renewal of ancient values, which Debray referred to as 'postmodern archaism' [...] (Parker, 2008: 337).

In the case of Argentina, Fortunato Malimacci found that the multiplication of beliefs within Catholicism, especially with regard to ideas of God, points to: 'a floating Christian culture that allows for multiple configurations and memories. We are not dealing with a process of De-Christianization but one of people moving away from the church' (Malimacci, 2011).

In Mexico, a survey conducted in three cities (Guadalajara, Aguascalientes and Mexico City) to provide insight on people's beliefs and devotional practices confirmed the existence of 'in-between' cults, which establish various frameworks of meaning. The survey authors concluded that new elements (including New Age beliefs and practices) are incorporated in a versatile and dynamic way to a popular and traditional religiosity that is unquestionably syncretic (De la Torre et al., 2015: 358).

In his study of differents neigborhoods in San Pablo, Brazil, Lísias Negrão (2008) has shown that today's believers are often affiliated to various religions at the same time and build their religiosity by selecting from different religious offers. The findings of these surveys and studies from across Latin America confirm that 'Catholics in their own particular way' generally describes the processes of de-institutionalization and a greater hybridization of beliefs that is often linked to the New Age movement.

However, the data gathered by these surveys contradict the findings of European surveys that noted contemporary trends in ways of believing which were depicted as universal. In addition to the example from Great Britain referred to earlier, we can mention the case of Spain, where the high rate of indifference to religion among the Catholic majority has been characterized as 'belonging without believing' (Mardones, 2005). Yet according to surveys like the one by the Pew Research Center also cited above, 92% of Latin Americans continue to belong to religious congregations (69% Catholics and 19% Protestants). These are believers who maintain their commitment or their bond by taking part in ceremonial practice; the change, then, is that their beliefs are no longer limited to their religious affiliation but are open to exploration and experimentation. This openness, however, does not force them to abandon or change their formal belonging.

To account for the complexity of 'Catholics in their own particular way', we conducted a multivariate statistical analysis to detect K-means conglomerations or clusters with data from the EPPCR 2006 Survey on Affiliation, Devotional Practices and Religious Beliefs in the state of Jalisco, Mexico.[6] On the basis of our ethnographic knowledge of the local religious field, we defined New Agers according to typical beliefs and practices (such as meditation, Tarot, karma, reincarnation), and found that due to the preeminence of Catholicism, there are twice as many Catholic New Agers as there are New Agers with no church affiliation (De la Torre and Gutiérrez Zúñiga, 2012b). Therefore, rather than speaking of a parallel spirituality, we are dealing with a spirituality that is particularly tied to Catholic affiliation.

The New Age and Popular Religiosity: Post-traditional or Re-traditionalized?

Returning to D'Andrea, we are interested in looking at the New Age movement as:

> A process that contaminates traditional religions (and scientific knowledges), making possible the emergence of a New Age Christianity, as well as a New Age Judaism, Buddhism and even a New Age Islam, in contrast to their traditional forms. As post-traditional appropriations of these world religions, Devekut, Zen and Sufi can be seen as new (or rediscovered) and expanded contemporary paths for the core development of the self, especially among Western/ized middle classes.
>
> D'ANDREA, 1998: 9

6 We included 50 of the 62 variables that make up the database and distributed as follows: beliefs (20 variables), practices (17 variables), values (7 variables), sexual morality (5 variables) and tolerance (6 variables). The general findings of this analysis can be found in De la Torre and Gutiérrez Zúñiga 2012.

According to D'Andrea, the New Age offers a framework for reinterpretation based on the holistic principle of the self, which sets in motion a 'New Ageing' of traditional goods and practices, creating a hybridizing tendency that he calls post-traditional. In this process, the traditional is reinterpreted as practices and rituals aimed at perfecting one's self, achieving harmony with nature and the universe, experiencing one's inner spirituality, holistic healing, etc. D'Andrea says post-traditionalizing consists of 'New Agers incorporating and hybridizing new and old knowledges, in the sense of satisfying existential and material demands and generating new meanings of life' (D'Andrea, 2000: 11). In our case, we shall view this as a process which contributes to reinterpreting deeply rooted Latin American traditions, many of which were proclaimed as ethnic and national emblems to sublimate the hybrid expressions of Latin American countries.

Now, the 'in-between' position of our study also allows for a 'cosmological' reinterpretation in conjunction with the appropriations made by popular Latin American religiosity. According to Pablo Semán (2008) and Pierre Sanchis (1994), Latin American popular religiosity also has a holistic character and, like the New Age, is a 'mother tongue' that subverts the official or singular meanings of hegemonic religions and cultures. Popular religion, as Pierre Sanchis noted, is 'phagocytic'. It provides an all-encompassing cosmological sense that goes 'beyond the distinctions between transcendent and immanent, or natural and supernatural' (Semán, 2008: 302), within which the meanings of cults are constantly being subverted. Popular cosmology resemanticizes the cultures of modernity (including Evangelical Christianity, Pentecostalism and the New Age) through miraculous, magic and occult forces, as a strategy for dealing with the uncertainties of economic crises and social conflict. In this regard, many of the cultural goods put into circulation by the New Age movement have themselves been resignified by popular cosmology and are constantly being turned into talismans for success or amulets to guard against bad vibrations: they have been taken up by specialists in magic and witchcraft healing, and have even been brought into ritual practice to amplify the virtues and miraculous powers of images and sacred forces.

New Age Transformations in Latin America

In general terms, we consider that the New Age is more than a repertoire of concepts and substantive symbols that can provide a framework and doctrinal coherence to beliefs. Rather, it is a matrix of meaning, a generative grammar, that creates and configures new interpretations of other, non-Western symbols and concepts (Amaral, 1999). At the same time we consider that it is not made from scratch, as the popular syncretism of colonial resistance in Latin America is a framework for assimilating exogenous cultures in and of itself (Sanchis, 2008; D'Andrea, 2000; and De la Torre, 2002). As we argued in the book *Raíces en movimiento*:

> Practices and representations of the 'autoctonous', the 'ancestral', the 'traditional', the 'pure', or the 'authentic' do attract the attention of New Age practitioners, but also tend to be used, reapplied and reinterpreted by persons or groups fighting for recognition of the contributions made by these practices to the cultural heritage of the region, the nation and the world. In some contexts they create new forms of ethnic or superethnic nationalism (…).
>
> ARGYRIADIS AND DE LA TORRE, 2008: 31

Nevertheless, as time went on, some scholars of contemporary religious transformations developed an interest in the continual displacements, itineraries and transcultural exchanges of the New Age. These researchers looked at the adaptations and resignifications of this religiosity among ordinary people and examined how it created new links with syncretic Latin American manifestations of popular religion such as traditional medicine, esoterica (or Neo-esoterica), popular magic and shamanism as soon as it appeared (Magnani,1999; De la Torre and Mora, 2001; De la Torre, 2000 and 2006; Siqueira, 2002; Guerriero, 2003; Sanchis, 2008; Mora Rosas, 2002; Teissenhoffer, 2008).

A feature of Latin America is the tendency to syncretize the myriad cultural elements of its traditions and religions. Emphasis on spirits coming from Kardecism for example, is 'a belief that has found fertile soil in Brazil', and can be found in different religious offers. Kardecism inherited this central belief in spirits from esoteric currents. In turn, it has had a significant impact in Mexico (and other Latin American countries) since the end of the nineteenth century, and currently exercises a considerable influence on the syncretic religiosity of Brazil (Hess, 1989), from Afro-Brazilian religions to Pentecostalism, Shamanism, and even the New Age. According to Otavio Velho:

> It is this that makes Pentecostalism surprisingly similar to 'New Age' religions and so-called esoteric and self-help literature (…). Also, it does not seem to be a simple coincidence that the emphasis on the spirit (and repeatedly also on energy and liberation)—an invisible agent

> responsible for dereification and the dissolution of oppositions—should reappear in different religious manifestations, from Pentecostalism to New Age.
>
> VELHO, 2000: 331

Nowadays, is important to take into consideration the impact of self-help literature on spreading Latin American versions of New Age. This can be seen in books by Paulo Coelho, which represent a New Age version of Evangelical Christianity (D'Andrea, 1998). His book *The Pilgrimage* (*O diário de um mago*) which became a best seller has served as a kind of guide to spiritual tourism for New Age seekers (Steil et al., 2014). Another important book is *Regina—Dos de octubre no se olvida* (1987) by Antonio Velasco Piña (currently the leader of the movement known as Neo-Mexicanism), whose main character, Regina, has become a sacred symbol for the spiritual awakening of Pre-Hispanic Mexico (De la Torre, 2008). Yet another significative contribution can be found in José Argüeyes's book *The Mayan Factor* (*El factor Maya*), which spread a supposedly ancient Mayan prophecy of the world ending in 2012, and interpreted this date as the beginning of the Age of Aquarius thanks to cultural industries like television and various Internet groups. This prophecy became a worldwide phenomenon which peaked in December that year. This phenomenon had an effect on Neo-Mayan spiritual tourism (Campechano, 2012), but also empowered the political movement of indigenous Mayan elders in Guatemala (see Bastos, Zamora and Tally in this book). Another example is that of a book by Clarisa Pinkola Estés, called *Women Who Run With Wolves*, used by women's groups as a guide to rediscovering the wild woman who is in danger of extinction in the modern world. Pinkola's ideas have been taken up by New Age feminists who are rediscovering their sacred inner femininity (Pinkola, 2009). Finally, it is also important to mention the effect of science fiction in literature on New Age conspiracy theories, such as the *Children of Matrix* by David Icke (2010), currently found in the theories used by Spanish Conchero dancers or 'Hispanekas' to resignify their appropriation and practice of a dance with Pre-Hispanic Mexican origins.

These links between the New Age and traditional cultures (ethnic or popular) are becoming stronger all the time, either because marketing has incorporated New Age sensibility into advertisements for its products (De la Torre, 2011) or as a result of the vigorous distribution of religious merchandise labeled New Age (De la Torre and Gutiérrez, 2005). Such merchandise is no longer found just on the shelves of bookshops, but also pops up on street markets and at esoteric fairs (Guerriero, 2003; Magnani, 1999). In other cases, the link is enhanced by spiritual seekers, who spread their cultural and religious beliefs in the *pueblos* they visit (De la Torre, 2011 and 2014), because tourism is exploiting native and ancestral spirituality (Aguilar Ros, 2008), or because the borders between magic, esoterica and the New Age have been permeable since the start of this movement (Michalik, 2011).

Such mediations are constantly provoking changes in traditional cultures, but they have myriad effects: while the New Age framework revives old syncretisms in new cultural hybrids, it also leads to the essentialization of ethnic identities, known as ethnogenesis. Likewise, although the New Age is presented as a matrix that resignifies and amalgamates existing traditions, folk religion also appropriates New Age goods for itself, and resignifies and recontextualizes them in syncretic processes of a longstanding cultural resistance.

Contributions to a Latin American Appropriation of the New Age

The syncretic and hybridized nature of popular, traditional religiosity in Latin America is fundamental for understanding the way in which New Age sensibilities have been incorporated in Latin America as part of a continuum. However, in order to understand the historical context and the extent of the Latin America appropriations and variations on the New Age, it is important to recall the historic and geographical origin of this movement in the Anglo-Saxon countries and its fusion with the hippie movement. It is also useful to acknowledge the channels where the New Age is promoted as part of overcoming personal challenges abd on therapeutic circults, not to mention the 'pollinizing' effects of spiritual seekers. Together, they produce constant exchanges that create new cultural hybrids where the New Age blends with popular religious and ethnic traditions. This dynamic, which has been favored by the contemporary exchange of people, objects and symbols across borders, creates interfaces between global and local, generating a constant renovation. In this process, narratives, symbols, rituatls and therapies become hybrid. This necessitates a historical and analytical distinction between the geneologies and histories of two matrixes of religiosity (the New Age and folk Latin American religion) that have produced a whole new syncretism. The goal is not to reify the cultural borders but to take into account the intersections, exchanges and especially the dynamics of appropriation, translationsand uses generated by the new hybrid expressions of this encounter.

This contents of the chapters of this book are at the crossroads where a New Age sensibility advances like an ecumene of worldwide spirituality without national, cultural or ecclesiastical borders. Here the New Age meets Latin America's syncretic religions, practiced by groups of people with African or indigenous roots, or based on a tradition of folk Catholicism, which have defended their position as bulwarks for the ancestral cultures and resistance against colonization. The New Age movement[7] and Latin American ethnic and folk religions[8] behave like two syncretizing and syncreticizable matrixes of meaning. Their intersection and the gestation of new traditional identities, or the traditionalizing of new religious movements, foster the convergence of academic research paths that had no former contact, as scholars usually stay in the same circles and take up positions in distinct networks of discussion and intellectual exchange. The fact that we have brought together these paths in a single book is an achievement in and of itself, not because the contributing authors share the same frameworks for debating concepts or because we all come to the same conclusions—to confirm this, see the discussion in Part I on the reach of the New Age as elaborated by Renée de la Torre, and its limits as described by Alejandro Frigerio. The points in common between the two opens up a rich debate with new questions and topics. We believe that this can provide the framework for a new field of anthropological study. How far is the reach of the New Age in popular traditions of Latin America? What new ways of signifying, living and experiencing religion is it creating with its new hybrids? Yet we also explore its limits.

As De la Torre explains in the first section, the New Age originally arose as a cultural expression in two of the most developed capitalist countries after the Second World War (Britain and the USA). They then evolved as a spirituality that inspired an alternative to the way of life of modern-day capitalism among the middle and upper class actors with access to art, science and cosmopolitan culture; their contact with indigenous cosmologies, popular knowledge, shamanistic magic and animistic or spiritualist experiences has generated cultural exchanges (and not just echoes in the globalizing homogenization of world culture). In fact, as the differents chapter by Campechano, Gutiérrez Zúñiga and De la Torre show, the Indianized New Age has also come back to Europe and the United States, in a direction opposite from that taken by the cosmopolitans.

7 York noted that 'the phenomenon of cultural appropriation is a fact, and this process of adoption/adaptation seems to be building one of the fundamental principles of the New Age' (York, 1999: 174).

8 According to Pierre Sanchis, syncretism is the characteristic feature of Brazilian society, and more generally, of Latin America as a whole. For this author, syncretism, a mixture of two or more religions, is based on resemanticizing one's own universe based on the relations learned from the Other. Syncretism is an incomplete dynamic in which social identity is continuously redefined (Sanchis, 1994: 7).

For this reason, unlike European and North American sociology, which approached the New Age from a globalizing perspective and focused on the goals of the cosmopolitan spiritual seekers, and their hybrid compositions of spiritualities of the self, we approach its reality by concentrating on ethnographic studies from the bottom up. This starts with popular practices, and encompasses the local but from a global perspective, in which the global is found in local society and the local is taken up by the global (Robertson, 1990). We will be looking at the circulation of teachers, symbols, rituals, knowledge and concepts; but also at processes of resignifying and of ethnic rooting, and the popular reappropriation of the New Age. As a result, in terms of academic literature on contemporary religion, our work provides insight into distinct ethnic and popular Latin American variations of the New Age, as seen in Brazil, Mexico, Guatemala, Peru, Spain, Argentina, and even among Guatemalans residing in Los Angeles, California. In such places, the New Age can be seen in the processes (though not in the products) of symbolic exchanges, cultural displacements (translocations and relocations of tradition), and in the production of new, neo-traditional, neo-ethnic, and neo-popular hybrid versions of syncretic ceremonies and religious movements.

The focus of this book is to describe the products and the new meanings generated by the meeting and symbolic exchange between New Age spirituality and traditional religions. This hibridizing process involves putting together the cultural remains of religious traditions, be these ethnic, Afro-American, or syncretic. They all have one thing in common: in recent years, they have begun to be valued and protected as bulwarks of the intangible inheritance of Latin American traditions. Examples include the Conchero and Aztec dances in Mexico; the movement of Mayan people in Guatemala; Santeria in Cuba; the Inca movement in Peru; the Wixaritari, the Mazatec and the Otomi in Mexico; and Candomblé and Umbanda in Brazil. At present, marked by globalization and intense transnational flows, these traditions are no longer the exclusive inheritance of certain traditional actors, but are practiced and enjoyed by various New Agers who have translocated and transnationalized.[9] At the same time, we are interested in the way in which popular religiosities have incorporated the symbolic goods put into circulation by the New Age, resemanticizing them in their cosmology of a magical and miraculous universe, linked to *Santeria* folk healing, popular spiritism and even indigenous political movements.

In short, we emphasize that the principal contribution of this book is that new syncretisms are being created by means of a multicultural encounter with

9 See Argyriadis, De la Torre, Gutiérrez Zúñiga and Aguilar Ros, 2008.

the New Age, which refers to the fact, as Sanchis says, that social identities are being redefined. This new syncretisms express a core characteristic of Latin American religiosity, as well as emergent features and a change in their scope. These identities are hybrid identities, the product of a transversalization of the new ingredients of a secular and universalizing spirituality, which is rooted in ancient traditions. As Silas Guerriero suggests in this volume, these new elements favor:

> The very permanence of native aspects—experienced now in new contexts by persons who were previously strangers—[which] may be understood on the basis of the creation of a common grammar, belonging to the spirit of the times. This is something like what happens with a language, which keeps its structure while receiving new elements, as the new elements come in from new forms of spirituality or are revived from the tradition, now with new meanings.
>
> GUERRIERO, in this book

The contributors to this book describe the genesis and the transformations of some of these new hybrid expressions, which are commonly called neo-ethnic, neo-traditional, neo-national and neo-religious, for a lack of better nomenclatures. The use of the prefix *neo* accompanies and requalifies the traditional new hybridations such as ethnic Neo-shamanisms (Rodríguez and Aguilar Ros); urban shamanisms (Magnani) and exo-shamanism (Galinier); Neo-Mexicanism, which hybridizes the Conchero rituals of the Mexicans (Gutiérrez Zúñiga; De la Torre and Campechano); and the Hispanekas, an appropriation of Conchero elements that recreates a hybrid identity of Neo-Mexicanism in Spain (Gutiérrez Zúñiga; De la Torre and Campechano). There is also the Andean New Age or Neo-inca (Molinié), the 'New Ageing' of the movement of Renovation of the Holy Spirit (Steil), the new Mayan spirituality (Bastos, Zamora and Tally), the eclectic Brazilian spiritualism of Valley of the Dawn in the city of Brasilia (Siqueira) and the New Age versions of some Afro-Brazilian ceremonies such as Umbanda, as well as the case of the Hare-Daimists (a hybrid of Hare Krishnas with the Santo Daimists) (Guerriero).

Contents of the Book

We have organized the contents of this volume in four sections, by theme. The first establishes a dialogue between past and recent theories on our subject, and relates them to the arguments presented in the book. The title of this section is 'Debates on the Interaction Between New Age and Local Latin American Cultures'. The second section contains articles on the subject of Neo-shamanisms in Latin America; it is followed by essays on popular medicine, healing and New Age therapeutic circuits. In the fourth section, we present chapters describing how ethnic traditions interact with the New Age. A final short chapter at the end of the book brings together the main conclusions of the writers of these chapters.

Taken as a whole, the contributions to this book deal with the intersection of traditional religions and New Age spiritualities. The effects of hybridization and appropriation of this intersection are emphasized throughout. However, we also want to reveal popular religion's capacity for resemanticizing: how does popular religion appropriate and incorporate the New Age signifiers into the cosmologies of the sacred and the world views of indigenous peoples? And finally, what are the new tensions provoked by this fusion? These are the questions that we address in our conclusion on this phenomenon.

Acknowledgements

This book was made possible thanks to the support received from Conacyt (*Consejo Nacional de Ciencia y Tecnología*, the National Council for Science and Technology) and from the *Agence National de la Recherche* (ANR). We also received the logistical and administrative support of CIESAS (*Centro de Investigaciones y Estudios Superiores en Antropología Social*, the Centre for Research and Advanced Studies in Social Anthropology) and El Colegio de Jalisco. We wish to extend our gratitude to the institutional authorities who not only believed in our work but also gave us invaluable encouragement to advance with the project: Virginia García Acosta (former Director of CIESAS), Susan Street Naussed (former Regional Director of CIESAS Occidente) and José Luis Leal Sanabria (former President of El Colegio de Jalisco).

The work brought together in this book was preceded most recently by the organization of a colloquium on 'New Age Reinterpretations of Syncretic Latin American Traditions'.[1] This meeting contributed to a focused and enriching discussion of the subject, especially with regards to collegiate decisions on the direction of the book. However, the colloquium was only the tip of an iceberg, in that it formed part of a more vigorous effort based on discussion groups and their contributions to the subject. A few of our contributors (Rodríguez, Juárez-Huet, Aguilar Ros, Frigerio, Gutiérrez Zúñiga and De la Torre) have been involved in '*Transnacionalización y relocalización de las religiones indo y afro americanas*' (Transnationalization and Relocalization of Native-Indian and Afro-American Religions), a research project coordinated by Renée de la Torre and financed by Conacyt No. 81926, since 2008. The same project was part of a larger project with a similar theme (the transnationalization processes of African, 'Native Indian' and Evangelical religions) and a shared geography, as evidenced in the title 'Transnational Religions of the Souths: Between Ethnicizing and Universalizing' (*Religions transnacionales des Suds: entre ethnisation et universalisation*), directed by Kali Argyriadis, and financed by the ANR. The specific objective of the project that our team of researchers was responsible for was to examine the translocation and relocalization of traditional religions. However, we also undertook to explore the New Age applications of ethnic traditions and determine the new position and the functional aspects of the New Age in Neo-esoteric circuits. Our aim was also to study the creation of new cultural identities and the contents of eclecticism

1 The colloquium was held at the offices of CIESAS Occidente, in Guadalajara, Mexico, from 21–23 September, 2011.

and hybridizing; to analyze the lively circulation of goods and services in translocal and transnational circuits; and to identify, when possible, the affinities of this dynamic with commercial logic. A final goal was to trace the New Age influence in the recovery of autochtonously pure cultural elements and calculate its contribution on the nativizing or essentializing of ethnic traditions.

Most of those of us who took part in writing this book had also met previously at various conferences and seminars where we shaped the subject matter. At these meetings, we shared our progress and worked together to build some of the main themes of discussion which are now included in this publication.[2] Another very important precedent was the co-ordination of a dossier on the subject of '*Religions amérindiennes et New Age*', which some of the authors of the articles in this volume took part in. This was published in one of the most renowned journals on this topic, *Archives de sciences sociales des religions,* No. 153, January-March 2011. In all of these projects, we successfully established an active network that has paved the way to including new themes in anthropology, such as the transnationalization of Afro and Latin American religions. These religions have surpassed their own ethnic, racial, cultural and national boundaries and moved in the opposite direction of the paths taken by missionary colonialism (see Argyriadis, Capone, De la Torre and Mary, 2012). We have also followed the fluxes and relocalizations of three ethno-national rituals: the Afro-American cult of Yemayá, original Wixaritari rituals, and the circuits of Mexican ritual dances (see De la Torre, 2012). The effort to maintain a perspective that addresses both the way a tradition is preserved and the way it reinvents and transforms itself at the same time was another important focus. Two special dossiers, drafted by several of the collaborators of this volume, deal with this subject; the journal *Cuicuilco* on 'Mexicanism and Neo-Indianism today', published in 2012; and issue number 21 of the journal *Debates Do Ner* about 'Rituals, new spiritualizations and transnationalization'.

Although each of our writers is responsible for his or her own text, we are indebted to colleagues who added their comments, advice and criticism

2 Cristina Gutiérrez and Renée de la Torre began to organize academic meetings on the subject of New Age spirituality in Latin America, at various national and international conferences. Some of these included the session *Religions amerindiennes et circuits de spiritualité New Age,* at the XXX Conference of the ISSR in Santiago de Compostela, Spain (30–31 July 2009); the round table '*Transnacionalización de prácticas religiosas*', at the XIII *Encuentro de la RIFREM*: Monterrey, Mexico, Colegio de la Frontera Norte, in May, 2010; and the round table '*Reinterpretaciones* New Age *de las tradiciones sincréticas*' at the XIV *Encuentro de la Red de Investigadores del Fenómeno Religioso,* Benemérita Universidad Autónoma de Puebla, Mexico, 6–8 April 2011.

during the various meetings we held, including Maria de Lourdes Beldi de Alcântara, Kali Argyriadis, Stefania Capone, Ari Pedro Oro, André Mary, Olga Odgers, Francisco de la Peña, Pablo Federico Semán, Margarita Zires, Hugo José Suárez, Manuela Camus, Jorge Durán, Isabel Lagarriga, Lorraine Karnoouh, Jean Paul Sarrazin, Paul Liffman and Ramón Sarro. We also received the help of research assistants who contributed to this job through their efforts and dedication: in particular, José Enrique Aceves, Rosario Ramírez, Verónica Briseño, Lizette Campechano and Gabriela Gil.

Numerous contributions made this volume in English possible. We would like to acknowledge the skilful translation into English by Nicholas Barrett of the original version of this book in Spanish. During the process of editing this edition with Brill, we received many helpful suggestions and as authors, we took the liberty of incorporating those which enhanced the original Spanish versions. We would like to especially thank Paul Heelas as a generous reader; Cristina Rocha and Steven Engler as members of the board of the collection Religion in the Americas (REAM); the thoughtful help provided by Maarten Frieswijk during the editing process; and the advice provided by Ingrid Heijckers and Henri Gooren.

List of Figures and Tables

Figures

Tables

List of Contributors

Alejandra Aguilar Ros

Ph.D. (2004), Manchester University, UK, is Professor and Researcher at the Center of Research and Graduate Studies in Social Anthropology (CIESAS Occidente) in Mexico. Her work and publications have dealt with embodiment and space in religion, ethnic responses to shifting religious contexts and contemporary Huichol shamanism. She is the author of the *Embodied religion: Religion and Identity in a Mexican Town* (LAP Lambert, 2010).

Santiago Bastos

Ph.D. (2000), University of Guadalajara/CIESAS Occidente, Mexico, is Professor and Researcher at the Center of Research and Graduate Studies in Social Anthropology, (CIESAS Occidente). His academic work focuses on ethnicity. He is the author of *Etnicidad y fuerzas armadas en Guatemala. Algunas ideas para debate* (FLACSO, 2004). His most recent book is *Dinosaurio Reloaded. Violencias actuales en Guatemala* (Fundación Constelación/FLACSO Guatemala, 2015).

Lizette Campechano

M.A. (2013), University of Guadalajara, Mexico, her principal research interest is in the social media data analysis project of Datcom Company. Her academic work is centered on internet media. She is the author of the articles: 'Apocalipsis maya: una creencia posmoderna en la era de la información' in *Revista Brasileira de História das Religioes* (2014) and '*El retorno virtual de Quetzalcóatl: una netnografía de la mexicanidad y neomexicanidad*' in Cuicuilco (2012).

Sylvie Pédron Colombani

Ph.D. (1994), Université Paris 10-Nanterre, is Professor and Researcher at Paris West University Nanterre La Défense, France. Her work is centered on conversion processes in Pentecostalism and the traditional 'Indian' cult of *Maximón* in Guatemala and its transnationalization. Also, religious transformations among Guatemalan migrants in the United States. She is author of *Le pentecôtisme au Guatemala. Conversion et identité* (Paris, C.N.R.S. Éditions, 1998). Her most recent book is *Maximón au Guatemala: Dieu, saint ou traitre* (Periplus, 2004).

Alejandro Frigerio

Ph.D. (1989), University of California, is Professor at FLACSO Argentina, and at The Pontifical Catholic University of Argentina. He is a tenured researcher at

CONICET (National Council for Scientific Research). His work focuses on the transnationalization of Afro-Brazilian religions and folk devotions in Argentina. He is the author (with M.J. Carozzi) of *El Estudio Científico de la Religión a Fines del Siglo XX* (Centro Editor de América Latina, 1994). His most recent publication (with Juan Renold) is *Visiones del Papa Francisco desde las Ciencias Sociales* (UNR Editora, 2015).

Jacques Galinier

Ph.D. (1985), University of Bordeaux, France, is Professor and Emeritus Research Director at The National Center for Scientific Research (CNRS). He has done field work in Mexico since 1969 with the Otomi Indians. He has devoted himself to studies of rituals, cosmology, Mesoamerican New Age and more recently anthropology of the night. He is author of 'The World Below—Body and Cosmos in the Otomi Indian Ritual' (Boulder, CO: University Press of Colorado, 2004). He is co-author with Antoinette Molinié of *Neo-Indians. A Religion for the Third Millenium* (University Press of Colorado, 2013).

Silas Guerriero

Ph.D. (2000), Pontifical Catholic University of São Paulo (PUC/SP), Brazil, is Professor and Researcher at the Post-Graduate Program of Religious Studies in the same university. His work and publications are centered on the Anthropology of Religion, especially New Religious Movements. He is author of *Magia existe?* (Paulus, 2003) and *Novos Movimentos Religiosos. O caso brasileiro* (PUC, 2006).

Cristina Gutiérrez Zúñiga

Ph.D. (2002), College of Jalisco (COLJAL), Mexico, is Professor and Researcher at the same institution. Her work is centered on the pluralizing of religion in Mexico, new religious and spiritual movements, and the transnationalization of the Aztec dance. Her most recent publications in English (with Renée de la Torre) are 'Chicano Spirituality in the Construction of an Imagined Nation: Aztlán/La spiritualité "chicana" dans la construction d'une nation imaginaire: Aztlán', in Social Compass, 60 (2) pp. 218–235, ISR, 2013, Sage, UK, ISSN: 0037–7686; and 'Analysis of the Emergence of Missionary Territorial Strategies in a Mexican Urban Context', in The Changing World Religion Map. Sacred Places, Identities, Practices and Politics, vol. 3 (Springer, 2015).

Nahayeilli B. Juárez Huet

Ph.D. (2007), Michoacan College (COLMICH), Mexico. She is a Researcher at the Center of Research and Graduate Studies in Social Anthropology (CIESAS

Peninsular). Her publications on the transnationalization of Afro-American religions in Mexico include *Un pedacito de Dios en Casa: circulación transnacional, relocalización y praxis de la santería en la ciudad de México* (CIESAS/UV/COLMICH, 2014).

José Guilherme C. Magnani

Ph.D. (1982), University of São Paulo, Brazil, is Professor and Researcher at the same university. His work has centered on urban anthropology, urban shamanism and Neo-esoteric networks. He is the author of *Da Periferia ao Centro: Trajetórias de Pesquisa em Antropologia Urbana* (Edit. Terceiro Nome, 2012) and co-author (with Lillian de Lucca Torres) of *Na Metrópole: Textos de Antropologia Urbana* (EDUSP/FAPESP, 1996). He is chief editor of the journal *Ponto Urbe* (http://www.pontourbe.net).

Antoinette Molinié

Ph.D. (1974), The Sorbonne, Paris, is currently Emeritus Director of Research at The National Center for Scientific Research (CNRS). She has published various works on traditional Andean societies in Peru and Bolivia, especially on their rituals. She has also published works comparing religiosity in Spain and America, such as *Celebrando el Cuerpo de Dios,* (Lima: Fondo Editorial de la Pontificia Universidad Católica del Perú, 1999). Her most recent book (with Jacques Galinier) is *The Neo-Indians. A Religion for the Third Millenium* (University Press of Colorado, 2013).

María Teresa Rodríguez

Ph.D. (2000), Metropolitan Autonomous University of Mexico (UAM-Iztapalapa), is Professor and Researcher at the Center of Research and Graduate Studies in Social Anthropology (CIESAS Golfo). Her research projects focus on the identity of ethnic religions, and on transnational migration. She is the author of *Ritual, identidad y procesos étnicos en la Sierra de Zongolica, Veracruz* (CIESAS, 2003), and co-author (with Odile Hoffmann) of *Retos de la diferencia. Los actores de la multiculturalidad entre México y Colombia,* (CIESAS/IRD/CEMCA, ICANH, 2007). Her most recent book (with Bernard Tallet) is *Historias de Hombres y Tierras* (CIESAS, 2009).

Deis Siqueira

Ph.D. (1984), National Autonomous University of Mexico (UNAM), is Professor at the Sociology Department of Brasilia University, Brazil. She is a Researcher at the The Brazilian National Council for Scientific and Technological Development (CNPq). Her research interest is in non-conventional religiosity and environmentalism and gender. Her most recent book is *Valle del Amanecer. Inventario Nacional de Referencias Culturales* (IPHAN, 2010).

Carlos Alberto Steil
Ph.D. (1995), National Museum, Federal University of Rio de Janeiro, Brazil. He is professor and researcher at the Federal University of Rio Grande do Sul, Brazil. His work is centered on Catholicism, Pilgrimage, and New Age and spiritual movements. He is the author of *O sertão das romarias. Um estudo antropológico sobre o santuário de Bom Jesus da Lapa—Bahia* (Vozes, 1996). His most recent book (with Rodrigo Toniol) is titled *On the Nature Trail: Converting the Rural into the Ecological through a State Tourism Policy* (Hauppauge, 2015).

Engel Tally
M.Sc. (2011), Lund University, Sweden. His research is about New Age tourism in Lake Atitlan, Guatemala. His first degree thesis *Turismo espiritual en tiempos posmodernos. El estudio de caso San Marcos La Laguna, Guatemala*, was used to produce the documentary *Tierra Sagrada* available at http://vimeo.com/15282336.

Renée de la Torre
Ph.D. (1997), University of Guadalajara/CIESAS Occidente, Mexico, is Professor and Researcher at the Center of Research and Graduate Studies in Social Anthropology (CIESAS Occidente). Her research has centered on contemporary transformations of religion in Mexico and the transnationalization of the Aztec dance. She is the author of *Religiosidades nómadas. Creencias y prácticas heterodoxas en Guadalajara*, Mexico: Publicaciones de la Casa Chata, 2013; and the chapter 'Religion and Embodiment: Religion and the (Latin American) Bodies that Practice It' in the book Controversies in Contemporary religion. Education, Politics Society, and Spirituality (Praeger, 2014).

Marcelo Zamora
Ph.D. (2011), Michoacan College (COLMICH) Mexico works at Instituto de Investigación y Proyección sobre Ambiente Natural y Sociedad (IARNA), Universidad Landívar, Guatemala. His research is focused on interethnic relationships in Guatemala. He is the author of the article 'Proyectos modernistas y reformulación de la ladinidad: el baile del Convite en Totonicapán, Guatemala' in *Revista Centroamericana de Ciencias Sociales* (FLACSO, 2004).

PART 1

Debates on the Interaction between New Age and Local Latin American Cultures

Introduction

The book starts with two chapters of theoretical reflections. They share the initial need to provide a framework for theoretical discussion of the term New Age. However they hold different positions.

In the first chapter, *Indo- and Afro-American Religiosities, and Circuits of New Age Spirituality*, Renée de la Torre revises the various definitions of the term New Age. The author highlights the processes and historical comings and goings that have permeated and molded different varieties of New Age, both in Europe, and in Latin America. Due to the changing, eclectic and diverse character of New Age, she has chosen a working definition, to conceive of it as a matrix of meaning, in other words a 'framework of interpretation', based on the 'holistic' principle that allows connections and analogies to be established between the part and the whole, the self and the cosmos, ego and Mother Earth, the human body and the noosphere. The author emphasizes that this aptitude is what characterizes New Age as syncretism in motion. She proposes the idea that its very hybridizing ability is what actually explains how this same matrix is reappropriated and reinterpreted by other syncretic matrices, that impress popular and traditional senses upon it, creating Neo versions of Latin American traditions such as the Neo-Indian spiritualities, Neo-shamanism, and Neo-magic. In these new currents two phenomena occur rather ambivalently: the New Age resemanticizing of Latin American popular traditions; and the popular appropriation and resignifying that magical, ethnic and nativist senses impress on the New Age. Hence the text opens up a debate as to whether it is possible today to speak of new, Latin American, versions of the New Age. In other words, whether the vigorous exchange between a New Age matrix of meaning and Latin American popular religiosity has resulted in new flows that impress new matrices on the New Age itself. The characteristic feature of Latin Americanization is to overvalue the holistic principle of the interpretive framework of this movement, which refunctionalizes and broadens the sense of a cosmopolitan sacred self, transforming it into a more social spirituality than one centered on the individual.

Alejandro Frigerio, in his turn, contributes a chapter on *The Logics and Limits of New Age Appropriation: Where Syncretism Comes to an End* and a greater emphasis is given to the need to place limits on what is meant by New Age. The author seeks to restrict indefinite and loose uses and abuses of the term 'New Age'. He therefore aims in his text to counter the growing tendency in academic studies, mainly but not exclusively from Latin America, to stress that 'everything mixes with everything' and to claim that these mixtures can be

 | DOI 10.1163/9789004316485_002

called New Age, simply by virtue of their being mixtures. Therefore the author attempts to establish the limits of the term, and also to clarify the various types of logic that concur in the religious hotchpotches, as well as the differential meanings the same symbols or rituals may acquire, depending on the social conditions in which they are appropriated. While he does not call for a substantive definition, he considers that the definition 'self religion' (Heelas and Carozi) is essential for understanding the New Age. In this way he seeks to clarify certain, not interchangeable, characteristics that make the distinction between what is and what is not New Age. For the author, not all syncretism and not all holism fall into New Age, as these are also developed in popular Catholicism or popular Esotericism. Frigerio advises us of the possibility of gaining a deeper understanding of the hybridizing and apparently omnivorous logic of New Age, through identifying the limits and degrees of appropriation by the New Age. These have been recorded as a matter of fact in the various ethnographic studies of the present volume, where there are clearly some ingredients that are 'excluded' from the New Age types of hybridization, in accordance with the distinctive national narratives and counter-narratives of countries such as Argentina, Mexico or Brazil. But he also warns that one should be alert to any misuse of the label New Age to catalog the presence of certain symbols, specific elements, or even specific practices, that the New Age had originally adopted from the East and have now been relocated, practiced and resignified in esoteric or magic circles, or in popular Catholicism, with semantic markers that are different or even opposite to those of the New Age.

As well as introducing the conceptual debate, both chapters present the questions that guide the reflections made in the book, such as: What continuities and ruptures can we identify between the Latin American syncretisms, practiced for centuries, and those that we see today in the ostentatious language and style of the New Age? Does it reduce to the idea of a 'syncretism in motion'? Can we define it on the basis of a different logic or grammar with respect to its appropriation and resignifying? And, can we distinguish nuclei of an interpretive framework that might give our analysis greater specificity and rigor?

CHAPTER 1

Indo- and Afro-American Religiosities, and Circuits of New Age Spirituality

Renée de la Torre[1]

Matches and Mismatches between Anthropology and Shamanism

The general theme of this book is the point of encounter between two worlds that appeared until a few decades ago never to contact: New Age, and ethnic religiosities (indigenous and African), on the Latin American continent.[2] There is no doubt that, as Ulf Hannerz had predicted they would, the cosmopolitans and the locals got in touch with each other thanks to the connectivity of globalization (1992). However, this is not altogether simple, because, as we know, globalization connects technologies and markets in the cosmopolitan capitals of the world with each other, but also disconnects villages and regions that do not fit into the global circuit (García Canclini, 2004). In the case of New Age spirituality, the connections that were made did follow the direction taken by globalization, but also, they reversed the course taken by the poles of neoliberal progress.[3] As the New Age was a countercultural sensibility, our cosmopolitan spiritual seekers propitiated the search for mystical experiences on the

1 This chapter is an extended version of the article 'Les rendez-vous manqués de l'anthropologie et du chamanisme', published in *Archives de Sciences sociales des religions*, No. 153 (56), 2011, pp. 145–158.

2 In the nineteen sixties, communities of the New Age network arose principally among sectors of the more enlightened middle classes, among artistic and intellectual circles of the metropolitan centers of the U.S.A. (with their epicenter in California) and of some European countries. They were oriented towards the forging of an alternative spirituality counter to the materialism of capitalist progress and the rationalism of modern times. Their quests were directed to importing techniques and examples of wisdom extracted from the old religions of the East, and opening up to 'cosmic' subjects such as: astrology, and tuning in to the presence of, or making contact with, extraterrestrial beings (see Melton et al., 1990).

3 The transnationalization of religiosities is to be distinguished from the one-way globalization of the historical great religions, so unlike the very different way in which small missions, ethnic ceremonies and subalternate religiosities have been transnationalized in the opposite direction, from the colonized peoples and nations to the centers of the colonizers. For more on this subject, consult Csordas, 2009 and Argyriadis, Capone, De la Torre and Mary 2012.

 | DOI 10.1163/9789004316485_003

cultural horizons that had been denied or deferred by the modern world: the Oriental, the Indigenous and Nature.

The first scholar to refer to the internal dynamics of the transformations in the religious life of modern society was Thomas Luckmann (1977), who proposed that the measure of secularization was not given by the unreligiousness of modern societies but by a change in the nature of religion in human beings. If religion is a symbolic place where the transcendental sense of the world is socially constructed, it is not that society has abandoned its needs for transcendence; what has changed are the channels of communication through which the ultimate meanings of societies are founded.

The main characteristic of contemporary culture is the complexity of its organization. We are dealing with a global village co-inhabited by a diversity of new tribes to identify with, that are formed through shared rites (Maffesoli, 1990). The referents of their tribal identity do not correspond only and unequivocally to the traditional forms of social organization, but are related to registers of identity of the mass media, that connect and relocate the local culture in networks of transnational globalization (García Canclini, 1995). Globalization profoundly modifies the processes of location of a culture, whose primordial dimensions are altered by new proximities and technified distances that affect the nature of daily life. But this situation is itself transformed by everyday social activity through which the mediated experiences received through the media are interiorized and resignified in the context of face to face social interactions (Tufte, 1997).

There is no doubt that one of the contemporary features of society is the globalizing or worldwide tendency of culture, as the processes of technifying information and mass communications have repercussions that fragment and deinstitutionalize religious beliefs. The churches that used to be the specialized institutions for administering the functions that defined what was religious—from the medieval period to the modern era—have to face a secular world today that competes, with other institutions, in the production and administration of beliefs in the supernatural, in sacralizing the group and in the diffusion of models of salvation and transcendence. But it should also be recognized that, when they lose their monopoly over social functions, this does not mean institutions are emptied of meaning, or that the religious passes freely through society. What can be affirmed is that religion has lost the exclusivity it had in certain social competencies, and now has to compete for production of the sacred and the transcendental with other, secular, institutions, where the communications media and cultural industries have an ever greater role as spaces for the production and practice of the sacred, the transcendental and occasions of having religious experiences.

Definitely a good description of the cultural complexity of our days is the one provided by Alain Touraine (1992), who pointed out that the diversity of cultural expressions, is largely due to the functionalist homogenizing and multiple fragmentation of referents of meaning. The last of these effects, an essential feature of postmodernity, is reflected in the multiplicity of points of view and voices; in people's unwillingness to believe in big ideological, aesthetic and ethical paradigms; in the weakening of traditional referents of authority, and, finally, in the emptying of institutions.

But it should not be forgotten that it is also a fact today that events from far away are integrated into individual and group experience in traditional contexts. That is, following Michael De Certeau, in the context of popular culture where consumption takes place through acts of combination and utility (De Certau, 1996). This is why, even in the new context of the age of information, experiences communicated through the media form frameworks of interaction and referents of group identity, which are present in contexts where the social activity of individuals is located. Just as the local is globalized, so the global also becomes local (García Canclini, 1995). The two poles are two aspects of glocalization (Robertson, 1990), and when both interact they produce effects of the most diverse and contrasting kinds. So although postmodernity proclaims a crisis in universal and universalizing values; there is at the same time a re-evaluation of specific identitites, and there are even examples where specifics whether local, national or religious, are exacerbated (Castells, 1999).

Hervieu-Léger (1993) explains the new trend of secularization as a process of 'fluidization of the religious through the length and breadth of modern society'. Contemporary religion is found widely disseminated in a multiplicity of modern forms of belief: new religious movements, civil religions, customized (*à la carte*) religions, new eclecticisms of believers (*bricolages*), profane religions, and so on. The new religiousness of modern times has been dubbed New Age and is marked by being mobile not static, individualized and not institutional, experimental not dogmatic, syncretic and not orthodox. As individuals we are affected by abstract influences that come largely from the electronic means of communication and that have a decisive effect on a new reorganization of social relations and of life styles.

Some writers, indeed, propose today that it is necessary to attend to imaginary societies, not because they did not use to exist, but because they now reach further and have more to say in the formation of identities. We see syncretisms that only a few decades ago would have been difficult to imagine, but have had no trouble in becoming real. For example, the impact on western societies of Oriental religions and philosophies, which, without causing ruptures, have been integrated into the great religions such as some versions of

Catholicism (for example Anthony de Melo and Teilhard de Chardin); or else that of Afro-Brazilian rites exported as far as Europe or to cultures like those of Uruguay and Argentina which though geographically close had seemed far away culturally, as they did not, apparently, share the same links to African societies; or consider the growth of new religions in Japan and their entry into countries like Brazil through the top echelons of business; then there are the New Age types of movement amalgamated to projects to save the Mexican soul that bring this feeling into a communion with Tibet or fuse it with traditional images of Catholic culture.

These religious manifestations are themselves the product of a counter culture which is opposed to the big institutions. They take the form of cosmic, not historical, spiritualities. The grand historical accounts of cultural civilizations and of the great religions turn up as bundles of fragmented tales, and the historical memory of these is reinstated in new religious identities. It is difficult to contextualize them in traditional notions of space and time. We find that the ways in which these macro stories are appropriated in syncretisms that make them unique turn out to be many and various, which is why they are called 'customized religions'. It is also difficult to place them in the social space of specialized studies, because, as Francoise Laplantine and Alexis Nouss (1997) remark, some of these new religious movements stem from science: whether physics (thermodynamics), medical science (dianetics), information science (the Mormons' microfilms), the conquest of space (Raelian movement) or quantum physics.

As religion is deinstitutionalized this (eclectic) process is one that favors the subjective, a shift which can be seen in several practices; for example, the loss of authority of the churches and of their hierarchical figures and their symbols of authority and the preference for mystical experimentation and ad hoc, *à la carte* or 'customized, religions; in the loss of belief and of respect for dogmas of faith, in favor of syncretisms of belief; in the change from a religious rationalization of society (Christian Humanism) to a contemplative experience of the sacred; and in the replacement of the universal value of truth to its relativization' (Mardones, 1996). It is however difficult to mark precisely where the new and the traditional separate, or how popular religion differs from New Age, as in some Latin American countries eclecticism and syncretism were around long before the New Age phenomenon and form an essential part of popular religious culture, combining elements properly of the Roman Catholic church with autochthonous cultures (having African or native American roots). It is therefore important to stress the syncretic nature of the supply on offer that combines Oriental learning along with esoteric knowledge and self improvement techniques. It takes place on the basis of a syncretism that already exists and gives a new dimension to the latest symbolical production as an extension of the syncretic logic of popular religion.

Anthropology and New Age

Pioneering studies of the New Age undertaken by sociologists of religion in the nineteen seventies and eighties realized that this movement had been born among cosmopolitans. Their earliest researches confirm this, dealing with utopian communities and circuits that offered alternative healing, and concentrating mostly on explanations of the phenomena of religious change that occurred in some of the major cities of the capitalist world, in England, Finland and the United States of America.

Around the same time, in particular during the nineteen seventies, anthropology, especially in America, debated with itself about which of two currents to follow. There was classical anthropology, concentrating on ethnic studies, folklore and traditions, which sought to set up fieldwork missions into the farthest reaches of civilization, and whose studies favored the most authentic and untouched cultures. These were the tribes and ethnic groups, whose identity was anchored in their roots, and in whose territories ancestral rituals and languages were kept up, which were valued for their primitivism and scarce contact with (more likely: contamination from) Western and Modern lifestyles. Indeed it was the anthropologists who served as a compass that led to the encounter of untouched spiritualities. Significant in this regard was the impact of work by Carlos Castaneda, a controversial anthropologist who narrated his shamanic experiences as an apprentice of Don Juan (a Yaqui medicine man), and whose books encouraged hundreds of New Ager spiritual seekers to follow the psychotropic path as a way of gaining access to one's inner life, and to meet with practicing shamans in order to experience new states of consciousness. However, the widespread diffusion of his writings also led titled anthropologists at the academy to view the study of magic and shamanism with serious misgivings. All the same, no matter how many ways there are in which Castaneda's work might be disqualified for its lack of anthropological rigor, it became the traveller's guide to shamanic initiation with American Indians, and has had enormous repercussions on the link between cosmopolitan New Agers and the Indians of native tribes on the American continent. But it was also this book that tempted young people into taking up the study of anthropology. Not that these distinctions ever became neat divisions, between those who were opposed to magic and shamanism as objects of anthropological research, and those who saw meeting the shaman as part of the ethnographic voyage. Octavio Paz, a well known Mexican writer who received the Nobel prize for literature, had the clarity to see this conflictive coupling:

> If the books of Castaneda are a work of literary fiction, they are so in a very strange way: his subject would then be the defeat of anthropology and the victory of magic; but if they are works of anthropology, then the subject is hardly less strange: the vengeance of an (anthropological) 'object', a medicine man, over an anthropologist by turning him into a witchdoctor.[4]

The idea of purity attached to native, distant and ancestral products attracted and seduced academician anthropologists in search of the 'village' (*aldea*) just as strongly as witchdoctor anthropologists and New Ager apprentices of the medicine men, searching for the springs of 'pure ancestral spirituality'. Anthropology saw what was still intact and adopted an essentializing view of the ethnic cultures, which it situated in spaces having self-contained borders; by contrast, cultural studies appeared that were interested in the new global and cosmopolitan cultures (Clifford, 1999), and were not very concerned with traditional identities. Currently, contemporary anthropology has had to accept that the pure object no longer exists and that the object of its study is no longer villages, but the cultures in the villages (Geertz, 1977: 33). Nonetheless, the bifocal view recommended by Clifford himself keeps the actual study of native tribes as the main interest of the studies, only now not looking just at their conservation strategies but also at their strategies for transcultural change and exchange. It is not enough to study them *in situ* unless their continual displacements and transcultural itineraries are also taken into account: hence not seeing them in isolation but as intensely mediatized by the market, the communications media, tourism, and migration (Clifford, 1999).

With regard to Brazil, here Catholicism cohabits with the Kardecist Spiritism inherited from Alan Kardec's movement, which had its heyday in the nineteenth century. Spritists believe their doctrine provides a synthesis of science, philosophy, and Christian morals. Spiritist practice involves the contact of mediums with spirits of the departed who are able to communicate with the living and appear to them. Some of their main beliefs, which are also cognitive bridges to the New Age, are the ideas of spirit, reincarnation, vital fluids, and cosmic energy. These conceptions are also shared by students of

4 Octavio Paz. Prologue to the book by Carlos Castaneda, *Las enseñanzas de don Juan*, taken from http://www.mercurialis.com/EMC/Octavio%20Paz%20-%20La%20Mirada%20Anterior%201.htm, consulted in February 2011.

parapsychology and by Gnostics. But above all, as explained by Hess (1989), spiritism in Brazil can be considered a vector running across different religious traditions, such as popular Catholicism[5] where practices include miracles and magic, and especially the syncretic religions denominated as Afro-Brazilian (for example, Candomblé and Umbanda) who practice possession by spirits and believe in the powers of mediums.

This tension made academician anthropologists delay before giving their attention to the impact that the New Age was having on the re-composition of beliefs and ritual systems among certain traditional ethnic communities in America. Which is the main theme of this book, and those of its chapters that are based on ethnographic studies take note of some of the transformations generated by the dynamic of flows and changes deriving from globalization, which are constantly cutting across the religious traditions commonly known as the 'native', 'tribal', 'traditional', 'popular' and 'ethnic' traditions of Latin America.

Until a few decades ago, Indian- and Afro-American religions were practiced in a restricted way by ethnic groups, linked to the ritual celebration of local festivals, in determined contexts and often incorporated into national folklores. Today, a larger public is fervently interested in them, and they are appreciated for representing paradigms of 'authenticity' and 'ancestry'. It is our hypothesis that this growth has contributed to relocating these religious practices in circuits of the New Age and as part of the quest for types of esoteric knowledge, that are themselves criss-crossed by the itineraries of cosmopolitan actors we recognize as 'spiritual seekers', who in their turn track down alternative springs of the spiritual life, creating a synthesis and establishing links between different traditions.

The New Agers: Cosmopolitans in Search of a 'Non-Western' Spirituality

At first the New Age was regarded by sociologists as a countercultural expression against Western modernity. It started in the U.S.A. in the historical context of the Vietnam War, where it gave origin to emerging subcultures opposed to war, racism, sexism, industrialism, the nuclear threat and damage to the

5 The word popular refers to the heterodox and syncretic sense of the Catholic religious system, as opposed to 'educated' or 'official' or 'institutionally orthodox' Catholicism, rather than to the social sector practicing it, because although it is mainly the practice of popular classes, it is also practiced by middle classes.

environment. As Heelas would say (1996), it provided a utopia for an alternative way of life. In her work *The Aquarian Conspiracy*, Ferguson (1981) succeeded in linking what seemed to be individual cases into a network promoting a change of consciousness which would be the engine for a change of life, with the power to spread its enthusiasm to the world and transform the planet into a harmonious whole.

In the 1990s, New Age became a challenge for the sociology of religions, which, in order to comprehend it, would have to deconstruct its concepts and leave behind substantive definitions, and adopt functionalist definitions that would allow religion to be thought of in a different way to that of institutional religions and that of the model of sects developed in Evangelical Christianity.[6]

Pioneering studies of the New Age were first produced in the U.S.A., and they stressed that the movement had originated in the sixties, in the Esalen community of California, where the Human Potential Movement was launched before going on to Europe and Latin America.[7] Alexander's study of the Esalen community emphasized the orientalist and countercultural orientation of their thinking and practices (Alexander, 1992). The New Age demanded a new universal awareness different to the modern Western type, one more oriented towards the spiritual rather than the material, towards intuition as against deductive knowledge, recuperating magic and shamanism as opposed to science, valuing the female pole over the masculine, and Nature in preference to industrial civilization. The New did not allude to the invention of beliefs and ceremonies, but to a utopian enthusiasm for renewing the world and its relations, through the recovery of traditions that had been denied or dismissed as worthless in the course of Western history.

The first utopian communities, founded in California and later in Europe, promoted an alternative sensibility to that promulgated by the principal Western institutions—church, family and State—which they endeavoured to

6 Discussion of the way the study of new religious movements should proceed became a theoretical challenge for the sociology of religion. The main debate on redefining the religious, where the choice was between continuing to use substantive definitions (deriving from the attributes and functions of historical religions), and creating functional definitions (open to the new capacities and actors of religion), was developed by McGuire (1987). In a similar way, European authors treated the same discussion as one between exclusive and inclusive points of view, and among them were Hervieu-Léger, 1993: 51–57 and Mardones, 1994.

7 Which does not mean as some scholars have wanted to say recently, that the early studies failed to establish a genealogical line to the New Agers as inheritors of the earlier development of esotericism, Occultism and theosophy. This is clearly shown by Melton, who offers an ample chronology for the New Age movement (Melton et al., 1990).

replace with something conceived of as 'vital force' or great unity: 'it was associated with a mystic East that was like a mirror image of the West' (Alexander, 1992 in Carozzi, 1999b: 11). Whereas Paul Heelas preferred to stress the subjective component of the inner search for meaning, and called it *self-religion* because of its emphasis on defending values based on personal freedom, the dignity of the individual, and personal responsibility (Heelas, 1996: 83). To start with the New Age communities established in California were for the most part identified with psychology, searching for inner meaning, and self-discipline. Later, however, British sociologists of religion drew attention to the subject of new religious movements, and noted their orientation towards the formation of social and spiritual networks that created a different model of belief. The new movements seemed to be interested in establishing priorities and transcendental ideas, as an alternative to the front presented by the great religions and also by the evangelical sects (Barker, 1989). While in France, the sociologists Hervieu-Léger and Champion denominated the phenomenon with the term 'esoteric nebula', highlighting its indefinite, fluid, non-institutional, anti-dogmatic and eclectic character. This way they resolved to see it as something nebulously esoteric, a fluid and invisible example of spirituality (Champion and Hervieu-Léger, 1990; Champion, 1995).

Some Keys for Defining New Age

Although the New Age movement is a dispersed form of spirituality, whose relationship to the sacred is strictly personal and not institutional, it operates as a system of informal networks, whose sympathizers share universal utopias that are to be achieved through the transformation of individuals. This notion rests upon the belief that the individual forms a part of the whole of cosmic energy (also thought of as God, love, spirit, goodwill or peace), and actions to reach perfection taken by the individual, will contribute to balancing the positive energies of the Earth and establishing a state of harmony between Man and the forces of Nature. Every individual is the creator of a new consciousness that will flow out into a planetary consciousness.

The New Age proclaims the end of a rational and material era ruled by the constellation of Pisces. It also brings to an end the Christian era—which has held sway on the Earth, it is believed, for 2000 years—as the stars of the next sign, Aquarius, move into the ecliptic and indicate the start of a New Age that is supposed to be marked by creativity, mystical experience and equilibrium with nature.

Because of its changing, eclectic and varied nature, it is not easy to define the New Age through its contents and beliefs. There are various definitions of its origins and the corpus of its beliefs, just as there are various discrepancies among them, but no agreement on using the term New Age (as many actors reject it), and there is not even a consensus about whether to consider it a religion, or, rather, a spirituality, or indeed, as Mardones called it (1994), just a sensibility of the times. In fact it has been easier to characterize the New Age by saying what it is not:

> A movement without sacred texts, without a teacher, with no strict organization and no dogmas. A sort of lay mysticism that invites the religious world to broaden its horizons and embrace the universe, science, and psychism, melting in a single embrace all the conflicting contrasts that have always affected the natural and the supernatural worlds.
>
> NATALE, 1993: 93, quoted in Mardones, 1994: 122

It has also been difficult to characterize its historical development. Although the New Age does not start, as such, until some years after the Second World War, and Wuthnow himself (1998) places the movement as successor to the disenchantment of the post world war generation in the United States, Melton (1992) points out that it did not arise from spontaneous generation but was heir to the occult and esoteric schools of the nineteenth century.

There are those who consider it to be a counterculture to modern times, opposed to material consumption and proposing an alternative life style, but it is a movement that has changed in its short life, and, as was demonstrated by Ferreux (2000), it has now been re-converted by merchandising into a form of consumption: something 'light', spiritual, and natural. In plainer language, it has been transformed into a spiritual shopping mall, as Hanegraaff (2001) categorized it. Paul Heelas—probably the scholar who has been following the behavior of New Age spirituality for longer than anyone else—has recognized a new transformation of the movement. He has developed a sequence of stages for observing its evolution, starting with its origins as a countercultural movement, passing through its linking up with ideals of success and material prosperity; and finally deriving in life spiritualities offering a renewed ethic against the de-humanizing materialism of the globalization process. Heelas does not cease to recognize the immersion of New Age in the general process of capitalist commodification and the generation of potent consumption for well-being among the middle classes of countries such as the USA or Britain, but he also warns about the need to conduct ethnographic studies and analyze the uses and meanings these commodities acquire in daily life and in the vital processes of the consuming subjects. From his point of view, New Age is a part of what he now calls 'Life spiritualities' that consist of spaces of subjective transformation and resistance against materialism and the dehumanizing of contemporary life, which on a small scale and through a gradual process are fortifying a humanistic ethic on a global scale, with a greater degree of acceptance than that of radical political movements (Heelas 2008). So, how do we characterize the New Age?

For the purposes of this book, we will take as our starting point the definition of one of the features of New Age put forward by Amaral:

> A field of various types of intersecting discourse, that works as a kaleidoscope, rearranging pieces of elements into different shapes, and constantly creating a kind of 'syncretism in motion'.
>
> AMARAL, 1999: 68

However, we cannot stick with this definition, as it does not respond to the principle of New Age identity, leaving any hybridizing principle at all, open to being considered New Age. So what turns a sort of amalgam of different cultural textures into New Age? Maybe what makes it a synthesis is not so much a unified discourse, but a matrix of meaning, or to put it anther way, an 'interpretive frame' based on the 'holistic' principle[8] on the basis of which a sacralization of the Self creates a sacralization of the cosmos, and projects of self-betterment acquire the potential to transform one's surroundings and the universal consciousness. The way it has of conceiving of the whole as being contained in its parts, allows the grammar of the New Age to appropriate, to translate and refunctionalize different cultural and/or spiritual aspects of the Other, and make them its own. The New Age is not only an assemblage of fragmentary contents, but above all a matrix of meaning that allows fragments of different discourses to amalgamate, under certain principles of signification. In this way it allows a global, holistic, generative unity, with a diversity of particular concrete applications that create a differentiated synthesis of holistic

8 The holistic principle, as popularly interpreted, allows connections to be made between the part and the whole, with everything inter-related, but at the same time has the parts containing the whole and the whole consisting of the parts. For example, in alternative therapies the physical and the mental are included in the spiritual dimension; the concept of transcendence finds the creative spirit in every cell of the individual; and with respect to the body, everything is related to everything else through the notion of chakras, centers of the channels through which energy is said to flow, and the human body, the earth and the universe are all related to each other through energy flows.

spirituality for every community and for every individual, although it takes selective remnants from distinct traditions, choosing examples that concur with certain basic New Age principals. For this reason it is good to define it as 'syncretism in motion', as Amaral does, as long as it is emphasized that as well as making and unmaking itself on the basis of a meaning-generating grammar, it is a matrix or framework of meaning that translates and resemanticizes practices as holistic (with the whole contained in the particular): whether therapeutic, to heal the spirit and the body, or else psychologizing, to guide one towards personal self betterment and to establish harmony with the cosmos and nature, or else as generators of energy flows and vibration potentialities connecting the inner Me to nature and nature to the Cosmos.

Is There Only One New Age?

Due to its power to make combinations, there is only one corpus of New Age beliefs—though, as mentioned above, it does have a generative grammar of hybrid, holistic and relational meaning. In the spiritual network denominated New Age, various philosophies, esoteric practices and religious beliefs that would normally diverge from each other, come together. A common belief is based on the coming of a New Era, the Age of Aquarius, which will be marked by a radical change of consciousness for individuals, that will provoke a universal change and reestablish harmonious relations with nature and the cosmos. This explains why spiritual seekers do not direct their search everywhere on the Earth but to those corners where the most ancient traditions are found, with their magical and esoteric knowledge supposedly intact and with their proximity to a harmonious relation with nature. As we said, the seekers borrow spiritual remnants and weave them into patchworks presenting new, hybrid and eclectic, versions that combine the oriental with the ethnic, and the esoteric elements of each historical religion with quantum physics, transpersonal psychology, metaphysics, astrology, psychology, etc.

However, although U.S. and European sociology placed an emphasis on the way subjective spiritualities were formed, calling them New Ager belief menus, and highlighted the eclectic accounts of their *à la carte* religiosities; for anthropologists with an interest in Latin America, the main concern has been to see how the New Age sensibility is changing the indigenous or native traditions of America, creating new hybrid currents of ancient ethnic traditions: the Neo-Indian (Galinier and Molinié, 2006), Neo-Mexicanism (De la Peña, 2001 and González, 2006, Rostas, 2008 and De la Torre, 2007), popular Neo-magicalism

(Parker Gumucio, 2001), Neo-esotericism (Magnani, 1999a; De la Torre and Mora, 2001; Mora 2002, De la Torre, 2006) and Neo-shamanism (Magnani, 1999b).

Can We Speak of a Latin American New Age?

We have been able to observe in the course of producing this book that although the New Age arose in industrially highly developed English-speaking countries, with the features of a dynamic movement, proclaiming a culture based on individualism and the Self, cosmopolitanism, universalism and cultural relativism; in the ethnographic studies produced in Latin America we detect that, as it adapts to the practices of popular religion, its features change: it takes root and contributes to recreating territories, it is practiced individually but celebrated collectively, it traditionalizes and re-ethnicizes, and finally it creates hybrids, which can contribute to relativizing frontiers and cultural differences, as well as to essentializing the ethnic, national and racial features of the various religiosities. However, we have also seen that not every country, and not every tradition, or every ethnic group incorporates it in the same way, or with the same force, or is equally receptive to it. For example in Argentina with its predominantly 'white' regime, the movement develops without losing its original character of regarding oriental spiritualities as exotic, and flows out mainly into a circuit of alternative healing. Whereas in Mexico, as a result of its fascination for the Native, the Indian and the Ancestral—on the one hand—it re-ethnicizes, creating new, 'neo-ethnic', identities; while on the other hand it is incorporated into the merchandising of popular magical religiosity, which changes it back into a commercial product, that implies emptying it of its life changing contents that were supposed to promote a New Age, and brings it into the circuit of Neo-esoteric practices (Neo because the logic of the market itself deprives the esoteric of its secretive nature and broadcasts it openly in an exoteric fashion, see Gutiérrez, 2008). For example, in Brazil the ethos of an eclectic religious multiplicity (as claimed in the chapters by Guerriero, Siqueira and Magnani), would seem to make the New Age another fragment of its historical dynamic of fusing the cultures to hand into a mixture of Catholicism, magic, spiritism, Indianism, with a touch of the African, though as Alejandro Frigerio himself demonstrates, there are consistent cultural boundaries in the amalgam with Afro religions. In short I believe it is important to keep in mind, as well as what is attractive from the exoticizing perspective of the New Agers, what it is each culture signifies in its national and regional context. Traditional religiosities are bulwarks for the defense of regional, ethnic and racial differences, and represent value in the patrimonialization of the national sense, and of differentiations and representations within the nation.

So what does the New Age distil down to? It is possible to identify distinct versions of the New Age today. We will focus on describing the modalities that this spiritual matrix has adopted in Latin America, undertake a revision of recent anthropological and sociological papers, and review the contents of the chapters in this book. The emphasis will be on the way in which the New Age hybridizes ancient syncretisms of popular culture, or even resemanticizes nativist versions of indigenous cosmologies and rituals.

An Imported New Age with Shades of the Orient

The Argentinian anthropologist Julia Carozzi detected as early as in the nineteen eighties that many groups in the city of Buenos Aires rejected the label New Age, and chose to call their movement an alternative global therapeutic-spiritual circuit that covered neopaganism, orientalism, self-help, female spirituality, new awareness and complementary therapies (Carozzi, 1999c). In Latin America the New Age developed originally in the capitals and other large cities (Mexico, Guadalajara, Buenos Aires, São Paulo, Santiago) as a network of workshops, therapies, conferences and groups that the author describes as practicing 'gestalt and humanist psychology' and that were 'linked to centers of The Movement and of the New Age in the U.S.A.' (Carozzi, 1999c: 170). In the case of Buenos Aires, those who took part were from the cultural elites: psychologists, artists and intellectuals. Carozzi lists the commonest disciplines found in the alternative complex: natural therapies, vegetarian diets, psychotherapies as distinct from psychoanalysis (which has a strong hegemony in Argentina), esoteric disciplines, oriental techniques of meditation through physical exercise, and alternative medicines, mainly oriental. And to a lesser extent, the growing influence of practices taking their inspiration from the American Indians of the United States, especially from Lakota ceremonies and shamanism (Carozzi, 1999a: 171). In short, we can appreciate from her description, the mark of imported spiritual-therapeutic alternatives, and the absence of local or ethnic options.

The New Age in Mexico was studied in the nineteen nineties by Cristina Gutiérrez Zúñiga, who conducted a pioneering study in the city of Guadalajara, and established that it had arrived in the city in 1970, with the foundation of *la Gran Fraternidad Universal* (GFU), the Universal Great Brotherhood, a New Age organization which linked itself to the countercultural expressions of hippies, psychedelia and rock music.

By the nineties there were already around 70 associations calling themselves New Age offering therapeutic or spiritual services, or that came together around ecological shopping and ecological movements. The greatest influence came from U.S.A. movements such as: Gurummayi-Siddha Yoga, 3HO (Happy, Holy and Healthy Organization), White Lotus Foundation, Elizabeth Claire Prophet and her Church Universal and Triumphant, Solara Star-Borne, and Native American groups from the Lakota tradition. There were also revivalist groups of the 'Sun Dance' (Gutiérrez Zúñiga, 1996: 36). In spite of the North American and Oriental hegemony, it could already be seen that the New Age network was becoming Latinamericanized, with the foundation of groups such as the Gnostic Anthropology Society (*la Asociación Antropología Gnóstica*), and in a most significant way when the GFU was ethnicized, changing into MAIS (*Mancomunidad Iniciática India Solar*, the Native Solar Commonwealth of Initiations) which chose not to look East any more but to search for the knowledge granted to initiates among various ethnic groups of America (Gutiérrez Zúñiga, 1996, García Medina, 2010; and García Medina & Gutiérrez Zúñiga, 2012).

Cosmopolitan Spiritual Seekers as Creators on Their Own of New *Mestizo* Tribes

As we have proposed, New Age agents shared a *habitus* with the new 'cosmopolitan' class that access to globalization brought about (travelers, spiritual seekers, explorers of alternative spiritualities). The New Agers looked for answers beyond the self-same, and directed their steps towards encounters with otherness, especially in those areas of life that had been unappreciated or even denied in the Western view: the East, Nature and the indigenous world.[9]

For the New Agers, certain indigenous traditions represented alternative ways of re-creating a novel sensibility of the sacred that included spiritual, natural, female and ancestral aspects. A species of religious counterculture

9 See Boaventura de Sousa Santos, who explains that the 'discoveries of the empire', which meant the imposition of the power of the West over the Other, had three different ways of differentiating the West from its Other. With the East, the Other was simply a different culture, seen as it were on the other side of a mirror and contrasted with that of the West; with the Savage, the best example was provided by the Indians of America, whose difference from Westerners was gauged in terms of their inferiority; and with Nature (expressing the exterior), the Other was thought of simultaneously as 'a threat and a resource' (Boaventura de Sousa Santos, 2009: 213–222).

that sought for a way out from puritan and institutional Christianity, and also an alternative to the coldness of rational secularism found in the intellectual circles of Europe and the United States. As described by José María Mardones, the New Age sensibility encouraged: 'an open type of religion, which finds traces of the sacred and of mystery on all the rough surfaces of reality' (Mardones, 1994: 162). The spiritual seekers or New Ager agents undertook their researches into esoteric secrets and Oriental therapies, principally from India and Tibet, and in parallel, through encounters with shamanic magic, at first with North American Indians and subsequently with those of the South.

The metaphor of religious pollination, *butinage religieux*, adapted by Edio Soares (2009) to picture religious experience in Brazil as a journey during which the religious process gains momentum, is highly suggestive because it illustrates the similarity between New Agers and the bees or hummingbirds who not only seek their food in flowers and create their own special dish of different types of pollen and nectar, but also pick up some of the pollen that they brush against, and, as they fly from flower to flower, take it from one plant to another, fertilizing some and creating mutations and hybrids between others. Like these pollinizers, the New Age seekers not only attend rituals and pick up remnants of the religious traditions that they visit in order to form their own *à la carte* menus, but also, through their journeyings, weave connections, create circuits and form networks of cultural exchange.[10] These circuits and assimilations create cultural transformations and exchanges, and new hybrids amongst the native groups and communities connected to the New Age network.

In this way, the pollinizers of a global consciousness and a universal consciousness, create holistic analogies as they practice their rituals and incorporate symbols and knowledge from different cultures: Celtic, Indigenous, Buddhist, Sufi, Pagan, or Esoteric; while establishing alternative circuits between distinct fields: astrology, medicine, artistic performances, psychology, religion and various alternative techniques for health and physical development (see the chapter by Cristina Gutiérrez Zúñiga).

An example of this mediation is that testified to by Alberto Ruz (Neo-Indian Cosmopolitan Mexican), who is currently the central actor joining networks of alternative consciousness and spirituality to a larger intercontinental connection (see De la Torre and Gutiérrez Zúñiga, 2011b). In his memoirs, Ruz tells of when he lived in California and belonged to tribes of the Beat generation, who

10 This idea is complemented by the proposal made by José Guilherme Cantor Magnani about the way in which the tracks followed go into making the circuits of Neo-esoteric consumption and a Neo-esoteric market (Cantor Magnani, 1999).

were the countercultural movement in the U.S.A. after the Second World War, and got into exploring psychotropic experiences in the late fifties. Soon afterwards he joined the Rainbow network in the U.S.A. and then went on to follow the path of spiritual seeking:

> When some members of the tribes got tired of walking the streets of the decrepit urban districts and of rolling down the long straight highways from coast to coast, they crossed over the tequila frontier into the north of Mexico and hitched themselves a ride, to the beat of the blues, to Mexico City. Hungry for new emotions they experimented with 'devil's weed' [thorn apple, Jimson's weed, *datura stramonium*] and with the 'seeds of the Virgin' [type of morning glory, *turbina corymbosa*, ololiuhqui i.e. seeds of the coaxihuitl] and discovered the ancient knowledge that comes with taking peyote and magic mushrooms. The 'Dharma Bums' began to walk the paths of the Hopi, the Navajo and the Lakota. They smoked the pipe of peace with the shamans, sang in the Temazcals (sweat lodges), and were initiated into the sacred ways of the American Indian Church.
>
> On their journeys of initiation, the new white Indians learned the way of peyote from the Huichol [Wixáritari] healers in the hills, and Mexican medicine women taught them the way of the 'heavenly mantle' [another type of morning glory, *ipomea violacea*, tlitliltzin], and of 'the seeds of the Virgin'. Eventually their journeyings led them to the forests of Amazonia, where the old men of the Tukano indians taught them the sacred uses of 'yopo' and 'ayahuasca'.
>
> The apprentices returned to their native lands much changed after their trip to the South. Now their culture was not just white and western, but had become mestizo (…) Some of them crossed the great waters and started their pilgrimage across the deserts of North Africa and Asia to spend time in the temples and mosques of Morocco, Turkey and India, as well as the schools of traditional knowledge in Japan and Nepal.
>
> RUZ BUENFIL, 1992: 76

From this brief first hand biographical account by one of the principal nodal actors of the most relevant worldwide New Age network, who in the course of his journeys has built spiritual bridges between United States hippies and Oriental gurus, between alternative communes—better known in the eighties as utopian—in California and in Europe, between Mexican New Agers and the chieftains of Indian tribes in North America and Mexico, between traditional Aztec dancers in Mexico and the larger Oriental spiritual community in Spain, between Tibetan monks and the Neo-Indian mestizos of America,[11] we can see two processes. The first is the dynamic in which the spiritual seekers convert themselves, after their contact with, and learning from, the native groups, into eclectic and hybrid tribes, and pass from being initiates to being masters. An example of this is the 'MAIS' tribes (acronym for *Mancomunidad de la America India Solar*, also known as *mais* or *maisales* belonging to the Indianist version of the GFU Universal Great Brotherhood), another, the Hispanekas (Spaniard-Aztecs) in Spain (De la Torre and Gutiérrez Zúñiga, 2011b; and De la Torre and Campechano, in this book); others are the *reginos* (followers of 'Regina') and the devotees of a Toltec lineage (synthesis of the races), the Neo-Indians, the Neo-shamans, the Neo-Incas, the Neo-Mayas, etc. Many of these cosmopolitan and *mestizo* tribes have designed their traditions and imaginary lineages themselves. The other dynamic, coming from the same contact, is found in the renewal of traditions, uses and meanings in those native communities that currently have intense interactions and exchanges with the New Age and Neo-esoteric circuits. These occur either because they have become sites of interest for spiritual tourism, as is the case of the Lakota in the U.S.A., the Huichol in the Western Sierra of Mexico, the Tarahumara in the North of Mexico, the Lacandona of the Mayan forest in Chiapas, the Incas of Peru and the Indians of the Amazonian forest, etc.; or else because their rituals, symbols and areas of knowledge circulate as merchandise in a large worldwide market of native New Age spirituality and of magical Neo-esotericism, where even Afro-American practices find a place, as happens with the ceremonies included in psychotherapy offered in France (Teisenhoffer, 2007). This is how the relocalizations occur, and with them the resemanticizing that these processes provoke (Argyriadis, De la Torre, Gutiérrez Zúñiga and Aguilar Ros, 2008). From their interactions new hybrids are generated, between the New Age and native or traditional culture. Hence the prefix Neo that they have been given, used to qualify the traditional subjects, the most studied of these being:

The Neo-Indians: Neo-Mexicans, Neo-Incas, Neo-Mayans and Neo-Afro-Latin Americans

All these are names used to recognize the cosmopolitan spiritual seekers who have stitched together an ethnic identity for themselves, and created an imagined lineage for their ancestral spiritual inheritance, while reviving the memory of rejected traditions in the name of rescuing them. The appropriation of some ancestral lineages is preferred to that of others, for example the Neo-Mexicans tend to universalize the cosmovisions and rituals associated with

11 See nodal actors in De la Torre and Gutiérrez Zúñiga, 2011.

'Pre-Hispanic' reminiscences, particularly through the practice of the Dance (De la Peña, 2001), the Neo-Andeans recreate Inca culture (Molinié), and there are the 'Hispanekas', Spanish hippies who have adopted the Conchero tradition of the Dancers (assumed to have been Aztecs). The name Neo-Indian stands for the movement of the mestizo actors which is:

> on the one hand, what makes up for the renewal of an obligatory inheritance, dissimulated in the urban fabric, in what Bonfil (1988) would call 'deep Mexico' and Valcárcel (1927) 'the telluric Andes', that is, everything that is reactivated from a tradition whose Pre-Hispanic origin is hidden, inhibited by the process of Westernization. Thus—and this is why the Neo-indian question is also complex—it turns out that among the new followers of the movement, some who proclaim themselves to be 'Indians' (in so far as their ancestors are authentic speakers of an Amerindian language) have chosen the path of return to the local and in this case, to learn again a language that had become foreign to them.
>
> GALINIER AND MOLINIÉ, 2006

Jacques Galinier (2005) also mentions that the Neo-Indian movement subtracts the Mesoamerican culture from its place, turning it into nomadic symbolic capital; and points out that it is contributing to a reinvention of the memory of 'high civilizations' recounted through a history ground into powder and reworked in the framework of a borderless New Age.

One of the questions that arise is: What type of ethnic identity is created by New Age reinterpretations? Do they contribute to politicizing or depoliticizing reality? Do they contribute to recovering lost memories or to fictionalizing reality? In a case study of the appearance of Andean New Age in the context of a ritual invented in Cusco, the author interprets the movement as a new way of colonizing and exploiting, and concludes with her answer: 'If the Andeans had their lands, their minerals, their work and also their history taken away from them through the Inca-izing of their traditions, now they have to offer their telluric energy and thereby transform themselves back into providers again, though this time of virtual goods only, but still generating the wealth of those who exploit them' (Molinié, in this book). For their part, the Mayan movement in Guatemala, in a very different way, give us their answer, in which the recovery of the millenarian vision of a changing era is shared by the New Agers and the Mayan tradition, and:

> represents an opportunity to think of a politically and cosmically possible utopia, that forms part of a greater, more important and more

> wideranging transformation. From the questioning, shared by Mayan activists, and proponents and followers of the New Age, of the modern Western status quo, comes an alternative political-spiritual agenda, of a personal or collective type, that makes it possible to change the current direction of humanity which will occur with the coming of *Oxlajuj b'aqtun*-2012.
>
> BASTOS, ZAMORA and TALLY, in this book

These two cases show us the ambivalence of the ideological and political effects that the New Age is having on ethnic groups.

It is important to note that not all the Indians have a spiritual attraction, just as not all the Oriental peoples were made out to be exotic by the New Age. Those who stand out are the Indians connected to the great empires of Pre-Hispanic America: the Mexicas, the Mayans and the Incas. Their ceremonial centers (like Machu Pichú, Teotihuacán and Chichen Itzá) and natural sanctuaries (cf. Lake Atitlán or the Wirikuta pilgrimage site) have recently been reconverted into new sanctuaries where Neo-pagan cults are practiced. For example, on the days of the solstices and equinoxes, millions of celebrants gather to 'get charged with solar energies'. In Cusco, Peru, Antoinette Molinié has discovered how the notion of 'energy' spread about by the New Age is translating and transforming the contents of Andean ideas, and she concludes that: 'The way globalization proceeds here is by homogenizing indigenous concepts'. Susanna Rostas studied a failed attempt to fuse Neo-Mexicanist Conchero dances with some Sufi dances (Rostas, 2008), while Renée de la Torre and Cristina Gutiérrez Zúñiga have looked into the Neo-Mexicanist movement and New Age circuits; analyzing particular circuits and nodal points of Neo-Mexicanism, which paradoxically stretch the whole distance from contact with Lakota traditions and their effects on the essentialization of the various versions of national and racial recovery of Aztec ancestry, to the opposite, in eclectic versions where Mexicanism can simultaneously experience hybridism with Tibetan Buddhism, which in turn gets a fresh look at itself from its meeting with the Lakota. In this book there is also a chapter on 'Hispaneka' Neo-Mexicanism, which has traveled the world wide electronic web not only to enlarge its information networks but also to practice its art (making an analogy between surfing the web and practicing the Dance of spiritual conquest) so as to contribute to its transformative evolution. As the authors explain:

> The dance was used as a matrix that would make navigating on the internet a metaphor for the Dance, as though it were a ritual activity making technology holy, linked to the notion of the noosphere, the network of

> light or of cosmic energy, the Planet Gaia as a field where flowers and songs are sown, and the idea of Four Winds or Four Directions, and so on. This idea, in the light of the holistic concept of a new era, contributes to the development and evolution of consciousness, whether internally (for the user) or cosmically (for the web).
>
> DE LA TORRE AND CAMPECHANO, in this book

Metaphorizing contributes to giving a new functional meaning to the practice of navigating on the internet, which it reinterprets as a way of freeing the networks of the web from their technological supports and transforming them into universal energy. Furthermore, this method of procedure is not closed to other interpretations, such as the interpretive frame of thinking of reality as virtual, which is capable of creating new narratives: one of them a belief in the Matrix. This belief readapts the meaning and the appropriation of reality through the fusion of certain spiritual techniques and practices incorporated previously into the New Age.

Nevertheless, although the postmodern eclecticism characteristic of Neo-Mexicanism and New Age appear to have no borders, in this book attention is given also to the tensions and the limits of the universalizing re-interpretation put into operation by the New Age matrix, because as it reanchors itself in syncretic practices and in the search for indigenous ancestral lineages, it comes up against the historical tensions accompanying the syncretic battles that set the limits of local and national identities in Mexico, Guatemala or in Peru. As Gutiérrez Zúñiga emphasizes, after comparing distinct therapeutic appropriations of the Mexican dance, the portability of the rituals is delimited by socio cultural contexts.

Neo-shamanism or Urban Shamanism

These names concern shamanic practices (of communication with the world of spirits) that were intimately related to the forms of transmitting knowledge of the indigenous communities, and have today been integrated into commercial Neo-esoteric circuits where magic is sold along with recipes for personal improvement (see Magnani, in this book). While traditionally, shamanism was a gift bestowed exclusively on certain members of a tribe or ethnic group, today it can be acquired through courses and workshops. Another difference is that Neo-shamanism follows the logic of magical efficacy and seeks to give quick answers to the problems suffered (as Magnani points out). One feature of Neo-shamanism is its de-territorialization, generated by the migrations and diasporas that relocate the shamans and take them away from their places of origin, thereby detaching them from the structural conditions in which the indigenous populations live (see the notion of exo-shamanism by Galinier in this book). Some of them, those most recognized by New Age practitioners, reside in ashrams and New Age communes in various parts of the world: Groisman, (2009) and Sarrazin, (2008) have studied the shamans of Santo Daime in Holland and the shamans of yajé ingestion in Bogotá, Colombia; and the export of sweat lodge rituals and the Sun Dance ceremony deriving from the Lakota Sioux tribes of North America have been studied by Csordas, (2009) and Arias Yerena, (2011). What Galinier notes is that these dynamics are decontextualizing the shamanic tradition, as it is taken out of its traditional role in settling local conflicts and powers.

The search for shamanic experience has induced an intensification of spiritual tourism to the villages of native groups, who are constantly being visited by New Agers and hippies in order to have exceptional experiences or to be intitiated as Neo-shamans. Examples of this are provided by the Huichol pilgrimages to the ceremony in Wirikuta of hunting for the peyote, and the Neo-Mexican reconversion of the Holy Week ceremonies of San Andrés Cohamiata (Aguilar Ros, 2008), which are having an impact on the hybridizing of the local traditions, as they induce the ethnic groups or their spiritual specialists to develop a tendency to adapt themselves more to the fictionalizing of their own rituals, which are no longer generated in accordance with the uses and needs of the community, but in order to be observed and experienced by the New Ager tourists. Once it has been placed on offer as another item of merchandise on the 'exotics' stand (Gutiérrez Zúñiga, 2008), or on the therapeutic circuit (as Gutiérrez Zúñiga shows in her chapter), the tradition no longer just lives alongside other traditions; it acquires other functional meanings and is reinterpreted in the light of certain ideas taken up by the New Age, such as: protection from bad vibrations, contact with spirits, the consulting of oracles, integrated and holistic healing, spells, balancing energies or the chakras, etc. (Magnani, 1999a; Mora, 2002 and De la Torre, 2012c). Many rituals have also been incorporated into the worldwide market of spa hotels where the guests are offered, as relaxing and purifying treatments, attending a Temazcal sweat lodge, or a choice of techniques of popular medicine from the massage menu (De la Torre, 2007). These mediations are not only relocalizing traditions in new territories, new fields and circuits; they are also dislocating them from their ethnic supports, because, as Rodríguez and Aguilar Ros show in their chapters, the new actors are initiated as specialists in the sacred or as neo-shamans and then compete with the old religious specialists. At the same time the intensity of their interaction with the circuits of worldwide spirituality is leading to re-signifyings, not only through the adoption of the tradition by cosmopolitan users, but also through the processes of adapting the performance at the core of the tribal ceremonies, where the ceremony is retouched to accord with the expectations of the tourists and consumers, that way creating an artificial sense of its theatrical essentialization, or the ritual is converted into something else by adapting the ethnic languages to an ecumenical, hybrid and eclectic language, with which a *bricolage* of universal wisdoms is concocted. Two examples of these processes are the adaptation by a Mazatec natural healer who wished to give herself a leading role in the council of thirteen grandmothers, studied by Rodríguez, and the case of a Huichol *mara'akame* who has worked with the Universal Great Brotherhood as a master of Huichol wisdom. Even though, as Aguilar Ros put it succinctly, in the case of interaction between the Wixarika *mara'akame*, or Huichol shaman, and the Neo-Mexicanist dancers in Tecate, Baja California, shamanism would seem to be a frame alignment (Snow, 1986), that is to say, a cultural element linking the New Agers and the Huichol on the basis of an appreciation of nature, spirituality and the supposed ancestry of the mestizos; nevertheless, in spite of the efforts that they made to join in with the Huichol tradition, the New Agers came up against barriers, tensions and contradictions, for example between their style of vegetarian natural living, and the ritual sacrifice of a deer. And correspondingly, this ethnography shows, that while for the Huichol the ritual of enrooting by the god Takutsi means vinculation to the line of ancestors, the Neo-Indians see it as an enrooting ceremony on a spiritual path that does not imply a lifelong commitment.

Neo-Esotericism

Separated by Cristian Parker into popular and magical, the Neo-esoteric is a current in which esoteric and New Age notions are re-signified on the basis of frames of interpretation belonging to Latin American popular syncretism (Parker, 2001: 8). As described by De la Torre (2007), popular Neo-esotericism 'is linked most strongly to a massive reformulation of the popular beliefs and practices connected to traditional beliefs in magic: herbal lore, magic, healing, spiritism, indigenous-popular Catholicism and sorcery. More than just offering a new life style, or an alternative life style (as the New Age originally proposed), it offers magic solutions to problems people suffer from (for example, with amulets, talismans and images of saints to give protection against the evil eye or to get a good job, or a spray for invoking spirits and getting the love of the man who is wanted).' The Neo-esoteric circuits combine objects and teachings having different religious and cultural origins, where items that are indigenous, or come from popular syncretic Catholicism, or popular medicine, live alongside Oriental ideas of karma, of yoga, or of reincarnation, and become an extra condiment for these notions. These circuits offer their wares mainly, but not exclusively, in cities, at esoteric fairs (studied extensively in Brazil by Magnani, 1999b and Guerriero, 2003), in supermarkets, folk remedy stores, herbal dispensaries, on television channels and on the internet (see De la Torre and Mora, 2001 and De la Torre, 2006). To illustrate the amalgams and surprising hybrids that New Age commercialization can make out of a key symbol of Mexican popular religiosity, such as the figure of La Santa Muerte (Holy Death), which has a syncretic origin in popular Catholicism and Pre-Hispanic Neo-paganism, Michalik (2011) explains how a recently invented symbol, but one that enjoys a great deal of popularity, has become a dominant symbol condensing various religious meanings, that appear to contradict each other. La Santa Muerte represents a symbol that is associated with Pre-Hispanic reminiscences, but is ritualized within the paraphernalia that belong to popular Catholicism and permit a syncretism with the Mexicanism movements, with Santeria and with New Ager seekers. Further, this symbol has been placed in a Neo-esoteric circuit that commercializes it as a symbol with magical and energetic potentialities exchangeable with other symbols on offer in the New Age spiritual market: divinations, protective amulets, energy cleansings, etc. The work published in the present volume on the cult of the Mayan Saint Simón, or Max Simón (Pédron), explains how popular religiosity appropriates to itself and resignifies certain symbolic goods that circulated as New Age or Neo-esoteric merchandise, but then came to be used and reinterpreted in accordance with the symbolic efficacy of magic, healing and popular Catholicism. These chapters show us the limits of the New Age. And the interest of including them lies in their making it plain that not everything that appears to come from the New Age—as Frigerio puts it—can be considered New Age. The various studies would seem to point out, that at the point where magic, popular Catholicism and esotericism meet, the New Age circulates in the form of an object, a good or a merchandise decontextualized from its own matrix of meaning. And they make it evident, as Sanchis (2008) demonstrated convincingly, that these syncretic molds of popular culture in Latin America retain their pertinence by collecting and recycling the elements that are present, in order to appropriate them in their own way and erase the original foreignness of the other. Finally, these works confirm that it is necessary to distinguish between the New Age and popular Neo-esoterica, promoted more and more as magical religious merchandise. This constant overlapping of a New Ageing of the popular, and a traditionalizing of New Age elements, is provoked in large measure because the New needs to anchor itself to instances of popular religious tradition but at the same time Tradition needs to make its roots looser in order to establish continuities in a changing world determined by mobilities (De la Torre, 2012c).

CHAPTER 2

Logics and Limits of New Age Appropriations: Where Syncretism Comes to an End

Alejandro Frigerio

This chapter starts with an observation and a doubt. The former is of how the New Age, which has been considered a paradigmatic example of contemporary syncretism or hybridism, systematically excludes several of the most dynamic forms of religion found in the different countries of Latin America. The long list of religious, spiritual or therapeutic practices that anthropologists and sociologists are prone to draw up in order to demonstrate the eclecticism (if not the nonsense) of the New Age, hardly ever includes Pentecostalism, devotion to popular saints, or Afro-American religions. It therefore becomes obvious that while some are invited into this variegated 'spiritual supermarket' (Van Hove, 1999), others are excluded.

The doubt that follows this observation is whether the blindness of academia to the syncretic capacity of the New Age—in a continent characterized by this cultural dynamic—has not led to its neglecting to study the equally real and important logics of exclusion, with the subsequent result of a 'conceptual overestimation' in drawing the specific contours of the phenomenon to be examined.

In the following pages, therefore, I will develop a reflection on why specific religious practices and beliefs appear to revolve outside the orbit of the New Age, or, following Champion (1993), say why they do not form a part of the 'mystical-esoteric nebula'. To synthesize, I will sketch a reflection on the *limits* of appropriation or reinterpretation by the New Age, with a special interest in its relation to the distinct Latin American religious traditions.

The Limits of New Age Appropriation or Reinterpretation

In this work I will argue that as academics we should not allow ourselves to be obfuscated by the apparently infinite capacity of what is usually called the New Age, to mix up and incorporate elements having diverse origins. Many times this potential for unlimited aggregation is the product of a weak construction of the object of study. As academics, we have grouped together practices that *seem to us* to belong to the New Age, on the basis of common sense

 | DOI 10.1163/9789004316485_004

rather than on the basis of a scrupulous and consistent academic conceptual construct. This makes it necessary to recognize the various efforts that have already been made to help find a workable and heuristically productive definition, and to go on from there to making a more coherent construction of this object of study, in order to be able to begin to think in a more specific and more detailed way about the types of incorporations that have occurred (or failed to happen), and about the types of passages and articulations, between elements having different religious origins, and the New Age movement. We will then be in a better position to understand the *logics* of New Age appropriation (of how it becomes a specific socio-religious movement) and above all to visualize, to comprehend and to distinguish also the *limits* of this mixture or appropriation.

We will be able, above all, to differentiate: appropriations (what really enters *into* the circuit on a more or less regular basis) from borrowings (the symbols or images from other traditions that come in only *sporadically* in the *bricolages* that only *some* of the practitioners make up) and the influences that the New Age may exercise over other religious groups—some of whose practitioners might adopt a 'New Age style' (Amaral, 1999), without their religious group entering the New Era circuit.

Especially in Latin America, it is necessary to distinguish 'New Age eclecticism' from the usual syncretism that is ubiquitous in the region. In a culture in which religious syncretism is a fact of life, it is urgent to comprehend better its New Age version. How is New Age syncretism to be distinguished from the syncretism that for centuries has characterized popular religion and Latin American folk healing? When would the syncretism before us be '*Latin American*', and when would it be a *New Age* syncretism? The construction of the object of study must be according to the strictest and most coherent criteria possible; otherwise we run the risk of seeing the New Era everywhere (every example of syncretism becoming a sign of the presence of the New Age), or of seeing it nowhere (so New Age no longer exists). Along with other authors who have studied the subject more exhaustively and with whom I will be conversing in these pages, I propose that there are certain features that distinguish the beliefs and practices of the New Age from those that do not belong so clearly to this movement.[1] The tenor of these features means that there can be New Age and Non-New Age versions of what nominally

1 Here we follow the insights developed by María Julia Carozzi in the various works found in our bibliography, comparing our point of view with that of other Latin American and European authors, and also considering the contributions made by those who took part in the seminar from which this book developed.

would be the same practice, just as there are *New Age uses* of therapeutic forms and religious forms (or of therapeutic-religious forms) that would not necessarily consider themselves to be New Age (e.g. reiki, or some schools of Buddhism).

I therefore wish to emphasize that the capacity for mixing, of what we call the New Age, is not unlimited nor is it haphazard—it is indeed *wideranging*, but clearly *heading in a particular direction* and therefore also *exclusive*. In the extremely long lists that we sociologists or anthropologists like to draw up of the various New Age practices, there is never any mention of Pentecostalism, Charismatic Renewal, Kardecist Spiritism, Afro-American religions, or devotion to popular saints as being part of the New Age circuit.

We may indeed have New Age ideas being diffused *within* some of these groups—as the work of Carlos Steil (in this book) on a charismatic group shows, and as the work of Jungblut (2006) shows for Pentecostals. However, as we have proposed so far, this would be better seen as an *influence*, as neither Charismatics nor Pentecostals entered the New Age circuit in Brazil—a fact which Magnani explains in his chapter in this volume, and which other articles, in the collection edited by Carozzi (1999a), have also shown to be true.

There might perhaps be a *borrowing* of some Afro-American image or symbol—which the work by Nahayeilli Juárez Huet in this book notes would seem to apply to the case of Changó Macho—but more generally it would just be part of the *personal* bricolage of some of the practitioners who, we can say, belong to the New Age circuit (always depending on how we define it). But these borrowings are few in number, and affect only a couple of Afro-American deities (generally Changó or Iemanjá) and not all of them.

All of these groups (Pentecostals, Charismatics, Afro-Brazilian) are certainly *not* within the New Age circuit. Hardly anyone claims that passing through one of these groups was part of the story of their personal growth: they do not provide New Age credentials. The work by Magnani in this book points this out clearly: in spite of their widespread popularity all over Brazil, they do not form part of the Neo-esoteric circuit that the author describes with precision.

Illusions of Homogeneity and Heterogeneity in the Study of Religious Groups and Movements

A number of scholars have discussed the difficulties involved in defining the New Age (Champion, 1993; Carozzi, 1995; Gutiérrez Zúñiga, 1996; Van Hove, 1999; York, 2001; and others)—and yet, some of them coincide more than is generally recognized in the way in which they characterize it.[2] There is no doubt that there are complications in trying to conceptualize the New Age as an object of study because of the number and the variety of religious and therapeutic groups included, which can vary not only from one social context to another (between countries) but also at different times in the same country, because as one discipline becomes fashionable, others cease to be popular (Carozzi, 2007; De la Torre, 2011). But let us remember, in case we should have to (and sometimes it seems that we must): any definition is not so much an attempt to reflect reality exhaustively as a working tool that makes it possible to comprehend it and analyze it better.

One should not necessarily need to cover absolutely all the practices and beliefs involved in the object of study, or agree with all the identifications made by different individuals—which would be impossible *regardless* of the religious group studied. Would any definition of Catholicism be able to cover the diversity of currents inside *just this one* institution? Or be able to take account of the extra-institutional beliefs of the majority of its adherents? Would any definition of Pentecostalism be able to include all the different types of belief and worship within it? Or account for the multiple variants branded as 'Afro-American religions'? This is a problem academics have with *all* religious groups.[3]

However, these religions do at least have certain features—including our academic preconceptions of them—that allow us to obtain an 'illusion of homogeneity' with respect to their practices and beliefs.[4] Principally, they have *centers* (using the word in a geometrical and at the same time organizational sense): churches or sects, more or less organized groups of people, which we can take as *representative* of the *whole* that we analyze under the name of

2 For example, in spite of having popularized the—in my opinion—misleading concept of a 'mystical-esoteric nebula', which tends to be taken as evidence of the indeterminate nature of the object of study, Champion (1993) offers a characterization of the term that shares some of the 'key features' proposed by York (1999) and some of the features listed by Melton (1990), Carozzi (1995, 2000) and Gutiérrez Zúñiga (1996).

3 It would be impossible to make a complete list of all the varieties of syncretism produced in the religions of African origin only in *Brazil*. For a long time academics solved this problem by taking a small group of places of worship—those considered 'pure', and representative of the surviving African tradition—as a model for what would be regional varieties: 'Candomblé', 'Xangô', 'Minas drum', 'Batuque'. The rest were ignored (or else scorned) as degenerate forms of little interest. On the construction of 'Nagô purity' see principally Dantas (1988) and Capone (1999).

4 A more moderate argument would be to say that they provide us with an illusion of homogeneity that is *excessively* out of proportion to the *real* degree of homogeneity found.

the religion. This allows us to analyze larger or smaller deviations from the center—in institutionalized groups like the Charismatic Renovation, or in groups having extremely variable degrees of relation with the Institution, as would be the case of popular Catholicism or 'popular religiosity'.

The individual *bricolages* that exist in *all* these religions (in some more than in others) may be ignored, or considered of little importance, as a function of this illusion of homogeneity provided by the institutional center.[5] We know from our day to day experience that the beliefs of most of those who define themselves as Catholics cover an unlimited variety that we ignore because of their *social* identification as 'Catholic'.[6] A *social* identification that, as I argue in another work (Frigerio, 2007), tends to not matter very much in the real life of individuals, in the scheme of their personal identifications, and *says nothing about their true* (in the sense of *effective* and *daily*) *religious practices*. Giving this diversity too much weight would of course make it almost impossible to say anything about it. Therefore we recognize, at most, the various currents within *the institution*—so as to be able to account for the diversity without making it unmanageable. But we should be honest and admit that this is simply an act of exorcism, excluding the vast and real diversity that makes up the social collective we call 'Catholics'.

In the case of the New Age, there are two things that preclude us from the 'illusion of homogeneity' which socially organized religions of the church or sect type provide. Firstly, there is no *institutional center* that allows us to anchor our perception of reality and use it as a synecdoche—naming the part to refer to the whole—, which is something we usually do in the study of other religions. Secondly, the organized groups that do exist in the New Age circuit do not generally fit the organizational type of sect or church. As shown by Magnani (1999a), the organizational forms—of various types of complexity, with different forms of sociability and levels of gregariousness—may be described better

5 It is clear that for those who participate in New Age circuits, personal syncretism is valued and encouraged, while for those who identify themselves as 'Catholics' it is not, at least by the institution. In the first case, there is an 'ethos of bricolage' (Van Hove, 1999), and in the second case, condemnation of any such thing. Which does not stop it from effectively existing in Catholic contexts everywhere—something we will have to take into account with greater precision if we are to produce realistic studies of our religious realities.

6 I prefer to speak of 'social identification' rather than 'social identity' because using a verbal form rather than the abstract noun gives a more exact idea of the contingent, contextual, strategic and performative character of the *acts of identification* (that are generally essentialized as 'identities').

as 'initiation societies', 'integrated centers', 'specialized centers' 'individualized spaces' or 'sales outlets'.[7]

Thirdly, the social identifications made by New Age individuals are even more slippery and unstable than they are found to be in the more studied groups. Many people with beliefs and practices that we can call New Age have never identified themselves as such, or chose to stop doing so when the name became more popular, and in some cases (Argentina, for example) acquired a stigma (Frigerio, 1993). When the expression gained currency, a number of practitioners of arts that were even more disapproved of, adopted it, because it held advantages over other options (witchdoctor healing, magic)—even though their practices would hardly be included in what is considered New Age academically.

I suggest that if the academic overvaluing of the concepts (and institutions) of 'church' and 'sect' have created an *illusion of homogeneity*, the large variety of forms of organization found in the New Age circuits (of each country) provide us with the opposite: an 'illusion of hetereogeneity' that hardly helps our understanding of the phenomenon. This excessive dependence of the theory on particular forms of social organization as providing the social support for what we call 'religion' also makes it hard for us to appreciate the *religious* character of New Age. Our usual definitions of religion—generally centered implicitly, as we said, on the typology of church or sect—underestimate the degree to which beliefs and practices are shared, and also their systematic coherence. Accustomed to relating religious beliefs principally to the organizational forms 'church' and 'sect' (or in the case of anthropology, to shamans or 'traditional' religious specialists), we find all others to be too imperfectly religious, and prefer to use the terms 'religiosity' or 'spirituality' etc.[8]

---

7 This is the way the author characterizes the groups forming the 'Neo-esoteric circuit' (a term he prefers to New Age) of São Paulo. Analysis of the relation between religious beliefs and the types of social organization that can support them and transmit them has for too long been conditioned by a preponderance of the church-sect typology deriving from European religious traditions (Campbell, 1978), in spite of the efforts by recognized scholars to transcend it and propose other classifications that can provide a number of terms that come closer to what we find in empirical studies of new religious movements. The notions of *audience cults, client cults* and *cult movements* held by Stark and Bainbridge 1979 and of *clinics* used by Lofland and Richardson (1984) might help with improving our understanding of the organizational forms found in the various circuits that serve to sustain the New Age movement. The (correct) idea that it consists of 'a network' (York, 1999: 74) does not however specify the *type* of associations that are *placed in relation with each other* by this means.

8 The frequent inclusion of New Age as a type of 'religion of mysticism' (Campbell, 1978), called 'radical religious individualism' by Troeltsch (1931: 377), leads to underrating the

For all these reasons, rather than dismissing the reality of New Age or postulating it as essentially ungraspable—if not *incomprehensible*—it is necessary to make an extra effort to conceptualize it, and especially to be academically coherent when applying our definitions to its study. The confection of a list of specific religious, therapeutic or esoteric *practices* that would make up the New Age does not seem a very profitable approach to the subject, because of its contextual and temporal variability. It would be more fruitful to identify the *underlying basic beliefs* that make it possible to put some or all of them to a determined use.[9] This New Age use of beliefs is distinct from other uses that might be made of the same practices, which would not be New Age. Pursuing the same argument, there are versions of astrology and tarot that are New Age, and there are versions that are not (Melton, 1992; Carozzi, 1995). There may be New Age uses of a shaman just as there are purely magical-healing ones.[10] In the latter case, only a physical cure is sought, while in the former, the aim is a healing that is conceptualized in a more holistic and integrated way as leading

existence of, and the need for, loose associations that the individual can circulate in and out of without necessarily having to become a member of the congregation, that are still very much indispensable for 'transforming the therapeutic, religious and pedagogical situations that they organize, in a consistent manner, (meaning that) these situations should be interpreted in a way that is different to the usual and is congruent with itself, as examples of self-knowledge and self-transformation' (Carozzi, 2000: 31). As the author points out, it is these multiple—albeit transitory—forms of organization found in the alternative circuit that manage to create new ways of interpreting and of organizing experience. The new meanings are not created solely through the discourse of the leaders, but also in the actions taken by the different groups processing the (religious or therapeutic) experience in the same direction as that proposed by the interpretive framework that they operate in (Carozzi, 2000).

9 A paragraph from the writings of York (2001: 363) gives an idea of the limited scope of substantive definitions: 'The phenomenon of the New Age is hard to describe and even harder to evaluate. It has been summed up as "a mixture of pagan religions, oriental philosophies and esoteric/psychic phenomena"' (York, 1995: 34). Williams Sims Bainbridge points out that the forms of religious movement most closely associated with New Age are the Esoteric, the Neo-pagan and the Oriental (Bainbridge, 1997: 386). For Hildegard Van Hove, the field of New Age spirituality is an inspired and eclectic mixture of Oriental religions, Western esoteric traditions and psychology, at times more integrated than at others (Van Hove, 1999). However, for the literary critic Harold Bloom, the New Age is simply 'a permanently entertaining saturnalia of ill-defined desires' (Bloom, 1996: 18).

10 As clearly pointed out by De la Torre (2006: 39), it is necessary to distinguish between 'New Age and Neo-esoteric supply, each with differentiated contents and each directed at a variety of consumers'. The same spiritual discipline can have different contents, emphases and objectives, depending on its orientation towards one circuit or another.

to an evolution of consciousness. To take another example, Zen Buddhism can also be used in a New Age way (as another tool in the multiple kit used for developing one's consciousness) or, on the contrary, it can be a new religious movement (or sect, in the sociological sense of the term), to which the practitioner is committed as the *exclusive* and *only* way to satori. Therefore it is not the presence—so to say, the nominal presence—of specific practices that indicates New Age hybridism, but the way in which they are used or recombined, in accordance with determined underlying common principles.

There are a number of features—about which there is more consensus than is usually admitted—that, taken together, make it possible to identify an interpretive scheme of the nature of Man and his place and purpose in the world, an interpretive frame shared—to a greater or lesser extent—by individuals who take part in religious/therapeutic circuits that have been denominated 'alternative' (Carozzi, 2000) or 'Neo-esoteric' (Magnani 1999a). The validity of this interpretive frame allows the circuits to be journeyed through in a specific way, forming a New Age movement that can (and should) be distinguished analytically from other religious or magic forms—and even from other ways of participating in the same circuits. The awareness of this frame makes it possible to order and comprehend better the beliefs, practices and experiences of those who benefit from an impressive quantity of religious/therapeutic expressions that are grouped by circuit—different circuits in each society—and are in turn refracted in different personal trajectories.

The acknowledgement of this interpretive frame allows for a better understanding of a 'New Age style' (Amaral, 1999) of appropriations and reinterpretations that is differentiated from others that are, more or less clearly, *not* New Age.

The Interpretive Frame of the New Age Movement

Referring to the work of Amaral (1999) that defines the New Age as a 'syncretism in motion', De la Torre affirms that this feature cannot be its defining particularity. She reasons as follows:

> We cannot rest with this definition, because (...) any hybridizing impulse could then be regarded as New Age. So what is it that makes a kind of amalgam of different cultural textures become New Age? Maybe what gives it the ability to synthesize is not so much a unified discourse, as a matrix of meaning, in other words an 'interpretive frame', based on the

> principle of 'holism', on the basis of which different cultural and/or spiritual aspects are appropriated, translated and refunctionalized from others, in order to make them its own. The New Age is not just a set of odds and ends of juxtaposed contents, but above all a matrix of meaning which allows the fragments of discourses to be amalgamated under certain principles of meaning. In this way it allows a global holistic creative unit, with a diversity of particular concretizations, that creates in each community, differentiated syntheses of holistic spirituality, and although it takes selective scraps from distinct traditions, it does so in accordance with certain basic principles of New Age ideology. Therefore it is right to define it, as Amaral does, as 'syncretism in motion', as long as it is also emphasized that it makes and remakes itself on the basis of a meaning-creating grammar. The New Age brings a matrix of meaning with which magical, indigenous, healing, psychological, spiritual and scientific practices are appropriated, translated, and resemanticized as holistic (whose semantic principle is that the whole is contained in the particular).

It is in the idea of a 'matrix', and a 'meaning-creating grammar' (see above), or of an 'interpretative frame' belonging to those who take part in the movement (Carozzi, 2000), that the clue lies to apprehending, with greater heuristic value, the character and originality of the New Age as a socio-religious movement. Instead of specifying from a list, which of various religious/therapeutic practices it is composed of, it is better to understand New Age as an interpretive frame that allows the individual to use the practices sequentially or simultaneously (Carozzi, 2000), or else, as an inner grammar that recombines them and gives them meaning *in a determined circuit*. It is not merely mixing certain elements (oriental or ethnic), but their *re-semanticizing* according to determined governing principles of the new configuration.

However, I suggest that although it is important to propose a holistic principle 'on the basis of which different cultural and/or spiritual aspects are appropriated, translated and refunctionalized from others, in order to make them its own' (see above) such a principle is not *specific* enough as a defining feature of New Age practices. For example, Pablo Semán (2001), has pointed out that popular religiosity *also* can be understood on the basis of an underlying holistic, cosmological and relational cultural matrix, and it could be argued that it is the character of some indigenous worldviews also, to be holistic.

I will propose three nuclei of ideas that I consider central for a greater comprehension of the interpretive frame underlying the New Age movement, ideas that allow its logics of appropriation (or not) of certain spiritual traditions to be understood.[11]

First Nucleus of Ideas of the Interpretive Frame: The Sacred Self

Following Heelas (1996) and Carozzi (2000), I consider that the principal nucleus of ideas belonging to the interpretive frame of the New Age—*that allows it best to be constructed as an object of study clearly distinguishable from others it has affinities with*, or from other practices that are most likely to be on its periphery—is made up of these postulates:

- The idea that there is a divine spark or a 'sacred self' within every individual.
- The idea of spiritual *development*, as a way of contacting or of displaying the *sacred self*, removing the barriers of the 'everyday ego' that hide it.
- A *holistic worldview* that postulates a necessary relationship between the *sacred self*, Nature, and the Universe, so that the development or the transformation of one of these affects the others.[12]

The idea of 'a good and holy interior' (Carozzi, 2000) that needs to be contacted or displayed through specific practices and techniques is key to distinguishing a New Age worldview from others that may also be holistic but propose a notion of the person closer to that which is current in traditional societies and, unlike that of the New Age, is not particularly appropriate for educated middle class urban sectors (Campbell, 1978; Heelas, 1996; Gutiérrez Zúñiga, 1996; Carozzi, 2000; Viotti, 2011).

The recognition of these central features is what makes it possible for there to be New Age versions of horoscopes, tarot and shamanism that differ from other, everyday, forms of these arts. In the New Age versions they are used as a way to *knowledge and personal transformation*—and not just as techniques for divining the future or curing physical illnesses. In the same vein, it could be said that a discipline commonly associated with the New Age, like reiki, also has uses that it would not be appropriate to consider as being relevant to a study of New Age; for example when it is used solely to cure a particular complaint. In fact, an individual receiving treatment might be making a *non* New

11 I follow the detailed scheme provided by Carozzi (2000), but on the basis of my own rearrangement of her list of features in three nuclei, which, for the purposes of this work, I consider to be especially relevant.

12 These three ideas are also highlighted by D'Andrea (2000) in his description of the New Age.

Age use of reiki even when the practitioner offers the service within an interpretive frame clearly linked to New Age.[13]

In similar fashion, attending to these basic features one can understand better on which occasions a traditional practitioner (shaman or healer) can become part of a New Age movement—either by being influenced by it or by being 'admitted' into the circuit. There are certain semantic markers that can show the degree of integration (or lack of it) of a traditional practitioner into a New Age circuit.[14] The practitioner is probably more integrated into the New Age circuit when he considers himself—or his followers consider him—to be a *Master* and not a 'healer' or 'witchdoctor'; when he conducts *Healings* and not just 'cures' or 'cleansings' and when he provides spiritual *Teachings*. Ideally, as we will see later, he should be able to claim to belong to some ethnic group or other. His exoticized ethnic character is precisely what gives him the possibility of having a *spiritual teaching* to offer beyond its strictly therapeutic qualities. To sum up, for a practitioner to belong (or to be able to belong in the future) to a New Age circuit, the emphasis must not be on generating 'magic', at least not in the most popular senses of the term—'black magic' or 'love magic', causing simple variations in the material life of individuals—but on producing some kind of spiritual *transformation* in the person, that does not just drive a physical illness away but *brings his spiritual quality to a new and better level.* In general the term 'healing' (*sanación*) is the one that manages to synthesise these ideas (Albanese, 1992).[15]

Second Nucleus of Ideas of the Interpretive Frame: Permanent Circulation

In her meticulous characterization of the New Age interpretive frame, Carozzi (2000) insists on another set of features that we might consider *a second nucleus.* No less important than the first set of ideas, which contained more

13 The lack of correspondence between the interpretive frames of supply and of demand (between the providers of services and those who receive them) ought to be studied better and is also one of the modalities of New Age limitations. In the chapter in this volume, for example, by Alejandra Aguilar Ros, a detailed examination is made of the different logics of relation to the spiritual world followed by a *mara'akame* and the members of a Dance group; that of the latter being more clearly New Age, and that of the indigenous specialist being more traditional and attached to a community. The tension between the two leads in the end to the dissolution of their relationship.

14 At any rate, these markers are mainly indicative and should be inserted in an interpretive frame containing, to a greater or lesser extent, the three nuclei of ideas developed here.

15 However, as shown in the work of Alejandra Aguilar Ros already referred to, these 'semantic markers' may be applied to someone who does not necessarily take part in the same way, in the interpretive frame underlying the New Age movement.

general propositions about the nature of the Holy, these would tend rather to explain the key organizational elements of the New Age. Principally, they allow us to understand the logic behind the circulation over a circuit of different practices—or, perhaps it would be better to say *the placing of different practices into relation with each other through the creation of a circuit formed by those who have this interpretive frame for religious reality, to a greater or lesser extent.*[16] If the circuit is the best *organizational* expression of the New Age—the organizational substratum that anchors it, according to Magnani (1999a), *this second set of features makes it possible to comprehend its creation and maintenance.*[17]

This second nucleus of New Age features, explaining mainly its forms of social organization, consists of:

- An affirmation of the autonomy of the subject, which is expressed in
- valuing permanent circulation and
- the continual establishment of ephemeral and changing relations and granting to them a central role in positive individual and collective transformation (all found in Carozzi, 2000:146, and, more developed, in Carozzi, 1999c and 2004).

While the first set of features defines the general outline of underlying beliefs, this second set justifies, as another basic feature of the New Age, the *circulation* between different groups, workshops and specialists.[18] It is the circulation that makes the New Age so difficult to grasp—it is a *self religion* but not just because it tries to develop or display an inner divine spark, but also because

16 As noted by Carozzi (2000) there is a self-perpetuating effect of circulation. The circuit is not formed only because some people have this interpretive frame, as participation itself leads to its being adopted. The new meanings do not come only from discourses but also from social (inter)actions.

17 Clearly this division into nuclei of features is merely heuristic. I emphasize them because the first nucleus allows us to differentiate New Age practices from other similar ones that do not have a vision of the *sacred self* (generally, more traditional practices), and the second enables us to distinguish them from others that do have the same vision but do not stress *circulation* so much as *permanence* within particular groups (Orientalists, for example). The third nucleus is especially pertinent to comprehending the selective appropriations made of non-Western religions.

18 'The alternative complex shaped by New Age ideas may be considered the product of an application of this changing anti-authoritarian trend towards personal autonomy, to the field of alternative therapies, psychotherapy, esoteric and religious therapies (...) The anti-authoritarian/personal autonomy tone of the New Age has been noted by both York (1995) and Heelas (1996) for the USA and England, and by Russo in her references to the alternative field in Brazil (Russo, 1993: 186 and ff.)' (Carozzi, 1999c: 20).

the individual (and not a specific religious group) *is the ultimate judge* of which practices work *for him*.[19] The emphasis on individual particularity and the multiplicity of spiritual paths separates the New Age from groups of people practicing Oriental religions in the West who usually consider it absolutely necessary (even if they do not say so in public discourses) to remain in their group, or for their work to be under the supervision of a *single* guru. In the New Age way of using these religions, circulation between different groups is not just positively valued but is an *indispensable* requirement for spiritual development.[20]

Third Nucleus of Ideas of the Interpretive Frame: Appreciation of Othernesses

To understand the limits of New Age appropriations, it is useful to distinguish a third nucleus of ideas that fit into its interpretive frame, mainly having to do with ideas of the Other (ethnic and religious, but also with respect to other minorities in the West). These make it possible to have a preference for certain religious/therapeutic practices. They consist mainly, as noted by Carozzi (2000: 146) of the following:

- An appreciation for suppressing established power hierarchies or inverting them
- An appreciation of nature and the role of an individual's connection to it, as engines of personal evolution and the positive transformation of humanity.

---

19 Here one must not exaggerate the degree of 'individualism' involved. As Carozzi (2000) has shown, it is to a large extent through participation in the many (loose) groups of the New Age circuit that self-authority becomes part of a *vocabulary of motives* (Wright Mills, 1940) *learned* in social interactions (see footnote 16, above)—and does not necessarily express an essential feature of advanced modern societies, as D'Andrea (2000) argues. Wood (2010) has likewise cogently argued against taking people's *accounts* of self-authority at face value, and also stressed the importance of the social interactions in which they take shape.

20 The 'spiritual wandering' (Amaral, 1999) of the New Age is not simply a reflection of the situation of religion in post-modern times. A special emphasis is made by the members of the different groups that form the circuit to *approve* of this circulation, seeing it as both *positive* and *necessary*—there is no aspiration for exclusiveness. On the other hand, as I have argued elsewhere (Frigerio, 2007), I doubt whether the offer of religion has ever been exclusively—or even mostly—made within church walls. The existence of '*à la carte*' Catholicism goes back longer than is currently recognized in the specialized literature—which is proved by how widespread 'popular religiosity' is.

Acording to this author, there is a recurring scheme in Western society that places nature and civilization in opposition, a dichotomy that applies equally to 'the sexes, the stages of life, the various cultures, ways of knowledge and of action, the body and the human psyche, and social relations'. The scheme may adopt the following form (Carozzi, 2000: 128–29):

Nature	Culture-Civilization
Past	Present
Magic/myth/ritual	Science
Art	Technology
Feminine	Masculine
Infancy	Adulthood
East	West
Indigenous peoples	Europeans
Body	Mind
Unconscious	Conscious
Intuition	Rationality
Receptivity	Critical faculty
Sensation/emotion	Intention/will
Pleasure	Effort
Gesture/movement/contact	Words
Spontaneity	Control
Direct manipulation	Machines and Tools
Rhythm	Tune

Although the valuations of these poles have occasionally changed (for example, when the image of the noble savage is preferred to myths based on the theory of evolution), the opposition of these elements has remained the same over the centuries and formed, as the author argues, a central scheme of modern Western culture. The preference shown, within the interpretive framework of the New Age, for the elements on the left, seen as the source for development of the 'sacred self', as opposed to those on the right which would, on the contrary, keep up an illusory 'exterior self' hindering positive transformations, expresses, as Carozzi notes, 'an evident change in relation to the sacralization of progress, rationality and technology, which was the ruling paradigm of urban culture in the nineteen fifties'. These preferences make the countercultural roots of the New Age movement evident. Nevertheless, the same redirection:

> [reaffirms] both a Western cultural scheme that counterposes Nature and Civilization, and, at the same time, the association of the two realms with particular individuals, activities and cultures. As a result, while it is counter-cultural in one sense, the New Age movement still reasserts one of the pillars of Western culture: the division between primitives or naturals (now healers and spiritual people), and the civilized (now those who have been contaminated, or limited or are ill), leaving women, children and those who take part in indigenous, oriental and African, non-European cultures, as representatives of Nature, along with the body, emotions, intuition, movement and physical contact, without historicity and socio-cultural influences.
>
> CAROZZI, 2000: 150

We can understand this *positively* valued continuity of stereotypes as a way of making such representatives of the human species from the 'Nature' side *exotic*. At greater depth this argument leads us to consider another limit to the New Age re-interpretations and hybridizations of non-Western religious traditions: their eminently *selective* nature. Even though it is obvious that not all non-Western traditions—any more than each and every Amerindian tradition—become part of this 'supermarket of religions' (Van Hove, 1999), the reasons for preferring them have not been evaluated enough, which is probably due to the insistence of academics on the unfettered eclecticism of the New Age.[21]

Exoticized Othernesses

Although some scholars (such as York, 2001: 368) believe that 'the New Age maintains the idea that all spiritual inheritances past and present are no longer private property, and belong in the new Aquarian Age to the public domain' and that there has therefore been 'an irresponsibly free accessibility to the spiritual traditions of the world', it is evident that *not all* the spiritual inheritances have been appropriated or form part of the repertoire or the circuit of the New Age (De la Torre, 2011).

It is necessary to possess an 'exotic otherness' to have the right to be considered part of the 'global supermarket of spiritual development' (which is *not* the sum of *all* possibilities, but *only of those* that are considered *worthy*). This status appears to be more easily attained by the Oriental than the Amerindian

21 Carozzi (2007) and De La Torre (2011) have drawn attention to this problem, but we do not, as yet, have enough studies on the subject.

traditions, and in the latter case by *some* and not by all of the options, which is clearly shown in the chapters by José G.C. Magnani, María Teresa Rodríguez and Alejandra Aguilar Ros in this book (see also De la Torre, 2011). It is hard for African, and even harder for Afro-American, traditions to be given the right to enter into this worldwide spiritual supermarket. There seems to be a latent evolutionism at work, placing some traditions above others: the Oriental above the Amerindian, and these above the African. Furthermore, certain technologies of the Self seem to be particularly suitable for developing the 'sacred self', as distinct from others.

The example of *The Council of Thirteen Grandmothers* studied in this book by María Teresa Rodríguez is particularly illustrative of this point. The only African member of the Council is a woman from Gabon, an initiate of the *Bwiti* cult of Fang, which uses a hallucinogenic bark, the *iboga*, as a way of gaining access to the spiritual world—quite a rarity in the context of African culture. The two representatives of 'Brazilian Amazonia' are members of the cult of Santo Daime, which also makes use of an entheogen—in this case, ayahuasca—as a basic part of its religious practices. It is a *mestizo* cult, which also does not, strictly speaking, represent the 'indigenous' traditions of Brazilian Amazonia. The appreciation of entheogens, irrespective of how representative they are of local spiritual traditions, as a way of gaining access to and of developing the Sacred Self shows the countercultural roots of the New Age movement and the *selective* appropriation of particular *technologies of the self* from non-Western spiritual traditions.[22]

For the case of Latin America, I suggest that the type of indigenous tradition that is appropriated or not by New Age circuits in each country depends also on *the place granted to the 'natives' in each of the dominant narratives of the nation.*[23] We might therefore understand the variations in the place held by local indigenous traditions in the New Age circuits of Mexico, Brazil, and Argentina, by attending to the different places given to the national indigenous peoples through myths of *mestizaje* (mixed racial origins), 'the three races' or

22 Although I do not claim that these are perfect examples, this would seem to be the case of meditation and yoga from Eastern religions and entheogens and sweat lodges from the Amerindian ones.

23 *Dominant narratives* provide 'an essentialized national identity, focusing on the nation's external boundaries and internal composition, proposing the correct and orderly placement order of its (ethnic, religious, gender) constituent elements, containing the present as they construct a legitimating past' (Frigerio, 2002). However, these narratives are not unequivocal and do not have an absolute supremacy, as they are confronted by counter-narratives or are subject to oppositional readings (as understood by Hall, 1993) that have an uneven degree of success or of social acceptance at different moments of history.

'whiteness' current in each of these countries. Perhaps the clearest example is to be found in Mexico, where the movement to vindicate the autochthonous cultures of *Mexicanism* has inspired different versions of the New Age that come together in what has been called Neo-Mexicanism, 'a syncretic circuit where movements of the spiritualist and esoteric current of Mexicanism, New Age networks, indigenous ceremonial communities and the Conchero dance all come together and are synthesized' (Gutiérrez Zúñiga, 2008, in the work by De la Torre and Gutiérrez Zúñiga,2011: 187).[24] In Brazil, as the chapter by Magnani in this book shows, the place held by local indigenous practices in Brazilian Neo-shamanism seems to be lower than that of the native populations thought to be 'more highly developed' (North American and Andean). In Argentina, the part played by indigenous natives in the local New Age is none, which is consistent with the invisibility of the local aboriginal populations (Carozzi, 2007: 352–354).[25] When they have not been made invisible, the local natives are still regarded as representatives of barbarianism that would hardly have any valuable belief to offer—even to the vision of well disposed middle classes. 'Native wisdom', for them, is found in other countries, never their own. In a similar vein, the work by Jean Paul Sarrazin in this book shows how in another nation where the presence of aboriginal peoples is not vindicated very much, the New Age revaluing of 'indigenous spirituality' is generic and does not have a strong basis in local cultures. While in Peru, on the contrary (see the article by Antoinette Molinié in this volume), the global and local appreciations of the Inca heritage make even the government tourist office want to emphasize the character of Machu Pichu as 'the magnetic centre of the world'.

I therefore propose that the *New Age appropriations of indigenous traditions generally only take place when there are exoticized outsider Others, or there are insider Others who are glorified within the country* (or included enough in the dominant narratives of the nation). *Or, at least, where the development of a counter-narrative of the nation is important enough for indigenous traditions to be valued.*

The case of Afro-American religions is particularly revealing, both of the latent evolutionist suppositions present in New Age appropriations, and of their not being considered as an exotic Other, either *externally*—in the '*global* supermarket of spiritual development'—or *internally*, in the New Age circuits

24 The *mestizaje* narrative in Mexico oscillates, according to De la Torre (2007: 123), 'between a *mestizaje* with an indigenous root stock and another kind tending towards a Mexican style of Creole Hispanicism' (in the work by De la Torre and Gutiérrez Zúñiga, 2011: 184).

25 Even though in absolute numbers and as a percentage of the population, they are more numerous than in Brazil.

of each country. In the first case, due to the evolutionist prejudice against the use of blood as a privileged means (not the only one) of communicating with the spiritual world and transforming the spiritual quality of people. In the second case, due to the invisibility of the populations descended from Africans, and of their cultural contributions in the majority of dominant national narratives in Latin America.

In Afro-American religions (at least in those of Afro-Brazilian origin) the concept of *orí* (head) could easily be assimilated to the idea of a divine spark in the individual. One might therefore expect that with a—not so arbitrary—exercise of 'frame-alignment' (Frigerio, 1999), it could be considered a kind of Sacred Self, and, as a Non-western hundred or thousand year-old spiritual tradition, the Afro-American religion might be appropriated by the New Age or come to form part of the circuit, thanks to its strong presence in Latin American countries with a black population and its expansion to other countries where it has been adopted by different social groups. However this has not happened, and a consideration of why not, gives us an interesting insight into the selective constitution of a New Age circuit and its appropriation of some non-Western spiritual traditions over others.

First of all we need to recognize that any exoticizing of 'Africans' or 'blacks' (now 'people of African descent') has always been related to their rhythm, musicality, cheerfulness or sexual potency and hardly as a function of their spirituality. This is a characteristic more easily attributed to 'Oriental' cultures, and with the arrival of countercultures, New Age and multiculturalism, to (specially chosen) Amerindian peoples and heritages.

In the global market of racial stereotypes, 'blacks' and 'Africans' are not valued for their spirituality. On the contrary, their spirituality was always labeled as 'magic' or 'witchcraft', because of the use of drums, dance and trance as the principal means of transforming (or substituting for) the Self. Even more so because of the profuse use of animal sacrifices or offerings in religious practices, which goes against the prevailing ideas in the West as to what is religion and what is magic or witchcraft. Any practice that involves sacrifices as part of the religious ceremony loses the status of legitimate religious practice *ipso facto*.[26] The custom also goes against the prevailing ecological consciousness of the New Age. All these reasons explain why there are no African centers of pilgrimage for New Age practitioners—in spite of their millenary age and the

26 It is no accident, as the work of Alejandra Aguilar Ros shows, that it was the sacrifice of a deer that proved decisive, leading to the split of the New Ager dancers from the Huichol *mara'akame*.

enormous variety of African religions, their practices and beliefs have not been appropriated by the New Age and do not form part of the circuit.

Even in Brazil, the Afro religions have been valued more as 'Black cultural heritage' (hence, 'ethnic') than as 'religions' (Frigerio, 2002). Not properly legitimized as religions even in their places of origin, their practice in new social contexts raises doubts and misgivings, especially if they are practiced by white individuals. As distinct from Oriental religions, which are considered part of the legitimate spiritual inheritance of humanity, African-derived religions are particularly stigmatized when practiced by white individuals, as they lose their worth (and precarious legitimacy) as an ethnic-racial heritage (Frigerio, 2002). For all these reasons it is difficult for them to qualify as an 'exotic Other', which would be necessary for them to be included in the New Age circuits.[27] New Agers interviewed in several articles think the energies handled by Afro-Brazilian and Afro-Cuban religions—because of the use of blood and the spirits that they invoke—are 'heavy' or 'dark' and are not really appropriate for the spiritual development sought for in the New Age circuit.[28]

There is, however, a social context in which there does seem to be a New Age reading of religious practices with African origins. In their special appropriation of Afro-Cuban Santeria, some North American practitioners (mainly but not only African-Americans) conduct some of the semantic operations mentioned at the start of this work, aiming to de-stigmatize their practices and beliefs and to reclassify them as part of the legitimate spiritual inheritance of humanity.[29] A number of the books published for the U.S. spiritual market

27 Up until recently, the same sort of thing happened in Cuba (Hagedorn, 2001).

28 The chapter by Magnani in this book provides several references to this point. Most clearly so when he says: '...for elements from the Afro-Brazilian tradition to be recognized in this universe, they must be renamed and explicitly recovered as a form of shamanism and not simply as Umbanda or Candomblé... (...)...the Afro traditions are linked to instinctual drives expressing a "basic self", heavy energies mobilized by the sacrifice of animals and by the beat of accelerated drum rhythms...'. See also the testimonies of some reiki practitioners in Havana, interviewed by Karnooth (2011:233) regarding practitioners of (Afro-Cuban) 'religion'. Her work shows that the 'complementary nature' of New Age and Afro-Cuban practices comes about more through an appropriation by *Santeros* of the former than through an appropriation by New Agers of the latter—it is more common for *Santeros* to complement their practice with reiki than the other way around.

29 There seem to be more, and less, universalist visions: the latter applying mainly to African-Americans or to those of African descent. A detailed examination of the question would mean overstepping the boundaries of this work. Here I would just like to use this example to show how the appropriation of their culture is easier for the New Age, just as it is in particular countries where the indigenous presence is more highly valued in the

show, in their terms and conceptualization, the intention of equating them to other legitimized traditions in the worldwide spiritual supermarket.

These are some examples:

Finding Soul on the Path of Orisa: A West African Spiritual Tradition—Tobe Melora Correal
The Altar of my Soul: The Living Traditions of Santería—Marta Moreno Vega
Teachings of the Santeria Gods: The Spirit of the Odu—Ocha' Ni Lele
The Way of the Orisa: Empowering your Life through the Ancient African Religion of Ifa—Philip Neimark.

In these titles we find semantic markers that reveal an interpretive frame that resonates easily with that of the New Age. The names of the books emphasize the fact that they are about 'teachings' or 'spiritual traditions', of 'ancient' 'African' provenance (even though nearly all the authors belong to, or started with, Afro-Cuban Santeria) that will 'empower' people. Emphasis on the word 'soul' (which is encountered or venerated through these religions) refers to a native idea that evokes the Sacred Self of the New Age. We mentioned earlier that the notion of *orí*—as part of the divinity in our own head—might, with the right kind of interpretive frame alignment, coalesce with the notion of a Sacred Self. This, however, is difficult in Latin American contexts, because of the low esteem in which the cultural and genetic inheritances of black people are held, and the little formal education possessed by a large number of practitioners of Afro-American religiosity who might otherwise be able to formulate the bridges or cognitive translations (Frigerio, 1999)—something that could be more successfully achieved in a different social context. In the United States, practitioners have more formal education (some with college degrees), and there is an African-American counter-narrative that stresses the relevance of African cultural inheritance and spiritual values.[30] For the market niche to which these books are addressed, Africa is not a barbarous place but a source

predominant narrative of the nation—or in some counter-narrative with a good level of acceptance.

30 It is instructive to compare these titles from the U.S. market with other Santeria books, found on the first floor of the Corona market in Guadalajara in Mexico. Here the names of the books were: 'Santeria for Relief from your Problems', 'Secrets of Santeria: How to Prepare the Santo Room', 'Manual of Santero Herbs and Ablutions', and 'Santeria: Songs and Prayers', showing a definite orientation towards ritual performance and the resolution of everyday problems. The semantic markers that might indicate a particularly New Age interpretive frame are missing here.

of spiritual wisdom. In this context it is possible to have a more New Age formulation of Afro-American religious practice—although it is probably hard to find an echo outside the racial-ethnic nucleus where it was formulated or to which it is directed.

With the (gradual) expansion of Afro-American religions to Europe, a new attempt seems to have been made, in some national contexts, to present some varieties in New Age language—this seems to be especially the case with Brazilian Umbanda. For example, an Umbanda temple studied in Paris by Teisenhoffer (2007)—as in other examples observed by Saraiva (2011) in Portugal—where the ideas of *balance, well-being* and *cures* seem to be key in the formulation of local interpretive frames. However, as the position of Umbanda in the Old Continent is nothing if not precarious, these seem to be examples of the *influence* of New Age ideas (or the strategic presentation of a new religious practice) rather than signs of the inclusion of Afro-Brazilian religion *within* the New Age circuit in Europe. With the exception of Portugal (and maybe in Spain) the number of temples of Afro-American religions in European countries is still small and these religions have for the most part been made invisible.[31] The line of argument pursued here is supported by the fact that the most visible and popular practice in Europe does not include the more controversial aspects such as the sacrifice of animals or Exú sessions. Also, part of the attraction seems to involve exoticizing Brazil, or in the Portuguese case—where the number of temples comes to around fifty—it becomes necessary to elaborate a counter-narrative for the nation, which, inspired in Luso-tropicalism, emphasizes the bonds between Portugal, Africa and Brazil as a culturally and historically related community (Guillot, 2009)—that way producing an exotic otherness, or its appraisal within a national narrative.

Conclusions

Rather than proposing a specific restrictive definition of the New Age, I have tried in this article to draw attention to the careful work of conceptualization that is necessary for the study of this social phenomenon, and its possibilities for appropriating and reinterpreting other religious traditions. I have emphasized the limits of such appropriations and suggested that the supposedly infinite capacity of the New Age to mix and blend traditions and practices, sometimes derives more from our weak construction of the object of study

31 If not stigmatized—as demonstrated by Birman (2000) examining the same temple studied by Teisenhoffer (2007), which was denounced as a 'sect' by some of its ex-members.

than from the features of the social phenomenon itself. I proposed, following Carozzi (2000) and De la Torre (in the current volume) that it is more productive to highlight the key components of its interpretive frame—about which there seems to be the greatest consensus in the specialized literature—rather than to make an exhaustive list of the disciplines it might be made up of. The idea of the existence of a Sacred Self and of the need to develop it or make it manifest, *within a holistic worldview* that allows for the transformation of the individual to combine with social change and the coming of a cosmic New Age, appears to be fundamental for pinpointing New Age beliefs, practices and appropriations. From the point of view of the *social organization* of the movement, the affirmation of personal autonomy and the value given to circulation allow us to understand the constitution of a circuit (and the need for it) through which the New Agers travel in search of their spiritual development. Its anti-authoritarian leanings (which are both modern and countercultural) set the individual, and not religious groups, as the final judge of what is best for his own spiritual growth through experimenting with different spiritual traditions.

I have argued especially that a better conceptualization of the phenomenon allows for its particularities to be noted with clarity, and precludes deception by the presence of symbols or disciplines considered New Age by academic common sense—because of their novel character or Oriental origins—but that do not really share the basic premises of the movement's interpretive frame. A more finely tuned appreciation of the phenomenon also makes it possible to note the existence of New Age *modalities* in disciplines that nominally belong rather to esoteric subcultures.

Aware of the importance of a *circuit* sustaining New Age practices and the presence (or absence) within it of certain disciplines and religious movements, I have stressed the need to distinguish between *influences*, *borrowings* and *appropriations*. Although multiple, there are less of these than is commonly thought, and they follow logics of appropriation derived from ideas found in the interpretive frame of the movement that are very specific and directed and can also be *excluding*. It therefore seems contradictory to maintain—as Amaral does—that 'there is a New Age *style* of relating oneself to the sacred', while also claiming that it 'implies a dynamic of combining *ad infinitum*' (99: 49) or that this is a 'kaleidoscopic religiosity' produced by an 'anarchic mix' (72).[32] I agree

32 Even taking into account the fact that she makes her claims—or perhaps just because she does so—within an academic subculture where 'syncretism is the way intellectuals formulate their representations of nationality', as observed recently in a review by Paula Montero of anthropological studies of religion in Brazil (1999: 357; see also Frigerio, 2005).

with Carozzi (2000) and De la Torre (in this book) that it is necessary to understand that there is an 'interpretive frame' or an 'internal grammar' that sustains and gives meaning to practices and beliefs that we can fruitfully conceptualize as New Age, and that also allows for the *selective nature* of its appropriations to be understood. The *specifically New Age practices* are found *inside* its circuit and provide the credentials (spiritual or professional) for the individuals circulating or practicing within it. *Influences* come in the form of particular emphases (generally on the importance of developing a Self conceived as sacred in terms similar to those of the New Age) with regard to certain groups that are *not* in the New Age circuit—such as Pentecostals or Charismatics. The *borrowings* consist of symbols and practices that may appear sporadically in the New Age circuit by virtue of the individual bricolages generated by the participants but in only a limited, occasional and irregular way. Borrowings are almost an irregularity, and sometimes their existence comes from a lack of rigor in the construction of the object of study by the researcher, who sees New Age where it does not exist. Alternatively, they may be the product of the very tolerance of the interpretive frame that allows a significant degree of flexibility but certainly not an unlimited one (as we have argued so far).

In order to understand the *selective* nature of New Age appropriations of particular spiritual traditions, I have suggested that it is necessary to consider the degree of *exoticizing* (or of stigmatizing) particular peoples and cultural heritages in the 'global spiritual market'—which certainly does not cover all the options possible. For the case of Latin America, New Age appropriation of local indigenous cultures seems to be related to the extent to which these ethnic groups are taken into account in the dominant narratives of the nation, or to the existence of counter-narratives that glorify them.[33] This would explain their strong presence in Mexico, along with strong movements of vindication of 'Indian' identity that reach into the middle classes, and their smaller presence in Brazil, their scarcity in Colombia and virtual non-existence in Argentina, where national narratives wipe out the presence and cultural importance of the aboriginal peoples more thoroughly.

33 One aspect I have not been able to develop in this work but deserves to be studied in greater depth is the degree to which its character as a particularly *middle class* expression of spirituality (which, as noted by Carozzi, 2000, reflects a *habitus* proper to educated middle classes with a certain cosmopolitan and multicultural sensibility) also intervenes in the New Age's possibilities for appropriating different traditions, so it discards those that do not have a sufficiently individualized notion of the person, or those that belong to popular culture—in national contexts where it is not very highly valued—and are therefore hard to exoticize (Viotti, 2011).

African and Afro-American religions are remarkable for their absence both in global and in local New Age circuits, with the exception of the United States where middle class Afro-American practitioners—or those who address this public—seem to be starting to develop versions that emphasize their character as a legitimate spiritual inheritance. The equally embryonic forms developed in Europe show more *influence* by New Age ideas on their religions than signs of their being accepted into, or included in, New Age circuits, and also show the need to present for the most part 'normalized' versions of an Umbanda expurgated of its more controversial features. The emphasis on notions of *well-being* and *cures* would also indicate that this articulation is made more on the therapeutic-holistic side than on the side of the spiritual development of the Self.

To conclude, and not wishing to replace excessively loose analyses with markedly rigid ones, it might be worth noting that the items proposed here for a necessary comprehension of the New Age interpretive frame (religion of the Self; holistic worldview; circulation; and the valuing of—certain—othernesses) are based mainly on studies conducted in large urban centres in Europe, or in the Southern Cone (Buenos Aires, São Paulo, Rio de Janeiro). To study the complex Latin American reality better (see Carozzi, 2007) one should take into account the inter-relation of these items and the fact that the greater or larger preponderance of one or another can vary in different countries of our continent, as a function—not excluding the relevance of other possible variables—of the various dominant narratives of the nation, the smaller or larger presence of urban middle class educated strata, the uneven reach of processes of psychologization and individualization and the level of development reached by different local New Age circuits. However, it is only through a more exact conceptualization of the object of study—whether that proposed here or another—that it will be possible to examine adequately these local variations and the limitations of the appropriations and syncretism that are produced in each national context.

PART 2

Latin American Neo-shamanisms

Introduction

The word shaman came into use in the West in the seventeenth century thanks to the accounts of archpriest Avvakum Petrov written during his exile in Siberia, and it acquired different meanings in the centuries to come. The word comes from the Tungusian used by speakers of Uralo-Altaic languages in the region, and spread through the world as having to do with the demonic, with charlatanism, madness, or possession by devils, as well as hysteria, epilepsy and psychosis (Martínez González, 2009: 198). It was not until the middle of the twentieth century that the canonic models of the shaman and of shamanism were erected in the first systematic book on the subject, written by Mircea Eliade (1951). According to Eliade, with whom a serious interest in the subject starts, one of the shaman's most emblematic specialities is the magic flight, an ecstasy unlike any other that consists of 'a trance during which his soul is believed to leave the body to undertake ascents into heaven or descents into the underworld' (1986: 23). The shaman communicates with the spirits but is not their instrument, and is chosen by descent or through a 'calling' (ibid.: 29). He is the great specialist of the human soul, an intermediary between the gods, the departed, and living humans.

According to this anthropologist, shamanism had formed as one of the continuities of culture covering Asia and America that derived from the migrations from one continent to the other in the Pleistocene. As Shepard (accepted for publication) points out, this premise, itself fertilized by the popularization of the term shaman all over the world, is what explains why 'certain West Asian traditions and similar Arctic and North American examples have been treated as original or more "pure" versions of shamanism than their Central and South American counterparts' (Eliade, 1986: 232). However, on the basis of the latest, controversial, archaeological findings, Shepard offers a vision that differs from the prevailing theory in Latin America of the diffusion of shamanism. In effect, he claims that, 'the native Central and South American shamanism should be seen not as derivative of or secondary to "classic" Asian shamanism, but rather parallel, largely independent, and equally ancient bodies of practice that have evolved and diversified in response to heterogeneous ecological, sociocultural, and historical conditions'.

In fact, shamanisms and shamans in Latin America do not necessarily stick to the model defined by Eliade, and their co-existence with other techniques of ecstasy, healing, or divination—and with the specialists practicing these arts, has created a great heterogeneity, sometimes without distinguishing between the uses and applications of such terms in Amerindian societies.

 | DOI 10.1163/9789004316485_005

These observations are emphasized by Galinier and Perrin, who propose a definition claiming to be more *ad hoc* and 'precise' for these geographical and cultural latitudes. They consider shamanism to be a system based on a theory of communication between this world, and another, which is thought of as a sacred space. Communication is established by a socially recognized person with the title of shaman 'who knows how to call up and dominate the will of relevant entities from the sacred space, generally classed as "auxiliary spirits", with the aim of fighting against misfortune' (Galinier and Perrin, 1995: IX–X). However, throughout the book published by these authors with I. Lagarriga, various cases of Latin American 'shamanisms' that are analyzed clearly show, whatever the authors' intentions, that it is impossible to have a clearly limited and precise definition of this phenomenon, because of its richness and complexity.

However, several of the authors metioned agree on 'healing' as a distinctive sign of shamanism in Central and South America, where shamans use medicinal plants, and enter into a trance with hallucinogens, narcotics or stimulants. Without covering all the details of such a vast field Shepard marks out its intrinsic mixing with popular Catholicism, as one of the regional differences between shamanism in Mesoamerica and the Andes region, and shamanism in the lowlands of South America. Which explains for example, why in Mexico and Guatemala as in Peru and Bolivia invocations are made equally to native spirits and Catholic saints (*ibidem*).

From the nineteen fifties onwards, techniques of shamanism began to be relocated in the fields of other sciences, like humanist psychology, as Eliade's transcultural model of neuropsychology was supplemented with the figure of the 'anthropologist-shaman'. As emphasized by Martínez González (2007: 124), this figure arises mostly in America, thanks to the experiences of researchers with indigenous peoples, which were set up as proofs that anyone can gain access to these states of awareness and thus obtain a therapeutic benefit. This kind of shamanism is then taken up as a new religious and therapeutic option for Westerners. The apparently positive evaluation it makes of the shaman did not however eliminate the figure of the 'noble savage' that underlies the exoticizing of an otherness originally associated with societies that were deemed to be archaic and primitive (Martínez González, 2009: 198).

With the rise of the countercultural movement of the sixties, shamanism gets to be discussed again and analyzed from very different angles (Adame, 2005: 78). The quests for alternative visions to that of Western culture, created by disenchantment with capitalism, various alternative urban cultures, such as those of the beatniks and the tribes of hippies and New Agers that followed them, undertook various searches that pointed to shamanism as a source of knowledge of exotic experiences and new states of consciousness. At the same time, psychotherapists sought to understand altered sates of consciousness. The hippies sought out shamans to experience altered states and new forms of extrasensory perception that their power plants provoked (ayahuasca, peyote, yajé, magic mushrooms, etc.). The spiritual seekers that make up the network of 'The Aquarian Conspiracy' sought to get from them contact and harmony with nature. Alternative healers wished to understand the curative power of their power plants and states of ecstasy. Initiates into esoteric teachings hoped to find in shamanism the source of mystery cult knowledge and the origin of extraordinary powers. Neuropsychologists saw in shamanism a technique for achieving personal betterment. Indeed, some postmodern anthropologists use shamanism as a way of seeing and perceiving the world that is able to encourage Pan-American sentiments.

These searches by westernized people looking towards shamanism began to create an awareness that this was a transcultural practice and therefore it was open for anyone who chose to do so, to become a shaman. This is known as Neo-shamanism, originally because its cultural and ritual frames were decontextualized, but then because novel functional senses were impressed upon it and its ritual practices were relocated in differentiated circuits. The phenomenon of Neo-shamanism does not imply only a change of subjects, but also involves changing the meanings and functions of the practice itself. In traditional shamanism it is a gift, a divine calling or a special charisma to be a shaman, but now it is possible to become a shaman through learning how to be one, in workshops and through initiation experiences. Neo-shamanism also contributes to de-mystifying the practice, as it is constantly incorporating shamanism into mercantile circuits such as New Age and Neo-esoteric consumption circuits. Neo-shamanism also makes teachings exoteric that were still esoteric until a century ago, that is to say, kept safe and hidden, and only allowed to be used by specialists. Another of the changes is, that its integration into magical quests for cures and for healing, gives it a sense of efficacy in the search for quick or immediate solutions. Finally, we can also mention the hybridizing of cultural meanings that Neo-shamanism creates by combining the teachings of particular native cultures with techniques and knowledge that have been cut out and removed from other traditions.

This section of the book does not aim to bring to an end the enormous amounts of discussion and analysis of shamanism in general and particularly in Latin America, but to bring to the table the continuities and changes of shamanism and its central figure for further discussion. We present four studies based on ethnographies that tell of experiences where shamanism (which incudes either shamans or their rituals) has been appropriated by the New Age movement in any one of two ways. Either through displacing it and incorporating it into new urban contexts in order to offer mystical or magical experiences; or, when it has been promoted by the mystical tourism that has invaded traditional spaces where Amerindian shamanism is practiced, presenting it as spectacle. We start with a chapter by Canto Magnani, who describes the process through which shamanism came to be included in the supply of Neo-esoteric mercantile circuits in São Paulo, Brazil; then we have Jacques Galinier, with a chapter in which he develops two new modalities of current shamanism: endo-shamanism and exo-shamanism; and questions the effects that translation and appropriation by the New Age have on ethnic systems. The third paper included in this section is by María Teresa Rodríguez, who describes the case of a Mazatec healer, who was incorporated, due to the fascination that New Agers have for María Sabina's magic mushrooms, into a cosmopolitan shamanic circle known as the Thirteen Grandmothers of the World; and finally, we present the work of Alejandra Aguilar Ros, who analyses the articulations and also the disarticulations between an eclectic group of Dancers from Tecate (in Baja California) and a Huichol *mar'akate*, with whose help they were hoping to find a way for their spiritual path to put down roots.

The Neo-shamanism that has arisen in Latin America may be considered one of the most obvious features picked up by the New Age movement in our sub-continent. Effectively, the continued presence of the figure of the shaman among various indigenous populations (in spite of an increasing social and territorial marginalization of these) speaks of the vitality of their role as mediators between worlds, and also of a common cosmology that has resisted colonization for centuries. The papers published here describe for us how the New Age spiritual seekers say they are able to imbibe from this source of ancestral knowledge in countries like Brazil and Mexico. This might be because of their traveling to out of the way places in search of new teachings and 'power plants' and intense experiences (already described and modeled on numerous occasions by other countercultural travelers like Carlos Castaneda). These are places where the Pre-Hispanic cultures of the indigenous populations that have taken refuge in them, carry on. And it might also be because of the mobility that the local specialists have acquired as a result of indigenous migrations to the city in search of new life opportunities. One such is the opportunity of displacement that the very Neo-esoteric circuits offer them, both nationally and worldwide. Through the work presented here our authors provide perspectives on answering the following questions: is the ancestral practice displaced to urban contexts still the same practice? How is the role of these mediators transformed outside their original ethnic contexts (Magnani)? What is it that integrates a spiritual supply of global aspirations for sale, which assumes that there is a universalist mold common to all traditions simply because they are non-Western indigenous (Galinier)? How are holistic psychological therapies and sacred ethnic ceremonies, as different as the sweat lodge and taking *ayahuasca*, integrated into the Neo-esoteric supply on offer, or into the conducting of cosmopolitan rituals by 13 guardians of ancestral traditions from different parts of the world working on planetary healing (Rodríguez)? What conflicts and tensions crop up (Aguilar Ros)? What conceptual tools do we have to distinguish between the shamanic practices of the original indigenous communities, and the phenomena of alternative spirituality that we observe in New Age circuits, which can help us to penetrate into their specificity and their significance in the reconfiguration of contemporary religiosities?

CHAPTER 3

The New Age Movement and Urban Shamanism in Brazil

José Guilherme Cantor Magnani

Introduction

The New Age movement in Brazil reached its zenith between the late eighties and the first years of the new millenium: endless talk shows on TV about meditation techniques, or about the properties of pendulums, crystals and pyramids, publishing material that flooded the shelves of bookshops with works by writers such as Paulo Coelho or Carlos Castaneda, offers of oracular divination services, massages of Oriental origin, ayurvedic medicine, not to mention workshops, talks and meetings that brought together people interested in subjects like past lives, the power of healing through the chakras, and so on: all these bear witness to the success of the Age of Aquarius in Brazilian territory, mainly in the big urban centers. Apart from all of that, it was possible to get your horoscope by telephone on the '*disque 900*' line from the Puerto Rican guru Walter Mercado, whose watchword was '*Ligue dja*'[1] (or something that sounded like that in Portuguese).

This movement, the place of convergence for practices as different as ancient arts of divination from various backgrounds (the Tarot, the I-Ching, Runes), and others ranging from therapies and exercises drawing their inspiration from the East (Tai Chi Chuan, Lian Gong, Shiatsu) to esoteric rituals, shamanic experiences, beliefs in elemental spirits, and many other modalities, still covers certain styles of seeking for spirituality beyond what conventional religions offer.

The phenomenon is complex and we know it has its roots in the countercultural movement of the sixties in the U.S.A., searching for alternatives to the Establishment in the fields of politics, aesthetics, morality and ways of life. As well as the obvious presence of oriental philosophies and religions, one could also detect the influence, amongst others, of late nineteenth century Spiritualism and Theosophy; it is also possible to cite gnosticism, hermeticism and other currents and occultist groups that are certainly there, in the remotest ancestry of the movement.

1 Answer next, answer now.

 | DOI 10.1163/9789004316485_006

To understand the particularities of the New Age as it developed in Brazil, and then its relation to the subject of these reflections, urban shamanism, it is worth looking for its antecedents by giving a brief historical account of the movement.[2]

Background

For the case of Brazil, we can find countercultural elements in the nineteen sixties. At that time, however, the agenda was markedly political, and young people at university, along with the unions and left-wing organizations, were more concerned about social inequalities than the signs that prosperity and academic modernism were coming to an end, which, it is said, would explain the disorientation of the baby boom generation, born after the second world war, in the United States.

In Brazil, the main trend of cultural agitation was for it to assume a more political point of view, and this was seen in the Popular Cultural Centers, in experimental New Cinema, and also in avant guard Theater and in popular music. It is only in the seventies, with channels of participation closed and popular organizations repressed, that conditions were created for the rise of the more mystical and individualized aspects of the new era.

It cannot be forgotten, however, that many of the elements that are usually linked to this phenomenon, such as Occultism, esotericism, and orientalism, had already been in the country for some time: leaving aside any speculation as to whether or not members of the Knights Templar were among those who disembarked from the galleons of the Portuguese navigator Pedro Álvarez Cabral, when he landed here in the year 1500, it may be stated categorically that some initiation societies have been operating in Brazil since at least the eighteenth century. Such is the case, for example, of masonry; the first society of masons that we know of was founded in the northern state of Pernambuco in 1797, by the doctor and veteran friar Arruda Câmara.

The first theosophical lodge in Brazil was established in Pelotas, a southern city in the State of Río Grande del Sur, in 1902, and was called Dharma, although theosophy had been mentioned earlier in an article by Darío Veloso published in Curitiba, in the state of Paraná, in 1896, with the title 'Theosophy and the Theosophical Society'. In 1919 the first Brazilian section of the Theosophical

2 Parts of this text take up subjects, data and analysis that appeared originally in works already published: data from Magnani 1999; 1999 b; 2000, and are presented here, revised and bought up to date.

Society, linked to The Theosophical Society with headquarters in Madras, India, was officially opened in Río de Janeiro.

The Esoteric Circle of Communion of Thought was founded in the city of São Paulo in 1909: linked to the publisher and bookshop O Pensamento (1907), and the journal with the same name, which was an important pioneering instrument for the divulging of philosophical-spiritualist ideas and systems, and whose orientation was adjusted to the prevailing beliefs and religious values of that time. The Anthroposophical Society in Brazil was officially founded in São Paulo in 1935, although there were followers of Anthroposophy in Porto Alegre as early as 1910; The Brazilian Theosophical Society, later called Eubiose, started in Río de Janeiro in 1916 and was officially established in 1969; Rosacruz Amorc is from 1956 and Rosacruz Áurea from 1957; all of these societies are still active and influential on the current new era scene.

Religions that are strictly speaking of oriental provenance, such as Buddhism in its different versions, have been in the country since the first decades of the twentieth century, and were originally linked to immigrants, mainly from Japan: the first Buddhist temple in Brazil, Kômyôji, was built in the city of Cafelândia, in the State of São Paulo. It was only after the end of the war and in particular in the nineteen fifties, that temples and societies were set up in various different parts of the country. For example, the Buddhist Sotô Zenshû Community was officially recognized on the 30th of November 1955, and had its first temple (Zengenji) built in Mogi de la Cruzes (São Paulo). The same thing happened with the so-called New Religions: *Seicho-No-iê* is from 1952, *Perfect Liberty* from 1958 and *Soka Gakkai*, whose organization was formally inaugurated in 1960, has had adepts since the fifties.

In the same decade, the practice of acupuncture, which had been limited to the Oriental Quarter of the *barrio* Liberdade in the city of São Paulo, began to spread outside the area of these immigrants and their descendants, through the courses given by Professor Frederico Spaeth, to Brazilian doctors. Some of his students went on to set up the first Brazilian association of this speciality and in 1961 they started the first institutionalized clinic, the Brazilian Acupuncture Institute.

There was a similar process for some of the modalities of martial arts: in 1959 the maestro Wong Sun Keung started to give Tai Chi Chuan classes in the Chinese Social Center; his example was followed by Chan Kow Wai and Chiu Ping Lok. In 1969, the latter founded, in the city of Santo André (State of São Paulo), one of the first martial arts academies to be registered in the country, the Tai Chi, Yoga and Kung-fu Academy. In Río de Janeiro there was also the Hermogenes Yoga Academy, which started around the same time (1962).

Even though these and other elements, institutions and practices have been incorporated into the New Age, they did not of themselves produce it: the spread of the phenomenon known by that name would depend on particular circumstances, which, as mentioned above, came out of the political and cultural agitation of the sixties and then expanded in the seventies. In the context of the agitation of that time there arose an artistic and musical movement known as 'Tropicalism', which opened a space for a position identified with the libertarian and Dionysian aesthetic of the counterculture: Caetano Veloso ('no handkerchief, no papers, nothing in my pockets or my hands' —as a line of one of his most famous songs ran), cheerfully celebrates rejection of the values of the system.

Gilberto Gil, another singer identified with 'Tropicalism' showed an affinity with some holistic ideas: his disc *Quanta*, from 1997, provides examples. But it was Raul Seixas who explicitly developed more 'mystical' aspects in his compositions, and even took part with his *partner* of the time, Paulo Coelho, in initiation societies inspired by the doctrines of the famous English occultist Aleister Crowley. The titles of some of his records (*Aeon* and *Gita*, the latter with music by 'Alternative Society') bear witness to this tendency. The raid on his house by the police in 1974 and his departure from Brazil (the same thing that happened to Gilberto Gil, Caetano Veloso and Chico Buarque, to name just a few of the most well known people) provide a sample of how far the 'years of lead' of the military dictatorship went, having started soon after John Lennon's famous phrase '*the dream is over*' started to gain currency. Many militants from left-wing organizations and participants in the cultural movement chose religious or alternative paths, such as those adopted by the writer and composer Rogério Duarte, who had been a member of the *Centro Popular de Cultura de la União Nacional de Estudantes*, the ex-militant and former political detainee Alex Polari (currently vice-president of Cefluris, one of the branches of the Santo Daime doctrine, a religion that uses the hallucinogenic plant ayahuasca), or the actress Odete Lara, now an adept of Zen Buddhism, and the playwright Fauzi Arap, and many others.

This was also when groups and associations like the International Society for Krishna Consciousness, more commonly known as Hare Krishna, arose and became part of the scene. The International Society for Krishna Consciousness was established in 1974 and three years later had 18 urban temples, and a rural community called Nova Gokula, in the municipality of Pindamonhangaba, in the State of São Paulo; the same thing happened at different times with Ananda Marga and with disciples of Bhagwan Shree Rajneesh, Maharishi Mahesh Yogi, and others.

However, what really gave the search for new paths its direction was the spread of what came to be known as 'alternative rural communities'. From the point of view of a more radical rejection of current values, those who took part in these, proposed the adoption of a life style based on other principles, diametrically opposed to the distortions of urban society and consumption: a communal life, frugality, spirituality in touch with nature, agricultural production without the use of insecticides or chemical fertilizers, and natural eating based on the ideas of macrobiotics, vegetarianism, etc.

Many of these alternative rural communties were inspired by the teachings of some spiritual master and followed a particular doctrine closely, as was the case of the Hare Krishna; others were motivated by their anticipation of catastrophes thought to be imminent, and more specifically, to protect themselves from the nuclear threat; others again established contacts, supposedly, with extraterrestrial beings. They spread all over, but some regions were preferred to others: in particular, the south of Minas Gerais, Chapada de los Veadeiros (State of Goiás), Chapada Diamantina (State of Bahia), Chapada de los Guimarães (State of Mato Grosso), Serra de la Bocaina (State of São Paulo), Planalto Central (Goiania and Brasilia). The reasons for these preferences had to do with the 'energy' of these places, their status as planetary chakras and other explanations taken out of the eclectic program of the New Age.

The extent to which these experiences spread (at that time encapsulated as 'alternative culture') was matched by the range of publications such as *Común-Unidad* (the organ for spreading news of the movement from 1980), *Transe, Pensamento Ecológico, Vida & Cultura Alternativa, Planeta,* and any number of home-produced pamphlets that disseminated and discussed the various experiences referred to.

The journal *Planeta*, founded in 1972 by a well known writer, Ignácio de Loyola Brandão, following the example of its French sister magazine *Planète*, which was run by Louis Pauwels and Jacques Bergier, lasted till 2000 as one of the main vehicles for alternative proposals in the fields of religion, therapy, personal education and development, linked to the subject matter of the New Age.[3] There were many other institutions in the principal cities of Brazil, that were pioneers in the areas that this seeking for new paths began to open up increasingly more of, such as the *Asociação Palas Athena* of 1972, and the Horus and Zipak bookshops, which were both founded in the mid seventies in the capital, São Paulo. Still the phenomenon was restricted, and even stigmatized; for many people it never got beyond the behavior it had inherited under the

3 It then changed its editorial line and became a journal commenting on curiosities connected to ecology, travel, health, etc. only very distantly connected to the New Age universe.

old banner of *hippy*. It was only towards the end of the eighties and during the nineties that it was consolidated enough to diversify, and following a world-wide tendency, become cosmopolitan and acquire the features of a Market: in the city of São Paulo, a survey conducted in 1992 recorded almost a thousand addresses of places dedicated to such activities. The 1993 edition of the *Seeker's Guide* noted 775 addresses, the 1994 edition had over a thousand, and the 1996 edition 1,300.

In effect, there was an increase in the demand in large urban centres for consumer products (food, medicinal plants, accessories and personal hygiene products) made according to principles considered 'natural', which in some cases meant not using toxic agro chemicals, in others it meant excluding animal based ingredients, or it might mean following the principles of a system such as anthroposophy, for example, in the course of production.

The size of the demand began to require a regular, uninterrupted, supply of quality goods that could no longer be dependent on sporadic deliveries, based on family sized establishments. There were organic food fairs, vegetarian restaurants, stores selling alternative products and even sections in conventional supermarkets, which started to obtain their stock from the larger producers, which was certified by bodies like the *Asociação de Agricultura Orgânica*, and there were establishments maintained by religious groups like *Korin Agropecuária*, (*Fundação Mokiti Okada*, linked to the Messianic Church) or else by philosophical groups like the *Instituto Biodinâmica*, in Botucatu (State of São Paulo), with an anthroposophical outlook.

This was definitely another scale of production, consumption and distribution, not just for these but for an infinite number of other products (publications, discs, videos, items used in alternative therapies and divination systems, objects of devotion and decoration, talismans, etc.) and services (congresses, meetings, talks, spectacles, training courses, celebrations, workshops, learning physical techniques, tourism, etc.), identified with the various systems that, broadly speaking, go to make up the New Age world.

Once the initial, more defensive phase, of radical rejection of dominant values, linked to a hippie and rural lifestyle, was past, the new tendency was to try to become prosperous, to discover and develop the individual's potentials, to search for a better quality of life, and institute a real 'lifestyle' that was recognized and visible in the big urban centers, this time without being weighed down by any stigma. The new tendency did not mean dismissing the 'alternative' communal experiences, lived in the countryside, but integrating them into the urban context and to the initiatives developed there: more frequently, properties located on the outsides of the big urban centres came to be used at weekends for meetings and worskhops. The circuit expanded, and a more diversified public started to join in, but the doubt was about how much and what remained, under these circumstances, of the old ideals that had produced the change that had started more than fifty years before.

The Research

The subject was, however, surrounded by prejudices: for some sectors of the mass media, for example, these practices amounted to no more than a jumble of superstitious beliefs (though they had a certain glamour, as they were aimed at middle class groups) conjured up by charlatans and false gurus on the basis of the consumers' good faith, and of an ingenuousness that was all too obvious in the stickers stuck to the windows of cars seen driving in the city that said things like 'I believe in fairies'.

In the field of religious studies, the scene was not much changed: on the whole (seen through the prism of fragmentation and a supposed absence of guiding principles, without a 'grammar') these activities taken together deserved to be labelled an *à la carte* religion: having no centralizing hierarchy, no revealed doctrine or unified body of ceremonies, they would get no further than being an enormous *bricolage*, the result of free choice by each of the participants, of sacred elements taken out of the most varied traditions and philosophies.

There was a challenge here: if the current theoretical frame discounted such modalities from being an object worthy of study, nevertheless those who used them still kept seeking them out, more and more intently, in different parts of the city, and the supply of services on offer adjusted to the growth of this demand. So the alternative was to tackle them, through their insertion in the metropolitan landscape, from the perspective of urban anthropology.

The first field trips revealed business models of management, the use of digital technologies, a more and more assiduous presence in the mass media, and the location of these modalities in middle class neighbourhoods. There did indeed seem to be a grammar organizing the way they were distributed through the city, their divulgation and the offer of their services. In this way, as the pole of analysis changed from the religious field to the dynamics of the city, it became possible to verify that beneath the multiplicity of proposals, systems and experiments there were guiding principles: in spatial distribution, in the programming of events that made up a calendar, and in a basic discourse. On the basis of this observation it was possible to identify the existence of a broader lifestyle that included, as one of the factors involved in developing personal potential and self-knowledge, the seeking out of new forms of spirituality and also of religion.

The anchor to hold this whole process is what I have called the Neo-esoteric circuit, a contiguous network in urban space that allows circulation through the most diverse systems, by means of the articulation of places used for courses, therapies, training and ceremonies, for the sale of products, and as meeting points, making a plainly recognizable whole in the urban landscape, that is accessible, open, and without mechanisms of exclusion or sectarian affiliation.[4]

Also according to this project, whose findings are in Magnani (1999), the underlying matrices of this system, that are invoked by its agents for the elaboration of the various discourses, reduce basically to five sources: religions and philosophies vaguely classified as 'oriental' (Buddhism, Hinduism, Taoism and others), intitiation or esoteric societies, indigenous cosmologies (shamanism, from Mircea Eliade's version of Siberian shamanism to the versions of the North American plains Indians, and those of the Andeans and Central Americans), pre-Christian rites from Europe such as those from the Celtic tradition, and even some readings of 'cutting edge' branches of some sciences, such as molecular biology, quantum physics and neurolinguistics.

Listed thus they seem to reaffirm the eclectic nature of some of the formulations current in the context of New Age; however, when the profile of the practitioners is analysed, for instance, here too the look 'from close by and towards the inside' (Magnani, 2002) spots differences: they do not form a homogeneous mass of credulous followers ready to see fairies everywhere; there are differentiations and at least three types of practitioner that the project was able to reveal: the 'erudite', the habitual participants, and the occasional participants. If the epithet ingenuous consumers can safely be applied to this last group, the first group, usually with the task of being 'facilitators', keep up relations of study and research into their areas. Certain yoga instructors, for example, do not treat their practice as just a form of physical exercise, but insert it into specific lines of Hindu cosmology; readers of Kabalah, specialists in astral maps, and appliers of Do-in, Tui na, acupuncture, etc. refer their abilities and practices to the medical, religious and philosophical systems they originally come from.

It therefore has to do with a particular form of expressing a relation with the sacred, which makes contact with other institutions that produce meaning:

4 The expression 'Neo-esotericism' was introduced and developed in earlier works (Magnani, 1999, 2000) to characterize the same phenomenon of beliefs, practices and institutions commonly termed mystical, esoteric or New Age; for a better contextualization of its use, see especially Magnani (1999: 13, note 7). Frequent use of the term 'Neo-esoteric circuit' is due to the fact that the study is not of the New Age as such but of its insertion in the city.

such as those concerned about ecology, the quality of life, respect for the Earth, healthy nutrition, care of the body, or the search for more contemplative spiritual states. I located these institutions in the sphere of the big Neo-esoteric circuit of the metropolis because, rather than their sharing a common base of dogma, what is observed is the establishment of a wide and unexpected system of exchanges; some authors, such as Leila Amaral (1999), refer to this passage as a sort of 'religious nomadism', or 'syncretism in motion' and use other terms to emphasize the transitional nature of these practices. To conclude, urban shamanism, which will form the subject of the next paragraphs, is not just a part of what the circuit is made up of, it is in itself a species of circuit derived from within it (Magnani, 1999:68).

Urban Shamanism

The term 'urban shamanism' or even 'Neo-shamanism' as it has been called, implies one question to start with: What frame of reference is suitable for understanding its scope? Can it be considered a variety of shamanism as described in classic anthropological texts? Taking as a source the native discourse—the literature that they consult, the systems that provide them with a base, and the objectives they pursue—in the Brazilian case the urban shamans, go on to look for inspiration and try to find a foundation for their practices mainly in studies and from writers in the areas of psychology, religion and comparative mythology. When they make references to indigenous cultures or the traditions of pre-historic tribes and civilizations, they reproduce an idealized vision, with an emphasis on a supposedly communal life in harmony with nature and in direct contact with the supernatural plane—a vision which clearly does not always correspond to what academic texts on these peoples have shown.

The findings from this transit over areas so different, responsible for an infinite number of proposals, accommodations and methods, open up a field of research for studies of an ethnographic type. However, it is necessary to have a previous demarcation and characterization of the phenomenon, even before establishing any dialog with the ethnologists studying shamanism in contemporary indigenous societies, or with their models of interpretation. Above all it is a matter of asking oneself about how specific this urban shamanism is, because, to put it plainly, it has only been possible to include it in the more general field of shamanism because the same word is used, though with different meanings, and this makes it possible in the world of common sense to use the term very broadly for labeling the most heterogeneous practices.

So with the objective of establishing a point of concrete support for its study, I have preferred to start with the particularity of the context where it is manifested, rather than accepting it immediately and without further ado, as a sort of variety of a generic shamanism: and this context is, as already mentioned, the current picture of the alternative paths in search of new spiritual, therapeutic, religious and even socializing experiences in the big urban centers. I therefore consider what is termed urban shamanism to be one of so many accommodations and syntheses produced on this scene, and in particular, on the circuit of Neo-esotericism.

Urban shamanism is not, however, just another fashion in this eclectic cauldron: in the highly cosmopolitan and globalized context of the Neo-esoteric world it is inserted into, urban shamanism represents, rather, an important aspect of the movement, along with religious practices and systems included in the broad category of 'oriental philosophies', as well as theosophical-spiritualist currents, European occultist traditions and some paradigms of ecological discourse. It is principally through versions of urban shamanism that the cultures of contemporary indigenous peoples and their ancestors, mainly in the Americas, are incorporated into the Neo-esoteric view of the world.

This is evident in the case of Brazil, where in the search for more proximate 'lineages' as a foundation for their practices and vocation, many of the urban shamans who completed their inititation in the United States, Peru or Mexico, or have kept up links with native masters living in those countries, have proposed founding a line of continuity with the traditions of the indigenous people of Brazil. In this way they begin, from a very particular reading, to discover, value and incorporate into their activities, elements of the *pajelança*,[5] of the myths, the dances and the pharmacopeia of many indigenous groups, which has resulted in countless meetings and workshops with *pajés*, leaders, and members of these groups who have schooling.

Urban shamanism in the case of Brazil amounts to an accommodation, to put it briefly, to another set of practices in the bosom of the Neo-esoteric world and, following the example of others in the same context, it is made up of an aggregation of elements with different origins, from different cultures and historical periods. The results of these agglomerations are not homogeneous: some are more elaborate and coherent, thanks to their having a more consistent degree of compatibility between their component parts; others, on the contrary, do not get beyond being a heap of fragments with little in common; which, naturally, does not stop them from being presented as the representatives of this or that tradition.

To sum up, in short, the aim is to understand the logic of this particular set of practices, in which the adjective 'shamanic' is sometimes more evocative

5 Practice of the *pajés*, an originally Tupi word to designate indigenous shamans or healers.

than really descriptive of an observable, specifically demarcated practice, seeking at first to show how it is inserted—through processes of production, circulation and consumption—into a context where it shows up recurrently and frequently, which is in the Neo-esoteric circuit.

Ethnography

The research which forms the empirical foundation of our reflection on urban shamanism was conducted in the following stages: (a) a survey with questionnaires in the city of São Paulo, of the network of self-styled shamans and the spaces where they act; (b) taking part in talks, round table discussions, and debates to establish a basic discourse, with its differences; (c) observation and recording of rites, celebrations, healing techniques, consultations; and finally, (d) being present and participating more intensively, in shamanic sessions, events and workshops, generally at weekends, some held in the city and most in properties on the periphery of the metropolitan region of the municipality of São Paulo.[6]

Before presenting data from the project, I will mention some of the institutions, places and events visited during the research, to give a more concrete view of this world: Paz Géia—Instituto de Pesquisas Xamânicas, Movimento Alma Xamã, Mekukrudjá—Atividades Indígenas e Ecológicas, Associación Arte e Cultura Idzô'huh, Instituto para Expansão da Consciência, The Four Windows Society, Centro de Dharma Shi-De Choe Tsog, and others.

Observations and recordings of celebrations, meetings, courses, rituals, and healing techniques were also made in the following places: Loja Amoa Konoya—Arte Indígena, Centro Cultural Illawasi, Espaço Momento de Paz, Espaço Tattersal do Parque Água Branca, Espaço Multidisciplinar Atria, Centro de Estudos Triom, Espaço Tattva-Humi, Iniciativa Gaia.

Among the events mentioned, five took place in rural properties close to São Paulo, and four in the city. Daniel Munduruku (of the Munduruku tribe) coordinated two meetings, with the title '*Oficina e vivência: a sabedoria que vem dos mitos*', both in la Chácara Florida, Cotia, SP. The first, which was held on the 1st of February 1997, had the participation as assistants of Siridiwé (Xavante tribe), Ana Vitória (independent shaman), and Mateo Arévalo Mayna (Peruvian shaman). The second took place on the 15th of March 1997, with the participation

6 According to figures from 2010, the city of São Paulo, capital of the State and central municipality of the metropolitan region, had 11,253,503 inhabitants and covered an area of 1,523 square kilometers, while the metropolitan region, of 39 municipalities, extended over 8,000 square kilometers, with a population of 19,672,582.

of Román Quétchua, Maria T., Ailton Krenak (of the Krenak tribe), as well as Siridiwé and Ana Vitória.

Kaká Werá Jecupé (of the Txukurramãe) conducted two workshops, one of them called '*A força dos quatro elementos na tradição indígena brasileira: o elemento terra*', that was held on the 2nd of March 1997, in a residence of the Morumbi neighbourhood of São Paulo. The other, '*Roda da Medicina Cristalina*', took place on the 24th of August 1997, in the property where he lives, which is now the headquarters of the Arapoty Institute that he directs in Itapecerica de la Serra (SP), and one of those taking part was Zezito Duarte. He in turn also conducted two workshops: the first was '*As sete flechas sagradas*'; it had Kaká Werá Jecupé to help and was held in the Sítio Anhangá, in Caucaia do Alto (SP), on the first four days (Thursday to Sunday) of May, 1997. The second was called '*Reacendendo o fogo sagrado da criança*', and was celebrated in a health center in the neighbourhood of Alto de Pinheiros, on the 12th of June 1997.

Alberto Villoldo, a Cuban American, invited and patronized by the publishing firm Editora Ágora and the Gaia Intitiative institution, directed the workshop '*Resgate de Alma no Xamanismo*' on the 26th and 27th (Saturday and Sunday) of April 1997, in a place situated in a neighbourhood called la Vila Madalena. Cecília Schmidt Oliveira (shaman and body therapist) and César Augusto Sartorelli (shaman and astrologer), offered a *Curso de Introdução ao Xamanismo* (eight classes) from October to December 1996, in the *Espaço Multidisciplinar Átria*, neighborhood of Pinheiros. And finally, Jorge Menezes, leader of the *Movimento Alma Xamã* organization, presided over an event called '*Iniciação Xamânica*' on the 6th and the 7th of December 1997, Saturday and Sunday, at the property 'Refúgio dos Índios', municipality of Mairiporã, SP.

Generally speaking the events,[7] whether those of the urban circuit or those that take place out of it, have the same structure: they start with a talk by the 'facilitator' about the dynamics of the occasion, and the basic course it will be taking; then everyone forms into a circle to introduce themselves, starting with the facilitator and his (or her) assistants, followed by the participants who explain the reasons why they have decided to sign up to the workshop.

The various activities during the day or a whole weekend consist of physical exercises that include relaxing, stretching, dances, sequences of a codified practice (yoga, tai chi chuan, liangong); teaching and practice of healing techniques, self-healing, massage, and self-knowledge, conducted in groups or in pairs; rites that include cleansings with tobacco, bonfires, making javelins, arrows, masks, body painting, and so on; specific practices to gain ASC (altered

---

7 To save space, I have omitted accounts of the events conducted by Kaká Werá Jecupé and by Jorge Menezes; they usually followed the same pattern as the rest.

FIGURE 3.1 *Sweat lodge in southern Brazil. Urubici-Santa Catarina, Brazil, January 2008*
PHOTO: ALINE FERREIRA OLIVEIRA

states of consciousness) or going on a shamanic trip by means of Temazcal sweat lodges, induced relaxation and in some cases, the use of a psychoactive plant (see Figure 3.1).

The differences and the particular emphases depend on the outlook of each facilitator and his group. For example, the events and the workshops conducted by Zezito Duarte, explicitly identified with the 'North American' line, all started with the *talk stick*, then followed with the drum and finally with the *sweat lodge*, as means of inducing altered states of mind, shamanic trips and meetings with your 'power animal'. References are always to rites, myths, legends and practices attributed in a general way to 'North American Indians', sometimes particularized as this or that tribe (the Cherokee, the Hopi, the Cheyenne, etc.). In spite of the reference to a tribe, other instruments and techniques currently used in the Neo-esoteric world would also be included, such as crystals, balancing the chakras, meditation practices and so on.

The events and workshops conducted by Daniel Munduruku, with the presence and performance of different indigenous peoples from all over Brazil, had as its base a generic discourse on 'The Indian', punctuated by references to one culture or another. Instead of healing rites, the stress was on going back to nature, and on contact with the typical elements of the ways of life of these peoples (the dance, body painting, and myths). The shamanic trips and the announced ASC were brought about at the end of these events by the use of ayahuasca, in a ceremony conducted in one case by a Peruvian shaman, and at the other event, by an 'independent' (woman) shaman. In the course of these two events it was possible to appreciate a clear separation between the part dedicated to activities like talks on indigenous culture and history, dances, or the telling of legends, and the other, given over to the use of the plant.

With regard to Alberto Villoldo, he belongs to a class of shamans who first contacted indigenous cultures as part of an academic interest (a dissertation or research project on psychology, and anthropology) and ended up 'converted', usually after a rupture represented by their experience with one of the 'power plants' with psychoactive properties. They go through a period of initiation guided by a native master, and then go on to hold shamanic sessions themselves, giving courses, writing books, and organizing excursions to 'places of power', always through some business structure, with everything duly divulged on internet sites.[8]

The best known of a generation of shamans and a pioneer among them, was Carlos Castaneda, followed by Michael Harner, Stanley Krippner, Foster Perry, Terence McKenna and others.

The events and the workshops of Alberto Villoldo that were held in São Paulo (with the help of a translator from English to Portuguese), and were an object of observation in the project, basically followed the typical discourse of Andean culture. Talks, and sessions to learn healing and self-healing techniques, took up nearly all the time of the event, as well as the visualizing of 'power animals' and a ceremony around a bonfire, where arrows made during the meeting were burned.

The event or workshop conducted by César Sartorelli and Cecilia Schmidt took on the character of a course, with eight classes. In spite of its being didactic, it presented the usual ingredients of the events: ceremonies (to open and close each session), talks, techniques and exercises for the 'shamanic trip', dances, relaxation, etc. finishing with an informal get together in a typical São Paulo pizza house and the promise of an initiation in a natural scene. Of the pair, César adopted the more 'brainy' role, quoting writers like Mircea Eliade, Joseph Campbell or Carl Jung and referring all the time to a 'speculative physics' type of science, with 'many planes connected by black holes', or 'levels of

8 The Foundation for Shamanic Studies, of Michael Harner http://www.shamanism.org and The Four Winds Society, of Alberto Villoldo, http://www.thefourwinds.com/, to name but two.

frequency'. Cecilia took the opposite, more 'intuitive' part. As they had both received their training in *la Paz Géia—Instituto de Pesquisas Xamânicas*, from Carminha Levy, their outlook was eclectic: César was constantly recalling his experience in Siberia, where he had gone on an excursion to Lake Baikal, in Buriatia, and his contact with Nadja Stepanova, a shaman he had met in Italy and later brought over to Brazil. Cecilia, who trained as a biologist but is a shamanic therapist, and exercises her practice in her own space in La Paz Géia, often referred to the 'matrix shamanism' that is commended by Carminha Levy.

Some Characteristics and Particularities

From the information gleaned by attending the events described above, and information picked up from other sources (talks, interviews, ceremonies, native literature, and consultations) it was possible to define certain common features that the various forms assumed by urban shamanism in the city of São Paulo possess.

In one way or another they all claim, whatever the specific culture each is affiliated to, to be the depositaries of a lineage with a long tradition, that of the oldest form of contact with planes of consciousness out of the ordinary. In some cases, recognition of an ancestral lineage goes back to time out of mind, the time of legends, marked by harmonious contact with nature and its forces, as can be seen in the first paragraph of the book *La conocedora de animales: viajes chamánicos y mitologías*, (The Knower of Animals: Shamanic and Mythological Trips) by Carminha Levy and Álvaro Machado, of la Paz Géia:

> At the Dawn of Time, when the Human Being slept in Eden and mingled with the world on the same undifferentiated field, some men and women discovered the power of waking up. Separating themselves from an initial, archaic, stage, where they were united with Nature in an 'Ouroboros' state, these special beings, who had the power to leave the body, inserted themselves into the Grand Current of Beings and reached the plane of the soul, where the archetypes lie. On their return to earth, they brought with them a vision of the Archetype of Divinity.
>
> LEVY, 1995:13

As well as being a search for ancestry, shamanism is understood, in these so-called urban versions, to be a capacity within everyone's reach that it is possible to awaken and develop.

This is an interpretation that gets farther and farther away from the more traditional view found in the literature, whether of anthropology or of the history of religions, according to which the shaman, a specialist in dealing with the plane of reality deemed to be outside the ordinary, has access to it as the function of a particular disposition, manifested by specific signs, that is approved and legitimized by initiation rites. To come into contact with this level of reality, impelled by the demands of the group he is joined to, it is important for the shaman to respect a series of taboos and precepts. In urban shamanism, however, anyone can cultivate this capacity, discover his guardian animal, possess objects of power and go on the shamanic trip: it is enough to learn, and to put into practice, specific techniques available during the countless courses, workshops and counsellings on offer in the network of Neo-esoteric institutions. And, in contrast to the prolonged periods taken for initiation in the classic forms, here the products are offered in a quicker way, adapted to the rythmn and the needs of modern life. This is how Michael Harner answered criticisms made of his intensive courses in shamanism after the nuclear accident of Chernobyl, in 1986:

> If the great nations of the world are working day and night on their own intensive programmes for our mutual destruction, we cannot afford the luxury of going more slowly in our work, which moves in the opposite direction. The slow learning that was possible in the ancient tribal cultures is no longer appropriate. The forces of nuclear and ecological destruction are advancing fast and we should also do so. It is necessary for people to wake up; otherwise, they may sleep for ever. And it is necessary not just that people wake up to ordinary reality, but that they gain a personal, deeply spiritual, comprehension of the interconnection between all that exists. We are working together and as fast as we can.
>
> TOWSEND, 1993: 120–121

Alberto Villoldo was more emphatic, at the event he conducted in São Paulo in December 1997, in stressing how fast results were obtained, when he said: 'what the Zen Buddhist seeks to attain during thirty years of meditation in a monastery, the shaman achieves in six seconds, in the presence of the Jaguar'.

Another common aspect that is seen at all the events, to a greater or lesser extent, is the combination of techniques, ceremonies and objects with far different origins; drum, sweat lodge, maracas, tobacco, herbs, cleansings, the making of arrows, bonfires, masks, and body painting, from the indigenous peoples; dances and physical exercises whether indigenous or oriental (lian-gong, tai chi chuan, yoga); and an emphasis on healthy nutrition, whether vegetarian or macrobiotic, when the event lasts for several days (see Figure 3.2).

And finally, last but not least (and leaving the list open), another typical feature of urban shamanism that also distinguishes it from traditional interpretations is the objective aimed at: the search is for personal perfection through techniques that lead to self-knowledge, to the development of personal capacities and to self-healing. As opposed to what happens in societies where shamanism is seen as a specific institution, in which certain specialists practice to help (or to hinder) members of the group, in the modalities that we are considering, shamanism is thought of as a kind of 'archetype' present in everyone and ready to be put to work as an access to the 'higher self', as César Sartorelli taught in his *Curso de Xamanismo*. This self-referring approach does not, however, exclude specialization: if someone feels they have a vocation to exercise their powers professionally, then (according to Sartorelli) they do need to submit to a more systematic process and, most importantly, be affiliated to a lineage, a specific 'ancestry', after all.

If so much concern about the aspect of personal growth and the perfection of one's potentials is a point of inflexion and of distancing from traditional shamanic forms, it is also off-putting to certain modalities of shamanism that occur in popular segments both in cities and in rural areas where systems with a high degree of syncretism combine elements of native cultures with religions of European origin, of the kind described by Sharon (1988) and Taussig (1993).[9]

The evils whose discovery is sought, and that are a recurring motive for members of these population groups to seek out the services of the shamans (or, to use different native terms that do not always coincide: witchdoctors, sorcerers, healers, and diviners) are in great part attributed to envy.[10] Difficulties and misfortunes in people's personal relationships, love lives or at work occur in networks that include relatives, neighbors, illwishers, acquaintances, colleagues, employers, or authorities: it turns out to be of fundamental importance to be aware of the dangers, to take preventive measures against an ambush, to counter attack and to know whom to blame, if one is to get through situations marked by a chronic shortage of material and financial resources.

9 This is probably also the case of the Kaxinauá shaman Carlito, in Rio Branco, capital of Acre, mentioned by Manuela Carneiro da Cunha: 'mixing techniques borrowed from the Jawanawa and the Katukina of Gregório and of Tarauaká, combined with rituals taken from Umbanda, learned in Belém and Manaus. His clients consist of his own large family and aged followers from the poorest *barrios* of Rio Branco' (Carneiro da Cunha, op. cit., 230).

10 As also happens with the *terreiros* of Umbanda (Magnani, 1980:43 and ff.).

FIGURE 3.2 *Urban shamanistic groups meet indians from Acre and Northeast for ritual with ayahuasca in Cotia-São Paulo, March 2011*
PHOTO: ALINE FERREIRA OLIVEIRA

But this is not what goes on in the versions of urban shamanism that are practiced on the Neo-esoteric circuit and are spread principally among the middle classes: here dangers do not come from others, but from inside the individual, and the prosperity one seeks will depend on knowledge of one's own potentialities or on the correction of interior perturbations. Illness is not the result of trivial disharmonies, of imbalances in networks of social relations, but comes form a cosmic level, from a lack of respect for the demands of Mother Earth, and disorder between the various levels of the universe that are also found in each individual, who is seen as a microcosm.

As distinct from what happens with Creole or Popular shamanism, here there is no ground formed by a network whose threads are: the opportunities for work, sustenance, help, and also the conflicts that arise where these population groups pass their daily lives. The communities that form, to learn and practice this other type of urban shamanism, are ephemeral, occasional, and formed in relation to having similar lifestyles (thus more on the plane of consumption than popular shamanism is), as opposed to those formed in the course of an everyday life marked by a scarcity of resources and opportunities. Which explains why in this type of shamanism there is no reference to 'attack' performances when the specialist takes the side of his client in a dispute that the client is having with an opponent, on the level of personal, affective relations, which is what happens with the 'demands' that are so common in Afro-Brazilian cults.

On the same subject, the relation of urban shamanism (in the Brazilian version) to such cults as these provides another facet of how it differs from popular beliefs and practices of healing. The research documented a meeting that illustrates the point: a symposium called *Encontro de Tradições: Budismo Tibetano, Candomblé, Povos Indígenas, Xamanismo Urbano*, held on the 9th of October 1996 in the Social Science Department of the PUC (Pontifícia Universidade Católica) of São Paulo, brought together a (female) anthropologist, a (female) urban shaman, some Tibetan lamas, a Siberian (female) shaman and a representative of the *Orishas* religion. The anthropologist gave her definition,[11] the urban shaman conducted the concluding ceremony, the lamas brought the voice of the old shamanic traditions of Tibet, of the *bon-po* previous to Buddhist times, and finally, to talk about Candomblé, there was an African postgraduate student from the University of São Paulo.

The fact that the representative of Candomblé should have been an African student and not a Brazilian Babalorixá or Ialorixá should not pass unobserved: it provides a clue to understanding the little contact there is between urban shamanism and the Afro-Brazilian religious traditions, which also fail to appear in the more general picture of Neo-esotericism, where they are regarded with some mistrust.

In the first instance, for elements of the Afro-Brazilian tradition to be legitimized in this universe, they have to be re-named and recovered specifically as a form of shamanism and not just as Umbanda or Candomblé: in the *Tashi Delê*, published by the *Centro de Dharma Shi-de Choe Tsog*, of the Tibetan Buddhist Gelupa lineage, the ex 'pai-de-santo' (Candomblé priest) now 'lama' Shakya Zangpo, is referred to as a shaman, and his system of healing is classified as an integration of 'principles and practices of Tantric Buddhism to Brazilian shamanism'.

It is interesting to note that while the indigenous cultures are incorporated and are valued for their links to nature and the creatures of the forest, the 'Afro'

11 'Shamanism is a social institution that, through ecstasy (provoked by various techniques, from meditation to the use of hallucinogenic substances), makes it possible to come into contact with the supernatural world (which is also defined in different ways by different cultures) and, from this contact, physical and psychic healing proceeds'. One of the monks asked Carminha Levy to give her definition of shamanism as well, and she said it is 'a technique of extremely rapid expansion of consciousness; a kind of high tec of the sacred' (1996).

traditions are identified with pulsations of the 'basic self', 'heavy' energies activated by animal sacrifices and by the accelerated rhythmic beat of the atabaque drums, as opposed to the monotonous single note of the traditional Siberian or North American shaman. It cannot yet be ruled out that this rejection is partly due to the fact that the root of the 'Afro' cults is popular and black, which makes it welcome in certain intellectualized sectors of the middle class, but not in that part that identifies with the proposals of Neo-esotericism.

Finally, there is one other argument for the separation of these types of devotion from each other, which is based on the distinction, still made in the most general writing on the subject, between two forms of altered awareness: if in the 'Afro' cults the altered awareness comes through being possessed by a spirit, in shamanism the general rule is that it comes in an ecstatic trance, in the shape of 'loss of the soul' or 'magic flight'. In the former, the spirit takes possession of the intermediary (the medium, or *iaô*) who serves the spirit as a vehicle, as an instrument; while in the latter, the agent maintains the initiative, as a soul that travels on the supernatural plane.[12]

In spite of this separation, one should remember that the Paz Géia institution—Instituto de Pesquisas Xamânicas, of Carminha Levy, is one of the few that refers explicitly to the *Orishas,* seeking a point of contact between the myths of the African deities and the practices developed in its halls. However, even in this case, the *Orishas* are accepted by virtue of their being reinterpreted as archetypes, guardians of natural forces, while their liturgy, beliefs and the offerings customarily made in the *terreiros* are discarded.

So when some elements of these cults appear in a Neo-esoteric context or as part of urban shamanism, they have passed through the filter of the dominant code. According to the code, a reference to Africa, where these cults came from with the slaves, gives them a mark of authenticity. The same does not apply to the syncretisms some of them (for example, Umbanda) experienced when they came into contact with other influences. When an element from one of these religions—generally considered as having lower vibrations because of the percussion instruments used, or because of their sensual dances, etc.—appears, it has to go through the filter, a kind of censorship. According to the filter, having an ancestry is a criterion for acceptance and in this case Candomblé, with its African associations, is considered more 'authentic' and therefore, acceptable. Whereas Umbanda, a more recent syncretic religion, from the early twentieth century (1920s), combining Spiritism, Christianity and indigenous cults, not having such a pedigree lacks prestige. This might explain why at the symposium described above it was an African,

12 For more information, see the discussion conducted by Pereira, 1992: 5 and ff.

who was a university student and what is more, at postgraduate level, who represented the *Orishas*. However, there is no such rejection on the other side: it is not unusual for there to be a *pais* and a *mães-de-santo* who incorporate into their discourse and their ritual or healing practice, elements typical of the Neo-esoteric world.

A variation of this question of contact between shamanism and Brazilian possession cults is one provided by a most unusual experience, as it concerns an ethnic minority within the Japanese community in Brazil: it has to do with the Okinawa shamans, first recorded, according to Professor Koichi Mori (2008)—who has studied the subject—in the nineteen fifties, when a woman from the community of emigrants from Okinawa living in São Paulo had health problems, and as no one in her community was able to attend her, went to take part in an Umbanda *terreiro*, where she received the spirit of *apreto velho*, a typical being of the Umbanda religion, but was also possessed by the spirit of an Okinawan forefather; thus she became the first Okinawan shaman (*yuta*) able to traverse the two systems. The contact was kept up and in the nineteen eighties Brazilian (female) shamans of Okinawan descent started travelling to Japan, and specifically to the isle of Okinawa, to receive training directly from the shamans there. Their guardian 'spirit' is no less than Nuestra Señora de Aparecida (Our Lady of Aparecida), patron saint of Brazilian Catholics, which widens the scope of this syncretism that, frankly, is miles apart from the New Age.

Urban Shamanism and the Logic of the Neo-esoteric Circuit

The Paz Géia Institute, which has the title to being the first school of Neo-shamanism in Brazil (*A primeira escola de neo-chamanismo do Brasil*), is an example of one of the types of shamanism that we are considering: with the crest of the wave of Neo-esotericism now past, it remains a reference and not only in the city of São Paulo. The institute holds regular courses of training and covers all the traditions, although it has developed a line called 'matrix shamanism' characterized by an emphasis on recovering the female side of this practice.

Those who have passed through its portals include exponents of globalized shamanism (Foster Perry, Nadja Stepanova, Rowland Barkley) with its innovations and contributions, introduced from the perspective of an ancient consolidated tradition such as that of the Buriate shaman, or from the point of view of a scientificist discourse like that of Barkley, which earns the adjective in a leaflet announcing one of his visits: 'Australian shaman who specializes in the reprogramming of subtle DNA, NLP [neurolinguistic programming], Time Line Holographic Therapy, Therapy of the Higher Self'.

The ceremonies observed during the regular programs of Paz Géia allowed other exemplary aspects of this eclecticism to be captured: a belly dance at the end of the year party, a celebration and talk on the Black Virgin on the occasion of the feast of Our Lady of Aparecida, given by a priest from 'the Old Catholic Church', and a meeting to discuss the diversity of sexual orientations and the freedom to decide one's own. This eclecticism reaffirms the point that the context of urban shamanism has less to do with localized indigenous cosmologies, and more to do with the frame of experimentation current in the wider field of contemporary spirituality and/or religiosity.

This impression was confirmed by the presence of elements of the most diverse origins in the discourse and the rituals, and even at the events and workshops that invoked indigenous traditions at the same time as notions like those of the chakras, the ordinary and the higher selves, the subtle body, holism, archetypes, and the employment of physical practices linked to oriental philosophies, the use of crystals, astrological symbols, etc. Some of the original terms from localized traditions or that are just associated with them, like the ubiquitous 'Pachamama', the 'council of elders', the 'Great Spirit', the 'sacred dances' and many others, circulated through all the lines indistinctly.

It must be concluded that this institute, which represents urban shamanism, lacks a reference to a specific cosmology that would give it a meaning, a direction and a legitimacy as in the indigenous societies where shamanism is a socially demarcated institution and structurally a part of the dynamics of tribal life; it also lacks the urgency that makes *caboclo* or popular shamanism a necessary tool for dealing with the harsh survival of everyday life. However, I am not saying that it is reduced to being just an aggregate of beliefs and gestures that are arbitrarily brought together, or separated from some of the traits of its users' ways of life: it is possible, beyond this fragmentation, to observe the presence of a common frame. To identify where its coherence lies and how its structural elements are organized, it was necessary to identify first the field in which it circulates (that of Neo-esotericism), and more concretely, which Neo-esoteric circle it is joined to.

The research undertaken to that end (of which studying urban shamanism forms a part) showed that, contrary to a common belief today (both in the communications media and in academic studies), the New Age movement is not an erratic and incongruous aggregate of beliefs, practices and doctrines of the most varied provenance, but shows regular features. Through having chosen to look through the lense of urban anthropology, regularities were observed most readily in its distribution over the *space* of the city, which is where it forms what I have called the Neo-esoteric circuit. However, the same regularities could also be seen over *time*, forming a sort of calendar of Neo-esoteric practices.

Thus, in spite of its particularites, urban shamanism not only formed a part of this world, but it was here that it found its sustenance, its conditions for development and its environment for barter. The research also showed that beyond eclecticism, which is the result of the reading and individual experience of its mentors, it was possible to distinguish the presence of a basic matrix, underlying the principal modalities found in the field. This matrix is the same one that provides a more general discursive support to the world of Neo-esotericism itself:

> At one end stands the Individual, in his various denominations and degrees of depth ('inner self/higher self', 'personal story', self, inner spirituality, self-spirituality, inner voice), at the other, the point where this indvidual emanates from, what he is part of and where he is going, in other words, the Whole (Transcendence, the Absolute, the Cosmos, the Higher Principle, Nature, or whatever the term). The history of humanity would be no more than a long journey, tinted by the idiosyncrasies of every culture, to reestablish full contact between the multiple and the one, and this was only possible because the former was always part of the latter. The social character of the life of human beings, however, puts a third party in between the Individual and the Whole, the Community, the depositary and the guardian of each particular tradition and the means for its members, in all historical contexts, to reach their true nature. The ideal model therefore says that there must be an indiviudal, seen in his integrity (of body, mind and spirit), that belongs to a community considered harmonious, in whose fold he perfects himself, with both the individual and the community immersed in and integrated to a more inclusive and complete reality that it is necessary to become aware of.
>
> MAGNANI, 1999: 93

At the pole of the Whole, what appears most frequently in the shamanic proposals is Mother Earth, Pachamama, the Planet, Nature; while the line of the Community is represented in various ways: first, by the indigenous peoples, sometimes through a vague reference but also in a 'realistic' way through the presence of one of its members at the events and shamanic sessions, which guarantees the 'authenticity' of these get-togethers; secondly, thanks to the trajectory of the 'facilitators', to the extent that they have submitted to an initiation process conducted by a shaman from a specific line and whom they consider to be their master, which gives the 'lineage' legitimacy. The third type of community, on this side of a triangle drawn to represent the Whole, the Community and the Individual, is made up of those participating in the events, members of a community that dissolves at the end of every workshop, with the possibility of reuniting or not, partly or wholly, at the next event. In this case, it corresponds to the usual idea of community on the Neo-esoteric circuit in general: as something ephemeral, transitory, and open.

The pole of the Individual (noted in studies of the New Age phenomenon, of contemporary spirituality and of alternative practices, as the dimension in which modernity has left its marks under the labels of 'psychologizing', 'reflexivity' and 'autonomy')[13] is particularly emphasized in the circles of urban shamanism. As we have shown, the shamanic capacity is a quality anyone can have: the rites, the techniques and the exercises developed in the various lines are considered means that are sufficient and are capable of modifying the direction of interior flows, of transmuting the weight of traumatic personal occasions, of redirecting negative impulses, of reaching the most hidden subjectivity.

At the same time, the space where it circulates and where it is sociologically significant, probably through the social inclusion of its members (basically middle class), or the objectives proposed and the infrastructure it makes use of (places, installations and equipment), as has been noted throughout this discussion, is that of the wider Neo-esoteric circle as it is spread over, for example, the city of São Paulo.

It is even possible to detect a scheme of connections: the shamans living outside the city who visit regularly, put into action before their arrival a network. This is made up of: the institute that has invited them and serves as a contact and as a place to sign up for courses, talks and small ceremonies; a property on the outskirts of the city, for events and weekend workshops; a clinic or surgery where private consultations are given; and local helpers, possessed of a list of e-mail addresses or telephone numbers to spread the agenda.

One example of several is that of Zezito Duarte, who comes to São Paulo on a regular basis from the Sítio Riachinho, in the Chapada Diamantina (Bahia), and put the following points of the circuit in action for the activities of his stay in August 1997:

---

13 See Russo, 1993; Heelas, 1996; D'Andrea, 1998; Carozzi, 1999d; Amaral, 1999.

(a) Event: 'A Dança Interior' in the Sítio Anhangá, municipality of Cotia (metropolitan region of São Paulo).
(b) Workshops: 'A Dança Interior', at the clinic of the *barrio* Alto de Pinheiros, and 'Contando histórias', at the Narayana Yoga Schoo, *barrio* Higienópolis.
(c) Round table: 'Super Homem: o mito', at the Spiro Bookshop, barrio de los Jardines.
(d) Round table: 'The Cure', at the Espaço Emanez, barrio de Perdizes.
(e) Workshop: 'Mandala Cristalina: uma roda de cura', at the headquarters of la Fraternidad Pax Universal, barrio de Santana.
(f) Workshop: 'Mandala Cristalina: uma roda de cura', at the Chácara Potira, Itapecerica de la Serra (metropolitan region of São Paulo).

One final question; does this logic, revealed by the 1997 research Project, still apply today? As generally happened with the Neo-esoteric movement, once past the apogee, only those institutions survived that were more solidly inserted and that depended hardly at all on the stimulus of marketing: many places, shops, sales points and so on that did not have much to sustain them, whether in terms of doctrine, or of logistics, closed their doors. In the case of shamanism, two examples of continuity are provided, by Carminha Levy with her Paz Géia—Instituto de Pesquisas Xamânicas, and Leo Artese with his Centro de Estudos de Xamanismo Vôo da Águia, which succeeded the Instituto para Expansão da Consciência.[14]

It is worth emphasising that Leo Artese includes the ayahuasca plant in his shamanic repertoire, and its use has been disseminated, it must be said, through the big urban centres of the whole country by affiliates of Santo Daime, União do Vegetal, and Cefluris e Barquinha, whose headquarters are in

14 A brief resumé available on his web page gives an idea of this person. 'Elo Artese: student of shamanism, has been initiated in the USA/Peru/Brazil, has been conducting ceremonies, rituals, study groups and shamanism workshops since 1990. Holistic therapist, acupuncturist, founder and director of Espacio Centro de Estudios de Chamanismo Vuelo del Águila. Founder and president of Centro Eclético de Fuente de Luz Universal Cielo de Luna Llena. Qualified Personal Professional Coach, certified by the International Coaching Council—Member of la Sociedad Brasileña de Coaching. Master Practitioner in Systemic Neurolinguistic Programming (*Programación Neurolingüística Sistémica*—PAHC). Motivation speaker, training consultant, specialist in marketing and sales. Executive Director of *L&C Asesoría en Desarrollo Social y Cultural* (Consultancy on Social and Cultural Development). Graduate in Business Management. Story teller. Teacher of verbal communication, techniques for presentation in personal marketing. Author of the books *O Vôo da Águia* and *O Espírito Animal*, Editora Roca. Owner of the web site www.xamanismo.com.br'.

the north of Brazil. The use of this plant within these institutions (deemed to be religions) is allowed and regulated by federal law. However, there have been a lot of disagreements about its more widespread use, often outside any religious context.[15]

Nevertheless, other institutional and discursive components have also been incorporated into urban shamanism. Kaká Werá Jecupé, who runs the Instituto Arapoty, in Itapecerica da Serra (on the outskirts of São Paulo) claims his company, dedicated to idigenous culture, develops social and cultural projects on the principle of 'eco-sustainability'. Further, the Institute follows the guidelines of a Social Organization (*Organização Social*, OS) through which the law in Brazil allows it to obtain public funding: the Institute was recognized as a cultural center ('Ponto de Cultura'), in a programme of the Cultural Ministry of the federal government. The same applies to the Instituto U'ka—Casa de los Saberes Ancestrais, run by Daniel Munduruku, that works for indigenous education and the production of publications with indigenous writers. Ciro Leãoo (Espaço Transformação), like Carminha Levy and Leo, keeps his orientation (healing rituals, consultations, courses, pep talks with companies) still framed in the Neo-esoteric circuit. So also do Dalton Campos Roque, Alexandre Meirelles, Hugo França, Wagner Frota, Akaiê Sramana, Samuel Silva, and others, who keep up their spaces and internet sites for divulgation.

Another reference to the national scale is provided by la Universidad Internacional de la Paz, which has been since 1987 a network with units all over the country. UNIPAZ is an OSCIP (*Organizaçao da Sociedad Civil de Interesse Público*) which according to the same legislation covers certain activities that are typical of the New Age, but in a more academic format, with training courses, symposia, etc. The *UNIPAZ del Rio Grande do Sul* is home to the organization 'los Guerreiros do Coração', with clear allusions to the shamanistic idea: of ancestral wisdom, valuing the feminine, etc.

To get a complete picture of urban shamanism in Brazil, there are other leads that need to be followed up. In cities located in regions with a good number of indigenous people living there, as is the case of Manaus, capital of the State of Amazonia, there are many experiences of 'shamanistic tourism': indigenous people from various tribes offering programs, mainly to foreign visitors, that include trips to the jungle, typical foods, dances, medicines and also shamanic sessions, either as spectacle or indeed for healing (see Figure 3.3). This is what happens, for example, in the Sateré-Mawé tribe's community of Sahú-Apé, in the municipality of Iranduba, near Manaus.

---

15 For more information see Volcoc et al. (2011).

FIGURE 3.3 *'Tucandeira' ritual of the Sateré-Mawé tribe of Amazonia, during which the initiate dances wearing gloves full of tucandeira ants (known as bullet ants). People from other tribes, and even 'whites' may take part. City of Manaus, Amazonia, Brazil, July 2010*
PHOTO: JOSÉ GUILHERME C. MAGNANI

Another case is seen on the Playa do Tupé, a beach on the edge of the Black River (río Negro), about 25 kilometres from Manaus, roughly an hour away by boat. This beach is the destination of many tourism programs for Brazilian and foreign citizens, who are offered a series of attractions: meals of local fish, the lovely beach on one of the rivers flowing into the Amazon, and two large, well equippped *ocas*, one of them with an attractive sign saying 'Núcleo Cultural Indígena, *Umuri mahsã wirã kuru opinión wi'i-tõ, õ, pa wi'idessana-tukana-tuyuka*' and the other, with a sign saying '*Umuri diro mahsã bayari wi'i bayiriko iw'i*', where visitors are offered, for a fee, exhibitions of ritual objects, rituals, ceremonies, songs and dances of the Tukano tribe.

Similar examples may be found in other indigenous areas, such as the Parque Indígena do Xingu, in the north of the State of Mato Grosso, in the central region of Brazil. Such situations as these offer a new field of study for researches into shamanism, where 'urban' has in a way moved out to spaces away from the big urban centers, in search, perhaps, of an environment judged to be more in keeping with the shamanic practices.

Conclusion

From all that has been presented and commented on here, some more general conclusions can be drawn, about the relations between urban shamanism and the New Age movement in the context of Brazil, with particular reference to the case of São Paulo. Firstly, it is clear that this movement at its apogee offered not only a discursive framework but also a concrete institutional circuit, which I have called a Neo-esoteric circuit, in the urban landscape, there to exercise its practice.

Urban shamanism in turn has left its marks on the New Age movement: it was through the mediation of urban shamanism that the Neo-esoteric context was able to acquire a type of wisdom thought to be contained in the gestures and beliefs preserved in orally transmitted primitive rites, within communities who were its guardians. In this way, urban shamanism did not just share the same model which served as a base and support for the multifarious varieties of Neo-esoteric discourse: because it also developed a similar dynamic for spreading and organizing itself in the city landscape, following those objectives (self-knowledge, seeking personal betterment, obtaining cures from outside the protocols of official medicine, and integration with more ample 'holistic' dimensions) that are common to other systems and proposals of this eclectic movement.

However, this shamanism was a rather special version, distilled from rituals coming principally from the plains Indians of North America, and from the Andean plateau, as well as the Yucatán peninsula and elsewhere in Mexico, rather than from the indigenous traditions of people in Brazil. Thus, so to say, its exogenous character is even more striking when there is seen to be little or no contact between urban shamanism in a New Age frame, and certain religions that are widespread in Brazil: that is, the Afro-Brazilian cults, that may also be thought of in the same key as shamanism; and there may even be rejection of the one by the other.

What is more, this is a globalized version of shamanism: names like Carlos Castaneda, Michael Harney, Perry Foster, Alberto Villoldo, Nadja Stepanova, Rowland Barkley, and others, freely go the rounds, whether as references or personally, in the best known shamanic spaces and institutions. Past their peak in the nineties, however, many of the more ephemeral shamanic experiences, without much real substance to back them up, disappeared. Those that were kept up, and supported a lasting circuit, were those with a more consistent discourse, offering training courses that lasted longer, establishing international contacts, and that had appropriate premises, in good locations inside the city and on the outskirts.

It is also necessary in the case of Brazil to mention the spread and the use of the ayahuasca plant in the context of urban shamanism. Originally cultivated, prepared and used in the nineteen thirties in the northern State of Acre as the basis of practices that were institutionalised as Santo Daime, la União do Vegetal, and Barquinha (strongly syncretic of Catholicism, Spiritism and Umbanda), it spread through the cities of the South-East in the seventies (Labate, 2004). However, it was in the peak years of the New Age that it came into the Neo-esoteric circuit and, more recently, it has become a therapeutic practice beyond the religious rituals (Mercante, 2009). There are also studies that show it has reached indigenous tribes and communities whose rituals and cosmologies do not orignally include the use of this plant (De Rose and Langdon, 2010).

Finally, it is worth noting the presence of certain new features in the exercise of shamanic practices: some of its representatives seek, beyond the frame of the New Age, an approximation to the current discourses on eco-sustainability, which also allows them to request money from NGOs and government bodies. This way a wider range of opportunities is opened up for the diffusion of shamanic practices, one of which is a kind of tourism in traditional indigenous areas, and so a closer contact with their reality. The struggles for delineating and legalizing their lands, the programmes of bilingual education, and the admission of young people with different ethnic origins to university, have made the indigenous presence more visible, and this has allowed their rites, their cosmologies, their healing procedures and their medicines to come into contact with present day experiments in the wider field of contemporary spirituality and/or religiosity, understood better as 'ways of life' or 'life styles' than as religions, strictly speaking.

CHAPTER 4

Endo- and Exo-shamanism in Mexico: Doctrines Disputing over 'Ethnic Spirituality'

Jacques Galinier

In this chapter an attempt is made to examine how, in Mexico, the hermeneutics of indigenous peoples have served as a background fabric for the elaboration of exegeses that feed into the rituals related to mystical tourism. But the aim is also, to see in what way do these peoples stimulate the elaboration of a standard and stable corpus of doctrine, in the service of a transnational orthodoxy. In particular, attention will be given to the controversial term 'spirituality', which has come up in academic conferences to refer to the types of knowledge and the worldviews of the native peoples of America, ever since the foundation in 1966 of the Inter-American Indigenous Spirituality Council (*Consejo Interamericano sobre Espiritualidad Indígena*, CISEI).[1] The strategic position this concept holds both in the discourse of the Mesoamerican New Age and in anthropological reflections, will be discussed. We will also consider the way in which 'spirituality' has found an echo in new theoretical interpretations of Freudian psychoanalysis.

The complexity of New Age thinking in its American Neo-shamanist version has been widely discussed, especially because of the hybrid, agglutinating character of its philosophical precepts, and the diversity both in time and in space of its original cultural sources. However, we can now see how a form of vulgate is being created, that combines some themes of urban ecology, museum folklore, and academic history with topics from the alternative psychologies that dominate the European and North American markets. Mexican Neo-shamanism is no longer a novelty, and it has started to form part of a heavy current, with its own public, its rules and its rituals. In particular, the appreciation of sacred sites or 'magic pueblos' expresses the dynamics of a single pattern, easily identifiable from one side of the American continent to the other, that expresses itself through a nomenclature of terms as widely spread as 'culture', 'mystic', 'harmony' and many others.

1 See Raquel Gutiérrez Nájera and Marina Villalobos Díaz (2000).

 | DOI 10.1163/9789004316485_007

Between Endo- and Exo-shamanism: The Ritual Return

Before exploring the nomenclature, and to put the semantic changes of New Age terminology in their places, it is necessary for us to make a distinction between what may be called endo- and exo-shamanism.[2] Endo-shamanism concerns ceremonial practices by members of an indigenous community, *in situ* or in places they have migrated to. There is not just one model that can encapsulate all the processes of resistance or of adaptation by the shamanic tradition, to the evangelization which has remodeled local Pre-Hispanic worldviews in a profund manner. Consider the Nahua, who have kept up continuity between the wisdom of the Aztec scholiast, which we know of from the chroniclers, and the contemporary shaman. It is a wisdom filtered through the codes of the Western tradition, and its autochthonous base still puts up a resistance. We can identify it both in public performances, and in exegetic sessions, in the shared wisdom of the inhabitants of an indigenous community as much as in esoteric glosses, in different parts of central and eastern Mexico. In the Otomi case I will be sharing today, the foundations of shamanic practice appear in the idea of an isomorphism between the structure of the body and the universe, or else in the polyvalency of the creatures of the other world, and in notions as complex as that of 'force', a kind of constantly running engine, which the specialist controls in order to favor the efficacy of the ritual activity. In the southern part of la Huasteca, the territorial limits of the shamanic market fluctuate as a function of the regional configurations of the demand for what it offers. They also respond to the cultural interpenetration between peoples in a multiethnic space, where the transfer of knowledge and the circulation of actors from one zone to another, are constant factors. Also relevant to the territorial limits of the shamanic market is the competition between the various shamans and against the representatives of salvation doctrines (the 'evangelists'). Endo-shamanism thus has an extensive topography, which is larger than the simple frame of the community. So it becomes necessary to take into account the intra- and inter-ethnic dynamics of the ritual practices, whether *in situ* or in the context of migration.

In Otomi endo-shamanism, the function of concentrating on a single point, the 'clear vision' or *nu mâho* of the world of the ancestors, is a requirement for reaching an adorational type of action. There are cases of the shaman personally falling into a trance, without involving the whole congregation: here there

2 We may also recall the distinction made by Cristina Gutiérrez Zúñiga, who uses the term 'exoteric shelves' to define the Neo-traditional dance in the context of 'spiritual consumerism' (Gutiérrez Zúñiga, 2008: 366).

is a kind of delegation of competences that is kept up from those attending, to the ritualist, who serves as a mediator between humans and the beyond, by means of these acts of possession (Fagetti, 2010: 17). The gift and the learning are connected to the vision; that is why a distinction between inherited shamanism and symptomatic shamanism is insisted on, these being the two great ways of initiation into the function of being a shaman. Dreams play a central role in communication between the territories where these 'forces' circulate; they are the space *par excellence* for performances of a mystical or spiritual type, that allow interactions with other worlds and provide access to an authentic spiritual transcendence. Unfortunately, these experiences are hard to qualify, because there is no suitable methodology, and there is also an almost total absence of references to them in the literature of Mesoamericanism.

Exo-shamanism, on the other hand, has to do with all those practices whose public is other than the native community, even when the expert is an indigenous person himself, the bearer of a cosmology with Pre-Hispanic origins. Thus exo-shamanism covers practices directed by native shamans, and performances organized by actors from North America or Europe, with devotees of mystical tourism, and *mestizo* populations, nearly all of whom are urban, and Spanish speaking. In exo-shamanism the dimension of exegesis is stressed, and it has a hermeneutics that completely saturates the field of interpretation, as distinct from endo-shamanism, which remits to an implicit knowledge.

In the New Age type of shamanism, reference to orthodoxy and an orthopraxis, is verified in the systemic 'cardinalizing' of the forces that serve as a frame for the representation of Mother Earth. There is, in fact, a transnational version of the *princeps* figure, ranging from *Mother Earth* among the U.S. Native Indians, to the Virgin of Guadalupe of the Chicanos, *Tlaltecuhtli* (in both the masculine and the feminine versions) and *Coatlicue*, and also including *Pachamama* of the Andes (Galinier and Molinié, 2006: 108). Whereas in the indigenous communities, the Earth is a kind of englobing entity which is confused with the active forces that are constantly modifying the relations between men and the creatures on the other side, from under the ground. It also serves as a kind of receptacle for all kinds of dejections, including particular words and foul speech in general which express a truly autochthonous spirituality. Among migrants, the figure of Mother Earth keeps up, like a magnet, a pole of reflection and for identifying with the ancestors of the matrix-community.

All over the continent the current demands of mystical tourism facilitate the acceptance of an ecumenical, transnational, version of Mother Earth, in spite of the contradiction that this representation expresses. There is a contradiction, because it nourishes a localist ideology, the vindication of a territorial base, as in El Valle de México, and at the same time its eugenic orientation is combined with an appreciation of the Anahuac Race, according to clichés linked to the stereotypes of a transatlantic New Age culture (Galinier and Molinié, 2006).

Ruptures and Continuities/The Dream of a Crystalline Theogony

More than ten years have passed since a continental (European) Aztec-ism started to develop in Spain, which was noted by Francisco de la Peña, who treats the Conchero dances as an example of 'alternative spirituality' (De la Peña, 2002: 71), as well as by Renée de la Torre (De la Torre, 2008a: 104). An exported Otomi shamanism has also been growing in France, as described by Denise Lombardi. She comments that 'when we speak of the relation between the shaman and the Western follower, we come up against a "nomadism of belief" where having recourse to accrediting the tradition is doubly useful: firstly in the political vindication that is directed towards a renewed valuation of the indigenous "being", and also in the presentation of an exotic otherness as a coherent system of beliefs which work as a kind of conversion in reverse, as the natives take the Word to the Westerners' (Lombardi, 2010). To illustrate this ideological to-ing and fro-ing, she adds that 'for the French New Agers', every Gallic specialist must at some point on his journey of initiation have a 'special relationship' with an indigenous practitioner, native America being one of the places still regarded as a 'reserve of primitivism', which would represent the '*structural equivalent* of the religious transcendence that customary Christianity defines as the ceremony of atonement' (Lombardi, 2011).

In exo-shamanism the search for a renewed autochthony is based on a process of cutting and pasting (both literally and metaphorically) in order to encourage an ideology of rupture, and invent alternative formulas in which the spirit of the environment can be captured through individual devotions that then re-emerge in *ad hoc* performances, as in Teotihuacán, in the Zócalo of Mexico City, or in Temoaya. This negotiation of a triturated and individualized spirituality, as we will be noting ahead, is located, willy nilly, in a global doctrine whose assumptions are interchangeable from one region to another, or from one continent to another. The extreme plasticity of these ritual tools paradoxically makes the atomization and reconfiguration of local Neo-shamanisms refer back to a collective pattern. The search for a maximum of otherness turns out to mean an appropriation of the common, of the shared, through a multiplicity of ideological convergences in a soft ecologism that is shared in all post-industrial societies: harmony, blending in with nature, protection of the environment as in the anti-nuclear movement, equilibrium, peace, and serenity. These new fictions are transnational creations, linked to an imagined Pre-Hispanic substratum, that is petrified as in a photographic image. Really there is no pristine shamanic purity to be found in isolated communities, as globalization has affected all indigenous peoples, so that exported endo-shamanism cannot now be distinguished from an exo-shamanism for local consumption.

To repeat: in exo-shamanism, it is documented that there has been a fetishizing of shamanic cultures under the apparently immobilized form of their 'primitive' configuration. Export shamanism is decontextualized, as it has eliminated the dimension of regulating intra-communal conflicts, controlling violence, and of politics in the community itself. It has been reduced to being a therapy for the individual that only regulates the relations between the body and the cosmos, without going through the dimension of society.

Now it is useful to remember the interactions between native exo-shamanism and endo-shamanism, in order to understand how catwalks have been put up between the two. If we are to take the case of populations that combine the two currents, such as the Otomi of Temoaya, then in concrete terms, the categories are not fixed. Exo- and endo- are flexible notions that simply remit to a topographic definition and not to a substantive one. We can contemplate a process in which erratic movements, distant from dogmas, are institutionalized, and are then crystallized in a globalized religion with universal concepts, in a new church of the New Age. There is no ethnic authenticity, in spite of the vindication of the most conservative factions of the movement, because it absorbs cultural schemes, symbols, images and discourses that belong to the global tradition. As a result, classical anthropologists need to look for new instruments to understand how values and standards circulate between the exo- and the endo-, and to evaluate to what extent spirituality is an outlook very distant from the religious life of indigenous communities, whose culture serves as a reserve of symbols, of myths and items in their kit of vestments.

Many varieties of exo- and endo-shamanism are developing in Mexico, and, through transatlantic migrations, in Europe. Certain sacred places appear as points where endo- and exo-shamanic practices flow together. Such is the case of the 'magic pueblos' in Mexico, where there is a strong match between the demand of international tourism, and the construction, for this market, of 'typical spaces', of mystic spots where ceremonies for expressing the new spirituality may be conducted. There is a consensus among the Mesoamerican emitters and the Western receivers that stems from the key concepts mentioned above, of harmony, purification, equilibrium, energy, vibrations, or worldview. The bureaucratic or institutional notion of a 'magic pueblo' therefore allows a connection to be made between certain places charged with

FIGURE 4.1 *Film set of Mictlán, place of the dead. All Saints Day in El Zócalo, Mexico City, November 1, 2008*
PHOTO: JACQUES GALINIER

expectations of a New Age type, and a renovated tourism, as at Real de Catorce or in Bernal.[3] In fact, the essentialization of the New Age movements, as we have witnessed it in modern Meso-America, is a typical tropism for all societies seeking an autochthonous existence who give Mother Earth a major role, as the vector of this dynamic. The local continues to be nourished by exotic images, reconfigured through the internet, in esoteric conclaves or in ritual praxis (see Figure 4.1).

The Migration of a Concept: Thoughts on Spirituality

So how are we to address the question of spirituality in the context of Mexican New Age? The term spirituality in medieval theology involves the idea of the spirit as an independent principle. Beliefs and practices associated with the soul, are combined with what is spiritual, something that is said to be like

3 http://www.pueblosmexico.com.mx/pueblo_mexico_ficha.php?id_rubrique=316 (Consulted: 15 July 2011).

'the reflection of a superior divine principle'. And according to a French dictionary by Robert (2002: 2480), this combination implies eventually a moral dimension. In this sense, 'ethnic spirituality' seems to be an adequate term for the hybrid cultural reality in which actors make use of the idea of spirit to deal with the convergence of demands coming from different cultural horizons. But why does this debate arouse no more than the annoyance of anthropologists? Flanagan answers this doubt with the following comment: 'As a term, spirituality betokens matters of the spirit world, issues of animism, ecstasy, magic and spells that sociology tends to treat with the utmost reserve, if not disdain' (Flanagan, 2011: 1–22). Surely the atmosphere of positivism in which sociological thought has been bathing for over a century must be responsible for this situation, creating an inability to answer questions such as those having to do with finding out who the bearers of this spirituality are, as the author emphasizes (ibid.: 2). Holmes in turn considers that the term 'spirituality' refers to a series of 'boxes' of discrete languages (Holmes, 2011: 25), in such a way that the traditional definitions of spirituality no longer work, and new ones have arisen to help guide us over the disciplines that manage them (ibid.: 26–27). In the Mesoamerican context, the question of spirituality facilitates a transition, from reflections on theology and Western institutions, to the definition of a new popular metaphysics, an assembly kit philosophy, a version of Turner's piecemeal exegesis. This then opens the way to a renewed reflection, contemplating the worldviews inspired in the New Age, though starting from the religions of the Book (Flanagan, 2011, 1–22.)

Now it behoves us to examine why this demand for spirituality is not merely a commercial artefact adapted to the requirements of mystical tourism, which, as pointed out by Gutiérrez Zúñiga, is a form of 'spiritual consumption'. In fact, the demand for spirituality is also an expression of the affects solicited during ritual perfomances. In the field, we can observe that the concept of 'spirituality' remits to a particular stage in the rituals, specifically to when the shaman is in an ecstatic state, and pleas are made to the entities that direct the lives of human beings. New Age spirituality actually concerns the link between alternative psychic demands. There is a demand for it to be a local, transnationalized, anchorage for the Neo-Indian Mexicans, and there are also emotional demands, originally from the first world. New Age spirituality has to do with a global religious framework, which is re-elaborated at a national level, but with operators in foreign parts, who are adepts of mystical tourism. Whether they are right or not, the European or Euro-American adepts come to Mexico with a vision of spirituality that derives from the great salvation religions.

The indigenous experience of spirituality, and that of the New Agers, come across each other in some of the ritual sequences, where different imaginaries are projected, and these are connected in the global network. The methodological problem we come up against is that we do not know how to define this phase of transition, which remits at the same time to the individualized experience of mystical activity in the West, and to the traditionally collective expressions in indigenous societies: given the fact that for the most part ethnographic literature does not take into consideration with due attention the private aspects of beliefs and religious emotions. For example, when it describes a prayer, it looks at the collective, functional or symbolic dimension and not at how it is related to the psychic motions of a particular actor. Academic ethnography does not go any deeper into this type of personal seeking, charged with authentic transcendence, while the Neo-shaman actors propose new hybrid models, for communion with beings from the other side, even though they might themselves be originally from indigenous communities that have been able to spread through the web (see Figure 4.2).[4]

In situ observation proves there has been a new 'Westernization' of the native philosophies, which does not nourish itself on references to doctrine but simply expresses the individual's demand for psychic atonement mentioned above. We can see that the concept of spirituality remits to a common signifier to denote experiences that are different in the Old World and in the New. All the same, how can the notion of spirituality be tanslated into the terms of native languages, and those of Mesoamerican categories of thought? What lived experience does it refer to? It is highly likely that for many of our colleagues this question makes no sense. It would appear that the European idea of spirituality has no equivalent in native cultures, as there is no word that could provide an immediate translation, at least not in the region I know. The challenge here is to show how New Age 'spirituality', theorized by Neo-shamans, remits to a socle of beliefs that is basically Mesoamerican and that is part of modern Mexican culture.[5] As I pointed out in another paper, 'in spite of the aporias that obstruct comprehension of their cultural assumptions, the New Agers are phased into the ethic of Meso-America before colonization, that remains as a cultural subsoil in the whole of Mexico, an ethic in whose name it is right to destroy without quarter in order to reconstruct the living' (Galinier, 2011: 32).

---

4 Among other examples, we may note that of Aztec Spirituality, Universal Spirituality (*Espiritualidad azteca, espiritualidad universal*) at http://resistenciaespiritual.blogspot.com/2008/03/espiritualidad-azteca-parte-3.html (consulted: 15 July 2011). For indigenous wisdom, see http://www.paraisomexico.org/?p=30 (consulted: 15 July 2011).

5 See the collective *Morir para vivir en Mesoamérica* (Báez Cubero and Catalina Rodríguez Lazcano, 2008).

FIGURE 4.2 *Individual cleansing and transmission of energies. El Zócalo, Mexico City, October 19, 2009*
PHOTO: JACQUES GALINIER

If ethnic spirituality is part of a transnational ideological kit, this is not only a media gimmick, and part of the corpus of the shamanic neo-language: it is also a product of history anchored in the socio-cultural reality of Mexico. The individual demand for spirituality, which forms the basis on which New Age ritual practices work, is adjusted to a collective phenomenon, not well studied by anthropologists who refuse to see the experiences of endo-shamanism in psychological terms. This is a problem that is accentuated by the implicit functionalism that animates the ethnographer's methodology, for example when it attributes to prayers an end that is strictly speaking of a utilitarian type, as might be, the relief of a patient. In indigenous communities, as we have said, it is hard to identify the elaboration of a personal spiritual quest for communion with the sacred, because the extreme ritualization of social life leaves little room for personal experiments of a spiritual kind. What is more, anthropologists conceive of social life as consisting exclusively of collective experiences (except in the cases of the people they are interviewing). We find it more productive to evaluate the concept of spirituality by reviewing the exegeses of the body and energies, expressed through a political language of opposition between forces, rather than trying to understand it in terms of an essentialist mystique supposed to be of Pre-Hispanic origin. It is better to take into account the ethnic theories that highlight the interactions between the inside and the outside, between the ancestors and the animal alter ego, stemming from which there is a relation of co-essence and co-presence. 'Force' is the principle that activates these interactions and takes into account the commitment of human beings to natural entities, through prayers, which allow emotions to be released and a spiritual quest to be put into words.

Spirituality and Godly Function/Capturing the New Age Phenomenologically

So far we have considered the indigenous peoples' wisdom as a central element of their worldview that is still active, even though in their communities, it does not really express knowledge of a personal kind. As for New Age spirituality, it has become a shibboleth, the catchword all over the world for the ecologists' *doxa* (socially unquestioned assumptions), that goes beyond the limits of popular Indianism. As distinct from what happens with indigenous communities, where social life is imbued with cosmological assumptions (relative to techniques, to nutrition, to trade and other things), in the pedagogic models of the spiritual masters of Neo-shamanism it is the symbolic dimension of social acts, which is inherited through the local tradition, that is reconstructed, as in the literature manipulated by New Agers. To tell the truth, postmodern spirituality is more suitable as a life project than as the reactivation of a religious practice shared by members of an indigenous community.

In the context of exo-shamanism, spirituality is a concept that is added to the concept of 'culture' that both the New Agers and the members of communities manipulate. It makes a connection between personal betterment and collective participation. While it has a long history in relation to mystical tourism in the United States, its expansion in the Mesoamerican world is more recent. Today spirituality is not only a signifier in the language of the New Age, but is also an idea that refers to the experience shared by those taking part in initiation ceremonies or rituals of a meteorological agrarian type, during a trance, in the context of local customs. Nevertheless, the question is still open as to how experiences of ecstasy circulate between leaders and the public.

In the course of the last twenty years, a psychological turn in anthropology has allowed researchers to pay greater attention to the role of affects in the construction of personality, outside the conventions shaped in the cultural ethos of the natives. We have not, however, advanced enough in studying the articulation of the psychic demands of indigenous people in their communities to those of New Age adepts, even though the role of the trance is appearing with greater intensity in shamanic type performances. There remains also the shadow of spirituality in the Catholic or Protestant ceremonial context, or as a private experience.

If then the notion of spirituality still remains today a *terra incognita* for Mexican anthropology, we cannot ignore the fact that in the field of psychoanalysis, there has evidently been a significant opening towards our discipline through a common interest in the subject of the deep, or the dark, which is the subsoil of Freudian meta-psychology. It is something we can address by means of other tools of analysis, in order to take into consideration a traumatic event, 'considering spiritual processes in their archaic state, in their universality, "on this side" of any belief or confession', as Véronique Donard put it in a recent work, *Du meurtre au sacrifice—Psychanalyse et dynamique spirituel* (Donard, 2009: 672). From a multidisciplinary point of view, she considers spiritual processes in their archaic condition, and how the Self adopts a sacrificial position with regard to traumatic experience, in the most archaic function of the psyche. A sacrificial fantasy appears in relation to this position, and Donard gives it a universal value, as one of the fantasies of origin. Religious ideas would be the result of this primitive organization of the psyche, and would support the subject in his emotional development. Also, the author comments, the originality of Freud's thinking lies in his insistence on the discarnate dimension, deterritorialized, in a way, from spirituality, when separated from the social base that the ritual perfomers who vindicate it are part of. In this sense we consider it to be the ideal way to reconcile mystiques coming from different historical-cultural horizons, Amerindian on the one side, and European on the other. Véronique Donard highlights the 'godly function' as a 'third function, bearing an ultimate sense' (ibid.: 630). She goes on to refer to 'this instance represented by the third function, that draws the trauma towards itself to give it a meaning, and that seems to us, still in a confused way, to occupy a real place in the psychic apparatus. This instance, the godly instance, seems to be an *empty place*, which, precisely through being empty, allows all the fantastic projections, that make what is lived spiritually and religiously possible' (ibid.: 630).

This hypothesis implies new debates with anthropologists in order to evaluate to what extent it fits in with a transdisciplinary point of view. Even now we can consider that Donard's thesis makes an original appreciation of the problem of articulation between the acts of a religious type that we have commented on (both in the space of native cultures and in that of the Mesoamerican New Age), and the deep functioning of psychism in general by means of a 'spiritual dynamic'. If in mysticism we see a relinquishment (*dépouillement*) of any type of representation (ibid.: 630), her idea seems to me to be a significant contribution to theorizing on the coalescence of cultural traditions that remit at the same time to societies without writing, to societies of the Book, and to the new ready made philosophies that have conquered the space of communications on the Earth.

Conclusions

Today the whole continent of America, native, *mestizo*, peasant, and urban, is consuming unrestrictedly notions such as 'culture', 'roots', 'identity', and consequently 'spirituality', a tendency that culminates with the progressive anthropologizing of the shamanic language of earlier times. Certainly the mysticism of traditional scholasticism has kept its essentially European and Middle Eastern historical base. However, it is now undergoing a process of de-localization. It receives nourishment from American mythologies that are remodeling their pantheon of divinities and highlighting some emblematic figures, such as the Indian of the Prairies. The internet has allowed a multipolar doctrine to be invented, to which any adept can integrate his own glosses and broadcast them, Wikipedia style. However, although the contents of Neo-shamanic exegeses have been diversified, there is a set of constants, that turn around a fantasized vision of the high civilizations or the 'mystical cultures' of a type like that of the Huichol. We have pointed out the difficulties, for an anthropologist in indigenous communities, to identify the personal manifestation of a communication with creatures from other worlds (from the supernatural world and from the world of the ancestors), considering the fact that any message is spread through shared experiences. We do not know the quality of a silent experience, just as we speak of silent reading, and the private experiences of the people we interview. We simply witness a process of transformation into ethno-categories of anthropological terms or of traditional European knowledge, which are now not only part of the New Age discourse, but also of a new indigenous vernacular language. This explains the flexibility of the concept 'spirituality' depending on the context considered, and the instrumental use made of it in the mind of the shaman, or the native ritualist, and in the Western market, that is to say, both in endo- and in exo-shamanism, with the intrusion through percolation of these same concepts into the ritual system of present day indigenous communities: till they reach the point of expelling the native beliefs, as in the case of the Otomi of Temoaya. The paradox in this municipality is that the exo-shaman does not receive nourishment from the native cosmovision, or from all the practices that are still actively engaged in by the local shamanism, but takes his inspiration from a reworked philosophy, from a supposedly Mesoamerican spirituality.

Finally, the notion of spirituality reflects the process through which erratic movements that are strangers to dogma, are institutionalized, as they are crystallized through a globalized religion, and through universal concepts, within a new *ecclesia* of the New Age, in tune with the tourist market. The New Age groups do not have any original affiliation to a community: they are the product of an individual type of demand that requires the applied knowledge of an expert in shamanism, who knows how to translate a cosmological language into the search for vibrations. In these conditions Neo-shamanism appears to be an ideal model for native groups on their way to a renewal of their ethnic existence, within the stable doctrine I have tried to identify. Following the thesis of Donard, we can consider that ethnic spirituality, through its capacity to free itself from the dispositives of cognition that nourish it, to 'strip itself of any type of representation', serves as an urn for alternative culture logics from the Old World and the New. It facilitates the circulation of Neo-shamanic assumptions in the context of performances without frontiers, in a hyperglobalized world, that is to say, one ever more dependent on the search for a local expression of the new modalities of belonging to an ethnic group.

CHAPTER 5

The Thirteen Grandmothers of the World: An Example of Cosmopolitan Shamanism

María Teresa Rodríguez

Introduction

The object of this paper is to describe and analyze the actions and proposals of an association called the International Council of the Thirteen Indigenous Grandmothers. This Council—made up of thirteen indigenous women from different parts of the world—declares that it is concerned about the current state of the world and believes the time has come to unite and be publicly recognized as 'guardians of the health of the Earth'. It proposes recovery of the indigenous traditions with respect to Nature, and protection of the spiritual practices of the aboriginal nations of the world.

The organization is projected on to the global scene through its insertion in a tissue of networks on an international scale, and forms a part of the new religious sociological phenomena of modernity informed by ideas of the New Age: it combines in its discourse and in its practices directions for transforming the individual, the veneration of Nature as sacred, physical and spiritual healing, and planetary consciousness (Carozzi, 1999c: 21). Further, it is based on an eclectic composition of fragments from various sacred traditions, with a holistic outlook (De la Torre and Gutiérrez, 2005). We can say that the International Council of Thirteen Indigenous Grandmothers is a particular response to the universal call for a new ethic of planetary responsibility (Beck, 2009: 36).

I propose to show with this ethnographic example—as explained in the Introduction to this book—that New Age spirituality has moved away from the Self of the individual, and proceeded towards a transformation of the universe, combining inner change with communication with the cosmos. Its evolving like this has led to a variety of links being formed between the New Age and traditional cultures. As De la Torre notes in her piece on the circuits of New Age spirituality (Chapter 1.1 in this book), the matrix of meaning or interpretive frame based on the holistic principle of New Age spirituality, allows projects for self-betterment to acquire a potential for transforming the surroundings. Appreciation of Nature and the connection of the individual to it, make for an efficient transformation of humanity and a positive valuing of othernesses, as is also emphasised by Frigerio (Chapter 1.2 in this book).

 | DOI 10.1163/9789004316485_008

According to Heelas (2008), New Age spirituality, nowadays, is part of the subjectivity that comes with different aspects of a culture of well-being. Spirituality, or the inner life, consumes, is used and is practiced with the idea of cultivating the awareness of being alive (op. cit.: 3). Heelas applies the term life spiritualities to contemporary, typically holistic, forms of belief, oriented to life affirmation. These assume that there is a need to find in oneself the sacred primary source, the thing that emanates from a 'meta empirical' search for life at this time and in this place. It is about being in touch with a deep spirituality, flowing through the inner self in order to integrate, 'harmonize' or 'balance' each of the aspects of the being, combining mind, body and spirit as a whole. Underlying this kind of wording is the proposal of a 'natural' spirituality that gives life fulfilment, as opposed to draining it which is what a consumer society requires (op. cit.: 5).

The case presented in this chapter is a clear example showing that this holistic orientation (*ibidem*) is a universal trend. The group of thirteen indigenous women from different countries is a metaphorical expression of the cosmopolitanism of practices oriented around mind, body, and spirit integration, that use ancestral knowledge.

The spirituality aiming at a kind of global sensibility that turns practitioners into citizens of the world, is implied in the fundamental standpoints of The Thirteen Grandmothers of the World. While they come from different traditions, they are united by a double mission: to enrich people's inner life through the subjective experimentation of spiritual connection with nature, and to promote concern for the planet applying ancestral knowledge based on care and respect for the environment.

The Council works under the aegis of the Center for Sacred Studies (CSS) with headquarters in California, U.S.A.[1] The CSS is part of a network of consultants, conference speakers, and therapists from different disciplines and with different orientations, who go to make up the alternative complex (Carozzi, op. cit.). The Center for Sacred Studies is registered in California as a Church dedicated to:

> [sustaining] indigenous ways of life through cross-cultural spiritual practices, ministry and education, and a commitment to peace and unity for all peoples. CSS activities include providing prayer services, ceremonies,

1 The main offices of the CSS are in Guerneville, California, in an area to the north of the San Francisco Bay. It also has an office in Sonora, California, at the foot of the mountains. The staff or administration of the Center consists of 13 persons (3 men and 10 women); one of them has the job of Spiritual Director, as we will explain ahead.

> and a variety of gatherings for worship, according to various traditions. The purpose of these offerings is to invite individuals, families, and communities to develop devotion, and to strengthen their relationship to the Divine.[2]

The Center gives courses, and runs workshops and other activities, integrating practices such as meditation, massage, tribal music, altered states of consciousness and other alternative therapies. It was in this context that the International Council of Thirteen Indigenous Grandmothers started in 2004. Most of the members of the Council, according to the short biographies available on the CSS web site, have a record of ethnic activism, cultural promotion and the application of knowledge of ancestral teachings from their respective traditions.

To give an example, according to this source Grandmother Agnes Baker-Pilgrim is one of the oldest members of the *Takelma Siletz* tribe in the South of Oregon, U.S.A. She has a degree in psychology, and is a historian, a cultural instructor and a 'guardian' of the Sacred Ceremony of the Salmon. She has received prizes for her work and has been honored as a 'living treasure' of her tribe, by the confederated Siletz tribes. Margaret Behan, the Cheyenne Grandmother, is a performer of traditional dances and has been the leader of a dance group in Oklahoma and at powwows across the United States. She sculpts, writes poetry and plays and has an active part as leader of her tribe. Mona Polacca is the name of the Hopi Grandmother from Arizona; she is the spiritual leader of the Havasupai, Hopi and Tewa tribes, and a member of the Arizona Inter-tribal Council.[3] She studied for a doctorate at the Department of Interdisciplinary Justice at the State University of Arizona and belongs to the World Indigenous Forum.

The Mazatec Grandmother Julieta Casimiro, presents herself as a continuer of the work of the great shaman María Sabina and as heir to the traditions of healing and conducting ceremonies with sacred plants, in accordance with the Pre-Hispanic path of sacred mushrooms or *teonanacatl*. The Oglala Lakota Grandmother, Rita Long-Visitor Holy Dance, is a guardian of the traditional Lakota forms. She lives with her sister, Grandmother Beatrice Long-Visitor Holy Dance, on the Pine Ridge reservation in South Dakota. The sisters Beatrice and Rita started the Council's Youth Ambassador program; they transmit to young people their sacred rites, the Sun Dance, and connection to the source of one's being (see Figure 5.1).[4]

2 http://www.sacredstudies.org/.

3 http://www.sacredstudies.org/.

4 http://www.sacredstudies.org/.

FIGURE 5.1 *Doña Julieta, the Mazatec grandmother, poses by her altar at the end of one of the sessions of the International Council of Thirteen Indigenous Grandmothers. She is with her daughter Eugenia and her interpreter. In the background, the logo of the Center for Sacred Studies and some members of the Center's directive committee. Anchorage, Alaska, May 2011*
PHOTO: MARÍA TERESA RODRÍGUEZ

TABLE 5.1 *List of members*

1	Agnes Baker Pilgrim, *Takelma Siletz* from Oregon, United States
2	Aama Bombo, *Tamang* from Nepal
3	Rita Pitka Blumenstein, *Yupik* from the Arctic Polar Circle, Alaska
4	Julieta Casimiro, *Mazateca* from Oaxaca, Mexico
5	Maria Alice Campos Freire, from Amazonia, Brazil
6	Bernadette Rebienot, *Omyene* from Gabon, Africa
7	Tsering Dolma Gyaltong, *Tibetan* (lives in Ontario, Canada)
8	Flordemayo, *Maya* from Nicaragua (lives in New Mexico)
9	Margaret Behan, *Arapahoe Cheyenne* from Montana, United States
10	Beatrice Long, *Oglala Lakota* from South Dakota, United States
11	Rita Long, *Oglala Lakota* from South Dakota, United States
12	Mona Polacca, *Havasupai Tewa Hopi* from Arizona, United States
13	Clara Shinobu Lura, of *Japanese* origin (lives in Amazonia, Brazil)

Most of the members of the International Council of Thirteen Indigenous Grandmothers live on the American continent, seven of them in the U.S.A., one in Canada, two in Brazil and one in Mexico; only two live outside, in Africa and Asia (Gabon, and Nepal) (see Table 5.1). Why do I consider it important to expound this case in a work about New Age in Latin America, given that only three members of the group come from this part of the continent?

While this organization is American by its genesis, it has proposed, ever since its original postulations, to validate ethnical wisdom from around the world. Mesoamerican and Amazonian representations could not be absent within this group of grandmothers, given that—according to the Council's statements—their goal is to share their knowledge and spirituality to the world.

We will see that, in our days, the transmission vectors in the religious cartography are not unidirectional. The International Council of the Thirteen Indigenous Grandmothers is evidence for a polycentric contemporary movement, focused on extending knowledge and its significance beyond the initial referent, with the dislocation of memory and religious practices from their diverse origins. As Rocha and Vázquez have observed, we are witnessing the emergence of a new religious cartography in which the 'Global South' plays the role of a protagonist (2013: 1).

Members of the International Council of Thirteen Indigenous Grandmothers

Through the organizing of meetings, events, workshops and other activities in different parts of the world, the International Council of Thirteen Indigenous Grandmothers is inserted in a framework of networks that in turn form circuits, whose functioning does not necessarily imply spacial contiguity between those taking part (Gutiérrez, 2008: 364).

The activities promoted by the Council imply processes of relocalizing and resignifying vernacular religious practices (Argyriadis and De la Torre, 2008: 16–22) that have been uprooted from their cultural settings. An ethnographic approach of this type allows us to find out what the values and symbolizing processes of contemporary society are, and to identify the new forms of sociability that have shown a certain degree of consistency and unity (Teisenhoffer, 2008: 54–55).

According to Beck (op. cit.), religious cosmopolitanism—as opposed to institutionalized religions—does not see other religions as a threat; instead, it admits that they bring elements that can enrich its view of the world. Being cosmopolitan is expressed in the universal duty of including the other culturally, and dealing socially with cultural otherness without hierarchical exclusions; ethnic differences are given a positive value. Further, this class of movement, as pointed out by Bartra, shows the modalities through which particular elites recycle and transfigure ancient traditions, seeking to connect persons to the spirit of the cosmos (2011: 85, 243).

Incorporation into the New Age network supposes the addition of a millenarian purpose, and awareness on a planetary and cosmic scale (Carozzi, op. cit.: 25). The significance of global risk is accompanied by a repertoire of new imaginaries and standards of behaviour. Even as new spheres of communication are established, there is a multiplication of transnational collective efforts in which networks take the initiative with movements of civil society (Beck, 2008). The International Council of the Thirteen Grandmothers approaches Nature as a *topos*, a rhetorical place of common interest (Haraway, 1999: 122); the feeling of worldwide pain that comes out everywhere after natural tragedies, is taken up by this organization to shape its horizon of meaning and the directrix of its operations on the international scene.

A visit to see a Mazatec woman—Julieta Casimiro, one of the Thirteen Indigenous Grandmothers—at home in Huautla de Jiménez, Oaxaca in November 2008, was the starting point for my approximation to the enigmas and veils of this organization. She—like other shamans and local healers—has taken up a position to deal with the inflow of tourists who visit the Mazatec Sierra in search of mystical, ecstatic or healing experiences from taking hallucinogenic mushrooms (which, for the Mazatecs themselves, have religious implications). Since she joined the Council—in 2004—Doña Julieta's experiences and activities have widened and now extend from the mountains of Huautla and its smoky kitchens, to environments totally integrated into cosmopolitan modernity. Today, a part of her symbolic and cultural world is available and lies open to a diversity of possible appropriations all over the world.

The information presented in this chapter derives from my observations on several visits to the Mazatec Grandmother at her house in Huautla, from interviews conducted with other inhabitants of Huautla, from my explorations in virtual space, and from my attendance at one of the Council's meetings, which took place in 2011, in Anchorage, Alaska.[5]

---

5 This field trip was undertaken with resources from CONACYT Project 81926: *Transnacionalización y relocalización de las religiones indo y afroamericanas*, coordinated by Renée de la Torre Castellanos.

Shamanic Tourism in the Sierra Mazateca

The Mazatec region covers approximately 2,400 square kilometres of the Eastern Sierra Madre, in the northern part of the state of Oaxaca, Mexico. Its topography ranges from low relief plains to mountainous knots 2,500 metres above sea-level. Most of the Mazatecan population is located in the federal state of Oaxaca, but there are also inhabitants of the same ethnicity in the south of the state of Veracruz, and migrants dispersed over other points of the nation and of the U.S.A. Nevertheless, it is the Oaxacan part of the Sierra that is the ancestral home occupied by the Mazatec, where they have lived for at least two thousand years. Until the fifteenth century, those living there were grouped in two dominions: Huautla was the centre of the Western dominion (*Poniente*), while Mazatlán was the central point of the Eastern dominion (*Oriente*) (Villa Rojas, 1955).

The municipality of Huautla de Jiménez (with a population of 30,004 inhabitants of whom 24,578 are speakers of the native language)[6] is the economic and political pole of the region and the place that is emblematic of Mazatec identity.[7] It is located between sixteen hundred and seventeen hundred metres above sea level, surrounded by humid tropical mountain forest and arable areas planted mainly with coffee, maize or beans.

The principal town of the municipality—with a population of 10,528 people[8]—concentrates the services, commerce and civil and religious powers. As pointed out by Demanget (2006: 18), in recent decades this place has become a plural and contrasting society where different types of actor live: single language peasants, traders, small coffee entrepreneurs, bureaucrats and national and international tourists. On this plural base different sectors make an exegetic version of the tradition (*ibidem*). The Mazatecs have become 'producers of their ethnicity' since a decisive event: when, in 1957, an article by Gordon Wasson, called '*Seeking the Magic Mushroom*', was published in Life magazine: in which the author tells of the discovery of the Mazatec wise woman María Sabina, and of the ritual use of hallucinogenic mushrooms (*Psilocybe caerulescens* and *Psilocybe mexicana*).[9]

6 INEGI, Censo General de Población y Vivienda, 2010.

7 See the studies by Boege (1988) and Demanget (2006) for more information on Huautla and the ethnic region as a whole.

8 INEGI, Censo General de Población y Vivienda, 2010.

9 There are a number of detailed studies that have been made of the circumstances relating to the discovery of Sacred Mushrooms by Gordon Wasson, the subsequent popularity of María Sabina, and the transformations in Huautla following these events. See for example: Demanget (2000, 2006) Marín (2010), Carrera (2000), Estrada (1977), among others.

The main feature of the following decades was the arrival to the mountains of Huautla of young people from Mexico and other countries, especially the United States, who filled the small town and its surroundings to the brim in order to get to know the Mazatec wise men and to take the sacred mushrooms. Well-known people such as John Lennon and other famous musicians of the time came to the town, and so did researchers from different disciplines, journalists, and hippies as well as other kinds of people.[10]

This period left a permanent mark on the Huautla society. The modest figure of María Sabina, and the sacred mushrooms themselves, became emblems of local identity from a process of resignifying tradition. The Mazatecs opened their reserved magical-religious space and commercialized the mushrooms, which up until then had had a ritual and curative use (Demanget, 2006). Shamanic tourism led to a process of re-elaborating ritual practices. However, the use of mushrooms is still a common practice among Mazatecs, in private rituals where illnesses are meant to be cured, and answers or solutions to social and personal problems are sought. These rituals are called 'veladas' (vigils), referring to their nocturnal particularity. In the Mazatec language, they are called *vi na choa*, meaning 'when one stays awake' (Minero, 2012); the intake of mushrooms—under the guidance of a ritual specialist or *chiota chiine*—is in order to search for solutions and cure illnesses by making a 'sacred trip' to the source of wisdom.

Even today the life of Huautla is still influenced by the arrival of tourists, especially during the rainy seasons of the summer. Although the number of visitors has declined from the peak in earlier decades, at these times of the year there is a proliferation of offers for visitors to experience 'vigils' directed by supposedly specialized shamans, and also the opportunity to obtain mushrooms that can be taken outside the ritual context.

It is in this setting that Doña Julieta Casimiro, one of the best known Huautec shamans, conducts her daily affairs. Like other ritual specialists, she receives Mexican and foreign travellers who come to her home to have the experience of an 'authentic' ceremony, in exchange for a previously arranged fee. She and her daughters (also dedicated to organizing vigils for tourists) pride themselves on knowing the secrets of the 'holy children' (the sacred mushrooms) and the Mazatec shamanic tradition. Doña Julieta explains that it was her mother-in-law who guided her through the first time she took mushrooms, and taught her the ritual procedures when she was young and only just

10 By the end of the sixties the visits by hippies had become unmanageable; they also took mushrooms without respecting the ritual prescriptions, and without moderation. The army intervened, first in the summer of 1969, to expel them from the region (Marín, 2010).

married; she is sure her knowledge of the mushrooms precedes the fame of María Sabina, whose popularity was more the result of chance than of her possessing a knowledge no one else had. With tourism at its peak in Huautla, Doña Julieta—like other shamans—made friends with foreign visitors. One of these friendships was with a North American woman linked to the Center for Sacred Studies, who visited her on numerous occasions. Through her, Doña Julieta was invited in 2004 to join the International Council of Thirteen Indigenous Grandmothers, then in formation.

The Thirteen Grandmothers of the World and the Center for Sacred Studies[11]

The Center for Sacred Studies with headquarters in California, is part of an alternative complex (Carozzi, op. cit.: 21) interested in therapeutic, psychotherapeutic, esoteric and religious fields. These ingredients mean it can be classified within the currents related to the human potential movement that arose in the West of the United States in the nineteen sixties. The countercultural movement of the time inspired the foundation of the Esalen Institute, and transpersonal psychology (Teisenhoffer, 2008: 60–61; Carozzi, 1999c: 20–23). A distinctive mark of this movement was the eclectic borrowing, by one discipline from another, and the proposal that individuals should have the autonomy that allows them to circulate between different groups (Stone, 1976: 94, quoted in Carozzi, op. cit.: 23).

The CSS gives training programmes in healing practices and in spiritual development under various modalities of payment. According to their web page, the people in charge of these programmes—in which the Thirteen Grandmothers take part—are qualified in transpersonal psychology, spiritual practices, meditation, massage and other alternative therapies. The courses are given on line, and are complemented by stays at a retreat center in California (at the Black Mountain Buddhist Retreat or the Padmasambhava Peace Institute). The founder and Spiritual Director of the CSS is Jeneane Prevatt (who uses the pseudonym Jyoti, meaning *light* in Sanskrit). She studied

11 Most of the information presented in this section comes from the web page of the Center for Sacred Studies and other complementary internet sites that are available, usually in English, for example: http://www.grandmotherscouncil.org/, http://www.earthandspirit.org, http://www.globalcommunity.org, http://www.stillpointfarmsfestival.com, http://www.intk.org, http://www.mothersgrace.com, and others.

psychology at the Jung Institute in Switzerland and *kundalini* philosophy in India.

The CSS is linked in various ways with other organizations in the U.S.A., Canada, and Europe. It receives donations from international foundations, American universities, civil societies and individuals. Through its belonging to a network of more than 30 kindred organizations in the country, the CSS is able to offer its services in programs directed by other similar organizations in different parts of the United States. I shall mention briefly the programs of the CSS:

The *Ministry Training Program* awards a title, Minister of Prayer, qualifying the holder to conduct ceremonies and study groups on the process of spiritual seeking. The course is taken on line for two years with five days of personal attendance.

The *Stargate Mystery School* is a programme designed for exploring extra-ordinary states of consciousness; it consists of five weekends of personal attendance for learning to 'listen to your body, your heart and the earth…to explore together the potential of subtle energy, which will allow us to follow our own psyche…'.[12]

The *Maitri Breathwork School* is aimed at discovering 'the art of hands and healing, understanding extra-ordinary states of consciousness, and developing a relation with shamanic music, plants and other healing aids'.[13] The training is for masseurs, therapists and cheiropractitioners.

The *International Council of Thirteen Indigenous Grandmothers* is one of the programmes developed by the CSS. The Council is co-ordinated by its founder and Spiritual Director Jeneane Prevatt (Jyoti). We are informed that Jyoti and some of the Thirteen Grandmothers had a vision that led them to take part in this Alliance, or knew of ancient prophecies that announced their joining. This is the case of Bernadette Rebienot, the Gabonese Grandmother, from the *Bwiti* tribe. Before the Council was started, Jyoti had travelled to Gabon to learn from Bernadette about her traditional knowledge; this was when the two women realised that they shared a vision for the need to bring thirteen indigenous grandmothers from around the world togther in a prayer for peace and the preservation of Mother Earth. Another of the grandmothers, Rita Pitka Blumenstein—of the *Yupik* tribe in Alaska—received a prophecy from her own great grandmother, who gave her thirteen stones and thirteen eagle feathers before she died, for her to deliver to each of the grandmothers when they should finally join up.

12 http://www.sacredstudies.org/.

13 *Ibidem.*

The International Council of Thirteen Indigenous Grandmothers was formally established in October 2004, in Phoenicia, New York, the ancestral lands of the Iroquois federation.

The original decree established that:

- The thirteen Grandmothers are concerned by the destruction of Mother Earth and the indigenous ways of life.
- The council is an Alliance for prayer, education and healing for Mother Earth, for all her inhabitants, for all children and for the next seven generations to come.
- The Grandmothers are worried by war and poverty, nuclear weapons and the contamination of air and water.
- They propose that the teachings of the ancestors be recovered.
- They propose to undertake projects that will protect cultures: lands, medicine, ceremonies and forms of prayer.

At the end of the conference, the grandmothers signed a declaration of the intentions of their global alliance.

> We meet to feed, educate and train our children. We meet to defend the practice of our ceremonies and to affirm the right to use our medicinal plants free of legal restrictions. We have come together to protect the lands where our peoples live and that our cultures depend on, to safeguard the collective inheritance of traditional medicines, and to defend the Earth itself. We believe that the teachings of our ancestors will illuminate our way...[14]

Three central elements stand out in this declaration: ecological concern, a feeling of planetary hurt, and the right to preserve ancestral knowledge—including the ritual and curative use of medicinal plants with psychotropic properties.[15]

From its creation as an International Council 'the grandmothers agreed to go back to visit their communities of origin, spread over the five continents,

14 *Ibidem.*

15 Among the proposals of the Thirteen Grandmothers, one refers to the need for regulations that allow the use of psychotropics for ritual and curative purposes by the indigenous peoples, such as those that already exist for the Mazatecs, for whom the taking of hallucinogenic mushrooms has been part of their ritual and curative practices since time immemorial.

FIGURE 5.2 *The Indigenous Grandmothers walking towards one of the Sacred Fire Ceremonies. Anchorage, Alaska, May 2011*
PHOTO: MARÍA TERESA RODRÍGUEZ

to pray for humanity to wake up and for Mother Earth'.[16] So far, there have been ten general meetings of the Council, six of them in the U.S.A. (including the state of Alaska), one in Mexico, one in India, one in Japan and one in Brazil. The Grandmothers also visited Italy and Spain at the behest of organizations there that they share interests and objectives with. At the time of writing, the locations of the next four meetings of the Council had been decided, as Montana, U.S.A. (2012), Nepal (2012) New Zealand (2013) and Gabon (no date as yet) (see Figure 5.2).

Each general meeting of the Council has had its own slogan and theme. For example, the Eighth Council which took place in Japan in October of 2010, concentrated on aspects of biodiversity. Before the meeting—which was held in Kirishima—the Thirteen Grandmothers put in an appearance at the Conference on Global Biodiversity, in Nagoya, where they stressed the need to take care of Mother Earth. The Nagoya protocol was passed, establishing

16 *Ibidem.*

among other things, that access to genetic resources should be granted with the permission of those providing the resources, especially in the case of indigenous peoples. From Nagoya, the Thirteen Grandmothers travelled to Kirishima, where the Eighth Council took place from the 23rd to the 26th of October. Then some of them (including Doña Julieta) went to Nagasaki to pray on the site where the atom bomb was dropped.

In addition to the annual meetings, the Council also organizes other activities in which the Grandmothers take part as individuals, or in groups of two or three. These jobs may take place in the grandmothers' places of origin or elsewhere in the world where they are invited by kindred associations. The thirteen grandmothers live their everyday lives in their places of origin or their places of residence, and keep in touch, by telephone, with the offices of the Center in California, where their calendars are organized and they are given their jobs. In the case of Doña Julieta, a young Mexican woman works as her personal contact and telephones her at home in Huautla on a regular basis to get relevant information through.

In exchange for their taking part in the Council meetings, in training courses or any other activity, the Grandmothers receive a financial incentive and the costs of their travel and accommodation are covered. Some of them are also invited to take part in events promoted by other organizations. For example, in August 2011, two of the Grandmothers, who reside in the U.S.A., attended the Mother Earth Festival organized by an ecological farm in Oregon (Stillpoint Farm), where others making presentations included artists, healers, and organic food producers. In the same year, four of the Grandmothers attended an event organized by a group called All Beings, in Montepellier, Vermont, in the North-East of the United States, where they helped to organize activities to celebrate the Winter Solstice, baby blessings, and a traditional Cherokee dance 'to build peace energy'. Grandmother Agnes Baker Pilgrim gave a course in Brienz, Switzerland, on the 'Healing of our Life Foundation Water', whose aim was to bless the water and make it well, and deepen the connection with Mother Earth. The same Swiss organzation (Kokoro Praxisgemeinschaft), invited Grandmothers Aama Bombo, Rita Long and Maria Alice Campos-Freire to come to the same place and teach them about indigenous ways of being healthy and looking after Mother Earth. With these examples of the travels of the Thirteen Grandmothers, I mean to emphasize the contrast with the times in which European explorers, *conquistadores*, and missionaries took their faith and their religion to the most remote areas of Africa, Asia and America (Rocha and Vásquez, *ibidem*). The role of these spiritual emissaries is proof of the new religious cartography in which they are settled, combining spiritual traditions from different parts of the world.

'Healing the Spirit from the Light Within': Sessions of the International Council of Thirteen Indigenous Grandmothers[17]

As already explained, by April 2012 there had been ten general meetings of the International Council of Thirteen Indigenous Grandmothers. Each of these meetings would last about three days; attendance by the general public is encouraged through the internet and through contacts with other organizations. The Council directive decides on the location of each of the meetings, and part of the organization becomes the responsibility of one of the Grandmothers, as one or other of their places of origin has been chosen to host the meeting. As they are in charge, they can get help through their connections to local authorities and state institutions, with obtaining funds and supports of other kinds. For example, amongst other things it is necessary to get a room for holding the sessions in and accommodation for those attending, to include speakers of the local language in the programme, and to have a space outdoors for conducting the Sacred Fire Ceremonies. Each meeting has its own slogan, which is a phrase or thought devised by the hosting Grandmother. The slogan for the Ninth Council, held in Anchorage, was *'Healing the spirit from the light within'* attributed to Yupik Grandmother Rita Blumenstein.

The meetings of the Council consist of two types of activity: closed sessions, restricted to those paying an admission fee (with the option of paying per session or for the whole day),[18] and the Sacred Fire ceremonies open to the general public.

There are strict rules for participating in either type of activity. For example, it is forbidden to take photos, make videos or make sound recordings. The Thirteen Grandmothers, the Staff and special guests, stay in a place separate from the others attending, who are basically just spectators. During the prayer ceremonies of the Sacred Fire, in Anchorage in May 2011, the former were in a special section with seats and under a canvas cover, while the rest of us had to stand or sit on the grass in a circle. In the closed sessions, the Grandmothers and the directors of the CSS were placed around a table on a platform, facing the public who were lined up on rows of seats. The sessions were conducted by the Spiritual Director of the CSS, with the support of members of the staff and

17 The information in this section is mostly based on observations made when I attended the Ninth International Council of Thirteen Indigenous Grandmothers, held in Anchorage, Alaska in May 2011. Descriptions and quotations are from my fieldwork notes—as recording machines were forbidden—and were originally translated into Spanish by me.

18 At the meeting of the Council held in Anchorage, the fee was 60 dollars a day or 30 dollars for half a day (otherwise 210 dollars for the whole event, or 360 including lunch every day). Those attending would have to pay their traveling, accommodation and food expenses, as well.

a master of ceremonies; the programme advanced—almost entirely in English—on time and in the planned order.

There were four types of activity that took place in the closed sessions:

- Formalities: acknowledgements, presentation of each of the Grandmothers, the directors of the CSS and local authorities.
- Ceremonies of collective blessings given by the Thirteen Grandmothers: 'Blessing for women and children', 'Blessing for the old and the young', and a ceremony in which 'men honour the Grandmothers' handing each of them a white flower.
- Collective motivation practices: song, dance, meditation, prayer, tears and laughter.
- Artistic presentations of dances and ethnic music.

There were two sessions a day at Anchorage: one in the morning and one in the evening. During the sessions the public remained in their places, except when they formed lines to receive the blessing of the grandmothers as part of one of the ceremonies; they came down off the platform only for this. Most of those attending the closed sessions (about 400 people) were North American women from the states of California, Michigan, Seattle, Chicago and Virginia, and some from Canada. There were some men present but they were evidently far fewer in number.

The fact that the majority of those attending these meetings were female is certainly a subject of interest sociologically and would need to be looked into later. For the moment I shall just hint at a hypothesis that it was because the Thirteen Grandmothers were represented as guardians of the earth, of ancestral wisdom and maternity. They have referred to the rise of a new wave of feminine power, in which women can rediscover and share their wisdom in order to guarantee the health of the whole planet and of humanity, by tapping in to an immense reserve of energy that runs underground.[19]

At the Ninth Council held in Anchorage a number of artists and activists from different parts of Alaska took part in the sessions, along with a delegation from Japan, a singer from the U.S.A. and another from Brazil. Larry Merculieff, a native Aleut from the Bering Strait and an indigenous activist, played the part of master of ceremonies. Also invited was Rosemary Ahtuangaruak, an indigenous Inupiaq from Barrow, in Alaska, 'an untiring activist for the health and protection of the people of the Arctic' and an executive member of the Alaska Intertribal Council. Shirley Mae Springer Staten, an Afro-American singer and

19 http://www.grandmotherscouncil.org/.

motivation workshop organizer took part with a musical presentation, as did Karina Moeller, a singer living in Alaska and a member of the tribal musical group *Pamyua*, who interpreted a song relating to femininity, and to the hope of being able to build a universe of peace and harmony where the voice of all the grandmothers of the world would be heard. Other highlights were the performances of three tribal music groups at different stages of the meeting: in addition to *Pamyua*, the *Yupik Eskimo Group Kicaput* and the *Sleeping Lady Drum Group*.[20]

The closed meetings were held at the Dena'ina Civic and Convention Center, a modernist building in the heart of Anchorage.[21] The windows of the room booked for the event allowed contemplation of the majestic range of snowy mountains that guards the city of Anchorage. The welcome to the Ninth International Council of the Thirteen Grandmothers was given by a member of the Tribal Government of the *Eklutna*, a Dena'ina Athabascan people from very close to Anchorage. Then the *Taarvaarnauramken* was presented, a Yupik purification dance performed by the *Yupik Eskimo Group Kicaput*. We are told that the native dances of Alaska tell stories through body and hand movements. The performance lasted only five minutes and then Yupik grandmother Rita Blumenstein was asked to speak and gave her welcome in English:

> I am Yupik and am here to help every one of you to find yourself. I am grateful for the opportunity to be able to help many people…my teachers taught me the power of the four elements of the universe, the wisdom to heal, respect for our roots so deep and for spiritual features. Thank you for coming to share in our culture; when you go back to your land and your country, share, share and share.

To end the first evening session, Doña Julieta—the Mazatec grandmother—was at the head of a ceremony, dressed in typical Huautec costume, accompanied by one of her daughters, and her translator, the young Mexican woman

20 These musical groups form part of a movement to revive the music and dance of the native peoples of the Arctic, who are organized into twelve regional corporations (*Alaska Native Regional Corporations*) and 200 local village corporations. Every town or villa has a tribal government. The number of indigenous people in Alaska is estimated at 119,241 and they represent 20% of the population of the state. They speak 20 different languages although the main language is Yupik with 14,000 speakers. The Yupik language belongs to the *Eskimo Aleut* family (http://www.lbblawyers.com/ancsa.htm; www.nativeco.com/).

21 Dena'ina (or Tanaina) is one of twenty languages spoken in Alaska. The name of the center and other elements of the urban landscape show that the local government is involved in gaining greater visibility for the native cultures of the Arctic.

who also works as her assistant. Doña Julieta moved to the front of an altar previously set up in the room where the sessions were held, with a Mexican flag and an image of the Virgin of Guadalupe, as well as flowers and candles. Doña Julieta spoke in Spanish, although her first language is Mazatec; and her words were translated simultaneously into English:

> Good night, brothers. I am going to pray for you and for Mother Rita; we are in her land, in Alaska, and I'm going to pray for all the people of this land, for the living and the dead and for the plants, because God needs it. We ourselves have caused harm to Mother Earth. Recently we were in Japan, and we went to pray where the bomb went off. We do not want war, we want peace for the children, the young, and the old like us. That is why we make a prayer for the earth. People use weapons, bombs, and everything that damages the earth, the animals and the plants. Little Virgin of Guadalupe, I ask for your forgiveness because we do not know how to look after your earth. We pray for love, for light, for the hopes of the grandmothers, to be worthy of being here, Mother Earth. Thank you Sun, thank you Air, thank you Constellations... Thank you Mother Earth, and thank you Father Sky, thank you the Elements, Mother Moon, Sister Star. We pray for love, for light, for the hopes of the grandmothers, to be worthy of being here, Mother Earth. Thank you Sun, thank you Air, thank you Constellations. [*translated here from Spanish*]

After singing and praying in her native tongue and reciting fragments of the Catholic Rosary in Spanish, Grandmother Julieta asked: 'that all of us here be strong. That we walk with devotion, that we make a prayer for Mother Earth, Lady Moon and Mister Sunshine... My father, I ask you fervently for there to be lots of fish, many little animals'.

When the ceremony was over she gave 'cleansings' to those attending who came up to her, sprinkling them with herbs moistened with blessed water, touching them on the forehead and the top of their heads with her right hand.

Before the evening session closed, the Spiritual Director of the CSS indicated that for the session the next morning the men attending should bring a white flower to give to the Grandmothers. The next day, while the men handed the Grandmothers flowers and received their blessings, Yupik songs were performed by the *Sleeping Lady Drum Group*.[22] Many people got up from their

22 The name of this group refers to a myth of origin that tells of the beginning of time, when the land of what is Alaska today was inhabited by giants. A beautiful young woman slept waiting for her lover, a warrior who had left her side to defend the land against a foreign

seats and swayed to the rhythm of the drums, with their hands raised up in the air in an attitude of prayer.

During the Blessings ceremonies that the Thirteen Grandmothers gave for those who came along in subsequent sessions, they came down from the platform while people filed past them: blessings for women, blessings for children and blessings for men; they touched the head of each person while saying a loving phrase, and a wish for well-being and health. Some women returned to their places visibly moved after these encounters.

One of the most moving events at the Ninth Council was after the presentation by a group of young people from Japan led by Yoshimaru Higa, who was introduced as a well known shaman of Okinawa. The Japanese guests asked the Thirteen Indigenous Grandmothers to offer prayers for the victims of the *tsunami* that hit their country in March 2011. Yoshimaru Higa said he was in possession of sacred knowledge and prayers from his ancestors; he felt that he should turn to the Thirteen Grandmothers to ask them for the power of their love and wisdom to help his people recover from the damage suffered as a result of the *tsunami*. He mentioned the radioactive leak from the nuclear plant of Fukushima and the death of animals, plants and all kinds of living things affected by this ecological disaster. A Japanese girl who accompanied the group sang in her own tongue, expressing consternation over what had happened in Japan. For some moments she spoke in English and with tears on her cheeks she asked: 'What has happened to us? The earth is the same for everyone and now we are suffering from a tragedy that reminds us of the victims of Hiroshima and Nagasaki. The fish are dying and the water is being poisoned'.

In a few moments feelings of consternation flooded the meeting; the invited guests from Japan and the Grandmothers and the people on the platform showed their sadness. Many women in the public also wept—either discretely or vehemently—over the tragedy suffered by the people of Japan. The guests from Japan compared the magnitude of the disaster with what had happened in the Second World War; but as well as regretting the loss of human lives, they lamented the damage done to the planet as a whole. Grandmother Julieta took up the microphone without anticipation while many people in the auditorium were sobbing. She said with feeling that she had visited Nagasaki, that place of destruction, that we have done a lot of harm to Mother Earth and that is why we are now suffering tragedies like those of the *tsunami* and the radioactive

invasion, in search of peace and the unification of its inhabitants. The legend says: 'When the sleeping lady wakes, all our people will be one'. http://www.ciri.com/content/history/regional.aspx/.

leaks from Fukushima. She spoke in Spanish while her translator strove to keep up with her in English.

In another of the sessions, the *Inupiaq* indigenous activist, Rosemary Ahtuangaruak, talked about the effects of oil exploitation in Alaska following the project of '*Oil Development in the American Arctic, 1999*'. She explained that with this project a drastic change came over the forms of life of the indigenous peoples: as violence and drugs came in. '*You cannot fish any more, the air is polluted and people are starting to get asthma. All of this goes against our traditions and our cultures*'. Once again, desolation and sensitivity appeared in the faces of the Grandmothers as it did among many of the public who were there. But there were also moments of happiness, euphoria and enthusiasm in the course of the sessions. One of these moments was during the performance by Allison Warden, an *Inupiaq* indigenous person, rap composer, poet, writer and performance artist. Dressed in Yupik costume, but wearing a baseball cap on her head, she sang to a rap beat and some of the Grandmothers came down from the platform to dance in the centre of the room, while the public joined in, though just with clapping and laughter.

The Circle of the Sacred Fire

It is in the Sacred Fire Ceremonies that one sees clearly the processes of resignifying ritual elements and cultural traditions that back up the work of the International Council of Thirteen Grandmothers. These events take place out of doors and are open to the general public. The display put on at these ceremonies is one that corroborates the work of each of the Thirteen Grandmothers and her sense of belonging to the group, in a clearly defined ritual framework. Fire is the dominant symbol (Turner, 1989, 30–37) for condensing and unifying the actions of each of them—in so far as they are representatives of a specific indigenous tradition—and of the participating spectators, who play a part in the ritual framework.

These ceremonies show the character of a *bricolage* that is typical of the age of individualization, onto which a new spiritual culture with borrrowed contents and practices from various traditions, is imposed (Beck, 2009: 36 and 59). Galinier calls this kind of process, in which alternative formulas are invented and expressed in *ad hoc* performances, a renewal of the autochthonous (see Galinier in this book). All thirteen of the Indigenous Grandmothers were able to connect distinct religious symbols out of their original context in a way that transmitted plausible messages.

The Circle of the Sacred Fire is a non-dogmatic ritual sphere, where each of the Grandmothers develops practices—which are supposed to be from their own cultural traditions—that aim to sacralize nature and transform the personalities of those attending. The ceremonies take one hour to perform. Taking it in turns, the Grandmothers give talks and perform ritual actions in front of the fire: they communicate their concerns about the ecological damage to Mother Earth, refer to the four elements as sacred entities (earth, air, fire and water), revive the cults of ancestors and of original teachings, and conduct prayers, songs and dances. In this hermeneutical circle there is a 'subjective cosmopolitanization' where traditional religious elements are mixed with new forms of religiosity (Beck, 2009: 136–137).

At the meeting of the Ninth Council, held in Anchorage, there were three ceremonies a day of prayers in the Circle of the Sacred Fire: from 8 till 9 in the morning; in the middle of the day, from 11.30 till 12.30; and at the end of the afternoon. In all there were eleven ceremonies over three and a half days. Each ceremony was conducted by one of the Grandmothers.

The Circle of the Sacred Fire was set up in Delaney Park, two blocks from the Conventions Center, and was precisely marked out in the form of three concentric circles. The largest was about 500 metres across and was outlined by a cord. A smaller ring, about 50 metres across, was marked by four stakes placed inside the bigger ring, showing the direction of the cardinal points. Next to each stake there was a bunch of flowers. The smallest circle, in the middle, was marked by a ring of stones within which the bonfire was made.

To get into the largest ring marked by the rope, it was necessary to use an entry in the East. The entry point was guarded by two people who held a smoking brand of sage, tobacco and other aromatic herbs, with which they perfumed everyone before they went into the circle, and also when they left.

A marquee or a canopy with rows of chairs in it was kept for the grandmothers, special guests and the directors of the CSS. To one side of the circle there were piles of firewood which kept the bonfire going for a whole week, protected by the Fire Keepers and the Fire Assistants; only they were authorized to feed the fire and to remove the ashes. At each meeting of the Council, the Sacred Fire burns for seven days and seven nights, and it is assumed that some ashes from the fires at previous meetings still remain in the fire place.

Those who had signed up to the event were given a program and also a basic protocol for staying in the Circle of the Sacred Fire: you are asked to approach the bonfire reverently and to respect the directions given by the Fire Keepers overseeing the development of the ceremonies. Out of respect for the privacy of the Grandmothers and the sacred character of the meeting, people are asked not to take photos duing the prayers. Gifts of tobacco and aromatic herbs like cedar and sage are accepted for the ceremonies. Part of the protocol is also a request to be alert to the needs of others and speak as little as possible so as to allow silent contemplation at the event. After midnight everyone is invited to pray in a contemplative way.

To start the event in Anchorage, the Sacred Fire was lit at an inauguration ceremony led by the hosting grandmother—the *Yupik* grandmother Rita Blumenstein—. At three on the dot on the first day of the meetings, the Thirteen Indigenous Grandmothers arrived in Delaney Park to take part in the opening ceremony; they all wore their typical formal dresses. They came on foot, as they were staying at the Anchorage Marriott Downtown hotel two blocks away from the park and very close to the *Dena'ina* Conventions Center. Some of them were brought in on wheel chairs.

Once they were all in their places, Grandmother Rita started the ceremony of lighting the Sacred Fire, with the help of the Fire Keepers. She faced each of the four cardinal points in turn, making invocations in her own language and then giving some words of welcome in English. A group of young people were playing Yupik tribal music, and they wore traditional costume. As Ambassador of the Grandmothers, Jyoti spoke briefly to say that with this ceremony the activities of the Ninth International Council of Thirteen Indigenous Grandmothers had begun. She invited all those present to attend the three ceremonies a day to be held in the Circle of Sacred Fire during the next three days. She said the Grandmothers would teach some of their wisdom and would transmit the love that they had cultivated in their places of origin, where they were respected and recognized for their knowledge.

The next day, activities began at eight in the morning with the second Sacred Fire Ceremony. In the open air and the cold of the Spring, Aama Bombo, the Tamang Grandmother from Nepal, stood out with her ceremonial performance. Dressed in white with a headdress of peacock feathers and with a ritual drum she placed between her crossed legs, on the floor, she enchanted the audience with her inspiration, her movements, her songs and her theatrical skill. She sang in her own language for an hour, playing her drum and with a baldric of bells crossed over her breast; the bells jingled to the strong beat of her legs and her whole body; at times Grandmother Aama semed to go into a trance. Suddenly she got up and without looking at anybody walked towards a tree that was outside the Circle of Sacred Fire. She placed a band of white cloth on one of its branches, bent down and embraced the trunk, and then tore off a bunch of fresh green leaves in her mouth. She went back into the Circle playing the drum and continuing her songs and rhythmic movements. The rest of the Grandmothers remained seated under the canopy, wrapped up in blankets, hoods and boots. The ceremony finished in just over an hour, when the Tamang Grandmother bowed in front of the bonfire with her hands on her breast, prayed softly and scattered tobacco over the flames.

Later it was the turn of Mona Polacca, the Hopi grandmother, to pray in the Circle of Fire; she spoke of the shortage of water in Africa, in the Andean regions, in Peru, and elsewhere, in Asia: 'Many people in the world don't have enough of this element, think about that. Here in Alaska you have plenty. I have brought some water from the Colorado River so we can all pray, because the waters of the Grand Canyon may get polluted'.

Standing by the fire, with a bunch of flowers, she asked the Grandmothers to all pray together for harmony, peace and the wisdom of the forefathers:

> Fire is the symbol of unity for the indigenous peoples of the United States. We should preserve these secrets of the indigenous peoples; they made prophecies about the disasters that Mother Earth would suffer. That is why this fire travels around the world, to those countries and peoples where truth is sought... The transnational companies take possession of our resources and of our indigenous knowledge in order to make medicines... When we went to Japan, people cried, the Grandmothers opened people's hearts and as a result of this prayer for the people who died in Hiroshima and their families, there was a shower of rain that night.

In turn, the Cheyenne Arapahoo grandmother, Margaret Behan, seated by the fire, pronounced a long speech which moved her to sobbing; she prayed for children, for peace and for the treasures of the grandmothers' knowledge to be kept up: 'Mother Earth, sacred elements, I ask you to forgive those who made the atom bomb. Grandmother fire, protect the female powers'.

Those who were with Margaret—three young Cheyenne—performed songs they had composed, accompanied by the Cheyenne drum. Grandmother Aama Bombo approached the fire, sang in her own tongue and went around the bonfire a few times. Then grandmother Julieta came up, and after making several obeisances to the Sacred Fire, sang briefly in Mazatec.

The afternoon prayer was conducted by the Oglala Lakota grandmother, Rita Long. She sang softly, accompanied by a man from her own tribe. The cold became more intense and it started to rain while they were performing the Pipe Ceremony. Joyti, the Fire Keepers, and the other Grandmothers, took part in this ceremony. They approached the bonfire and took it in turns to smoke the sacred pipe.

After each of the ceremonies conducted in the Circle of Fire, those people who wished to do so drew close to the fire, bowing reverently and taking a pinch of tobacco (from a bowl placed there specially) to scatter over the flames.

They stayed there in a meditative attitude for a few minutes, trying to draw smoke towards themselves.

Doña Julieta, the Mazatec grandmother, took part in the Circle of Fire at different times. In her interventions she made recurrent use of a bowl of water and a flower, with which she sprinkled those who were there, as is the practice in certain Catholic and indigenous ceremonial contexts of the Mazatec region.

During the final ceremony held in the Circle of Sacred Fire, which was also the closing ceremony of the Ninth Council, grandmothers Pauline Tagore (ambassadress grandmother from New Zealand) and Agnes Baker Pilgrim (of the Takelma Siletz), conducted a joint prayer and asked for applauses and blessings for each of the Grandmothers. The hosting Grandmother, Rita Blumenstein, also took part, and blessed those attending, with a ceremonial feather, skipping happily to the beat of the Yupik drums. With a flower in her right hand, Grandmother Julieta sprinkled water and spread smiles among those who were there.

The ritual atmosphere of the closing ceremony was marked again by folk dances and songs of the Yupik. For the first time since the Council started, the afternoon was warm and sunny. Some thirty chairs were placed in the Sacred Circle so those attending could take it in turns to be blessed by the Grandmothers. They put on cheerful traditional costume. Some women cried emotionally after receiving their blessing. The women attending also sported colorful dresses and skirts; amongst other clothes they wore Yupik outfits and Mazatec blouses that had been on sale during the meeting. The atmosphere of the last Fire Ceremony was cheerful and emotional, and had a taste of farewell to it.

The meeting dispersed once it was clear that the Thirteen Grandmothers had gone; the seats were removed, and so was the rope used to outline the ceremonial space, and small groups came together to chat and say goodbye. But the Sacred Fire stayed alight; a long queue formed and many of those attending drew close to the bonfire to say farewell with bows and prayers. The Fire Keepers distributed ashes from the Sacred Fire to some of those attending, who had acquired a special box for the purpose, with the logo of the CSS on it. Some of the energy that had emanated from the Sacred Fire was held in these ashes.

Final Comments

The activity of the Thirteen Indigenous Grandmothers on the international scene transmits the idea that people from different traditions share the same convictions about subjects of interest involving the whole population of the Earth. As Beck notices, expressions of cosmopolitan compassion are characteristic of an experience of universal neighborliness without frontiers (2009: 48). This particular organization proposes discourses and practices that show feelings of planetary grief, initiatives with a pacifist and ecological orientation, devotion to the ancestors and to the female side of things, and a return to original knowledges. Members and directors of the group intertwine a diversity of meetings by taking part in networks that connect them to other groups, institutions and individuals, through circuits of economic and symbolic exchange. To do so, they take up ethnic components and traditions as instruments having the flexibility that allows them to be projected on a worldwide scale; in these spaces of relations both the users and the contexts are mobile (Argyriadis and De la Torre, op. cit.: 11–22).

The International Council of Thirteen Grandmothers is inserted in a network of organizations whose supply of spiritual goods on offer is available simultaneously in the new density of world communications, without borders (Beck, op. cit.: 56). The current forms of operation by network between individuals and between groups, or between groups and individuals, make it possible to have meetings with specific aims for limited periods of time (Riechman and Fernández Buey, 1994, quoted in Carozzi, op. cit.: 23–31.)

In the case presented here we should ask how the practice of Doña Julieta, the Mazatec grandmother, is reflected in her original environment; that is to say, how the dynamics of the interface between global and local are expressed for her (Argyriadis and De la Torre, *ibidem*). She clearly has advantages over other members of her community who do not have the possibilities provided by mass media. Her membership of the Council of Thirteen Indigenous Grandmothers has contributed to her fame in Huautla and outside it, hence to the increased number of tourists wanting to take part in a Vigil presided over by her or by one or other of her daughters, who have followed her steps in the shamanic practice. As Galinier points out with reference to the process he denominates endo-shamanism (Chapter II.2 of this book), the shamanic market in Huautla varies according to the demand there is for interpretation by ritual specialists through their relations with particular classes of actors in the framework of inter-ethnic and intra-ethnic dynamics. Still, we should mention that the exo-shamanic practice[23] of Doña Julieta does not seem to be reflected

23 For Galinier the term exo-shamanism refers to practices where the public is alien to the native community (and might consist of urban inhabitants or mystical tourists) even when the expert could be an indigenous person bearing the cosmology of a Pre-Hispanic tradition (see Chapter II.2 in this book).

in direct or indirect benefits for the rest of the Mazatec community; according to what my enquiries showed, there have been no programs, projects or local events that have been promoted in line with the objectives stated by the Council on their media platform.

Other actors in the Huautla society, however, have recently promoted novel strategies to project themselves, this time on a wider scale; for example, organizing an Annual Festival to commemorate the birth of María Sabina, as well as the formation of the Association of Healers of Huatla, established by the Municipal Council and the House of Culture. Grandmother Julieta refrains from taking part in these activities as she belongs, she says, to an internationally recognized organization of the greatest importance (personal communication to the author). An expression of the same distancing was also seen during the meeting of the Third International Council of the Thirteen Indigenous Grandmothers, which took place in Huautla in May, 2006. She and her co-workers organized the reception for the members of the Council and other people attending the event who came from different latitudes. Interaction with the rest of the Huautla community was reduced to a minimum; and even the Sacred Fire Ceremonies—which are usually open to the public—were conducted in the inner patio of the family house (personal communication to the author).

Nevertheless, as with other, similar associations, in the cosmopolitaan framework of overcoming hierarchies and pre-fixed frontiers (Beck, op. cit.: 62), this group of women, the Thirteen Indigenous Grandmothers, is committed to offering meaning at the present time when global risks are paramount. They are indeed committed to the construction of a flow of universal meaning through decontextualized but unifying practices. Finally, ecological concerns and the attempt to preserve and transmit inherited knowledge codified in the indigenous cultures of the world, reveal the adoption of a planetary consciousness, with motivations that bring together people having the most varied origins, though in a selective and transitory way.

CHAPTER 6

Strategies for Resistance and the Negotiation of Cultural Goods in Wixaritari Shamanism: Processes of Articulation[1]

Alejandra Aguilar Ros

Introduction

One of the most attractive ideas of the new era or New Age, is the promise of personal access to sacred experience (Heelas, 1996). It offers an easy way in to non-visible reality, and an easy way out, should it be required. The sensibility of the New Age has democratic elements, with an emphasis on the search for techniques and spiritual development through individual endeavour. For some authors such as Heelas (1996), these individual efforts form the basis of spiritual growth. Other writers however, do not agree, as beliefs can always be changed to suit the practitioner's taste without the need to go any deeper into a religious tradition (Clark, 2006: 34–37).

Although New Age practices appear at first sight to be very eclectic, for those who join in and live them, what matters is their complementary nature. What is sought is a transformation of consciousness in order to perceive realities beyond the material world, a transformation that it is not too hard to gain access to and one which practitioners can approach by distinguishing 'ego' from the 'real being'—of inner, pure or non-material energy—and detaching themselves from desire (Clark, 2006: 30–31). The objective is also another form of knowledge, which is not necessarily based on scientific reasoning, but can be helped by it. This way of knowing is one that questions science and the scientific way of explaining the world, while offering certainties that have to do with immaterial realities.

In Mexico in particular, practices related to the New Age are related to an exaltation of subjectivities in the sense of finding individuation[2] through cultivating a sense of one's own spirituality, but this is done within relatively

1 The present article and the fieldwork undertaken were made possible by the project: '*Transnacionalización y relocalización de las religiones indo y afro americanas*' financed by CONACYT 081926.

2 A term derived from transpersonal psychology, from which many practitioners take up pieces.

 | DOI 10.1163/9789004316485_009

stable community organizations, which is very important. While examples of personal spiritual development are important, New Age practices are also anchored in groups with an alternative emphasis on community, as in the case of Mexicanism. Movements such as this aim to bring back to life the Pre-Hispanic culture of Anáhuac in central Mexico, recreating what they consider to be ancient Aztec dances and seeking for a cultural reconnection with the *Mexica* past. Some of them incorporate into the philosophical base of Mexicanism a search for roots, hence for ritual contact with indigenous people in order to broaden their knowledge and experiences of the Indian world. To this end, they seek out indigenous subjects whom they consider to be authentic—either because their parents were indigenous or because they live in Indian communities, or because they speak a native language—thus rooting their quest for the spiritual Indian in concrete traditions.[3]

The Huichol or *Wixaritari*[4] are one of the indigenous groups in Mexico most strongly fixed in the national imagination as 'untouched' Indians. Their religious specialists, the *mara'akate*, are thought of as authentic transmitters of a millenarian cosmological and healing tradition, who have kept up an ethnic identity linked to a mythology and religious practices of their own, in spite of Catholic evangelization. Because of this image of isolation and authenticity, and with the popularization of New Age practices in Mexico, encouraged especially by Mexicanist groups, the *Wixaritari* are now in great demand on the part of spiritual seekers and it is important to document the way in which relations between the *Wixaritari* and the seekers have transformed both parts. This concern is expressed in the context of a larger study[5] that I have participated in, in an attempt to understand the way in which the Wixaritari seek to

3 Here I will be using the term 'spiritual Indian' or 'mystic' to refer to the representations and imaginaries of the original peoples, that are held by groups and individuals who wish to exalt them as examples of spirituality, of union with and care for the earth, of community forms of organization and above all, of people holding native rituals. This type of representation tends to blur the differences between ethnic groups, and the conflicts within them, linking indigenous people to a kind of common wisdom that manages to stay in harmony with its surroundings, and places them in the position of being non-violent and not materialistic (Sarrazin, 2008).

4 In the last few years, the preferred policy of the *Wixaritari* has been to call themselves *Wixaritari* (pronounced Wirráritari); I will therefore try to keep to this name, changing back to 'Huichol' when giving the point of the view of the dancers or of others who still call them by that name, without any unfavorable connotation.

5 First, in the project '*Translocalización y relocalización de lo religioso (México, Cuba, Colombia)*' (2006–2008) and then in a macro-project entitled '*Tansnacionalización y relocalización de las religiones indo y afro americanas*', financed by CONACYT from 2009.

negotiate and assume a stance in the representation of themselves during the process in which their identity is being globalized. The macro-project has shown in several cases (Gutiérrez and Aguilar, 2008), how the processes of religious hybridization are differential, occurring at different speeds, and are frequently interrupted, do not work or may even be cancelled.[6]

In this article I will be exploring an interesting case of association between an Aztec Dance group and a *Wixarika mara'akame*, or Huichol shaman. Of particular interest is how the relationship broke up. The case contains elements that seem to me to be crucial for understanding connections in a discourse on the mystical Indian, and finding what the breaking points of the discourse are in concrete socio-cultural situations.

These connections are not only made at the level of beliefs and interpretive and conceptual frameworks (Frigerio, 1999). Frigerio (see his example of Afro-Brazilian religions in Argentina) shows how beliefs are adopted in non-traditional contexts through the use of 'mechanisms of *presentation* (rather than of adaptation) that make their reception easier (...) without necessarily implying big changes to doctrine and practices' (1999: 5). This is achieved by means of cognitive bridges between 'the systems of beliefs and values' (1999: 5). In this way it may be possible to provide interpretive schemes for the orientation of new experiences, based on previous beliefs. The concept of an interpretive frame helps with the comprehension of how symbolic resources are mobilized, and with understanding the processes of conversion, but leaves to one side more detailed, important aspects: such as the symbolic charge of these elements, or the power, class and ethnicity games that come into play, as well as elements of an emotional type, such as taste and bodily habits (Csordas, 1994).[7] Using frames of reference puts a greater emphasis on gnosis than the emotions or the body, but it seems to me that this does not cover all that happens when choosing religious practices. The practices are not only bridges of passage based on the representation or conceptual understanding of beliefs, but have much denser cultural forms, which include emotions, the body, history, and power relations of ethnicity and class.

6 Here we distinguish three types of limiting factor in the process of hybridization: the original intentions of the actors, their relative positions attained in the religious fields, and the national and political contexts in which these processes develop, which are of great importance (Gutiérrez and Aguilar, 2008: 394).

7 Frigerio (1995 and 1999) would call this relation one created by 'cognitive bridges', thus denoting the prevalence of gnosis over emotions or the body. However, this relation does not only happen at a cognitive level; furthermore, when an articulation or a disarticulation happens in religious practices, it is the last part of a process.

There are basically two, interlinked, ways in which the connection between dissimilar religious practices is made. One has to do with elements of a cognitive, symbolical, or semantic type; which would include objects or concepts with symbolic ceremonial charges, as we will see below. The other way in which the connection between different religious practices is made, concerns the processes that these objects are found in. These have to do with emotions, and with collisions between classes, and ethnicities, as well as differentiated historical-cultural positions. Both types of connection are mediated mainly by actors who in the bigger project have been called 'nodal', through being connectors between circuits in a wider network.[8] However, this expression might not be able to cover all that is alluded to in terms of power and class relations. It might not be suficient to account for how the actors' mediations objectify the symbolic, the religious and the historic. Beyond the intermediation that these actors achieve, their identity is plural. It is situated in the network that they manage to articulate in partial, temporary and polysemic forms, created through their associations in a transitory way (García and Romero, 2002: 48).

Here I will refer to the concept of articulation, which Hall defines as a 'form of connection that can produce a unity out of two different elements, under certain conditions. It is a union that is not necessary, determined, absolute or essential' (Hall interviewed by Grossberg, 1996: 140). He establishes that there is a 'relation between elements such that their identity is modified as a result of this practice' (García and Romero, 2002). By 'articulation', I understand a process of relation between different identities, which is effected at various levels. It is a link that points us towards the *relation* between the parts, towards subject/subject and subject/object relations, and helps to reveal power relations and asymmetries.

An analysis of articulation implies considering the human and non-human *collectives* mobilized in each case, and including the semiotic-material practices of a group of people, as well as their material, institutional and symbolic contrivances. The mobilization of these collectives includes the possibilities (or impossibilities) they may have of forming a relation (García and Romero, 2002: 59).

I will explore these articulations in the particular case of the mobilization of a (human and non-human) collective made up of a group of New Age style Aztec

8 In the project '*Religiones Transnacionales del Sur*' (RELITRANS), we have preferred certain terms such as *nodal actors*, and *cognitive networks* or *bridges*, to others that are used here. Although I will be using these terms, I would also like to include the point of view of articulation that comes from Marxist discussion. The case I present shows inequalities between actors, which are not reflected in the idea of networks as such, as this model posits actors on the same level without adopting a critical stand.

Dancers, a Huichol *mara'akame* and his family, and a Huichol deity. The Aztec group is called Chicahuac Ollin, from the city of Tijuana, Baja California, who followed the 'Huichol way' after appropriating a *Wixarika* deity that was offered to them through a *Wixarika mara'akame*. For this work I will first offer some reflections on what has been called Huichol Neo-shamanism, and then explain what I mean by articulation. I will deal with the articulating elements which I have found linked the Aztec dance group to the 'Huichol tradition'. Then I will describe the ensuing disarticulation, in order to show how these links were made, along with encounters and disagreements on different levels.

These working notions will provide the leading thread of an analysis of the processes of appropriation that allow, and facilitate, the circulation of symbolic goods in the adjudication of the Huichol tradition by groups interested in them. These concepts will also show us the limits of the circulation of these goods.

Wixarika Shamanism or *Nierika* as an Illusion

The Wixaritari, or Huichol, live mainly in the north of the state of Jalisco and in the state of Nayarit, in Mexico. The large area they have traditionally occupied—and held onto with some difficulty over the years of the Spanish colonization and then under the regime established by the Nation State—allows them to live for some months of the year from harvesting maize and small-scale hunting. However the seasonality of maize and the need to search for other means of survival, has taken them outside their traditional lands, to tobacco plantations in Nayarit, or as migrants to the United States, or else, to sell crafts all over the country, sometimes in combination with farm work. The presence of the *Wixaritari* and especially their particular style of crafts have made them recognizable in Mexico wherever they go. Their wandering has also given them platforms for forming relations with various social groups: from members of non governmental organisations (NGOs), to government officials, anthropologists and cultural promoters, and, of course, followers of the mystical native.

Weigand and Fikes (2004) take note of the works that helped to propagate the stereotype of the *mara'akate* as *individuals* specializing in the use of peyote to reach unparalleled mystical experiences. They show what they call the 'sensationalist diffusion' of studies that set out to be anthropological but only served as the basis for a 'false' image of the Huichol people, especially in the writings by Peter Furst. For these authors, the *mara'akate* portrayed in the studies mentioned are urban Huichols, so they consider them as alienated subjects dissociated from their cosmology, which is intimately linked to the ceremonial cycle of agriculture within the Huichol communities (2004: 53–54).

To understand this type of Neo-esoteric diffusion, we should consider the impact of a type of literature that has been crucial to placing and representing the indigenous peoples as transmitters of a revealed, esoteric wisdom, handed down to our days from Pre-Hispanic times. According to this literature, such knowledge is only accessible through direct learning, working with a shaman to whom the apprentice must join himself. Of course, the main author here is Castaneda, who first published his Ph.D. thesis in Anthropology in the nineteen sixties, which tells of his meeting with a Yaqui shaman whom he calls Don Juan; the shaman takes him on as an apprentice and reveals to him the secrets of the 'power plants' (or hallucinogenics) for taking control of one's personal energy and transforming one's consciousness. Although Castaneda made it clear that his character was a Yaqui, his Don Juan has been thought to be like the Huichol *mara'akame*.

His books have been taken up quite often over a period of several decades, but now, with a boom for the New Age and ecological sensibility, the ideas in them have found a fruitful resonance in the discourses of those who call for 'a new human consciousness'. Such enthusiasts portray the native groups as bearers of an ancestral wisdom, who have managed to relate in a sustainable way to the earth and from whom we should learn this relation anew (cf. Soares, 1990 on Santo Daime in Brazil).

The idea that the Indian groups have kept their beliefs untouched, maintaining the 'true indigenous tradition', has allowed an interesting relationship between non-indigenous groups, and natives, based on a particular reconstruction of the past combined with New Age beliefs (for the Huichol, see Aguilar, 2008 and Durín and Aguilar, 2008; for the Otomi, Farfán et al., 2005). This amalgamation has its equivalent in some strains of Mexicanism as expressed in the Aztec dances, whose practitioners claim that the truly Indian has been preserved through them (De la Torre 2008a; Gutiérrez 2008). For them, the original, ancient Pre-Hispanic indigenous knowledge lies beneath the surface, covered by a syncretic Catholicism, and is only transmitted through the teaching of the dance.

While Weigand and Fikes (2004) and especially the latter (2009)[9] have specifically criticized the shamanism represented by Castaneda,[10] they were actually trying to open the debate as to what Huichol shamanism 'really means'; however, their critique leaves important aspects out. Firstly, Fikes and Weigand argue that the shamans who have been the spokespersons of Huichol shamanism to

9 In fact, Fikes makes a similar sort of apology for *Wixarika* shamanism (2009), but he is at times so insistent that his is the authentic representation of the subject, that one begins to think his representation may be as open to doubt as that of the Neo-shamans he criticises.

10 Fikes even wrote a letter to the ethics committee of the American Anthropological Association accusing Castaneda's publications of amounting to a fraud.

the West, did not live close to their communities and so will not have participated in the ritual life of the Huichol agricultural cycle. If their teachers have not participated in the communities, then the learning by their *mestizo* followers is put into question, and the representation of shamanism that has been made to them must be 'erroneous'. Either those who taught them were not shamans, or what they learned cannot have been authentic. For these critics, what the ceremonial practices have against them is that they were not conducted within the traditional ritual cycle and what is worse, that they were transmitted to people who were not members of *Wixaritari* tribe.

But if we take into account the fact that while a third of the Wixaritari are estimated to live outside their traditional communities (Durín, 2003) the identity that they subscribe to is still Wixaritari; we cannot just discard as unauthentic one or more of the *types* of shamanic practice that derive from Wixaritari tradition. The fact that these *mara'akate* have lived for a long time outside their own communities selling crafts in the big cities, does not make them any less important or any less Wixaritari in the eyes of their own communities; even if they are criticized for not participating in communal rituals.

The *mara'akate* who are willing to teach their techniques to *mestizos*, or just conduct healings in esoteric centres, are part of what is going on in the Huichol world and we cannot just throw them into the fraud basket. In the argument as to whether these are fraudulent practices or whether some shamans are more authentic than others, we lose sight of the anthropological work: of documenting the social, analyzing processes and understanding how the actors give their practices meaning.

An anthropological project would be one that sought to understand how the *Wixaritari* slot in on the borderline with New Age practices and relate to them. This tells us not only about subjective practices in the *Wixarika* world—an aspect that seems to be hard to reflect on in Mexican anthropological writing—but also about how certain strategies come into play in the indigenous world in order to relocate globalizing discourses. The *mara'akate* who are willing to provide shamanic services to *mestizos*, although tolerated, are certainly not kindly regarded in the *Wixaritari* communities; however, these services are ancient, dating from Pre-Hispanic times (Liffman, 2012) and their provision today outside the community is not an exception.

Here I will present one of the best-known exponents of this type of *mara'akame*: Don Pablo Taizán,[11] who, to my mind, is at one of the extreme points in the range of shamanic services. Taizán was expelled from his

---

11 Pablo Taizán de la Cruz, born around 1936 (his original Huichol name being *Yauxa*), lived in *Taimarita*, in a settlement near *Tuapurie* (Santa Catarina). His cousin, José Benítez, is an internationally renowned Huichol artist (Negrín, 2008).

community over problems having to do with land, and is unable to return to Huichol territory. As a *mara'akame* and preserver of the ritual cycle, he has founded his own community on a plot of land near Las Varas, Nayarit, which he has called Taimarita. Here he receives hundreds of non-Huichol followers to whom he teaches what some think of as 'the Huichol way'.[12] The annual event, where new followers are recruited, is the pilgrimage to Wirikuta, the *Wixarika* sacred place *par excellence*, in the East of the holy land of the Cerro del Quemado in the state of San Luis Potosí. On this pilgrimage many followers of Indian ways have converted to a Huichol way of life, ordering their existences around the ceremonial cycle Taizán style, faithfully keeping their promises to him and baptizing their children in this tradition.

Pablo Taizán rose to fame in the world of native spirituality thanks to his participation in the community of Teopantli Kalpulli,[13] a self-sufficient community in the countryside, which strives to be nourished from indigenous roots. Domingo Díaz Porta, a Venezuelan, and ex-member of the GFU, founded it in 1983,[14] and today he is the leader of an organization called MAIS,[15] that seeks to rescue the traditions of the original peoples.

12 The understanding of some of the followers is that they are learning how to become a *mara'akate*.

13 The community arose after the separation of its members from the Grand Universal Fraternity (*Gran Fraternidad Universal*, or GFU) and is located on the southern edge of the Primavera forest, near the town of San Isidro Mazatepec, in the municipality of Tala, in the state of Jalisco. They cultivate four main 'indigenous' traditions: Mexica, Lakota, Huichol and Yoga. Currently it has 105 persons living there. The way it is organized is through councils, and they use consultation and consensus. The economy is family based and organized in production co-operatives made up of groups of members of the community. The area covered is 37 hectares (i.e. 0.37 square kilometers or 370,000 square meters—around 90 acres); of which 30 hectares (300,000 square meters) are kept for agricultural use and as an environmental reserve. They grow maize, soya, other beans, sunflower and squash, using techniques of organic agriculture. Seven hectares (70,000 square meters) are for the residential area; of these, three hectares are divided into 55 lots measuring approximately 500 square meters each, and four hectares are for common use (Ríos Levi, n.d.).

14 The GFU is a movement that defines itself as searching for the spiritual and individual growth of human beings, based on a combination of science, art, philosophy and Occultism, with the aim of promoting consciousness and health (see their web page: http://www.gfu.org/2012/index.php).

15 MAIS, or Commonwealth of Solar Indian America (*Mancomunidad de la América India Solar* in Spanish), broke off from the GFU, as a separate movement. It defines itself as a bridge between different native cultures, thereby promoting mutual spiritual and cultural understanding.

In 1988, at an inter-tribal ceremony called 'Kanto de la Tierra'[16] that brought together the most important ancient guardians of the continent in the Kalpulli, Pablo Taizán was one of those invited. The relation of Don Pablo to 'El Kanto' brought him many connections and a continuing relation with Kalpulli. Don Pablo thus became a nodal actor, connecting leaders and groups of the alternative spiritual movements that are now very important to members of Mexicanism (see Figure 6.1).

Many of those interested in alternative ways of life would come to Kalpulli, and so it was that members of what is now the Aztec Dance group Chicahuac Ollin, 'Strength and Movement', arrived and began to follow Taizán on his trips in the desert. This group is based in Tijuana, Baja California and is linked to indigenous traditions like those of the Pai Pai from northern Baja California, the Lakota Sioux tribe from the U.S.A. (through Tigre Pérez), and the *Wixaritari* or Huichol of Mexico, as well as organizations like MAIS, and the GFU. Furthermore, its individual members have influence over, and contacts with other spiritual movements, like Wicca,[17] or musical ones like the Solar Fest. Its spiritual leaders are Tata Cuaxtle and Arturo Meza, leader of *el Camino Rojo* (Red Path) of the Mexicayotl movement. It was not long before they invited Taizán to preside over *híkuri*,[18] peyote vigils for them in Tijuana.

During one of these vigils, after 'taking the medicine', Don Pablo made a drawing which he then gave to one of the leaders, the one he had the most confidence in, as he was the first to have made contact with him in the Kalpulli. The drawing was of a Huichol deity: the god that represents the energy of the Dance, according to what members of the group said. This deity had asked Don Pablo to let him come down and stay with the dancers; thus, Don Pablo asked the group if He might. Duly impressed, the Chicahuac talked it over and came to an agreement to take in the deity after the main leaders of the time had accepted.

From then on, the Huichol deity Tatutsi Tsramurahui in the form of a wooden sculpture made by Don Pablo, accompanied them wherever they went: to their dance performances—at that time they did public shows,—or

16 Kanto de la Tierra is an inter-tribal vision organized originally by Tigre Pérez, a renowned North American tribal leader (cf. http://www.llamadodelcorazondelatierra.com/nosotros/historia.html). Originally called Kanto del Pueblo, then Kanto de la Tierra, and nowadays Raíces de la Tierra, it gathers native spiritual leaders from all over the world in order to perform ceremonies to heal the earth (cf. http://raicesdelatierracolombia.com/raices-de-la-tierra/historia/).

17 Wicca though an Old English word refers to a neo-pagan religion with Celtic origins, of a mystical and initiation type, based on belief in the forces of nature and control of them.

18 *Lophophora williamsii.*

FIGURE 6.1 *Pablo Taizán waiting for the unrooting ceremony to start, with a member of Chicahuac. Samurawi ceremonial complex, Tecate, Baja California, Mexico, January 2010*
PHOTO: ALEJANDRA AGUILAR ROS

to radio and television broadcasts. Having been adopted by Tatutsi, they would also have to follow the tradition and the forms that the deity liked: the ceremonial cycle of the Huichol would have to be started up in Tijuana.

After two years of trying, the group could not keep up with the ceremonial demands made on them and decided to separate from the Huichol tradition as a commitment of the whole group. We will now explore how this dance group adopted and then abandoned the Huichol way, which will allow us to observe processes of articulation and disarticulation and of circulation between traditions.

Articulation: A Political Concept

The Chicahuac group can be classified as cross-border because of its location and the participation of its members at various levels in trans-border[19] activities.

19 Transborder or *Transfronteridad* is a concept useful for understanding how on the border between Mexico and the USA, there are different levels of cultural and political experiences of the frontier; in other words, different levels of exchange, dependence, frequency,

This gives the Chicahuacs a particular slant other groups do not have, because while they hold to the ideology of Mexicanism, they are also connected, as we have mentioned, to other transnational and indigenous traditions. Also, a number of its members are psychologists following their own spiritual quest based on broadening their knowledge through the reading of texts related to understanding indigenous cultures. At the same time, some members of the group practice alternative activities linked to New Age: reiki, pagan practices, indigenous music, vigils and Aztec dance. Rather than being an end in itself, the latter is a medium through which to come together, and seek opportunities of self-growth. The Chicahuac is a group that values knowledge and many of those in it have read not only Castaneda but also transpersonal, and Jungian psychology. They consider indigenous knowledge to have roots in an ancient and superior wisdom above rational scientific knowledge, although they do not exclude the latter. One of the group's outstanding features is the degree of individuation possessed by members of the group. In a way not seen in other dance groups, each member has his or her own activities (to match their 'own spiritual path'), and they all come together in Chicahuac.

A number of them said that they believed indigenous people to have a superior wisdom mostly in their relation with 'Mother Earth'. They understood that in this, there is an important role for reciprocity and caring for others, but at the same time they did not consider all indigenous practices to be valuable. Gender relations, hierarchical obedience, and some indigenous customs made no sense to them, and they simply did not see the need to follow them. Explanations of this kind appeared after the break from the Huichol tradition, something I will take up again in the reflections on disarticulations.

I understand this process, and the relation between the dancers and Taizán, as being permeated by an eco-indigenous discourse that represents the indigenous pole as bearers of ancestral wisdom, intimately linked to the earth, the possessors of an alternative and much needed knowledge for surviving present day uncertainties. The 'Huichol way' of the American *mara'akate* apprentices (the 'false prophets' of Weigand and Fikes), exalts objects and ceremonies related to the *Wixaritari*, in a single, whole discourse, where differences with historical and structural processes are blurred.

In the particular process of the Chicahuac and Taizán there was a work of translation, popularization and transmission of both versions of what their joint project meant for tradition. On the one hand, the Chicahuac, looked for elements in their own beliefs that had a power of articulation, so they could

directionality and meaning in social exchanges on both sides of the border with the United States (Iglesias, 2008).

find an echo in the *Wixarika* system of meaning. On the other, for Taizán and his family, finding followers of the *Wixarika* way allowed them to keep up their ritual cycle as *Wixaritari*, even though they were not living in traditional communities anymore.

To understand this process I will work here with the notion of articulation, a term used since the nineteen seventies to make it possible to think of the contradictions and differences between identities that at the time were not being considered: neither by feminism and the left in general, nor in discussions of race and class that were critical of colonization (García and Romero, 2002: 45). Articulation, in this literature, is a word with a charge of political resistance in which differences between identities is their constituent problem: it is what makes the articulation possible or impossible (Butler, 1997, quoted in García and Romero, 2002: 46). To enquire into articulations is to ask about the exclusions and acts of violence from which forms of community were created (García and Romero, 2002: 47).

Laclau and Mouffe (1987: 119), give the name *articulation* to any practice that establishes a relation between elements such that their identities are modified as a result of their practice. Nevertheless, there are 'material limits that condition possibilities for articulation' (Hall, interviewed by Grossberg, 1996: 146); in this case, not only those marked by ethnicity and class, but also those marked by historical and contextual configurations of meaning. Here the discourse is not just linguistic but also has to do with the 'materiality of discursive structures' (García and Romero, 2002).

Articulation should therefore be understood as:

> ...the form of connection that can produce a unity of two different elements, under certain conditions. The union is not necessary, or determined, absolute, or forever essential. One should ask under what circumstances it can be produced or forged into a relation. Thus the so-called 'unity' of a discourse is really the articulation of various specific elements that can be re-articulated in distinct forms, as they do not 'belong' to each other. The 'unity' that counts is a link between this articulated discourse and the social forces it can connect itself to under certain historical conditions, though it does not have to.
>
> HALL INTERVIEWED BY GROSSBERG, 1996: 140

Here I understand historical forces within a cultural analysis of *symbolic forms* (Thompson, 1998), in structured contexts, studying their constitution of meaning and their social contextualization. These should be approached from '...the study of actions, objects and meaningful expressions of various kinds in relation to the historically specific and socially constructed contexts by means of which the symbolic forms are produced, transmitted and received'. That is, from the analysis of socially structured contexts and processes (Latour, 2008).[20]

In this frame, the universe of discourse is made up of the 'Huichol way', structured as a field of relations within which the two traditions acted together due to having practices in common, that appeared to have a shared meaning, but would soon reveal their complex contradictions.

The concept of articulation allows us to ask questions about the nature of these connections in a way that permits us to understand within them the politics that link the human to the non-human elements[21] (Haraway, 1991) in the collectives, and how these relations are developed. That is to say, in these collectives (networks) there are human beings and actants, objects with the capacity of 'objecting' (*objetar*) (García and Romero, 2002: 48), that may form part of the 'functioning set' of the collective and on many occasions do mark the limits of its possibilities.[22]

Here *the network* will be understood as the alliances that allow symbolic and material resources to be mobilized for those who are linked to the actant, and in this network of relations, Agency is distributed over the network (Latour, 2008); there is no single subject who puts it in action, thus provoking transformations in it. In this sense, any action producing a transformation makes the actant suffer and perform another action, in such a way that the possibility of being subject and object is integrated into himself (Greimás and Cortés, 1990).

20 For Latour 'the social' does not have an ontological status of relation only between persons, as it is the result of material interactions between elements that are not considered social: he seeks a sociology of associations, not of the social, as a result of the theoretical focus on actor-networks (2008).

21 García and Romero remind us that the term can also be used as an epistemological or methodological tool (2002: 58) that allows dualisms of closed and essential identities to be discarded, actors in the network to be singled out, and non-human elements to be granted agency, 'generating contingent articulations'. These articulations are situated where there is room as much for an analysis of the differences and connections between the various articulated elements, as there is for paying attention to the form in which such differences and connections are constituted as such.

22 Let me say that this was the role of Takutsi in the whole process. It is not that I consider the *Wixarika* god to be on the same level as human actions, but that the deity's weight in the network, linked to that of Don Pablo and to the process for acquiring his 'energy', cannot be eliminated from the collective. Rather, if we take it into account, we put an emphasis on the differentiated symbolic charge and how this actant can work for each group in its articulation, but also as a disarticulator, depending on the charges of power of the actors.

Articulation also makes it possible to ask about the politics that actants hold, the conditions making it possible or impossible to get their demands met, what the common elements are, and in an important way, what meanings are excluded (García and Romero, 2002). Thus, in the case we are concerned with, we must now ask ourselves: which are the articulations that allowed such a close relation in such different actants, and why did it break up.

Discourses and Articulating Elements

The Chicahuac group entered fully into the relation with Don Pablo principally because he was going to teach them contact with the Earth by incorporating the worship of *Takutsi* into the agricutural cycle, as is natural in his worldview. One of the members of the group offered to donate a plot of land in the countryside to conduct the rituals and sow maize; they named it Samurawi (see Figure 6.2). Don Pablo then asked them to make a Kali Huey, a temple for the god for which they obtained the materials. This was a very important process for all those involved as they took part in the construction of a complete ceremonial center. One of the most significant aspects of this grand ritual was the burying, in various 'vortices', of personal offerings to the Huichol deities, thus putting themselves on the 'Huichol way', as ceremonial members of an ethnic group. For the Huichol, the metaphor of the root is very important, as this is the metonomy for the system of *Wixarika* kinship (Liffman, 2005). It is by means of roots connected to the different hierarchical positions of the ritual fires that the *Wixaritari* are united as members of the same group of kinship and can take part in the same cosmogonic system. For the Chicahuac this metaphor did not mean joining themselves to a Huichol genealogy—that is to say, it does not link them to the ancestors, as in the *Wixarika* religion—but setting themselves on a path of spiritual learning; which in turn has an equivalence with the notion of *yeiyari*, the *Wixarika* way of the heart.

For the dancers, the generic term 'indigenous' indicated a relation with the Earth and a tradition through which there was a possibility of getting closer, of (re) connecting with the indigenous, from the position of being a *mestizo* in Mexico. In the present case, and not in the case of other groups, it was a question not only of adopting practices loosely, but of literally *taking root* in them. So the process was not based on correspondences intrinsic to religious systems, but on links created by the actors themselves in search of objectives elaborated with elements thought to be similar.

Within this discourse, what helped the Chicahuac to commit themselves to the 'Huichol tradition' was the pre-existing symbolic forms in the narratives they shared, as Don Pablo had managed to articulate them; that is, the idea of the untouched Indian as a source of wisdom in the ecologist discourse, and the idea of the Indian as a means of gaining access to esoteric gateways, taken from literature written in the style of Castaneda. The specific types of articulation that the beginning of the operation of the link entails, are not however made only as bridges from the cognitive, as they are produced from social forms charged with cultural, historical and emotional content.

In the Chicahuac/Don Pablo relationship there were elements of this discourse, which are those that 'extend the field of play and meaning infinitely' (Laclau and Mouffe 1987: 129). The articulating elements connect a 'discursive chain not because of its lack of meaning but, on the contrary, because of its excess of meaning': 'the articulation is configured…as a practice of partial fixations that stabilizes certain nodal points just for a short while' (García and Romero, 2002: 50).

The elaboration of articulations was made possible by the following elements, which we find to be the main ones:

- 'Objects' that remit to ritual/symbolical concepts and possess multivocal meanings with a big historical, literary and emotional charge. The holy objects circulate among the circuits of those taking part, and are

FIGURE 6.2 *Panoramic view of the Samurawi ceremonial complex, Tecate, Baja California, Mexico, January 2010*
PHOTO: ALEJANDRA AGUILAR ROS

ceremonially charged goods, while at the same time condensing cultural forms; however, they are charged with *differentiated meanings*, and are not necessarily found at the same level on the network (Frigerio, 1999; Escobar, 2008).
- Ritual processes which when experienced created emotional links and anchorages for identity: vigils, pilgrimages, taking part in a sacrifice, agricultural ceremonies, the 'Huichol way' with its agricultural cycle, and later, the disconnection that occurred for various circumstantial reasons as we will see: processes in which the sense that had been given to the objects was influential, and which ended in a ceremony of disarticulation.
- Nodal actors and actant leaders or cultural promoters: these are Don Pablo, the moral leaders of Chicahuac, and Takutsi as energy and as god.

None of these elements can be separated from any of the others, and in fact we should understand them in a context where thanks to the social forms that already existed, they could be articulated in such a way as to make sense for members of the collective—which, as we will see below, once the meaning ceased to apply, produced a disarticulation.

In the first year of the dance group's commitment to Takutsi, Chicahuac experienced the phase of articulation; after the consecration of the Kali Huey, they all took part in sowing maize and different associated ceremonies that Don Pablo indicated to them. Some members of the group even visited *Taimarita*, in Jalisco, the ceremonial plot where Don Pablo lives, for some of these festivals.

One of the important figures that connect New Age style practices is that of energy, a concept that covers a large number of semantic meanings in which various concepts of supernatural action find room (Bordes, 2006). The term 'energy', and practices associated with it such as 'reiki and magnetism', also acquired a considerable power of evocation among the Chicahuac. Following the schism, the translation that the dancers make today of Takutsi is that it was the 'energy' of the god, which wanted to be with them in their dance. Thus, it is not given hierarchical agency as a deity, but is regarded as an influence which they can choose to use or not.

Another important figure is that of the *híkuri*: for the Chicahuac as for the *Wixaritari* it is a sacred plant, but for the former it is considered above all as a *means* of attaining altered states of consciousness that will allow them to advance individually in their spiritual progress. Whereas the *Wixaritari* have a complicated relationship with the *híkuri*: it is not just a medicine, a mediation, but is in itself Maize and Deer, two of their central deities, as well as being a means of communication with the ancestors, who provide a reminder of how to live as the true people, and who can be asked for good harvests and health.

For the Chicahuac, maize is wedded to the Indian peoples, and these are related to the cultivation of the land. For them it was a privilege to have a more direct connection with a real Indian who would teach them how to relate to Mother Earth. The same thing happened with the idea of the root, which as we stated has a matrix of much broader meanings for the *Wixaritari*; for the Chicahuac it helps them to put down roots on a spiritual path, without committing to them for life—not an option for the *Wixaritari*. The idea of Mother Earth has wider connotations where both traditions are able to meet: for the New Age sensibility it remits to Gaia the Earth as a living creature we all should respect, learning how to do so from the indigenous groups.

In the first year the Chicahuac all took part in working the land, and harvested an abundant crop of maize. For the second year, Don Pablo demanded more time, more dedication and a greater commitment to this path; he therefore had to travel to Tijuana more frequently to teach them the ritual cycle. First, he would come with an assistant who soon became two and eventually there would be five of them. Each trip by Don Pablo was paid for by the group and so, if he needed more assistants, they paid for them as well. The commitment meant accommodating the group for the time they stayed in Tijuana and looking after them in order to help them sell their crafts.[23] The rituals, of course, involved expenses and preparations, such as making the *tejuino* (a fermented drink made of fresh maize dough with brown sugar), so some of the Chicahuac took to learning how to do it. All of this, added to the cost of the temple and the amount of time spent on the rituals, began to be very onerous; less and less Chicahuacs stayed, until there were only a few to carry on with performing the ritual agricultural cycle.

As mentioned above, for the Chicahuac, a key element of their articulation to the *Wixaritari* was the idea that being in touch with a real Indian would connect them to the elements of nature. Things changed when, as part of the ritual cycle of harvesting the maize, Don Pablo requested the sacrifice of a deer as a sign of the *Wixarika* ceremonial cycle (it might have been for the feast of *Tatei Niwetzika*). The Chicahuac went through the labor of obtaining it, feeding it and keeping it on the ceremonial plot of land, with the idea that this was an element of Mother Earth both for the *Wixaritari* and for the dancers. However,

23 All the same, Paco, the dancer closest to Don Pablo and second in command of the group, managed to negotiate with him: 'it is good that the Huichol gods want to bring five of you, Don Pablo, but the group can only take two'. On that occasion three of the *Wixaritari* had to go back to Taimarita.

for the dancers, who were vegetarians, the mere fact of considering an animal sacrifice proved to be too much. They themselves have given an account of how one of the children present at the ritual, a girl, had dreams for months because of the sacrifice, and others remember vividly how Don Pablo was angry with them because they did not cut the animal's throat cleanly and quickly (as the knife was blunt). After the sacrifice, they had to collect the blood and paint their faces with it, and finally skin the animal as they do in *Wixaritari* rituals. The family that owned the ritual plot, *Samurawi*, decided not to take part in the ceremony, as they were also vegetarians. Weeks later, when they walked near the area, they skirted it so as not to get close to the place of sacrifice. This ritual was etched into the perception of the Chicahuac as a limit to their relationship.[24]

Rituals as an articulating element were important here, as vigils, pilgrimages, agricultural ceremonies and making sacrifices all resonate in the matrix of meaning of Mexicanism. But the sacrifice of a deer, and suffering this exaction as required by the *Wixarika* ceremonial cycle, were important breaking points.

The third element that managed to articulate the network was the articulating leadership. In the alternative world of the New Age in the state of Jalisco (cf. García Medina, 2010), the nodal leaders have the important task of articulating the indigenous traditions to those that they themselves have been linked to or that they are interested in spreading. Mediation by a leader who has, additionally, been initiated by indigenous masters is much better for gaining the prestige necessary for the articulation of these traditions; that is, not all the adepts of New Age Indian practices will be able to live directly with 'literal' Indians, only with the translations that the leaders make of them. The 'explanations' of the indigenous customs and beliefs, and the translation of the indigenous language into that of 'energy', is the work of the leaders. The daily living with indigenous customs is much easier to translate if it is done by someone who is considered a 'master' through having been close to some indigenous group or having lived in close proximity to one of the healers or shamans, and has understood their message. Some of these subjects will follow the path of apprentices to the shaman, depending on the degree to which they are involved in the practice. However, for the majority of those taking part, who come from the intellectualized middle class, the constant ritual practice of the

24 During the final stage of this decisive ceremony, Don Pablo brought down another god and offered it to the group, who rejected it. Only one of the Chicahuac, who wanted to be an apprentice *mara'akame*, did accept it.

indigenous groups and the vicissitudes of their daily life will sometimes be unintelligible.

Don Pablo in particular, but also to a lesser extent the leader who made the original connection to Don Pablo and who was the first in command of the group (*la Primera Palabra*, literally the First Word), may be understood as nodal actors. They had connected different religious movements together, provoking processes of relation between different networks.[25] The term actant, in my view, from the theory of articulation, broadens the definition of nodal actor to include both it and all the other *elements* that are able through their 'excess of meaning' to extend their meanings to different points of the network, allowing them to be appropriated at various points of the network. The actants can be understood on the basis of their process of articulation, immersed in the processes of power: not as subjects in their 'total' identity, but with regard to the identity they possess at the moment of their articulation, which is finite and strategic and is configured within a network of relations.[26] I use the word actant in order to put into the same category entities that are hybrid and contingent, not to describe essences or natures. These nodal actors put into play strategic identities that have obtained successful articulations. They may also mobilize other, non-human actors. An important actant here was Takutsi,[27] who integrates the concept of energy (object) with ritualized ancestor (subject) at one and the same time. Bearing in mind that not all the actors in the analysis of articulation are human, we can see that Takutsi reveals the saturation of meanings that finally splits the two groups.

The network of relations and articulations cannot be understood as perfectly equal: although all the elements can mobilize meanings, they have different weights, for the structural power an actor has in the network is not horizontal, due to issues of class, power and historical relations. In the case

---

25 Cf. Relitrans, 'Réflexion comparative': http://www.ird.fr/relitrans/?Reflexion-comparative&var_recherche=noeuds.

26 Escobar (2008) proposes making a distinction between dominant Network Actor and junior-ranking Network Actor in order to make out in a network the differentiated weights of power. Hierarchical structure distinguishes the first, and forms of self-organization the latter. While this suggestion is very interesting, precisely because it is a political proposal in the sense of showing the different weights of power, in this work I stay with just the model of articulation proposed above, as my intention for now is to pick out the symbolic and emotional bonds that had a lot of weight in this case, though without ignoring questions of class.

27 As other *elements* that go beyond their own meaning might, but in this case, the actant Takutsi is bound to Don Pablo and his legitimacy as a *mara'akame*, so Takutsi's agency is very important.

presented here, the network does not have the appearance of being hierarchical at first glance, but the process of disarticulation allowed inequalities to be seen, especially between members of the Chicahuac and Taizán, as they both occupy differentiated positions in the structure, whether of education, or of class.

The different weights in the network were due to the imposition of meanings on the articulations. These meanings, given for the most part to objects, were not given just by one actor, but by the network of relations itself; that is, while a member of the Chicahuac might wish to treat Don Pablo as an equal and in fact did so, in the end the historical, racial and class meanings would impose themselves and propitiate the disarticulation which was to undo the discourse of the mystical Indian. The relation itself was not completely broken, because what the Chicahuac wished to keep up was the process of getting onto the Huichol way as a spiritual path.

Disarticulation: The Rationalization of Cultural Forms

The actants in this case (nodal actors and actants in general) provided translations between different systems, in which cultural misunderstanding was often handled obliquely, in order to achieve the articulation. The articulation consisted of historical cultural forms, symbols that were common to some extent to both, but did not necessarily have exactly the same meaning. On the other hand, they did have some semantic equivalence and historical, contextual and corporeal discursive predispositions, achieved through a space of shared meaning in which the positive motion of the relation was made patent and the articulation was secured. When the articulation is not needed any more—in this case it really sought not to become necessary—the misunderstanding comes to light; it is rationalized and the break-up ensues. So the disarticulations show that the flows of meaning are not so 'fluid'. One breaking point between traditions comes from the problem of committing to a single practice, which was described as constricting for this kind of mobile religiosity.

While these processes appeared to take place within a system of coherent and agreed practices, we could point to zones of friction or disarticulation, both at a symbolic and at a social level; and even though it might not have been obvious, also from class habits. In the present case, when extreme points were reached in the senses granted to the experiences of shared rituals, or when positions of power became explicit, there were splits that accelerated the process of individuation and the reinterpretation of meanings even more. The rupture in this case came on several fronts. Though the Chicahuac were keen at first to make the ritual commitment of sowing the maize, feeding their tutelary deity and finding the money to bring Don Pablo and his assistants to Tijuana whenever there was a ceremony, there were elements in which the articulations and cultural misunderstandings manifested themselves, as mentioned above with reference to the increased burden of rituals, and even a new tutelary god.

The Chicahuac leaders were often the ones to absorb this burden; at times Taizán's assistants would stay for over a month in the home of one of the leaders, who said that while 'she had a lot of respect for the Huichol as an indigenous group and for their traditions', she could not stand the *macho* way they treated her, and eventually she exploded one Sunday and went and fetched them to do the washing up. Another crucial incident, which further smashed their perception of the indigenous people as mystics, was the imposition by Don Pablo of the Huichol notion of ritual and sacrifice, which the Chicahuac had translated into the Catholic sacrificial complex: when Don Pablo explained the illness of a very dear member of the group, and the possible spread of it among others, as being the consequence of not having done the rituals as Takutsi wanted them, the group rejected this idea totally:

> Don Pablo, I am not a practicing Catholic precisely because Catholics act out of fear and threats...if you don't confess and take communion.... And let me tell you just one thing, in all frankness, we are not Huichols; what we do, we do because it caught our interest, because we like sowing, we like the interior and personal work each of us does with the medicine, and having you as family, but if that means we are going to live in fear, then that's it for me![28]

The ritual tasks that were shared out among less and less members of the group, added to the deer event and the growing understanding that to be an Indian in this way was not for them (as one of the Chicahuac said, there wasn't enough time for them to 'be Huichols'),[29] made the previous articulations unnecessary. So the small group of followers who were left at the end decided to finish their commitment to the rituals, though not their personal relationship with Taizán.

Even when they agreed with Don Pablo to conduct a ceremony of 'uprooting', the Taizán family saw this as a grave offence to them. The ceremony consisted basically of opening the 'vortices'—to use the language of the Chicahuac—and unearth the offerings and burn them. After the unearthing,

28 Interview with Alejandra, member of Chicahuac, April 2010, by Alejandra Aguilar.

29 Interview with Claudia, member of Chicahuac. April 2010, by Alejandra Aguilar.

Don Pablo sang three rounds and finally asked the Chicahuac to present themselves and declare that they thought ill of the process they had shared. Only the Chicahuac closest to Don Pablo dared to speak, and thanked him and his family. Some negotiations between the leaders and Don Pablo followed, to leave the Takutsi as before, without the ritual obligations of having to take Takutsi with them whenever they moved, which objectifies clearly the transhumance that this framework of religiosity requires in practice. Don Pablo did not want to, but finally agreed. Offerings were made to Takutsi—*tejuino*, fruits and *tamales*—and Don Pablo forbade the taking of *híkuri* on this occasion. After a while, he went off to bed, with his assistants, visibly upset. On the other hand, the Chicahuac danced for joy, their shoulders clearly relieved of the ritual burden, and they celebrated the whole night, taking *tejuino*, powdered *híkuri*, and dancing.

Conclusion

The dancers of the Chicahuac group, like other groups who have linked up with the Huichol, elaborated a series of articulations that bound them to the Huichol tradition. Through their participation with the *mara'akame* in his rituals, they managed to join themselves to a tradition of living Indians, who were 'authentic' to them.

It was the set of articulations based on the imaginary of pre-existing symbolic forms (Thompson 1998), that made it possible for the Chicahuac to commit themselves to what they called 'the Huichol tradition'. These social forms have their basis in the imaginaries and a global consumption of the New Age notion of ecological or mystical Indian (Galinier, 2008), but are also found in the mythical social forms of a nationalistic type referring to the historical Indian as structurally subordinate. They are also made from emotions and practices related to charity and imaginaries towards indigenous groups. In the present case, the dancers found 'ethnic' and not 'mystical' Indians, with all their problems, whom it was difficult to live with from the point of view of class and from a differentiated structural position.

By encountering a real Huichol, the self-same articulations allowed the dancers to rescue their own identity ('we are not Huichols'), and also to rationalize the difference between them. With the removal of elements that did not correspond to social forms the group is made of—vegetarianism, equality of gender, individual and collective seeking of knowledge—the articulations became unnecessary and the viability of the alliance was rationalized. It was at this point that the ritual, and the uprooting, unraveled the differences of 'habitus' of class and of points of view. Cultural misunderstanding places itself on the negotiation table, and those taking part cease to hide it, because the articulation is no longer necessary. Just as the original articulation starts in an emotional and cognitive fashion, based on pre-existing social forms whose senses can be negotiated.

Legitimizing discourses, and a mystical literature supporting the articulation, form the basis of the spiritual quest, just as the indigenous ancestral practices provide the necessary spiritual authentication for them to be accepted as true and 'pure', free of all mercantilism and any stain of the market: the category of the mystical Indian allows this approach. Due to the intellectual education of these dancers, there is a rationalization of their own practices, especially when confronted by indigenous customs, which do not fit in with the elaborate configuration of their own ecology and human rights based spirituality.

Taizán in his turn is the representative of a type of *mara'akame* that provides us with an example of the articulation of shamanic practice outside the traditional *Wixarika* region. By being a nodal actor, he can adopt a position both in the imaginary of the spiritual Indian in the performance of the *Wixarika* ceremonial cycle, and in that of the dancers as a new ethnic-spiritual community. This allows him to keep his spiritual leadership while at the same time he can continue mediating with the *Wixaritari* gods. Don Pablo the *mara'akame* could not exist without these actant deities who give him the power to connect others with the gods. Thus, it is important to stress that in the metaphor of the network, inequalities of power and class can be concealed, and it is only by differentiating the weights of each actant in the network that it is possible to understand their part, whether the actant is a god or a human being.

Finally, we cannot forget the social context in which these religious processes and recompositions operate, where the question of identity is fundamental. The location occupied by the dancers in land bordering on the U.S.A. implies an area with its community referents in crisis mode, influenced by the American way of life, which enhances individuation (Gutiérrez and Aguilar, 2008). The idea of 'history' in the tradition of the region itself, is short-spanned, and has few indigenous references, that would anchor historical references to a traditional past. The Tijuana frontier provides a key to understanding the 'mobile' religiosity that the Chicahuac dancers perform. It is also an area of conflict, of symbolic and actual danger to society, because of the war by the Mexican State against drug trafficking, which on the one hand forces society to fall back, but also forces novel forms of socializing and of communal relations.

Thus, the idea of articulation brings us to consider this type of shamanism: it propitiates the formation of a network of connections through rhizomes towards the mediatic Indian, blurring his economic reality and exalting his spiritual virtues, rather than to an Indian fixed to historical structures of exploitation. This does not mean, however, that in the particular case of Don Pablo, shamanic practice must be a false articulation. We can see from this case, that as identities associate by means of different elements, they articulate in accordance with the history of their relations. We can also understand *how* these associations, that show us the circulation of meanings, were made, and this case shows us how the assembly of shared meanings in movement, contributes to the expansion of the network and at the same time, at some point, to a disconnection from it.

PART 3

Popular Medicines, Healing and New Age Therapy Circuits

∴

Introduction

> Popular religion at any time is not simply the subversion or the free use of official notions but their decline in terms of another mother tongue whose relevance to interpretation should be kept in mind. We relate socially and politically, we get ill and get better and we join ourselves to totalizing and superhuman instances according to the concept of person written into that mother tongue.
>
> PABLO SEMÁN (2001: 54)

The third part of this book brings together a group of ethnographic papers that provide an analysis of the interactions between the holistic and universalist matrix of meaning of the New Age, and another aspect of the religious landscape in Latin America (which is as rich as that of the Shamanisms with their ethnic roots): the aspect of popular Catholicism, also known as popular religiosity, so widespread in the subcontinent and strongly linked to the formation of its national and religious identity. The process by which it was installed, through the Iberian conquest, created syncretisms of varying degrees with preexisting (indigenous) beliefs and practices, and later it cross-bred with the traditions that came over with people from Africa who had been forced to migrate to the Americas by transatlantic traders, creating a great variety of cults, devotions and popular practices for curing and for resolving a large number of the problems of daily life.

To this 'religious subsoil' in Latin America there was added, at the end of the nineteenth century, Kardecist spiritism, the elements of which are still active today, and have led to the development of various other syncretisms. In the twentieth century this complex religious panorama was further augmented with the New Age movement as it adapted to the diversity of religious contexts that is characteristic of Latin America, and especially of its most important urban centres. The New Age movement brought not only hope for a new golden age for humanity, but also the possibility of access to new therapeutic discourses of healing and personal transformation, among which the outstanding are the psychologies that are open to spiritual experience (Transpersonal, Gestalt) and those of various Orientalisms through notions such as those of reincarnation, karma, and chakras understood as energy centers of the body and of the planet. It was possible in the early stages to trace its diffusion through specific spaces and sectors of the urban population, among those of middle income with an education and cosmopolitan aspirations.

 | DOI 10.1163/9789004316485_010

However, it soon spread into more popular environments, and with new notions, objects and practices it fertilized popular specialists of the old school, like medicine men and women, herbalists, Santeros, witchdoctors and spiritual healers, contributing to the reproduction as well as the renewal of popular medicine, which is a central part of Catholic religiosity in Latin America (Seman, 2001).

Health clinics, markets, folk remedy shops, bookshops and esoteric centers have ceased to be simply the providers of objects, practices and symbols to meet the specific demand of a particular community of believers. Today they form in places of mobility and juxtaposition, spaces where a potential hybridation is created with fragments of various religious traditions, that are now available to subjects on a quest for the spiritual or for alternative life styles, or else in need of remedies for problems of health, money, love or other anxieties (De la Torre, 2006: 39). Images of angels and traditional Catholic saints cohabit today in these spaces of hybridation with Buddhas, *Orisha*, interstellar landscapes, dreamcatchers, runes, ointments, herbs and pyramids, thanks to translocal and even transnational networks of production and circulation. Not only do religious specialists of the old and the new guard drop in to get their supplies, these places serve for the creation and learning of conventions of ritual usage in cleansings, divinations, healings and all kinds of magical treatments.

We can say that the production and circulation of specialists, services and religious objects/merchandise have acquired transnational and even global dimensions, transforming the ways in which local societies cure themselves and keep well. All of this was energized in a contemporary context marked by intense physical and virtual mobility (migration, tourism and access to the internet) which has caused a great variety of processes of transnationalization and even a 'reversion' of the colonial flows, generating new meanings on the geopolitical religious map of the world today.

The aim of this section is not just to observe and analyze the impact of the New Age framework of meaning on this aspect of Catholic popular religiosity in Latin America, but also to focus on the dense Latin American cultural subsoil, as a framework of meaning itself: it consists of a broad spectrum of syncretic beliefs and practices with their own specialists, spaces and circuits that has revealed itself as a 'cosmological, monist and relational' universe (Semán, 2001) having its own boundaries, and a great capacity for resistance over the centuries of Latin American history. This resistance finds itself linked to its 'phagocytic' capacity of devouring new elements, but is also undergoing today a new transformation in the light of globalizing cultural flows.

The studies in this part of the book take as their starting point and object of research not the globalizing impetus of the New Age framework of meaning, but concrete practices, of religiosity and popular medicine, or of a popular Catholic space, that have come into contact with New Age circuits, in order to be able to produce an ethnography of their interactions. In this way the focus turns to Guatemalan devotions to San Simón in a folk remedy shop in Los Angeles, the Aztec Conchero dance displaced to Spain as a therapeutic practice, the hybrid trajectories of Mexican diviners and healers who have incorporated Santeria in their clinics, the community of the Valley of the Dawn in Brasilia where spiritual treatments are given with elements of New Age, Kardecism and Umbanda, and the practices of transformation/liberation of a charismatic Catholic group in Porto Alegre.

To what extent are popular religious traditions incorporated into New Age therapeutic language? And where, in turn, does this find its limits? Under what circumstances are the religious traditions activated? Can we speak here of two matrices of syncretic religiosity living together and generating flows in both directions? What is the margin for action and what the strategy of the various actors and even of the Catholic church in these hybridizing processes? What cultural and collective senses organize these hybrids in the particular national and transnational contexts where they occur? Articles in this part of the book offer elements for answering the questions in this far ranging reflection and thus take account of the selective and varied character of the different levels, appropriations and influences of New Age sensibility, in the light of a diversity of complex sociocultural contexts.

For the case of Brazil, Steil analyses a group of charismatic Catholics in Porto Alegre, making it possible to show how the dynamics articulating contiguous religious regimes to each other, occur; in this case the articulation of charismatic Catholicism to New Age and Kardecist spiritism. It is however an interaction that is fundamentally built on a Catholic tradition which functions as the main pole of meaning. A meaning that is anchored in the institution but at the same time passes over it. The interaction between these regimes unveils personal and community experiences in the contemporary world of religion that go beyond conversion and religious transition, and incorporates in a primordial manner the therapeutic dimension as one of the elements that allow cognitive bridges to be built between 'foreign traditions'. Today, having access to therapeutic resources and making use of them, or appropriating symbolic elements from different 'traditions', does not necessarily imply a commitment of faith to an affiliation or to a community, but it does make plain the tension that there is between tradition and innovation, between agency and structure. Fields for negotiation are thus raised up as intense, and new forms of religious 'institutionalization' are energized with new ways of belonging. Adopting the point of view of Bhabha, the author of this chapter points out how, in these 'in-between' places, there is the possibility of gaining access to alternative types of therapy and belief regimes which, without breaking off from the Catholic institution, have introduced hetereodox elements into their rituals.

The national and local particularities of beliefs and practices concerning spirits, and communication with them, are also left unveiled in this article which shows, along with those of Juárez Huet and Gutiérrez Zúñiga for the case of Mexico, the construction of bridges of meaning stemming from these doctrines, not only in the field of popular religiosity and in that of the most 'traditional' institutions, but above all in the area of therapy.

The piece by Gutiérrez Zúñiga shows clearly the complexity inherent in the therapeutic dimension, from a comparative analysis of two cases on the basis of which she describes how the Aztec Conchero dance is incorporated into the New Age movement as a therapeutic resource that allows it to be reanchored in the most dissimilar of contexts, thanks to the holistic garb it has been dressed in both on the level of the individual and of the planet. However, transnationalization of the Aztec dance and its resignification as a New Age therapeutic practice does not neutralize the historical contexts of its origin (in Mexico) or of its arrival (in Spain), but produces new imaginaries of cultural contact, traversed by a memory of colonial conquest.

Further, her article highlights the role played by what the author terms 'shelves of exoteric merchandise' (2008), which incorporate into their wares not only the Dance but also many other practices and symbols from a variety of traditions, in an enormous market of spiritual and therapeutic goods and services, and of Neo-esoteric and neo-magical circuits. All of which occurs in a contemporary context in which the idea of revaluing and revitalizing 'traditional wisdoms' and 'native cultures' has been gaining greater legitimacy, as many of them have been declared the heritage of humanity (whether national, cultural or non-material). The context which has been obvious in Latin America, especially since the nineteen nineties, has been a condition for making a 'legitimate' recognition of other religions or 'native cultural expressions' a possibility, even if the latter are not always indigenous, and these also have been transnationalized, for example in the case of the 'religion of the *Orisha*' (Yoruba, Santeria, Candomblé, etc.) as explained in the article by Juárez Huet.

Most of the writers assembled in this section, in particular Gutiérrez Zúñiga, Pedrón and Juárez Huet, take into account the importance of the circulation—with more and more transnational dimensions—of practices, symbols and teachings, in so far as it contributes to transfigurations and re-semanticizings of them. These are then adopted by consumers and spiritual seekers. The 'traveled' saints or pilgrims, for example, who may in certain places have been regarded as a cultural heritage or a symbol of national, regional or local identification, are transfigured, or re-semanticized, in the course of their journey into new contexts, and might end up differing completely from the meaning or the representation they 'originally' possessed. To give an example, the Mayan aspect of San Simón is eclipsed in his relocation within the context of migration from Guatemala to Los Angeles—a United States city in which the regional referent of San Simón, in this case as Central American or indeed as 'Latin', acquires a greater value with regard not only to his representation but also in the forms of his worship: which is clearly shown in the ethnographic study produced by Sylvie Pedrón—. Or there is the case of Changó, taken up by Juárez Huet—the *Orisha* of Santeria that has in the course of his transnational circulation been transformed into a 'holy talisman' bearing an iconographic representation of Oriental extraction, and has come to form part of a repertoire of personal protectors who have dis-located him from his original ritual and religious matrix. However, the case of devotion to San Simón among Central American immigrants to Los Angeles explained by Pedrón Colombani, and that of the practitioners of divination and healing with links to Santería described by Juárez Huet, show, to begin with, the existence of limits to the process of hybridation between these practices and the New Age. Not only does the New Age have limits to its omniverous capacity, as Alejandro Frigerio suggests at the start of this book, but, adopting the analytical point of view of this section, which addresses popular practices and propular medicine, we can appreciate a corresponding selective incorporation, by practitioners of popular religion, of some of the ideas introduced by the New Age—for example, that of the chakra, or that of a spiritual guide—without having to change their traditional praxis or traditional social role. We therefore have new notions, new practices and new objects that were originally spread by the New Age, appearing in the spaces and specific circuits of popular medicine, where the cure is mediated by the knowledge the practitioners have of remedies, power plants and magic rituals; and this produces a resignification of New Age via popular cosmology.

The case of *El Vale do Amanhecer* in Brasilia provides a particularly good illustration of this point: it starts as a model residential community under the charisma of a medium, Tía Neiva. Its discourses and its landscape combine particular fragments of different cultures and traditions such as those of the Mayan and Incan empires, considered by esotericists as reserves of ancestral wisdom, with extra-terrestrial narratives, and the mixture is offered to a popular sector of urban inhabitants in Brazil as an alternative way to that of the ideology of Western modernity. Although it is open to hybridation and its discourse contains a series of references to reincarnation or cosmic spiritual energies that are easily identified with the New Age matrix, we can see in the community's therapeutic practices, with the laying on of hands, charges of energy and spiritual surgeries, the predominance of a popular subsoil based on magic and miracles. The subsoil is expressed in a popular Brazilian version of spiritism, with its roots in Kardecism but syncretized with Afro-Brazilian religions. The link between them is the practice of possession by spirits that both these traditions share.

We will see how in the processes of new uses or the re-semanticizing of some of its symbols or elements, boundaries are established that help us to understand better the limits of both the (apparently) 'omnivorous' phenomena of the New Age, and the popular religiosity of Latin America.

CHAPTER 7

Catholicism and the New Age: A Cure through Liberation and Finding Oneself, in a Charismatic Catholic Ritual

Carlos Alberto Steil

The concept of religion in modern society is facing a crisis. The generally agreed definition among Christian and civil institutions has been considerably shaken by the practices and experiences of spiritualities denominated, for want of a better term, as New Age.[1] The hegemonic conception of religion as a system of belief articulated and maintained by autonomous communities in the setting of a plural society does not seem to cover the practices and models that the New Age has impressed on its social expression. The separation between the natural and the supernatural orders that we as moderns thought had been definitely established, after a long movement of secularisation, seems to be failing, with energies and avatars from traditions that have impregnated the lives and visions of the world of countless people. The transcendent theodicy that places God outside the world, is countered today by an immanence that insists on placing God not only in the public realm but, particularly, in the intimacy of contemporary subjects.

Beside the religions of transcendence, founded on the revelation of a God that is placed outside the world, we now see rising a movement that runs across religious institutions and traditions and places God inside each person, making Him accessible through experience.[2] This movement towards immanence is not restricted, in fact, to the field of alternative spiritualities, as it crosses over traditional religions, leaving many of the principles that support their dogmas and doctrines, re-defined in its wake. It is possible to speak of a

1 The rise of the New Age in the nineteen sixties produced a transformation of the religious field in the West which put the concept of religion itself into check. Parts of this transformation include the possibility of going in and coming out of different religious traditions having a variety of origins and geographical backgrounds, rejecting the term 'religion' and replacing it with 'spirituality', and assuming a lifestyle that is unlike that of the religious groups who are identified by their belonging to a specific religious institution.

2 Here we take New Age to be not so much a religious institution as a grammar that generates meanings, which can both be expressed in specific religious groups or institutions, and also impregnate traditional religious forms, producing transformations in their belief systems, ceremonies and practices.

 | DOI 10.1163/9789004316485_011

'spirit of the time' disseminated in a multiplicty of practices and experiences that arise on the edges of the great religions.

The data we supply from the context of our ethnographic research were obtained in the area of charismatic Catholicism, from a particular group in Porto Alegre, Brazil: the Grupo São José. Our aim here is to show the transformations that have been occurring in Catholicism as it gets closer to the New Age, an approach that takes place on its edges, creating zones of escape from orthodoxy with regard to its established meanings and beliefs. The conterminous position of these escape zones turns out to be an ampitheatre for negotiations between distinct regimes of belief.[3] It is from this place, on the periphery of Catholicism, that we shall be able to refer to religious syncretism.

The analysis that we make here aims to catch the heterogeneity of the religious within Catholicism, which as a great tradition has been able to incorporate differences into its constitution and its dynamics. Our concern, therefore, is to observe how the diversity of the religious field today is reflected in Catholicism, allowing other languages and forms of spirituality to emerge in its own bosom.[4] In this sense we can think of these languages and spiritualities as counter-narratives that make a rent in the Catholic identity which the hierarchy seeks to define as a homogeneous and substantial unity. While on the other hand, the syncretism that appears in the ethnography of the group we study keeps up a disjointed relation between the elements activated in each of the regimes, making a play in which the Catholic hierarchy seeks to mark the bounds of Catholic identity and the directors of the group seek to place themselves within such demarcations so they can interpret their practices as being within the parameters of the traditional code.

Before we move on to the ethnography of the Grupo São José, we would like to show some of the signposts guiding our intepretations. The first has to do with a paradox that could be formulated as a 'departure' from Catholic orthodoxy through the assertion of Catholic identity. In the utterances and attitudes of those we interviewed we were able to observe a repeated defence of their belonging to the Catholic church, while at the same time they had joined a system of beliefs and practices that are opposed in principle to the church's orthodoxy. Because they are Catholics, they can drink from many fountains.

3 Pierre Sanchis says that this zone of negotiation is a characteristic of Catholicism or a '*habitus* (history made into structure) of porous identities and ambivalent values in a tendency, always frustrated, but permanently taken up again, towards a conjugation of the multiple in a unity that is never reached' (Sanchis, 2001: 45).

4 In the empirical case to be analyzed here the following languages can be identified: Pentecostal/Charismatic, Spiritist, Afro-Brazilian and New Age.

In other words, there is an attempt to assume a new religious *habitus* without having to stop being a Catholic, even though this will leave you on the edge of the institution.[5]

The other marker is associated with a point of view of performance that sees the presence of these peripheral groups within Catholicism not as dissidences, but as events claiming a place in the very heart of the dominant narrative of Catholicism. In this way a creative articulation is formed between orthodoxy and heterodoxy, in a play that internalizes the borders between different religious languages. This remits us to an environment of religious plurality, which in some way makes it possible for incommensurable differences to become compatible.

The affirmation of Catholic identity referred to becomes indispensable for rubbing out the internal differences that stay latent in the dominant narrative of Catholicism. On the other hand, the 'difference that will not keep quiet' reveals the ambivalence that there is inside Catholicism itself, crossed by the disjunctive othernesses of the different belief regimes that go to make up the contemporary religious field. In this sense, what we will find in the field is a syncretism that takes us back, less to religious transition and more to a repeated attempt to get the beliefs and rituals of other institutions to be inscribed and included in the Catholic narrative. The experience we shall analyze is therefore situated in a frame of references, that while seeming to appear within Catholicism, possesses a degree of autonomy with respect to Catholic orthodoxy. It concerns an in-between place that emerges as the *locus* for negotiations between different belief regimes, bringing practices and rituals from other religious traditions closer to the Catholic narrative and inscribing them in it.

The Grupo São José in the Context of the Charismatic Catholic Revival in Porto Alegre

The earliest researches into *Renovación Carismática Católica* (RCC) highlighted its ideological profile and took it as a homogeneous whole, marked by a conservative bias among the forces disputing for political and institutional space in the bosom of Catholicism. In this sense, there are frequent comparisons between the RCC and the Ecclesiastical Base Communities, which would

5 The term *habitus* employed here refers to the conception held by Bourdieu, who defines it as a universalizing mediation that is invested with a double function: as a principle generating practices—in its relation with objective structures—and as a unifying principle, in its relation with a complete repertoire of social practices (Bourdieu, 1977: 83).

represent the opposite pole to conservatism (Oliveira, 1985; Prandi and Souza, 1996). Other studies, such as that by Oro (1996), note the competition in the religious field, and point out the strategic use being made of this movement by the Catholic Church in order to 'retain its followers and impede the advance of the Pentecostals' (Oro, 1996: 108). More recently, we can reccord some studies in line with the pioneering research of Thomas Csordas in the U.S.A. (Csordas, 1996), that have sought to relate RCC with processes of constructing subjectivity, and the role of the body in religious experience (Maués 2002). Along with this reflection we wish to show, on the basis of the scheme proposed by Troeltsch, how the RCC approximates to the 'mystical model': one of the models through which Christianity has limited itself historically (Steil, 1999; 2001; 2006).

The Catholic charismatic movement in Porto Alegre appears to be divided into three main currents. First there is the central nucleus, which has the official recognition of the archdiocese and of the National Council of the RCC in Brasilia. It is organized in sections such as the State Council, the Diocesan Office and an extensive range of prayer groups, life and alliance communities, secretariats, a radio station and projects (Oro, 1996: 108–117).

The second nucleus, named after Saint Martin (São Martinho), is organized around the parish of the same name and has the support and the structure of the parish priest. This group is closely connected to the official movement, but enjoys a certain degree of autonomy, keeping its own projects and its particular orientation. This nucleus also has a radio station, and a network of prayer groups and independent missionary communities.

The Grupo São José, the object of study in this chapter, appears as the third nucleus with a visible presence in local Catholicism. However, its identification with the RCC is more in the type of worship and in the forms it adopts than in an organic link to the movement. As the priest in attendance for the Group says: 'In spite of the fact that the Grupo São José is not joined to the official Charismatic Revival, it does not stray outside it in terms of subject matter. Maybe the methodology is different [...] It is a group that has its own way, that is not the way of the Revival, even though it shares some points of convergence with it'.

It is the use of ceremonies from the Charismatic Catholic Revival, like speaking in tongues, the laying on of hands, prophecy and exorcism that brings these religious practices closer together in the breast of Catholicism. One can also perceive a common *ethos*, shared by those who are accustomed to using these places of worship. Such affinities have not, however, guaranteed recognition, by the directors of the RCC, of the Grupo São José as part of their organization and structure. For M.A., as we can see from her autobiographical account, the

Grupo São José arose from a demand that was not being attended to by the RCC: 'I started in the charismatic movement; when I began to hear voices, I sought out the movement and went to many of their meetings, but their style, right from the start, seemed different, to me, it was not in tune with me, so I left'.

At any rate, those running the Grupo São José recognize as many things in common as differences between their practices and those that are used by the RCC as a whole. As M.A. tells us: 'we sing the same hymns and the prayers are very like each other, the laying on of hands is the same'. The fundamental difference would be in the 'ancestral lineage', which, according to our interviewee, consists of establishing a line of influence over the present life of each human being, from the ancestors.[6] In another portion of her testimony, M.A. evokes the recognition given to Father Jonás, and his authority as one of the central figures of the RCC in Brazil, in order to express the inspiration and charismatic identity of his movement.[7]

> The first time I saw Father Jonás, who is an extraordinarily charismatic person, […] I told myself: 'here is someone who understands me'. I went to his place for breakfast and got the notebook [with a record of her inspired words] and took it with me. I arrived before the meal and said: 'Father Jonás, read this and tell me what you think' […] He read it and told me: 'my daughter, go ahead, this is pure Holy Spirit. Carry on and don't mind anything anyone says to you'.

Having been institutionally marginalized by the archdiocesan office of the Catholic Charismatic Revival and by the Catholic hierarchy, M.A. tries to find a legitimization of her group in the recognition given to her by a charismatic authority. While the ecclesiastical hierarchy recognizes a link between the Grupo São José and the Charismatic Catholic Revival, it sees it more as a convergence of themes and style than in terms of methods employed or of doctrinal basis.

6 I have covered the subject of the 'generational demons' more extensively and more systematically in a piece called *Los demonios generacionales. Herencia de los antepasados en la determinación de las elecciones y de las trayectorias personales* (meaning approximately: 'Generational demons and the part played by ancestral inheritance in making choices and in determining the course of one's life'), published by Luiz Fernando Días Duarte in the book *Família e Religião* (2006).

7 The figure of Father Jonás, and the Canção Nova movement, were introduced in an article by Braga (2004).

Belief or Belonging

The Grupo São José was created in the late nineteen seventies by M.A., an upper middle class woman from Porto Alegre. The group has approximately five thousand people who take part in the services and over two hundred directors who are cast as 'sensitives', intercessors and liberators.[8] Their headquarters is in their leader's own house, a comfortable buiding in an upper middle class district of the city. The services are attended by middle class people, nearly all of them women. Even though it is not necessary to say one is a Catholic to take part, the directors, the 'sensitives' and the singers, as well as their principal leader, M.A., make a special effort to declare that they are Catholics. As M.A. says in the interview she granted us, 'I have always been Catholic, Apostolic and Roman, ever since I was in my mother's womb. I had a very solid upbringing, which is rare among Catholics. I have always been active in the Church and never went to other religions, so you cannot say that what happened to me is because of making contact with other religions…' There are two references in this comment which deserve to be highlighted. The first is related to what originally made her a Catholic, which she traces back to the womb and not to the sacrament of baptism.

As we shall see below, considering the phase of human existence passed in the womb as a moment of choice when each person's destiny is determined, is one of the central postulates for sustaining the theory, of a psychological nature, that members of the group share. The existence of an autonomous life in the womb which can at a later stage be intervened in through techniques of regression and spiritual liberation, is presented as an agonizing moment when the decisive combat between the forces of good and evil, between God and the Devil, takes place. The presence of psychic forces and spiritual entities, that can be controlled, and submitted to therapeutic and ritual procedures, is projected onto this intra-uterine space. This is the perfect field for the directors of the group to act in, where Catholic priests feel they do not have the competence. As Father R.P. said,

> on the postulate of a past life, of life in the womb, which has to do with the creation of the soul and the possibility of a regression, I do not have anything to say. The Church also has no doctrine on the subject; it is a subject for Psychology.

8 Those who are called 'sensitives' are people who have the gift of being able to perceive and to reveal what the participants in the service are feeling. They have a role in the ceremony just as the intercessor or the singer does.

The second point she refers to has to do with M.A.'s concern to make her loyalty to Catholicism clear and to distance herself from any belief in entities associated with magic or mediumistic religions. When she mentions the course of her life, she says 'I never went to other religions'. She makes this statement in response to frequent criticisms, and insinuations that her group has incorporated a kind of syncretism between Catholicism, New Age, and Spiritism. Hence her insistence on showing she has always been a Catholic and is completely faithful to the Church, which works as a safe conduct granting her group its ecclesiastical character, something that is reinforced by her constant criticism of changing from one religion to another.

On the other side, the Catholic clergy is ambivalent about the orthodoxy of the group. There is a hope in the discourse of some of the priests whom we interviewed that the Grupo São José may effectively help to keep the faithful in the bosom of the Church, to the extent that it can offer those who go to it what they would otherwise be searching for in New Age spiritualities and in Spritism if they did not have access in their own parish, to rituals of healing and of communicating with the ancestors, through the Grupo São José. As explained by the parish priest of the Iglesia de Auxiliadora (the Church of Mary Help of Christians), where a large number of the faithful who are linked to the group meet every week:

> We do not have specialized people in our parishes, a specialized group equipped to deal with these special cases. So if there is a group that can do something to help these people with all their problems…then it should. What Doña M.A.'s group does, does not come under the rubric of the *Apostolado de la Oración* (The Apostleship of Prayer), *la Congregación Mariana* (the Marian Congregation: Congregation of Marian Fathers of the Immaculate Conception of the Blessed Virgin Mary, or: Marians of the Immaculate Conception), the Vincentians (a lay ecclesial movement) and other traditional or more modern groups. What the Grupo São José is offering in the modern context of competition between religions, becomes fundamental to making sure it is possible to keep them in the Catholic system.

To sum up, according to the view of the priests who make room for these cults in their parishes, the group is responding to a spiritual demand that is present in society, which neither the parrochial nor the apostolic movements are capable of meeting. So, for the hierarchy, the group assumes a supplementary role in the work of the church. As a result, there is an attempt to cover the otherness of the Grupo São José by way of internalizing the borders between Catholic orthodoxy and therapeutical practices. This attitude provides recognition by the institution of the ritual practices of the Grupo São José and gives legitimacy to the beliefs shared by its affiliates, as is reaffirmed in another part of the same interview, where the priest explains that those taking part in the Grupo São José 'have the facility of language and are conducting ceremonies for people who are into the New Age or Spiritism' offering them 'what the Catholic Church does not have to give them'. And he concludes, 'If the Church does not provide this and the Group does, until the Church can provide something better we cannot prohibit it. It is wise to let it act'.

The *Amorizacao* Service

The Grupo São José offers a number of services which vary according to the proposed objective, the public they are directed to, and the places they are held.[9] There are services whose aim it is to attend to the day to day demands of people seeking relief from their pains and an answer to the anxieties of the soul. These are regular weekly services, frequented by an assiduous nucleus of directors, singers, 'sensitives' and initiates, and by a fluctuating public of the faithful and sympathizers, who are the object of the cares of the former. The first modality, open to all those who want, is called the *cult of loving*. The ceremony begins with a welcome for those attending, who are asked to sit on rows of chairs usually arranged in concentric circles. This part is performed to the beat of a guitar played by a musician who sings songs from the Catholic charismatic movement, and songs that we might call *world music*, whose aim is to create an atmosphere of silence for meditation. In between the songs there are short readings from the Bible and interventions by the directors who give teachings and offer reflections.

Next, participants are invited to say out loud the petitions and demands they have brought to the ceremony, and to thank God for graces received or the general well-being of their daily lives. After this expression, the directors lay their hands on each of those attending, praying 'in tongues' or babbling. This rite is considered the high point of the service; it may effect the healing of small ills of the soul or the body, for those attending or their relatives. The latter, while not physically present, are brought to the service by means of the memory of the person who is praying for them. Another effect can be the revelation of a more serious physical or mental problem that the participant or

9 With regard to the places of worship, the services may be held in the buildings of a Catholic parish, in chapels, in Catholic colleges, in private homes or in the home of M.A.

someone in his circle of family and friends is suffering from without yet knowing about it.[10]

In the case of a psychic diagnosis, the participant is advised to look for other alternative therapeutic resources, especially in line with the method of 'direct access to the unconscious' proposed by Renate Jost Moraes, a psychologist and friend of M.A. According to this method, therapy should take place on two levels: on that of the 'psychic unconscious' and on that of the 'spiritual unconscious'.[11] The first has to do with becoming aware of the negative conditionings that have been inherited from our ancestors since our time in the womb, and taking action to deal with them. The second has to do with the combat in the spirit between good and evil, between God and the Devil, for possession of the subject. There is thus established a separation of functions between the therapist who is going to work on the inheritance of the ancestors, and the mystic

10 Csordas establishes a relation, which helps us to understand the ritual we are interpreting here, between glossolalia and prophecy, the two forms that occur in the RCC. He asserts that in this sense 'prophecy contains a semantic component of a more sacred type, as prophetic utterance is understood as a message straight from God. The speaker is not entirely passive, as he must discern when, where and whether to proffer the inspired words, but the address is invariably in the first person, with God supposedly the one that is speaking. Charismatic prophecy rarely tells the future, instead of which it establishes, in ceremonial fashion, a state of affairs in the world, saying, for example that "you are my people, I am doing great work with you, devote your lives to me"' (Csordas, 2008: 133).

11 According to the therapeutic method proposed by Renate J. de Moraes in her book *O inconsciente sem fronteiras*, the 'complete cure consists of the closest approximation of man to his originally healthy and perfect structure' (1995: 40). The process of healing in this therapy works on two levels. The first consists of becoming aware, in the realm of the Personal Self, and then through this awareness modifying negative conditionings accumulated in the same area of life, that are the results of bad choices generally made in the mother's womb and in early infancy. The second level is reached through an experience of living faith, through which it becomes possible to identify a divine reality, always present in the human being but not confused with it. 'The Personal Self that identifies the light', says Moraes, 'indicates another dimension to us that we call the spiritual unconscious' (Moraes, 1995: 40). It follows that while the negative charge that we inherit from our ancestors, mentioned by M.A., passes through the mediation of inherited devils (*demonios generacionales*), with Moraes' approach of 'direct access to the unconscious' (DAU), our inheritance is described as '*mnemic* traces of the ancestors in our unconscious in the most incredible detail. So it is not difficult for a patient to feel he is *living* as if he were that ancestor, especially when the *conscious* mind has been obliterated' (Moraes, 1995: 42, italics in the author's original text). There is therefore a process here of incorporating a therapeutical narrative that is produced on the periphery of the dominant debate in the area, into a religious narrative that is just as much on the periphery of the Catholic tradition.

who will have to face the demons, first defeating them in the area of his personal experience and then exorcizing them from the bodies of those searching for the liberation that the demons are fighting against.

Liberation as a Personal Experience

Before presenting an ethnography of the liberation service as such, we shall comment on the personal experience of liberation lived by those who attend the service, in the liberation rituals: an experience which is a required condition for those who perform the services to be allowed to do so. The data interpreted here derive from the interviews we conducted with M.A., in the course of which she tells the story of her life as a mystic and as a liberator. Hers is an exemplary case, covering both the ritual-therapeutic process and the mystical-spiritual. In the first case the 'generational demons' are identified and expelled, demons that show up in the lives of all human beings as bad inheritances from their ancestors. This inheritance is supposed to have a strong genetic component that is passed on from the ancestors to future generations through bad genes that can be identitifed in people's DNA. In the second, mystical-spiritual, process there is an attempt to confront the Devil in person as an entity opposed to God. The body of the mystic thus becomes the field of battle for a dispute between these entities over his soul. This dispute is presented as a component part of his vocation established by his role as an exorcist.[12]

As will be clear from the parts of M.A.'s account we have chosen to look at, these two dimensions, the ritual-therapeutical and the mystical-spiritual, are interwoven and remit to a single process in which psychic intervention goes together with the spiritual. In effect, it is not that a spiritual process follows a therapeutic process, but that the two are simultaneous and feed into each other. The mystical experience that makes M.A. an exorcist also gives her therapeutic capacity. However, a hierarchical relation is observed to exist between the two, in the sense that the first includes the second (Dumont, 1992). So the

12 This indissoluble relation between the mystical and the therapeutical, in turn, permits us to speak of a psychic-mystical religious regime that is established in contemporary culture as a controlled environment or a corporeality that ends up redefining the very concept of religion itself (Champion, 1989; Lambert, 1991). It is just such a change in the regime of the religious that we observe in the Grupo São José, but it can also be identified with other practices that are going on in the heart of the Catholic church, that allow therapeutic and mystical practices to be incorporated into the Catholic system by widening the boundaries of its orthodoxy.

mystics are allowed to intervene as therapists, identifying the type of genetic inheritance from the ancestors that is making life difficult for people who have chosen to submit to the liberation ritual, but those who are only therapists do not have the necessary legitimacy to conduct the liberation ritual as part of the service.

The account by M.A. of a divine calling that legitimizes her as an exorcist already has this mixture of elements that remit to an association of the mystical experience with the psychic. The 'voices she hears' may equally well be interpreted as a symptom of schizophrenia, or as the 'divine voice' that calls her on a mission. It is important to note that when she gives her account of this divine calling, M.A. defines herself as one of a long line of prophets, saints and mystics who received their missions directly from God without going through the institution as an intermediary.[13] And here is the best way to see how the style of her narrative corresponds with the way in which receiving a calling is described in the Bible, for example in the cases of Abraham, Saul of Tarsus, Mary and Jesus. In M.A.'s own words:

> It has been 25 years since I began to hear voices that said... 'I have need of thee', 'I need thy hands because my children are suffering'. [...] I was worried, but kept hearing and seeing these *flashes* and I was afraid because no one else saw them. So that's when I thought I was schizophrenic... Then I went for help to a psychologist friend, Renate Jost de Moraes, who has a practice in Belo Horizonte. She gave me a therapy and I think the therapy is another stage on the evolutionary scale. Then I ended up doing TIP, dealing directly with the unconscious. A series of relaxation techniques that go straight to the unconscious, without hypnosis. You can call it a kind of regression. The therapy is to deal with everything wrong that has happened.

In this account there is a relation between psychic symptoms and mystical experience that is actually much more complicated than a simple choice between religion and therapy (Rocchi, 2003: 179). The search for a therapeutic solution to the disturbance she suffers from is associated with a perception that her illness transcends the realm of therapies, even if the therapeutic treatment is taken up. Thus a continuity may be seen between therapy and mysticism that makes these two dimensions of experience ambivalent, where therapeutic treatment is associated with regression. The next part of the interview that we have transcribed

13 The tension between charisma and institution is a component of the experience of Catholicism and can be observed in many of its historical expressions.

expresses this relation between the psychic and the spiritual in the clearest possible way:

I did the therapy to see my psychosomatic condition. After the therapy, Renate told me my problem was not mental, or physical, but in the light of what I had experienced, could only be spiritual. Then she told me to do what the voice asked me to. I even went to see a priest, but received no understanding. He questioned me and said who did I think I was to be hearing the voice of God.

These two parts of the interview with M.A. show a boundary area that is established in the Grupo São José cult, where a heterodox Catholic doctrine is linked to a psychological theory that is also heterodox. Specifically, the belief in the generational demons and the possibility of exorcism through the regression to past lives, is associated with psychic symptoms that remit to a disturbance in which the Self is disassociated and can be treated by means of therapeutic techniques. These heterodoxies, in turn, begin to make sense and legitimize themselves as part of a wider context in which there is a dissemination and a hegemony of the *religions of the self*, which share a common lineage with the *psychologies of the self*. In the case we have been looking at, we realize that M.A. submits to the therapeutic process in order to come to the conclusion that the origin of her disturbance is of a spiritual order. In brief, what we see here is a kind of articulation between mystical experience and therapeutic practice that indicates, as Leila Amaral says, an implicit desire for 'radical transformation', which becomes synonymous with the terms 'cure' and 'salvation' (Amaral, 2003). The account transcribed below presents us with this experience of transformation lived by M.A. in a most convincing manner:

> I had knowledge of the devil as a real being. There are obviously the devils you create yourself, but there is also Lucifer and the struggle for the soul. I experienced the force of the King of cunning and that is why I believe. Because of what I went through I can believe in people and can talk with this confidence; if I didn't have experience of the arts of the other, I would not believe it. There I experienced the Devil [...] But I have knowledge through experience; the Lord said: 'I try you to try what cannot be tried. Thereby to make the foundations strong, with solid bases'. I have the knowledge of experience, hence my confidence and the authority with which I act.

The art of curing and of liberating has been forged in the experience of the fight of good with evil, of God and the Devil, which is lived in a person's interior. An experience marked by atrocious suffering experienced as a critical moment of affliction that leads, at the same time, to an encounter with yourself, also gives you the ability to go down into the depths of the soul and meet the ultimate origin of all illness. It is in this center of one's being that the cure of all physical and psychic suffering should take place, along with the liberation from the negative conditionings of the ancestors, and the salvation of the human subject, through overcoming evil and reconciliation with the good. Here the idea of curing and salvation is inseparable from the sense of an encounter with oneself. The efficacy of the curing and liberation ritual requires those administering it to have passed through the experience of suffering and pain at the deepest level of themselves.

The Liberation Ritual

The liberation ritual takes place in M.A.'s home in a space separate from the private space of the family. The whole of the ground floor, made up of different environments, was deliberately adapted for the performance of rituals. Those to be helped generally spend a long time waiting, from the time their names are included on the list, to the ritual itself. Those who decide to go through with this ritual have generally participated previously in the *cult of loving* service or have heard a talk by M.A.; on these occasions they will have been diagnosed as needing to attend a liberation ritual. There are, however, some people, who come straight to the liberation ritual, who have been signaled out by the directors and 'sensitives' who help M.A. in running the group. In these cases, personal relations count for a lot in getting the paperwork done and reducing the time participants have to wait. The ritual itself is in several stages and a participant may be asked to come to more than one session. Through the whole process there is a group of auxiliaries with M.A. who might be in the room where the service is conducted, doing the job of 'sensitives', or they might stay in an adjoining room in a prayer vigil. A short passage from the interview with the priest attending the Grupo São José provides a vision of what happens in this modality of the service:

> She places a person in the middle. She is a sensitive so she can conduct an analysis of the person's problem in the past, from his ancestors. Naturally it is possible to do this because we have a spiritual unconscious. All this formation from our ancestors is in our unconscious, and she can have access to it. To do that you have to have special charismas. Obviously it could be something natural or something supernatural; I don't say which. But this reading she makes of the forefathers of the

person who is being liberated, has sometimes been interpreted as a paranormal phenomenon.

Before analyzing the central objective of this ritual, which consists of liberating the participants from the negative influences of their ancestors, by neutralizing the action of the 'generational demons' over their lives, we should like to direct the reader's attention to what the priest says, which recognizes to some extent the power that M.A. has to get in to people's unconscious, where there are vestiges of their ancestors. Further, while the cult of liberation seems to want to get closer to the Spiritist rituals of communication with the dead, it also seeks, in terms of the group's own theory, to mark a fundamental difference, when it says that belief in the 'generational demons', and regression to past lives practiced as a therapeutic resource by the sect, does not require as a premise, belief in the reincarnation of the dead. Though tenuous, the difference between regression and reincarnation is constantly being affirmed as a border for identifying oneself with Catholicism or spiritism.[14] This insistence on marking out the border is due to a great extent to the fact that a large number of Catholics in Brazil transit between these two beliefs.

As a matter of fact, belief in 'generational demons' implies a sophisticated theory of family bonds between one generation and another and between the living and the dead, based on a mystical-psychic referent whose fundamental premise is the belief that we inherit from our ancestors, through our genes, patterns of physical and psychic illnesses that affect us. Associated with this belief is the promise that these bonds can be untied and our inherited problems dissolved by means of the ritual process. In the final account it is a matter of offering participants the opportunity of a ritual through which they can assume control of the past as a function of the present. Consequently, the aim is to reconstruct a sequence of the generations that make up the participant's family history and his own biography, so as to give him an opportunity to undo the knots that imprisoned those who preceded him physically and psychically, and are stopping him from reaching his full human and spiritual potential. In this kind of interpretation, pain and suffering become a necessary condition

14 Figures from the census for the year 2000 reveal that the population of Brazil was of 170 million people. By 2010 this number had gone up to 190 million, but the data for religions had not, at the time of writing, been divulged, so we have had to work with the figures for the year 2000, with a majority made up of Catholics (73.6%) and just 1.3% who were Spiritists. Nevertheless, later surveys agree that 12% of the people in Brazil believe in reincarnation of the soul. The second largest religious group in the country is that of the Protestants, who account for 15.4% of the population.

both for reaching psychic and physical health, and for advancing to a higher level in the spiritual order.

In another part of the interview with M.A. it is possible to see how radically she assumes the task of liberating the individual through the Cure, going down into the depths of the human soul.

> We search for the root of the evil and we can see it perfectly. [...] The Lord allows us to go into the world of spiritual purification and see the levies of slaves tied with chains, ropes and umbilical cords, that is, the generations. We go to where the disorder first started. So there are physical, mental and spiritual illnesses, and it is necessary to see the various patterns. [...] I went through all I had to go through in order to be able to do what I do here, because we are a group of liberators. So it is a characteristic of the Grupo São José; that is why we are liberators, we are going to free people from the conditionings that come from back there.

This is a good moment to reflect briefly on the category of 'liberation' that appears in the language of the Grupo São José, and might be countered by the category 'conversion' observed in the language of other groups in the Charismatic Catholic Revival as a semantic resource for characterizing the process of change that occurs in the life of the individual when he joins the Charismatic movement (Maués 2002). The choice of the category liberation as opposed to conversion denotes a significant difference between the group and the orthodoxy of the Charismatic Catholic Revival. The point being that while conversion stands for accepting a revelation as the objective source of truth, liberation refers to an experience of the radical nature of suffering and pain as a way in. So it is not a question of converting to a new way of being Catholic in the sense of adopting a new identity that is built around a subjective acceptance of the institution, but of asserting an objective Catholic identity that authorizes members of the Grupo São José to introduce New Age beliefs and practices into the world of the Catholic tradition.

However, the passage we shall reproduce now shows that the ritual of liberation covers more than the psychic field of the individual in the present. The liberation is not only of those whose illnesses had been diagnosed as having been produced by the 'generational demons', characterized as 'super-empirical entities' (*entidades supra-empíricas*) (Lambert, 1995), but also of the dead, who had turned into vehicles for transmitting suffering and pain to the living.

> There are incredible things in the spiritual world, incredible things that happen because you never only free a person, you also free the ancestors.

> Because when we see the ancestral line where the problem comes from [...] I began to see that there were more things behind. So today we take the light to the origin of the problem. I have been praying for twenty-five years and the Lord has been preparing me a little at a time. And very often what originally caused the disorder is a prisoner in horrible places. Horrible! The symbol that it gives us, is darkness. You have to be very brave to get there. Anyone who is not spiritually prepared will be unable to get to that place [...] People walk through caves and go on to dark places. The ground is slippery and the hands of those purgatories of life, imploring, big hands that try to grab you and beg for some help... Horrible, horrible, horrible... And the Lord lets us see the people who are generally the original cause of some great family disorder, imprisoned in places as it were caves and one has to make the prayer of liberation there. And in the spiritual part we see what we call generational demons; it is as though one passed through the ovum or the spermatozoon, we see them as black, then you can tell you are passing through a spiritual problem, and it is there the liberation is effected in order to cure the disease.

As one can see from the language used, the inner psychic world of people may be inhabited by 'generational demons' that affect them through genetic reproduction. The images and categories employed to describe this world, however, remit to a Catholic-Biblical culture, in which evil is hypostasized into demons that have left the darkness of the inferno and penetrated the labyrinths of the souls of the living or who periodically visit purgatory to torment the souls of the dead.

The practice of liberation achieved in the rituals conducted by M.A. establishes a discursive superposition of one imaginative field over another—of the alternative therapies of the Self over traditional Catholic culture—and thus creates an 'in-between' area where these two regimes cross paths and establish a relative autonomy with respect to each other. A brief remark by a Catholic priest who runs a parish in which the Grupo São José holds one of its weekly services is revealing in this sense. He says: 'they are beyond traditional Catholicism and under official Catholicism'. So if the demons of generation cannot be placed in the pantheon of Catholic creatures because they do not fit into the imaginative perspective of Catholic theology and tradition, they can, all the same, be dated back to 'a system of mystical-psychic referents to the senses and faith' (Lambert, 1991: 81). This boundary situation of the Grupo São José becomes, then, a point of escape, which allows Catholics to incorporate another religious system into their own without having to formally stop being Catholics.

The sacramental efficacy of Catholic rites performed by priests is an important resource for liberation that can reach both the living and the dead. The efficacy formulated in the Catholic doctrine of *ex opere operato* gives the sacraments a natural efficacy that comes just from following the correct procedures. The same logic seems to govern the therapeutic rites performed in the liberation service that are based on the *power of illusion* of the symbols and the language, that has been authorized by the experience that was acquired in the mystical process of gaining victory over the Devil. The strategy adopted by the Grupo São José is, therefore, to compose and add up the virtues and the powers that are present, and act in each of the religious regimes. In this sense liberation coincides with the cure, which must be processed on the three levels on which the human being is structured: the psychic, the emotional, and the spiritual. A *transformation of the self* must be made beyond the limits of the living world. As we can see in the transcription below of our interview with M.A., liberation is for those taking part in the service and for their ancestors.

> So I have to bring here a person whom the ancestor is holding captive and who needs the pardon of the priest; but I can't give that; you must pray for this person instead of me. Because the blessing is for the soul. The body is of no interest, the body is transformed into a corpse...but the person stays the same...so you are going to give her your blessing. And it is given. The soul is freed. And when the soul is liberated, it has the symbols that you have placed in my hand, the links to the descendants...you understand...it leaves the conditionings and brings people to do the most absurd things...

Expressed here once again is the communion of the saints as a central dogma of Catholic-Biblical culture. The possibility for the members of the church militant (i.e. the living) to influence the destiny of those suffering (the souls in purgatory) acquires a new connotation in the context of the liberation service. It is not simply a case of prayers, vigils or offerings for the dead, but a ritual gesture that has in itself the power and the strength to free the ancestors from the pains and the residues of the evil that they did in their lives and have transmitted genetically to their descendants. With this Catholic dogma adopted by the mystical-psychic liberation service, the idea which keeps recurring in this context, that illness is an external event that it is necessary to fight against, receives a further emphasis. However, where it differs from the secularized therapies, is that here the principal cause of illnesses and suffering has to be sought in a maladjustment in the spiritual order. Thus the process of healing only comes to an end when the subject goes beyond the stages of a physical and a psychic cure, and attains spiritual liberation.

Conclusion

By way of a conclusion I should like to reflect on the metaphor of the *revolving door* that one of the priests suggested to us when we asked him if the Grupo São José could be a way in or a way out of Catholicism. This was his reply: 'Well, I think (the Group) is on the border. But it is also important to have borders [smiles]. We cannot all stay locked in the middle or at the nucleus. And it's true: it is a doorway out but it is a doorway in. I would say that it is a revolving door [smiles]. Some go out and some come in'.

The metaphor lets us imagine contiguous religious regimes as compartments of a revolving door, where people on the way in or on the way out interact with each other or rub up against each other. On the central axis of this revolving door we find the Grupo São José, which links different religious regimes, and gains its own legitimacy as a dispenser of symbolic goods that respond to the differentiated individual demands that are present in society: for beliefs, rituals and cosmologies. So what attracts people to the services of the Grupo São José is the possibility of gaining access, without having to make a commitment to a faith or a community, to fragments of religious and therapeutic regimes that are able to respond to the search for physical and mental well-being. In this sense it is not appropriate to speak here of a process of conversion or of religious transition, as what we really have is the chance to gain access to alternative therapeutic modalities and belief regimes that can introduce heterodox elements into their ceremonies without breaking away from the Catholic institution.

As a further, and final, point: we will comment on what the other priest we interviewed said about the Grupo São José being 'under official Catholicism and beyond popular Catholicism'. This shows that the boundary position of the Grupo São José is useful to the institution. By keeping it in an in-between spot, it becomes possible to include inside the boundaries of the Catholic Church, and to place in a hierarchy, significant New Age practices and beliefs that many Catholics share. Keeping these zones of ambiguity in the bosom of the Catholic Church ends up assuming an important role, as it allows the Church to continue to exercise hegemony over the religious field. The 'frontier pastoral work' as one of the priests interviewed called it, is what has made it possible to increase the supply of religious goods on offer that did not traditionally form part of the Catholic repertoire, in response to current demands in society.

From looking at the beliefs and rituals expressed in the services of *cult of loving* and of *liberation* we should like to draw attention to the boundaries that we observe between the Grupo São José, Kardecist Spiritism and New Age. We see in Kardecist Spiritism a narrow frontier between reincarnation and the therapy of regression to past lives. We might say that M.A. reinterprets belief in reincarnation, in the key of regression. As in Spiritism, in the Grupo São José it is also possible to communicate with the dead. However, the ritual contexts and the services in the two cases are very different from each other. In the services of the Grupo São José there are many more elements that remit to a Catholic repertoire of beliefs, symbols and gestures than there are in Spiritism. Further, while the ceremony of laying on of hands approximates the ceremonies of the Group to the passing of hands in Spiritist sessions, the remaining elements involved in the Spiritist service are marked by a liturgy that is charismatic and aesthetic, with a strongly Pentecostal connotation.

From the New Age, the Grupo São José has recovered experience as a source of knowledge, and therapy as a way of getting in to the Self and the sacred. However here, as in its relations with Spiritism, inscribing the personal experience of liberation into the mystical tradition of Catholicism is what distinguishes the Grupo São José from the majority of New Age institutions and groups. The process of overcoming the hang-ups and conditionings of the Ego, lived as an inner struggle, is common in the New Age as a source of legitimacy and for instituting religious guides and gurus. In the case of the Grupo São José, however, though we can identify the same process in the accounts of M.A.'s mystical progress, the style and the references woven into her story are profoundly anchored in the Catholic tradition.

CHAPTER 8

Santeria and New Age: Interactions, Limits and Complementarities

Nahayeilli B. Juárez Huet

Introduction

Santeria,[1] like other Afro-American religions, began with the transatlantic trafficking of African slaves that went on for nearly four hundred years from the sixteenth century to the nineteenth. According to Roger Bastide (1971), these religions emerged in guilds (*cabildos*) and lay brotherhoods (*cofradías*), mutualistic associations organized under Catholic patronage and established in each city by Africans and African descendants with the same ethnic background. Ultimately, it was in these spaces that distinct varieties of Afro-American religions were born, and their individual particularities became much more prominent in the nineteenth and early twentieth centuries.

Santeria began in Cuba and is considered to have a Yoruba base,[2] although in the course of its formation it also incorporated elements of Kardecist Spiritism, a set of beliefs that was most influential in the nineteenth century. Santeria also took up elements from other cults of African origin[3] and spread widely in the American continent after the Cuban Revolution (1959). From the outset, it was a 'racialized' religion, in that it was characteristically associated with African people and people of Afro descent, although Santeria broke away from such 'ethnic borders' quite early on (cf. Argyriadis and Juárez Huet, 2007). Furthermore, until just before the Cuban Revolution, Afro-Cuban cults were regarded in Cuba as 'witchcraft' and were associated with a 'primitive intelligence', supposedly a vestige of African heritage. This idea is exemplified in the first works of Fernando Ortiz—the father of Afro-Cuban studies—who analyzed these cultural expressions under the influence of the positivism and

1 Leaving aside discussions of terminology, I use the word Santeria in this text to refer to the set of complementary modalities that it consisted of originally (Spiritism, Catholicism, Palo Monte, worship of Ifá). Argyriadis notes that in Cuba this complementarity is called *La Religión* (1999).

2 Category applied to an ethno-linguistic group in West Africa, living mainly in Nigeria and Benin.

3 Principally Bantu and Arara.

 | DOI 10.1163/9789004316485_012

social Darwinism fashionable at the time, from the point of view of criminology (Menéndez, 2002; Hagedorn, 2001: 174). Ortiz considered the 'black race' to be harmful for Cuban society, arguing this race had transmitted its 'superstitions, its organizations, its languages and its dances' to the Cuban population at large (Ortiz, 2000: 5).

Thus, at the start of the twentieth century 'every trace of Africanism, especially to do with magical-religious practices, was mercilessly attacked' (Argyriadis, 2000: 651), and indeed, various campaigns against these so-called atavisms had led to legislation, as early as during the colonial period, suppressing all music of 'Afro' origin (Moore, 2001–2002: 178). It was only more recently that African heritage was 'legitimized and re-valued' as part of Cuban miscegenation and Cuban culture, thanks to the 1920s Afro-Cuban movement and the influence of European intellectuals and artists who made 'black' and 'primitive' art fashionable (Brandon, 1993; Menéndez, 2002; Agyriadis, 2006). 'Appreciation' of Santeria's aesthetic aspects, especially its music and dance, has persisted, and since the 1990s, Cuba's tourist industry has heavily promoted Santeria, and it is now a very popular emblem of Afro-Cuban culture (Hagedorn, 2001: 8, 221; Knauer, 2001: 23). But the legitimacy that Santeria enjoys today in Cuba does not transfer to new contexts (see Frigerio, 2004: 41–42), something that has also occurred with other Afro-American religions (such as Voodoo, Candomblé, Umbanda and others). While Santeria has existed in Mexico, at least in part, since the late nineteenth century,[4] it still lacks a positive social status.

Santeria in Mexico does not represent, nor does it claim to represent, the legacy of a longstanding Afro-descended population. Instead, as is the case in many countries outside Cuba, Santeria is a contemporary phenomenon. Furthermore, while Mexican *Santeros* rarely identify themselves as descendants of Africans, some of them like to call themselves 'Yorubas'. In this sense, the identity is not ethnic, but more of a 'spiritual' identity anchored in lineages tied together by religious initiations.

Although the practice of Santeria is indeed contemporary, it has flourished in Mexico largely thanks to what J. Galinier calls a 'cultural substratum' (see his chapter in this book) that includes non-Spanish, non-indigenous elements. African and Afro-American practices and beliefs were energized in part by the campaigns against superstitions, the extirpation of idolatries, and inquisitorial witch hunts and prosecutions (Quezada, 1989; Solís, 2005). But Afro-American religions also formed in spaces of negotiation, dialog and complementarity,

4 For the case of Guadalajara see Esparza, 2002; 2003. For the case of Veracruz see Argyriadis and Juárez Huet 2006; 2008, and for the case of Mexico City, see Juárez Huet, 2007, 2009; González Torres, 2008.

at both the collective and individual levels, among Spanish, indigenous and African religious practices and beliefs. Today, their complementarities serve as the basis for 'new' interactions.

In other words, Santeria does not constitute a new phenomenon, but, as Sanchis argues, '...the universalism of the syncretic process does not stop some in the syncretism achieved from being fundamentally "more equal than others"' (1994:10). These dynamics cannot be understood without considering socio-historical contexts marked by relations of power. African contributions to New World culture during the colonial period, especially in the field of 'magical religious' therapy, though made invisible in the discourse of a *mestizo* nation, did not disappear, and today these contributions undergird the cognitive bridges (cf. Frigerio, 1999) that make Mexico a fertile, receptive socio-cultural field for contemporary Afro-American practices like Santeria.

The Santeria Worldview in General Terms[5]

In Santeria, destiny and daily human activities are understood to be influenced by spirits, deities and the 'power materials' associated with them (Espinosa, 1996: 78). To please these spirits, or to invoke them and make oneself worthy of their protection, believers may use a number of ritual practices including displays of reverence, care and attention through offerings, animal sacrifices, ceremonially charging objects with power (*aché*), as well as the use of herbs, and cleansing and purification rituals (see Figure 8.1).

Practitioners also use different methods of divination (oracles), and these constitute one of the basic tenets of Santeria. Divinations are the essential way of establishing communication with the *Orisha* and other spiritual entities, and through these rituals, it is possible to hear the advice and instructions they give. The ultimate goal is to achieve 'development, health and tranquility' in the order of life, and to fend off the deathly forces that 'upset' the harmony of everyday activities (Argyriadis and Juárez Huet, http://www.ird.fr/relitrans/?Santeria,304).

5 While it is true that in the course of its history Santeria has been the object of a great variety of appropriations, in this section we review the general picture of its practice in the case of Cuba where it originated. In methodological terms, this will allow us to better comprehend its 'relocalizations' in Mexico.

FIGURE 8.1 *Altar to honor the Orisha. In the middle is the tureen of Obatalá, the tutelary Orisha of the lady whose altar it is*
MÉRIDA, YUCATÁN, JULY 2012 (PHOTO: NAHAYEILLI JUÁREZ HUET)

The oracles are based on interpreting signs, aiming to make a 'diagnosis' of the situation of the person making the consultation and to determine the actions to be taken, if necessary, to 'stabilize' the person and ward off 'misfortune'. However, initiates' techniques for communicating with spiritual beings are not limited to Santeria oracles (coconut, seashells and Ifá). These practices are often complemented by other methods that come from other spiritual or esoteric traditions which form a part of the life history (before or after Santeria) of the subjects of my study (spiritual masses; being a medium; clairvoyance, various divinations, etc.) (*idem*).

In Santeria, ritual kinship is established through various initiation ceremonies. The person who teaches the basics, or the 'secrets' that correspond to them, will be considered a godfather or godmother, and those receiving instruction will be their godchildren. These networks are bound by religious genealogies: networks of kinship that allow the circulation of material, symbolic and other goods within a great variety of spaces. Ritual kinship networks are organized around hierarchies of seniority (number of years since initiation), gender, and ritual age. At each level of the hierarchy there is a ritual authority in a field marked by struggles for power.

The Arrival of Cuban Santeria in Mexico[6]

It is true that parts of Santeria's symbolic universe, including music, dance and its deities, had circulated Mexico since the late nineteenth and early twentieth centuries thanks to networks of artists and later, the music, theater, and film industries. But Santeria did not yet constitute a religious option in Mexico, where only aesthetic representations had been disseminated. The Santeria aesthetic was 'exoticized' through performances of statuesque 'rumba goddesses' in films and by the musicians who accompanied them. This phenomenon was particularly emblematic of the late 1940s and early 1950s, when rumba dancers were at the height of their popularity. This period can be considered the first moment of the transnationalization of Santeria to Mexico. Then, the 1959 Cuban revolution and the waves of migration that followed, especially from Cuba to the United States, mark the beginning of a second stage of transnationalization. Santeria was no longer circulating in a fragmented way. Unlike the 'tropical' shows in transnational circuits of spectacle and entertainment in the first half of the twentieth century, Santeria no longer circulated in this fragmented way. After 1959, Santeria emerged as a religious option that was spreading to other countries like the U.S.A., where the largest community of Cubans in the world resided.

It was not until the 1970s that most of the first Mexican *Santeros* were initiated, either in Mexico City by Cubans who came mostly from Miami, or else in the United States, also by Miami Cubans. The expansion of Santeria at this time was accelerating, and it came to public attention in the late 1980s due to the scandal of so-called Narco-Satanists in Matamoros, in the northern Mexican state of Tamaulipas.[7] This event also revealed the growing number of Santeria initiates and consultants, and I argue that this marked the close of the second stage of the transnationalization of Santeria.

Beginning in the 1990s, and especially by the middle of the decade, there was a change in the socio-economic background of both initiates and those

6 Elsewhere (Juárez Huet, 2007 and 2009) I have argued that the presence and spread of Santeria in Mexico may be understood and analyzed as a transnational religious process that connects people and places to each other, thus forming a transnational social field (Basch, Glick-Schiller and Blanc Szanton, 1994, Glick-Schiller and Fouron, 1999).

7 In this city on the border with the United States, *Santeros* who were allegedly linked to drug trafficking were accused of conducting 'human sacrifices', and this unleashed a series of fantasies in which the rituals of this religion—and of other Afro-American devotions—were reduced to merely indecent, Satanic cults, and were henceforth loosely connected with delinquency and drug trafficking.

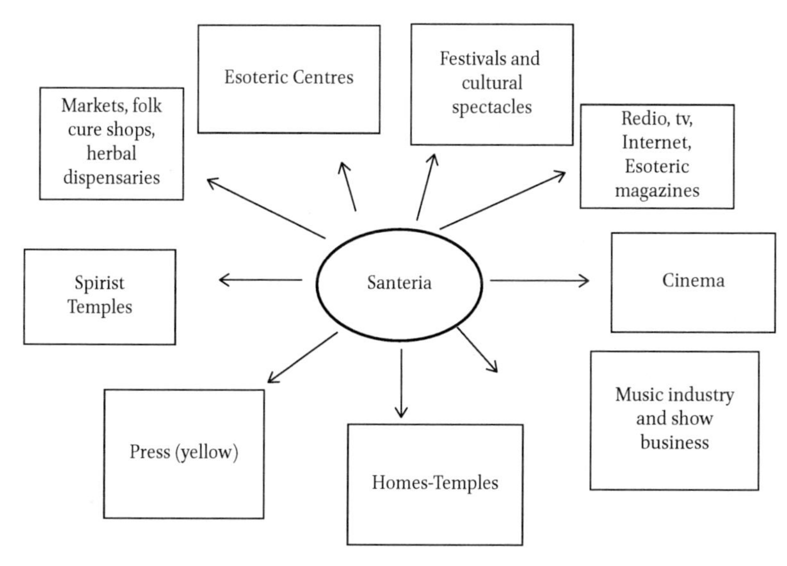

FIGURE 8.2 *Areas of circulation and cultural consumption of Santeria in Mexico*

consulting them,[8] previously limited to members of the middle and upper classes but who were now clearly more diversified. Parallel to this change, the circulation of Santeria simultaneously expanded and intensified as it spread to ever more heterogeneous areas (see Figure 8.2). This has had an influence on the nuances of its representations and 'reformulations' (in terms of its practices). This chapter focuses on this third phase of Santeria's transnationalization.

Interactions and Complementarities of Santeria in Neo-esoteric Circuits

The practice of Santeria in Mexico is often complemented by other practices and belief systems, some with roots in the past and others that only began to circulate more recently. These include: (1) 'traditional indigenous' (also called *mestizo*) medicine, which can be understood as a 'generic name used to designate the combination that results from a whole multiplicity of beliefs, concepts, techniques and practices having to do with health, illness, life and death, which still reference, after 500 years of cultural syncretism, to a remote indigenous past' (Gallardo, 2002: 14; cf. also Aguirre Beltrán, 1980: 2); (2) Trinitarian Marian Spiritualism, a millenarian type of popular religiosity aimed at healing

8 People consulting *Santeros* who are not themselves initiates.

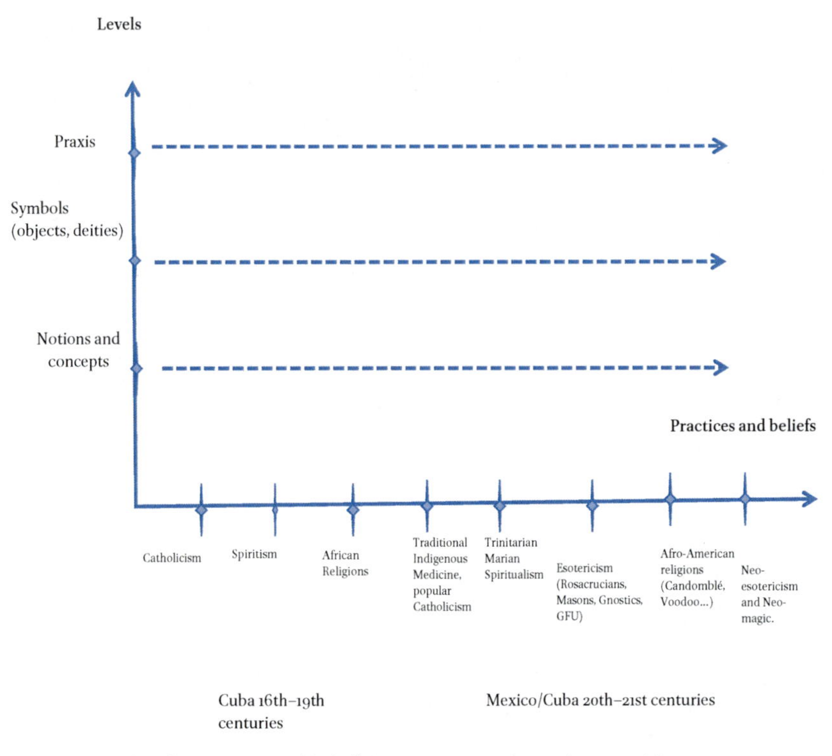

FIGURE 8.3 *Levels, practices and beliefs: interactions and complementarities*

through possession and the practice of traditional medicine (Lagarriga, 1991, 2008; Lagarriga and Ortíz, 2007); and (3) alternative forms of New Age-style 'spiritual healing' and ancient esoteric and magical practices from both the West and the East, inherited by this movement and then exotericized (see Gutiérrez Zúñiga, 1999b) (see Figure 8.3).

These continual processes of interactions and complementarities take place at different levels and move in different directions, so it might be more useful methodologically to consider the matrices of meaning through which complementarities acquire 'form and content' with particular limits and possibilities. In this way, certain interactions are deeply rooted while others remain on the symbolic and aesthetic surface (for example, between deities with similar attributes). Still other elements coexist without fusing into one another. Santeria in Mexico can be seen, then, in terms of multiple dimensions of a single process with particular logics that reflect not only a permanent 'syncretism in motion' (Amaral, 1999), but also its limits, limits that are sometimes insuperable (see chapter by Alejandro Frigerio in this volume).

Several studies of religious diversity in Mexico, especially in urban population centers, have shown the disjuncture of belonging, belief and practice as well as the remarkable simultaneity of credos coming from different cultural matrices, that are accessible in the field of religious praxis and trajectories (De la Torre, Dorantes et al. 1999; Gutiérrez Martínez, 2005).

Santeros are no exception to this phenomenon, for they may simultaneously identify themselves as Catholics, Spiritists, witchdoctors (*brujos*) or Paleros (adherents of Palo Monte); be able to read the Spanish deck or Tarot cards, know numerology, do meditation and reiki, have had some experience with Rosicrucians or be Masons; and believe in some of the precepts of Buddhism. These multiple skills and identities exist in a historical and socio-cultural context strongly marked by Catholicism and shaped by the presence and the expansion of Spiritism and Trinitarian Marian Spritualism since the nineteenth century.

During the twentieth and the twenty-first centuries, this 'cultural substratum' has incorporated New Age currents. This occurred first with 1970s New Age, the inheritor of the esoteric and occultist schools of the nineteenth century (see the chapter by Renée de la Torre in this volume), and then in the 1990s, when these elements were exotericized and broadcast to the masses in a fragmented way through the mass media and in Neo-esoteric circuits (De la Torre, 2006; Gutiérrez Zúñiga, 2008).

The New Age's matrix of meaning promotes the idea that the individual, rather than an institution, 'builds, on the basis of newly available techniques, doctrines and occasional adherences, from his own subjective frame of interpretation' (Gutiérrez Zuñiga, 1996). In other words, there is a strong tendency towards autonomy, leading to New Age being called a religion of the Self, which Carozzi (1999c) identifies as a distinctive feature of New Age (*idem*). In Mexico, New Age not only recovered the ethnic dimension of initiation knowledge but also spread to and connected with what is known as 'alternative medicine' (Gutiérrez Zúñiga, *idem*; García Medina, 2010; De la Torre, 2011: 151). As a field of 'spiritual healing' this encompasses,

> [technical] training offered in courses, manuals, and demonstrations, therapeutic services (massages, therapy sessions), components of a tool kit (crystals, perfumes, needles, massage tables), and products to create a certain atmosphere (like incense, decorations, and musical recordings). It also offers a sustained incentive to improve as new techniques of healing emerge, [and finally] it encompasses the publication of self-help manuals.
>
> HERNÁNDEZ, 2005: 23

This supply of goods is promoted and provided by a wide variety of specialists in herbalism, reiki, meditation and other practices (*idem*). Thus, it is important to recognize the impact of advertising, marketing, the mass media and the publishing industry on this 'alternative consumerism with a New Age seal' (De la Torre, 2006). In effect, as De la Torre puts it, the New Age 'ceased to be an alternative countercultural movement and was transformed into a successful cultural industry, spread through the network of communications media, in which the movement was resignified as a specialized consumer product offering a life style identified with a certain type of consumption' (op. cit.: 33. See also the chapter by the same writer in this volume).

During the same period in which New Age expanded and transformed, Santeria was spreading to several Mexican cities through the same circuits of merchandise that incorporated it, or at least some of its elements, into a vast supply of products that apparently dilute Santeria. It is no coincidence that many scholars insist on distinguishing between the traditions and practices that make up this market. For example, De la Torre has made a useful distinction between New Age and Neo-esoterics. New Age offers a lifestyle directed at urban middle and upper class cosmopolitans who from their position of comfort may experiment with alternative practices as part of their sophisticated consumption. Neo-esotericism has more to do with the 'massive reformulation of popular beliefs and practices related to traditional magical beliefs: herbalism, magic, healing, Spiritism, popular indigenous Catholicism and witchcraft' (2006: 39).

On the other hand, Magnani (in this volume) conceives of the Neo-esoteric circuit as a network articulated in urban space that facilitates circulation through various systems of practices and beliefs in an accessible way without sectarian mechanisms of membership. According to the author, these systems draw from five different main sources: Eastern philosophies, esoteric societies, pre-Christian European practices, indigenous cosmologies, and scientific texts (such as neurolinguistics and quantum physics). Beyond questions of terminology, what is clear is that the many consumer products and symbolic resources of Neo-esotericism and New Age converge in a huge market, coming together and even overlapping. Nevertheless, they do not become a 'Mystical-Esoteric nebula' (Champion, 1993). Rather, the circuits in which Santeria circulates constitute a space for exchanges between popular Latin American religious beliefs, which are holistic, cosmological, and relational (Semán, 2001), and exogenous spiritualities that are adapted and resignified. As Semán affirms, this allows the 'exercise of a compatibility that organizes world views and specific arrangements of sacred powers'. This should not be confused with the homogeneous diffusion of a pluralistic experience of the multiplicity of religions (Semán, ibid.: 58).

In this way, just as the occultist dimension of the New Age is exotericized and resignified by popular religion, the many 'secrets' contained in Santeria's ritual framework are revealed. Deities, paraphernalia, and symbols intersect in tune with a syncretic, hybrid and/or complementary dialog. Thus, various Santeria practices can be sold as 'recipes for cleansings' in do-it-yourself-type manuals, and Santeria philosophy and practice can be made relatively accessible through specialized workshops. In particular, aspects that are linked to other methods of divination and communication with spiritual beings circulate widely as another choice in Neo-esoterical circles, in which the power of 'magic' or of divination techniques predominates. Its paraphernalia are transformed into merchandise that can be ritualized by 'authorized mediators' who are not necessarily *Santeros*.

In the late 1960s and 1970s, Santeria began to spread in Mexico alongside the New Age movement. Gradually, some of its elements were incorporated into Neo-esoterical circles increasing the dissemination of the Santeria elements and symbols that today circulate on a massive scale alongside various religiosities and/or philosophies that also interact with Santeria in a wide range of spaces created by large networks and consumption circuits. These spaces of diffusion and revitalization generate points of interaction between symbols and practices which open the way to 'new functions', resignification, or, in Appadurai's words, 'indigenization' (1996: 67) on various levels and with various meanings (see Figure 8.4).[9]

Many of the places where these interactions occur in Mexico, such as herbalist shops, markets and esoteric centers, have long promoted such confluences of alternative religious ideas and practices. In these places, Santeria and its elements can be obtained as products that acquire other symbolic attributes in the context of other ritualizations that are not properly part of its 'original matrix of meaning'. In the same vein, esoteric centers allow Santeria or its elements to be interpreted in New Age terms. As De la Torre and Gutiérrez Zúñiga have pointed out (see the introductory chapter to this book), New Age contains a hybrid, holistic and relational syntax. What I seek to emphasize, however, perhaps because the New Age core predominates in interactions with Santeria, is that part of the grammar and much of the vocabulary and

9 A wide ranging and fruitful discussion of the conceptual framework of networks, consumption circuits, transnationalization and relocation of the religious, which has influenced this chapter, is in Argyriadis, Aguilar, De la Torre and Gutiérrez Zúñiga, 2008.

FIGURE 8.4 *Passage in the popular market of Sonora where there is an enormous amount of basic material and paraphernalia from various Mexican and foreign traditions*
MEXICO CITY, MAY 2010 (PHOTO: JORGE SALGADO)

many of the products of New Age (energy, cosmos, chakras), have permeated the Santero world. These elements can then be renamed or repurposed with an analogical and complementary reading. I will illustrate this with three representative portraits of such interactions in the context of matrices of meaning that may or may not allow for complementarity.

Three Ethnographic Portraits

Case 1: Rubí
Santeria as a Matrix of Meaning in the 'Reading' of New Age Notions Popularized by Neo-esotericism

Rubí was born in the mid-1960s in Mexico City. She says she came into the world with the 'gift' of second sight and mediumship; she heals with her hands, is a Santera and also presents herself to those who consult her as 'a servant of God'. For Rubí, contact with Santeria came only when she was an adult, and this has meant strengthening and broadening some of the interpretive orientations (cf. Frigerio, 1999) on 'spiritual and esoteric' matters that she had previously established. In her family, contact with spirits and second sight were quite common, and in her home they read the cards. Her grandfather was a Mason, and her mother was a 'contemplative medium' who would help people not by communicating with a spiritual being as mediums usually do, but through prayer and 'contemplation' learned from Capuchin sisters, according to Rubí. She became familiar with Hinduism and Buddhism and later, after meeting Marian Trinitarian Spiritualists—'the little brothers' as she calls them—she was able to 'accept and recognize' her gift for mediumship. It was when she was with the Marian Trinitarians that she first encountered Santeria and Tomasa, her dead figure, first appeared to her. Tomasa was someone who appears to have been a Santera when she was alive. For Rubí, it was not strange to hear of oracles, spirits and protecting guides at her first meeting with Santeria practitioners. Thus, over time she has been learning more and more about the spiritual world from which she receives 'guidance' to help others and also to help herself.

In addition to using shells, Rubí casts the Spanish deck of cards that she learned to read first. For her, reading the cards refers to 'projections' but she says 'my dead spirits also speak': these are the spirits that protect and accompany her. They are Tomasa, who is Afro-descended, and also a Gypsy woman. Rubí says these spirits are 'very chatty' as they add to the information Rubí learns from the cards:

> [...] I don't just cast the cards *any old way*, sometimes the dead make me put them down in particular ways, although I do have a method [...] My dead figure lives in the real world, I just have to say what is here. [... whereas] with the shells, you know what is coming and how you can prevent it [...].[10]

During the divination process, we can observe the complementary nature of the two methods. For example, Rubí lights a candle for Tomasa, her dead figure, to give her light, and in exchange for her help with the reading, a similar offering is made to the dead, just as in Spiritism, Spiritualism and Santeria. She proceeds to make libations of water 'to refresh (cleanse) the house and the cards' as *Santeros* do, and she recites the same invocation that is used in Santeria—at the beginning of a reading of oracles—to pay homage to the ancestors and elders, whether alive or dead. And even when using the Spanish deck, the universe of Santeria (and all the complementarity of its origins) has a much greater weight in interpretation and in praxis. In other words, it is the

10 Interview with Rubí Alba, Cancún, Quintana Roo, 16 June 2006.

predominant matrix of meaning even though Rubí came into contact with it later in her life.

But in the course of her consultations, Rubí also speaks of an 'energy field' (when this 'opens' in the person consulting her, the dead and the saints speak more easily); of 'chakras' (these for her are the same 'energy points', such as the head and the breast, that are 'marked' on the body of the person consulting her when the reading of the cards or of the shells begins); and of 'karma' (as the law of cause and effect). Accumulation of knowledge here becomes a kind of 'spiritual synergy' where there is 'strength in unity'. The unifying elements that produce this congruence correspond to different levels and poles. For Rubí, it is the dead and the saints (*Orisha*) who remain as the central figures of her devotion, and are given priority in her religious practice, and by extension, in the primary matrix of meaning. This stands in contrast to Rubí's integration of notions and vocabulary from the East such as 'chakras' and 'karma', and 'energy', which have spread on a massive scale thanks to New Age 'circuits of spiritual consumption and of alternative health' (Gutiérrez Zúñiga, 2008: 365). We could say that these Eastern notions have not been incorporated into spiritual praxis, but instead remain at the level of correspondences or symbolic associations.

Although Rubí has kept up her contact with Buddhism and Hinduism throughout her spiritual journey, these religions did not 'grab' her in the same way as Santeria and Spiritualism did. She says that Buddhism does not match her own philosophy, as she explains, 'because I am a materialist, I like the good life…', an attitude contrary to a Buddhist principle of austerity. But she believes that Hinduism has many similarities with Santeria, though in reality she may be referring to the possibility of correspondences between Hindu deities and the *Orisha*, on the basis of their aspects and physical and symbolical attributes. In other words, she interprets these deities within the matrix of Santeria:

> If you are involved in Santeria, *Ganesh* [revered as a remover of obstacles] is *Eleguá* [an *Orisha*], who opens doors and paths; I have a connection with *Ganesh* since I saw him in India […] *Lakshmi* [according to the picture of her that she has at home] is in the sea, has four arms and is on a lotus flower; that's *Yemayá,* [because] the lotus flower is life, and *Yemayá* is the mother of everything and is the one who gives you life, that's how *Lakshmi* is […] they are the same […].

In other words, in the specific area of divination methods, while it does seem possible to build cognitive bridges from Santeria to these rather common and increasingly 'global' notions,[11] the semantic threads suspending these linkages do not enjoy the solid foundations of other forms of devotion and worship of spirits, saints and the deceased that resonate with practices deeply rooted in Mexico. These resonances create the conditions in which points of interaction allow for a 'deeper' level of complementary appropriation: in this case, the level of religious praxis.

Case 2. Ramiro
Santeria from the Perspective of Neo-esoteric Circuits (Changó and Santa Muerte)

This process develops in a context marked by a significant expansion of symbols and teachings in distribution mechanisms (markets, esoteric shops and centers, herbal dispensaries, folk remedy stores and others) which make it possible for elements from endogenous and exogenous traditions to converge and be inserted into esoteric industries on a global, or at least transnational scale. This context stimulates the proliferation of innovations that take material form in symbols that are resemanticized in cultural worlds distinct from the 'original matrix' (cf. Guillot and Juárez Huet, 2012). In other words, while we observe some interactions that bring about aesthetic and symbolic mixing, at the same time some of these objects or symbols are resemanticized in accordance with other worlds of meaning (see de la Torre and Gutiérrez Zúñiga, 2005).

This is illustrated by the *Orisha*, Changó (or Shango), a Yoruba thunder god, venerated in Santeria as an *Orisha* warrior, who began to circulate in Mexico as *Changó macho*, the 'spirit of good luck' and was given a tray instead of the axe that was his primary attribute, and seated in a lotus position (*padmasana*, the classic yoga pose). The figure of *Changó macho* is as likely to be found in Mexico City as in Caracas, Barcelona, Mallorca, Madrid, Miami, New York or Los Angeles, and he has acquired mass appeal to such an extent that it is difficult to say precisely what the origin of this innovation was. Along with this Hindu-style *Changó macho*, there is another version with breasts. She is said to be the female avatar of Changó in his 'African version', just as his Catholic female 'cover' would be Saint Barbara, patroness of thunder and lightning. Thanks to books sold in exoteric shops[12] described by Cristina Gutiérrez (2007), Shango has become an accessible object of devotion that has reached places where

11 See Argyriadis and Juárez Huet, 2007.

12 '[...] traditions and disciplines supposedly maintained as esoteric, are exotericized and placed within the reach of any consumer with a certain amount of purchasing power. [Hence] "Esoteric" describes nothing more than the aura of mystery and authenticity

Santeria has not spread, and yet its symbols are resemanticized, in this case in terms of the matrix of traditional medicine and popular Catholicism integrated into Neo-esoterical circuits.

The intense circulation of religious merchandise from different cultures in distribution outlets (markets, folk remedy stores, herbal dispensaries, esoteric centres and others) has created exchanges and interactions that promote various resignifications. In the case of this particular *Orisha*, the original world of its semantics and the double male/female aspect of Shango among the Yoruba, are reconfigured with the creation of 'new forms', this time in a 'Hindu style'. *Changó macho* and his female version, are increasingly well-known representations in markets and folk remedy stores in various cities where Santeria, or its elements and paraphernalia, are made 'accessible' in spaces of commercialization through which it circulates and creates particular forms.

Ramiro is an emblematic example of this process in which Santeria is neither the ritual framework nor the main framework of meaning for the person who adopts its elements. This man, in his forties, is the owner of a shop selling medicinal plants in Chetumal (Quintana Roo, Mexico), near the border with Belize. Ramiro defines himself as a healer (*curandero*), an 'empirical profession' that he first learned from his mother and then completed with studies of herbalism in Mexico City. In his shop, he has an examination room where he receives between 40 and 50 people every week. In the 1990s, Ramiro encountered Santeria through the sale of his products, including esoteric and religious articles as well as herbs and literature on occult sciences.[13] It was from magazines and books about Santeria that he first learned about Changó, with whom he identified because of his 'dual nature'. For this reason, on his personal altar he has a figure of *Changó Macho* in his female incarnation with breasts, in addition to *La Santa Muerte*. Ramiro says that his Changó 'has been sanctified' thanks to a ritual that he performed himself, based on his experience as a healer and incorporating elements from Santeria. Ramiro transformed this Changó-object into a kind of holy talisman and assumed the 'spiritual authority' to offer it to patients who want 'one like his'. He buys the figure in Mexico City, and 'to prepare it and charge it' he follows a procedure that includes prayers, lighting candles, herbal infusions, and a ceremony in the river or else a cleansing on the Mayan pyramids. He says he inherited this knowledge, which he has made his own, from his ancestors, but as a 'researcher' he does

---

that these commercial choices use to mark up the symbolic value of their merchandise' (Gutiérrez Zúñiga, 2007: 17).

13 He has a catalogue of 4,000 products, the vast majority of which were purchased in Mexico City.

not look only to 'custom'. Ramiro is not interested in being initiated into Santeria, but he has made Changó a symbol that represents his invisible world.

According to Ramiro, the most important characteristic of Changó is his 'dual nature', always having an alternative or a complementary side. Changó has the ability to be 'a man for six months, and a woman for six months', which would correspond to *yin* and *yang*: 'when one cycle ends, another begins. It is like death: it is the end of everything and the start of something else. Death and life are a duality. *Santa Muerte* and *Changó* represent metamorphosis, changes, transformations'.[14]

Case 3. Falokun (A Babalawo 'Accused' of Being Esoteric) New Age Elements Viewed from the Matrix of Santeria/ Yoruba Religion

Falokun is a *babalawo*[15] from the United States who was initiated in the late 1980s in the city of Ode Remo in Nigeria, a country that is home to the sacred city where the Yoruba religion and its transatlantic varieties (like Santeria) originated. He lives in Mexico City and has initiated various Mexicans, and also holds workshops on different aspects of the Yoruba religion, which he has linked to elements of the Hindu tradition.

Every initiate into Santeria is the child of a specific *Orisha*, and is ceremonially and symbolically crowned by having a figure of the *Orisha* placed on his head during an initiation ceremony called 'coronation of the saint'. Initiation into Santeria marks a symbolic birth in which there is an 'imposition of the *Aché* (*áshe*)' (Menéndez 2002: 121). *Aché*, or *Ashe* in Yoruba means 'let it be so' (Chief Fama, 1996). But it is also the strength and the power with which Olodumare (God) created the universe, and everything that there is in the world is 'made of *Ashe*. The *Orisha* are the repositories of Olodumare's *Ashe*. All the invocations, propitiations and rituals in Santeria are performed in order to acquire *Ashe* from the *Orisha*' (González-Wippler, 1994: 5). It is a positive energy that circulates and is transmitted in religious ceremonies in Santeria

14 Interview with Ramiro O., Chetumal, Quintana Roo, 23 March 2008.

15 The *babalawo* (father of the secrets, in Yoruba) is a hierarchical title usually reserved for men (in theory heterosexual) and tends to carry the greatest prestige, as devotees use the oracle of Ifá, considered by many to be the 'most complex' of the Yoruba religion's divination systems. The divination system has 16 basic figures, whose combinations give a total of 256 signs called Odu, that are related, just as the shells or Dilogún used by *Santeros* are, to a set of myths (cf. Kali Argyriadis, Nahayeilli Juárez and Stefania Capone, http://www.ird.fr/relitrans/?Ifa,309).

and in Yoruba spirituality. To receive *Ashe* implies receiving grace, blessings, and the strength of the *Orisha*.

According to Falokun, the American *babalawo*, 'initiation (into this religion) does not consist of you getting something inside yourself from the outside [...] but of opening up something inside yourself to the outside. You cannot be given something in the initiation that you were not born with. All I can do is to open it, to unbind it in your interior'. This is what he calls 'letting the *ASHE* through'. The body, he says, has particular centers of energy or points where the chakras are located, and these are associated with the energy, the *Ashe*, of specific *Orisha*.

1. In the head, the crown chakra corresponds to Obatalá (*Orisha* of wisdom).
2. Eshu, the messenger Orisha of God (Olodumare) on Earth, resides in the seventh vertebra.
3. Yemayá, lady of the waters, corresponds to the throat area.
4. Ogún, the god of metals and iron corresponds to the heart area (Anahata chakra).
5. Oshún, lady of the rivers, would be found at the height of the navel.
6. Oyá, lady of the doors to the cemetery, beneath Oshún.
7. Changó corresponds to the base chakra or sexual organs.

For this *babalawo*, to be initiated means 'cleansing oneself of obstructions' in each of these chakras:

> If you cling to anger, fear, spite...childhood traumas...that is an obstruction that does not allow you to connect to the spirits. If you initiate people or conduct a ceremony where they have one or more of these chakras blocked, the *Ashé* will open the chakra, will push the obstruction out and make you feel emotions related to the transformation of one's Being.

Here, the elements that can be identified as part of the core of the New Age as defined by Frigerio are read in the light of the matrix of 'Yoruba religion'. The Yoruba conception of body and spirit are seen as two related areas reinterpreted under a New Age holistic vision. Initiation is a way to heal the spirit by unblocking the points in the body that allow the flow of energy or *Ashe* that makes up the universe and by extension, the individual. The center supporting the religious praxis of this particular *babalawo* remains within the Yoruba religion, but its semantic field incorporates correspondences of meaning with notions of the transformation of the self and healing. The ideas of chakras and energy channels combined with those of the *Orisha* and the *Ashe* acquire meaning in the body and in the rituals practiced upon it.[16]

Final Notes

As I have noted in this chapter, in these processes of interaction and complementarity, exchanges do not occur in just one direction: they go from the places of origin to those of relocation, and from there they return to the places of origin. Today in Cuba, even the most 'traditionalist' *babalawo* incorporates into his practice the notions of chakras and energy, makes astrological correspondences with the signs of the oracles, and is in contact with the diversity of options forming part of the global esoteric market under the prism of New Age.

Santeria in Mexico has come to enrich its original complementarity: it complements other religious and esoteric practices that were already in the country and interacts with more recently emerging religious practices. Nevertheless, as the ethnographic cases presented show, not everything that meets in the Neo-esoteric fields and circuits interacts in a 'positive' or 'successful' way, and at times it seems unlikely, though not impossible, for cognitive bridges to be able to link Santeria and certain aspects of the New Age ideas and practices.

Thus Santeria appears to have found much more fertile ground in Neo-esoteric circuits, than in a New Age lifestyle. But this does not negate the fact that part of New Age language, and much of its vocabulary circulating in Neo-esoteric circuits, has permeated the Santero world from which it is inclusively re-interpreted. It seems that until recently, as Frigerio affirms, the Afro-American world in Latin America has tended to be excluded from New Age praxis. But the opposite is not true, and that process also warrants mention as a model of the multidirectional nature of making distinct world views compatible, as described by Semán.

What has been explored here is not exclusive to Mexico. In this book, Silas Guerriero explains how the New Age circuit in Brazil expanded its horizons in the search for exotic traditions and began to include popular religions with African roots. S. Capone, referring to Teisenhoffer's fieldwork stresses that African-American cults are often re-interpreted by Europeans—as well as by

16 The *babalawo* says that the number of chakras he mentions is not the same as the number of chakras in India: 'those I mentioned were those that correspond most readily to some of the *Orisha*. In Ifá there are at least about 30 chakras...'.

U.S. Americans—from a 'New Age perspective', through 'compatible' analogies among elements from both worlds, such as the notion of 'cosmic energy' which corresponds to the notion of *Ashe* from Yoruba based cults (2001–2002:10). The close relationship of their cosmology with nature facilitates interpretations such as 'ecological' religions. The cult's divinities, associated with diverse elements from nature, are beings worshipped on altars that achieve a balance between elements of the cosmos as it 'passes through a rebalancing of energies' (*idem*: 11).

Taking the case of Brazilian Umbanda in Paris, Viola Teisenhoffer (2007), shows how the logic of accumulation, and the mobility and plasticity of their rituals, is shared by the New Age world with which it connects. Teisenhoffer explains how members adapt both worlds under the logic of 'all is one', regardless of whether the religion has been popularized in Europe or not.

In the case of Cuba, Lorraine Karnoouh (2011) and Emma Gobin (2014) explore the New Age world through the prism of its relationship to Afro-Cuban religious practices, and they also show distinct forms and levels of appropriation of meaning linking the two worlds. Gobin's ethnographic cases include a man who is initiated not only into Santeria and the Ifá cult, but who is also a practitioner of reiki. Instead of performing animal sacrifice, he feeds his 'ritual objects' with 'energy' rather than blood, creating compatibility between apparently 'incompatible points'. These findings lead Gobin to ask if we are observing an Afro-Cuban New Age (Gobin, 2014). Regardless of the answer, it seems to be only a matter of time before we can speak definitively of New Age Afro-American cults.

CHAPTER 9

The Journey of San Simón from Guatemala to the United States: Processes of Reappropriation of a Popular Saint of Guatemala

Sylvie Pédron Colombani

San Simón or Maximón is a controversial popular saint,[1] whose cult has developed exponentially in Guatemala in the last few decades. This complicated character inspired authors such as Miguel Angel Asturias, awarded the Nobel prize for Literature, who wrote *Maximón, divinidad de agua dulce* (Maximón, Divinity of Sweet Water) in the nineteen forties, and the poet Hugo Carrillo, whose play *Las orgias sagradas de Maximón* (The Sacred Orgies of Maximón) was performed in several countries of Latin America. Today he has considerable importance nationally. Maximón is exhibited in museums, in offices of the Guatemala Institute of Tourism, in tourist leaflets, on postcards and stamps, and is recommended as the object of excursions. The indigenous figure of Maximón appears as an element of the Guatemalan national identity, and at the same time as a symbol of Mayan traditions. But his cult is not limited to this emblematic dimension. There is popular fervor around the Saint, and even more, around the mestizo figure of his character (San Simón). Thus, as with many 'traditional' religions,[2] the cult of Maximón/San Simón, which was identified just a few decades ago with a single territory, a culture, even an ethnic group—the Tzutujil Mayans—, entered a process of translocalization and of transnationalization.

I shall try in this chapter to examine the process of translocalization of this cult and its current inscription into California in the U.S.A. First I shall explain the principal elements that make it possible to understand the particularity of the San Simón cult in Guatemala. Then I shall analyze its transformation and

1 The history of the Saint is marked by episodes of conflict with the Catholic hierarchy. In Santiago Atitlán, where Maximón originated, the earliest ethnographic observations were made in the nineteen twenties by S.K. Lothrop, who reported that when a Catholic bishop arrived in 1915 to celebrate Easter he was horrified to see that his congregation worshipped this figure. He tried to burn it but the natives of the village rejected him violently (Lothrop, 1929: 23). A similar episode, this time with repercussions at national level—even the president of the country intervened—occurred in 1951 (see Mendelson, 1965; Tarn and Prechtel, 1997; and Pédron Colombani, 2005).

2 For more on this subject, see Argyriadis, De la Torre, Gutiérrez Zúñiga and Aguilar Ros, 2008.

 | DOI 10.1163/9789004316485_013

resignifying in the context of the city of Los Angeles. We shall see how the cult is relocalized and resignified, on the basis of networks of Guatemalan migrants and the very special world of folk remedy stores (*botánicas*), in order to enter into new spiritual circuits of a New Age or, more precisely, of a Neo-esoterical, type—using here the distinction established by Renée De la Torre (De la Torre, 2006),[3] in an attempt to see to what extent the cult has integrated the logic of these circuits into itself.

The Figure of Maximón in Guatemala

Maximón is a many-sided character, half saint and half god, originally from Santiago Atitlán, a pueblo in the mountains in the West of Guatemala that is on the edge of Lake Atitlán and whose inhabitants are mostly Tzutujil-Mayan descendants.[4] He was born on the periphery of popular Catholicism, in the system of guilds. In the mind of the indigenous people, belief in Maximón is almost an inseparable part of the Catholic religion that they learned from the Spaniards. At the same time, many of them insist on the Mayan heritage woven into this cult.

In fact, Maximón is a deity that transfigures itself. Among his many personalities there are Catholic saints like Saint Peter the first Apostle, Saint Andrew, and the archangel Saint Michael. But another of his characters is Judas Iscariot, the disciple who betrayed Jesus.[5] Another of his personalities is that of Mam,

3 As Renée De la Torre notes in her article on the mass media circuits of Neo-esoteric merchandise in Guadalajara, we can make a distinction between the New Age type of services on offer and the Neo-esoteric, which form two distinct circuits with differentiated contents and are directed at separate publics and consumers. Neo-esotericism is more linked to a massive reformulation of popular beliefs and practices related to traditional magical beliefs: herbalism, magic, healing, popular Catholicism and witchcraft; and not so much to the offer of a new or alternative liefestyle, which is what the New Age provides. What Neo-esotericism offers is magical solutions to problems (De la Torre, 2006: 38–39).

4 The principal language today of the inhabitants of Atitlán is still Tzutujil, which is closely related to Cakchiquel, Quiché, Rabinal and Uspanteca. Together these form the Quiché group of Mayan languages.

5 In some pueblos where we can find figures of Maximón, he looks very like a realistic image of Judas Iscariot. For example, in the guild of Saint George of the Lake—another pueblo on the edge of Lake Atitlán—just Maximón's head is guarded in a special place and annually there is a 'dressing' ceremony. What happens is, that after the celebrations of Holy Week have been completed, the Saint's body is taken to pieces so the head can go back to being locked in a special trunk belonging to the guild. The head is a mask like those used by the indigenous people in their Moorish dances; it has moustaches and a distinctly funereal expression, as its

the old Mayan god that the ancient Mayans worshipped during the Uayeb—the last five days of the Pre-hispanic calendar, which mark the change from one year to the next.[6] For this reason, as I have shown previously (Pédron Colombani, 2006), in Santiago this is a deity who guarantees fertility and life in the community, especially during the rituals of Holy Week.[7]

Maximón sometimes also becomes a particular historical person. He may be Pedro de Alvarado, conqueror of the indigenous people of the region. Or the mestizo president: many people relate San Simón de San Andrés Itzapa to President Estrada Cabrera, who ruled the country between 1898 and 1920; it was his liberal politics that allowed the massive entry of foreign companies—like the United Fruit Company from the U.S.A. He might also be a soldier, or a policeman. And the Saint turns out to represent a religious figure that is completely rooted in the history of the country, as it refers to the major events the Indians of the region have had to pass through, and in particular the Spanish domination; also the recent history of Guatemalan populations—the political violence of the ninenteen eighties, for example.

The indigenous people of Lake Atitlán turn to him when they want to be cured of a disease, or want to protect a woman from falling into temptation with another man, or want success in their business, protection for the crops, or they want to attract a woman. They bring him various offerings and quite a lot of money to guarantee their petitions are granted. And they worship him giving him spirits to drink through a hole where his mouth is, into which they also stick lighted cigars and cigarettes. Like the great Mayan lords, Maximón smokes cigars and cigarettes. He uses them to cure, but also to inflict madness on certain members of the community—adulterers, for example. What stands out is the dual nature of the figure. His identity manages to integrate miraculous Saints and at the same time the characters of enemies or traitors. The faithful respect him, reverence him and fear him, because he is able to personify both the best and the worst. Those who wish their enemies ill also turn to him because he has a reputation for remedying injustices.

features show the grimace of a hanged man. In Nahualá, a municipality of the department of Sololá, Maximón also appears with his mouth open and his tongue hanging out.

6 Mam is the feared god of evil, whom the Mayans only allowed out of his subterranean home at particularly critical times. According to Bishop Landa and other sources, the ancient Mayans worshipped him during the last five days of the pre-Columbian calendar, the Uayeb; a period marking the transition from one year to another. 'The Indians were afraid of these days, believing that they were unlucky and brought with them danger of sudden death, plagues and other misfortunes', as explained by Lopez de Cogolludo (Thompson: 1975, 361). This period is not only one of grief and tension, but also the prelude to a new cycle of life.

7 For more on this subject, see Pédron Colombani: 2006, 289–314.

Spread of the Cult

As Pilar Sanchiz Ochoa (1993) has already pointed out, there is a proliferation of figures of the Saint in a large part of the land of Guatemala. Several temples have recently opened their doors. With the demand for cultural exoticism coming from tourists, who are more numerous and more important to the country's economy since the ending of the civil war, the number of temples in touristic towns like Chichicastenango or la Antigua has increased. In these places the authenticity of the 'traditional cult' is always guaranteed by having 'Mayan priests' to hand. The rites, the petitions and the congregations vary, but reference to an indigenous Mayan tradition still persists.

Many Guatemalans also have their own effigies in their homes or businesses. Traders have appropriated the divinity in order to be protected, because the Saint is also patron of travellers and of traders. At present, the 28th of October—feast day of Saint Simon—is the occasion for many festivities across the country. In Panajachel, a Lake Atitlán town dedicted to tourism and the sale of crafts, fireworks and marimbas can be heard all day. The town has a number of tradespeople who organize fiestas around the figure of Maximón to guarantee the prosperity of their businesses. This dimension is put into high relief in the current context of the country's opening up to mass tourism, which makes for a multiplication of businesses of every kind (travel agents, transport services, crafts, hotels, etc.) but also makes for severe competition between sellers. So, many traders have their own special altars.

The Figure of San Simón

In the course of this spread of the cult and its appropriation by new sectors of the population, the farther we get from the Lake Atitlán region, the more Maximón is transformed into 'San Simón'. His effigy is so changed that at times it is difficult to establish any relation between the Maximón of Santiago Atitlán, and the figures we find in other places. But the faithful assert that in spite of the different name and the many variations of the cult, Maximón and San Simón are the same person.

The San Simón of San Andrés Itzapa—a town located some fifty kilometers from Guatemala City—is an interesting version of this transfiguration and of this process of admixing the figure. Here the manikin worshipped by the faithful has nothing to do with the indigenous figure from Santiago Atitlán, which consists of a piece of wood approximately 1 meter 30 centimeters high wrapped in pieces of cloth and maize leaves, wearing the typical clothes of men in the area, with a wealth of neckerchiefs. The head is formed of a piece of wood, or a pumpkin, with a mask, also made of wood, placed upon it.

San Simón de San Andrés Itzapa, by contrast, is a big statue of a white-skinned person with a moustache, wearing European style clothes: a white shirt, a tie and sunglasses. Here the Saint has his own temple and is completely separate from the guilds. Also, while in essentially indigenous communities such as that of Santiago, Maximón is seen with many other figures of Catholic Saints and especially with the recumbent Christ, in San Andrés Itzapa all these images have disappeared. Only Saint Judas Thaddeus, the patron of hopeless causes, is kept, to the left of San Simón. The temple—built in a modern style—contains several tables where the faithful burn candles and cigars, once they have been presented to San Simón and put in touch with him. While in Santiago an indigenous, ethnic and local religion has been developed, the Sanctuary of San Andrés Itzapa attracts a large number of pilgrims, especially mestizos and Central Americans. Here in Itzapa where the congregation is mostly urban, the cult is more open to international cultural elements[8] and seems to have adapted to the requirements of the modern world. All the same, the 'Mayan priests' officiating in this place make references to the Mayan tradition in order to legitimate their practices. On many occasions in Guatemala I have heard people appealing to the authentically Mayan character of the cult and its strongly ethnic aspect.

The Travelers' Saint

San Simón also crossed the borders with the Guatemalans who emigrated to Mexico or the U.S.A. This is not fortuitous, because in Guatemala, he has always been associated with journeys and business.

In Santiago Atitlán, he can pass as a traveler. A number of legends have him traveling the roads of the country, usually on foot but sometimes on horseback.

8 The crowds of pilgrims around the temple have encouraged the appearance of indigenous and mestizo street vendors, who sell colored statues of the Saint, San Simón amulets, protections for the car, San Simón soap or perfumes...but also the New Spiritist Prayer Book (*Nuevo devocionario espiritista*) by Allan Kardec, and various books on black or white magic, Caravaca crucifixes, statues of Saint Gregory or of El Rey Pascual (San Pascualito), little statues of the Buddha... Some women—who have taken up positions on the steps of the temple or are sitting on the ground in the street—offer services of divination through Tarot cards. Some musicians are playing Mexican music...

Maximón comes out at night and the faithful fear his irruptions.[9] This particularity appears to be anchored in Mayan thought. J. Eric S. Thompson says that the ancient Mayan sculptors would keep their idols in pitchers for fear they might come out at night (Thompson, 1954: 254). And Pilar Sanchiz Ochoa stresses that the black face of the San Simón of San Lucas Toliman—near Santiago Atitlán—can be related to the black Mayan god of commerce of the Ek Chuah (Sanchiz Ochoa, 1993). The latter was both the god of commerce and the god of cacao, possibly because the seeds of this plant were used as money, hence as the base for all commercial transactions in Meso-America. He generally appears in the codices painted black with a pack on his shoulders and sometimes with a stick in his hand. Diego de Landa—chronicler of the Conquest in the Mayan world[10] relates that travelers would take incense with them and burn it to Ek Chuah asking him to allow them to return home safe and sound (Thompson, 1970: 370–372). San Simón thus appears as the patron of those making journeys.

With his having a record like this, it is hardly surprising that those who are about to travel or emigrate come from all over the country to consult him, and obtain his blessing and protection. Many specialists in the cult—who usually call themselves 'Mayan priests'—take charge of the ceremonies. I came across a woman in Panajachel who had come to consult a priestess before starting the paperwork for emigrating to the U.S.A. After a divination ceremony using cigars, she told her client that San Simón was in agreement, and she would get her green card for going. It is not uncommon in some of the centers of worship for the Divinity to be dressed, for this kind of ceremony, in the uniform of a soldier, a policeman or of the border patrol, that is to say, with attributions of the authorities. Sometimes those planning to cross the border illegally also carry with them an effigy of San Simón. I was told many stories in Los Angeles of 'miraculous' crossings of the border thanks to the intervention of the Saint. Here San Simón joins other Mexican figures of secular saints such as Jesús Malverde and Juan Soldado, who are regarded as patrons of migration or border Saints. Thus as noted by Miguel Olmos Aguilera (2008, 50–51), these

---

9 Mendelson (1965) says that for some of those he spoke to—midwives—the birth of some children with deformities was linked to Maximón. He also tells us of the case of a married girl, whose husband was away on his travels, who dreamed that her husband was lying asleep beside her, but when she woke up she remembered he was away. She lit a candle but couldn't see anyone. Later she gave birth to a child with the shape of Maximón, with a big chest, short legs and a wrinkled face. Other people who spoke to Mendelson did not believe in Maximón's children because, they said, 'if Maximón slept with women, they would go mad and die immediately'.

10 Diego de Landa, *Relacion de las cosas de Yucatán* (1566).

characters have the peculiarity of coming from a mestizo environment, and yet they show up looking like a white skinned man. San Simón dos not escape this rule. The figure that has crossed the borders is not the one from the Indian world of Lake Atitlán, but the mestizo figure from San Andrés Itzapa.

San Simón in Los Angeles

We can find the character of San Simón in many folk remedy shops (*botánicas*) in the city of Los Angeles. These shops are at the same time spiritual centers, places to buy religious objects from various backgrounds, and alternative health centers. Here we can find all the material that is needed for ceremonies of popular Catholicism, for Santeria, for the Mayombé rod, for Spiritism, and Voodoo, but also medicinal plants, etc. As emphasized by Polk (2004)—author of a book of photographs of the *botánicas* of Los Angeles—these folk remedy shops are a means for Latin Americans to guarantee the continuity of the traditions from their countries of origin, and this, in a context of migration, diaspora and exile.

For José Murphy (1988: 48), these shops are refuges from the sometimes hostile outside world, a visible place where the consumer is free to express his beliefs. But it seems to me that they are also a crucible for hybridation[11] open to a great diversity of influences. Many of the owners of these shops aim to preserve traditional practices originally from the countries they come from, but they also experiment with new ways of contemplating the sacred, and bring in new practices. In the context of an *à la carte* religiosity, businesses like these—*botánicas*, herbal suppliers and popular markets, and even some kinds of supermarket—form consumption routes allowing individuals to design their own belief menus. It is no accident, then, that San Simón should have

11 The concept of hybridation refers to processes of intersection with transactions that make a variety of inter-cultural mixtures possible. García Canclini defines it as 'socio-cultural processes in which discreet structures or practices that existed separately, combine to make new structures, objects, and practices. One should also be clear that the structures said to be discreet were themselves the result of hybridizings, and cannot therefore be considered pure sources' (García Canclini, 2000: 8). He proposes this category as a way to get over syncretism, in so far as hybridation allows the inclusion of elements not covered by the latter term, which, he says, is generally used to refer to a fusion of religious beliefs, in the framework of the movement of traditional symbols (García Canclini, 1989).

taken up his abode there, along with other 'informal' Saints, as they are called by Piotr Grzegorz Michalik.[12]

In Los Angeles, the first people to open folk remedy stores were from Cuba and Puerto Rico, in the nineteen fifties (Polk, 2004: 31). In the following decades it was Mexicans—in the sixties and early seventies—, and then people from El Salvador and Guatemala—in the eighties and nineties. Many of them converted old herbal dispensaries, selling plants and remedies of popular medicine, into *botánicas*. Afro-Americans and Americans of Oriental extraction also opened their shops. But today, most of the owners of *botánicas* in the south of California are originally from Mexico and Central America. These businesses have adapted to consumer demand. The success of this kind of folk remedy store may be explained by the large numbers of Mexicans and Central Americans living in the city. I came across a Cuban woman who owned a *botánica* in a largely Guatemalan neighborhood. She sold little figures of San Simón without really believing in him, just because 'it's what the customers ask for'. Others say they change the supply of goods on offer in their folk remedy shops, as the neighbourhood evolves. So most of the *botánicas* in the city sell statues of San Simón along with all the material needed for the worship of this miracle working Saint who has the reputation of being able to solve many problems, especially those to do with health, business and migration.

The *Botánica* of San Simón de los Llanos

A number of the owners of folk remedy shops, who were from Guatemala, reconstructed an altar in the corner of some of their shops. In the *botánica* of San Simón de los Llanos, the owner went so far as to build a temple to one side of his shop, with a statue like that in San Andrés Itzapa, enclosed in a glass case (see Figure 9.1). Other figures such as those of the crucified Christ, la Santa Muerte, the Mexican, syncretic, Our Lady of Guadalupe, a Hindu deity, Saint Judas Thaddeus, Saint Anthony of Padua, and the Buddha[13] began to turn up

12 Referring to popular Catholicism in Mexico, Piotr Grzegorz Michalik makes a distinction between informal saints and half-formal saints. The informal are said by the faithful to be Saints even though they have not been canonized. San Simón and Jesús Malverde fall into this category (Michalik, 2011).

13 Our Lady of Guadalupe is a famous syncretic Mexican figure belonging to the Catholic world; *la Santa Muerte* is an unconventional figure from Mexican popular Catholicism; Saint Anthony of Padua is a Franciscan Saint of Portuguese origin, popularly known as 'the Saint who is looking for love', and whose cult has developed recently in Central America. Judas Thaddeus, 'patron of difficult cases' is a major figure of popular Catholicism

FIGURE 9.1 *San Simón in his chapel, Los Angeles, California, October 2008*
PHOTO: SYLVIE PÉDRON COLOMBANI

beside him. The Saint Simon, who rules in this temple, was made in Guatemala. When I asked him, on the basis of my experience of the cult in Guatemala, whether the figure had been made by a 'Mayan priest', the owner of the shop, Carlos, looked at me, surprised, and said No. It had just been made by someone who makes Saint Simons. This is an important detail for understanding the relocalizing of the cult in California. Here, specialists in the cult do not guarantee the ceremonial production of the little figures as sacred obects. Their manufacture is disconnected from the circuits of believers and has entered globalized commercial circuits. Some of the little figures come straight from Guatemala. But others are produced locally and show significant physical changes. Such as the addition of a rifle to replace the traditional stick which was a symbol of power among the Guatemalan guilds. We came across a Phillipine company located in Los Angeles that makes plaster statues of San Simón for the *botánicas* of the city, in response to increasing demand. During this process of commercializing the popular Guatemalan Saint, many very

in Latin America. These figures more than anything set the place they occupy in the framework of popular Catholicism, whether conventional or not. The figures of the Buddha and the Hindu deity—that appear as a minority interest and not as central—testify to the co-existence of these with other symbols from a diversity of traditions.

stereotyped manufactured products also appear, such as: soaps, perfumes, oils, medallions, and amulets for the car. There is a San Simón soap just as there is a Jesús Malverde soap, soap of *la Santa Muerte* and soap of the Seven Powers. They are used by the faithful in private ceremonies, without precise codification, in order to feel better, to propitiate a petition to San Simón, to expel bad influences or to purify oneself. Merchandise of this kind, made in Venezuela, is distributed all over Hispanic America. They are now to be found in several places in Guatemala, including San Andrés Itzapa—the center of worship that is most open to international influences, due to the many foreign pilgrims that come to visit. There are also sites on the internet dedicated to the sale of this type of goods. Thus the Saint originally from Guatemala has come into circuits of Neo-esoteric goods for sale on a worldwide scale, as a symbol endowed with magical power. And its uses are homogenized. The presence of San Simón in this universe of *botánicas*—which favors the circulation of the symbols and the products—thus transforms his worship, putting him in touch with new consumers, who are going to be able to use all these products in rites of purification, of '*sanación*', used for their greater personal well-being, far from all the restraints related to the cult of San Simón in the native temples of Guatemala. This presence also connects the saint to the sphere of influence of New Age circuits and to new ways of envisioning the relation of people with the sacred.

In Carlos's *botánica*, the story told by the faithful to explain the origin of San Simón seems to be foreign to the version given in the indigenous zone of Guatemala. In Santiago, legends tell of how the ancients created the Divinity with a sacred tree and prayers to protect their community—and in particular their women—whenever the men were away.[14] In Los Angeles, people speak of

14 There are several legends existing at the same time to explain the creation of Maximón in Santiago, but they all refer to the need to save a sexual order, which has been endangered by frequent adultery among the original inhabitants. Some elements are repeated in every account. Firstly, the ancestors of the pueblo created the manikin in order to protect the women who were left alone in the village as a result of the commercial activities of their husbands. However, once the idol had been made, its powers may have grown immoderately, and as he could become a man or a woman, and he not only terrified adulterers by assuming the shape of their loved one, only to reveal himself and drive them mad, but also managed to couple, indifferently with boys or girls, thus becoming the principal factor in breaking up the order for whose preservation he had been created. And finally, the image had been destroyed, which explains the current form of the effigy of Santiago (without arms and with bandy legs). For Pilar Sanchiz Ochoa, all of these legends reflect an unresolved problem for the indigenous people after their contact with the Spaniards: the insertion of Christian morality, in the area of sexual relations, into a dualistic vision of the world, where categories of right and wrong are not well defined and

a man who really lived sixty or seventy years ago. He was a young doctor from Italy who had emigrated to Guatemala, to the town of Zunil—where an important cult devoted to San Simón developed—with plenty of money, and he decided to help the local people. They say San Simón chose this place because of the poverty of its inhabitants, and that he became very popular because he gave people medicine, money, vaccines, etc. He was like a protector of those who suffered. Which did not fail to arouse the jealousy of the authorities. And those who envied him wanted to kill him. To discredit him they said he was not a medical doctor but a witch doctor. The Indians protected him and tried to hide him. He escaped and undertook a journey to the capital, in the course of which he stopped in a place where an old man offered him a cup of coffee. The beverage transformed him miraculously into San Simón. The place where this happened was San Andrés Itzapa. For this reason, many of the faithful I came across in Los Angeles wanted to go there or had already gone there on pilgrimage. The story told by Carlos highlights the migratory dimension of the character, and the way the cult is rooted in Guatemala. San Simón appears as the migrant who comes to the help of the people. He becomes a real man who is able to change the lives of those who suffer. In this he approaches once again the other saintly figures on the edges of the Catholic institution, such as Jesús Malverde and Juan Soldado.[15]

Carlos, the owner of the folk remedy shop *San Simón de los Llano*s, came to Los Angeles in the nineteen eighties, and is from Samayac, a town in West Guatemala whose traditional medicine men are famous all over the country. He has been practicing for over 30 years, and opened his first folk remedy shop in 1994. In the course of our interviews he told me he worked as a medicine man to solve problems of health, alcoholism, relations between couples, and economic difficulties, to help with crossing the border and getting the papers in order. To do so he works for the most part with San Simón who appears as his principal contact. The Saint guides him, appears in his dreams, and appears

---

where man is not responsible for his final destiny. This is how, in a Christian context, Maximón becomes the traitor, the fallen angel, capable of doing good but also bad, of protecting and healing but also of harming men.

15 The use of these figures of popular Saints, consulted by a growing number of followers in Central America and the U.S.A. whose ceremonies include identical commercial elements that circulate in a transnational market, is being homogenized. One can still see the mutual influence of one figure on another. Thus for example, the figure of Jesús Malverde, formerly only available in the form of a bust, has recently started to be sold in nearly all the folk remedy stores of Los Angeles in the shape of a man seated on a chair, exactly like San Simón. The shopkeepers explain this modification as being due to the demand of their customers.

to him to make diagnoses, and to give him indications for looking after his patients, and so on. He also performs black magic with San Simón, as they do in Guatemala.

But in the office where he receives his patients, the objects present show how hybridized his practices are. He has included several elements from outside and does not hesitate, for example, to call on *la Santa Muerte*—who is so popular in Mexico. In an advertisement for his temple, he wrote 'The Indian from Samayac, medicine man from birth, astrologer, parapsychologist, spiritual counsellor'. It says in the text that he can do all kinds of work for love, for luck and for protection. 'Cards, coral tree beans and tumbler readings'. There is a photo on this poster of San Simón, and one of Carlos, a drawing of a North American Indian and a statuette of the Buddha.

In this way, Carlos has broadened his traditional knowledge of herbal medicine and popular Catholicism to include other techniques such as reading cards, diagnosing at a distance with photographs, using merchandise brought from elsewhere (figurines of the Buddha or Egyptian pyramids), making talismans to get the money flowing or amulets to counter bad energies at home or in the car. The hybridized nature of his practices can be observed in this inclusion of new techniques and objects originally from other religious traditions, but also in the way he defines himself as a medicine man and at the same time as a parapsychologist, an astrologer and above all, as a spiritual guide. Alejandro Frigerio indicates that there are semantic markers which suggest the degree of integration of a traditional specialist in the New Age circuit. A good example would be the fact that Carlos defines himself as a 'spiritual guide' and not as a '*curandero*' (natural healer) or '*brujo*' (medicine man) as all the specialists of the cult in Guatemala do. It seems to me to shine a light on the reconciliation with a New Age logic. The fact that he has expanded the scope of his activities to include parapsychology, spiritual advice and a whole set of practices intended to bring a greater sense of well-being to the individual, and what is more, adopting a global perspective, also points in the same direction.

In spite of this, his practice has nothing to do with Buddhism, for example. The Buddha is just a figure. Carlos's practice stays principally tied to the figure of San Simón. The other figurines appear more as magic fetishes that can help with the performance of miracles. They are used because they have a reputation for being effective and because customers of the shop know them and trust them. That is why the statue of *la Santa Muerte* is there, standing to the left of San Simon in the temple (i.e. on his right), and receives her tortillas or bread every day (without taking part directly in Carlos's ceremonial practices). All these figures are connected, and live together, but are not really fused into each other. In the end, Carlos's practice is part of a framework of wide ranging circuits of a Neo-esoteric type, but it has not completely redefined the internal logic of its curative action, which is that of a traditional medicine man from Guatemala who works with the figure of a popular Saint.

The Feast of San Simón in Los Angeles

In Guatemala, the 28th of October—Saint Simon's day—is the occasion of many fiestas across the country. In Los Angeles, the faithful also organize private celebrations. And Carlos organizes a public event, which he calls 'Saint Simon's birthday'. He associates himself with a local group called 'the Saint Simon guild'. This group, which is completely independent of Carlos's temple, has its own effigy in a minute temple built in the yard of a family house—the son of the family, Oscar, also being president of the guild.

The day of the feast turns on 4 periods that we can revise quickly:

(1) First moment: Dances in the San Simón de los Llanos folk remedy shop. Starting at dawn, some of the faithful dance before the statue of San Simón, making him various offerings of food, spirits and money. This part of the feast is very like what is now done in many temples in Guatemala. Some of those taking part wear typical Guatemalan dress, but the rest are dressed in Western clothing. Their dances are not like any collective ceremonial dance. Each one evolves individually to the beat of music with influences from Mexico.

Carlos is dressed for the occasion in a white suit bordered with very colourful emblems of flowers, birds and people,[16] a belt from Guatemala, a turban—like those worn by Mayan priests in Guatemala—, a rod that stands for power in the guilds, and numerous necklaces of red and black seeds. The whole display, such as I had never seen in Guatemala, evoked Guatemala and the world of the guilds and the Mayan medicine men, in a completely original scheme. Carlos gave his imagination free rein to construct a person that he called a 'spiritual guide'. By choosing this expression, 'spiritual guide', Carlos is inscribing his activities into a universal tradition. But at the same time his aesthetic composition underlines the anchoring of his activities in the Indian and Guatemalan world, which legitimates his practices. But he does not focus on a particular Mayan identity—the identity that would legitimize the cult in Guatemala—so much as on a more generic Indian identity.

16 This costume has nothing to do with typical Guatemalan dress but some of the embroidered figures are inspired by those that indigenous women in certain communities traditionally stitch on their blouses.

(2) Second moment: The visit to the San Simón guild. Here the faithful eat, prepare portable altars to take out into the street, and dance, but this time with the divinity in their arms.[17] Here direct contact with the divinity, without intermediaries, is the rule. Today this is also done in some places in Guatemala. But this way of relating to the divine is new. And I think we have to relate it to the comings and goings of the faithful between Guatemala and the U.S.A. In Santiago, the *telinel*[18] plays an important part and still serves as an intermediary between the divinity and the faithful. In Los Angeles, a direct individual relation is established.

In the yard, a group of dancers have been asked by the organizers to come and perform Conquest dances, but in a very special way. Their dances do not evoke episodes from the Spanish Conquest but have the dancers dancing round in circles. Here the Conquest dances have nothing to do with evocations of the grandeur of the Spanish Christians or with an indigenous parody of the same. Even their costumes showed the original meaning of the dances had been lost here in a North American context. They did indeed wear the masks of Spanish conquerors. But their costumes belonged to no codified tradition, only to a hybrid folklore. They wore long colourful dresses with figures of Indians adorned with feathers, or of the Virgin of Guadalupe.[19]

(3) Third moment: The procession through the streets of Los Angeles. This procession has been officially recognized for seven years. Today the organizers have a legal permit to file through the streets, and a police escort that they seem to be very proud of. They obtained the permit on the grounds that they were following Guatemalan religious tradition. Having official recognition seems to them to be a real sign because it means that San Simón has opened a border—the subject of crossing the border is primordial among the faithful in Los Angeles. Carlos also insists on the fact that the visitors who come for consultations are from all over the world: from India, Israel, Russia, or France… He speaks constantly of the international dimension of his shop.

The procession consists of a parade through some of the streets of Los Angeles, in the Pico Avenida quarter, which is home to many people from Guatemala. Those participating take it in turns to carry San Simón as they

17 This way of showing one's devotion, by carrying the Saint, seems to be spreading. The same thing is now being done in Mexico with *la Santa Muerte* or Saint Jude (Judas Thaddeus).

18 The *telinel* is a specialist in charge of the worship of Maximón for a year. He belongs to the Santa Cruz guild that looks after Maximón, and he works as a medicine man.

19 Their dress is like that of the Chinelo dancers in the state of Morelos, Mexico. Once again we can verify the influence of Mexican culture.

FIGURE 9.2 *Fiesta of San Simón in the streets of Los Angeles. Portable altars carried in procession. Los Angeles, California, October 26, 2011*
PHOTO: SYLVIE PÉDRON COLOMBANI

would in processions dedicated to Saints or the Virgin in Latin America. In the Saint's retinue, many of the faithful also carry their own statues of San Simón in baskets. Each basket has a special sign to show the owner: a Mexican cowboy hat, a Guatemalan fabric, or a Pre-hispanic mask (but not necessarily of Mayan origin; it might be an Aztec or some other mask). All combinations seem possible (see Figure 9.2).

The Parade starts with the flag of Guatemala carried proudly by a woman, and a censer spreading the fumes of copal. Then comes Miss San Simón, chosen specially for this occasion, who is exhibited in a pick-up truck, followed by women wearing typical Guatemalan costumes.

During the preparations I asked them what the origin of their blouses (*huipiles*) was. Their blouses are traditionally worn by Guatemalan Indian women and they represent a particular pueblo according to the type and clour of its design. None of them could tell me. 'I don't know. I'm not from Guatemala', they would say. In fact many of them were from other countries in Central America, and just wore this dress for the procession. Some of them even counted on me, as an anthropologist who had worked in Guatemala, to tell them where their costume was from. I was also able to observe in the parade a number of Guatemalan flags, paintings of the famous quetzal—the emblematic bird of the nation—also T-shirts with a picture of a Bank of Guatemala banknote printed on them, etc. So whatever the identity of those taking part, everyone played the game of dressing up as Guatemalans, from the country San Simón came from, on this his 'birthday' when he was to be honored.

(4) The fourth moment is a night of honoring San Simón, with food—traditional food from Guatemala and Honduras—, games, spectacles and dance. This fourth period gives the occasion a festive dimension and clearly shows Mexican and U.S.A. influences. Los Angeles is city in which Mexican culture prevails, and they invited *mariachi* musicians and imitators of Mexican singers like Vicente Fernandez and others. Many prostitutes and transvestite men turned up, as they would do in San Andrés Itzapa.[20]

Between the Influence of New Age and Processes of Identification Among Central American Migrants

Studying Saint Simon's Day as it appears in Los Angeles highlights three elements:

1. First there is a hybrid dimension to the practices, which we can prove from the wealth of combinations on the private altars brought by some of those taking part. The cult adapts and evolves without stopping. So, for example, Carlos gets San Simón to smoke and drink a considerable amount, as they do in Guatemala. This practice has its roots in the ways the ancient Mayans worshipped their gods. However, Oscar, president of the guild—who was born in Los Angeles, is young and works in an American government office—does not do this and wants to eradicate this aspect of the cult. He has never really known how the figure of San Simón is worshipped in Guatemala, and says he is worried about the image the cult presents to U.S.A. society. He therefore rejects the consumption of alcohol and tobacco. The *bricolage* he delivers himself up to seems to get farther away all the time from the Mayan world where the cult began. While trying at the same time to reform an institution

---

20 In Guatemala, Maximón is also closely related today to sexual deviation and in Santiago it is said that he was at one time married to a prostitute. Some of the people interviewed reported that Maximón has a woman, called Magdalena or María Castellana. Mendelson also says that the *telinel* (specialist responsible for the cult during a year)—one of the people he interviewed in the nineteen fifties—asserted that 'yes, he walks the streets with his girlfriend, who is a prostitute, a whore woman'—María or Magdalena Castellana—, and that 'he must sleep with her' (Mendelson, 1965: 130). Many of the prostitutes of the capital—women but also men—make the journey to San Andrés Itzapa to offer him worship.

according to the pattern of the guild, Oscar insists on everyone's freedom to worship San Simón in his own way 'following his heart'. He says that he is in connection with the saint. And, to establish contact with him, he favors internal dialogue over respecting codified rites springing from the tradition of Guatemalan native popular Catholicism. This communication brings him a form of knowledge that guides his daily life, and a personal transformation that makes him better and better adapted to his environment. Oscar's quest is not only for a cure or miracles, but for another way to envisage man and his relation to the sacred. Alcohol and the tobacco would be obstacles to this personal fulfillment. We could make a parallel between this way of conceiving his relation with the saint, with an emphasis on the interior, free of ritual restraints, and the notion of 'sacred self' developed by Alejandro Frigerio in this book as a characteristic of New Age currents. We can still see the influence of the New Age matrix on the cult of San Simón as it is expressed in the context of California today.

Another of the faithful is Antonietta, who came from Guatemala about thirty years ago. She says she has a special relationship with San Simón, who keeps her company in the course of her daily life, looks after her house when she is not there, and comes with her when she goes to an interview for a job… She entrusted me with many of her prescriptions for solving all kinds of problems (of love, of work, of physical or mental health) in which she combines many products offered for sale in the folk remedy shops, mixed with medicinal herbs, or minerals… What she does, underlines the commercial side of the cult. She only approaches others in the cult for the feast day of the 28th of October. But for the rest of the year she develops her own domestic cult on her own altar, using merchandise that is also consumed by the faithful in many other urban centers all over Spanish and Portuguese speaking America.

2. Then there is the universal dimension of the cult. This dimension can be found at various levels: in the legend set in motion to explain the origin of the Figure but also in the statements made by the protagonists. In his opening speech for the feast day, the president of the guild did not attempt to inscribe the cult in any particular Pre-Hispanic tradition, but stressed its spiritual and human dimension. He spoke of this feast as the only 'authentic' one to be conducted in Los Angeles; a feast day 'close to each human being, rich in feeling'. He called on everyone to let their feelings show, to sing, to dance, to shout, or to cry 'because that is what being human is', he said. He reminded those taking part of the need for harmony between people. He invited them to form a queue and have the good fortune of dancing with San Simón and sharing his energy. The use of all this language shows new notions, linked to the New Age, have been incorporated into the cult.

3. Finally, the fiesta and the procession present a collective, cultural and folk dimension. For this, referring to Guatemala as the place from which the cult originates appears to be quite central. Everything happens as if the procession were a way of proudly affirming in public in a city like Los Angeles, a Guatemalan cultural identity, formed to a great extent by emigrants from there. Religion is the element that allows them to assert this identity. This Guatemalan origin of the cult allows the faithful to be joined up to a recognized lineage of belief. It gives them legitimacy.

In Guatemala, many of those who are active in the cult of San Simón refer themselves to an identity linked to the Pre-Hispanic past of the country. This dimension is relevant in the current international context that is sensitive to ethnic diversity, and to the assertion of the rights of the indigenous peoples; and the country has to face a request for cultural exoticism on the part of tourists. We have seen the number of priests claiming to be 'Mayans' who devote themselves to the cult has increased considerably over the last twenty years.

In Los Angeles, the Mayan origin of the cult is not so central. They do not deny it. But neither do they insist on it. Those taking part refer themselves to a Guatemalan national identity—and more broadly to a Central American one—which seems more meaningful to them. In fact, the cult was adopted by Central Americans from different countries who have experienced the same migration problems and have had the same difficulties of fitting into the U.S.A. context.[21] The cult of San Simón, with its origins in a country of Central America, its history of a migrant who has come from a far away land, and its inscription in popular Catholicism and in the world of the peripheral Saints who help illegal immigrants, forms a religiosity that is closer to these migrants from Central America. It allows them to mobilize new community referents. Nevertheless, the references to the Indian world are present, and the identity showcased throughout the festivities dedicated to San Simón makes reference to an Indian origin, but in a perspective which is not centered on the Mayan ethnic peculiarity. It leans rather on a generic Indian identity disconnected from the Mayan world. The reference to what is 'Indian'—in the dances, or the costumes—highlights this form of otherness according to a process of positive exoticizing which, if we follow Alejandro Frigerio, is necessary for the full appropriation of a religious tradition by New Age currents. We could then imagine that this work of cultural valuation can one day change the nature of the interactions between the New Age and this revisited religious tradition.

21 In this procession, the most numerous are participants from Guatemala and El Salvador.

Conclusions

I have shown that the cult of San Simón suffered a large number of modifications in the process of being relocalized in the city of Los Angeles. The local populations changed; the rituals and their meanings changed also. Even the story of San Simón and the whole imaginary that undelies the cult, evolved. Because, as emphasized by André Mary (2003), religious mobility also brings itself up to date in the imaginary of the religious actors.

On the one hand, we see a process of commercialization and at the same time of hybridation of the cult, which takes up a position in a Western world dominated by a regime of individualizing beliefs and practices. With its entry into the system of *botánica* folk remedy stores, the ceremonies, the teachings and the symbols linked to the cult of San Simón circulate as items of merchandise in a giant globalized market of New Age spiritualism or Neo-esoteric magic, which in their turn influence the cult. With new uses, new ways of conceiving one's relation to San Simón emerge, and now the faithful can establish a direct intimate relation with him, which transmits positive energies that are associated with other figures whose followers use commercialized products to help with success and personal well-being.

On the other hand, followers of San Simón do not hold to a new or alternative life style, which in New Age spirituality they would do. The festivities organized around his figure do not contest a vision of life anchored in the world of popular Catholicism. For the faithful, San Simón clearly appears as a popular Catholic Saint. For this reason, the procession is organized as a copy of the model followed for Catholic Saints in the countries the participants come from, even though there are differences of form. There are many elements that contribute to showing that the logic of popular Catholic religiosity and of miraculous resources still operates, in association with a popular religiosity that has incorporated terms, objects and metaphors that circulate among New Agers. The cult of San Simón is not translated completely into the New Age matrix, as it proposes magical and miraculous solutions for the concrete difficulties of daily life. And the procession of the 28th of October finally reveals an eminently collective side to the cult. We find many national and 'Latin' symbols in the parade, that make it look more like a civic ceremony, a way of claiming a space in Los Angeles society, of putting a national minority up on the stage to be seen; but it is re-ethnicized as Latino or Hispanic, incorporating the Mexican, the Salvadoran and the Honduran, as parts. And what stands out here is its inscription in a logic that belongs, in the end, to popular Latin American Catholicism, resignified in the context of migration.

Finally, this work brings us to thinking about the relations of the New Age with the cults stemming from popular Catholicism that are very influenced by native cosmologies. It allows us to see that the interactions can be numerous without speaking of a simple appropriation by New Age circuits. In his article, Alejandro Frigerio underlines the limits of the capacity of appropriation by the New Age movement, noting that there is never any mention of devotion to popular saints as being part of the New Age circuit. Our work comes to the same conclusion. In this case, we see very clearly how the cult of San Simón is influenced by New Age currents. Its presence in *botánicas*, the evolution of the specialists of the cult in the multicultural frame of the city of Los Angeles, their adoption of a universalist vocabulary and hybrid practices, the vision of the sacred that certain followers have, which seems to get closer to a holistic vision and to integrating the notion of *sacred self*, all give evidence of what Alejandro Frigerio called—in this work—the influences of the New Age currents, underlining the importance, according to him, of *distinguishing* the appropriations, the borrowings and the influences that the New Age may exercise over other religious groups without the religious group actually entering the New Era circuit. The cult of San Simón has exchanges with the New Age universe but there is no real interpenetration.

CHAPTER 10

Post-colonial Narratives: The Resignifying of the Aztec Conchero Dance as a New Age Therapeutic Practice in Mexico and Spain

Cristina Gutiérrez Zúñiga

Like other traditional practices such as Santeria or taking ayahuasca, the Azteca-Conchero dance has been dislocated from its original context—the popular religiosity of Mexico—and legitimized on a universal scale as a holistic therapeutic practice. This then facilitates new processes of relocation for such practices in places that might be at the antipodes of where they originated, and their incorporation into a market of spiritual and therapeutic goods and services.[1] The crucial point for getting these practices into the New Age version of therapy is its holistic conception of a link between the energy of the individual and the energy of the cosmos, from which comes the orientation towards individual work to achieve personal balance as a way of contributing to planetary change in a period considered axial. It is this link that makes it impossible to think of the New Age as centered on personal subjective well-being, and explains how from its very beginings its spiritual expression has been joined specifically to ecological and countercultural social movements.[2] Paul Heelas, author of the term 'Self Religions' (Heelas, 1996) has observed this holistic dimension, and recognizing the actual immersion of new age provisions and services in the capitalistic schemes of consumption, has created the term 'Spiritualities of life' (2008) to emphasize how these inner-life activities contribute to personal and multicultural relationality, and to a 'politics of the good life' as opposed to mere consumerism.

From a wider point of view than that of studies of religion, it has been suggested that the New Age movement or sensibility is one of the most important matrices of local/national cultural decontextualization, and for the remaking of an authentically cosmopolitan global spirituality (York, 1999: 174; Renée de la Torre *supra*). This matrix would 'absorb' local practices, that are converted

1 On the subject of the transnationalization of the dance, see De la Torre, 2007; De la Torre and Gutiérrez Zúñiga, 2011b and 2012. Other findings from the collective project I form a part of, referring to the transnationalization of the dance to Spain and the U.S.A., have been accepted for publication.

2 See Ferguson, 1981; Carozzi, 2004; Gutiérrez Zúñiga, 1996; and Frigerio, in this book.

 | DOI 10.1163/9789004316485_014

through their inscription-cum- reinterpretation into components of a multicultural, hybridized, collage available for consumption by spiritual seekers almost anywhere in the world. Once inscribed into the New Age, the formerly local traditions circumscribed to a time and a place, that operated using the criteria of a specialized authority in their original context, would now express the maximum degree of 'portability' and 'transportability' proposed by Thomas Csordas. The 'portable practices' are those that can be easily learned, that need relatively little esoteric knowledge, and are not considered as belonging to or as necessarily joined to a specific cultural context, and may be practiced without having to commit oneself to an elaborate ideological or institutional apparatus.[3] Whereas the concept of 'transportability' refers to the fact that the basis of attraction contained in the principles, premises or promises of a religion can be anchored in distinct linguistic and cultural contexts.[4]

According to these points of view, because of its eclectic and universalist dimension the New Age matrix would neutralize or make invisible the boundaries of the places of origin of the traditions, and appeal to a cosmopolitan and authentically global spiritual consumerism nourished by 'new' exotic ingredients.

However, the study of the transnationalization, into European contexts, of practices that originated with American ethnicities, as a result of the processes of contemporary spiritual seeking, has alerted us to the possibility that far from the creation of a transcultural and geopolitically 'neutral' spirituality, what has been generated is new geopolitical meanings of this transnational cultural flow. Indeed, the reversal of cultural flows from the colonial metropolises to the edges has been observed as a constant in the post-colonial era.

3 The original version of Thomas Csordas's definition calls portable practices 'rites that can be easily learned, require relatively little esoteric knowledge or paraphernalia, are not held as proprietary or necessarily linked to a specific cultural context, and can be performed without commitment to an elaborate ideological or institutional apparatus. The many forms of yoga are perhaps the archetypal instances of portable practice, explicit bodily practices accompanied by more or less spiritual elaboration and which may or may not form the basis for communal commitments or transformation of everyday life' (Csordas, 2009b: 4).

4 Csordas explains a transposable image thus: 'the basis of appeal contained in religious tenets, premises, or promises can find footing across diverse linguistic and cultural settings. I prefer the notion of transposability to those of transmissibility, transferability, or even translatability in part because its definition encompasses several of these ideas and also in part because it includes the connotations of being susceptible to being transformed or reordered without being denatured, as well as the valuable musical metaphor of being performable in a different key. Whether a religious message is transposable and in what degree depends on either its plasticity (transformability) or its generalizability (universality)' (Csordas, 2009b: 5).

Csordas himself considers this reversal to be one of the 'intersubjective modalities' in which the globalization of religions is currently taking place (Csordas, 2009b: 5).[5] The New Age is not foreign to this dynamic, on the contrary: in some similar cases of transnationalization to Europe of indigenous practices like that of ayahuasca or Santo Daime, which run in the opposite direction to the colonization flow of the past and which imply an appreciation of such traditions as authentic sacraments or ways of access to the sacred for cosmopolitan citizens of European origin, it has been noted how they are inscribed into a holistic and global sense of 'cosmic and cultural reparation' of the destruction and plundering that occurred in the colonial past. According to Peter Beyer, such an act of reparation would be inscribed in a new dynamic of the remission of sins that would include cultural and ecological damage, in order to obtain contemporary salvation, to whose redefinition the New Age has had a very important contribution to make.[6]

What are the features of the incorporation of the Aztec Conchero dance as a therapeutic practice into the holistic, eclectic and universalist New Age matrix, in the national contexts of Mexico and Spain? How does the memory of the colonial past between these two countries influence the process of transnationalization of the dance from Mexico to Spain? How is this memory re-inscribed into the practice in a post-colonial era? Does the holistic and universalist matrix of the New Age operate effectively to wipe out the historical asymmetries between the contexts of origin and destination? Or does it provide a sense of 'reparation' within the dimension of seeking for a balance of energy on a planetary and personal scale, which is typical of the New Age? To what extent does the New Age matrix itself form a new opportunity to create post-colonial narratives that reformulate, instead of neutralizing, the historically asymmetrical relations between the places of origin and of destination now relating to each other through New Age circuits?

What I will do in this work is to explore and compare narratives of the Aztec Conchero Dance, where its resignifying as a therapeutic practice has been perceived in the two national contexts. These narratives come from the circuits of

5 The other three are Pan-Indianism, the reglobalization of secularly global religions, and the formation of hybrids with the imaginaries of technology and the world economy.

6 'These processes also include incorporation of contemporary forms of religiosity, resignifying salvation in the New Age performative field, and in an attempt at cosmic and cultural reparation. In the contemporary project, the idea of remission of sins is not abandoned; however; instead of sacrifice and charity, redemption is to be found in a search for knowledge and for what Beyer (1994) has called adequate "eco-environmental" relationships'. (Groisman, 2009b: 198).

the dance[7] and of alternative spirituality articulated by two nodal actors from different circuits who have been crucial to the process of transnationalizing the dance: Francisco Jiménez 'Tlacaélel', spiritual leader of Mexicanism and one of the main promoters of essentializing the Aztec Conchero dance to accord with a particular version of Indo-American identity, and Emilio Fiel, 'Miyo', leader of alternative spiritual movements in Spain and founder of the dance group *Mesa de la Cruz Espiral del Señor Santiago de Hispania*.[8]

From the Dance as a Practice of Popular Religiosity to the Dance as an Indianist and New Age Practice in Mexico

The dance has long been a practice in Mexican popular religiosity that makes up 'a form of worship parallel to the Catholic, involving many aspects of Pre-Hispanic religion' (González Torres, 2006: 12). It is in many ways an example of what we understand as the syncretic result of a process of evangelization. In it we can both, observe how the sense of belonging to the Catholic religion is affirmed, and, catch reminiscences of a ritual of the Indians from the central zone of Pre-Hispanic Mexico. The complex of the dance as a ritual practice includes a cycle of festivities around figures of devotion such as images of Christ, Saints and Virgins, a repertoire of praises, music and garments, and an organization based on a hierarchical structure with military discipline. The Conchero dance is an obligation to the Deity and a mutual commitment to one's own and to other Conchero groups.[9]

The importance of the dance does not lie only in its expansion as a practice of popular Catholicism, but also as part of a process of reconstructing the

7 I am using the concept here of a circuit proposed by José Guillherme Cantor Magnani: 'a pattern of distribution and articulation of establishments that allow the exercise of sociability by habitual users, that does not necessarily imply a contiguity in space, but does imply articulation through typical practices' (Magnani, 1999a).

8 These narratives have been recorded in the course of several projects: '*Transnacionalización de las prácticas religiosas neo-tradicionales (a partir de México y del Caribe)*', financed by IRD, Université Paris-X Nanterre, CIESAS, and El Colegio de Jalisco, (2005–2008); '*Religiones transnacionales del sur: entre la etnización y la universalización*' coordinated by Kali Argyriadis (IRD-France) and financed by ANR and AIRD (France), (2008–2010); and '*Transnacionalización y relocalización de las religiones indo y afro americanas*', directed by Renée de la Torre and financed by CONACYT (clave 81926), lasting three years (October 2008—October 2011). They have adopted the method of following circuits, identifying nodal actors and polar actors, which was suggested by Kali Argyriadis and Renée de la Torre, 2008.

9 See González Torres, 2006; and the pioneering studies by Stone, 1975; and Stenn, 1990.

memory of the nation and within that, the predominant image of the Indian in modern Mexico.[10] In this process the Mexicanism movement, and later the Neo-Mexicanist movement created through an eclectic dialogue with the New Age, have played a fundamental part (De la Peña 2002: 96; De la Torre and Gutiérrez Zúñiga, 2011), as we will be able to see in the narratives of their circuits shared by one of their intellectuals.

Narratives of the Dance in the Tlacaélel Circuit

Francisco Jiménez 'Tlacaélel', and several other intellectual leaders of the contemporary Mexicanist movement,[11] discovered the Conchero dance and conceived of it as '*chicontequiza*', meaning a living indigenous practice that has come out of the dark, where it was hidden in the context of the conquest, but preserved by means of guardians linked from one generation to the next, until the arrival of the age of Mexica restoration, the Sixth Sun;[12] its reproduction as a traditional practice overlaid with Catholicism will have kept secrets concealed in its non-verbal aspects, such as the salutation in four directions, certain rhythms, steps and dance movements, and will have allowed it to survive as a form stripped of explict indigenous cosmological meanings for the dancers themselves, but full of clues that might be reconstructed by these intellectuals. Aware of the imminent arrival of the moment when Anahuak (Aztec Empire) would be restored, it was decided by these people to undertake a work of raising conciouness of the tradition and purifying it among the groups of Conchero dancers in different parts of the country. Tlacaélel's pupil Rosalío Albarrán, who adopted the *Náhuatl* name of 'Olpamitzin' as part of assuming his indigenous identity, chose this mission among traditional dance groups in the city of Guadalajara, starting in the nineteen eighties. With another dancer

10 Galinier and Molinié (2006) have coined the term 'Imperial Indian' to describe this representation. The terms Neo-Indian and 'Imperial Indian' are also explained in the article by Galinier, 2010.

11 Mexicanism (*la mexicanidad*) or *mexicáyotl* is a contemporary nativist movement characterized by an affirmation of the Mexican autochthonic, through the reinvention of Pre-Hispanic traditions and by reinterpreting the Mexican past. It is not made up of indigenous people but mainly of urban mestizos who aspire to the restoration of an idealized pre-Columbian civilization and a re-indianization of the nation's culture (De la Peña, 2001). A description of the important activity of Tlacaélel can be consulted in De la Peña, 2002.

12 See the principle element of the 'prophetic corpus of Mexicanism', the rallying cry of Cuauhtémoc (De la Peña, 2002).

from the same circuit, 'Mizcoatzin', he found out how difficult it was to work with these groups because of their resistance to changing their practices, so the two of them combined their work of teaching indigenous traditions, with the foundation of numerous Aztec dance groups in the city, and other activities linked to their Indianist cultural activism. Olpamitzin is also a consultant in indigenous herbal lore, and Mizcoatzin a craftsman who makes cloths painted with glyphs from *Náhuatl* cultures, which are very popular among the dancers themselves, and alternative consumers in the city. His unceasing work is particularly visible in public on occasions like the equinoxes and solstices in places in the city that have vestiges of Pre-Hispanic times, such as *el Cerro de la Reina*, Tonalá and especially in the park of *Los Colomos*, one of the green areas in Guadalajara that function as ecological-territorial reserves, where he offers his teachings, significantly, to passers-by who are searching for contact with nature in the middle of the city (see figure 10.1). This is how Olpamitzin states his approach to the 'rescue' of authentic indigenous dance:

> The original Dance has been kept in the lines of the Concheros, who confuse it with the 'Aztec' dance (...), now we take away the ostrich feathers, the little kilt; we build on what they have given to us and are very grateful, but now we are cleansing it, to show it as it is...we have been readjusting the dress and adjusting the ancient things so they remain in a purified dance.
>
> ALBARRÁN, 2012

The dance is presented from this point of view as a mechanically repeated practice, virtually empty for the dancers themselves of meaning from previous centuries;[13] this condition, combined with its form of master to pupil transmission and, until recently, no formally written record of the dance movements or of their musical and poetic repertoires, makes it a particularly malleable vehicle for the Mexicanism intellectuals, and as such is open to being joined up with different matrices of meaning, as we will see in the other narratives of the various circuits of the dance.

On this reinterpretation of the dance as a practice empty of explicit meanings for the traditional Conchero dancers, Tlacaélel and his followers have superimposed a mythical interpretation of the origin of the cultures of America

13 The Conchero dancers frame their practice in the system of meaning of popular Catholicism, but this is seen by the Mexicanist intellectuals as a meaning imposed through the need to hide its 'authentic' meaning, which would be that of its indigenous Pre-Hispanic roots.

FIGURE 10.1 *Olpamitzin, 'sowing the name' and celebrating the Equinox. Cerro de la Reina, Tonalá, Jalisco, Mexico, March 2006*
PHOTO: RENÉE DE LA TORRE

called 'the theory of the four arrows', according to which all the cultures of America have the same millenary Toltec (Pre-Mexica) origin: following a devastation due to natural causes, survivors from the Valley of Guadalupe in the center of Mexico spread out in four directions 'to invite' all the indigenous nations of the continent 'to form a great confederation'. In this way the solar religion came into being, and maize, beans, squash and chilli were taken to all the ethnicities of America to form the basis of a common culture.[14] This myth is the foundation that allows the dance to be completely unlinked from the complex of Mexican popular Catholicism (as an occult indigenous tradition) and for it to be reinvented in accordance with the findings and interpretations of current dance and ceremonial practices of various indigenous groups both in Mexico and in the United States, principally the Lakota or the Sioux. Thus we can see how the dance practiced in the circuit of Tlacaélel has adopted songs from that tradition, the dancers' dress is simplified using only a minimum of ornamentation and only natural fibers and colors, while in general terms a good part of the Conchero ritual apparatus has been weakened: the

14 Taken from Aldo Daniel Arias Yerena's interview with Tlacaélel, 26 December 2009 in San Martín de las Pirámides. For a complete version of this mythical account, see González Torres, 2010.

importance of traditional commendations transmitted orally and its references to the Catholic world—with its Virgins, its Saints and its emphasis on sacrifice—the propitiation rite of a vigil held the night before a dance, the system of mutual obligations between *mesas* or *conquistas* to hold feasts for each other, and the almost military type of organization within each *mesa* and the duty to maintain an oratory. Further, the practice of the *temazcal* is revived along the lines of the Lakota sweat lodges, the Dance of the Sun or Sundance is brought over and naturally the percussion forbidden by the church is revived with a whole gamut of musical instruments having various origins in America.[15]

It is in this decatholicized circuit of dancers, disposed to innovation of a re-indianizing type, transnationalized and open to the north, that we see the word 'medicine' appear in a particular way in narratives of the dance. Mizcoatzin says: 'The dances are not quick. We are creating *medicine* with the energy we ask for from the cosmos and the earth. We ask for it for ourselves and then for the circle. We do it together and it is distributed to those who are watching and from there to the whole world. This is work we do now'.[16]

The dance itself appears as a process that causes pain but cures:

> The dance is slow, it is like starting to walk, sometimes it is painful, there may be tears, but it is about gradually freeing, letting everything go, smiling when you are really tired, and then suddenly you feel you get a second wind given to you. Everyone can offer their tiredness, so everyone knows, and you keep taking the medicine that the dance is making, so you can go on for hours. We have to think what the step we find the most difficult to take is. We have to think why our grandparents created it. If you get tangled up you need to find out how to untangle yourself, find the thread to get you out of there… If you do things the way they were taught, as they left them for us to do, it is a medicine that is made and handed over as a whole, and we all make use of it, and what is more it fans out to everyone there and to the whole world.[17]

In this short passage we can highlight certain notions or concepts that link the sense of the dance practice to New Age therapeutic practices. Firstly there is the implicit idea of an illness to be cured: it is something in the person that

15 On the mixture of Lakota or Sioux tradition with the Aztec, see Hernández Ávila, 2000. For Tlacaélel's contacts with the North American Indians, see De la Peña, 2001. On the subject of how the Sun Dance was relocated to Jalisco, Arias Yerena, 2011.

16 Interview with Mizcoatzin by Cristina Gutiérrez Zúñiga, 20 October 2005.

17 Interview with Mizcoatzin by Cristina Gutiérrez Zúñiga, 22 October 2005.

needs to be freed, let go of, something blocked inside that prevents well-being. The cure or the medicine is a universal energy, that is invoked or generated by a collective group operating as a circle whose action is not directed only to the healing of individuals but to the collective itself, and as energy it transcends the occasion, to benefit 'the whole world'. The collective action that creates the medicine is the dance, which does not consist of any old magical rite or healing act, but has the specific character of being an inheritance from our Indian forefathers, that was left to us with the intention of healing. So not only is the practice effective, it also has the value of being an affirmation of a tradition of our ancestors. How does it work? In keeping with the idea of the illness to be cured as a 'block' which needs to be released, we will see in this circuit of practitioners that the healing action of the dance is explained as a way of achieving 're-connection'. Reconnection to what? The dance is explained as a way of relating to the natural surroundings and to the indigenous past, as we can appreciate in the following statement by Mizcoatzin himself:

> To dance is to be there and not be there...You have to pay attention to the dance itself, but you have to look inside and outside at the same time. We have to elevate ourselves, but *we have to be conscious that we are below, and not disconnect ourselves, we have to be in communication, and not drift off... The thing is you dance and you are in contact and you begin to see your natural brothers*.... The Chichimeca dance is performed to honor the forefathers who went out to the four compass points to teach the other tribes... You go round, you pay attention, pursuing knowledge, there are always forefathers who are there, you have to pursue them, find them...[18]

Olpamitzin says something similar when he speaks:

> The step with which you ask permission from the four winds, known as the *Nahui Ollin*, or the sign of the cross of the Concheros, is taken in a very harmonious way, slowly, *being conscious of every move as a move that connects* to different cardinal points, to the brethren (of scales, of hair, of feathers, of leaves). (...) their harmonious movements evoke the movements of the stars, the movements of cycles, of climates, of the seasons of the year... Really the dance is cosmogony, *the dance is feeling all the creatures of the universe.*
>
> ALBARRÁN, 2012

18 Interview with Mizcoatzin by Cristina Gutiérrez Zúñiga, 20 October 2005.

Although the achievement of a cure or reconnection is presented as a very pleasant experience, there is no hiding of the fact that it is the result of a struggle that demands a considerable effort from the dancers. It is a struggle that has an energetic character in the circle itself: during the process the dancers come up against resistances, external attractions, weariness, or a loss of concentration, which are interpreted as indicating the presence of negative energies, even 'dark' forces or energies, that must be overcome by the dancer himself or herself. Thus the traditional idea that the meetings of dancers to celebrate the main feasts are 'battles' that need to be prepared for through what are called vigils (*velaciones*), as they are an 'ornamental war' (*guerra florida*), is transformed in the context of New Age circuits into a struggle whose outcome affects not only the circle itself but its surroundings and may even acquire cosmic proportions.

So far we should be able to assert that the therapeutic perspective of the dance in this circuit is composed of various notions: there is an illness, perceived as a 'block', that can be released or unraveled through an interior attitude that the dance facilitates, and with the intervention of the 'medicine' that the collective dance itself generates. The dance circle is a therapeutic space of an energetic kind. The cure that is given is linked to the experience of reconnecting to nature and to the ancestors who handed the dance down to us. In other words, while it is clearly a therapeutic approach allowing the subject to cure his illness, it does not stop there: the approach is in fact linked to a cultural project that reclaims contact with nature and the recognition of a specific cultural heritage that joins us, the heritage of the Mexican Indians.

This particular Indianist reclamation has been very conflictive: in the imaginary of the state, the Mexican nation has been forged as a mestizo nation, and in the imaginary put forward by the Catholic church it is a nation of Indians converted culturally and religiously to Catholicism, that is to say, forged out of de-indianizing.[19] To change this archaic indigenous figure, disdained and stigmatized, into an Exotic Other takes a considerable amount of elaboration of the discourse (according to Frigerio in this book it is an 'exoticized otherness'): a different being, covered by an aura of mysticism and ancestral wisdom that appears, in the light of the failures of modern times, to be an alternative for the future.[20]

19 For more on this cultural conflict, see the work of Bonfil Batalla, 1995; and for reflections on his work see De la Torre, 2007; De la Torre and Gutiérrez, 2011.

20 It is still possible in the context of Guadalajara, to trace, in attempts to recover indigenous traditions, conflicts within the organizations that are identified with the New Age—and

We find as a fundamental part of this claim, in the narratives of the dance, a constant affirmation of its value from a universalist and rationalist point of view, which is a feature of Western modernity. The teachers scorn representations of the dance as the product of an atavistic past or as being exclusive to the indigenous peoples, and they affirm the universal value of this heritage, and its opening without restrictions of religion or nationality. What is more, far from being archaic, as the adoration of a deity may seem to be to modern rational thought, especially if it is totemic or specific to a people or a clan, they say the dance is performed to a life generating principle:

> The salutation we make…is a salutation, not worship. We are saluting the brethren in all four directions, and upwards to the creator, of whom there is no image, who is just one, father and mother, *Ometéotl*, duality. Of *téotl* there is no representation. It is a generative principle. If we salute the sun, it is the strength of the sun that makes life possible we are saluting.
>
> Beyond is God, or *Téotl*, the generative principle, as our forefathers thought. It is all the same: Theos, Deus, it is global, it is universal, it is just one family, one should not get stuck in regionalisms.[21]

In his turn, Olpamitzin says:

> The dance, which the Spaniards saw as idolatry, is not a dance to the gods—that is what the priests and the text books in the schools want to teach; that's all a fantasy they invented themselves. Our culture is alive with the old people who have kept it for centuries, and they give it to us in small bites, a little at a time, until we are well enough prepared to receive it. The dance is mathematics, it is astronomy. Here is the center, here you learn how to measure distance; we keep count, we keep order; we are conscious of space, and of time. Here you learn to co-ordinate yourself.[22]

On several occasions in the course of the field work we were able to observe how the dancers establish the dance as a fruit of ancestral wisdom that is compatible with scientific advances. The dance thus becomes a practice that can be

---

are strongly inclined towards the Orient (García Medina 2010; García Medina and Gutiérrez 2012).

21 Interview with Mizcoatzin by Cristina Gutiérrez Zúñiga, 20 October 2005.

22 Ethnographic observation of the Celebration of the Equinox, and the Sowing of the Name, in the park of Los Colomos, Guadalajara and on Cerro de la Reina, Tonalá, 21 March 2006. Renée de la Torre and Cristina Gutiérrez.

sustained through a modern and rational discourse, following the lead of other ancestral or archaic practices, such as yoga, which was separated from Hinduism and from certain Tantric variations hard for the European public in general to gain access to, and was transformed into an ethereally 'spiritual' practice of great benefit to physical and mental health; in other words, it became 'hygienic' in the course of its translocalization to the West.[23] In a similar way, it is not surprising that in the narratives of the Aztec Conchero Dance, the legitimate image of 'internal discipline' and 'meditation' should be adopted, as in other previously transnationalized traditional practices, especially Oriental ones:

> You don't just move your feet, you have to move the whole body. You have to look for *physical co-ordination.* The dance is to get you to concentrate. It should be done in accordance with the pulse of the heart (...) It teaches us to concentrate on the space, and to be inside. *The dance is a discipline that allows you to be inside and outside at the same time* (...) The dance is not difficult, it is we who are difficult.
>
> The dance mobilizes energy. *It is co-ordination between the body and the mind, meditation in movement.* It is on the same level as Chi Kung and Tai Chi. We make the mistake of thinking that we Mexican people don't have these disciplines.[24]

To confirm this new legitimacy, reference is made to the vision from abroad, and we are invited to forget the prejudices that come from the 'Malinche' side of our national culture when we look at ourselves: 'It is a shame that Europeans value the dances and ask permission to dance—including even the Spanish; Catalans are trying to learn the dances, which happens in Compostela, while we Mexicans are ashamed to dance' (*ibidem*).

We can see in this quotation a first reference to how the interest of Spanish dancers in the tradition is viewed.

Narratives of the Dance in the Circuit of Hispanekas

The dance was brought over to Spain as part of a spiritual and cultural project, Puente Wirikuta, set up between Mexico and Spain around the celebration in

23 For the case of yoga, see Van der Veer, 2009.

24 Ethnographic observation of the Celebration of the Equinox and the Sowing of the Name, in the park of Los Colomos, Guadalajaraon and on Cerro de la Reina, Tonalá, 21 March 2006. Renée de la Torre and Cristina Gutiérrez.

1992 of the 500th anniversary of the discovery of Columbus. The aim of this project was:

> To spread in Europe *la mexicayotl*, the great American tradition based on an encounter with 'the harmony of each and every thing' and to awaken, as a consequence of this tradition, the mysticism of Christianity. An esoteric Christianity of initiation, far from the Catholic orthodoxy and linked to the Way to Santiago, a pilgrimage that represents for these groups the deepest of European spirituality.
>
> DE LA PEÑA, 2002

As a consequence of this initiative, the captain of the dance group Insignias Aztecas, called Nanita Jiménez Sanabria, raised the standard of the Conchero dance to Emilio Fiel 'Miyo', nodal actor of alternative spirituality in Spain since the nineteen seventies, which had been nourished by spiritual currents from the East and the recovery of Celtic reminiscences, and he then became captain of the *Mesa* la Cruz Espiral del Señor Santiago en Hispania ('Division' of the Spiral Cross of St. James in Hispania). According to one of the principal Mexican actors in this process of transnationalization, who was a nodal actor in the alternative spiritual movement in Mexico, Alberto Ruz, the meeting between Miyo and *la Nanita* could not fail to have as a backdrop the colonial history of the two nations:

> And, well, who knows what went on there; it was like a falling in love in both directions, immediate, instantaneous, which made me see almost from that moment on, the one I had always felt was *like the new conqueror*, Christopher Columbus, Cortés, on his knees to *la Nanita*. (...) Something really important happened here: this well known guru, whom I had met in the desert, comes and *submits himself to the orders and to the service of a grandmother of the tradition* (...) And there this wonderful work started, of going from the tradition to the creating that the *mesa* of *el Señor Santiago* then undertook, the spiritual conquest, as la Nanita called it, a *conquest.*

In effect, from the point of view of the Conchero spiritual leader, this diffusion of the dance would mark the start of 'the spiritual re-conquest of Europe, not through the use of force this time, but by the force of love and of the heart' (Ruz Buenfil, 2002). Which she proclaimed in the very Cathedral of Santiago de Compostela in 1992. And so from that year onwards, Miyo undertakes what was called the 'Awakening of Europe' (*Despertar de Europa*) forming local groups and *mesas*, trying thus to recover the sacred Geography of Hispania, and even of all Europe (De la Torre and Gutiérrez Zúñiga, 2011b).

The context of the Spanish alternative spiritual movement shaped the way the Conchero dance was received in those lands; it was incorporated into a large menu of practices by a nucleus of spiritual seekers in the circuit of Miyo himself, of whom only a few define themselves as dancers. In fact:

> Currently, the Conchero oratory is integrated into the Chrisgaia School, where Conchero Dance is offered and practiced as a choice of spiritual therapy together with others. The place was designed to house different stage sets that would re-create various ceremonial centers from different spiritual traditions: Iberian, Hindu, Vedic, Lakota, and among these the Nanita Tower (*Torre Nanita*) has been built (a kind of spa hotel)[25] and there is an ashram of Universal Conchero Dance. A species of multiple 'spiritual-scapes'[26] to provide a setting for the different initiation rituals of the school.
>
> DE LA TORRE AND GUTIÉRREZ ZÚÑIGA, 2011b

What does the dance mean to the Spaniards? In the course of ethnographic expeditions, conducted with Renée de la Torre to learn about this case of transnationalizing the dance,[27] we held in-depth interviews and made an ethnographic observation of the feast of Santiago in the Cathedral of Santiago de Compostela, which included the ritual of a vigil the night before, and I will be drawing the narratives, to analyze the significance of this practice, from that field work, along with fragments of a speech by Miyo to Mexican and Spanish dancers in Mexico City.

The general sense of celebrating the dance during the feast of Santiago by members of the *mesa* is to activate planetary chakras: so it is completely in the matrix of the New Age. In an axial age 'It becomes more important to work on activating the Chakras of Spain. This (the chakra of Santiago) is the main one, and on a planetary level…' This is not because it is on the site of the Catholic basilica, but:

25 In honor of Conchero chieftain Nanita Jiménez Sanabria.

26 We apply the concept of landscape creation as an expression of transterritorialization, contributed by Arjun Appadurai (2001).

27 The vein of activity of this Hispanic leader in the digital networks and its resignifying on the web itself is analyzed and described later on in this volume by De la Torre and Campechano.

> [due] to its primeval, original, rocks. All this area is on a layer of primeval rock. Hence its power. The Way to Santiago is in fact a reflection of the Milky Way. If you notice, it's beside the constellation of the Dog, its faithful companion, like the faithful companion of the Apostle...its power comes from before, because they are where the energy lines of the planet cross...in fact Christianity covered them up.[28]

In other words, although the Feast of Santiago is a feast of official, popular Catholicism in Spain, the participation of the Dancers has no antecedents in Catholic devotion. The 'Hispanekas' who introduced it, started from this re-interpreted sense of an ancestral traditional practice, recovered by the New Age matrix as a spiritual discipline and a discipline of personal and planetary balancing of energies. However, having chosen Santiago as the central symbol of the *mesa,* their participation in the fiesta did have to detach itself from the connotations acquired by the Saint and his cult during what is known as the Catholic 're-conquest' of Muslim Spain in the sixteenth century, and from his role as the Patron Saint of Spain under Franco. And they did it through subscribing to a Pre-Christian sacred Geography, which is what we can see partly reflected in this version of the Road, that Miyo expanded on:

> Santiago is the humble pilgrim who walks the roads, and who can fly over the fields of the soul by means of this humble way...he walks the paths of power. The Way of Santiago is a path with a special telluric energy (...). Lord Santiago is the one who dissolves the rock when he comes to Spain; he is the Lord of the winds and has a Sea Shell on his forehad or on his breast; 'the Lord of the Four Winds', the Christ sense par excellence (...) which means the capacity to understand that good and evil are the same thing in this universe (...) it is called Christ consciousness when the two corners of a duality are in your consciousness in the same way.[29]

In 1992 the contact between Mexico and Spain was in the context of the celebration of what was called the 'Encounter of Two Worlds': that is, facing the historical memory of the two countries. Also, the foundation of the Hispaneka division took place at the time of the Puente Wirikuta; it is therefore possible that for the Spaniards, adopting this originally indigenous practice might

---

28 Interview with Carlos Caballero by Cristina Gutiérrez Zúñiga, 18 July 2009, Santiago de Compostela.

29 Interview with Emilio Fiel, by Renée de la Torre and Cristina Gutiérrez, in 'Torre Nanita-Chrisgaia', Zaragoza 10 June 2009.

have—facing the historical memory mentioned—the meaning of 'purification of spilled blood' (De la Torre and Gutiérrez Zúñiga, 2011b). For example, Miyo himself has stated that his own spiritual campaign meant a reversal of the sense of a military conquest: in reference to the known Spanish war cry '*¡Santiago, cierra España!*' (Santiago: close ranks, Spain!) he said: 'And that is why the cry in nineteen ninety-two is: *Santiago, open the heart of Hispania!*'

However, during the ethnographic observations made in June and July 2009, we did not find any recollections of this particular meaning. Rather, the ritual of the vigil that we were able to witness was very rich in narratives that would make it a therapeutic or healing ceremony, while at the same time we observed the will to recover some of the elements of the Conchero tradition that the Mexicanism movement itself had 'purified'. The keeping of the vigil during the whole night—as it happens, in a Catholic chapel—as well as the preponderance of hymns having a Conchero origin,[30] were some of the most outstanding observations.

To see how this rite has been resemanticized, it is necessary to remember that the meaning of the ritual of a vigil in the context of Mexican popular Catholicism is one of preparation before a dance in a traditional feast; the participation of the dancers in the feast is understood as the fulfilment of an obligation assumed by the group to the Saint or Virgin who is being venerated, as well as to the dance group sponsoring it; to be able to fulfil the obligation, a petition is made for strength to be given to the spirits of the dancers that are represented on an altar, because—as noted above—the dance is thought of and lived as the fighting of a battle, part of an 'ornamental war'. During the vigil, the groups brought together through their relations of reciprocity, assemble in the place of the host group's *Mesa*, and they prepare an offering of flowers, the *Santo Súchil*, all night, while intoning the traditional Conchero praises of Saints, Virgins, and Christ figures. Using the flower arrangements prepared, two rods are made up for conducting a cleansing or a purification of those attending, thus bringing their preparation for the dance the next day to an end.[31]

Found on the altar of dancing spirits—far from being circumscribed to the Conchero tradition—were a wide range of religious and spiritual figures from

30 *La Mesa de la Cruz Espiral del señor Santiago* have published various hymn books from collections of the Conchero tradition followed by *Insignias Aztecas*, but adapted to their New Age vision. A detailed critical analysis of this process of Conchero resignifying can be found in an on-line document entitled 'Más línea que linaje' (more Line than Lineage) written by Eduardo Montaner, an original member of the *Mesa* of the Hispanekas: www.scribd.com/doc/12340024/Mas-linea-que-linaje Consulted: 25 April 2012.

31 For a description of the Conchero vigil ceremony, see De la Torre 2012.

a large number of spiritual traditions, represented by candles of different sizes that were invoked in the course of the ceremony. One member of the group explained it to those of us who were attending for the first time:

> Tonight is a purification, a preparation for the dance. In front (of the altar) are the illuminated beings who have transcended this duality: Gautama Buddha, everyone, tons of them from the European tradition and chieftains of the Mexica, Mexican, Aztec tradition. (For these) the very small candles; and the big ones for our tradition, the European; the Sufi, the Celts…invoking these souls to help us and protect us in all we are about to do.

The second stage, which consists of arranging the flowers for the laying out of the form and of the *Nahui Ollin*, is explained as a work of mandalas, pertaining to the Tibetan tradition, for the integration of the male-female duality. In other words, reference is made to this Buddhist way of working, and to other Oriental concepts that the Spanish seekers feel more familiar with—the Oriental teachings having arrived in the nineteen seventies—for making this fundamental part of the Conchero rite accessible:

> We will make the lay-out of the form, with flowers, some mandalas of flowers. To the left of the *súchil* which is the eight pointed cross, with eight arms, and is the male aspect or principle. We will be making an integration, throughout the ceremony, of the female and the male principles; although the ceremony is a female place, it has male elements in it, because the yin is in the yang, and the yang in the yin, and all that.
>
> On the right we will make the *Nahui Olllin* which is duality, like a yin-yang. The lay-out expresses us as when we are born into this world, where the cross represents all we have to live and experience and learn, and duality shows us that we are always divided into duality as man/woman, night and day, cold and heat.
>
> ANONYMOUS HISPANEKA, 18–19 June 2009

The flower work was done in separate groups of men and women. In the end, when the forms were laid out in front of the altar and before taking a rest, the captain of the *Mesa*, Emilio Fiel, invited us to focus our energy on both shapes. Before trying to introduce the elements of indigenous philosophy that the Mexicanist intellectuals see expressed in this ancient Conchero ritual, the Hispaneka leader proposes a completely novel point of view, but as in the case of the Mexican dancers, it is one that appeals to modern and even to scientific thought: the male and female forms would be 'genetic archetypes' that explain the symbology of this and many other universal rituals, and are thought to represent the 'genetic code':

> He is God, you are Goddess, a while ago we decided that if we say to ourselves 'You are God' that implies also the Goddess within. And with flowers, we go first to the Goddess, then the dancing spirits, conquerors of the winds, then us. Here, we have planted. Planting means the incarnation of life. We have planted two forms of sacred geometry that we were taught by the ancients…those which most raised the *ancient archetypes* and *the genetic archetypes* that we all have. We have before us two forms that evolve everything, that sum up the very essence of duality…(The Nahui Ollin) *is the symbol of the genetic code*; many strands of this code were still blocked, but now with a change of energy, with the nourishment of the sun, with love, the waxing moon and the waning moon awaken, till everything in our lives is equivalent for us.
>
> EMILIO FIEL, *'MIYO'.* 18–19 June 2009

At the third stage of the vigil, the laid out forms are raised in the shape of a cross. Among the esoteric Christian keys of this group, the cross is found to be full of meanings, one of which, as Miyo already pointed out to us, is the Christ principle, of overcoming duality. This process is represented by the flower arrangements:

> This cross that was on the ground is placed on poles and lifted up, and it symbolizes the *awakened Christ*; when you have awoken *your inner self*, and you have a light for the world; that is why there is a candle that will be lit, and there is a mirror in the middle, which is a heart.
>
> Then this duality that was on the ground; from this duality on the ground, the parts come together and they turn into two flowering rods, which means, at that moment *you have already transcended duality*. They become the arms of God. And they have the power of healing.
>
> ANONYMOUS HISPANEKA, 18 June 2009

The fourth stage is the culmination of the therapeutic process, which is known among the Concheros as cleansing with flowering rods, and among the Hispanekas it is explained as an energy healing (see Figure 10.2). The same member of the group went on to explain more:

> Placing the cross in the middle and with these two rods, we are going to conduct a cleansing of all the people who have taken part; the rods will

FIGURE 10.2 *Cleansing in the Hispaneka vigil. Chapel of St. Mark, Santiago de Compostela, Spain, June 18–19 2009*
PHOTO: RENÉE DE LA TORRE

> be passed over the body to make an *energy cleansing of the spirit*, because it is charged with the power of the spirits, and the intention of all of us taking part, with the energy of everyone; it is a moment of inner healing, connection at a spiritual or energy level; if you connect to your inner self, at that moment any disease, any thing, can heal, it's impressive… Once you have lit the flowery cross and you have awakened and you have become a master, then the liberated souls and all the rest are no longer needed, because you have become an illuminated being; here the vigil ends.
>
> ANONYMOUS HISPANEKA, 18–19 June 2009

We can see that the ritual vigil is experienced as an individual therapeutic process, that is however made possible through the collective, helped by the energy that all the other people put into the ceremony, and in concrete terms, into the energy work of arranging the flowers to make the shapes and then the rods. The process is lived as 'overcoming duality' and clearly resonates with notions found among Mexican dancers, like that of spiritual energy connection to your inner self, which nevertheless is part of an energy that flows and is universal, or cosmic.

The process of healing does not finish there, but is part of a larger ritual whose meaning is an offering of energy, by means of the Santo Súchil and the dance itself, to a power point of Gaia-Earth, which Santiago's Cathedral is thought to be on. In the vigil ceremony we can perceive that the first stage is indeed centered on inner healing, but only as a step on the way to its culmination and full meaning. As one of the members of the group told us, before the dance in the forecourt of the Cathedral: 'We dance for ourselves, to offer our dance to Santiago and lay the Santo Súchil on the altar…because it is charged with energy from the vigil and by depositing it at this power point, the energy radiates out from here to everybody, and the more, the better'.[32]

The sense of the collective in the ceremony offers a clear link to narratives of the dance in the circuit of Tlacaélel. However, the cultural project of Indianist reclamation within which the dance is performed in the context of the Mexicanist movement, and especially its dimension of national reclamation, is completely erased from the practice in Spain. So much so, that when I insisted on making a reference to Mexico when observing the ritual, I was told in no uncertain terms by one of the dancers: 'You should understand that the dance is not from Mexico and does not come from Mexico. It was always a fusion, and now is the age of fusion. It is a discipline to get in touch with the body, and put the body in touch with the energy of the Earth, which you have to get flowing'.[33]

The tradition which the *Mexicayotl* movement detaches from Catholicism, is itself caught up in a project that goes on to become an awakening of the Sacred Geography of Europe, and seeks to become universal. This it does by accepting help from any tradition anywhere in the world, and inserting it into a global collage that nourishes a cosmopolitan spiritual journeying. As Miyo puts it:

> We are happy with what we are; we come to offer our energy to the Earth and to life. And what difference does it make that here it's called Montserrat, or Guadalupe…in another place, Los Remedios, and somewhere else, El Rocío or El Pilar de Zaragoza… I can always distinguish: it's the same. *I don't care what anybody calls it, where we are, it exists; it is the*

32 Interview with Claudio by Cristina Gutiérrez Zúñiga, 19 July 2009, Santiago de Compostela.

33 Interview with Carlos Caballero by Cristina Gutiérrez Zúñiga, op. cit.

energy that illuminates my cells and the energy that lives in the heart of our Mother Earth.[34]

Comparison of Therapeutic Narratives from Mexico and Spain

We may observe in the narratives assembled, how the therapeutic discourse, in which curing or healing illnesses or physical weaknesses and emotional conflicts is the main subject, becomes a powerful matrix to provide a pseudo-scientific legitimacy and a universal value to a practice that was originally rooted in popular Mexican religiosity. We could evaluate whether the dance 'travels well' or 'travels badly' in particular cultural and even international contexts, but could not say this of a particular quality; rather that it went through a concentrated process of resignifyings; and that through this process, it is turned into a body practice[35] that helps, according to the notion of a mind-body-spirit unity, to reestablish flows of the individual's energy, and establish a re-connection with his inner self, and to universal energy.

In the cases considered we can see that in various ways the illness to be healed or treated is adjoined to the idea of a block, a hang-up, or of being disconnected. The cure or the healing is understood basically as a *re-connection* and thus becomes an integral part of participating in rituals inserted into a larger collective project, which transposes the same idea of healing onto a planetary scale, thinking of the Earth as a body whose energy channels should be—as in the individual—unblocked, activated or *reconnected*, in just the same way. The metaphors used here remit to the notion of movement, connection, flow and transparency as features of health; as a result, blocks, being disconnected or stuck, obstructions, and opacity, all mean illness. These metaphors become more and more plausible in a world of growing geographical mobility with a multiplication of inter-cultural experiences.

Just as the holistic therapeutical matrix, that covers both the individual and the planet, is a powerful vehicle for disembedding the practice of the dance from the original context of popular religiosity from which its practitioners started, so it is important to stress the continuity of its character as a collective ritual. The collective dimension is to be found both in the conception of healing or curing itself—the medicine or energy is created through the participation

34 Emilio Fiel at the presentation of his book: 'El sol que mora en las tinieblas' (The Sun That Dwells In The Shadows), Centro Cultural España, Mexico City, 10 June 2011.

35 The embodiment perspective has been proved very useful in interpreting the Conchero Aztec dance. See Olga Olivas 2013.

of everyone—and in the objective of the rituals that this conception is woven into: sending medicine to the planet, activating its powerful chakras.

However, contrasting the cultural senses that this collective action is organized by, and practiced with, in the case of the actors of the circuit of Tlacaélel in Mexico, and that of the people of Emilio Fiel in Spain, the discontinuities between them become apparent.

The meanings of the practice in question cannot be thought of only in terms of *message transposability*, like 'a tune or melody performable in a different key' (Csordas, 2009b: 5). Instead of just seeing 'portability' and 'transposability' as an intrinsic quality of the practice itself, making the message of the dance a hard core that might or might not be capable of being translated or reproduced in other cultural contexts, we find it interesting to analyze the process through which it is resignified as a result of the journey. In this way we can observe that its significance in the context of traditional Catholicism is practically abstracted and transformed in order to be able to travel, and when it travels, its success depends pretty much on the context it is taken to. In fact we observe that the dance is practiced with different cultural meanings in each national context, coming from its own historical density and its own 'regime of differences':[36] in Mexico, inevitably, the relation of the dance to indigenous traditions remits afresh to the problem of the original mixing of races in the formation of the nation, and it takes the road of ethno-national vindication in the wider context offered by the spiritual globalization of the New Age; whereas in Spain, it is added to an eclectic menu of de-contextualized ancestral techniques for activating the planet.

In most of the cases addressed, the matrix of holistic therapy fails to homogenize the meaning of the practice and *allows the dance just as it is practiced to be inscribed with different meanings in each context.* This general matrix allows the dancers from both contexts to *converge* in shared collective rituals, which has in fact happened at the various spiritual events around the 500th anniversary of the Encounter of Two Worlds, and continues to take place on the pilgrimages organized by Emilio Fiel to the sacred places of Europe, or at the Conchero festivals in Mexico that the Spaniards have mutual obligations with, as well as in other Regina-ist ceremonies (see De la Torre and Gutierrez Zúñiga, 2011b). But even in these, the presence of particular participants is signified also in a specific and distinctive way. The link between Spain and Mexico is a subject of discussion between the different groups, and remits infallibly to the

36 Segato, 2007: 20. The application of this term to interpreting the transnationalization of the dance between Mexico and the U.S.A. was very useful. See De la Torre and Gutiérrez Zúñiga 2012.

significance of the relation between the two national contexts through the mediation of a past of conquest.

The Mexican dancers felt that the interest of Spanish seekers in the Aztec Conchero dance implied its re-evaluation, but after the experience of its being planted in Spain, where we might say it has only spread as a part of the collage that the Chrisgaia Schools provide to spiritual seekers through workshops and pilgrimages—we already said that the Spanish seekers are not converted into dancers but experience the dance—the founder of the Spanish version recognizes that he had not been aware of the implications of accepting the obligation of captaining a *mesa* of the dance in the Conchera way of understanding it. Even from the new holistic matrix that he has inserted it into, he considers it to be, more than a tradition to be kept alive, a tradition to reinterpret in a way that implies its improvement. In a way that recalls the vision of Conchero dancing held by the Mexicanist intellectuals themselves, Miyo explains to the Spanish and Mexican practitioners, why he is going to dance in the Sanctuary of Chalma, at one of the main festivals for Conchero-Aztec dancers:

> Why do I stop off in Chalma? Why am I with *people who think three hundred years before my thinking* and why do I dance with them? And why when I come here do I sing even to Christ's nails? ... First, because I have seen that this tradition will still be around after 2013—if not, it would not have lasted till now; secondly, because I needed a shower of *humility* when I had just become the most important guru in Europe, and the only way to do that is to get in touch with the wise ancients...what I mean, then, is, why I'm here is because there are people with a magnificent heart (...) there is nothing in our tradition that is not wise, so one should understand!: every human being is born in the sacred zone of the sacred, where the fire of Christ is, also called the second god, the serpent of fire (...) This is why I am with these people, this is why I have come to Chalma to make an offering as so many years ago, in the name of my country, but also in the name of this spiritual reconquest...

When interviewed, he is even more emphatic about his vision of the Conchero tradition as a sort of unconscious source of knowledge that needs to be interpreted, and specifically about Nanita:

> Nanita is a woman with a young spirit, but is old, and her scheme is a scheme of time...she channels and loses consciousness; while channeling she receives messages from other planes, but *she withdraws and is not even conscious of what these consciousnesses say through her* so she leaves

> her material in the hands of other entities and this is an ancient form of channeling.[37]

During the vigil, an inner ceremony of the Hispanekas, he also speaks of the cultural representations that mediate between Mexican dancers and Hispanekas:

> This religion is so magnificent that we have been taught by a few Mexicans performing the dance, who look awful, who don't take a proper step... who have no rhythm, but, what pride when they end! (...) The truth is that sometimes people who do not seem to have had any training (...) their joy when they end, because they have done what they had to do, they do not have to apologize to anyone and...they don't even know what their dance is called and we don't even know if what they did was a dance or...but it is enough: they have made an offering. End of story. So this moment has come for us to recover our innocence more than ever before. Faith is what can heal us and faith shows us this is not something foreign to us, but faith is energy that, between all of us, we move.

Alberto Ruz in turn, makes the following balance as a Mexican, in which he does not speak of sources and interpreters, but of the construction of a brotherood, as a new turn in the history of Mexico and Spain:

> By nineteen ninety-two, then, we had concluded this first stage, the stage that implied the passage of warriors coming here, the passage of emerging warriors from here going to Spain, traveling in Spain, performing ceremonies, holding Temazcal sweat lodges, visiting the sacred sites here in Mexico with groups of Spaniards: Hispanekas now. Because this was creating this *new fraternity, this fraternity that came to give a whole new turn to history*. Here we have returned to find in the midst of the ornamental battles (...) these battles of Teotihuacán, these battles of Chalmita where Miyo, here in the *Zócalo* itself—when he came in for the first time with his dance group and met the different dance groups and met the different captains who would say 'What are these Spanish conquistadores doing coming here to profane our sacred sites', the same thing that happened in Chalma—; that is, really interesting battles, that were important, transcendent, that have been gradually changing the history of this country,

37 As a mater of fact, we can relate these impressions of Miyo's to the practice of channeling in Marian Trinity Spiritualism, a movement that Nanita belonged to.

> of Spain and our relationship, and precisely pointing in the direction...of *a new consciousness of countries, of nations, of religions, of theories, of colors...this new Rainbow nation that between us all we are building up.*[38]

The initial aim declared when the Puente Wirikuta started, seemed to encourage the idea that a transnationalization of the dance would amount to a reversal of the conquest; however, it is necessary to point out—again—that the significance of the relation between Mexico and Spain in the context of a transnationalization of the dance is to a great extent different for the Spanish practitioners and the Mexican dancers: the sense of reconquest is more important to the Mexicans than for the Spaniards, who see in the dance, through their model of eclectic spirituality, an exotic ingredient, yes, but one to be combined with others in their process of spiritual seeking. The fact that the dance comes from Mexico not only is not an opportunity for 'reparation' of the colonial period, as it would be in the case of transnationalized ayahuasca previously mentioned, but it even lacks importance for the Spanish dancers in the model that promotes reinterpretation of a large number of traditions for the creation of a new model of planetary spirituality. Their narratives are not constructed on the basis of a memory of the colonial relation, an element that would seem to continue to be central among the Mexicans.

Conclusions

The portable and *transposable* nature of a practice is not simply an intrinsic quality of the practice itself, it is more the result of a process of resignifying. The case of each of the two nations analyzed here turns out to be exemplary: in the case of Mexico it is a question of resemanticizing the originally indigenous practice through a conflictive process—that even causes splits between the Mexicanist and Neo-Mexicanist movements—in which the indigenous traditions first stigmatized are then made exotic and mystified, using for the purpose a re-evaluation based on looking in from the outside, and an appeal to modern rational discourse to convert it from archaic to ancestral, from a relic of the past to a resource for holistic well-being with which to build an

38 Alberto Ruz is referring to the first encounters between Mexican dancers and Spanish practitioners at the festival of Chalma and at events organized by the Neo-Mexicanist movement Regina, which was started by Antonio Velasco Piña in the *Zócalo* central square of Mexico City at the presentation of the book by Emilio Fiel: *El sol que mora en las tinieblas*, Centro Cultural España, Ciudad de México, 10 June 2011.

alternative future. The language of therapy is in itself a powerful legitimizer that both detaches the dance from the practices of Mexican popular Catholicism, and makes it possible for it to be inserted as one of the global therapeutic body techniques on offer for the individual and the planet. But paradoxically, for all its universalizing character, there persists among Mexican practitioners a cultural sense that directs the practice as one of reconnecting with a heritage that is at one and the same time denied and very much one's own, the inheritance of the indigenous forefathers (or 'grandparents', *abuelos*). This cultural sense is seen to be non-existent in Spain, where indeed attempts are made to neutralize the Mexican origin of this tradition.

Attention to therapeutic language and its ability to incorporate local practices into the holistic, universalist matrix of the New Age, should not obscure the specific processes of the relocalizing of the practices. These processes are historically and geopolitically marked both by their original context and by that of their point of arrival, forming the possibilities and the limits of the resignifying.

Therapeutic language displaces the dance and produces new possibilities for expanding and resignifying it in new cultural contexts, and even creates possibilities for cosmopolitan ritual convergence. Beyond other self centered techniques, the New Age with its holistic component makes the individual isomorphic with the planet and creates therapeutic activities that are personally experienced but have planetary and cosmic transcendence; in this way it allows both global action and taking up the practice from any geopolitically specific place. Even in the ritual convergence of cosmopolitan practitioners (rituals in nodal places), the place of origin of the practitioners constitutes a mark and is in its turn resignified in a particular way: for the Mexicans, it means recognition of what has been denied, a reversal of the conquest, fraternity between formerly unequal parties; for the Spaniards, it is a tradition from a world in agony that is still alive, and like others, forms a spiritual source for building the future, a resource to be reinterpreted in the almost omnivorous holistic matrix of the New Age.

Even incorporated into the circuits of New Age spirituality, the dance keeps features of the process of resemanticizing that were acquired in the distinct national contexts. These processes produce differences in the meanings of the practices, and in the interpretive schemes on the basis of which the presence of the other is interpreted in the spaces of ritual convergence, in the transnationalized circuits of the Conchero Aztec dancers who are preparing for the arrival of a new era.

CHAPTER 11

Unconventional Religiosities and the New Age in Vale do Amanhecer (the Valley of the Dawn), Brasilia

Deis Siqueira

Introduction

The birth of Brasilia was accompanied by two grand creation myths: the Utopian City and the Promised Land (Siqueira and Bandeira, 1997). The former is found in the urban planning and futuristic architecture of the Pilot Plan. This myth converges with another, mystical one, based on the prophecies of Don Bosco, the Salesian saint from Italy who had a dream-premonition that a new civilization, the Promised Land, would be born in the territory where the capital of Brazil was later built. These two myths form the basis of a mystical-esoterical phenomenon that calls Brasilia the mystical city, and capital of the third millenium, or of the New Age.

As it happens, Don Bosco's prophecy is coming true. There are a growing number of unconventional religiosities in the capital and in the region. These groups give themselves many different titles; for example, they might call themselves an Association, or consider themselves Knights; they might be a Center, a City, a College, a Space, or a Faith. They might be called Children, a Fraternity, Forces, a Foundation, or a Group; or refer to themslves as an Institution, a Legion, a Movement, an Order, a Bridge, a Sanctuary, a Society, or a Temple (Siqueira, 2002, 2003 and 2003a). They are unconventional because they do not claim to be religions; they declare themselves to be anti-clerical, anti-hierarchical, and especially, anti-institutional. They do not classify themselves as Catholics Protestant, Spiritist or Afro-Brazilian, that is to say as belonging to any of the four varieties of religion institutionally recognized as such in Brazil.

Theirs is a religiosity that has been described as a broader religious field, a diffused religion, a free floating-flexible religiosity or religious identity, a new religious space, or as new forms of the sacred in contemporary society. It has been referred to as a new mystical-esoterical sensibility, a non-religious holiness; also as a sacralization of individual relations of transcendence. It has been described in terms of a new syncretic religiosity, new religious movements and new forms of religion, and has been regarded as a mystical-esoteric nebula with

 | DOI 10.1163/9789004316485_015

diffuse creeds, a heteredox nebula, and as a secularized religiosity. It has been placed in the category of secular religions, and has been called inorganic religion. It has been referred to as a diversity of identities, or as diversity in New Age ways of esoteric-holistic belonging; and has been called a multi-value and versatile Mystical-Esoteric nebula (Champion, 1990; Heelas, 1996; Hervieu-Léger, 1993; Mardones, 1994; Piette, 1993; Carozzi, 1998; Rodríguez, 2000).

It has been established that in spite of the difficulties in defining New Age, there is a consensus that it began in the 1960s, in the United States, as a small counter-cultural movement reacting against the hegemonic values of modern Western culture and society. This tendency, then, based on the possibility that a New Age might appear or be created, was part of a wider movement of discontent and opposition that included the recovery of pre-capitalist and non-western values, practices and beliefs, that had been denied or devalued by modernity. The movement included the search for new unconventional religiosities, but was not limited to that. At any rate, this search for unconventional religiosities is one of the tentacles of the movement and is in turn associated with many, not necessarily or directly, religious, mystical or esoteric practices (such as therapies, diet and health care regimes, massages, meditations). Thus, according to Magnani (1999:10), the New Age movement includes currents deriving from Eastern religious traditions, as well as from the encounters between contemporary science and ancient cosmology, indigenous traditions and new environmental proposals.

The New Age movement can be understood as a non-centralized group organized primarily in networks, which unites a variety of Western and Eastern cultural traditions (Siqueira and Torre, 2008). Its practitioners may not always identify themselves as followers or New Agers (Possamai, 2001), given that they may be only occasional adherents and also that beliefs may be exchanged, substituted or combined, according to the tastes of each participant (Clark, 2006). Fundamentally, the movement seeks to recuperate a sacred and spiritual experience, to such an extent that New Age customs are often referred to as spiritual practices: Guerriero (2014) and Heelas and Woodhead (2005) refer to the New Age as a Spiritual Revolution.

To understand the sacred from a New Age perspective, it is important to understand the three key elements of its beliefs: (a) its critical, counter-cultural, anti-dogmatic, anti-doctrinal, and anti-institutional posture, (b) its holism, and (c) its presupposition that the divine is to be found in the interior of the person, rather than being external to the self, distant, absolute and powerful. New Age philosophy is not only based on a critical perspective of modern, Western capitalist reality, including its hegemonic religious institutions, but is also characterized by an ongoing quest for new or unconventional religious perspectives.

As the subject existed but there had been no sociological research into it, at the end of 1994 the Sociology Department of the University of Brasilia started a research project into the sociology of affiliations: Mystical and Esoterical Practices in the Federal District. The Valley of the Dawn, *Vale do Amanhecer*, was one of the unconventional religiosities that formed the object of study of the first phase of the project (1994). There is also the fact to be taken into account that this unconventional religiosity has been growing exponentially. Apart from the headquarters of *Vale do Amanhecer*, which are in Brasilia, there are currently over 600 temples of Amanhecer in Brazil and abroad (see Figure 11.1).

While Brasilia was still being built, another unconventional religiosity also arose, apart from *Vale do Amanhecer*: the Eclectic City. Although they are both very syncretic, the latter continues to be a group that is very closed in on itself, with only a small increase in the number of adepts. Most of the unconventional religiosities that were born or made their appearance in the 'mystical capital' and elsewhere in the region, have a smaller number of followers than

FIGURE 11.1 *Front view of the Temple of Doctrine of Vale do Amanhecer (Valley of the Dawn). Brasilia, Brazil, February 20, 2006*
PHOTO: MARCELO REIS

Vale (Siqueira, 2003, 2003a). Scholars of religion in Brazil recognize *Vale do Amanhecer* as one of the most syncretic religious experiences in the country. Its representativeness seems to be undeniable as a reflector of the contemporary search for new forms of religiosity in the West, and in particular in the capital of Brazil. Apart from having been born in the 1960s, its main claim to be representative comes from its preparation for the New Age or the third millenium. Its identification with the New Age provides clues to the 'spirit of the times'.

The key question guiding the discussion here has to do with the forms of dialog with, and of transit between, The Valley of the Dawn and the New Age movement. The aim is to contribute to understanding how New Age is used by popular and traditional cultures; in other words, how it changes and is resignified by them. And also to enquire into the way in which the New Age's matrix of meanings contributes to valuing and resignifying practices, symbols and rituals belonging to the ethnic and/or popular traditions in Latin America. In order to answer these questions, I start by describing the origins of *Vale do Amanhecer*, emphasizing the diversity of elements that came together in the formation of the community's religiosity and identity in the context of Brazilian culture, and then go on to describe the dynamics of its rituals for healing the spirit. On the basis of this information I will contrast the characteristics found, with the elements that have defined New Age conceptually in the context of its origins: in particular the ideas of individual autonomy and perfecting the self. This will make it possible to develop a proposal for explaining a popular example of this movement, which evolved specifically in Brazil, placing a greater emphasis on those features that have linked its collective and popular religiosity historically.

The Valley of the Dawn

Vale do Amanhecer, the Valley of the Dawn, is inhabited by a socio-religious group called the Christian Spiritualist Order, incorporating beliefs that range from reincarnation to communication with extra-terrestrial aliens. *Vale do Amanhecer* and its doctrine were created by Neiva Chavez Zelaya, known as Tía Neiva (Aunt Neiva) (1925–1985),[1] a prophetess or incarnation of the holy (Rodrigues and Muel-Dreyfus, 1987: 111).

---

1 'According to the adepts, Tía Neiva was clairvoyant because she had universal mediumship, that is she had the privilege of being able to use all mediumistic faculties, having unrestricted access to different planes of existence, 'clear sight' of things from the past and the ability to

In 1957 Neiva Zelaya began to have her first experiences of recurring visions. The first spirit to reveal itself to her was an indigenous chieftain wearing white feathers and speaking Spanish: Pai Seta Branca (Father White Arrow). Gradually, Tía Neiva 'accepted her mission' and began to mark out the ways that led to the installation of the doctrine of *el Amanecer*, which has White Arrow (Seta Branca) as the spiritual leader of the teachings, understood here as a set of beliefs, principles and norms that guide, and at the same time reproduce the practices of, the group. Seta Branca is a super-human creature, also known as the supreme leader of the Dawn, who in one of his previous incarnations was St. Francis of Assisi. As Seta Branca had a great mission to perform on Earth and could not incarnate again, he chose Tía Neiva as his replacement for the creation of a doctrine, based on spiritual healing, that would prepare humanity for the coming of the third millenium or the New Age.

In 1964 Tía Neiva had received direct instructions from him about the urgent need to start 'the indoctrination of the spirits' before the third millenium. Starting in 1969, her doctrine came to maturity thanks to the joining in of Mario Sassi, Neiva's companion and 'intellectual' mentor for the messages received by her in their raw form. Sassi would contextualize them and try to give them 'scientific' backing, especially in Kardecist molds.[2] The *corpus* of doctrine and ritual orchestrated by her and by Sassi has remained relatively stable since then.

In 1969 the group set up in Vale do Amanhecer, which is the city of their headquarters, occupying about 1,000 hectares (roughly 4 square miles), with approximately 25,000 inhabitants, some of them adepts and others not, located about 50 kilometers from the Plan Piloto of Brasilia. At first all the people living there were adepts. Then some lots were sold, and a town called Vila Pacheco, with a low-income population, was built on land adjoining the *Vale*. The city has the usual problems of Brazilian settlements lacking infrastructure (robbery, murder and a shortage of health services). Currently most of the population are adepts but not everyone is. During the week, several rituals mix with the toing and froing of people going about their daily business, and at weekends

foresee the future—this both on the mundane plane as well as on the spiritual level: and a special channel of communication with the 'spirit worlds', with the sphere of the holy' (Reis, 2004: 76).

2 Mário Sassi knew many traditions and versions of esoteric thought as well as Kardecist Spiritism. The original Kardecism is defined as being based on three dimensions: the philosophical, the scientific and the religious. Its founder, the Frenchman Alan Kardec, did not stress the latter, which developed very strongly in Brazil, a country that is recognized today as the 'the homeland of Spiritism'.

there is a concentration of activities, which demonstrate that the city is the headquarters of the doctrine, with residents of the Federal District and from other places coming in. One of Tía Neiva's children is the city administrator. The cupola of the doctrine, that he is a part of, coordinates and organizes the religious and doctrinal practices of the place (see Figure 11.2).

As for their creation myth, the cosmology of *Vale do Amanhecer* goes back 32,000 years, as a project of energetic, physical and planetary reorganization. The mythological planet Capella (Capela), or Monster Planet (Planeta Monstro), is thought to be the point of origin of the human species, where all the ancient civilizations came from and where all the 'indoctrinated' spirits will go when the third millenium arrives. Making the Earth a planet of transition and expiation.

(1) In the beginning, in the Andes, there was a Phalanx of Equituman Missionaries, who were androgynous giants, and after two thousand years they disappeared, as the result of a cataclysm caused by the approach of an alien spacecraft, the Shining Star (*la Estrela Candente*), originally from 'planet' Capella. The return of this vessel to the world wrought changes, even where

FIGURE 11.2 *Panoramic view of the religious city of Vale do Amanecer (Valley of the Dawn). Brasilia, Brazil, February 20, 2006*
PHOTO: MARCELO REIS

the Missionaries lived, near what would later become Lake Titicaca, which is, according to this plan for 'spiritual colonization', a creation of the Capellans. Pai Seta Branca, as Equituman Master, commanded the Shining Star on this mission. The extermination of the Phalanx was explained as having been necessary because of the 'distortion' of the principles of the mission: the giants had become ambitious and competitive.

(2) The second group to arrive was the Tumuchís. They came from Capella five thousand years after the extinction of the Equitumans. They settled in an area that is now almost entirely covered by the Pacific Ocean. Their objective on Earth was to continue with the preparations initiated by the Equitumans for receiving a new civilization, as they could handle cosmic energies with their advanced science. The stone heads on Easter Island, the Inca city of Machu Picchu and the pyramids of Egypt are among the achievements attributed to the Tumachís. Seta Branca was the leader of this mission, as the Grand Tumuchí.

(3) Finally, twenty thousand years ago, having by then the same physical structure as now, and being highly populated, the Earth welcomed the Jaguars.[3] They came with a mission to 'regulate the populations of the world'. The Jaguars originated a number of civilizations that came after them: the Chaldeans, the Syrians, the Persians, the Phoenicians, the Aztecs, the Greeks, the Incas, and even the forms found today, whose destinies will converge again, through the Valley of the Dawn, in Capella, their home planet. In this account Seta Blanco was also part of the command, as Chief Jaguar.

The peculiar nature of this religiosity is to be seen on many scales in the sacred space of the Valley.[4] The space hosts a disconcerting religious hybridation with symbolic frontiers that do not have very precise demarcations. As for the buildings, these include the Jaguar waterfall, the Delphic oracle, the Pyramid, the Turigano, and the temple of the Mother. The latter was built of stone, in the form of an ellipse, with a covered area of 2,400 square meters. In the initiation complex built in space open to the stars, called the Solar of the Mediums, or the Shining Star, there are artificial waterfalls, a body of water in the shape of a star with a radius of 79 meters, lakes, stone staircases and straw huts.

3 Jaguar is a name taken from one of the sacred tales of the adepts. Also used is the expression 'Jaguar Tribe' (Reis, 2004). In everyday speech the word Jaguar is used by a Master to refer to another, but it is an identifier of the group itself, as all its members, men and women, are Jaguars.

4 The term 'sacred space' is considered on the basis of Eliade (1998: 295): the *locus* where 'hierophantics' (manifestations of the sacred) occur, when ruptures with the profane take place, to a greater or smaller extent.

Ceremonial spaces are organized according to a mythical, and in some sense also a 'multi-ethnic', geography. Thus, for example, the Turigano, a circular ritual space adjoining the main temple, refers to the Roman Empire; the Pyramid, a site for concentrating energy which serves as a plant generating energy to be distributed through various rituals, expresses a relation with Egypt of the pharaos; the waterfall of Mother Iara refers to the indigenous peoples of Brazil; and the Gateway and Temple of Stone, to the Mayans.

The principal celebrations held by the community, and their titles, also create an impact on visitors due to their singular nature. The calendar is marked by various daily rituals, and consecrations (Ecstasy, Phalanxes of Mastery, Missionary Phalanxes, Consecration of Associates, and of the Indoctrinators), some festivities, and other activities such as meetings with the mediumistic body or specific segments of it.

With regard to the main superhuman entities invoked, the amazement these produce is no less. Apart from Pai Seta Branca, there are, among others, the Queen of Sheba, grandfather Indu; the Knights of Light, of the Black Lance, of the Golden Lance, of the Blue Lance and the Green Lance, of the Middle Kingdom; Ministers, Caboclos (spirits related to the woods and connected to indigenous/*mestizo* spiritual power), Space Doctors, Mermaids, the Three Kings, the Divine Master Lazarus, Angels and Holy Spirits, and the Brethren (the sick, the little ones that have died, Reis, 2001).

The dress worn is if anything the most extraordinary sight of all: the men wear maroon vestments with a protection for the neck. The women wear very colorful clothes that float in the wind, with various layers of very fine material; many adornments in their hair and on their arms; many embroidered symbols and natural elements. Hundreds of people are observed wearing the uniforms of their particular phalanxes, some of them moving on foot, others performing ceremonies in small groups in various parts of the sacred precinct, and others again taking part in rituals with a large number of adepts, either in the Solar of the Mediums, or in the Temple of Stone.

The rite has an indescribably large scope in the sense of individual effort to make sense of the inner and outer world, because it is during this (sacred behavior) that in some way the conviction is born that the religious conceptions are true and the religious norms are correct. In the ceremonies, 'the dispositions and motivations induced by sacred symbols in men, and the general conceptions of the order of existence that they formulate for men, meet and mutually reinforce each other'. And in the ritual, the lived world and the imagined world mix, through the mediations of a set of symbolic figures (Geertz, 1978: 70). In this sense there would be a fusion of the lived and the imagined worlds, penetrating each other through the power of the ritual. In the Valley of the Dawn, the ritual element does not seem to have been reduced to the realms of the sacred. The religious rites seem to be intertwined with social rites: they exist together, are associated, and create each other.

Many visitors have commented that the landscape seems to be that of a carnival. It has to do with an imaginary world, but one that makes sense of reality for those who believe in it. According to the faithful, the costume makes it easy to 'connect' to their spirit/past lives/sacred stories and to identify with their original phalanxes.

In *Vale*, an alliance between the symbolic and the imagined becomes visible. There is a pact that allows the individual to appear in public, and at the same time order his existence. So much so, that the definition by Geertz of religion may be seen to refer to a system of symbols that acts to establish rules and motivations through the formulation of concepts of a general order of existence, redressing these conceptions with an aura of objectivity, in such a way that these dispositions and motivations appear to be realistic (Geertz, 1978).

Identity

Vale do Amanhecer can be seen from the point of view of sociocultural studies, as a privileged space for creating and reconfiguring identity performances. Reflecting on this as being strictly speaking religious, and broadly speaking cultural, an important dimension having to do with identity is perceived, which is the result of representations forged to a large extent by the founder, and belonging to *Vale*, even though they contain religious signs that have been valued traditionally in Western culture, especially the Judaeo-Christian.

These representations unify the imaginary of the followers and give them a mark of identity, to the extent that the Doctrine of the Dawn is also mentioned, but less frequently than the Doctrine of the Jaguar. One can understand this concept as a stimulus to self-classification, that is, to the process of seeing oneself as a member of a social group, so typical of religious communities (Smith and Mackie, 1995: 176). Further, everyone's spirit has the experience of many incarnations, that is, of thousands of years already lived, and so the Dawn exists to revive people's spiritual memory, meaning, to put them in contact with their 'spirit'.

There are many occasions on which, and situations in which, the faithful recognize themselves from times out of mind, in the vestments and in ritual discourses: a recognition of identity on the basis of a group memory informed by the sacred, with the aim of infusing, into the dimension of collective imaginaries, components of a tradition that is vigorous enough to legitimize their actions. According to Catroga (2001: 48), there is no collective memory common to people who do not have the support of memories shared ceremonially, even if the traces show no signs of materiality. Hence the origin of the performances and the living of an 'enchanted' everyday life. These elements are fundamental to understanding the social imaginary of the Valley.

It is common to have recourse to 'ideas and images of the collective representation' (Pesavento, 2003: 43), which construct meanings and organize the world through the continual exercise of memory on the part of the faithful, especially those who lived with Tia Neiva.

Modernity shows itself in the effectiveness of reason, and in the appearance of the human subject as freedom and action: a subject that affirms itself in the will to act and to be recognized as an actor. In this way, subjectifying is expressed as the penetration of the subject into the individual, which consolidates the superiority of one's own virtues over one's social roles, and of moral conscience over public judgement (Touraine, 2002). The construction of new identities and new spiritualities seems to indicate a crisis of established models of identity, and the construction of a new collective being (Castells, 2000). *Vale* makes it possible to think of the strengthening of subjectivities, and the proliferation of groups claiming to integrate identity (Geertz, 2001).

The doctrine allows everyone, whether an adept or just a practitioner, to make a free composition of symbolic elements from the teachings, the practices and the rituals. The doctrine is integrated by a symbolic system of meaning; that is to say, there are individual compositions, but they are not haphazard. The composition becomes meaning, while religiosity passes to the sphere of subjectivity (Bittencourt Filho, 2003). This is an important and novel freedom, either for the individual or for the collective, and it is a central characteristic of the New Age and of the Valley.

These unconventional religiosities, including the Valley, are not only 'religions of the self' (Andrade, 2002); after all, they move around the imaginary construction of a new social group: values and also emotions are shared. Therefore one cannot generalize saying New Age communities are communities 'without essence', which is what Amaral does (1999).

The Expanded Religious Field

Recent studies by Negrão (2008) show that the roads taken by *religiously mutant agents*, of dual beliefs, affiliations and experiences, are multiple or ambiguous in respect of institutional affiliation or religious tradition in Brazil. The principal ecclesiastical teachings and institutions continue to be the source of symbols and beliefs, but the aspect that stands out is the dimension of subjectivity in the construction of the religious, and the growing individualization of religiosity. What is chosen is what makes the person feel good, what answers his questions or even what suits him in terms of his socioeconomic or educational level and his own needs.

At the same time, one's 'own self' cannot be considered in isolation. Perceived as constructions, identities are not fixed, and immutable, but relative, and they change (Woodward, 2000). Subjects and communities are signified by their differences: by 'being' and also by 'not being', even if this proposal does not translate into a polarized, reductionist, reading of the complex reality of *Vale*. Jovchelovitch (1998: 69) postulates that without recognition by the other, the production of meanings and their correlations, that is, the symbolic forms, language and identities, would not exist. This is, after all, a symbolic-religious multireferential. Identity is constructed both by denial and by incorporation of the other. It is therefore worth remembering the concept of appropriation of Chartier (1991: 190): categories must be built in the discontinuity of the historical trajectories. One of the key notions in the case, is that of cultural circularity (Baktin, 1987), and another, that of continual intercultural dialogue, which motivates identity to search for stabilization, and at the same time, ambiguously, makes it live under the sign of displacement, of sliding.

And the mythical world of *Vale do Amanhecer* seeks to revive elements of lost civilizations by putting down roots or making connections to sites, peoples, and different moments: the Mayan, Inca, Egyptian, Greek and other societies considered for one reason or another as being of universal mystical interest. That is, it provides, in itself, pluralism, and traffic.

Healing

The dynamics of the cosmology of *Vale* are organized principally around the performance of ceremonial activities for spiritual healing, connected to the idea of spiritual development, which is fundamental in the doctrine of Kardecist spiritism. Tia Nieva and her disciples consider healing through psychopictography or spiritual treatments should benefit everyone's development, because the Earth is a planet for the rectification of spirits.

For adepts, the final aim of the Valley would be this healing. There is a constant search for the cure of spirits, whether incarnated or not. Therefore the effort to preserve the physical body is largely due to the requirements of the spirit inhabiting it. The healing is a service absolutely free of charge. No money is taken for the therapy, and although it is common for patients to be advised not to stop seeing their doctor, they are told to come back and continue with their treatments. This is how many of the 'adepts' came to *Vale*, looking for cures for physical problems.

Vale do Amanhecer has hundreds and even thousands of visitors every day, who are called 'patients', and the problems they come to be cured of may be addictions, imbalances in social relations, or an illness. The cure is effected through cleansings and recharging their energy, but also through spiritist surgeries. There are operating theaters where patients are treated by spirits. These services are provided free by the *apará* (trance mediums), who are guided by the *pretos velhos* (spirits of old slaves) and *caboclos*. The mediums establish communication, through possession, with the spirits causing the disturbance in the client. Introvigne explains that:

> There is a whole hierarchy of dangerous spirits, from the truly evil to the simply confused, again with similarities to both Brazilian Spiritism and Umbanda. Once the spirit passes from the body of the client to that of the *apará*, the *doutrinador* teaches him or her the doctrine, and guides the spirit to stop disturbing the client and go on towards the realm of light, where good principles will continue to be taught. The client is freed from one or more spirits, and can proceed to the second castle, where the *apará* channels again his or her benign spirit guide, whose words are interpreted by the *doutrinador* for the benefit of the client. While *pretos velhos* appear to be good conversationalists, *caboclos* limit themselves to a few words. The client receives common sense advice, and the OEC [Christian Spiritualist Order] emphasizes that in case of physical illnesses the patient is always counseled to see also an 'earthly' doctor and follow the corresponding prescriptions. But to the client it is also normally suggested that they come again—one session is rarely enough to solve the problem—, and to consider developing the mediumship which everybody naturally has. The final solution of all the client's problems lies in fact in joining the movement, which automatically means becoming a medium, either an *apará* or a *doutrinador*.
>
> INTROVIGNE, 2013: 196

These spiritist practices, which are rather like those of Brazilian spiritism in general and of the religion of Umbanda, are labeled as witchcraft by Evangelical and Protestant churches, who have banned them. In fact over thirty evangelical churches have set up around *el Vale do Amanecer* and compete against each other in conducting exorcisms on customers of *Vale*. The practice of mediumistic chaneling is used in *el Vale do Amanhecer* to favor the curing of psychological, emotional and physical illnesses and complaints that are caused by negative energies and especially by the harm brought about by dark spirits.

Illness is generally defined as disorder or imbalance in the physical, intellectual or social conditions of a person. In the cases of *Vale* and of mediumship, the mission is to attend to the transcendental realm, although the problems deriving from this manifest themselves on physical, mental or social planes.

Illnesses are divided into two groups. Some are the fruit of obsession and take the form of alcoholism, madness, or problems with social relations (of affection or to do with the family). The entities that make up the Valley's pantheon are grouped into Spirits of Light and Spirits of Darkness (the Obscure). The latter include the obsessive spirits, who are considered to be the principal causes of illnesses. Another group of illnesses consists of karmic diseases, which are cured by the expiation of debts acquired in past lives. There are therefore 'programed' and 'unprogramed' illnesses.

According to Gallinkin (2008), the 'adepts' and the 'patients' who go to *Vale* have different readings of what the cure is; the commonest being: (a) interpretations connected to the particular ritual called the Cure (an anchor of the doctrine); and (b) the partial or total remission of physical symptoms, which to a large extent motivates the seeking in *Vale*.

For Gallinkin, the process of healing implies a three-point relation linking (a) the patient with the obsession (an illness caused by spirits), who may transmit the problem to others as well as suffering from it in his own person; (b) the *apará,* the mediator between the human world and the spirit world, who classifies the symptoms, anchored in symbols of the doctrine, and (c) the indoctrinating medium who not only decodes the spiritual messages and symbols for the patient, but guides the spirit causing the obsession towards the Higher Astral.

Psychic healing or a spiritual cure are effected through the patient's subtle body; there is no need for physical contact between the healers and the sick, because the curing is actually conducted by 'space doctor' spirits who attend the work of healing through the medium.

Bricolage and Syncretism

Associating symbolic elements and historical references from the most diverse expressions of distinct civilizations, the Valley of the Dawn seem to qualify for Strauss's concept of *bricolage,* which corresponds to the production of an object from fragments of others (Chauí, 2000): elements from different religious traditions that form a new arrangement.

Most of the unconventional religiosities incorporate into their *bricolage*, emphatically, the fundamentals, the values and the religious beliefs of the Orient[5] (specifically from India, China and Japan; Siqueira, 2003, 2003a). In the case of *Vale*, there is a rich *bricolage* (from Greece, Egypt, India, Rome, and pre-Columbian cultures) and what stands out is Kardecist spiritism and Afro-Brazilian religions, especially the entities from the Afro-Brazilian cult of Umbanda, as we saw in the previous section of this chapter, on healing.[6]

According to Carvalho (1999: 8 and 12), even though Tía Neiva and many other religious leaders started out *ignorant of theology*, following the steps already taken by various lines of Umbanda, they were led to spiritualist doctrines, with roots in Brazil for over a century; thus,

> [a] point of semiotic complexity and rational intelligibility beyond which it was hardly possible to go…was able to extend the spiritualist worldview beyond Alan Kardec, the founder of the teaching, and even beyond Francisco Xavier, its major exponent in Brazil…[to a level that they] could never have imagined… What most fascinates me in the Valley of the Dawn is the symbolic imagination exercised there.

Thus Tia Neiva acted as a 'collagist', as she composed a system with a completely new meaning from various mixed elements. The teaching uses fragments from different sources, but only after reorganizing them, and reorchestrating them in a new compostion and a new structure. Each element is reformulated and readapted, which creates a new significance in the new model. Thus there is, in a way, a concealing, a denial or a marginalizing of the model and the ethos of the systems from which these elements were extracted to compose the mythological *corpus* of the new doctrine: systems that have left only a trace, a vestige, a style or a trait. The relation established by the doctrine between the two ways into the sacred, syncretism and revelation, is extraordinary.

Therefore this fusion of symbols does not appear to fit the theories of syncretism that are based on the stability of the symbol. As has been pointed out

---

5 Campbell (1997) even wrote about a 'process of orientalizing' the West.

6 The principal superhuman entity in *Vale*, Pai Seta Branca, as well as having incarnated as St. Francis of Assisi, also incarnated as a *caboclo*. Carvalho (1999) constructed a typology of Afro-Brazilian religions dividing them into groups: the more orthodox, Afro-centric, more or less 'reproducing' African culture; and the more syncretic religions, which also include non-African entities, originally from the Americas, one of which is the *caboclo* (essentially a person of mixed indigenous and black descent).

by Carvalho (1992), where else has there been a real dissociation from the tradition in the hopes of a new design? An alternative meaning? The entities that are placed in a new context keep their identities but leave their historical characterizations in suspense (Catholic Saints, Spirits of Light, entities of Afro-Brazilian worship) (see Figure 11.3).

The Religiosity of Brazil

In addition to the singularity of the capital, there is the religious particularity of Brazil, well known for its constituent *bricolage*; thus we can start to come to possible explanations for the existence of the Valley of the Dawn. The founding religions of Brazil are Catholicism, Protestantism (both of them with recent diversifications and a notable growth of Neo-Pentecostals), the Afro-Brazilian cults in all their varieties, and Kardecist Spiritism. Today there are transits between all of them, of followers, of values, and of practices—even between Evangelicals and the rest, although to a lesser extent. After all, such transits are

FIGURE 11.3 *Ceremony for the 'Consecration of the Glowing Star' at the Solar de los Médiums, Vale do Amanhecer (Valley of the Dawn). Brasilia, Brazil, February 20, 2006*
PHOTO: MARCELO REIS

marked by conflicts and ambiguities, which are more obvious in the case of the Evangelicals, who refuse to incorporate Afro-Brazilian practices. In the case of a number of these confessions, even though the entities that form the pantheon of African religions are identified with 'evil', there is a symbolic appropriation of their contents: the white dress, salt, rue (a plant of spiritual 'cleansing'), and even the same nomenclature used for the spirits of the Afro-Brazilian cults, has been adopted by the Universal Church of the Kingdom of God. There is an assimilation in this case of a religious attitude that converges more with a process of individualization which is typical of contemporary times and of the New Age. What predominates is the tendency towards a more private faith, without however meaning that the practitioner discards institutional affiliation. At the same time, his loyalty is limited by the sense he finds in the religious group, which may also be quite ephemeral.

At any rate, a movement has been identified that draws apart from the orthodoxy of traditional Protestantism, which is retained by Evangelicals in general, and also includes an approach to the traditional religions of the East. Fonseca (1999: 7) goes so far as to refer to a 'new evangelical age'.

New Age

Movement of Contestation

The teachings of the Valley of Dawn were born at the same time as the New Age, anchored in the need to prepare for the approaching new era. There is nothing more exotic than a Sunday in *Vale*, with the faithful walking through the streets, or seen in restaurants and in sacred places, all wearing clothes that refer to their previous incarnations. The clothing with its gaudy look evokes gypsies, and Indians from India and Mesoamerican Indians (long skirts, of many colors, made with big transparent materials, with sheen, everything very bright). The multi-religious show reminds one as much of Disneyland as of the Brazilian Carnival. In the words of Cavalcante (2005: 168):

> The Valley of the Dawn speaks of Andean Indians, of Mesoamericans, Brazilians and United States Americans, all exposed to a strong mythical aura, who seem to have arrived through systems such as tourist agency leaflets and souvenirs bought on trips, as well as through Umbanda, New Age religiosity and also cowboy movies shown in the cinema and on television. Curiously, in The Valley, the Indians themselves refer to spaceships, creatures from other planets, pharaohs and Egyptian pyramids, and other things.

It is worth pointing out the symbol of the ellipse, which represents the feminine deity: according to Tía Neiva, this will be the cross of the third millennium, which corresponds to the scientific period of Christianity.

The mystical experience of the Valley, like many others, is based on a way of experiencing the sacred that is characterized by the development of a cosmology of its own. Its practices and techniques have been extracted from a series of elements of popular Brazilian religiosity, along with others taken out of their original contexts and used as *performance*, as happens with the New Age. This dynamic is characterized by a fluidity allowing the person who practices it to deal with the sacred with greater freedom in the mystical experience.

Re-evaluation of Pre-enlightenment and Pre-capitalist Times

This revaluing incorporates both: visions of the world from before the Enlightenment, and magical practices, regarded as though they were elements of the natural, physical, sciences. One of the main beliefs refers to Gaia: the Earth as a living organism to which we are all connected in various complex forms (the holistic approach, getting closer to natural sciences). Through esoteric, mystical practices, one is said to be able to have access to spiritual energies and superhuman or infrahuman realities. The search for holistic healing found here is an alternative to hegemonic forms of diet and health. It has to do with another kind of knowledge that is not necessarily based on scientific logic, because this it questions, even though sometimes it leans on it. Various communities were established along with the movement, as alternatives to the system, whose objective was, rather than the unchecked exploitation of nature, a more harmonious life, respectful of the environment, using only what is necessary.

El Vale is a young city but combines many cultural and religious forms from before the arrival of the Europeans in America, including elements from a mythical time before the Christian era.

Eclecticism and Transits

New Age practices are linked to having recourse to eclectic practices that arose from distinct cultural traditions (but especially the Oriental), or from ecology, environmentalism, and peace and holistic movements, and others. It is a decentralized movement, organized in networks, with a lot of movement between practices, methods and beliefs. And in effect, the New Age covers a large variety of practices and of representations. Amaral (1999) uses the expression 'New Age wanderers'. And for Magnani (1999), the different spaces and their practices can be read as a circuit, which the practitioners can transit, creating their way for themselves.

The adepts of *Vale* have a relation to the doctrine, i.e. a relation of adherence, and to a considerable extent, a relation of membership. The practice of transiting between other traditional religions or unconventional religiosities, typical of the New Agers, does not exist here. After all, the doctrine itself cannot be more eclectic than it is. Whatever his previous religious education, a visitor will find familiar signs and symbols (such as the cross, Solomon's seal, the pentagram, the seven pointed star, the crescent moon, the dove of the Holy Spirit which is also the symbol of Ojalá—the principal deity of the Umbanda tradition—, woven ribbons, the eye of the pyramid, feathers, and arrows).

The typical 'wandering' of the New Age, identified by Amaral (1999), gives way, for the followers of Tia Neiva, to a spiritual quest centered on a new way of experiencing the sacred, which creates a new habit, a new form of perception, and acquires importance because it is based on shared values, on emotions brought to life in inter-subjective experience.

Spiritual Seeking Based 'On Oneself': Perfection of the Self, and Self-Development

Spiritual experience and development are centered on a seeking that is lived on the basis of individualities. More important than belief is experiment. In spite of constant references to spirits and master-guides, the aim is, above all else, to have a spiritual experience: personal access to the sacred, the perception of realities beyond the material. For which it is necessary to distinguish the ego (the personality, or social masks) from the true Self or Real Being (also called the Higher Self, the Christian 'I', the Divine Self); also called the inner, the pure or immaterial energy: in effect the divine, also the cosmic truth, which is in every person and not outside him or her, as people are a 'micro' version of the Whole.

Even though the Christian dimension is very strong in the doctrine, with its concepts of charity, solidarity, and compassion, there is a priority having to do with self knowledge, the self development of the adepts. The first step for the neophyte is to attend a course for beginners who are trained to identify their origin, their phalanx, and their past histories. And one of the poles of the doctrine is the education of the indoctrinator (the missionary aim being to prepare a new man for the New Age, and insisting on the centrality of inner experience, through one's own mediumship).

The subject himself is responsible for everything that happens, whether positive or negative. Therefore each individual must assume his own 'karmically' accumulated debts, and these will be paid through an interior 'perfectioning' and by practices of interiorization. On the one hand there is the need to prepare humanity for the third millenium, and later, for its return to the 'planet' it came from originally, Capella. On the other, there are the right (ethical or exemplary) actions directed towards the Other (help one another) which have donations as their guiding thread.

Anti-institutionalism and Holism

Another feature of the New Age is its non-institutional, anti-clerical and anti-hierarchical attitude, as a quest based on the inclination of the practitioner, without going deeply into a religious tradition. The legitimacy of traditional religious institutions is broken. The religion being sought is no longer the Christian-Biblical, but a religiosity based on a variety of sources, especially oriental and indigenous ones. This means that methods to improve physical and mental health (such as shiatsu, bio-energy, or homeopathy), are combined with spiritual techniques (yoga, tai chi chuan, or shamanic rituals), and divination skills for developing paranormal capacities (Spiritism and Occultism) or in order to understand the laws of nature and to predict the future (astrology, tarot, and telepathy); all of these in association with modern psychology for interpreting and explaining the mystical and esoteric practices. The objective is the transformation of consciousness, reaching reality beyond the material, reaching spirituality not isolated from the other dimensions of life, and reaching life that is more harmonious in all its aspects, such as health, relations, education or nutrition. In other words, a 'lifestyle' different to the hegemonic lifestyle of Western society: whether dealing with spirituality or the body, with materiality or personal development.

In spite of the undeniably charismatic leadership of Tia Neiva and the existence of a hierarchy worked out by her, her followers, who call it the Christian Spiritualist Order, do not identify it as a religion. The spiritual and mediumistic dimension is far more important than doctrinal texts in the development of the adepts. It is a lifestyle rooted in another time, much more elastic in terms of past and future. The devotional experience of the Jaguars indicates the identity the adepts can claim to belong to and has the mark of collective reincarnations, with their requirements for moral behaviour.

The Privileged Strata of Society, and Popular New Age

New Age activities have become increasingly popular especially among the younger generations and the more privileged strata of society, with higher levels of education. But *Vale* has a peculiarity that distinguishes it from the New Age movement. In general, alternative or unconventional practices identified with the New Age are not used (health, body, psychology); mainly because in most cases, members of *Vale* come from the least privileged ranks of society, with few economic resources.

It may be thought, in line with Guerriero (in this volume) that the New Age is a movement of the spirit of the times, as there are deeper changes in society influencing the beliefs and practices of citizens and vice versa. In this sense, the practices often classed as New Age would just be the tip of the iceberg.

But why is the New Age movement so visible? Maybe precisely because it is lived, for the most part, by people from the middle ranks of society, with more access to communications media and other social and cultural goods. It should be noted that Carvalho (1994, 1999) refuses to include *Vale* in the movement, especially because, he argues, the majority of its followers belong to popular strata and not the middle class.

But at any rate, *Vale do Amanhecer* remits to the fundamental elements of this spirit of the times, critical of Western modernity, as well as explaining the particularities of the capital city and of the religiosity of Brazil.

The preparation of the 'indoctrinator' for the new age, the mainstay of the teaching, is guided by the development of mediumship[7] (on Kardecist-Christian principles). However, the practices of *Vale* cannot be identified with an individualism that has no concern for others, which is a generalized feature of New Age practices. On the contrary: Christian charity is fundamental to the doctrine.

The protest movement of the nineteen sixties did not last long, but the religious movements that arose at the time continued during the following decades. In this process they left behind the aspects of a strong rejection of the community dimension and finally integrated social values into themselves. However, they kept the features of a new religiosity. This is most clearly seen by comparing them with later examples of the New Age that have a strong degree of adhesion to the hegemonic social values, such as individualism and financial success.

Back to Concepts, So as Not to End

The New Age has a date of birth. According to Carozzi (1999: 186), the movement would seem to have some characteristics that allow it to be classified as

7 Mediumship is one of the capital notions of the doctrine, as it is also for Kardecism. The principal faculties of mediumship are: second sight, the capacity to listen to spirits, premonition, healing, incorporation of spirits, and 'psychography' (the medium works as an instrument for writing messages transmitted by spirits). According to one of the leaders of *Vale* (Silva, 1999), 'the medium is the intermediary, who makes the connection between what is objective and the subjective, which, thanks to the medium's intuition, and through extremely refined connections, connects one plane to another, allowing an exchange to take place between the material word and the spiritual world'.

'the religious wing of the macro autonomic movement that started in the sixties'.

It is a movement that includes the growing 'de-traditionalizing' of the religious sphere in Brazil (Pierucci: 2004). However, the tradition is still present, because it constantly reinvents itself, as pointed out by Giddens (1997). The religiosity of the new era may be seen as something more than a simple syncretism; it is an eclecticism, because there is no synthesis, only a juxtaposition of diverse elements, proceeding from different religions.

In *Vale*, the fusion of symbols amounts to a real dissociation from the tradition in the hopes of finding a new, alternative, re-elaboration (creatures with their own identities situated in a new context, leaving their historical characterizations in suspense).

As noted throughout this work, the search for a 'native self' seems pretty constant, at least in the West (Clark, 2006; Possamai, 2001; Mulcock, 2001). In this sense, here it is possible to identify a return to the 'native', which implies a return to Mother Earth, an 'ecospiritual rebirth' (Mulcock, 2001), and the indigenous traditions do tend to be grouped around a common root. In Brazil it is a matter of indigenous and African traditions that are already mixed in popular religiosity, and include Christian elements as well as Kardecism, introduced in the nineteenth century.

On the one hand, analytical emphasis should be on intersubjectivity mediated by values and emotions and not by institutional supports, although these elements cannot be dismissed if we are to understand the movement. But, on the other hand, the object of our study is broader and may be considered popular New Age, one that can be detected both in the Valley of the Dawn and in other practices, such as Mystical Umbanda, the Goodwill Legion, Santo Daime (and other religious practices that involve taking *ayahuasca*), and even in Neo-Pentecostal confessions like the Universal Church of the Kingdom of God.

Therefore we propose as a hypothesis that there is a popular New Age that might be considered a recomposition of New Age style religious practices and discourses, reinterpeted, and articulated to beliefs and practices found in popular Brazilian religiosities.

And the confirmation is, that the New Age, far from being a block or a homogeneous movement, is made up of a series of diffused practices, some religious, some not. And in Brazil, it appears to have acquired the features of possibly a *popular* New Age in constant dialog with and transit between already existing religions in their respective fields, with the formation of composites of discursive interpenetration and cross-overs that include oriental and occidental elements of popular religiosity.

And one of the aspects that can be highlighted in this hypothetical *popular* New Age remits to the fact that present in it are religious subjectivity, a centering on the self, and the search for self perfection and self development. Nevertheless, they are present in a particular way with respect to what might be called *classical* New Age, because these aspects are not the basic supports of the popular New Age, in which intersubjectivity gains more importance and the self becomes collective.

While the possibility of individual choices is important, these are made objective through collective routes, and shared values. There is autonomy, but the collective is also important, especially in *Vale*, with a strong belief in reincarnations by the group of followers. Individualities are articulated, and resignified, in the collective. Here the sacred is experienced on the basis of the development and construction of one's own cosmologies, a dynamic that offers more freedom in handling the sacred, typical of the New Age, but also takes into account the Other, especially with Christian charity as a reference.

Brazilian religiosity is characterized by much more than polarizations. What stands out is what has to do with relations, the transit between more official and more marginalized religions, which taken together form a gradient or a continuum. Therefore, New Age has influenced and been influenced by both groups: religions and religiosities. Hence, as Guerriero (2006) has said, any attempt to classify it must be limited and restrictive.

PART 4

Ethnic Traditions and New Age

Introduction

The fourth part of this book contains work from several countries in Latin America, these being Brazil, Peru, Guatemala and Mexico.

In the chapters of this part of the book, the aim is to give an account of the complex cross-overs between, on the one hand, the individualized and eclectic religiosity of the New Age movement, that portrays a postmodern sensibility, and on the other hand, the Pre-Hispanic or Pre-Columbian ancestral traditions of these nations. The diversity of approaches and of scales in this section is itself eloquent of how ample this phenomenon is and how important it is in Latin America.

Some of the authors have chosen to explore to what extent the concepts of the New Age, originally from English speaking countries, and those from European sociology about contemporary individualized spirituality, are useful to us for explaining the new expressions of hybrids that have been recorded in the dynamic religious field of Brazil. The chapter by Guerriero provides us with a full introduction to exploring the syncretism and hybridizing that are particularly characteristic of Brazilian culture. His study notes the cross-over between religious traditions of Brazil—Pentecostalism, and Umbanda or Santo Daime—and the new spiritualities that are part of an ethos which overtakes and reconfigures the limits between the religious and the secular.

These studies suggest how we can use the most classical of the New Age concepts to illuminate the porosity and the generalized fluidity between religious matrices that are operative in one of the paradigmatic religious fields of Latin America.

Other writers in this part of the book concentrate on observation and critical analysis of the processes of cultural invention and of re-ethnicizing that have been generated in the context of an intensification of the flows of cultural tourism to places that are symbolic or representative of Latin American ancestral cultures, such as Lake Atitlán of the Maya of Guatemala, and Machu Pichu, sacred site of Inca culture in Peru. The former is studied by Bastos, Zamora and Tally, and the latter, by Molinié.

These ancient places are currently being resignified as New Age ceremonial centers and are becoming sacred nuclei in a new Geography of the cosmos, in which these places are chakras or special energy centers for the healing of the planet, as well as landscapes that objectify the new value that the New Age movement in Latin America gives to Pre-Columbian civilizations, just as the same movement once did for European Pre-Christian and native North American civilizations: seeing them as reserves of ancestral wisdom, threads

 | DOI 10.1163/9789004316485_016

for the construction of a new memory that makes it possible to envision an alternative utopia to that of Western modernity.

This cultural inflection in turn is providing a unique opportunity locally for reinventing the ancestral and ethnic tradition in a post-colonial context, which is also a novelty for the indigenous movements and for the nationalist resistance movements that are seeking to find in these traditions a basis for their political vision and struggle.

So what is the political effect of a re-evaluation of indigenous ancestral traditions where they intersect with the cosmopolitan spirituality of the New Age? The study by Molinié no less than those of Bastos, Zamora and Tally shows us the importance of attending equally to the processes of reinvention and of fictionalizing the traditions at a time when these places are being inserted into the worldwide circuits of tourism and merchandising that have been particularly active during the millenarian effervescence of the year 2012, as well as considering the processes of re-ethnicizing, of political usage, and of creating new Indianist and environmental identitites. The new ways of exploiting cultural and natural resources—water, minerals, and biodiversity—which are concentrated, not coincidentally, in several areas of refuge for ethnic groups, suggest new scenarios for the reconfiguration of resistance movements, in which the sacred notions of Pachamama—who is now being reconceptualized as Mother Earth, as a result of these intersections—are becoming new nuclei, potentially for the convergence of new and old political actors, who might be local or global.

The common thread of the analysis in the chapters of this part of the book is their focus on contemporary processes of invention and cultural creativity that seek, as new uses and meanings are given to the ancestral ritual practices, to make sense of previously unheard of experiences, recreating the tradition and giving it a new viability. The same approach is adopted for a new area of study in the chapter by De la Torre and Campechano, in which they explore the displacements of worlds of meaning created by the dancers of Neo-Mexicanism, who are connected through a cybernetic network of Spanish speaking New Agers. We can see from this study how the dance becomes a matrix that turns virtual navigation on the web into a metaphor and even makes the experience of being connected, made possible by technological means, into something sacred.

CHAPTER 12

The Process of Resignifying the Traditional Religions, and New Spiritual Currents in Brazilian Society

Silas Guerriero

The proliferation of new religions at the end of the twentieth century and at the start of the twenty-first, among these, New Age practices, is just one of the visible aspects of deeper changes that have been going on in the field of religion. Maybe the most significant of these is the very transformation that many traditional religions are undergoing. As with wider social changes, present day religious forms are, more and more, assuming the characteristics of individual and subjective experience. It is true we have not yet reached the future envisaged by Durkheim in which he contemplated the possibility of 'the day when the only cult there is will be the one celebrated freely by each person in his own inner sanctum' (Durkheim, 2000: 30).[1] However, in the case of Brazil we have noted an increasingly common process of resignifying for the great religions. Our objective is to understand how the particularities of the religious field in Brazil stimulate these transformations.

Firstly, we shall continue the discussion of new forms of spirituality, set in motion by certain authors who have taken an interest in them, and then we shall describe the situation of Brazil's traditional religions, and explain what makes this country an interesting field for studying the changes mentioned.

The concept of new spiritualities has been used, over the long term, in the sense pointed out by particular writers, such as Hanegraaff (1999a), Heelas and Woodhead (2005) and others, who identify as new forms of religious association not only those related to an appreciation of subjectivities, but also those that have the characteristic of being detached from institutions. Among them there are some that have a more formal institutional character, but in these the degree of individual autonomy in search of spiritual enlightenment is very great. For Hanegraaff (1999a), the new spiritualities are particular interpretations of religious-symbolic sets. It should be clear that the word spirituality used here does not have any mystical or theological connotation in the most traditional sense.

---

1 Author's translation from the Portuguese.

 | DOI 10.1163/9789004316485_017

The Process of Resignifying and the New Forms of Spirituality

The new forms of spirituality, and among them New Age practices, are gaining more space and visibility all the time. Although the New Age arose specifically in the last decades of the twentieth century, many of its central features date from before, for example the centrality of subjective experience, the autonomy of the individual and the possibility of hedonistic seeking. The exaltation of hedonism came, according to Campbell (2001), from the subjectivist tendency of the Romantic movement in the nineteenth century. According to him, the roots of twentieth century spiritual movements can already be seen in the century before. Neither is the attempt to fuse scientific and esoteric knowledge a novelty. Perhaps what is most striking at the moment, is the fluid state of boundaries and the constant exchanges that the social actors allow themselves to make between one and another of the religious-magic systems that are around, whether new ones or traditional ones. Just as the New Age has started to use elements from traditional Brazilian religions, the latter have started to present ever more elements and practices that could only be seen before in the new forms of spirituality. This phenomenon is possible because there is a wider transformation in society at present that is leading to a new ethos. We agree with Heelas and Woodhead (2005) that this transformation can be characterized through its definition as a theory of subjectivity, in which personal experience of the holy has a direct impact on life and subjective well-being.

In practice there are no pure religions. They all play a part in a constant dynamic of change, of flows and of cultural exchanges (García Canclini, 1997). This chaotic appearance acquires meaning when analyzed from a more elaborate point of view. Then the underlying logics can be seen and we can detect the energy of appropriations and resistances which allows territories to be built. Change and resistance become elements of a process of permanence for the most varied groups. If some decades ago popular traditional religions and the religions of native groups were limited by their ethnic or local contexts, today they gain prominence and are sought out by practitioners living in the big secularized urban centres.

It is well known by now that the New Age has a real appreciation for native religions. In its first years, the seeking went from the most traditional religions of the East to pre-Christian paganism and the shamanism of North America. All of this was seen as a way to have profound experiences through traditions perceived as being more authentic, as they were not contaminated by the evils of Western society. It is interesting to note that at this early moment in Brazil, practitioners on the New Age circuit did not value popular religions. Many of the practitioners were from the more prosperous echelons of society and had a higher degree of education. To go back to the popular religions of Brazil, including Umbanda, was regarded as a regression to primitivism. What was valued, was the exotic. And to be exotic was to be far away in terms of time and space. In the same period, according to Teisenhoffer (2007), the adepts of these new forms of spirituality on European soil sought out the wizards (*brujos*) of Brazilian Umbanda. She shows how Umbanda was remade, far from its original home, on European soil within the world of New Age: as something exotic for the Europeans, though not for the people of Brazil.

Defenders of a sort of traditional purism hastened to state that the New Age was deforming these religions, and using them in a superficial manner for consumption that was only of interest to certain segments of the well to do classes, who were looking for exotic adventure as a pastime. Even the terms used, like esotericism or mysticism, were seen as a cheap simplification that had nothing to do with real mysticism or erudite esoteric thought. It is true that the New Age experiences, whose origins were in far away practices, had almost nothing in common with their original sources. They were lived within a determined grammaticality belonging to certain urban groups. In the end, how do you classify Siberian shamanism practiced in a flat in a city like São Paulo? And at the same time, how can you say such practices are not legitimate and have no meaning for their practitioners?

As is happening now, the transformations occurred rapidly. The New Age circuit widened its search for exotic traditions. Contacts made between native populations and many alternative groups that settled in rural communties from the nineteen eighties onwards, began to change the situation in Brazil. Then, popular Brazilian religions started to be incorporated into the circuit, including those with African matrices. Today there is a relatively large group of indigenous Brazilians from different tribes who give conferences, courses and workshops to anyone interested in seeking the perfection of his being and spiritual elevation. Mantras, reiki and *pajelança*[2] form part of the same repertoire, though they all have different origins. Thus, in the same way as the New Age incorporates natives from traditional religions into itself, so these present a new language belonging to their circuit, that joins cultural elements which are different but acquire sense and meaning within a logic common to the environment. The most interesting thing however might be to look at the other side and realize that the mainstream religions have also been modified. Signs are coming in from all sides that Catholicism, Pentecostalism and other traditional religions of Brazilian society have incorporated New Age elements into

2 *Pajelança* is a term used in the shamanic rituals of many indigenous Brazilian peoples, rituals that are directed by the shaman of the group.

themselves, and even an ethos (cf. Jungblut 2006, Labate 2004, Stoll 2002). This is a two way road, a hybrid in which the parts penetrate each other and leave their marks.

The New Age rescues traditions of the past and of the present. With those of the past it undertakes a process of remaking. To those of the present it gives a new meaning. It is impossible however in this process to avoid altering present day religions, because many of their practitioners end up adopting the New Age way of dealing with the sacred. In all this transit and migration, these practitioners end up going back to their original religion with baggage made up of new ideas and concepts. It is a very rich and dynamic process. You might see a young Hare Krishna person who was originally a Catholic and might even be a member of the ISKCON,[3] venerating a picture of Saint Francis wearing *vaishnava* clothes.[4] Or young Catholics who take part in prayer groups and have started to practice sacred dances after coming into contact with New Age groups.

So far we have been looking at the New Age as if it were a form of religion, as though we could see it as a new religion. The immediate problem is how to distinguish between what is, and what is not, a religion. Like Amaral (2000), we consider New Age to be more an adjective than a noun. It would be difficult to understand it as a solid movement with defined borders and fixed contents, with the rules of belonging clearly established among its members. In fact it is even difficult to say who its members are. As Champion (1989) would say, it is a nebula with uncertain boundaries. However, instead of trying in vain to find its borders we can describe it much better as a fruit of the spirit of the time. Deep changes in society act on the beliefs and practices of citizens. The transformations that traditional religions go through are reflections of this moment of history. The practices generally classified as New Age are the tip of an iceberg, the visible part of a different style of handling spirituality, the body, and personal development.

It is in this sense that we can comprehend the exchange and the fluidity of the boundaries. There is a grammaticality in these experiences, and the elements do not matter very much as long as they fit the underlying logic. Forms of religiosity are examples of the transformations suffered by Western society not only in the religious field but in its culture in general. Beliefs and ceremonies from traditional native regions are now experienced on the basis of new

3 ISKCON, International Society for Krishna Consciousness, is the institution of the Hare Krishna movement.

4 These are the vestments of celibate Hindu monks made of a single piece of orange colored cloth.

references centered on subjectivity. Then again, the new meanings and practices of pre-modern traditional religions can be comprehended as hybrid articulations made by actors included in a postmodern urban dynamic, who value a non-institutional religiosity, subjectively experienced.

It is the existence of a new ethos, a spirit of the times, that makes the different religions and the practices of new forms of spirituality part of an integrated symbolic system, and allows them to make exchanges with each other and the other forms of religiosity that there are, and to be intelligible to each other and to them. It is an ethos for the new forms of spirituality. This does not mean that the traditional forms are being undermined or gradually abandoned. In fact we are facing a new situation in which the diversity of beliefs and systems of meaning is ever more active. In a continual process of secularization of beliefs, rationalizing of attitudes, and individuation, become distinctive markers.

Much has been said of the New Age as an expression of syncretism (Amaral, 2000), but it is not the old syncretism. We should think of hybrid situations, in which the ancient and the new, the traditional and the postmodern, live together and exchange elements forcefully and across borders that are more fluid all the time. There has been a profound transformation seen in social aspects and in the cohabitation of religious worlds. We are no longer dealing with the former model in which identities were clear, and easily recognized. Today we share an extremely broad view of options. We are dealing with transformations that have been going on for some decades. There have been changes in the role played by religious institutions in the organization of societies. Which does not mean that we have come to the end of traditions, but reflects a change in the direction adopted by individuals.

The divine came to be seen as a prerogative of the individual. Now the mystery is to be sought inside each of us. That is to say, the great mystery today consists of everyone finding his own way. Many people acccept the old traditions, such as Christianity, but do not see it as the only way, so it becomes just one of the possible experiences leading to transcendence.

A Catholic is always a Catholic; but is becoming more and more accepting, now, of beliefs that originated in other matrices. This always was a feature of Brazilian religiosity. What is new at the moment is the content of these hybrid formulations. In a society where boundaries are permeable and combinations depend more and more on the autonomy of individuals, it is really difficut to say what their agents believe.

The new values are not limited to those who practice new religions to the exclusion of others, but also penetrate common sense and are absorbed quite naturally, which shows the course being taken by a wide transformation of the view of the world held in society.

The beliefs and the values that are spread through the practices of the new forms of spirituality are evident in the broadest sense of culture, modifying habits and provoking changes in the view of the world of urban society. Traditional values are not simply abandoned but mix in with the new. No inhabitant of a big urban nucleus has failed to come into contact with some form of spirituality that is an alternative to the traditionally established types. Certainly the degree of contact varies enormously, as does the response of each individual to a new world of beliefs. It is no longer a question of aspects of a radical or exotic posture being maintained by some young person of the counter-culture, but one of something habitual that is widely accepted in the social milieu. We can see this diffusion in how naturally these subjects appear in the communications media, either through soap operas or in advertisements or even through personalities who speak of their beliefs and practices in public.

Although these values and beliefs have come to be part of prevailing common sense, they are not perceived in a homogeneous way. The more the population get in touch with the new forms of spirituality, which can even take place through the mass media, the greater the extent to which the system of their beliefs and values is transformed. This change affecting basic values is accompanied to a greater or lesser extent by transformations of beliefs and attitudes. The new beliefs are spread through other mechanisms, such as the printed press or television, and not just through people's access to the new forms of experimenting with religiosity. Even if they are accepted, to begin with, as part of a fashion, staying with them and holding to them shows they have a stronger meaning for the practitioners. The natural way in which they act and absorb the new beliefs suggests that the transformation noted by Campbell (1997) is fully active.

The world of these beliefs is very heterogeneous and therefore difficult to define. We can find elements that point to changes in the image of a higher truth, a personal God, the creator, towards the idea of an impersonal divinity that is like a universal spark and is present in nature. There is also the problem of the relation between these beliefs and science. There are some who have the idea that there is a reality that has not yet been explained by science, and that science should change, and ally itself with forms of spirituality, in order to be able to comprehend other dimensions of our existence. For many, what science denies today and places in the field of the supernatural will come to be accepted as a legitimate part of the scientific knowledge of tomorrow. Old beliefs are recovered and they undergo a strong process of divulgation, for example belief in mental powers and the transmission of thought. New beliefs are incorporated into the process, among them the belief that the Earth is being visited all the time by alien creatures, who in some way have power over us; also observed is the vulgarization of aspects of science such as quantum physics and genetics.

We are going through a reorganization of beliefs that is generated by a varied combination of religious, magical and scientific elements. Distinctive elements that once belonged to other systems form a part of new compositions that, strictly speaking, escape what we understand by religion, magic or science. The believing subject is not even aware of possible contradictions, because what counts is that these new orders guarantee a psychological, and principally affective, coherence.

For the social agents who adhere to these new beliefs, the great systems of explaining the world, science and religion, tend to be considered insufficient. A new system is built on the basis of assuming that it is possible to bring the spiritual closer to the rational by broadening scientific knowledge in a more intuitive sense, which would be able to reveal the most hidden secrets and the big questions of human existence.

There is an important point that needs to be made here. We are speaking of a new vision of the world, but there is no rupture or radical transformation from one minute to the next, when the former vision of the world is abandoned and the new one comes to take its place. We note that there is a transformation going on, and that particular elements, which originated in the context of the new forms of spirituality, begin to form a part, along with the others, of the world view, and of a broader cultural brew. This also means that the people who share this view are not necessarily the carriers of identitites that are clearly defined by the new religious practices. It is not necessary to be a Zen Buddhist to practice meditation. There is a cultural backdrop that nourishes a new ethos and a new vision of the world. The new forms of spirituality cover a wide range of elements that can be exchanged with all society. These elements can come from religious contexts, for example figurines or blessed amulets, or they may derive from a secular context, as shown by Hanegraaff (1999b), for example, the category of 'energy', and appeals to quantum physics. What they say does not seem absurd or exceptional to members of modern society at the start of this twenty-first century. It is all in the mass media and in informal conversations, even if it is treated in a funny tone of voice or as a childish joke. These symbols and ideas permeate society. However, in this world the degree to which they penetrate may vary. People join the symbols together in various ways, creating different syntheses. So it is possible to observe that the system of beliefs shared by the agents and promoters of the new practices is not distinct from the whole set of beliefs that society covers, but takes from the whole set what it finds interesting and places it in an intelligible and comprehensible order. Thus a whole is formed, as though it were a special sub-system that needs to be examined with a very keen gaze.

It should also not be forgotten how porous the borders are between the religious denominations that make up the identities. No one in anthropology would deny that there are no pure cultures, and syncretic combinations are the general rule. However, the term 'syncretism' retains a negative connotation, related to the situation of domination and the passive incorporation of the colonizers' gods by black slaves. Many writers prefer to use other concepts, like flow and hybridizing, and assume that these are more appropriate for translating what goes on in the context of advanced modernism, with its unending transits and resignifyings (Leopold and Jensen, 2005; García Canclini, 1997). Some time ago Pierre Sanchis proposed that syncretism exists in the realm of the biggest societies and not specifically in the religious field. He tries to show how the case of Brazil has always been exemplary, in terms of constant uprooting and the formation of a typical pre-modern syncretism. However, he points out that the Brazilian way of being religious is a phenomenon very like that which seems to have invaded the social spaces of advanced modernism, for example the deep 'de-institutionalization' of religion seen in Europe (Sanchis, 1995). There may always have been syncretism or hybridization but today they have assumed a scale that was previously impossible to imagine. It is worth emphasizing that in the present context the changes are more intense and more constant all the time, and that the limits and boundaries allow an uninterrupted exchange, without risking an identity crisis for the subject manipulating symbolic religious goods. These elements might originally have come from traditional Brazilian religions or from foreign religions that now come in renewed, that is to say in combinations with what is taken as science, from which a new universe is formed where traditions are being invented all the time.

Beyond the boundaries, and essential to the broadest cognitive system of society, we find common elements, and in this specific case, many of them point to changes related to the new beliefs. The transformations that society is experiencing today may be understood on the basis of two separate works that deal specifically with the transformations of the Western view of the world. One of these is the empirical study by Paul Heelas and Linda Woodhead (2005), who co-ordinated a research project in England into the ever increasing importance people give to spirituality as opposed to religion. For these writers there is a real spiritual revolution going on, which aims at a subjective experience of religiosity.

If the individual's references were formerly inclined towards external institutions, like a traditional religion, now they are directed towards internal, subjective matters, like interior states of consciousness, physical experiences, the relation between body, mind and spirit, and others. In their study they establish that terms like spirituality, holism, yoga, feng shui, New Age and inner god are beginning to be more common in general culture than the traditional Christian lexicon. The research showed a strong reduction in Christianity and an increase in the number of people who preferred to identify themselves with some form of spirituality related to inner growth and well-being.

It is important to highlight the perception of the authors that there is a massive change of direction going on towards subjectivity, that is, towards an appreciation of subjective experiences. An alteration is noted in the values and impositions created by outside sources, such as the family, the nation, tradition, corporations and religion, towards inner values based on one's own experience. In these transformations there is a strong appreciation of the body, of emotions, of dreams and of feelings. Subjectivity is transformed into the top source of meaning. In this sense the importance of external authorities is reduced and the individual is motivated to transform himself into his own authority, and to forge his subjective life.

This subjectivity of life has modified the panorama of Western cultural development. In the former model, life was ordered hierarchically by the authority of institutions and their representatives, like the teacher, the doctor, the politician and the priest. Now everything has centered on the individual: education is focused on the student, health care on the patient, the market is focused on the consumer, and also religious experience is focused on what the believer expects and wants.

On the basis of these changes, Heelas and Woodhead establish the difference between religion and spirituality. Spirituality is not the same as the traditional experience of Christianity where, for example, what defines it is devotion to God and an intense relation with the divine through a mystical attitude. The new spirituality is centered on autonomous inner experience and the dissolution of traditional forms of committing to the sacred (Heelas and Woodhead, 2005: 12–32). It is more about experiencing an inner path around a founding myth that says we are all divine beings with the potential to attain fullness. A path has to be trodden and everyone has to tread it on his own. Salvation is inside everybody and depends on the individual's choices and the experiences that follow from them. As mentioned above, in so far as the New Age is the spirit of a time, it would fit nicely into the definition of spirituality proposed by these writers.

A different reading of the transformations Western society is going through comes from a fertile article by Colin Campbell (1997). The British sociologist says the vision of the Western world is undergoing a process of Orientalizing, which does not mean the presence of oriental religions in our society—although this is one of the most evident features of the new forms of spirituality. What it means, is a profound change in Western theodicy. For him, Orientalizing is not simply the entry of cultural products from the East, like spices, clothing, therapeutic practices, religions and other things. All of these elements could have been incorporated into our society without necessarily provoking changes to the system. That would be the most ordinary and the most anticipated course of events. But according to Campbell, this is not what is happening. It is in the field of values that this oriental theodicy is perceived. Less narrow beliefs, and ideas such as monism, the unity of body and spirit, enlightenment, intuition, ecstasy, and spiritual and mystical religiosity now make up the larger universe of Western belief systems. That is to say, without being restricted to isolated groups, oriental cosmology may be perceived at various levels of Western society. In the same way, it can be said that the values of the new forms of spirituality, whether from the East or not, are present in society in a broader way. They appear in the discourse of people in the big communications media, they form a part of advertising campaigns and are included even in educational programs or in new scientific paradigms. Seen in this way it can be stated that they form a part of common sense. Once again, use of the category 'energy' is illuminating. As well as being a category that remits to the world of science, it is also susceptible to being manipulated by agents who may feel the 'energy of an environment' and can 'control the energy' to their own benefit.

For Campbell, the cultural paradigm or theodicy that has sustained the practices and thinking of the West for two thousand years is now undergoing a process of being replaced by a paradigm that traditionally characterized the East. Some categories distinguish the two styles from each other: on one side, we have the quest for synthesis, a vision of the whole, an appreciation of subjectivity and of intuitive and deductive knowledge; on the other, there is an emphasis on analysis (which made the whole advance of Western science possible), a fragmented vision, and a search for objectivity and for a rational and inductive type of knowledge. In this short list, we can see that many of the new forms of spirituality stress aspects attributed to what Campbell called the oriental model (1997: 8). One of the most apparent aspects of this change can be perceived in the concept that everyone has of ultimate reality. From a dualistic vision, with a divine creator, perfect and separate from the rest of the world, we have passed to a monist vision in which there is no separation between the sacred and the profane, as the whole universe, including human beings, is seen as something bearing meaning. Another aspect has to do with a lessening of the importance of the religious institution, and with the rise of a mystical type of religion that is more individualistic, syncretic, and relative, and has a strong belief that spiritual elevation may be attained by means of the effort of each individual, like a perfection of the self.

Although the new religious expressions are clearly marked by a consumerist connotation, they are just part of a much larger process of change. Maybe they are what Heelas himself called a religion of the Self (1996), the religious expression of a society centered on the individual. But the new forms of spirituality do not make up a world separate from the rest of society. In this sense, other religious expressions should also be undergoing these changes. And this is what we can see in several movements inside the big traditional religions, in which the faithful are looking for their own ways to live their religiosity, without submitting rigidly to ecclesiastical authorities. If the process is obvious in the new religious expressions and principally in those called New Age, the same process is beginning to be seen in the traditional religions.

In present day society, there is a significant set of practices and services that promise well-being to their adepts and that highlight the triad of body, mind and spirit as a central component of their discourse. Many of these activities originated in distant exotic religious traditions, such as oriental religions or indigenous shamanisms. For many of their followers, especially those who claim to profess no religion, these practices are not religious in any way, although they are profoundly spiritual in the sense that they seek spiritual development. A good example is the practice of yoga. Coming from a religious world, it is practiced today as a physical technique that provides spiritual well-being. For many of its practitioners there is nothing to suggest that it is a religious practice, and many do not even imagine its origins, linked to Hinduism. However, many, even the erudite, see yoga as one of the most widespread practices of what is commonly called the New Age movement. In this sense Hanegraaff can help us. For him, one can even think of secular religions, of which the New Age is a case (1999b).

Hanegraaff (1999a) proposes a new view of the concept of religion and applies it to an analysis of the New Age field. For him, the forecast by Durkheim of interiorized religions, made a century ago, has been confirmed in the spirituality of the New Age. In order to analyze what he calls secular religion (and the New Age, which is a good example today), Hanegraaff orders a critical revision of the idea of religion elaborated by Geertz. The latter defines his concept of religion thus: any symbolic system that influences human actions through the provision of ceremonial forms of contact between the world of everyday reality and a more general meta-empirical framework of meanings (Hanegraaff, 1999b: 147). This formulation of the concept, says Hanegraaff, applies to the notion of religion in general, but should be analyzed so we can appreciate the forms that are actually manifested in society. To do so, two sub-categories are required: that of 'religions' in the plural, which are always manifested through a specific religion, and that of 'forms of spirituality'.

Religion (singular) can be manifested (and frequently is) in the shape of religions (plural), but does not necessarily have to do so. Religion can also be manifested as what the author calls 'a spirituality'. For him, a form of spirituality is any human practice that keeps up a contact between the everyday world and a more general meta-empirical framework of meanings, as mentioned above, by means of individual manipulations of symbolic systems, while religions are always institutionalized.

For Hanegraaff, this concept of a form of spirituality is fundamental for interpreting the New Age movement. Although knowledge in a formal religion appears in a systemized form in doctrines or theologies, these are less important for preserving the community of the faithful, than the narratives and fundamental images shared by its members. This is what he calls collective symbolism. The same thing occurs with the forms of spirituality. There is also a symbolism shared by a group of believers, made up of images and stories that have a strong moral influence on individuals. These are stimulated by images according to a code of group conduct. Although this is easier to see in the case of religions, among the forms of spirituality the same process goes on. In this way we can comprehend how individual experiences are also framed in wider social contexts, as the symbolism is collective. According to Hanegraaff, forms of spirituality can exist in religious or secular contexts.

Similarly, we can remember what Heelas (2008) points out is an ethic of humanity internalized and experienced within the individual, but always in harmony with the wider humanity. Its difference from secular humanism is precisely the source that feeds this ethic, in which humanity is regarded as a sacred inner source. Life and nature as a whole, are seen as sacred.

Individuals can interpret and experience a collective symbolism derived from a religion, and can do the same with non-religious symbolic systems. Such is the case of New Age forms of spirituality. In this sense, we can understand the use of positive visualization in the processes of healing practiced by New Age adepts. Many of the elements that go to make up the idea of visualization (images and narratives) are taken from a scientific or para-scientific world. They do not come from religious systems. As an example of secular collective symbolism, Hanegraaff uses quantum mechanics—as it happens from the field of science. Few of the people who use the images and the narratives of quantum mechanics, like that of interference by the observer in the behavior of the object observed, the idea of a particle as both wave and matter, the notion of energy, etc., know exactly what they are talking about. They have at best a vague notion, and for the most part hardly more than an assumption, that quantum physics explains the fact that consciousness interferes with reality, or they may just have an idea of other possible applications of this science. For many New Age practitioners, quantum physics explains the existence of other dimensions of reality and makes it possible for the spirit to be elevated through exploring these worlds. A group of people can unite around these ideas in the full conviction that they share a common cause which is in the service of a good for all humanity. What we have here is not exactly a science but a set of myths of science that serves as a basic collective system.

For the laity, scientific discoveries sound like fabulous things. For New Age adepts and defenders of a change in paradigms, the new science cannot be tied to models of modern science, as these models are seen as materialist, whereas the new science should try to get closer to a form of spirituality.

It does not matter much to what extent the people who embrace these values understand scientific thought. For Hanegraaff, contemporary society is not based on scientific rationality any more than pre-enlightenment Christianity was based on Christian theology. Few people at the time engaged in theological discussions or understood them, just as few people today have mastered the world of particle physics. In one way or another, anyone can personally recompose some collective symbolic system, religious or not, and create a form of spirituality of his own. This would explain the growth in beliefs and religious experiences that are more interiorized and individualized all the time.

A form of spirituality can arise from a religion that already exists, but it can also arise from outside that world. For Hanegraaff, the New Age is an example of a form of spirituality that arises from a pluralist secular society. This secularization can be noted in the degree to which forms of spirituality that are ever more autonomous and disconnected from a religion, confront institutional religions. The confrontation between them implies a competition for formulating new syntheses that give individuals the possibility of staying in touch with a meta-empirical picture of meanings. Through this contact, which is often of a ceremonial type and implies images and ideas, people give their everyday experiences meaning. In a secular society, religion does not disappear, but faces competition from other collective symbolisms, now formulated autonomously by social agents.

The New Age uses both religious symbolic systems (preferably those farthest off from existing institutions) and non-religious systems. An example is the case of quantum physics mentioned above. The world shared by the New Age, which would be a set of beliefs and symbols, does not originate in an existing religion, but in a large number of symbolic systems coming from various sources that are reconfigured through the advertising of the mass media, as in the case cited by Hanegraaff (1999b), which has incorporated elements of science.

In so far as there is no common authority or established structure, the individual is free to evaluate the religious implications of the symbolic systems available. Heelas and Woodhead (2005) pointed to a process of individualization of religion and autonomy for the individual. This phenomenon does not happen only in religion, but appears in several processes of social life. The New Age expresses, in this way, the characteristics of a broader phenomenon.

Otavio Velho (1998) emphasizes the change of an old cultural paradigm in progress. Although it is rooted in a Gnostic tradition, Velho states that it is not necessary to go to the ancient traditions for the gnosis of today which is presented in a diffuse manner, as a product of the spirit of an age. In this sense, it is similar to the perspective of a 'cultic milieu' (Campbell, 1972). This spirit of the times would be influencing the way ancient religions are experienced, without necessarily forming new cults or religious groups. The term de-traditionalization attempts to account for this phenomenon. There is a true decline in the force of tradition, whether religious or not, in guiding the individual's behavior (Velho, 1997). For D'Andrea, groups from the traditional religions incorporate derived practices and worldviews of the New Age universe (D'Andrea, 2000).

These new spiritualities do not require a rigid institutional control. Away from the traditions, there are numerous possibilities for new compositions, including the creation of new mythologies with secular elements. The New Age can be understood as a strange mixture of secular and non-secular elements. The autonomy of the individual in it may be comprehended better by saying that followers of the New Age do not allow others to tell them what they should or should not believe. They start from the principle, and this may be understood as the symbolic center of the New Age, that the Self undergoes an endless process of spiritual evolution, through which it learns from its experiences, in the greatest variety of combinations produced by the individual himself.

But if the composition of these new spiritualities is given by secular elements, how can we tell whether we are dealing with a religion, or simply with a set of physical practices whose aim is well-being? To understand this situation better, it is useful to provide some examples, considering the fact that the New Age is composed of an extremely varied multitude of beliefs, practices and even affiliations. What could be religious about a course of *feng shui*, when this millenarian practice from China merely deals with a configuration of energy flows? Would Tai Chi Chuan not be just a form of physical exercise, like so many others practiced in the gym? Does reading a self-help book, that delves into knowledge of neurolinguistics, and is found on the shelf of a small shop selling incense, crystals, natural products and little figures of gnomes, frequented by characters belonging to the New Age environment, have something to do with religion? Following the position of Hanegraaff (1999a), we can understand this world, which at times has only secular elements, as a form of spirituality, or rather, as a religion (in the singular), as it has an influence on human actions, through the provision of forms of contact between the everyday world and a more general meta-empirical picture of meanings. The meta-empirical picture includes the founding myth that each of us has within himself the greatest cosmic potential, that God is in everything, and that the goal and the mission of everyone is to reach full enlightenment. This enlightenment comes through an endless spiritual evolution, and is attained on the basis of the lessons that each of us apprehends from the experiences we ourselves have created.

New Forms of Spirituality and Brazilian Society

One of the most outstanding features of the new forms of spirituality, as we have seen, is the central position in them of the individual. The perception that the divine is found inside the subject led to a lack of trust and to a break with the traditional models that were centered on the institution, and especially to a breaking away from traditional ecclesiastical forms. For some, the old dichotomy between sect and church would be running out of time because what was at first a movement in effervescence would now be a mystical type of religion (Campbell, 1997). Institutions creating meaning would lose their power, and the individual would find himself with less ties all the time, and so be able to build a world of beliefs by himself. However, we have come to realize gradually that even within the new forms of spirituality, we can also find a contrary position. Wandering and interim affiliations are being, or have been, replaced by permanent adhesions, or at least ones that are considered permanent for as long as they last. Many individuals insist on staying in traditional institutions, but their ethos imposes alternatives to the way they belong to that religion or feel it.

It seems that in Brazil, the process of atomizing religions, and of transit between religions, has taken forms that do not exist in other countries. The historical development of religion in this country, with official Catholicism and the practice of a multiplicty of expressions, provokes a peculiarity in religious trajectories (Negrão, 2008: 266). We are used to saying that Brazil is a fantastic country for students of religion, because we find a wide and varied range of religious experiences here. What is this peculiarity? Maybe the answer is in the culture itself, and the way in which Brazilians cope with traditional values. The expression of a popular religiosity, independent of the official one, has been quite evident ever since Brazilian society was formed.

We may note that the Brazilian person is prone to establishing new religious hybrids. It is worth remembering that some sociologists, such as Lísias Negrão (1997), had already pointed out the existence of a set of common elements in most of the traditions found in the field of religion in Brazil (whether Christian or not) that makes it possible to belong to two or three religions, and also allows mobility between them. Changing from one religion to another, which in the end guaranees greater religious pluralism, does not require any rupture or conversion. It might be a simple adhesion motivated by casual factors linked to the life history of the subject that transits from one religion to another.

This peculiarity of religious transit in Brazil shows that the institutional bonds were never very rigid. So the appearance of new forms of spirituality had the effect of a transit by the followers of traditional religions, not only to other religions but also towards new experiences. The response was immediate. The traditional religions, having a less rigid structure than elsewhere, also began to incorporate new elements.

In the Catholic area, the first signs came from the Charismatic Renewal Movement, which challenged the church hierarchy through its much greater emphasis on charisma. A distinctive and prominent feature of this group is the willingness of its members to have an intimate and direct experience of the presence of God. Constant tension between the heterodox and the orthodox led the hierarchy to impose disciplinary control, on many occasions. However, this was never enough and this movement is the one with the biggest growth of all the segments of the Catholic Church in Brazil. Categorized as having a conservative disposition, it contrasts with the Ecclesiastical Base Communities (EBCs) who have always been more concerned with politicizing the faithful than with devotion. It is common today to see groups of young people taking part in activities that used to be linked to the EBCs: conducting energizing practices, sacred circular dances and devotions to Nature at specific phases of the Moon. There is a transit among charismatic devotees that makes many of them attend holistic events. These are all attitudes typical of the New Age that could not have been imagined in a Catholic environment until recently. There are many different groups today belonging to the Catholic church that cultivate mystical devotion of an emotional nature, centered on the individual; examples of these are the New Song, groups of Catholic *Axé* (an Afro-Brazilian style of music) and the so-called 'Christoteques' (*cristotecas*), which can all be found in the dissertation *Dançando para Deus*[5] by Luisa Sena (cf. Sena, 2011). For the

5 Dancing for God.

charismatics, the God every individual feels inside is no longer the Being of absolute transcendence that the Church proclaims. We can observe that there is a transformation going on in the consciousness of a constantly larger number of expressive sectors within Catholicism.

In Pentecostal Protestantism, the process appears to have started earlier and to have acquired greater dimensions. Jungblut (2006) perceives a Gnostic vein in the relation of believers to God. He called it the 'New Ageing' of sectors of the Pentecostal world. This process is characterized by the detraditionalizing of religion, which led to the adoption of practices and cosmologies in tune with those of the New Age. He also cites, as a typical element of this process, a particular reading of the theology of prosperity, which makes the Pentecostal believer assume postures of enrichment, hedonistic personal pleasure, and the search for self-help within schemes very like those of the New Age set. In the case of some Pentecostal churches, their discourse is very like that of the new forms of spirituality. An in-the-world salvation is sought and any suffering is to be avoided.

Kardecist spiritism is also not left out of these changes. Although the centralizing organizations like the federations do not like the look of it, many spiritist centers provide a variety of activities that were originally New Age, like reiki. Seen by many as being like the famous 'pass', it is a process of laying on of hands in which the medium acts as a channel between the spirits and the patient, getting the flows and energies to act in favour of a cure. Apart from reiki they practise color therapy, radiesthesia, healing through crystals, pyramids, tarot, and other things. In the discourse of these new mediums, there arises the idea that knowledge should be channeled to accelerate personal evolution. A radical change, typical of the New Age, can be appreciated in the ethic of caring (charity), so important in the spiritist doctrine, that is now starting to be discarded to make way for personal prosperity. One of the greatest publishing successes in Brazil is that of the books by Zíbia Gasparetto, a spiritist who has distanced herself from the orthodox doctrine and works on the subject of self-help. Here also, there is a strong debate with the theology of prosperity. Stoll (2002) identifies two tendencies in this spiritist environment: on the one hand, an approximation to science, or para-science, through studies of 'projection-ology' and 'consciousness-ology';[6] on the other, towards what

6 '*Proyecciología*' (projection-ology) is the term used by those who share a reading, considered scientific, of Spiritism for out of the body experiences or astral projection, when the subject is deliberately and consciously aware of the spirit leaving the body. '*Concienciología*' (consciousness-ology) is the term used by the spiritist doctor Waldo Vieira for a new science dedicated to the study of consciousness independent of the body.

is more identified with the New Age circuit and that of self-help. All the same, as far as our analysis is concerned, they are both of them reflections of broader cultural changes that are going on at the moment.

In Umbanda, we also find a somewhat analogous situation. Umbanda is a Brazilian religion *par excellence*, but has relatively few followers (cf. Concone, 1987). It started out at the beginning of the twentieth century as the fruit of an amalgamation of elements from devotions with an African origin, the native religiosity of the Amerindians, the spiritual tradition of a Kardecism popularized by then, and a rustic Catholicism lived by the least favored sections of urban populations who were starting up in the South-East of Brazil. Since then it has undergone a rather conspicuous diversification, with a pluralist and eclectic liturgy.

Possessed of a wealth of elements of belief and magic, Umbanda inherited from spritism a moralizing tendency, principally related to charity towards one's neighbour, as well as the notion of reincarnation and communication with the 'guides' or spirits through mediumship. Syncretic from the start, but restricted to the most marginal groups of urban populations, Umbanda went through a change, starting in the nineteen seventies. The better educated and better off sectors of society began to attend their places of worship. As the fruit of this influence, some Umbanda groups adopted new elements that came from the echoes of the counterculture. Thus was formed a new concept, that of Esoteric Umbanda, based on Oriental Occultism, combined with Rosicrucian and Theosophical studies. Although the term Esoteric Umbanda had been around since 1960, with the teachings of Magno Oliveira, who defined Umbanda as deriving from the Hindu term *aumbhandan*, meaning 'combination of divine laws', the great leap of differentiation from Africanized Umbanda came in the environment of New Age. This was when various branches arose, like the Umbanda of Inititation, with the synthesis proposed by the *Pai* Rivas Neto.

Unlike traditional Umbanda, which remits to Afro-Brazilian roots, Esoteric Umbanda takes its marks of identity from the mythical civilizations of Atlantis and Lemuria, as well as the Oriental exoticism of ancient India. According to Rivas Neto (2002), the original Umbanda is the primary source of wisdom and should be rescued after having suffered every kind of deformation. Esoteric Umbanda is certainly very different from the traditional version, principally in questions that require a more intellectual type of study and are only considered by a few. However, it does keep similarities in doctrine that make it preserve its identity as Umbanda. Aiming for deep knowledge, it ends up discarding much of the more pragmatic magic that is common in Umbanda. Here, magic is transformed into the search for deep universal knowledge. Does this make it poorer? Maybe. But on the other hand it acquired forms that did not exist before. All recent quantitative measures signal a reduction in the number of Umbanda adepts in Brazil. We may ask ourselves whether such a reduction might not be due to the lack of an elective affinity with society at the start of this, the twenty-first, century. Could Esoteric Umbanda be a postmodern way out for Umbanda? From our point of view, any affinity would come from the cultural mix that traverses relations in the first years of this century. An appreciation of the centrality of the individual makes the mystical quest quite reasonable. The fight to get Umbanda recognized as a religion among others in a plural and secular society has established some interesting initiatives, like the creation of the Faculty of Umbanda Theology, following an esoteric line, which hopes to be approved by the Ministry of Education and by the academic community as an association promoting an intellectualized type of knowledge.

Another interesting religious tradition that should be noted is that of Santo Daime. It was born in the Amazonian region at the start of the twentieth century, and is the fruit of syncretism between native rituals, popular Catholic beliefs, and spiritism. In spite of a strict control of behaviour and the requirement of obedience to the master and the doctrine, it spread through the big urban centers from the nineteen eighties onwards and today is part of the New Age circuit, with places of worship in several countries. We might consider Santo Daime to be a Christian religion, because one of its pillars is the experience of a popular Catholicism natural to the inhabitants of the interior of the Amazonian forest at the start of the nineteen thirties. Today, this religion has dozens of centers and communities scattered over the whole territory of Brazil, and thousands of adepts in over twenty countries of the world including the U.S.A., Holland, Spain, France, Germany, England, Argentina and Japan. One of its central features is the use of ayahuasca, a herbal infusion of indigenous origin with psychoactive properties. For adepts of Santo Daime, the drink is more than simply receiving light and energy, and they treat it as a form of mystical experience which can only be spoken of by those who have had it. The drink is regarded as a divine being, capable of transmitting knowledge. The current view of ayahuasca cannot be understood on the basis of how the ancient indigenous people saw it, or of how it is seen by indigenous people today—as many indigenous groups do still make frequent use of the plant. The conceptions presented today are undoubtedly based on a grammaticality from outside the origins of Santo Daime, which was gradually adopted as the cult penetrated the big urban centres in the nineteen eighties, already within the logic of the new forms of spirituality.

After the death of the founding master, one of the representatives at the time broke away from the group and started a new association and went to live in a commune (Labate, 2004: 70). In the late seventies and early eighties, with the alternative movement, as it then was, booming, some young urban wanderers searching for an alternative to the life they were leading, joined the community. In 1982 the first church of this type was set up outside the Amazon region, in a large metropolis of South-East Brazil: Rio de Janeiro. Six years later it reached São Paulo. Some celebrities from the world of television and the arts affiliated themselves to Santo Daime and that was when the first attacks arose in the press, mainly related to the use of ayahuasca. It was already in the big urban centres, where it had been tried by an ever wider spectrum of individuals in search of self-knowledge, and ayahuasca came out of the limits of the rituals imposed by the Santo Daime religion and started to be used in other spaces, like therapeutic consulting rooms, and in the vindication of other traditions (Labate, 2004: 91). In all of this, a mythical reference can still be observed to the symbolic space of Acre, in the Amazonian region. New unions are possible, from the experience of urban shamanism to hybrids like the Hare-Daimians (*hare-daimistas*).[7]

Labate points to an urban network of ayahuasca consumption that includes a variety of elements, many of them close to the New Age circuit. There can be found in it, Osho meditation groups, body therapies, events, collective healings, the use of flower remedies and other, similar, practices (2004: 31). Typical of a new form of indepedent spirituality, which is separate from institutional religions, this new use of ayahuasca inclines towards self-knowledge and spiritual self-development. Any resembance to the New Age is not just a coincidence. Alongside these new experiences of taking the drink there continue to exist, in ever greater numbers, traditional Santo Daime centers. The uniformity and strictness of the ritual, the division of men and women, and the contents of the songs, which turn out to be quite traditional and conservative, collide with our postmodern vision, of autonomy for the individual and a loss of values. The most interesting point is that the adepts of this religion in the big urban centres, have nothing to do with the traditional past of the Amazonian forest, except for a mythical and symbolical relation. Some of them cross over into other affiliations characteristic of the New Age, although a certain rigidity remains to their boundaries.

To sum up, we have in this field, of the ritual use of ayahuasca, two examples of experiences that appear to be opposites, but form part of the same logic. If we continue to observe the institutional boundaries of the religions, we shall keep seeing Santo Daime on one side, and keep looking for the New Age on the other. If we comprehend them as two sides of the same coin, we can understand

7 The term is used by natives to refer to the followers of the Hare Krishna movement who use Santo Daime.

both the existence of the two, and the constant fluidity of symbols, values, beliefs, elements, and, mainly, social agents.

These different symbolic systems are not autonomous systems nor are they closed. There is a principle of conmensurability between them all, provided by a wider variety of culture. The apparently fragmented experiences form an ordered whole, if thought of from the point of view of the individual and not of institutions. Not that we are eliminating the external dimension with this. The external dimension exists, and marks the difference in personal choices. In a dialectic relationship, it offers what the agents demand, but at the same time it influences this demand by offering particular types of products.

As Stark reminds us (1985: 27–30), in the past, religious controversies found their privileged space in institutional discussions and they aimed to replace one institution with another. Today the panorama is different. Individualized, the new forms of spirituality do not replace each other, they complement each other. Adhesion is much more the result of personal decisions than the imposition of institutional norms. In this way, many different combinations become possible. Elements generated in a specific environment can quickly migrate to another. Any attempt at an interpretation on the basis of definite institutional forms, turns out to be inadequate. It is necessary to comprehend these compositions from the point of view of the individual, not in the postmodern sense of there being an absence of meta-narratives, but on the basis of there being a profound change in the idea of the universe and in the comprehension by the individual of the world. Thus the new ethos penetrates all consciousnesses with greater or less intensity, and it is impossible for the faithful of traditional religious institutions not to be affected by it.

The introduction of new elements, and their combination with the traditional ones, as well as the very permanence of native aspects, experienced now in new contexts by people to whom they were previously foreign, can be understood on the basis of the creation of a common grammaticality, proper to this spirit of the age. It has to do with something that is like what happens to a language that keeps its structure but can receive new elements, in this case either coming from the new forms of spirituality or else revived from tradition, though now with new meanings.

This new ethos shows an immense cultural dynamism. We are not dealing with homogeneous units that mix purely and simply, but with admixtures, ruptures, contradictions and new constructs. It has to do with something dynamic, carried by its own agents through the porousness of the social fabric.

The case of Brazil provides determining elements in the current transformation of the religious field. The reduction in institutional ties, allied to the Brazilian habit of constructing unofficial religious trajectories of religious experience, makes the country a challenge to traditional theories for analyzing the new forms of spirituality. The central problem in addressing the subject of transformations that have occurred in the religious field, on the basis of the established religions, is that the majority of cultural concepts define the culture itself and regard the New Age and the new forms of spirituality as things in themselves, without managing to comprehend the view that the producers of these new religious forms have of them; that is, the point of view of men and women of flesh and bone. To observe these transformations on the basis of these subjects may mark the difference. It is necessary to incorporate the notion of creative individuals.

CHAPTER 13

The Invention of Andean New Age: The Globalization of Tradition

Antoinette Molinié

From its very beginning, the New Age movement was receptive of beliefs and rituals alien to its Western origins.[1] Its holistic approach allows the movement to absorb foreign concepts. Furthermore, its tolerant nature opens the way for infinite variations since its principles are sufficiently vague to admit adaptations. One should also bear in mind the colonial flavor of the relationship that the New Age entertains with other cultures it calls 'traditional'. The New Age freely draws from these cultures since its clear conscience is based on principles of harmony and brotherhood. Thus in recent years in Latin America, a whole galaxy of New Age movements has been invented. They combine an amazing variety of local traditions to build a global ideology. This process reveals a marvelous creativity. In all Andean countries, but particularly in Peru, New Age movements show remarkable dynamics and originality. After a long process of de-Indianization of the Andean culture, especially by means of the folklorization of its traditions,[2] a general trend towards re-Indianization and even a Neo-Indian movement can now be observed in Peru (Galinier and Molinié, 2006; 2013), particularly in Cuzco, the ancient capital of the Inca Empire. The Neo-Incaism that originated there at the start of the twentieth century with the development of Nativism has gradually mingled with the New Age current.[3] This gives a special shade of color to Andean traditions that were believed by many observers to have been stable since the merger of Christianity with Pre-Hispanic cultures.

It can be argued that we are witnessing a worldwide phenomenon, and, in accordance with current fashion, one can brandish expressions such as 'globalization', 'transnationalization', 'internationalization', and the like. One can also use expressions such as 'syncretism', 'admixture', '*mestizaje*' or 'hybridization'. It is obvious that all these terms are, in fact, redundant and tautological, because there is no purity of any culture. The real problem brought to light by these discussions is the genesis of a culture, with the peculiarity that efficient

1 For an overview of the New Age, see De la Torre (2011).

2 For more on this process, see De la Cadena (2000).

3 For a first study of this process, see Molinié (2009).

 | DOI 10.1163/9789004316485_018

communications accelerate the process. However, a general theory of cultural development would be useless without specific data. Here, on the basis of ethnography, we will observe a culture that is being elaborated before our eyes (Galinier and Molinié, op. cit.). While indigenous societies have developed gradually since Christianity was grafted onto the Pre-Hispanic culture, and a 'World System' could then be re-appropriated with the creation of 'cosmologies of capitalism' (Sahlins, 2002), Neo-Indian cultures are forming at the speed of modern means of communication, which accelerate borrowings, cultural ambiguities and fusion. This accelerated pace allows us to observe *in vivo* and, in an almost experimental fashion, a concrete process of ethnogenesis. However, this cannot be generalized, because precise data can only be gathered for specific processes. For this reason, we will study a ritual that we observed in 2002 in the region of Cuzco in Peru. At different stages of its celebration, the ceremony reveals the ingredients that make up its substance. On the basis of this concrete case, we will later be able to define some of the cognitive procedures of the invention of the Andean New Age.

We will begin by showing how Neo-Indian rituals have adopted the traditional Andean form of offerings, the *despacho*, while introducing imported elements. Next we will observe the 'Inca-ization' of tradition: indeed, some historical and archeological knowledge about the Inca empire has been injected into the healing session that we are studying. We will describe the Incaist context in which Neo-Indian ceremonies are currently being invented (Galinier and Molinié op. cit.; Molinié 2009). Next we will analyze the transformations of traditional rites in the framework of the Andean New Age. For this purpose we will compare Andean beliefs with those of the New Age, in particular, with reference to sacrifice. Andean messianism, as revealed through the myth of the impending return of Inkarrí, is now expressed through the global search for a universal Inca. This quest takes the form of mystical tourism. We will attempt to ascertain its scope, meaning and relevance.

Sacrificial Offerings: The 'Savage' Dimensions of a Rite

After walking for several hours, we reach the foot of Picol, one of the most sacred and most imposing mountains in the region of Cuzco.[4] The ceremonial

4 The Andeans practice the cult of worshipping the mountains, and traditional medicine, which often consists of making offerings to these divine beings, who have their own hierarchy and kinship relations. See for example Ricard Lanata (2007).

space is idyllic, beside a river, facing a waterfall. The *paqu*[5] is not a native of the local communities, as we used to see in our earlier visits, but a person from Cuzco who likes to conduct his healing sessions here. For convenience we will call him a Neo-shaman. We will explain the meaning of this expression later on. His patient has arrived earlier this morning by plane from Lima. He suffers from depression and has great hopes in the 'traditional' cure that we will now describe. The procedures combine several cultural registers as well as the emergence of a Neo-tradition with features that we can recognize in various semantic fields of the Andean culture. Ultimately, this rite reveals the dawn of an Andean New Age, which we will study in more detail.

The first stage of the cure consists of a *pago* also known as a *despacho*, that is an offering to the local god of the mountains (Apu). This ceremonial offering is made in traditional Andean communities at specific times of the year, at the beginning of August or at carnivals, especially to ask for a particular gift or to cure an illness. The first step is to lay out on a special cloth a number of objects arranged according to a specific code.[6] This collection is offered to the Pachamama (divinity of the Earth) or Apu through prayers, and finally, the specialist will burn it in an appropriate spot. Twenty years ago, these rites were practiced in secret in the city of Cuzco—people did not wish to display their origins, and one could only reveal in intellectual circles that one had consulted a *paqu*. Today this practice is valued: it is seen more as an act of autochthony than an act of idolatry. Even official organizations celebrate *despachos* today, for a football team, to open a monument, to pass an exam and even for the success of a bank or supermarket. While a few years ago a *despacho* was held in some hidden neighborhood on the outskirts of a town, now the preference is for sites that are impregnated with 'Incaism', ruins such as Sacsayhuamán, for example. The Imperial dimension of the myth thus transmits its power to the indigenous dimension of the rite. In this case, one does not call upon a *paqu* from traditional communities—who are not aware of the prestige of these ruins—but instead on urban specialists who have not followed any traditional course. These Neo-shamans generally say they were initiated by an indigenous master, and sometimes that they were struck by a bolt of lightning that designated them, in accordance with tradition. Their 'authentication' therefore

5 The Quechua word *paqu* denotes, in a general way, a specialist in mediation between the natural and supernatural worlds, able to appease the gods of the mountains or the divinity in the Earth. He has some therapeutic power but less than the *altumisayuq* who can summon the gods of the mountains at night to come to a ritual table and is generally considered by anthropologists to be a shaman.

6 For a study of the traditional *pago*, see Molinié (1979).

makes use of the 'savage' background even when they have no contact with any indigenous communities. They generally use paraphernalia of their own, a personal item that gives them their reputation, for example a bottle of water from a sacred glacier, a puma claw or an archaeological object, proof of their direct link to some ancient deity.

The *despacho* we describe is addressed to Apu Picol. The Neo-shaman first offers 'altar wine' (in Spanish, *vino de misa*)[7] and then *quintos* of coca leaves (clusters of three leaves) to each Apu of the region. Next he prepares the *despacho*, placing each of the ingredients in its proper place. We recognize the different elements of traditional *pagos*: llama fat, coca leaves, various dried wild plants, rice, sugar, peanuts (the Apu's favorite snack), gilded and silvery aluminum foil (*qori libro* and *qolqe libro*), a skein of rainbow-colored threads, pieces of cotton, sweets, grains of maize, confetti, soil from sacred places... The Neo-shaman wraps all these items in the paper they have been placed on, and burns the parcel, with prayers for the offering.

These days, Neo-shamans celebrate their *despachos* not just for the citizens of Cuzco, as we have seen, but also for tourists. In luxury hotels, in addition to having a bar, hairdressing and massage services, one can ask a specialist to make an offering to the sacred mountains. The people with the best reputation for such cures are the Q'ero, who have become the Incas' heirs through the fantasy image of Cuzco's Neo-Indians.

The Q'ero live in the north of the Cuzco region, in an isolated area that borders on the tropical forests. They were discovered, or rather 'invented', in 1955 by an expedition of academics from Cuzco, who decided both to study them and to free them from the almost feudal exploitation they suffered from, working on an enormous hacienda. The expedition's publications contributed not only to the expropriation of the hacienda in 1963, but also to the reinvention of Neo-Incaism. The Q'ero had several characteristics that enabled them to transform themselves into the Incas' heirs in the world of Nativism, and to provide the 'savage' side of the Neo-Indian. Firstly, they lived in a region that was difficult to reach, on the Eastern side of the mountain range. It is assumed that they had remained 'clean' of any *mestizaje* (racial mixing), an indispensable condition for being Inca. Also, even today, the Q'ero still practice agriculture in various ecological zones that resemble the model of a Pre-Hispanic vertical

7 This expression plays on the two meanings of '*misa*': one that refers to the Catholic rite of the 'mass', and the other to a table (*mesa*), which speakers of Quechua pronounce *misa,* meaning the ritual space of the offering, which is generally a piece of cloth specially made for the purpose.

archipelago as defined by John Murra (1975).[8] Until now, this system of production made their society relatively autonomous and free of outside influence. Furthermore, the Q'ero are the last ethnic group in Peru to live in this manner, and this peculiarity has been accentuated by the anthropological work of the Indigenists.[9]

Before the 1955 expedition, an earlier study, by Luis Yábar Palacio, had been published in 1922, in which he presented the Q'ero as 'the legitimate sons of the Sun', and identified them as descendants of the Inca. Many people, and even some anthropologists, have taken up this tradition from Cuzco (Flores Ochoa, 1984). The Q'ero themselves do not claim to be descendants of the Incas, but a people who were defeated by them. Their rituals may have originated in the tropical piedmont, as suggested by the *ch'unchu* garment they wear in religious ceremonies. However the Inca identity that has been attributed to the Q'ero appears to be a belief that is stronger than the historical evidence, as it is based on the violent 'telluric' environment described by Luis Valcárcel (1927), one of the fathers of Peruvian Indigenism. It is as though the extreme landscape of the Andes and ethnographic aspects of the Q'ero had contributed to create an Inca autochthony. The people of Cuzco like to adopt this autochthony through rituals of which the Q'ero are said to be specialists.

One of the ways in which the Neo-Inca tradition is being invented stands out clearly. The Q'ero, the most miserable serfs of an almost feudal hacienda, were identified in the 1950s as descendants of the Inca, based on a fantasy that they have features of autochthony. Thus they gradually became the depositories of a Pre-Hispanic ritual knowledge for the Neo-Indians, who used the Q'ero so that they would be able to become Incas again: they ask for 'shamanic' rites, 'messianic' myths, and 'esoteric' initiations. But at the same time, for the Neo-Incas of the city, the Q'ero still remain dirty, drunken and archaic Indians. One day they are brought to hotels in Cuzco to celebrate *despachos* for the tourists, and the next day they are thrown out of the hovel where they had taken their lodgings in Cuzco. They then return to their communities where the women have been tending the animals and crops. Many Q'ero live by going back and forth between their community in the mountains and five-star hotels in Cuzco. Their existence reflects the ideological schism of the Neo-Incas who

8 Their settlement is between a plateau at five thousand meters above sea level and the upper ranges of the tropical forest at an altitude of two thousand meters. They combine the pasture of Camelidae on higher grounds with the cultivation of roots on the middle ground and maize on the tropical level.

9 For a study of the relations between Cuzco Indigenism and the image of the Q'ero, see Le Borgne (2005).

use them to realize their fantasies of autochthony. The Neo-Indians oscillate between the exaltation of retrieving their ancestors and the sense of failure that comes from the recognition that these people represent what they despise most in the world: Indians who are more Indian than anyone proclaiming themselves to be Indian. The anthropologist feels something of this hesitation between fascination and disgust in the classrooms and halls of Cuzco, a feeling connected to the schizophrenic autochthony of the Neo-Incas who have usurped the identity of people they despise. The promotion of the miserable Q'ero to the status of Incas is a metaphor for this autochthony, a split between the noble imperial Indian and the ignoble contemporary Indian.

The Neo-Inca ideology we have just detected in the Apu Picol *despacho* forms part of the ideological framework of today's Neo-shamans, and more evidence for its existence emerges during the next stages of the healing session we will now observe.

The Imperial Body of the Patient: The Inca-ization of Tradition

Once the offering has been burned, the patient lies down on the ground. The Neo-shaman binds the body of the patient with two threads, winding them around several times as though he were wrapping a piece of meat. One thread is red and the other is white, the first being male and the second, female—as are the two carnations, the Neo-shaman adds, which make up the *despacho*, and the two colors of the Peruvian flag. The patient's body is completely tied up. The shaman observes that the red and white threads are *ceques*, which explains the name *ceq'esqa* given to the ritual. This reference to the Inca system of *ceques* is interesting and calls for an explanation.

In the Inca temple of the Sun of Cuzco (Coricancha) there was a convergence of 41 alignments (*ceques*) of 328 sanctuaries (*huacas*). The orientations of these alignments of sanctuaries or *ceques* were determined by astronomical observations. These lines were displayed around the temple of the Sun according to the positions of the stars: thus the *ceques* corresponded to months of the year, forming a giant calendar around the city of Cuzco that was both sidereal and synodic (see Figure 13.1).[10] Rites were celebrated in the sanctuaries aligned with the *ceques* on the corresponding calendar dates. They were the responsibility of

10 The system of *ceques* has been described by Tom Zuidema (1964; 2010) on the basis of information collected in the seventeenth century by B. Cobo ([1653] 1956). More recently, B. Bauer (2000) determined a very precise cartography of the system through archaeological excavations.

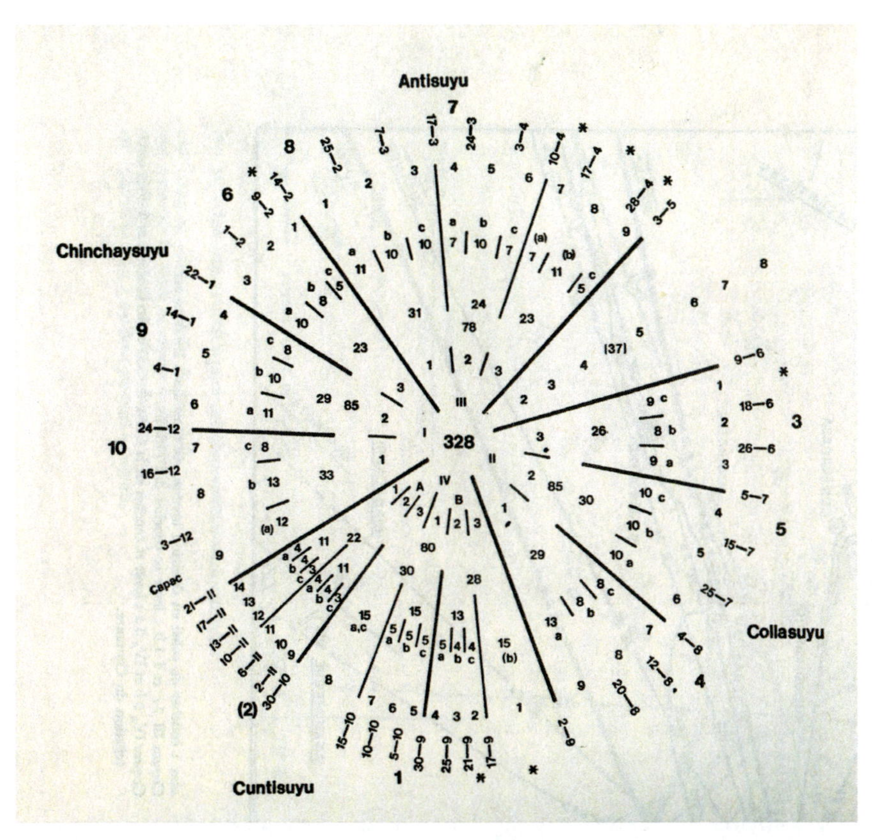

FIGURE 13.1 *The Calendar of Three Hundred and Twenty-eight Days of the* Ceques *System. Outer circles 1 and 2: Classification of the* suyus *and of the groups of three* ceques. *Circles 3, 4, 5: the number of* huacas *in the* suyus, *the groups of three* ceques, *and the* ceques. *Circle 5: the names of the* ceques: (*a*) *'principal' Collana;* (*b*) *'secondary' Payan;* (*c*) *'original' Cayao. Circle 6: the sequence of the* ceques *according to the order of* suyus *I, III, II, IV. Circle 7: the calendar; each* huaca *is represented by a segment of the circle, each segment corresponding to one day. Circle 8: the numbers and the *: pre-Inca* panacas *and* ayllus.
ACCORDING TO ZUIDEMA 1986, P. 94

each of Cuzco's social units, and these served such and such a *huaca* in such and such a *ceque* of which the group had to take care. The alignments of the sanctuaries were, then, not merely a giant calendar around the imperial city; they were also references to geographical locations in the territory of Cuzco, and a register of its social units, because it was among these that the services conducted in each of the aligned sanctuaries were shared. The system thus organized the imperial space, regulated time through the ritual calendar it formed, and ordered the society that conducted the services of worship.

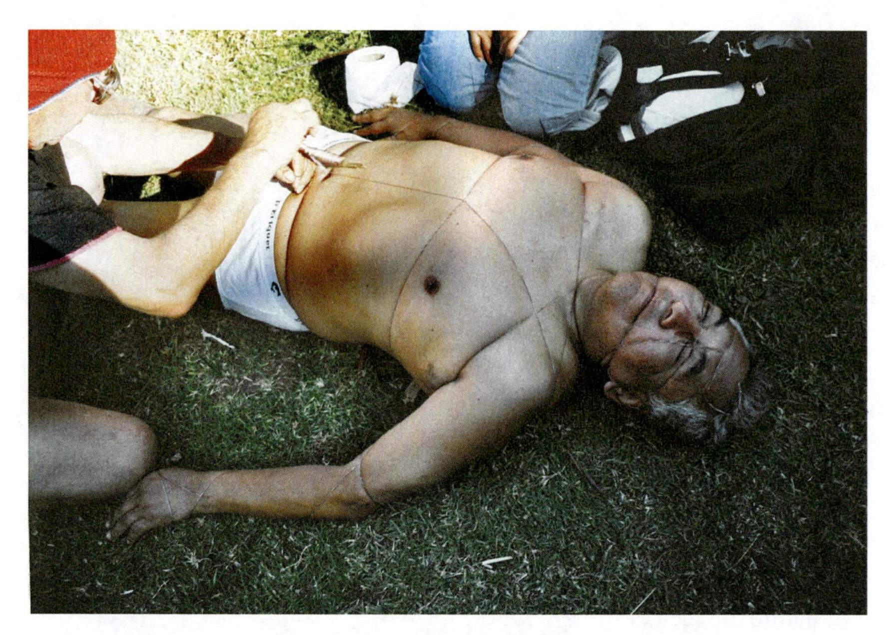

FIGURE 13.2 *Inventing the ceq'esqa ritual. The threads the shaman winds around the body of the patient represent the ritual lines (ceques) of the Mayan calendar and his navel stands for Q'osqo, the Pre-Hispanic capital. The body of the patient is thus brought into a homologous relationship with the Inca empire. Cuzco region, Peru, June 2002*
PHOTO: ANTOINETTE MOLINIÉ

We will now return to the healing ceremony we were observing (see Figure 13.2). It would seem that the Neo-shaman is drawing a replica of the *ceques* system on his patient's body. He calls the sick person's navel *qosqo*, and indeed Inca Garcilaso de la Vega (1960 [1609]) claimed that *qosqo* means 'navel' in Quechua.[11] The city of Cuzco has been called Qosqo since 1990,[12] when the mayor of the time decided that this was the Pre-Hispanic name of the capital of the Tawantinsuyu; he was inspired by references to an imperial past and the wish for 'authenticity' and autochthony that is typical of Neo-Incaism.[13] In the Neo-Quechua language, '*qosqo*' means 'solar plexus, integrating pole of the world and organizer of the forces that make up the Andean world'. This word also means the 'social and political solar center of civilization' as well as being that 'preternatural category with which the Kuraq Akulli organize their

11 According to Itier (1997, p. 152) its etymology cannot be traced in the Quechua language.

12 Municipal Agreement 78 (Acuerdo Municipal 78), June 23 1990.

13 For more about Neo-Incaism see Molinié, 1996; 2004; op. cit.

spiritual world, on the basis of which they perform their beneficial work in favor of their fellows' (Núñez del Prado, J.V. 1991, p. 7 and p. 30).

Thus the city of Qosqo has a new name, and it also has a new flag. The seven colors of the rainbow it displays are supposed to correspond to the Inca deity Kuychi. The municipality of Cuzco made it the city's official emblem in 1978. For the citizens of Cuzco, it really is the flag of the Incas, who they believe (without any evidence) must have held it aloft in their wars and ceremonies.

Qosqo has also had a coat of arms since June 23rd 1986, in order to 'proscribe any heraldic device imposed by the Spanish conquest' (Municipal Agreement 63). It is a copy of the 'Echenique plaque' given to President Echenique in 1853 by a descendant of the Inca, whose name has unfortunately fallen into oblivion. It thus enjoys a mythical autochthony, although the original 'Echenique plaque' is now in New York. It is a disc of gold showing a stylized feline face and is now considered characteristic of Inca art, though it clearly has features that correspond to the Pre-Hispanic civilization of the Huari, who dominated the Andes before the Incas.

In possession of a flag and a coat of arms, the city of Qosqo now only needed an anthem. The Municipal Agreement 17 of June 11th 1984 elevated the 1944 composition by Cuzco poets Luis Nieto and Roberto Ojeda Campana to be its official anthem:

Qosqo, Qosqo willkasqan sutynki	Cusco, Cusco is your sacred name
Inkapachaq Tayta Intin hina	Like the sun of the immortal Inkario
Teqsimunun ahasqonpi apqsunki	Everybody bears you in their breast
Haylli taki unanchanta hina.	As a song and a triumphal flag.
Mana llallin sanankia pukaran	Invincible bastion of your race,
Llaqtakunan much'ankusunki	The peoples salute you standing upright;
Sunutaqmi ayllunkiwan samisqa	And the fatherland that is honored in your offspring
Mat'inkiman pilluta churan.[14]	Places a laurel on your forehead.

It is evident that the hymn to Incaism adopts the style of a national anthem, thus showing, like many other Neo-Inca symbols, that the representations of the Peruvian nation's autochthony originated in Cuzco.

14 The spelling is given by the municipality of Cuzco.

This apology for the Inca empire is clearly part of an attempt to raise the status of the Pre-Hispanic past.[15] The indigenous culture that nourished this movement has already been transformed and urbanized by an apologetic revitalization that began in the twentieth century. The genesis of the Andean New Age cannot be understood unless Neo-Incaism, and especially its rebirth in contemporary Cuzco, are taken into account.

At the start of the twentieth century, the Indigenist movement assumed the task of finding for the Peruvian nation a respectable ancestor who would allow the historical autochthony of the Andean natives despised by the Creole elites to be surpassed. This movement imparted to the nostalgia for the empire the dimension of a founding myth in which the whole nation should be united to build its identity. Feeling for the nation is thus presented as something contaminated by nostalgia that has been transformed into autochthony.[16] The Indigenists celebrate the Imperial Indian. This representation clearly has a European origin. As early as 1763, in Leblanc de Guillet's tragedy, Manco Capac the Inca, is presented as a model for the French enlightenment, and it is claimed that the Inca state stands for 'the nature of benign and egalitarian man'. *Les Incas* by Marmontel, published in 1777, a year before Jean-Jacques Rousseau's death, presents the Inca government as 'almost institutional and filled with a generous love'. The intellectuals of the Peruvian left in the 1920's merely reinvented the myth of perfect government: what the Incas had invented was nothing less than socialism, and the need to return to this grand age was both a nationalist credo and an essential condition for establishing the Workers' International. For these Peruvian professors, the Inca Empire was 'a socialist state organized in accordance with the characteristics of a modern state'. According to them, it corresponded to a 'consciousness of the indigenous' carried by faith in popular government and communal fraternity (Sivirichi, 1946, p. 21). Thus, while the myth of a perfect and bountiful Inca State was elaborated, and the cult of a solar divinity was reinvented in Cuzco with the ceremony of Inti Raymi, the Indians rebelling in the haciendas could be safely ignored.

15 For a study of the Neo-Indian movement, see Galinier and Molinié, op. cit.

16 Such a nostalgia is undoubtedly linked to the image of the 'sadness of the Indian' that was typical in the sixteenth century (Estenssoro, 1992). The principal representatives of Peruvian indigenism, which cannot be studied here, are Mariátegui (1928), Uriel García (1973) and Valcárcel (1927). For an analysis of the myth of the Inca, see Burga (1988) and Flores Galindo (1986). For a history of the Indigenism of Cuzco, see Tamayo Herrera (1980).

This Neo-Incaism began to acquire new features about twenty years ago (Galinier and Molinié, op. cit.; Molinié, op. cit., 2009). In Cuzco, some recent architecture is reminiscent of monumental Inca constructions. Monuments have been erected in memory of mythical ancestors such as Pachacuti Inca. Pachamama is venerated, after being celebrated by the Indigenists of the twentieth century, and is now ready to embrace the Mother Earth of the New Age. Little is known of a Pre-Hispanic Pachamama. In traditional communities she now appears as a deity who is both very local and ubiquitous. Recently she has become a worldwide divinity, venerated not only by the New Age International but also by ecological movements, the United Nations and NGOs, giving rise to terms such as 'Pachamama-izing' and 'Pachamamaism' (Lambert, 2011). The children of the Age of Aquarius celebrate the generosity of this goddess with the same enthusiasm as the Indigenists of the twentieth century, in complete ignorance of the indigenous Andean version of a voracious deity hungry for sacrifices. The present-day Indianist movements have taken their inspiration from twentieth-century Indigenists to shape this maternal representation of the Earth goddess, and merged it with the Mother Earth of the New Age. This synthetic image has become popular among indigenous Andeans, and they frequently act as informants for anthropologists. Ultimately, the anthropologist receives the product of these alterations as the synthetic image of a generous Pachamama whose origin can be found in the Indigenist movement, tinted by the New Age, and which is then returned to the indigenous Andeans who have endowed it once again with its original sacrificial dimension.

Moreover, the Neo-cult of the Sun, the Inti Raymi, celebrated at the June solstice, attracts huge crowds who are convinced that it is an authentic ceremony of their Pre-Hispanic ancestors. Invented by Indigenists in 1943, this ceremony has been presided over since the 1990's by an Inca, who is not, for once, an actor but a true descendant of the lineage of Inca Roca. He has formed a Council of the Tawantinsuyu that filed claims for official recognition.

This return of the Incas is not only observed in the Cuzco region. For about twenty years, it has taken on a national dimension in Peru. For example, the President of the Republic, Alejandro Toledo, who governed from 2001 to 2006, presented himself on various occasions as an Inca sovereign. Before his election, he appeared at a meeting in Sacsahuaman, where the Inti Raymi is usually celebrated, wearing the royal headdress of the *mascaypacha*. However, what gave President Toledo an Inca dimension was, more than anything, his enthronement in the majestic ruins of Machu Picchu, considered today both as the cathedral of the Incas and as one of the centers of New Age spirituality in the world. Some shamans from the region contributed to the coronation ceremony, which acquired an international scale, since the presidents of various Latin American republics attended, along with the foreign minister of Israel and the Infante (crown prince) of Spain.[17] One of the shamans who conducted the rites was none other than the rector of the University of Cuzco, who was an esteemed high-ranking specialist.[18]

It turns out that he was the same Neo-shaman who conducted the *ceq'esqa* healing that we were observing near Apu Picol, where we discovered in the patient's body the system of *ceques* from the Inca calendar. Knowing this, we can understand the role played by intellectuals and academics on the Neo-Indian scene better. As we will now see, they have also played a fundamental role in the invention of the Andean New Age.

Coming back to the *ceq'esqa* healing, we asked the Neo-shaman what the Inca *ceques* had to do with his patient's body. He found our question absurd. How could we not understand that the *ceques*, the alignments of sacred places, while indeed forming an immense Inca calendar, are really 'lines of energy'. For him it was quite obvious that these 'lines of energy' would heal his patient. The threads he had bound around the patient's body would create circuits of energy, just as the *ceques* around the Pre-Hispanic imperial city did. This energy, inherited from the Incas, is what would heal the patient.

Clearly, in a traditional healing session today, not the slightest reference is made either to Incas or to *ceques*, and even less to the notion of energy, which comes straight from the New Age. We can thus observe two procedures invented by the Andean New Age that have been added to the traditional *despacho* described above: first the Inca-izing of a ritual that would otherwise have been stained by its 'Indian' origins, and secondly, the transformation of the Inca reference by a New Age theory. The first stage of the ritual, the *despacho* offered to Apu Picol, corresponds to the 'savage' part of Andean culture, to an 'authentic' offering made to an 'Indian' deity, merged, of course, with elements of Christianity, whereas the second stage of the rite provides an extraordinary example of the invention of tradition.[19] It proceeds by

17 In December 2005, the President of the Republic of Bolivia, Evo Morales, took part in a similar ceremony in the ruins of Tiahuanaco near La Paz. In the north of Peru, the Neo-Mochicas already celebrate the Lord of Sipán (el Señor de Sipán) in a ceremony organized close to the museum (which is actually a sort of a pantheon) that presents excavations from his tomb.

18 I would like to pay a posthumous tribute to Aurelio Carmona who contributed a great deal to my research.

19 In the sense of Hobsbawm and Ranger, 1983.

creating a structural homology between the patient's body and the Inca calendar, that is, through the isomorphism of the spatial dimensions of the patient's body with the space of the Inca empire. The patient's navel is, in relation to other parts of his body, what the city of Cuzco was to the Empire: the center of a system of alignments, in the first case of threads placed by the Neo-shaman, and in the second case, of Pre-Hispanic places of worship—with the exquisite detail that the new name of the city of Cuzco is Qosqo, which means 'navel' in Neo-Inca Quechua (*qosqo.*) Thus we can see a reference to the Incas, this time through their calendar, borrowed from the work of Zuidema. What we find of even greater interest is that New Age interpretations have been imported into this neo-ritual, since the *ceques* of the Incas have become vectors of 'energy'. In this way, Qosqo, the new name of the Inca capital, corresponds to the *qosqo* of the patient, that is, to the New Age name of his solar plexus. At this moment in the ceremony, the indigenous and local idea of the sacred assumes the worldwide scale of New Age beliefs through the interposition of Incas. We may note the cognitive procedure: an item from Inca history is picked up (here, the sanctuaries aligned with the *ceques*) and taken out of its Pre-Hispanic context; then it is cut out and pasted into an indigenous practice (in this case the *despacho*); and finally, the New Age notion of energy is brought in to recycle the local ritual in a global theory while borrowing from anthropological knowledge. We will see in due course how other Neo-shamans in Cuzco use the *ceques* system in their ceremonies, a good example of the Neo-Indians' reappropriation of anthropological knowledge.

Suddenly, with a brusque gesture, the Neo-shaman cuts the threads crying '¡*Kutiy*! ¡*Kutiy*! ¡*Kutiy* carajo!' just like indigenous shamans do in their healings. In this cry of '¡*Kutiy*! ¡*Kutiy*!' the Quechua verb meaning 'to go back' can be recognized; while *carajo* is a vulgar interjection in Spanish. The Neo-shaman explains that this is how he repels negative energy, more or less as in the expression 'Get thee behind me, Satan' (*¡Atrás Satanás!*) used in ancient times. In fact, he is referring to a traditional ritual called *kutychi* that consists of an offering for the return of a soul captured by the *soq'a,* the negative and lethal figure of a pre-human ancestor (Molinié, op. cit., 1979). However, this element of the indigenous culture is out of place here. The Neo-shaman merrily explains that the last phrase of the ceremony can be understood by English-speaking patients to mean '*Cut it! Cut it!*', alluding to the brusque movements he makes to cut the threads around the patient's body. We will never know whether he was joking or if he was speaking of an ingenious adaptation of the Andean rite for clients from the United States who come to Cuzco to capture the energy of the Incas, as we will now see.

The Energy of Tradition: The New Age Inversion of Sacrifice

Many New Age prophecies have announced that the imminent entry into the Age of Aquarius will be accompanied by profound changes as described in the Revelations of Saint John. A cataclysm will bring us a 'Great King' whose coming will be like a return of Christ and will open a new Golden Age. This New Age belief is extraordinarily similar to an Andean myth. There is a tradition that Inkarrí, i.e., the Inca King, was decapitated,[20] by foreign invaders and will return some day to restore a new empire.[21] From his head, which is buried somewhere in an unknown place in the mountains, his entire body will start growing back little by little, and when it is complete, Inkarrí will come back to life and take power to restore Indian society for some, or the empire of Tawantinsuyu for others. This myth appears in various forms. Some versions tell of how Inkarrí vanquished Jesus Christ, personified as his brother, who was called Sucristu or Españarri depending on the version. The latter hid the Inca King's head, but

> [the] blood of Inkarrí is alive in the depths of our Mother Earth. It is said that the day will come when his head, his blood and his body will be joined. That day the sun will rise in the evening, and reptiles will fly. Lake Parinacochas will dry up, and then the beautiful grand Pueblo that our Inkarrí was unable to finish will be visible again.[22]

The Andean and New Age visions of history are curiously comparable.[23] For the Andeans, history is not linear as it is for us, but is formed by different *pacha*, universes of space and time that are separated from each other by *pachacuti*, that is, inversions expressed by cataclysms. This notion of *pachacuti* chimes in well with the New Age. Like the Andeans, the children of the Age of Aquarius have a cyclical view of the future. For them, each cycle consists of four successive ages, of gold, silver, bronze and iron, and humanity has come to the transition to a New Age. As the age of iron ends with the latest millennium, a Golden

20 And not hanged as historical documents say.

21 There are variations of this myth. The first was collected in Cuzco in 1955 (Núñez del Prado, 1973). The Quechua version was published by Arguedas (1968). A book edited by Juan Ossio (1973) brought together various versions from different regions of Peru. See also Burga (1988), Valderrama and Escalante (1995) and Ortíz Rescaniere (1973).

22 Ortiz Rescaniere, op. cit., p. 139 (our translation).

23 For data about the Andean New Age, see Cumes and Lizárraga (1999); Jenkins (1997); Parisi Wilcox and Jenkins (1996); Sullivan (1999).

Age is opening for us now and will last for another 2,160 years. Three qualities of the sign of Aquarius (Air, Masculine, and Uranus) will allow cloudless happiness. Like the time of the New Agers, Andean time 'works in a bipolar and cyclical fashion' (Vernette, 1993 p. 26). These two visions of time include a messianic dimension.

Other New Age ideas are so close to notions that have been studied by Andean anthropology that one may ask if the latter was not established under Aquarian influence. The notion of *yanantin* expresses the opposition of contraries that are also complementary, such as female-male, up-down, etc. This is a 'symmetrical relation as in a mirror' (Platt, 1978 p. 1098). The same idea is found in yin and yang, i.e., the ideal of complementary parts applied not only to the sexes but also to colors and temperaments. The Neo-Indians interpret this idea as the notion of *ayni*. Originally it refers to the mutual exchange of labor; but in today's urban environment, the word has come to mean any type of reciprocity and complementary activity. It is claimed that the ideal Andean society would apply reciprocity in all areas if it were not contaminated by our mercantile civilization. In this way, *ayni* has reached a New Age ideal by itself. So the very local notions of *yanantin*, *pachacuti* and *ayni* naturally find a place in New Age worldwide cosmology.

Moreover, the notion of energy, transposed from the New Age finds an echo in certain Quechua concepts such as *sami* in which the New Agers recognize 'refined energy', or *poq'po* which is equivalent to the aura, and *kausay* which stands for 'energy suspended in the world'. We can see how the same term 'energy', imported from the New Age, when combined with an adjective, expresses a wide variety of Andean notions. Globalization proceeds by homogenizing indigenous concepts. For example, to 'eat and digest heavy energy' you have to activate your *qosqo*, the solar plexus, a notion that is important for the New Age but unknown to the indigenous people of the communities. For New Agers, it is a kind of spiritual stomach that allows one to digest the heavy energy emitted by people who generate 'negative vibrations'. Each of us should learn to locate our *qosqo*, and practice concentration exercises so as to digest negative flows. We have already seen the importance of this concept in the *ceq'esqa* healing session we studied in detail.

If there has been a transformation of the New Age notion of energy in Quechua terms, one can also observe a recycling of traditional Andean rites, especially that of the *despacho*.

In their New Age versions, the *despachos* are celebrated by 'masters' during short courses given in California, Baltimore, northern Italy, Scandinavia and Catalonia. Sometimes they are accompanied by Q'eros, who are exhibited on these occasions as descendants of the Incas, as we have seen. If it is common

FIGURE 13.3
A New Age mystic receives the benefits of a 'payment' from the hands of a Neo-shaman in the Inca ruins of Pisac. This offering is not dedicated to the hill behind the initiate but helps the believer directly through physical contact with his body. Ruins of Pisac, Peru, June 2002
PHOTO: ANTOINETTE MOLINIÉ

practice of the *Runa*[24] to burn the *despacho* as a sacrifice to the divinity, the New Agers prefer have it placed by the Neo-shaman on their heads or on their solar plexuses (see Figure 13.3). One can then feel 'the energy that penetrates from your head to your feet' or 'a burning sensation in the head' or 'a very strong emotion of communing with your neighbor', or, also, 'the feeling of being transformed into a serpent'. Others have had visions 'of a group of Tibetan monks crossed by a silver ray' or indeed 'of a solar eclipse with a ring of gold and a space ship moving in a very warm environment'.[25]

The New Agers and the traditional Andeans have a completely different view of the *despacho*: while the latter make an offering to the deities of the mountains or the Earth, the children of the Age of Aquarius, on the contrary, capture their energy for their own benefit. The *Runa* give in order to receive, while the New Agers take in order to live better. In the first case, the *despacho* is a vehicle for giving to the gods; in the second, the *despacho* contains the sought-after benefit in its very substance. In the Andean tradition of exchange, the objects that make up the offering are intended to nourish the gods. In the New

24 *Runa* is what the indigenous people of the communities call themselves.

25 Eyewitness reports from members of a group of mystical tourists in June 2002. The information collected at that time may have changed since, as New Age ceremonies are typically unstable and permeable.

Age version, these elements are charged with 'energy' that is captured by the master of the 'Andean tradition' (Nuñez del Prado J.V., 1998, p. 78) which millions of Indians take part in, thus converting themselves into vectors of energy.

There is another difference: while the composition of the indigenous *despacho* varies according to what is being asked for and in accordance with the divinity appealed to, that of the New Age is specific to the individual making the offering: everyone has his own magic stone or *khuya*, which has been given a small personal touch and a special ingredient no one else has. This individualism makes sense, since, in contrast to the *Runa* who serve their gods, the New Agers serve themselves. Globalization and individualism thus invest in the Andean sacrificial circuit: instead of making an offering, New Agers make a capture, following a predatory logic.

It is necessary to highlight the flexibility of the *despacho* rite that allows for extremely diverse practices: it can be offered for the fertility of the earth, prepared for the inauguration of a bank or a public garden, celebrated during a ceremony held at the university, accompanied by the petition of the high priest during the Inti Raymi, and indeed displayed during the enthronement of the President of the Republic.... This ritual tool shows its extreme flexibility, playing in turn the role of an offering to the Apu, a breathing in of light energy, or a blowing away of heavy energy. This malleability allows it to be adapted to all occasions and for them to be multiplied *ad infinitum*. The technical simplicity of its elaboration helps it to be so widely spread. The variety of its composition allows for combinations and adaptations of its ingredients, which depend on the relation between the person making the offering and the context. However, all these variations on a theme are only possible if an essential factor of this traditional practice is ignored: the special power of the indigenous specialist who elaborates a *despacho* in a specific cultural frame, the divine character of the talent he exercises, and the coherence between this special power and its divine origins. Rituals are evidently considered more effective by New Agers when they are performed on the very site from where they originate: at the Pre-Hispanic ruins where the energy of the Incas is preserved, and during festivals with the participation of modern-day Indians to create good vibrations.

In Search of a World-Wide Inca: The Globalization of the Andean New Age

The 'route of initiation' that we will now observe, like the *ceq'esqa* healing we studied, is evidence of a real invention of tradition. It was created by a former professor of anthropology at the University of San Antonio Abad de Cuzco, who claims he has followed different stages of initiation all the way to the top grade of shaman.[26] His teacher showed him the rite of 'crowning a sacred king' (Núñez del Prado J.V., 1998, p. 45). On the basis of his experience, Núñez del Prado created an initiation route whose stages (most of them on archaeological Inca sites) are those of discovering the future Inca who will rule in the new era foreseen by the New Age movement. This ritual cycle, between pilgrimages and initiation ceremonies, is a good example of the meeting of the Messianism of the New Age and the Andean myth of the return of the Inca. It also shows the role played by anthropology in local re-elaborations and reappropriations of the New Age.

The initiation route begins in the cathedral of Cuzco where an appeal is made to the *hanaqpacha* (the world above),[27] addressed to two divinities of local Catholicism: *la Virgen de la Natividad la Antigua*, who welcomes the faithful at the entrance and receives the blinding light of the Plaza de Armas; and Taytacha Temblores, who is highly revered in Cuzco and implored among countless lit candles amidst the murmur of Indian supplications. It is not a case of the invention of new icons, because these two divinities have received the prayers of thousands of people from Cuzco for centuries,[28] but it can be noted that the Andean New Age retrieves not only a Pre-Hispanic past invented by the Neo-Incas, but also local Catholicism, the fruit of a fusion with Pre-Hispanic beliefs, as well as the vibrations of Indian rituals.

This is not all. Here, in the cathedral, the group of New Agers directs itself to a strange divinity that is probably more ancient than the two Christian images: it is an ovoid stone that is used to wedge the massive door to the Plaza de Armas. It has a diameter of around one and a half meters at its widest and is sixty centimeters high; it is meticulously polished and there is a cavity in the middle, about ten centimeters deep. This *khuya* (see below) is able to absorb the negative energies (*hucha*) brought in by the New Agers. Núñez del Prado calls it Hatun Taqe Wiraqocha, that is, he gives it the name of the principal

26 I would like to express my warm thanks to Juan Núñez del Prado for his contributions to my research.

27 Generally speaking, according to anthropological tradition, the Andean world is divided into three parts: *hanaqpacha* (world above), *kaypacha* (the world of here and now, the world of human beings), and *ukhupacha* (the underworld), though the indigenous people really only consider the last two.

28 The people of Cuzco have a great devotion for Taytacha Temblores, especially on Easter Monday. He is treated in prayers and ceremonies as a god of the mountains (Valencia Espinoza, 1991) and as such may even appear on the ritual table of a high-ranking shaman who has the authority to summon him.

deity of the Inca. However, this stone is also an object of devotion for the Indians. Until a few years ago, it had been relegated to the corner of a chapel in the cathedral. On various occasions the priests tried to get rid of it, but protests from the Indians forced them to put it back again, this time as a doorstop. This does not discourage people from distant communities from coming in with offerings, especially in August when the Earth is open, and especially at dawn, when the cathedral doors are opened and there is no one aound to see them. They often come to an agreement with the sacristan so he leaves the llama grease and coca leaves they have offered close to the sacred stone. Most people in Cuzco know nothing of this cult, as those who follow it are few in number and only raise their hands with a murmured invocation and the look of affliction that is so typical of the Indians of Cuzco. Here we witness the abrupt move from an indigenous cult to a New Age cult without going through the 'Neo-inca-ization' we have observed in other situations, whether in the *despachos* or in the folk dances or in the Neo-cult of the Sun. The Indian *khuya* became a New Age *khuya* after it had been relegated to a position against the door. Will the children of the Age of Aquarius return to the *Runa* a deity that had been rooted out by the priests? While Núñez del Prado was explaining to us how you have to rub this *khuya* stone to free yourself of your 'heavy energy', an old woman knelt down, removed her hat, and, murmuring prayers, gently rubbed the whole stone with the llama grease she had brought with her. Here, as everywhere, the Indian and the New Ager have an inverse relation with the sacred: the former makes an offering while the latter discharges his negative energy. In the end, the *khuya* of the Indians located in the cathedral, and identified by some Neo-Incas as the supreme deity Wiraqocha, changes its function from being a doorstop to that of a garbage can for negative New Age energy.

The second stage of the initiation route brings us to Q'enko, Inca ruins near Cuzco where the New Age mystics gather on a 'platform of light' to shed any excess of heavy energy through a *despacho* performed by the 'maestro' of the group. Then, in the cave of Amaru Macha'ay, the initiates are supposed to imagine their own conception in their mother's womb. In this way they manage to 'transfer the umbilical cord of energy from their mother to Pachamama'. This then makes them 'brethren' since they have become children of the same Mother. Later they continue to travel to Lake Huacarpay, a few kilometers from Cuzco, a place that they have been told is the birthplace of Huascar the Inca, the last sovereign of Tawantinsuyu, with whom they are to be connected. Afterwards, the initiates are to devote themselves to the spirit of Pachacuti, in the midst of the Cyclopean blocks of the citadel of Sacsahuaman. The group then takes the path to Pisac and climbs over the majestic Inca buildings.

Here, like the shaman of the *ceq'esqa* healing session which we analyzed above, the New Agers use the Inca calendar with its system of *ceques* (Zuidema, op. cit.), only this time to absorb the energy of the surrounding mountains. One of the rituals celebrated by today's mystics consists of 'capturing the energy of the *ceques*' which, according to them, lies within the niches of the Inca walls facing the mountains, as if certain New Age *ceques* had established a mysterious relationship between, on the one hand, the Inca niches in the ruins and, on the other, the Apu living in the mountains today. There is an explicit relationship between the Inca ancestors and contemporary indigenous gods. In the New Agers' prayers mumbled in the niches of the ruins, we can glimpse the outlines of a genealogy, with an additional scientific reference to the system of *ceques*. The New Age culture, with its anthropological backdrop, gains much of its coherence here: from the *ceq'esqa* healing session celebrated by a Neo-shaman from Cuzco, as we saw above, to the New Age mystics with their initiations, the notion of *ceque* that was taken from anthropological writings acquires an extraordinary symbolic efficiency.

We follow the trek as far as Ollantaytambo. Again, the New Agers seem not to be impressed by the amazing beauty of the site. They concentrate on opening the eye of their throats to enter into the body of the spirit of the Wind that precipitates itself in gusts in the Wayrapunk'u (Gate of the Wind) opposite the magnificent snow-covered Mount La Verónica. The mystics allow themselves to be penetrated by this wind that is considered beneficial while pressing coca leaves in their hands. Finally, when the breeze has freed them of their 'heavy energy', they throw the coca leaves over their heads. The wind lifts them up, they flutter towards the rocks and disappear into the void. During the entire ceremony, the 'maestro' blows on his *misadespacho* (offerings table) to recharge it with *sami*, i.e., with 'light energy'.

The initiation continues in Machu Picchu, which has been assaulted by esoteric groups that squabble over its temples, just as priests from different churches have fought in Jerusalem to hold mass over the tomb of Christ. Some groups come in at night, and inevitably become victims of accidents due to the steepness of the site. Archaeologists complain about the irrevocable damage they cause by doing this. The 'maestro' here identifies sanctuaries that are unknown to archaeologists.[29] He enters the temple of the Condor declaring that this bird represents the collective spirit of all Andeans. According to the 'maestro', the Americans from the US carry the spirit of the Eagle. One must therefore use the *yanantin* energy emitted by the pair formed by the Andean condor and the American eagle.

29 Very little is known about the history of Machu Picchu.

The final stage of the initiation circuit is the gigantic temple of Wiracocha, a few kilometers from Cuzco. We know the Spaniards believed this deity to be equivalent to God the Father, thus opposing his worship to that of the Sun, which was considered idolatry. This theory seems to have been adopted by New Agers who claim to be in the temple of Yahweh. If in Cuzco they 'worked' with *kaypacha*, the world of here and now, and in Machu Picchu with the subterranean world of *ukhupacha*, they are now dealing with *hanaqpacha*, i.e., the world above. The maestro says the twelve royal families would meet in this temple, to choose from among twelve candidates who was to be the Inca, indicated by the supernatural splendor of a sixth grade priest. Here the Sapa Inca and his Qoya will appear one day. They will make a triumphal entry into the cathedral of Cuzco and will be resplendent with mystical New Age light. This final age of Sapa Inca coincides with the Golden Age of the New Age.

We can see from this initiation route how messianism provides a possible convergence between Andean tradition and New Age ideas. As we have seen, the notion of *pachacuti*, as generally analyzed by anthropologists, fits very naturally into New Age millenarianism. And as we have also seen, the return of the Inca is expressed in the Andes through his successive incarnations: Inkarrí in the myth, Tupac Amaru in the anti-colonial revolt (O'Phelan, 1995), the Inca of the Neo-cult of the Sun in the Inti Raymi, and Alejandro Toledo as president of the Republic... Only the New Age Inca is still to come. It was an anthropologist, an ex-professor of the University of Cuzco, an academic acquiring the functions of a shaman, and as we will see, of a tour operator, who created him.

Marketing Tradition: Mystical Tourism

This ritual tour in search of the next Inca can be booked on the website http://tonebytone.com/hatunkarpay/o.shtml or through travel agencies in Cuzco.[30] The guides are presented as 'indigenous masters of the Andean tradition'. The Q'ero are exhibited as the last descendants of the Incas and are shown dressed in ponchos that they never wear in their communities, in an advertisement that says 'Develop your Personal Power in the Inca Tradition of the Q'ero Indians of Peru', standing beside a tall, fair-haired guide. He claims that in 'this way he honors with his work the lineage of the maestros who preceded his initiator'. We learn that he has a network of half a dozen priests around the world, who act at the same time as both mystical and financial intermediaries. He has given lectures all over the world, as indicated by *Wiraqocha Fonde*

30 For more on mystical tourism, see Flores Ochoa (1996).

Skandinavien on their website. A promoter of esoteric tourism explained to us that he could practice Andean rituals in Austria and in the north of Italy, where the mountains are high enough to produce energies like those in the Andes.

Esoteric tourism has gained in respectability thanks to international meetings of mystics. As early as 1992, the Intiq Amarunkuna Institute and the World Community of Solar Indian America (*la Comunidad Mundial de América India Solar*) organized a World Congress of Andean Mysticism to celebrate the 'return of the x Pachacuteq' and 'to drink at the sources of Andean wisdom'. This event was patronized by the local government of Cuzco, the National Culture Institute (*Instituto Nacional de la Cultura*) and the University of Cuzco. The same year, the imperial city was the site of the first International Holistic Meeting (*Primer Encuentro Internacional Holístico*). The program included ceremonies of offerings to the gods of the mountains, visits to the medicinal baths of Machu Picchu, the accompaniment of Andean music, and lectures on themes such as 'To die is to return to yourself', 'The way of true initiation', 'How to live in the light', 'Initiation and counter-initiation in modern times', 'The mind in matter and matter in the spirit', etc. In 1995, an International Peace Conference was organized in Carleton College in Northfield, Minnesota by the International Institute of Integral Human Sciences Inc. This event offered an encounter with Tibetan Gyuto monks, as well as a day in the company of Willaru Huayra from Cuzco to speak about the 'message of the Inca prophecy', the prophecy being that when the Condor of the South meets the Eagle of the North, 'the spirit of Mother Earth will awaken'.

It is remarkable how little interest New Age mystics show in ordinary tourism, especially the local folklore which is so rich and colorful. It seems that they would rather avoid the 'true Indians' because the latter might upset their meditations in the Inca ruins. They thus participate through an agency in the pilgrimage to Quyllirit'i, where numerous indigenous communities come with their dancers, but none of these spectacular ceremonies have any interest for New Age mystics. They wait until the end of the fiesta, impatient for the indigenous pilgrims to leave, so that they can go and 'catch the good vibrations' that 'the Indians' have generated. It is as though the landscape in its telluric materiality had picked up something of the sacred character of these indigenous rites, so that this holiness can now be captured through New Age rites.

The mystical tourists are not interested in Neo-Inca rituals either, except to inspire them in their search for the future Inca. Such is the case of the Neo-cult of the Sun in the Inti Raymi, which has spread among the traditional communities of the region and also in the central Andes. In the ruins of Moray, near the pueblo of Maras (Cuzco), an Inti Raymi copied from the one in Cuzco is celebrated. Pupils from schools in the area are dressed up as soldiers of

Tawantinsuyu, while for this occasion the local Inca dresses in the mantle of his colleague from Cuzco, woven with the wings of bats. A traditional shaman comes from the communities in the hills to offer a *despacho*. The mayors of the pueblos are transformed into the Inca's ministers, wearing ponchos like those of the Indians they despise. The latter come from their communities to attend the ceremony because they have been told that this is what their ancestors did: they invade the ruins of Moray to take part in this new ritual. And this is not all. In these very ruins of Moray, once they remain empty after the Neo-Inca ceremonies, New Age mystics arrive to meditate and catch the vibrations of the historical Incas. In the same exceptionally beautiful place, perhaps at the same time, one can find oneself confronted with Indians looking after their sheep, adepts of the solar Neo-cult, Pre-Hispanic armies, shamans from the communities in the hills, and Californian New Agers in meditation.

From this prodigious accumulation of periods, spaces and cultures arises the Andean New Age. It reaches beyond the limits of Peru, of course. It draws its legitimacy from the national tourism agency that comments on its virtues in numerous leaflets. The tourist promotion agency FOPTUR (*El Fondo de Promoción Turística*) presents Peru as the magnetic center of the world, the mountain range of the Andes and its shamans having taken up the energy of India and her gurus. In particular, Machu Picchu has become a planetary *chakra* towards which mystics from all over the world should direct their steps (Longato, 1991, p. 25, quoted by Pilares Villa, 1992, p. 36). FOPTUR is not content merely to praise the merits of the ruins: it also sells a more or less reinvented traditional culture. In the section on Andean religious cosmology ('*Cosmovisión religiosa andina*'), it offers an incredibly chaotic list of supernatural entities, like stalls in a market. In 1995, The director of the National Institute of Culture for Cuzco, INC (*Instituto Nacional de Cultura de Cuzco*) did not conceal his attachment to the new Andean 'cosmovision', and in his writings, he presents himself as 'a scholar and a mystic of the Andean Church, a living and applicable faith that forms the fundamental touchstone of our autochthonous, our very own and true spirituality'.[31] He published a book on the 'mystical interpretation' of the Sacsayhuamán site (Altamirano, 1993) that leaves no doubt about his orientations. Altamirano's considerations about the chakras through which the energy of this site is supposed to enter, and the joint flight of the condor and the eagle, or the serpent of cosmic light, are all the more disconcerting as he is the director of the institution to which the archaeological remains of the region have been entrusted and since the damage caused by groups of mystical

31 'Iglesia sin nombre. La fe milenaria de la Iglesia Andina. Entrevista a José Altamirano, presidente del INC del Cusco, conocedor del tema' (*Caretas*, April 12, 1995, p. 54 and 81).

tourists, whether here in Sacsayhuamán, in Machu Picchu or at other sites, is irreparable. So it is that the State, through its two ministerial offices (FOPTUR and *el Instituto Nacional de Cultura*), and the University with its anthropologists, have definitively institutionalized the Andean New Age in Cuzco.

Conclusions

For the last decade or so, from the United States to Tibet, thousands of New Age followers have been waiting for the return of the Inca. The local myth of Inkarrí has been transformed into the worldwide *doxa* of an Andean New Age whose invention we have analyzed through a specific rite observed near Cuzco.

We are witnessing the genesis of a culture that is above all ritual, and takes root in two areas. Firstly, there is the Andean culture that is heir to five hundred years of fusion between the Pre-Hispanic and Spanish corpuses. This Andean culture, which used to be localized in rural communities, has been 'Inca-ized' by urban Neo-Incaism: first through the Indigenist current at the beginning of the twentieth century, and twenty years ago by a broader Neo-Indian movement (Galinier and Molinié, op. cit.). For example, in a *despacho* ritual, a Neo-shaman adds a basis of archaeological provenance to ennoble the scene. Conversely, contemporary indigenous gestures and elements are added to reinvented ceremonies such as the Neo-cult of the Sun in the Inti Raymi. These gestures, which are Indian by their origins, acquire an imperial dimension through their Inca-type approach. This involves inventing iconographies that are intermediate between the Andean tradition and the figure of the imperial Indian, in such a way that the former is given nobility and the second is given autochthony. It is remarkable how these representations have been nationalized to lend reality to a mythic autochthony of the Peruvian nation, one that represents the State Indian. The enthroning of president Toledo in Machu Picchu by Neo-shamans from Cuzco provides an eloquent example of this process.

Then there is the international current of the New Age that picks up these traditions, constructed on the basis of indigenous culture by Cuzco's Neo-Incas. Little by little, they elaborate intermediate concepts between the two corpuses, essentially based on ideas of energy and messianism. One can thus observe a genuine factory of rituals in Cuzco, mostly aimed at international mystical tourists, organized not only by travel agents but also by state offices, just as the folklorification of Andean culture was supported by official organizations nearly a century earlier. Neo-Incaism has been progressively de-nationalized and dissolved into a global New Age, thus creating new inventions of tradition. In the long course of history, the invention of the Andean New Age is no more than the latest stage of an ethnogenesis: the Indigenists imperialized the tradition, the Neo-Incas nationalized it, and the Neo-Indian followers of the New Age have given it a global range.

Now that the magnetic center has shifted from the Himalayan to the Andean mountain ranges, it seems that the resurrection of the Inca has recovered the cosmic dimension of Inkarrí invented by a defeated and colonized people. For centuries, the Andeans had their land, their mineral wealth, and the product of their work taken from them. Last but not least, their history was also taken from them through the Inca-ization of their traditions. The Indians are now compelled to offer the telluric energy that they generated in the course of their long history. This telluric energy has a feature that deserves to be emphasized: it is more than a mere merchandise, since it is a virtual wealth. In this sense the telluric energy is comparable to financial assets that are traded on the stock market. This is how the energy that is harnessed by New Age mystics through their tour operators becomes part of free-market capitalism.

CHAPTER 14

The Reinterpretation of *Oxlajuj b'aqtun* in Guatemala: Between the New Age and Mayan Reconstitution

Santiago Bastos, Marcelo Zamora and Engel Tally

In the classical period, the Mayans developed a system of measuring time with at least three different types of calendar: the *cholq'ij* or *tzolkin*, the *haab*, and the so-called 'long count' calendar that would end on the *oxlajuj* (thirteen) *b'aqtun*; a date that corresponds in the Gregorian calendar to the 21st of December 2012.

As this date approached, political and cultural events leading up to it went well beyond regarding it as merely a historical or an archaeological anecdote, to considering it a time when the cultural persistence of contemporary Mayans traversed the re-creation of their identity with political contents and New Age mystical interpretations, and spiritual tourism.

Since the mid 1980s different proposals for what we might term Mayan New Age have been created, reappropriating and reinterpreting the various findings and understandings of archaeologists and anthropologists, and the political-spiritual revindication of the Mayan movement in Guatemala. Among all these, the most widespread para-scientific and Mayan New Age theories forecast a new 'Awakening' of humanity, of a mystical-millenarian character, due with the arrival of the year 2012, a forecast that can be seen in the numerous books, articles, and web pages that have been produced about it.

The Mayan New Age interpretations of *oxlajuj b'aqtun* are a phenomenon deserving closer scrutiny, both with regard to the occurrence of this event and in terms of anthropological interpretations of the various manifestations of New Age in Latin America.[1] The particular case of the Mayan variation of New Age can also help us to understand the way in which a religious form with Pre-Hispanic roots is brought up to date in the context of post-modernism, late capitalism and the current economic, ecological and socio-cultural crises of the modern Western paradigm.

1 Following the suggestion of spatial phenomenologist Peter Sloterdijk (2003), New Age is defined here as a resource and an existential attempt to rebuild inhabitable spheres after the spatial-existential breakdown and destruction provoked by modernity and the excesses of post-modernism.

 | DOI 10.1163/9789004316485_019

In this article we shall therefore review the way in which the date of the end of the *oxlajuj baq'tun* has come to be the proposal we now know of; from its beginnings as part of the calendar of classic Mayan dynasties; through its appropriation and resignifying by the New Age and the reconstituted Mayan thinking of today; to being a symbolic date that everyone has now heard of.

Mayan Calendars and Their Historical Continuity

The Calendar of the Long Count

One of the fundamental concepts defining the religion of ancient Mayan societies is the long count calendar, which marks days on 5 general levels, the longest of which is the *baq'tun* while the others are *katún, tun, uinal* and *kin*, as shown in Table 14.1. It is a vigesimal system for organizing time, except the *tun*—for solar timing—, and following the Mayan system of numbers, there are thirteen *b'aqtuns* in all.

The long count starts on a mythical day that can be calculated—within a margin of error of days—to have been in the 'Gregorian' year of 3114 B.C. The date is mythical, because there are no monuments that were built at that time.

During the classic period (250–900 A.C.) Mayan political administrators used the long count to mark the days of their own time, and to build up the historical record of their rulers and political and religious alliances. Thus the long count may be understood as a part of State ideology, an institutionalized form of religion and politics used to run the dominions of the classic states. Seen as a form of domination, the long count will have created a historical sense—in terms of the imposition of myths of origin and continuity—and, supposedly, the control of war cycles and astronomical cycles through its

TABLE 14.1 *Table of cycles of the long count*

Cycle	Equivalences in the long count	In Gregorian calendar years
Baq'tun	20 *katuns*	144,000 days, or 394.52 years
Katún	20 *tuns*	7,200 days, or 19.73 years
Tun	18 *uinals*	360 days
Uinal	20 *kins*	20 days
Kin	1 day	1 day

SOURCE: ELABORATED BY MARCELO ZAMORA FROM VARIOUS TEXTS.

relation to biological cycles and the life of the ruler (birth, coronation, marriage, death of ancestors, death of ruler, etc.).

During the post-classic period the long count was extinguished from all known calendar records. As it was directly connected to a state religion, it did not last any longer, except in some centralized states, and then it disappeared entirely after the late post-classic. By the time of the colonial period, references in the long count have disappeared, and it is no longer mentioned in generally known ethno-historical and ethnographic studies of modern Mayan religiosity and traditions.

Calendars of the Short Count

The *cholq'ij* and the *haab* appear in the historical records of the steles from the classical period, within the long count, with their own autonomy, and refer to regional ritual processes—the *haab*—, and communities—the *cholq'ij*.

The *haab* is a solar calendar of 365 days that organized the processes of ritual events held by the guilds, such as dances, pilgrimages and offerings. Although its use appears to extend to Non-Mayan societies, like that of the Mexica, it has a very different look in each region. In the Low Lands of the North during the pre-classic period, it seems to have kept alive the traditions and the rituals belonging to the political elites. It is possible that although the long count celebrations were interrupted, the *haab* was an important replacement that united political entities over the region during the post-classic period.[2]

The *cholq'ij* or *tzolkin* is made up of twenty 13-day periods.[3] It is the calendar of Pre-Hispanic origin that still has most relevance to Mesoamerican indigenous spiritualities, for it is linked to vital cycles and the 'energies' that some *K'iche'* specialists say are represented by the numbers. Once a person's date of birth according to the *cholq'ij* is known, it is possible to know the dominating *nawal* and the 'energies' that some *K'iche'* specialists say are represented by the numbers.

As an everyday calendar, the *cholq'ij* was active after the collapse of the classic period and lasted in the records found in codices made by post-classical societies in the Low Lands of Yucatán. It was also used, known and documented during the colonial period, as revealed by documents found in certain palces in the

2 The everyday strength of use that the *haab* possessed once the colonial period had begun, according to accounts of Yucatán by bishop Diego de Landa in the sixteenth century, is quite surprising. Landa speaks of celebrations of the civil calendar—the calendar associated with the agricultural cycle—with connotations relevant to the cult of monthly bearers and the social organization of the guilds: warriors, sculptors, healers, hunters, fishermen, priests and witch doctors.

3 *Cholq'ij* is the name in the Maya Kíche language that is spoken in Guatemala; while *Tzolkin* is used in the Mayan of the state of Yucatán in Mexico. In this article we will use mainly the first term, as the commonest in Guatemala.

Guatemalan High Lands (Romero, 2000; Weeks et al., 2009). So it appears to have survived in popular knowledge and in other more esoteric types of knowledge, to judge from the training of religious specialists—osteopaths, herbalists, and spiritual healers, as well as individual and collective bearers (see Tedlock, 1982).

Thus for contemporary interpretations of the *cholq'ij* we have the Yucatán tradition (which epigraphists have used to nourish their interpretations) and the local Mayan *K'iche'* tradition shown by the presence of ritual specialists practicing among the activities of daily life. In Guatemala there have been and still are a large number of *aj q'ijab'* dispersed all over the country, especially on the western plateau.[4]

It is important to mention that after the European conquest, the dominant calendar was the Christian one and it was important for ritual specialists to find a way to link birth dates to the *cholq'ij* directly. Specialists like epigraphists have also managed to find correlations between the Gregorian calendar, the long count and the short count of contemporary, post-classical, and classical Mayan societies.

The Goodman-Thompson-Martínez correlation (GTM) is a calculation that dates the start of the long count in the Gregorian calendar through a conversion table created by the combined work of three specialists.[5] From this moment onwards, epigraphists were able to create a documentary source for studying the political history of the classical period during the years 250–900 A.D. which are the dates referred to in the monumental records of the steles and hieroglyphics in general. This way the date fixed for the first day of the long count is the 13th of August 3114 B.C., and the date on which the final cycle of the 13 long *b'aqtuns* comes to an end coincides with the 12th of December 2012 in the Gregorian calendar.

Mayan Calendars as a Mystical Proposal

Following the 'positivist' archaeological and anthropological accounts of ancient and contemporary Mayans and their calendars, parascientific proponents of the

4 In the context of Guatemala we use the term *aj q'ij*, or *aj q'ijab'* in the plural, to refer to spiritual guides, the counters of days and specialists in historical enrootedness, who belong to the Maya of tradition and custom and work with the *cholq'ij*.

5 In 1905, on the basis of astronomical measurements, Joseph Goodman proposed the date of the 11th of August 3114 B.C. as the first day. In 1926, the Yucatecan mathematician, musician and Mayan scholar Juan Martínez Hernández, published his date for the first day of the long count as the 12th of August 3114 B.C. It was the American archaeologist J. Eric S. Thompson who picked up the works of Goodman and Martínez and in 1927 proposed the GTM2 correlation.

New Age have built alternative narratives that provide a better explanation in the context of postmodernity and late capitalism. According to these authors, the ancient Mayans left a message of great importance and relevance for our time which is to be found encoded in Mayan hieroglyphs, in the 260 day *cholq'ij*, the texts of *Pop Wuj* and the *Chilam Balam*, as well as in the Mayan ritual ball game and temples with astronomical alignments.

The New Age View: José Argüelles and 'The Mayan Factor'

José Argüelles has been one of the principal and earliest New Age commentators on the Maya and 2012. His most notable book, *The Mayan Factor* (1987), makes a mystical intepretation of Mayan numbers and the *cholq'ij* available to the English speaking public.

For Argüelles, the ancient Maya were not simply a civilization with distinctive architectural and intellectual achievements, but the emissaries of a 'Galactic Federation' whose mission was to 'awaken', alert, and orientate the human species with regard to its potential and inevitable spiritual evolution through stages on the calendar. Mayan numbers represent a particular 'tone of creation' that may create harmony or dissonance with musical notes. Through this scheme Argüelles develops his Mayan numerology with original calculations and reasonings, whose most complex formulations tend to be not very logical or coherent. Nevertheless, his numerological criteria allow him to draw out mystical patterns 'woven' into the *cholq'ij* and taken as a whole he calls them 'The Mayan Loom'.

> The Loom is the analog or hologram of the operating principle of the galaxy itself as a total self-contained system. Keeping in mind that the numbers represent symbolic qualities, which describe the potential of our reality, then we see that everything is interactive, interdependent, that all cycles feed on themselves, that nothing can really be described without describing everything, that the whole is indeed contained in the part. The Loom of Maya and the Harmonic Module woven by it comprise a genuine resonant keyboard for our use in toning or dialing up galactic frequencies whose wave formations lie within our very being.
>
> ARGÜELLES, 1987:93

Even though the Mayan New Age cosmic-numerological meta narrative starts specifically with the *cholq'ij*, its interpretation goes beyond it by conducting an exercise of recuperation, reappropriation and reinterpretation of the long count calendar. According to Argüelles, in the course of human history since 3114 B.C., every time one of the 13 *b'aqtuns* has come to an end humanity has taken a step towards its illumination and perfect synchronicity, but not without first passing through the dissonances of materialism, individualism, consumerism and ecological destruction of the planet. Thus the *oxlajuj baq'tun* represents a climax at which the human species will attain a state of perfect harmony and synchronization with nature and the universe, when all the organisms on the planet will be transformed into bodies of light. This is the point of origin and return of the universe—our final destination—where there is neither time nor space only absolute synchronization with everything.

The New Age View: John Major Jenkins and Cosmogenesis 2012

The independent writer John Major Jenkins provides a more elaborate explanation of the year 2012 based on archaeological and anthropological studies of ancient and contemporary Mayans. Although he mentions on several occasions that his proposal is strictly scientific, the final result is a comprehensive reinterpretation of different sources combined under a criterion of his own that is indisputably situated in the New Age spiritual current.[6]

In line with the New Age cosmic tradition worked out for the year 2012, Jenkins takes up the idea of a planetary and galactic alignment, but he adds new elements and brings new evidence to the discussion. Scrutinizing the *K'iche'* Mayan creation myth, the *Pop Wuj*,[7] with care, Jenkins says he has identified astronomical aspects of the myth that include the 'celestial crossroads' of the Milky Way, the ecliptic[8] and the dark rift (Jenkins, 2009). The point C of Figure 14.1 shows exactly where the Sun will be aligned for the winter solstice of 2012 with the centre of the galaxy, and Jenkins proposes that the Mayan cultural elements: the creation myth of the *Pop Wuj*, the Mayan ball game and the temples—are only metaphorical expressions of this galactic alignment, which is reached in 2012 at the end of the 13 *b'aqtun* (Jenkins, 2009).[9]

---

6 His arguments, based on the interpretation of elements taken from Hinduism, Buddhism, Christianity, Astrology, Astronomy, Archaeology, Anthropology, Epigraphy and Conspiracy Theories were used to elaborate an intricate unified para-scientific meta-narrative of 2012.

7 Specifically, the translation by Dennis Tedlock that includes interpretive notes based on information collected during several years of fieldwork with *aj q'ijab' K'iche'* Mayans in Guatemala.

8 The ecliptic is an imaginary circular line to trace the annual passage of the Sun through the heavens with the Earth spinning around it in its own orbit.

9 In this way, the '*Xibalbá b'e*' or 'Road to the underworld' that was taken by *Hun Hunahpú* and *Vucub Hunahpú*—and then by their sons *Hunahpú* and *Ixbalanqué*—to face the Lords of the underworld according to the *Pop Wuj*, simply symbolizes the dark rift dividing the Milky Way. Similarly, the section of the tree where the head of *Hun Hunahpú* was hung by the Lords of the underworld and from which the twins *Hunahpú* and *Ixbalanqué* were engendered, represents this same dark rift.

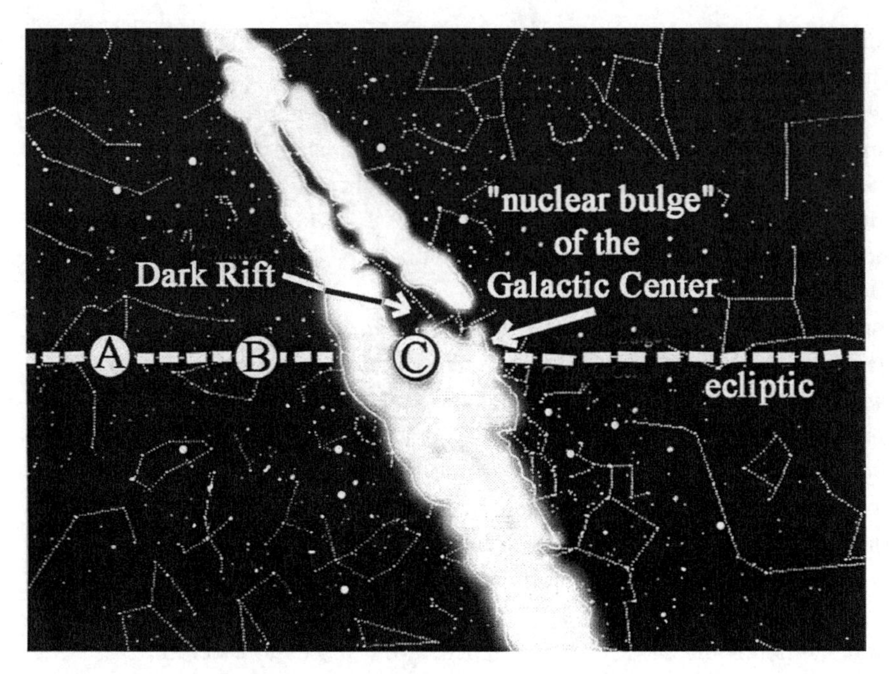

FIGURE 14.1 *The Galactic Alignment of the 2012 Period*

Thus the deep meaning of the symbolic allusions to the dark rift in the *Pop Wuj* and their realtion to the 13 *b'aqtun* are—for Jenkins—a point and a stage of transformation from one paradigm and Age to another.

> The end of a 13-Baktun cycle, as recorded at Quiriguá and elsewhere, is the end of an Era, otherwise known as a Sun or an Age. These Ages, or World Ages, belonged to a World Age doctrine that, as a mythological construct, is described in the Maya Creation Myth (Te Popol Vuh). In this way we can see that the Long Count's 13-Baktun cycle and the Maya Creation Myth are both expressions of an underlying World Age paradigm. One is calendrical and the other is mythological, and as we will see they both encode astronomy.
>
> JENKINS, 2009

The relevance of Jenkins's interpretations lies in the way he extrapolates the deep meaning of cosmic and mythological events to contemporary society. Described in a few words, the death of the Lords of the underworld represents the extermination of their contemporary homologs: the huge capital of transnational corporations, politicians of bad faith like George W. Bush, and the destructive egotism of the consumer society. Inversely, the resurrection of Hun Hunahpú is the renaissance of a new harmonious humanity, with a sense of solidarity and unselfishness, which will arrive in the New Age when the 13 *b'aqtun* comes to an end.

Finally, this far reaching cosmic, mythological and sociological interpretation would not be complete without the provision of certain concrete recommendations as to what to do on the eve of the ending of the 13 *b'aqtun*. Jenkins suggests taking up a position of spiritually centered political activism that resists and peacefully opposes the influences of modern egocentricity, the culture of consumerism, the fantastic version of reality processed by the mass media, corrupt politics and the destruction of the environment, and others (Jenkins, 2009). He also recommends adopting methods and techniques that can help to free one's identity from ego, such as meditation, the use of sacred plants (peyote and hallucinogenic mushrooms), exercises of shamanic healing, devotional prayers and doing social work (Jenkins, 2009). With this, human beings will be able to open themselves to a trans-ego and trans-rational perspective, which will finally flow into a global unity of consciousness that change to a New Age will propitiate anyway.

The New Age and the *Oxlajuj baq'tun* in Guatemala

The proposals for 2012 made by Argüelles and Jenkins have come to form a part of the 'body of doctrine' of the New Age that is available to any cosmopolitan spiritual seeker. Attracted by the mystical experiences of cultural perspectives denied by modernity, as argued by De la Torre (2010), tourism becomes an ideal practice for spiritual seekers as they explore these different, exotic, not modern, horizons.

In the case of Guatemala, New Age spiritual seeking goes back to the arrival of hippies in the 1960s and 70s. Lake Atitlán on the western plateau of the country was their favored destination and many hippies made it their permanent home. Permanent residence in Lake Atitlán led to an interrelation with local Mayan culture and to the development of a Mayan variety of New Age that gained in strength at the end of the 1990s and in the first years of the new century.

Currently New Age spiritual tourism in the municipalities of San Marcos and San Pedro la Laguna is emblematic, with the offer of short courses on the Mayan calendar and the Maya *nawals*, an introduction to Mayan Neo-shamanism, Mayan therapies and the celebration of Mayan ceremonies, as well as others (Tally, 2006; 2007).[10] Such spiritual goods are offered by Mayan practitioners of New Age spirituality and by the local Mayans themselves.

10 See also the documentary *Tierra Sagrada* inspired by the investigative reporting of Tally (2006). http://vimeo.com/groups/guatemala/videos/15282336 (9 April 2012).

With the approach of 2012 and the commercial potential this particular event could generate, official and private tourist services were offered in great quantities. The year 2012 had become a touristic item within a bigger packet that offered 'nature, culture and spirituality' (Robinson, 2003) into which a 'sanitized', purified and idealized vision of the Guatemalans as 'witnesses of an ideal past' fitted nicely.

The spiritual instruction of Mayan New Age practitioners is based to a large extent on the teachings of *aj q'ijab'* by Mayans living locally or within the country, as well as ideas from writers like Argüelles and Jenkins; their discourse is mixed with other spiritual and esoteric currents. The training period of the *neo-aj q'ijab'*—from Guatemala, Latin America, Europe and the U.S.A.—may last for two years, and ends with receiving the 'rod', a symbol of authority, and spiritual and moral legitimacy, according to traditional Mayan customs.

This is how Mayan New Age spiritual leaders such as Tata Chus came to prominence, he being a Guatemalan-Mexican ex hippie who gives talks on the calendar and Mayan spirituality to Guatemalans and foreign tourists at El Remate, Petén, as well as being a member of 'Mayan Unity' (*Unificación Maya*).[11] Asked about his knowledge of the ancient Mayans and the final consequence of the closing of the 13 *b'aqtun* in 2012, he said this:

> The ancestors said: 'we start from a beginning and we return to the beginning'. And we are returning to the beginning of the galaxy. That is why there are changes on the planet, because we are part of a consciousness that is in turn part of another consciousness; we are returning to the beginning of our galaxy, to the galactic womb. And this center is sending a ray, it is sending a vibration, it is sending a wave to our Sun and our Sun is receiving it. That is why our planet is changing. It is not only because we have polluted our atmosphere, it is not only because we have made holes in the ground and sucked the blood out of our planet, not only because we have taken all the treasures.

To complement this, a Ladina (not indigenous) *neo-aj q'ij* woman from the City of Guatemala, who also received guidance from Tata Pedro Cruz (see Figure 14.2) and devotes herself to giving talks to tourists in San Marcos la Laguna under a sign for *Cosmic Mayan Tours,* makes the following comments:

> Now that a change of time is coming, the great change of time, what is going on? The count of 0, 0, 0, 0, 0. A new dawn. What is going to happen?

11 www.unificacionmaya.com (9 April 2012).

FIGURE 14.2
Tata Pedro Cruz, Tz'utujil aj qij' from San Pedro La Laguna, Guatemala, April 20, 2011
PHOTO: SANTIAGO BASTOS

> We can see that human beings have become unbalanced because of the times we are living through. We are in a period when we are experiencing the expansion of the universe. We are the universe. So when we expand there is a disintegration. What does this mean? The Moon is what creates gravity in us. And with this same expansion, the Moon is getting farther away from us these days. So that's why we have this disintegration. But if we are aware of the natural cycles of time, of what is happening with time, we know that this is exactly the right moment to work on integration so we do not disintegrate completely. Integration, unity, a return to being at one, at one with oneself and at one with nature. The spirit of the great Ajaw lives in everything that exists.

Last but not least, a French *Neo-shaman* from San Marcos La Laguna interprets the arrival of the year 2012 and the ensuing cosmic transformations in the following way:

> The Mayans are clear. This is a passage to a new world, a new way, but it also means there is an opportunity to change your consciousness, to make a leap forward for the evolution of Man… What is happening is that this alignment produces a resonance between the energies coming in, that pass through the Sun and the Earth and ourselves: so, bombarded with these energies, we are going to discover new things. Only, the energies

coming in are all of the same type, but they enter into our bodies and cause mutations, but mutations calculated by the Creator and not by a twist here or there. So it is a divine plan that is unfolding, that gives us new possibilities. And it happens to all the quanta and [it so happens that] the Mayan calendars know all these things.

The Political Re-creation of the Maya, and Magical Thought

The process of expanding New Age thought coincides with the 'indigenous emergence' (Bengoa, 2000) in Latin America, which is taking place in Guatemala after the tragedy of the genocide perpetrated by the Army (ODHAG, 1998; CEH, 1999). The peace process provided the context for the Mayan People (*Pueblo Maya*) to reclaim a historical and cultural continuity with the classical Mayans, and start up a dynamic for recreating the contents of this identity label in order to adapt it to present day reality as a basis for political rights (Cojtí, 1997; Warren 1998; Fisher 2001; Bastos and Camus, 1993, 2003).

Sacred Acts in Mayan Politics

When Mayan reclamations began to be heard in public at the end of the 1980s, the subject of 'Mayan religion' was not an important component of the definition of Mayan, based mostly on language as the epitome of cultural difference.

In the following decade, elements of spirituality began to be institutionalized. The *Pop Wuj* turns into the '*k'iche'* bible', the 'canon' of identity (Morales, 2007) through continual quotes and invocations. The 'Mayan ceremonies' become habitual at political, academic or festive activities having to do with indigenous peoples, and they develop a unified ritual (Morales, 2007). The figure of the *aj q'ij* is institutionalized as 'the' religious specialist, also by antonomasia.[12] Historical leaders with the most varied ideological and religious origins appear in public as these *aj q'ijab,* now in charge of giving shape to new expressions of the 'spirituality' which has renounced its title to being a 'religion' while at the same time it has been institutionalized. All this is done in a way that 'creates' a new form of Mayan spirituality, even more differentiated from the 'custom', the form in which this spirituality had subsisted in the colonial context of the last few centuries.

12 Historically there has been a large diversity of ritual and therapeutic specialists related to Mayan spirituality in its various manifestations: *aj q'ij* (counter of the days), *aj q'un* (healer) and *aj itz* (sorcerer). Currently it is the *aj q'ijab* who stand out and are consulted in the local and national spiritual arena.

The introduction into the agreement on the identity and rights of the indigenous peoples, *Acuerdo de Identidad y Derechos de los Pueblos Indígenas* (AIDPI) of the subject of 'Spirituality and Sacred Places' formed the basis for a definitive institutionalization of Mayan spirituality.[13] The organizations of spiritual guides fortified their position, negotiating an agreement on spirituality and sacred places (*Acuerdo sobre Espiritualidad y Lugares Sagrados*), and gained recognition for places previously ignored or stigmatized (Bastos and Camus, 2003; Morales 2007). But the definition of this spirituality slipped out of their hands when the Minister of Culture was left in charge of declaring which sites were or were not sacred, and of handing out tags saying who is and who is not officially *aj q'ij*; also when 'Mayan ceremonies', as shown in Figure 14.3 started to appear at government events, of cooperation, culture and tourism; and when politicians and various personalities, anthropologists and non Mayan tourists also started to figure on the list of *aj q'ijab'* who have been given their wand. This process has led to a politicizing of spirituality, when the sacred is used to legitimize the actions of the Mayans, of the State and of other subjects.[14]

The Sacralization of Being Maya

While demands for political insertion in a multicultural nation were being made, there was a move from the concept of people-as-a-nation, claiming autonomy within a state, to the conception of an original people claiming the right to self-determination beyond the political realm: because it was not claiming to be a nation opposed to a nation, but a civilization against a civilization. The sense of difference becomes greater.

A sector of the Mayans—calling themselves such—have been involved in a process of seeking elements of 'their own' that define them as Mayans, passing from external cultural elements—their language the most evident of these—to their 'cosmovision', as their purest possession and the most untouched by centuries of Western colonization.

> [Our cosmovision] is the form of interpreting, explaining, reacting, feeling and thinking which our ancestors and ancestresses developed for

13 The agreement on the identity and rights of the indigenous peoples, *Acuerdo de Identidad y Derechos de los Pueblos Indígenas* (AIDPI), signed in 1995 as part of the Peace Agreements between the guerrilla and the government of Guatemala, assumed a recognition of the multicultural character of Guatemala (Cojtí, 1997; Cayzac, 2000; Bastos and Camus, 2003).

14 The Vice President is 'blessed' by the ancients of Chichicastenango, a presidential candidate declares that he has received the *aj q'ij* wand, or Mayan ceremonies are conducted to legitimize mining projects that have been refused by the population (Bastos, 2007).

FIGURE 14.3 *Mayan ceremony, Guatemala, November 24, 2010*
PHOTO: SANTIAGO BASTOS

> living and for relating to the Universe. It is about understanding from life and from the world of the Mayab People.
>
> UK'UX B'E, 2009: 11

Their worldview includes the relation to nature and to the universe or cosmos, through which it is sacralized, as it closely approaches and is blended in with the relation to 'spirituality'. 'This way of interpreting the *mayab'* reality can be described as a fact of the sacred universe, from which social and natural order are derived' (Uk'ux'Be', 2009: 11).

At the level of identity, all this implies that the choice of being 'Maya' instead of 'indigenous' is no longer an ethnic or political question, but has become a matter of a spiritual or religious kind, thereby entering into a new dimension. The belief in the sacred elements that make up the character of this identity, becomes in effect a requirement, something indispensable to being Maya: 'the *Mayab'* identity is a collective construct (in a cosmogonic and not merely a social sense) (Uk'ux B'e, 2009: 20).

Thus, during the course of recent times, the Mayan has come to be considered more and more as a quality over and above the cultural, reaching the spiritual, the sacred. And the non-rational aspects, the 'supernatural', have been installed in Mayan politics, that are conducted in the name of, and justified by, arguments that are not human or rational, but connected to outside forces, far from any possibility of being socially controlled.[15]

The Cholq'ij and the Oxlajuj B'aqtun

In this process of seeking what is their own, the sacred calendar of 260 days, the *cholq'ij*, has assumed a central role. The ability to measure time that defined the classic Mayans is attributed to this calendar, which is also an obvious sign of cultural continuity:

> The *cholq'ij* is the greatest expression of the universe: space and time. It is the comprehension of interdependence, of unity, of energy and of movement. The Lunar Calendar is the result of a study of the universe, of the development of the life of the person, and is synthesized in 20 signs.
> VÁSQUEZ, 2001: 11–12

The *cholq'ij* is used, as the *aj q'ij ab* always have used it, as something that gives special meanings to, and conditions, human activities, through the value of each *nawal*:

> The principals and elementary bases determining the experience and the application of *Mayab'* cosmic knowledge ('*cosmocimiento*'), correspond to the 20 *nawals* of the *Cholq'ij*: each principal of the *Cholq'ij* has an energy that forms a part of our living essence.
> UK'UX B'E, 2009: 29

Compared to continuity in the use of the *choq'ij*, the long count calendar which contains the 13 *b'aqtun* was recovered through the work of archaeologists and epigraphists who started to reconstruct Mayan script half way through the twentieth century, and has been appropriated by Mayans with access to this type of knowledge. At first it was used in its 'lay' form, to show the depth of the roots of Mayan culture.

---

15 So it appears when the *Asamblea de Representantes del Pueblo Maya* has proposed that: 'Holding an office in the Assembly must last for 7 years, corresponding to the vision of time according to the Sacred Mayan Calendar... The community and local authorities should take possession of their offices on the day established by the *Ajq'ijab'* specialists. Further, applicants must have been born under the sign or *nawal* of *Batz'* or *Kan*' (quoted in Morales Sic, 2004: 70–71).

In this context, the symbolic date of the *Oxlajuj B'aqtun* has gained constantly more attention on the scene. It may be found in the 'Oxlajuj B'aqtun Series' which is how Uk'ux B'e denominates his texts. It may be seen in a group of 'indigenous revolutionary militants' who were reunited in 2010 in the Oxlajuj B'aqtun Political Council to 'take up again the revolutionary aspirations that originated the insurgent movement' (Ceto, 2010: 34); or at a Conference of Mayan Studies under the heading 'Oxlajuj B'aqtun: A Change of Cycle and Associated Challenges'.

The ways in which this date is understood are associated with a change, normally one corresponding to a superior and unknowable order, which will occur in a fashion that is above our wills, as the Mayan ancestors had said. The 'catastrophism' of a social, economic and climate crisis getting worse all the time, which announces that we are reaching the end (some say of the world, others of the Age), is combined with the promise of a radical change—often a renaissance of the explicitly Mayan. It is from this idea of a 'new dawn' that the political dimension of *oxlajuj b'aqtun* is drawn.

> Those of us who form the National Council of Mayan Elders, Xinca and Garifuna of Guatemala...are here in fulfilment of the Mayan Prophecies of the 13 Baktun and 13 Ajau. We believe firmly in the prophecies announcing the Change and for this reason we reaffirm that it will have the full support of the population through this National Council of Elders.[16]
>
> We therefore as the Mayans of today have the responsibility of being decisive actors in this new 'Majawil k'ij' [New dawn] creation in the direction announced by our grandparents and confirmed by modern thinkers and events. Now we have to participate energetically in the conducting of History and fight together to gain recognition for our equality among the peoples (De Paz, 2010: 85, 112).
>
> We are ending a cycle. From Mayans we went to being Indians, and then we were indigenous people, peasants, and now we are going back to being Mayans again. From resistance we go on to recovery and now reconstitution. It is the closing of a cycle, and we have to prepare ourselves for the new time.[17]

16 Don Cirilo Oxlaj, President of *el Consejo Nacional de Ancianos Mayas, Xinca y Garifuna de Guatemala*, words spoken during the act of assuming office by Alvaro Colom as President of the Republic of Guatemala, 14 January 2008.

17 Don Leopoldo Méndez, personal communication to Santiago Bastos, 22 July 2011.

Added to the perpectives previously described of the various actors within the Mayan movement are also the contributions of important academic figures like the well known Jakalteko Mayan anthropologist, Víctor Montejo, who proposes in his book *Maya Intellectual Renaissance* his 'b'aktunean theory'.

> This millenial or b'aktunian movement responds to the close of a great prophetic cycle, Oxlanh B'aktun, the great prophetic cycle of 400 years in the Maya calendar... If we review ethnohistorical books such as the Popol Vuh, the Chilam Balam, El Q'anil, and others, there are passages that give the people hope for a return to their roots at the close of the millenium. The messages in these books have given the Maya optimism for the struggle to achieve a better future for the indigenous peoples of the Mayab' region. This b'aktunian theory responds to both the global and the cosmic meaning of the cyclical period of the thirteenth b'aktun, at the beginning of which we stand.
>
> MONTEJO, 2005:121–122

Versions of the Maya in San Pedro de la Laguna

To end this section in the same way as the one before, we shall see some versions of the *oxlajuj b'aqtun* proposed by Mayans living in San Pedro La Laguna, on Lake Atitlán. In these we shall see that elements from the different traditions noted, are combined. The president of the T'zutujil lingusitic community of the *ALMG* (Academy of Mayan Languages of Guatemala) in San Pedro la Laguna gives an interpretation that includes cosmic and ecological rather than political elements:

> Just imagine if the changes with the alignment of the planets should come, and the new Sun comes in, for example, what happens in practical terms in this case is that the technology will collapse. If the solar rays were to be stronger the technology would not be able to cope and the satellites that keep the telephones, the television and the digital networks running, would all be in chaos. But at the same time we will have the opportunity to start again, to relate to nature, to be more conscious that it is not just us humans living here but plants, animals, everything we know. In other words, it is the greening of the planet.[18]

18 Pedro Culum Culum, personal communication to Engel Tally, 12 July 2011.

One of the most recognized social commentators in San Pedro la Laguna, who is best known through his weekly radio programme, offers a deeper Mayan cosmic discourse when he mentions the following:

> We know very well that the Oxlajuj B'aqtun ends on the 21st of December 2012, precisely on the day of Ajpub'. This is the Mayan symbol that represents the Sun. … However, the Oxlajuj b'aqtun is the culmination of a period of time and the beginning of another b'aqtun. The change started in 1992 with the alignment of the planets. I don't know if you remember in 1992 there was an alignment of the planets when first Venus came out in the morning, then the Moon and then the Sun; they appeared in the same part of the sky. So that is when the change of time began. Not only did the change of time arise from the changing astronomical phenomena, but it also changed the mentality of people. As though there was an effect produced by this astronomical change, a change of time.[19]

We cannot end without giving some space to *Tata* Pedro Cruz, the *tz'utujil* Mayan *aj q'i* who is a point of reference in custom-based Mayan and Pan-Mayan spirituality in the area, especially for New Agers in the nearby municipality of San Marcos La Laguna (Tally 2006), and deserves to be mentioned on his own merits. He has trained various foreigners as *aj q'ijab* and celebrates Mayan weddings in places as far away as Slovakia and Norway.

In an interview with Tata Pedro Cruz about his interpretation of 2012, he argues the following:

> They say I am crazy because I make invocations, because I talk to the stones, talk to the wood. No, I am not crazy. I talk to the wood because I know wood has a spirit. I talk to the stone because I know stone has a spirit. I talk to a mountain, to the hills, because they are sacred temples, because they have a spirit. I call on the cloud, I call on the storms because everything has a spirit. It is the god, it is the god that is here inside. I ask that we unite our minds, that we come to understand we are a single spirit. We are of the same blood, we are of the same race. Our colours have nothing to do with it, we are all human beings. All of us who live on this earth are children of an Ajaw, of a God, of a Yaweh, of a Jehovah, we are one…

19 Vicente Bosel, personal communication to Engel Tally, 15 July 2011.

> For 2012, this event which is approaching us, it is to be commemorated, to celebrate, for us to embrace each other, but an honest embrace. This is the change that is approaching us, this is the awakening of consciousness that we are bringing all over the world. We have to awaken consciousness... There will be an important change, there have to be changes... Guatemala needs a revolution, a revolution of consciousness. I have always been a revolutionary, but of consciousness. What we need is the revolution of the awakening of consciousness... There has to be a new generation that will come and end all this.

The *Oxlajuj b'aqtun* and the Critique of Modernity

The historical review we have made of the system of Mayan calendars and the date of the Oxlajuj B'aqtun in it, is an example of how Indo-American religions can be recreated historically. Starting as State religions, they survived in the colonial period as spaces of resistance that had found a place in the official Catholic religion, resulting in de-institutionalized forms that still managed to keep up some continuity, as happened with the use of the *cholq'ij*.

This is now reunited with the long count calendar in frameworks that have in common a 'magical' view of the world, like the New Age and the political reconstitution of the Maya. Both of these movements seek to find their initial 'purity' but they give it new, contemporary, content. They are both forms that are critical of Western thinking, and arose with postmodernity and the crisis of capitalism, which is where the current success of the *oxlaqjuj b'aqtun* must be placed.

In this way the symbolic date of the *oxlajuj b'aqtun* is present in Guatemala as something inseparable from tourism and all the commercializing of Mayan culture associated with it; but it gets above this and percolates through into the everyday life of the people of Guatemala. The same discourse combines New Age elements with those of Mayan recovery.

A superficial study of the discourses of the various actors has shown us that these tend to coincide more than they differ. Arguments about cosmic alignments and their impact in the form of a change of human mentality, towards unity and universal harmony, are tightly linked, as are environmental concerns and the 'existential anguish' of the modern human who finds himself in a state of disequilibrium and disharmony. To a great extent all this also reflects—in varying degrees and measures—the underlying assumptions of Argüelles (1987) and Jenkins (1998).

The New Age type of meta-narrative has infiltrated Mayan political discourse, and inversely, Mayan political discourse has permeated New Age discourses. But the relation is not a simple one like that of colonialism, which is what one might have supposed from reading only Galinier's chapter of this book. Both discourses arise and evolve at the same time on different fronts; and come to a partial interpretive accord that makes it extremely difficult to discern the elements proper to each posture.[20] There is evidence for this in the interpretations of Mayan activists like Maco de Paz, who says in his book '*2012. La quinta era en la historia del pueblo maya*' (2012. The Fifth Age in the History of the Mayan People) that:

> The prophecy of Nostradamus, made in the sixteenth century and interpreted by scientists in the twenty-first century, accords with the prophecies of the Mayan People, of the Egyptians, of the Hopi and the Hindu, who prophesied many centuries before. They also all discovered the future of Human History, in the heavens.
>
> DE PAZ, 2010: 110

The growing presence of spirituality in the contemporary construction of the Maya is an example of something more widespread, as is the spiritual dimension in the *reconstitution* of the Mayans as an original people. Within the process of thinking of themselves as an original people, the same actors have been looking for elements that make them special and unite them with other peoples of Abya Yala while differentiating them from the 'West'. And as what is one's 'own' is sought out from among the aggregated elements of centuries of colonization, an ideological nucleus of 'the Mayan' remains intact, whose best expression is in its spirituality, the part that survived, de-institutionalized and hidden among superimposed Catholic elements. This is the basis for the recovery of 'one's own forms of knowledge and action', a task undertaken inwardly more than outwardly. According to Uk'ux B'e, reconstitution arises from:

> [the need] to recover, revalue and recreate our cosmic knowledge and our reconstitution so as to be able to face cognitive injustice through decolonization...only our cosmic knowledge will allow it to be, for us, in itself and for itself a process of revindication of our Mayan vision and logic.
>
> UK'UX B'E, 2009: 1

20 General agreement does not preclude disputes, like the one between John Major Jenkins and Mayan activist Gaspar Pedro González over the appropriation and interpretive legitimacy of 2012 (See Jenkins, 2009), which take place in very limited spaces and without further consequences.

Understanding scientific reason to be a part of the special epistemological-political development of the West and therefore related to capital and colonialism, the other types of knowledge generated elsewhere in the world—and hidden by the colonization of knowledge—are related, through their opposition, to non-rational knowledge: 'Comprehension of the world is far greater than the Western understanding of the world' (Santos, 2005: 153).

> We are living through a change of Age, not an Age of changes. The Industrial Age is over. The paradigm of Newton, the view of the world of Cartesian reason is no longer appropriate for understanding the socio-political phenomena that the planet is passing through.
>
> DANIEL MATUL, EL PERIÓDICO, 21 December 2006

Hence a vindication of the 'enchanted' as a way to understand their relation to nature and the very society of the indigenous peoples as original inhabitants rather than Westerners. The *Mayab'* way of thinking is considered magical. Facts and processes occur through forces that escape our rational comprehension, and are related to nature and especially the universe (*'el cosmos'*, hence the insistence on 'cosmic knowledge', *cosmocimiento*, as opposed to *conocimiento*, meaning simply, knowledge). A process of self-knowledge and self-creation, as the 'recovery' of what is one's own, in a radically different context from that in which it originally arose, and with different intentions to those originally possessed, has turned the result into something new, a product of the twenty-first century.

This ties in perfectly with changes in the forms of belief and religiosity, which have been passing everywhere from the powerful monolithic historical religions, to de-institutionalized, syncretic or openly hybrid types, recreated personally, and thus closer to the concept of 'spirituality', and suchlike. The greatest expression of these changes is in the New Age movement, this seeking out of alternative spiritualities that nourishes the quest for a new way of relating to the world, to nature and to the supernatural.

Mayan New Age meta-narratives consist of reinterpretations and appropriations that appeal to a wide public in post-industrial and post-modern countries, in response to the present and growing 'existential anguish' of many people, especially in the so-called 'first world' in the context of postmodernism and late capitalism. In these versions a new twist and a new meaning is given to the romantic notion of the 'noble savage' of Rousseau, to mysticism, to the anti-capitalist ethic, to the 'counter culture' and to concerns about the environment, consumer culture and exacerbated individualism.

In spite of their having so evidently a 'Western' origin, from the 'center', these ideas have found niches with local reinterpretations both in the tourism sector and in Mayan Neo-tribal and Neo-shamanistic circles of the region, and from there they have come to the same discourse as the Mayan movement activists in Guatemala. Thus it is not just that Mayan spirituality is one of the sources from which the New Agers seek pure and uncorrupted wisdom, such as that of the Aztecs, that of India or of Buddhism; but also that chronologically speaking they have been building together, with actors who have moved between the two worlds, for example the big chiefs of the native Americans.

So we are not speaking of a relation back and forth between New Age forms and popular religiosity, but a relation between more, and less, developed political sensibilities. The current construction of Mayan and New Age discourses responds in part to similar projects, with a common cultural, social, economic, ecological and human political ethic. In both cases we see processes, that coincide historically in the crisis of Western modernity, which began to be forged in the nineteen sixties, and to take clear shape in the nineties. We might say that the rediscovery of the 'enchantment of reality' by the Mayans corresponds to the search for what is one's own based on getting farther away from the Western, whose rationality had hidden 'other types of knowledge' with non-rational bases. This critique of modernity has also provided the basis for other developments, such as the New Age movement that seeks a utopia of universal love through personal choices.

For both of them, the date of the *oxlajuj b'aqtun* represents an opportunity to think of a political utopia that is possible in cosmic terms, inserted into a larger transformation that is more important and more ample. The questioning of the modern Western status quo, shared by Mayan activists and New Age proponents and followers, reveals an alternative spiritual-political agenda, of a personal and/or of a collective type, which makes it possible to change the current march of humanity, which will happen with the arrival of the *oxlajuj b'aqtun* of 2012. This symbol settles into place in a context that combines extreme environmental degradation with the 'civilizing crisis' (and the economic crisis), and the symptoms of a renovation in which the same actors are protagonists. This is what gives it its meaning.

CHAPTER 15

The Conchero Dance and the Conquest of Cyberspace

Renée de la Torre and Lizette Campechano

Introduction

The aim of this work is to attend to the appropriations, resemanticizings and uses provoked by the interaction of the Conchero dance in its Neo-Mexicanist version (a hybridism that has created a narrative synthesis between postulates of the New Age and essentialist Mexicanism), and cyberspace. This places our study in line with anthropological studies of religion and the media. The media are producing new displacements and reconfigurations of the religious phenomenon. Religion and media are not incompatible at all, as they both have the same primary function: of connecting and binding. Today the mass media and the internet are both being used to inform the public of religious events and news, which is consistent with the aim of turning these means of communication into instruments that will benefit the missionary and proselitism activities of these groups. The new communication technologies have helped to increase the range and the reach of various missionary activities, to create virtual communities, to connect transnational diaspora communities and to propitiate exchanges between networks that make it easier for new transnational religious movements to exist. But cyberspace has also become a place where new religious forms are developed, and these have been categorized as *online religion*. It has become increasingly common for the media to supply the support for 'virtual' rituals or liturgies, that are transforming the traditional ways of acceding to grace, to a miracle, to blessings, to purification, to transcendence, to protection against the evil eye, ways of making contact with the spiritual world, conceiving of the transcendental and even of interacting with the divine (Cowan and Hadden, 2004). Hence every day the supports provided by communications media are valued and used as a new territory for missions, not just to increase the reach by various churches and religious movements of their proselytism, but mainly because this area has become a new stage for religious experience and knowledge. In short, it can be said today that the new technologies, among them the internet, are creating mediatized forms of producing, experiencing and perceiving the religious. They are also causing a displacement of the religious emanating from the habitual institutions (churches),

 | DOI 10.1163/9789004316485_020

by de-centering the reach of religious authorities (priests, ministers, shamans or gurus), and relocating the religious in cultural industries that produce for massive wordwide consumption, in which the teachings, the images and the rituals belonging to religion are mixed with entertainment and even with fiction.[1] The impact of this situation has been to deregulate the monopolistic management of specialized fields (Bourdieu, 1971) with which the modern world had ordered, compartmentalized, and ranked the workings of the social sphere. But the biggest impact has been on cognitive and, especially, sensitive mediation of the religious fact, that is, 'on the ways in which apparently traditional religious rituals and rites suffer significant changes, thanks to their mediated representation' (Stolow, 2014: 152).

We are interested, most of all, in accounting for how the internet interacts with, and mediates in, the construction of new imaginaries and new practical, narrative and metaphorical orientations for the performance of a Neo-pagan ritual known as the Conchero Aztec Dance. Due to the fact that the ritual Conchero dance is a performance, valued as ancestral, when it was originally taken up by networks of practitioners of alternative spiritualities, commonly known as New Age, this provoked a territorial and functional displacement of the dance, taking it out of the forecourts of Catholic churches and getting it performed in Neo-pagan and Neo-indigenous ceremonies, such as the dance to purify and activate the energy of the sacred Geography of Mother Earth. And more recently, the network of paractitioners of an alternative spirituality have widened their interpretive frames to include the new New Age conspiracy theories of the Matrix, a representation inspired by cultural industries producing science fiction that has now become a worldwide narrative about a way of understanding the universe that concords with New Age conceptions of the Cosmos. On the basis of this narrative, a movement of dancers in Spain have hybridized the inherited tradition of Pre-Hispanic Catholic ritualism and turned it into another esoteric item on the bulging shelves of Neo-esoteric goods. This group has undertaken to activate cyberspace through the dance, no

1 An example of this was the phenomenon of Mayan Millenarism, which proclaimed that a change of Age was to occur in December 2012. This belief had been circulating among networks of the practitioners in New Age circuits even earlier than the year 2012, but in 2012 it began to be broadcast by cultural industries (especially in films, video clips, published works of fiction, and documentaries), transforming its neo-pagan millenarian content into an apocalyptic belief predicting the imminent end of the world. This idea was propagated *en masse* all over the world, and motivated followers to create spaces and virtual communities on the internet to face the disaster that had been announced (Campechano and De la Torre, 2014).

longer regarding cyberspace as a technological medium but using New Age sensibility to turn it into a metaphor.

Our methodology is based on the description of three spheres of action, each with its own universe of meaning: (1) Neo-Mexicanism and the Conchero dancers tradition; (2) the network of Spanish speaking New Agers; and (3) the conceptions (cf. the Matrix and cyberspace) created by experimentation with the technological spaces developed on the internet. Our analysis is based first on describing the types of knowledge and the rules of each universe of meaning, and then on analyzing the 'metaphorical displacement of such concepts, by means of which metamorphoses of disciplines are managed' (Mier, 2002). Metaphors are hermeneutic instruments in a process of reinterpretation that works through analogies to form a language capable of creating a new and a particular conception, and of configuring new openings and boundaries for the universes of meaning 'from the most structured disciplines to those with more uncertain boundaries and notions' (Mier, 2002: 90). In our case, we will see how the narratives, when removed to other spaces, metaphorize the other symbolic universes, and thus contribute to resignifying and modifying their uses, with perspectives distinct from those of their original identity.

The three universes of meaning to be developed in the course of this chapter are:

(1) The Conchero dance and Neo-Mexicanism. Here we will see how the dance has been modified, in its form (aesthetics), in its content (cultural identity) and also in its use (change of places where performed and meaning of the dance practice). The ritual of the dance has been traversed by the incessant and ambivalent play of 'demonstrating the continued existence of groups that hold on to a tradition and at the same time revitalize it and renew it' (León Portilla, 2002: 13). Even though the Conchero dance is a syncretic tradition, which kept itself assimilated to festive Catholicism, it has held on to certain, semi-hidden, cultural elements, belonging to the Pre-Hispanic peoples, that were prohibited for being 'idolatrous', 'witchcraft', 'pagan' or 'diabolical'. This led to the Conchero dance being seen as a safeguard for the pure ancestral tradition, and although it is supported by a closed and hierarchical structure, it was open to interactions with other ideological, artistic and cultural currents, due to the fact that it contemplated a project not just of cultural resistance but of cultural conquest. It is to the polysemic sense of 'the conquest' that we will be directing our attention in order to show the projects and uses of the rituals.

(2) A 'netnographic' approach to the alternative spirituality networks of Spanish speakers forming a territory on the web. Having explored this dense network, we study the main web pages of groups with an online and an offline presence (referring to virtual reality, and physical reality, respectively), and attention is directed to a hermeneutic analysis of the passage of the Conchero dance, reinterpreted by the New Age matrix of meaning of the Reginos and the Hispanekas, towards the conquest of territory in cyberspace. We analyze the way in which metaphors create an analogy between the space of Conchero rituals, and the web, seen as a living, sentient, organism that forms a part of the cosmos, considering, as De Certeau (1996) does, that these are tactics to appropriate cyberspace by means of ritual and performance.

(3) The metaphor of the Matrix in the offline world. We will expound the case of Chrisgaia and Emilio Fiel, leader of the Hispanekas (New Agers from Spain who borrowed the Conchero tradition) (De la Torre and Gutiérrez Zúñiga, 2011), and we have re-elaborated it under two matrices of meaning: the New Age, and one based on what was learned from the narrative of 'the children of the Matrix'. Our study deals with the way in which the very notion of cyberspace has itself been turning into a matrix of meaning, constructed on the basis of media intertextuality and that of social networks, thus influencing a new current within the New Age networks, that of The Matrix. We ask: What are the cognitive bridges that allow contact between traditions that appear to be so unlike each other, and their assimilation? What new explanations and narratives are being created? What is the role played by the Conchero dance, whose performance has the capacity to transform the space of a territory, in this new way of making sense of one's relation with the internet? And, how does this mediation transform the concept and the practice itself of a traditional ritual such as the Conchero dance?

Evolution of the Dance: From Pre-Hispanic Paganism to Its New Age Expression

The ritual dance of Mesoamerican peoples was not just the dancing, but had a holistic sense and formed an essential part of a ritual system through which the dance operated as a way of establishing a direct relation between man-society-god-nature (Sten, 1990: 69). For the Amerindian peoples the dance also worked as a pole linking the social, political and religious life of these societies: the warriors danced before going to war; there was a dancing rite to prepare for the sacrificial offering, and in nearly all of the feasts of the Aztec ritual calendar, the dance was present.[2]

During the conquest and the colonial period, the dances were forbidden because the Spaniards thought they were idolatrous practices, but at the same time, the friars had the ritual Aztec dance replaced by the dance of Moors and Christians, thus introducing their own ritual system, where the dance was used to represent the triumph of the Spaniards and the Catholic Church over the Moors (now the indigenous people). Then, during the colonial period, these spread as conquest dances (Warman, 1972). The indigenous people seemed to accept and practice the cult and worship of the new images, but they concealed behind them the meanings of their previous gods, giving it a syncretic and at the same time, esoteric, character (Gruzsinki, 1990). Gabriel Moedano, a Mexican anthropologist who pioneered the study of Conchero dances, defined them this way: 'There is obviously syncretism in them, maybe even actual concealment. The persistence of indigenous symbols and beliefs and indigenous ceremonies with many different origins (…)' (Moedano, 1986: 63).

We will now review the most significant cultural and stylistic re-elaborations of the Conchero dance, and the different meanings that the practice has acquired.

The dances known as Conchero were styled Aztec in the 1930s. They were also considered Conquest dances, as the dances were performed in order to reclaim the memory and practice of ancestral rituals in the spaces where colonial Catholicism had erected itself over the indigenous temples. Conchero dancers have considered themselves a front of resistance against Westernization, conceiving of the dance as a 'combat' against the cultural enemies of Indian roots (González Torres, 2005).

In the period following the revolution, when Mexican nationalism came in, the Conchero dance was taken up again as an expression of Mexicanism and turned into folklore by the State. Revalued by popular urban sectors as the most legitimate source for recovering an indigenous sense of the 'Aztec', it was brought into show business and suffered aesthetic transformations recognized as Aztec-izing (*aztequización*), turning the dance into spectacle as a way of recovering national folklore. The Aztec-ized aesthetics of the Conchero dance, were later taken up as a banner for the Mexicanist movement (De la Torre, 2008), which has contributed to the creation of a narrative concerned with

2 A detailed historiography of descriptions of the dances in the chronicles of the conquest and in indigenous codices is that of Yólotl González (2005). In it the customs, the dress, the devotions and the ritual uses of the dances performed by the natives of Meso-America can be found.

radically essentializing the Aztec, rejecting its syncretism with Catholicism and Hispanicism (De la Peña, 2002: 96).

Starting in the 1980s, the dance also became a source of mystical inspiration for the New Mexicanism (González, 2005; De la Peña, 2002; De la Torre, 2007; Rostas, 2008). Conchero dances were valued by sectors of the middle class who were sympathetic to the New Age spiritual movement, as a way into the universal wisdom of a civilization, able to share religious and philosophical conceptions with other spiritual manifestations, from the East. This markedly hybrid and eclectic current has kept up a dialog with the New Age matrix of postmodern spiritual sensibility.[3] The Neo-Mexican dance is integrated into a worldwide project whose aim is to awaken cosmic consciousness. There are some who have collated it with 'transcendental' meditation practices or 'yoga in motion' (Gutiérrez Zúñiga, 2008). But it has also been reinterpreted as a ritual for raising inner awareness and to harmonize with nature (De la Torre, 2012). The most important precursor to this movement is Antonio Velasco Piña, who wrote the famous novel *Regina*, which has been valued by his disciples as the historical testimony of a sacrificial act to awaken the Indian and Feminine spirituality of Mexico. In terms of narrative, his book contributed to establishing a 'frame alignment' (in reference to interpretive frames)[4] between the New Age and Mexicanism (González Torres, 1997: 29). The Reginos,[5] as followers of this movement are known, have learned to be Conchero dancers, and situate their dance practice on the spiritual paths with a mission to purify the chakras

3 The dances have been considered by New Agers, for example, the Reginos, as syncretic refuges for indigenous wisdom and popular magic. The Huichol *mara'akate* and the Mazatec witchdoctors, described in this book by Aguilar Ros and by Rodríguez, and valued by New Agers in their seeking as masters of shamanism, were displaced from their popular spheres and inscribed in cosmopolitan circuits and even in global New Age networks (as is the case of the old lady Nanita who founded the movement of the Hispanekas); in much the same way, the captains of the Conchero dance have been recognized as the guardians of the Pre-Hispanic tradition of Mexico, and therefore a source of initiation on the Red or Mexicayotl path.

4 Frame alignment (Snow, 1986) translated into Spanish by Frigerio as 'cognitive bridges' refers to a situation where 'two frames of interpretation that are ideologically congruent with respect to a particular problem, but were structurally disconnected, meet' (Frigerio, 1999: 9).

5 Participants in this group are known as Reginos, referring to the novel *Regina* by Velasco Piña. It tells the story of a young Mexican woman who comes back from Tibet—in 1968, no less, the year of the student movement—where she had acquired esoteric knowledge of one kind and another, and starts a movement for the spiritual awakening of the nation. She undertakes a search for the guardians of the traditions of Mexico, who start showing her the sacred tracks that would allow the energy pathways of Mexico City to be unblocked (De la Torre, 2005).

of Gaia (Mother Earth) and awaken consciousness. One reinterpretation of the dance is based on the New Age sensibility that announces the coming of a new spiritual civilization: including the idea of reincarnation, and the conception of the Earth as a living organism that works through its chakras, with the ritual of dance activity providing a kind of reiki for Mother Earth.[6] This is why the dances are important for the Reginos, because they believe that their rhythms and sounds can transmit codes to awaken a genetic memory, both in the case of individual consciousness and in the case of a connection to, and an awakening of, Mother Earth or Gaia.

As we said, these rituals are sustained by the New Age belief that Planet Earth is a living creature, and as such has nine chakras where its cosmic energy is concentrated, one of these being in Mexico. The therapeutic function of the ceremonies is to free the energy of the Earth. Among these rituals are also to be found those peformed at the (Mexican) pyramids, which are considered to be 'cosmic machines' that have to be reactivated in order to awaken Mexico;[7] and ceremonial marches along the old routes of Catholic pilgrimages, as the faithful believe that on these tracks is to be found 'the hidden energy line', left to us by the Pre-Hispanic civilizations of the zone. They also join the dance groups at the principal religious feasts, as they consider the places where they meet to be neuralgic points (*nadis*) for liberating the feminine energy of the Earth.

Finally, it should be noted that the dance has been transnationalizing in two ways: the first is through migration from Mexico to the United States, where it was imported as folklore, and adopted during the nineteen seventies by the civic movement of the Chicanos, who impressed it with a renewed cultural and political significance that served to sustain the creation of a mythical spirituality which in turn serves as the basis of the concept of an imagined nation, that of Aztlán (De la Torre and Gutiérrez, 2011). The second way is by a kind of pollination effected by New Age spiritual seekers, who hope to appropriate

6 As Gutiérrez Zúñiga shows in this book, the dances were taken up by spiritual seekers who then went on to include them in the therapeutic services they offered, along with other techniques of interior awareness and of relaxation and alternative healing. The way it was incorporated into esoteric merchandise and therapeutic circuits has created hybrid interpretations of the dance such as those that treat it as an equivalent to yoga or reiki.

7 This is illustrated in the novel *Regina*, when Uriel, who had been a dance captain, and guardian of the tradition, goes to Monte Albán on the 21st of March 1968, and there discovers that the pyramid was 'a gigantic machine which transformed cosmic energies with a specific purpose: that of propitiating the harmonious workings of human nature. Surely in times past it must have been the most advanced therapeutic center on earth. A hospital of bodies and souls to which people came from far off lands to recover their lost equilibrium' (Velasco Piña, 1987: 46).

FIGURE 15.1 *Hispaneka dancers in the forecourt of the Cathedral of Santiago de Compostela, Spain, August 18, 2009*
PHOTO: RENÉE DE LA TORRE

ancestral shamanic knowledge and then become masters themselves, forming belief menus on which the traditions are reinterpreted (De la Torre, 2011).

For the purpose of this chapter we will concentrate on this second way, which began in 1992, due to the interconnection of two distinct but convergent projects. In the first place it was exported by a countercultural movement to redefine the discovery of America. The Mexicans, led by an elderly Conchera chieftainess (Guadalupe Jiménez Sanabria, known as 'Chief Nanita', captain of the dance group Insignias Aztecas, from Mexico City), undertook the reconquest of Europe, with the aim of commemorating the 500th anniversary of the 'meeting between European and Indo-American cultures', in 1992. This project was undertaken by a pilgrimage of Mexican Conchero dancers on their way to Santiago, in Spain, which: 'gave a start to the spiritual reconquest of Europe, not by force this time, but by the force of love and of the heart' (Ruz Buenfil, 2002: 178) (see Figure 15.1). Thus these masters translate the contents they have learned to new geographies in the world, including their circulation in virtual spaces. This is the case of the Reginos (a Neo-Mexicanism born in Mexico) and of the Hispanekas (Spanish Conchero New Age), who have created a new 'conquest of territory in cyberspace', generating a circuit of alternative spirituality, in which the dance serves as narrative support to naturalize the space of technology in a cosmic spiritual space.

The Neo-Mexican Dance in the Constellation of New Age in Cyberspace

Michael De Certau mentions that stories are a way of practicing space, but also 'produce geographies of actions and drift towards the commonplaces of an order' (De Certeau, 1996:128). Taking into account this performative conception of narration in the generation of territory, we will provide a description of the way in which the network of Neo-Mexicanist dancers, linked to the constellation of Spanish speaking New Agers, configures the territory of cyberspace and gives it meaning.[8]

According to Escobar, the term cyberspace alludes to the growing networks and systems of environments mediated by computers, or a network of specialized interactions such that cyberspace comes to be seen as the 'equipment of a shared presence and complete interaction by a multiplicity of users, that allows a going in and a coming out, to and from the human sensorial field, from which it obtains the faculty to perceive virtual and physical realities, the remote collection of information, control through presence-at-a-distance and a total integration and intercommunication with a complete range of products and intelligent environments in real space' (Escobar, 2005: 15).

Cyberspace consists mainly of web sites, which will be the objects of our study. Two aspects that we wish to study, of the internet as a space where religious beliefs circulate and are redefined, are these: the worldwide networks made possible by the internet; and 'the age of media convergence, based on the fusion and integration of the media, making forms of communal rather than individualistic reception possible' (Jenkins, 2008). The internet provides easy access to information and easy diffusion of the same through it, and encourages the formation of a multiple rhetoric based on a fusion of languages (Galavis, 2003), which contributes to hybridizing and creating narratives, *bricolage* style, and the revaluing of images as narratives of identity.

To start with we will describe the ways of transiting, designing spaces (blogs, web pages and forums) and forming connections (links used between pages and forums), thereby to reconstruct the way in which the circuit of practitioners and followers of the Neo-Mexicanist movement is practiced and given shape in cyberspace. Then we will conduct a hermeneutic analysis of the

8 The study presented here is based on research conducted by Lizette Campechano, that was presented as a dissertation for a first degree in Philosophy and Social Sciences, during which she conducted a netnographic study of Mexicanism and Neo-Mexicanism circuits in cyberspace (Campechano, 2010). Netnography conceives of the internet as a field in which to conduct an ethnographic study, with the aim of constructing an explanation of the cyberculture investigated by means of a new way of being there in cyberspace (Del Fresno, 2011: 68).

metaphorical uses with which Neo-Mexicanism names and appropriates the web, observing the narratives of its action and the redefinition of the web as a 'ritual domain' (Turner, 1974). In this sense, we will attend to the performative act in the way the symbols and meanings belonging to Neo-Mexicanism adjust metaphorically, creating a semantic and functional redefinition of ritual domains.

Cyberculture began to be considered by these movements (in the first decade of the new millenium) as a space of empowerment, construction, creativity and community online (Rueda, 2008). Different groups, networks and movements with the common feature of practicing Neo-Mexicanism have created their blogs, their websites, and their social networks, to broadcast their activities, keep members of the network informed, and promote their wisdom teachings and rituals in the form of 'esoteric merchandise' (Gutiérrez, 2008) for seekers after unconventional spiritualities. Nevertheless, being online does not stop them having foundations offline and in the territoriality of a tradition; indeed Neo-Mexicanism remits to the tradition as a form of legitimacy. The offline experience does not create the dissolution or the delocalization of a specific faith from a territory, rather it expands this faith to unsuspected places with a marked tendency to conquer space by performance, as territory for spiritual rituals. Like the concept of Castells' 'space of flows' as 'the technological and organizational possibility of organizing the simultaneity of social practices without geographical contiguity' (Castells, 2000: 14). In this case the dance, recognized by the dancers themselves as one of 'conquest', is a tale and a practice that is used to generate sacred geographies that allow space to be resymbolized and the landscape to be symbolically redefined, for example, by transforming the Zócalo in Mexico City into an Aztec ceremonial center, or following the route of a Catholic pilgrimage as a ritual to revitalize one of the chakras of Mother Earth. In what way is the metaphorizing of internet use as dance, and the redefinition of cyberspace under New Age notions, contributing to the conquest and symbolic redefinition of the web? And, apart from that, what role does the traditional anchorage of the Conchero dance have, in granting it realism and enrooting virtual networks offline?

We have found that some of the main web pages forming the fabric of the constellation of Hispanic New Age spirituality belong to the Ibero-American Light Network, *la Red Iberoamericana de Luz*: these are la Red Anahuak, la Red Luz, Red Mexicana de Conciencia and la Casa de la Red (see Figure 15.2). These sites were considered 'nodal points'[9] of the Spanish-language alternative

---

9 We understand by nodal point a place 'multipracticed' by different actors with different national, cultural and religious backgrounds (Castells, 2006: 446–448). On the internet,

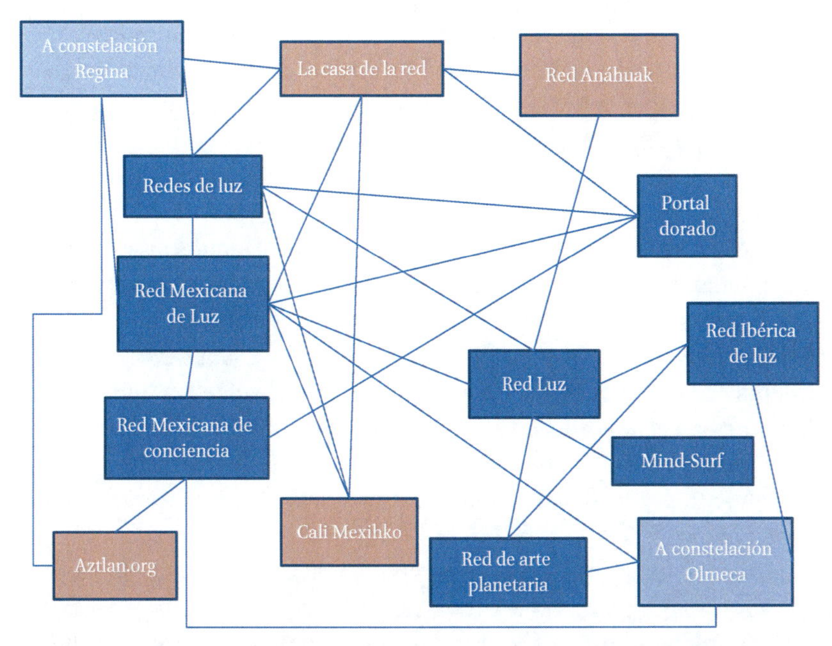

FIGURE 15.2 *Ibero-American Light Network* (Red Iberoamericana de Luz)

spirituality network, due to the fact that they concentrate and maintain links with each other, and form a circuit of spirituality and Neo-esoteric knowledge, that in diagram form looks like this:[10]

One of the narrative strategies for appropriating cyberspace as a territory of the cosmic network,[11] is the design of the web page itself, which is constructed,

we consider nodal points to be those that are created as a consequence of the flow (of visits and links to other pages).

10 In all, over approximately four months (December 2008—March 2009), 324 pages of Mexicanism and Neo-Mexicanism were recorded; of these 144 were web pages or sites, and 180 were forums, personal pages or blogs. To characterize the nodes, classifications were developed: matrices, filials, and sporadic modules or users, which can be distinguished by noting: the links, the quantity, the size and density of connections a site makes, the activity on the page, its services and web technology resources.

11 When this research was developed, Facebook had only started to make its powerful entrance into the internet. However when the links were revised and some of the places that hosted the studied web sites were upgraded they showed the dynamic features that the web imprints onto its contents: change, continuous and fast. Some of the platforms fused themselves, like Miyo's blog (www.elblogdemiyo.com) and Miyo's web site (www.emiliofield.com). However the fact that you can (now) find the actors studied here on Facebook attracts attention. It is something that didn't happen when the data was first

designed, and named through the application of certain iconic codes that are possessed, but whose use is also regulated through the establishment of certain rules. For example, on the site of *Redes de Luz* (Retrieved from http://redesdeluz.blogspot.com), there are 'rules for communication on the network' that provide guidance for proper participation on the network, which is in effect a way of humanizing, standardizing and urbanizing the space.[12] In possession of the ability to name or symbolize the space, the creators or webmasters hand a metaphorical guide to their users, who go through it and practice it, that is to say, create a particular way of constructing the meaning of the space. The users, who cannot transform the space directly (not having access to the webmaster), adapt it, as they use it, to their everyday needs, altering the norms and meanings (Salcedo, 2008). This is achieved through their interactions, their practices in cyberspace, following instructions or disregarding them, or generating new dynamics for ways of presenting information and ways of interacting.

The Implementation of Narratives and Metaphors in Pursuit of the Neo-Conchero Conquest of Cyberspace

The web is valued as a space that allows the objectives, activities and services offered by these groups to be strengthened, spread, and exchanged. At the same time, its sites and its links make it possible to amplify networks formed between

collected. Today Facebook has become a handy tool for managing these nets, since it enables the creation of networks in a simpler way. Not only for the user, but also for web managers since it has an impressive hypersegmentation for publicity. This helps the site to reach a wider audience that might be interested in the topics that each group is promoting. But also the technical features of this platform develop new dynamics for the appropriation of cyberspace.

12 Some examples taken from the page are these: '1. Always bear in mind that on the other side of your screen there is a real human being, with his own ideas and feelings. Always write as though the two of you were looking each other in the eye. Never write anything that you would not tell another person face to face. This is perhaps the most important rule you should always have with you. 7. You should know and use the little expression faces to help transmit certain feelings, especially if you are using humor or sarcasm. 13. CAPITAL letters may be used instead of accents or to make an emphasis, but DO NOT write everything in capitals as this will be interpreted on the network to mean YOU ARE SHOUTING! 15. Be tolerant. Remember the "Delete" key which will allow you to erase and ignore any undesired message'.

these groups, and movements that are kindred to the Conchero tradition and to the network of alternative (New Age) spirituality in the Spanish speaking world, as also to reinforce internal communication and the sharing of information between members of the groups. Among the objectives set out on a web page are these: 'The page aims to fulfill a twofold purpose: to let those who have started to delve into Conchero know what it is, and at the same time, to serve as a useful and quick internal communications device among the Concheros of Spain' (http://web.jet.es/planetagaia/mesa.htm).

The language and signs brought along by the New Age holistic vision generate an esoteric-mystical symbolic domain on the web that gradually builds up a circuit of informal networks to exchange information, and for communication between Spanish speaking people living in different parts of the world, where their sympathizers share universal utopias that it will be possible to realize by transforming lifestyles. For example, on the site: http://web.jet.es/planetagaia/mesa.htm, the page of *la Mesa de Danza de la Cruz Espiral del Señor Santiago* (created by the group of Hispaneka Concheros) we find an apology for their presence on the web:

> Who said we Concheros couldn't submerge ourselves in cyberspace; that the new technologies were at odds with the tradition? Who set the roots clinging to the Earth against the branches solacing themselves with new airs? concheros.com will show the world that we move the 'mouse' with no less precision and affection than the 'arms' in our ceremony; that we do not wish to waste the possibilities that Heaven has given us to sow songs and flowers, also in the virtual world of '*Interné*'.[13]

In this text, as the terms of the Conchero identity are adapted to the internet, space—represented by the allegory of 'branches solacing themselves with new airs'—in which 'we move the mouse' is practiced and transformed (creating an analogy with the movements of the dance accompanied by a tambourine). For the Concheros, the weapons of conquest are their musical instruments; here the 'mouse' is introduced into the narrative as a weapon of conquest that will contribute to redrawing the landscape of the internet.

This Conchero group from Spain, which calls itself 'Hispaneka' (a compound of *hispanica* and *azteca*, referring to its hybrid character as part Spanish and part Aztec), is also linked to a dense network of alternative spirituality, definable as New Age. However, their discourse does not lose its Conchero identity,

13 Retrieved from http://web.jet.es/planetagaia/mesa.htm.

as it proceeds with terms that are very specific to the Conchero dance and are linked to Neo-Mexicanism, for example calling the webmaster 'chief' (*jefe*, the leader of the dance group), or describing sections of the web page as the 'four winds' (the four directions, or cardinal points), or saying that the web page is perfumed and beautified by the users' ideas (in reference to a practice during the vigil, at the moment of ritual cleansing). Let us see:

> Visit the new web page, mark it as one your favorites and contribute your ideas to it to perfume it and beautify it. Our Webmaster the chief of this electronic platform, Kepa, will register your offerings (...). After he has reached the home page, the visitor is presented with four winds, four possible directions (...). concheros.com will make available to those who are interested the secrets of a tradition that marked a before and after in our passage through the Earth and will also provide us with an efficient means of communication between ourselves.[14]

On their own page, they interpret their presence on the web as being a part of the commitment they assumed with the tradition to conquer new adepts culturally, and to strengthen relations of ritual godparenting (*compradazgo*): the sign of greeting among dancing 'godparents' (*compadritos*) is an embrace.[15] On the page of *la Mesa de Danza de la Cruz Espiral del Señor Santiago* they define their transit over the web as being equivalent to going on a pilgrimage, so the space of the internet is transformed into a place that can be cleansed by them and their ritual:

> And in this effort to widen our embrace more and more, to establish ever more robust, broad and capable points of union, arose the intention also to go on a pilgrimage along the trails of the new millenium: along the cybernetic paths of the internet. With a little daring and a lot of hope, along with a lack of knowledge, we launched ourselves onto it trusting, as always, in a little push from the Spirit. At the end of the day, as we often like to say 'Él es Dios' ('He is God') and everything serves in the carrying

14 Retrieved from http://web.jet.es/planetagaia/mesa.htm.

15 Within the Conchero tradition, relations like those of godparents are established, and these have to do with initiation into the rite. Among Concheros the greeting is '*compadritos*' ('my little fellow godparents') and it is symbolized by an embrace in which arms are crossed to form the shape of a cross and the hand of the *compadre* or *comadre* is kissed.

> out of His Plan on this our Earth (…) we now wish to present our new baby to society from the platform provided by Planet Gaia.[16]

The discourse on their page is laced with the lexicon of the Concheros but also includes elements of New Age sensibility. The cybernetic paths of the internet are conceived of as the route of a sacred pilgrimage, through which, with their constant use of metaphor, the Concheros apply a narrative tactic for the appropriation of space. That is why space is liable to be described and represented in images of their cosmovision.

In this sense the presence on the web of a group from the Conchero tradition, contributes to bringing to light, or making public, certain secrets or ritual practices that are meant for more private or restricted spaces. It also allows them to be broadcast 'to the four winds', and to be relocated to the New Age tradition as one more product of alternative spirituality on offer. However, the Conchero group, which has offline support, allows the virtual community to maintain connections and roots to an ancient tradition.

New Age Resignification of Cyberspace

When cyberspace is represented and described in images from the Conchero dance or Neo-Mexicanism, it enters into a field of representations, that is, of interiorized relations more or less distant from individuals and groups in space (Herin, 2006). We will take up the notion of frame alignment (in reference to frames for interpreting reality) proposed by Frigerio (1999: 7) to describe the way in which 'cognitive bridges' are built and 'interpretive frames are amplified' in the flowing together of three distinct matrices of meaning, which were formerly disconnected, but have started to interact with each other on the network: New Age spirituality; Conchero rituals of Neo-Mexicanism; and technological representations of the network and the internet.

To detect the narrative figures that allow cognitive bridges to be built between the system of New Age beliefs, the system of Neo-Mexicanism, and technological representations provided by the internet system, we look for the topics pertaining to this narrative: 'spirituality, nativism, nature, energy, development of consciousness, planetary consciousness, healing and alternative therapies inspired in techniques from the east, and shamanism, etc'. We found

16 Retrieved from http://web.jet.es/planetagaia/mesa.htm.

those recurring most frequently to be: the Earth as a living being, energy, healing, and the holistic conception of unity and totality.[17]

The web pages are presented as being part of a network, and even more broadly as part of a communal construction for 'the illumination of a New Earth and the New Humanity that is dawning'. For example, 'Unity in diversity'[18] is one of the slogans of 'this interwoven multi-dimensional platform of service, articulation and publication' meaning the pages of www.casadelared.org and http://redesdeluz.blogspot.com-. Especially on these sites it is possible to find a definition of what the internet represents to their promoters, as it is not only valued as a tool for providing and receiving information, but also as a space to be conquered and transformed into an 'international corridor'. *Casa Atzingo-La Casa de la Red*, is defined as: '(...) a private space that is still open to all social actors with a specific project they have developed and wish to share (...) All those taking part are promoted on the global network and are invited to travel on an intercontinental corridor'.

The ambivalence of the definition of private and at the same time open space, is the product of contradictions and paradoxes that form an inherent part of the social dynamics of space. However, the actors circumscribe it, looking for certain reservations as they open themselves up to those individuals or groups that coincide with the aims of their own group. All the same, much of what they are and what they do is open to the public on the web. The distinction between public and private implies different forms of access to those of offline reality, because on the web, the borders are more vulnerable and dynamic. But both aspects, the public and the private, seek to flow together towards the same objective. The objective of their pages is to use also this new (virtual) platform provided by 'Planet Gaia', along with other, offline (physical reality) resources, as we can read on *Casa de la Red*: 'The project is philanthropic and is conceived of as a physical and virtual platform for publishing and linking humanistic, scientific and artistic efforts that have the aim of helping with the evolution of the consciousness of the human species. It is located in Cuernavaca, in the state of Morelos, Mexico (...)'[19]

---

17 We had tried to find New Age topics from the scheme proposed by Carozzi: the past, magic, art, the feminine, the East, the Indian, the body, the unconscious, intuition, receptivity, emotion, pleasure, performance, spontaneity and rhythm (cf. Carozzi, 1999).

18 This idea is based on a holistic principle of the New Age that the whole is contained in the particular, and the particular forms a part of the whole, on the basis of which it can be said that interior spiritual development can have consequences in the transformation of the cosmos.

19 Retrieved from www.casadelared.org and move to http://lacasadelared.blogspot.mx/.

Using the Web in the Service of an Evolving Planetary Consciousness

We should point out that here also a term associated with New Age makes its appearance: 'consciousness' (*conciencia*), which is noted on this web page as one of the ends to which the efforts of these networks are directed. From the perspective of the New Age: 'individual consciousness amplified becomes planetary and cosmic consciousness...the incorporation of this also supposes the addition of a millenarian proposal to expand consciousness: the installation of a new era for humanity' (Carozzi, 1999b). Thus by assuming a role in the evolution of human consciousness, the *Casa de la Red* commits to change towards a new era, not only as the group but by transforming the internet, and resignifying it, which is also part of this new consciousness, and is not only a personal or social task but extends through all the media and along all paths that can reach this far, and over the internet as an instrument and a space for it, through the articulation of individuals and groups that meet there, that take up a position or can be assimilated as a part of this change.

www.casadelared.org claims to be a 'physical and virtual platform', while the *Casa Atzingo-Casa de la Red* is the 'physical' (off-line) version, in a specific geographical location in Mexico, of the Global Consciousness Network, *la Red Global de Conciencia*. This evolution of consciousness does not only take place in the physical realm but also in the virtual, according to their holistic vision. The pages mentioned have an offline presence (of groups, movements and communities) as well as an online presence (of virtual networks and cybercommunities), both of them connected by having the same aims, of encouraging the development in each other of consciousness through the spread of information, seminars and events, most of them to be attended in person, which are also announced on the web, and in many cases reports on these events are actually reviewed on the web.

Invitations to activities that take place offline can be found on the page or in physical world pamphlets, but there is also information on the web page for studying, thus creating a kind of virtual library with 'resources on the web'. So the limits of space are diffuse, as they cover both the virtual and the real, but they also have universal pretensions, as they cover certain geographical nations such as Mexico, Argentina, Spain, Venezuela, and others. But neither is it circumscribed to circuits whose boundaries are formed offline, as there are many subjects on the web who constantly transversalize this space and extend it to other pages, links and specialized circuits.[20]

20 These topics might be political, artistic, therapeutic, esoteric, scientific or ecological, for example.

By setting out to be a philanthropic project, www.casadelared.org[21] was distinct from other pages that do consider themselves to be commercial, as the main aim of the commercial sites is to 'provide services'; whereas the former page wishes to be a means of connecting forces whose aim is to help in the evolution of the consciousness of the human species—though it does not exclude certain commercial aspects, especially those having to do with workshops that cost something to attend; however this is not their main aim, unlike for example the page www.iluminado-tours.com, which only offers commercial services and links to other pages.

Red Planetaria is set up like a matrix containing important ties with other pages for exchanging information, and also participates in an important way in two other circuits of pages on Neo-Mexicanism: that of *Casa de la Red* and that of the Olmeca circuit. In the section 'Who We Are' (*Quiénes somos*), written by Dante Oliver and dated 'Monday, 31 December 2007', the following information can be found:

> It is a Network created by Man that represents a form of communication that to begin with had never been dreamed of. This Network will continue to evolve as time passes. When a certain frequency of vibration is reached, the physical cables that form this Network will be changed into light and it will be transformed into a Network of Light that will connect us to everyone, in emulation of the Universal Energy of the physical kingdom in the fifth dimension. After a while, this light will be integrated with patterns of thought.[22,23]

The narrative expressed in the paragraph quoted above, is extremely interesting for understanding the New Age resignifying of the web, and finding the cognitive bridge, generated by the meaning given to the practice as a therapeutic task (just as the dance becomes a reiki type of practice for the planet). According to the discourse above, the digital network is a technological resource, and then by saying it is made by Man, these groups reconfigure it as a sentient being, in much the same way as they conceive of the Earth as Planet Gaia. The web, the human body and the earth are all living, sentient, creatures, that are connected to energy, and are capable of evolving through vibration practices created by the users—a principle that is similar to that of the dance purifying the chakras of the Earth, or the rituals and marches of the Reginos to

21 Now at http://lacasadelared.blogspot.mx/

22 We have picked the concepts that redefine the web from a New Age matrix of meaning.

23 Retrieved from www.redplanetaria.com.

awaken consciousness—which will transform the 'physical cables' into a 'Network of light'. In this sense, technological resources are naturalized by a holistic conception of cosmic energy, and are made into part of the evolutionist destiny in which material is transformed into energy. Just like Planet Gaia, the technological network is given the properties of a living, sentient, creature. Hence it can be transformed in the project of developing universal consciousness. Also it is made to join a millenarian programme, characteristic of belief in the close approach of a new era, that proclaims the new times of transformation of consciousness and energy. Here also, elements of an evolutionary transformation are to be found: light that will reach the very confines of the universe. The slogan on this banner page is actually 'A Single Planetary Nation in Contact with the Infinite'.[24] It can be seen that this discourse is like that of *la Casa de la Red*. Its diffusion is not vertical but horizontal, hoping different pages will interact, so it is not hierarchical, although the trajectory would appear to begin with a subject, the Self. The internet is seen as a technique for provoking change and for the evolution of inner consciousness and of energy flows for the cosmos. It connects to the 'Self' by offering courses and materials that help with introspection and self-knowledge, through therapies or workshops, conferences, ceremonies, etc. But at the same time, it generates an interactive network to the extent that it establishes contacts and creates circuits with therapists, consultants, conferences, masters, etc., in such a way that the information and the social networks of the internet contribute to expanding cosmic consciousness.

The Naturalization of the Internet and the Use of It as Energy Transformation

New Age spirituality is conceived of, and works as, a Network of networks (Gutiérrez, 1996) in a way that is analogous to the internet network. In this sense, the *Red Planetaria* ('Planetary Network'), makes its spiritual posture explicit, resignifying the internet network as a spiritual kind of activity:

> It is the energy of Heaven creating magic on Earth (…). The Basis of the Network is Spirituality. Now, what does the word 'spiritual' mean? It is normally associated with some type of religion or religious practice; in reality it has a broader connotation: any activity that gives human beings an impulse towards some form of development—physical, emotional,

24 Retrieved from www.redplanetaria.com/.

> mental, intuitive, or social—if it is ahead of their current state, is essentially of a spiritual kind. According to this definition, every word, every thought and every action is potentially spiritual and has a capacity for improving the human condition.[25]

With this approach, the practice of using the net is conceived of as an activity promoting the development of humanity, that is, the search for spiritual transcendence. The concept of energy is a basic constituent of this spiritual project. According to the New Age conception, the transformation of energy leads to personal transformation and the spiritual self-improvement of each individual, which 'will contribute to a new cosmic consciousness that allows communion with Mother Earth and an experience of unity with the cosmos' (De la Torre, 2006: 32). This spirituality acquires a global character, within a holistic conception of existence. The part is identified with the whole, as the working principle of holism and the holographic principle are applied, based on everything being found in the part, and each part together with the rest forming the whole. It is at the level of consciousness and individual experience that the identity of identities is woven.

On his blog, Miyo (Emilio Fiel)[26] provides a reflection on the role of the internet in the world, where we can find the metaphors it awakens:

> Furthermore the internet is like the reflection of the inter-relations of all of us in a single field of consciousness. We have access to all the secrets of creation that are hidden in our cells and dimensional bodies, we are creators and a manifestation of the wisdom of God, we can share

25 Retrieved from www.redplanetaria.com.

26 Emilio Fiel, known as Miyo, was the guru and founder of the *Centro Sadhana de San Sebastián* where the first teachers of yoga, kundalini and meditation in the Basque Country were trained. In 1978 he became the guide of the Rainbow Community (*la Comunidad del Arcoiris*) which was at the head of the Hispanic and European community movement until his retirement at the Convergencia Armónica in 1987. From the end of 1988, Miyo focused on the shamanic view of a return to Mother Nature, and created the Clans of Quetzalcoatl (*los Clanes de Quetzalcóatl*), which consisted of a search for shamanic experiences. In 1993 he became the Hispanic heir of the Mexican ancestral lineage of Concheros, through transmission from its Major Guide Guadalupe Jiménez Sanabria, and since then has assumed the title of Captain of *la Mesa de Danza del Señor Santiago*, participating as such at the Councils of Elders of 'Amerrikua' (*Consejos de Ancianos de Amerrikúa*) and at their Planetary Ceremonies (*Ceremonias Planetarias*). He founded the Chrisgaia School, where the center of Universal Conchero Dancing was built, in the Zaragoza region of Spain.

> everything in a single instant and we choose our reality through the beliefs we choose to be conscious of.[27]

The Web and Enlarging the Reach of the Offline Network

Offline and online activities are part of what defines these groups. It is useful to understand that there are 'different degrees of involvement with and commitment to the movement, which go from consuming certain products, practices, symbols and beliefs identified with the movement, to being active members of New Age communities and networks' (De la Torre and Mora, 2001: 232). On some pages there is an emphasis on offline activities, for example, *la Red Iberoamericana de Luz* started with their meetings in Monterrey, Mexico. In the case of *la Mesa de Danza de la Cruz Espiral del Señor Santiago* the emphasis was on the meeting between two spiritual leaders: for Spain (Emilio Fiel) and for Mexico (Alberto Ruz),[28] who had undertaken a plan they called the Puente Wirikuta back in 1988, that is: 'a pact to begin a spiritual bridge between both sides of the Atlantic'. These leaders are very active and may be considered nodal actors offline and online, as they head important New Age learning centres, offer courses and workshops all the time, and are in charge of significant spiritual activities with a wide appeal among New Age networks. They are both promoters of books, but also keep an up to date record of their actions and reflections, on the internet, making themselves into an ideological and symbolical point of reference for the New Age, especially among Spanish speakers in America and Europe.

Each of them has his own page, but they both converge, not only through having the same ends but by creating this large network together. This way they consolidate the links of community-belonging between Chrisgaia (in

27 Retrieved from http://www.elblogdemiyo.com/?p=2213 consulted 10 March 2012. This blog was then erased and he also wrote about that on http://www.emiliofiel.com/2012/03/10/10-de-marzo-la-maestria-de-la-red/.

28 Alberto Ruz Buenfil (who uses the pseudonym sub-coyote Alberto) is founder and promoter of the Rainbow Caravan movement (*Caravana Arcoiris*). In 1982 he came back to Mexico and stayed in Tepoztlán, in the state of Morelos, where he founded the first eco-village ('*ecoaldea*') in Mexico, an alternative lifestyle ecological community known as Huehuecóyotl (Ruz Buenfil, 1992). This community has had an influence on getting the village of Tepoztlán to be currently recognized as the national center for New Ager groups. Tepoztlán is one of the main centers of utopian life, where different rituals have been celebrated linking hippyism, and the search for shamanic experiences, to oriental disciplines, ecologism, New Age, Mexicanism, and nativist traditions, etc.

Zaragoza, Spain) and Huehuecóyotl (state of Morelos, in Mexico). Their alliance is reinforced by face to face encounters organized by them, and in projects where they share events and activities in common. For example, the *Red Planetaria* page explains one of these network encounters like this:

> Members of the Network had occasion to share the process of unity. And [this] where the same has already acquired the characteristic of being an annual event. With the intention, of contacting more groups that are in a position to combine forces for this initiative and establish other alliances on the Network in order to take the light-information beyond the organizations and spiritual groups of the region, to environmentalist associations, perma-culturists, ancestral and indigenous culture societies, new economy and community money associations and other civil organizations for minorities and community services, human rights, etc. As also the search for financing so as to be able to continue and expand the services of the Network.[29]

This paragraph tells us of new senses of belonging, where the possibilities of exchange and coming together of different elements are laid out, where ancient esoteric teachings are revalued, and backing is given to an integrating sensation of diversity, and the rescue of the world through ideals that are generated by the creation of points of light to spread the spiritual energy of the universe through this esoteric work. For Miyo, to be heading the change of consciousness is intimately linked to managing the technology of the networks:

> It is incredible when a new consciousness collective can use Skype to communicate without having to pay, with words and images, even though we are in the four quarters of the world. Today it is more and more impossible to be at the head of a change of consciousness without being at the same time a leader in applied technology. You have to immerse yourself in all the networks and use them with enormous precision, in an efficient manner and using all their capacities to the maximum.[30]

The pages http://lacasadelared.blogspot.mx/ and redesdeluz.blogspot.com interconnect, are part of *la Red de Luz Iberoamericana*, and in the terms of our analysis they form a single matrix (along with the mailing lists). These two

29 Retrieved from www.redplanetaria.com.

30 Retrieved from http://www.emiliofiel.com/2012/03/10/10-de-marzo-la-maestria-de-la-red/.

pages have a wide ranging theory about networks, from texts formulated by the actual founders of the sites, to references to sociologist Manuel Castells or the World Health Organization. For example:

> Use of the word network to designate a set of organizations is not new. In fact, organizations have had relations with each other for some time now in order to reach common aims, but as Castells points out, they acquired a new life in the so-called Age of Information, making use of the new information and communication technologies like the internet.[31]

A diversity of authors, and points of view like this, allow a multiplicity of aspects to be included in the pieces published on the page, which range from subjects like 'the family as the first network', to the legal side of networks. In this matrix there is a wide ranging self-reflection on its role as a 'network' (*red*), a condition both pages assume even in the names of their websites: *casadelared* (network home) and *redluz* (light network). Apart from this, they also form a large network through their connection with other groups, which is to be seen in the links. Compared to other groups registered on the web, this is one of the networks with a more theoretical self-analysis of how they use the internet to achieve their aims.

The large section of self-reflection on this page on the web mentions other networks, not just on the internet but in several types of social organization; in either case the 'networks' are intimately linked to the site's own cosmovision and those who run it even go so far as to make explicit some of the mythical-imaginary elements that make up their vision. For example, on the page *redesdeluz.blogspot.com*, where there is an extra explanation of networks, of how they understand space, and of how they define their identity in it. It is remarkable that between the two of them they manage to complement a large amount of information on the vision and mission of this matrix on the web and in the physical world. On *redesdeluz.blogspot.com* we find more efforts to redefine the historical horizon of the current era according to the properties of technological advances and using the terms accepted by the New Age sensibility for conceiving of the cosmos. Let us see how the following discourse is supported by elements of such a worldview:

> New options for human communication have been made unexpectedly easier for us thanks to the new technologies and it now turns out that from the Industrial Revolution we have moved on to the Information

31 Retrieved from http://redesdeluz.blogspot.mx/2008/12/el-desafo-de-las-redes.html.

> Revolution and now we are in the Cyberspace Revolution, which implies the death of the concrete and an interaction with all human experience of life in a kind of fourth dimension which connects everything with everything else, as in the Cosmos and Nature. The mythical noosphere envisioned by de Chardin in the first half of the twentieth century, the last century of the millenium, offers us the magical possibility of activating new frameworks [not 'bars' (*rejillas*) as a literal translation of the English word 'grids' would suggest] of the old planetary system of electromagnetic networks that form the material stored in the new living library of the planet. The Earth is growing another 'brain' and like the layers of an onion is providentially recreating her conscious plane through a new reticulum which keeps everything and projects it, as though it were a collective vision propelled by the force of experiences, memory, intentions and the focus of their keepers.[32]

Internet connects everything to everything else just as the New Age planetary movement does. Every record, every flow on the internet can be compared to energy, and to the chakras or energy points found in human beings, or on the earth, the sacred geography. 'The Earth like the individual is conceived of as a living organism, with seven chakras, located where the cultures that have allowed the progress of humanity flourished. One of the most important is Mexico' (De la Torre, 2008). The subject of chakras is another version of the energy that was spoken about before, and it recurs in Neo-Mexicanism, especially in the constellation of the Reginos, who conduct their dance rituals in the belief that they are thus contributing to a reactivation of the cosmic energy system as a whole, to a reactivation of the chakras. And as we have tried to show, the fact is that the cybernaut Concheros navigate the circuits on the web and establish links between the matrix pages of Spanish speaking alternative spirituality; and they ritualize it as though it were the sacred geography of a living organism, hence aware, and capable of being transformed through their online and offline ritualizations.

The Conception of Cyberspace in the Resignifying of New Age: Children of the Matrix

In the case studied, we have shown that the New Age operates, as Leila Amaral so clearly defines it, like: 'A field of varied intersecting discourses, that works

32 Retrieved from http://redesdeluz.blogspot.mx/2007/12/los-nuevos-entramados-mallamados.html.

like a kaleidoscope rearranging pieces into different shapes, constantly creating a sort of "syncretism in motion'" (Amaral, 1999: 68). We were also able to attend to the way in which the incorporation of the Conchero dance practice into New Age has contributed to appropriating cyberspace (under the metaphor of Gaia, the noosphere, and sacred tracks) as a living organism, because the ritual practice (of transits through the network) allows one to join the worldwide movement with the aim of raising the level of planetary consciousness and developing inner spirituality.

Now, as Galavis (2003) has pointed out, development of the new digital technologies not only allows new things to be done, but is also able to modify cognitive patterns, ways of seeing, and mechanisms of contact with social reality and with our personal imaginaries. Two of the characteristics that best define the discourse on new digital technologies and the vehicle or space through which the discourse is manifested, are: their hypertextuality (a communication resource for defining a new way of making and perceiving information) and cyberspace (a virtual place where this occurs). Turkle maintains that experience with virtual interactions is based on effects simulating reality, which are affecting our minds and ways of thinking about ourselves (Turkle, 1997). This is reflected in the appearance of new religious movements projecting a radical change on Earth, of divine origin; other types of narrative that emphasize the existence of UFOs, and other 'exotic' or esoterical beliefs, that would have been unthinkable some years ago; and in others again (such as the one we will be expounding) that conceive of present day reality as being something like the Matrix.[33]

While the older generations would think of their present as being based on the past, now life is being thought of on the basis of a future in which imagination, naturally, plays a fundamental role. This creates a breaking apart of forms of understanding and relating to the world, whose values, norms and models will have to be revalued. It is therefore necessary to reflect on the way in which the imagined worlds of the mass media provide general conceptions of existence (Ríos, 2000: 135). In cyberspace, discourses can mutate or be hybridized to become signifiers in other contexts, so they turn into new spaces for religion, like relinking, because in cyberspace this conception

33 According to David Icke, author of Children of the Matrix, who is considered to be the principal spreader of conspiracy theory inspired by a current of New Age networks, the Matrix is the system of control, found everywhere, inside and outside individuals, that rules perception of the world, implanting a false perception or a perception that nullifies access to the real world. According to Morpheus, in the film of the Matrix: 'it is the world that has been moving your eyes so you don't see the truth' (Icke, 2010: 541).

acquires power through the connections and collectivity it makes possible, with its own cosmology structured on notions of time and space, and reflections on human nature, where the notion of life is redefined (Calil Júnior, 2008). The point being that 'Internet has modified our way of "thinking" the world because it has modified our way of "being present" in it', as Turkle (1997) pointed out.

We have detected that in the offline world the representation of the web as a dense cobweb, and the way our being in the world is conceived of as a virtual representation, are not just widening the reach of the expanding network of alternative spirituality, and of new era followers, but also resignifying the narratives and the rituals adopted by New Age alternative spirituality. Contents found on the internet have resurfaced offline and are then projected into cyberspace, however, now, more and more, offline reality is picking up narratives of virtual reality, and metaphorizing the relation of man to reality with the metaphor of the Matrix, which contributes to a new frame for ontological explanations of the human being and a guide for proceeding in the offline world.

As a sample, we can return to the movement of the Hispanekas led by Emilio (Miyo) Fiel, who was, as mentioned above, a recognized guru for Oriental spiritualities in Spain in the 1970s, and was later designated first Conchero captain in Spain. Currently, he has built a Center of Universal Conchero Dancing called Chrisgaia, where they also give courses and workshops designed to generate a development of consciousness, drawing on different traditions for the purpose (see Figure 15.3). In an interview he gave us, Miyo[34] explained that the different workshops seek to find the paths that make it possible to break with the illusory world we live in and raise the levels of our consciousness so we can free the human being from 'the Matrix':

> The techniques that we develop seek to awaken the genetic code in the body, not just so as to have a better body than what we have, but to provoke the union of the real earth with the illusory earth, which can be achieved by going into certain places of power in the earth itself or connecting to particular energies of hers. What matters is that the creators of the Matrix [referring to lizard people or reptilians] wish to enslave other creatures but they themselves serve the spirit, and the spirit has much bigger plans.

Miyo considers that we live in a reality constructed by the Matrix, like a kind of illusory and virtual world, through which all of us as human beings perceive

34 Interview with Emilio Fiel, conducted by Cristina Gutiérrez and Renée de la Torre, Chrisgaia (Zaragoza, Spain), 11 July 2009.

FIGURE 15.3 *Sacred objects on the altar of the Conchero center in Chrisgaia, Zaragoza, Spain, June 18, 2009*
PHOTO: RENÉE DE LA TORRE

the world in a distorted way, and our experience and perception is one of living in an unreal world that we consider to be real. Quoting Miyo:

> And as there was no way to reach this freedom because the reptilians were destroying all the humanoids, an illusion called Matrix was created so everyone could kill and be killed without killing, so the souls would not die—because some weapons destroy souls (within a certain radius nuclear arms do not just destroy bodies they have so much energy that they destroy souls); and these creatures are very fond of plasma weapons, nuclear weapons, having destroyed many planets, many solar systems, [so] an attempt has been made to create conditions in which those who were fighting could arm themselves and this they all arranged and this is what we have, only the Matrix is over and it's time for it to break to pieces.

The first cognitive bridge we established to understand the narrative of The Matrix was with a science fiction film called The Matrix,[35] which like other

35 The film The Matrix, which eventually came out in three episodes, was written and directed by Larry Wachowski and his brother Andy, and produced by Warner Brothers in 1999.

science fiction films and books has not only produced followers but also ritualizations and meta-theories to explain the reality that nourishes certain forms of belief inspired by virtual reality.[36] The film conceives of The Matrix as a system of virtual simulation in which human beings participate throughout their existence, believing it to be real. According to this theory, in 'reality' humanity has been captured by machines and is being used as energy for their subsistence. When asked about the similarity between his discourse and that of the film, Miyo admitted there was a connection, and said:

> Well, yes, the Matrix is The Matrix. The only problem with the Matrix film is when the human beings come out of the illusion created by the machines, the machines are in the same world they have just come out into; that is the only thing wrong with the film, really [what you see in it] is creatures linked in the dark to the secret government of the world; the point is, we are not straw we are cattle. They are two different things, we are cattle for some and for others we are straw for the cattle.

After the film we came across the book *Children of the Matrix* written by journalist David Icke (2010),[37] considered by Robertson to be one of the most significant spokesmen of 'contemporary millenarianism' and the main promoter of the conspiracy theory current of the New Age. Children of the Matrix makes claims for the theory of a race of reptilian humanoids, an interdimensional race, which has been controlling the world for thousands of years, creating the illusion of a real world, by means of a range of frequencies that has imprisoned our perception of the real. The book combines different ideologies and narratives creating cognitive bridges between conspiracy theories about world power, and revealing hidden truths of world esotericism, recurring to ancient history and the disappearance of Lemuria and Atlantis,

36 Virtual reality is understood to mean computer simulations of the real world, which is effected through three dimensional images and external components. The users move around virtual reality as though they were in the real world.

37 Icke was born in London, England, in 1952. For many years he worked as a journalist both in newspapers (e.g. The Guardian) and on television programs produced for the BBC in London. Until the nineties, he was an important promoter of New Age beliefs. Now he has written a best-selling book to add to about 20 others. He goes on world tours (and has been to over twenty countries) giving talks and workshops attended like rock concerts by thousands of people. For example, in October 2012, he spoke for ten hours in the Wembley Arena in London in front of an audience of about six thousand followers (Robertson, 2013).

reaffirming the idea of the domination of extra- and intra- terrestrial creatures on Earth, and claiming that 'reality is only the product of our 'imagination', or that what we live is an illusion (p. 541). This notion is perhaps based on various scenes from the Matrix movie (see Icke, 2010: 545–546).[38] The book has a large number of followers today, but it is through the internet that the content is most widely distributed, as followers on the web join in the denunciation of political and economic leaders of the world (such as Hillary Clinton, Hitler, the Bush family, etc.) as reptilians disguised as humanoids who are dominating the world. We even detected a belief in the reptilian conspiracy in connection with the millenarian phenomenon of 2012, which was based on this writer's ideas.[39] The theories of a reptilian conspiracy have attained a worldwide diffusion no one expected. To get an idea of the scale of this phenomenon, we can mention that just the site of David Icke (http://forum.davidicke.com/) has over three million visitors, and is counted one of the 10,000 most visited sites in the world (Robertson 2013).

It is obvious that this subject needs a deeper analysis, which, however, the length of the present work does not allow us to make. All the same it is considered worthy of mention that The Matrix is working like a key concept for the resignifying of practices, teachings, rituals, symbols and in-the-body experiences that were previously amalgamated and resemanticized by New Age spirituality. For example, in Chrisgaia, Miyo trains his disciples, a group of young people who live at the school, in various disciplines aimed at passing through the Matrix and establishing contact with real reality (the one we do not normally accede to). An experimental, practical and theoretical education is offered, inviting participants to share the process of personal growth

38 Nick Bostrom was dead on when he suggested that the film Matrix might be thought of as having repercussions, in that people would propose to themselves that they were probably living in a reality that is basically a computer simulation, and that therefore the brain, or the way we perceive reality, would also be part of the simulation (Bostrom 2003). The more everyday experience of virtual reality there has been, the more this imaginary has extended. One should also mention that another attribute of virtual reality is its connectivity, a rationale that is always present in conspiracy theories that have been gaining currency (even though they have always existed), and are widely distributed on the internet. Virtual reality provides the possibility of being and projecting oneself as one would like to be, even if this does not correspond with material reality, and for this reason it might be an option for people with utopian and creative horizons.

39 In a recent book, Icke sees in 2012 an opportunity for humanity to free itself from the domination of the reptilians, and their conspiracy, and see freedom return to this planet for the first time in many years (Defesche, 2008).

and the development of higher levels of consciousness. There are therapies and workshops that contemplate: 'deep meditation to draw oneself up to higher levels of consciousness'. Some of the elements learned, that were taken from oriental traditions, are today thought of as being strategic for getting through the Matrix, such as: deep meditation, kundalini yoga for sexual awakening; the tantric rule of one act of sexual intercourse per day without ejaculation in order to maintain optimum levels of energy, and energizing with crystals. They even had ceremonies of going and giving crystals back to the Earth, on pilgrimages passing through the most important sanctuaries in the world, 'because they belong to her and are necessary for her working'. They also prepare themselves in workshops on such things as experience of the dark, and the ability to dream consciously and contact real creatures in one's dreams. This is based on the fact that the first law for getting out of the Matrix is: 'control of the mind, anyone who does not achieve interior silence can never know he is in a Matrix'—according to Miyo. For example, he explains that it is in your dreams that real creatures present themselves and invite you to come to their worlds. That is why it is so important to learn to manage the visions and to wake up when asleep as a practice that allows you to get onto other planes of reality and to develop an evolution in levels of consciousness (a technique developed and promoted by Alejandro Jodorowsky), that is, to have an awareness guiding your being in dreams, where the dreamer sees himself as acting under his own will; and learn to relate to these creatures that are present in other dimensions—not imaginary. The point is that being trapped in the world we perceive in the Matrix, we have to get free of The Matrix, and also we have to get onto its inner levels in order to pass through it, which is why sometimes his discourse has a counter-cultural tone, adopted for example to challenge the current movement of the indignant.[40] For example, this piece of writing appeared recently on his site:

> [remember] that for as long as you consider you need to work eight hours a day to survive; that social security have a bed ready for you to keep you company on your final voyage; that it is better to go through the church to get your relation with your spouse sanctified; that a nation cannot be

40 *Indignados* is also the name given to the 15-M movement formed by citizens protesting pacifically for some days in May 2011 in Spain, demonstrating in favor of a Real Democracy Now, '*¡Democracia Real YA!*', worried by and indignant at the economic, political and social outlook for Spain.

> governed without politicians; that private property is a gift from God; or that love and the common good are an unrealizable utopia, it is you, through your thoughts, beliefs and actions, who is sustaining the structure of the matrix of dependence we are immersed in. The bad guys in the film are not the ones who are drowning our most elevated dreams, but you have your chain in place and you formulate it at every moment. Come out of the old schemes and stand up, to shout out the change not so much of the indignant as of the awake.[41]

The Matrix, finally, is also a matrix of meaning that contributes to translating the symbols and the meaning of the Conchero rituals under this logic. For example, Miyo does not value Catholic symbols or those with Pre-Hispanic roots for what they are supposed to represent, because for him 'they are not symbols (referring to the Virgin of Guadalupe and the Apostle Santiago) but living presences that allow the levels of consciousness in the Matrix to be passed over' (ibid. interview). The holy *súchil*, in turn, that is made during the ceremony of the vigil of the Concheros, to plead for the protection of souls (*ánimas*), has been resignified by the Hispanekas as a genetic code containing hidden knowledge for deciphering the way in which we were designed genetically. This remits to another belief based on the idea that 'we were created by genetic engineers', and that it is there that clues to the liberation of the human being lie.

In his convocation to the 'Council of Guardians of the Earth (Ancient Youngsters)', *Convocatoria al Consejo de Guardianes de la Tierra* (*Jóvenes Ancianos*), of the 1st of December 2011, Miyo puts out a call through the internet in which he mentions the elements that make up the whole amalgam of actors that converge around his practices, and who are the prospective recipients of his message:

> Dear friends all: Veterans of a thousand battles in the Rainbow Community; *Comadres* and *Compadres* of the Hispana Division of the Conchero Dance (*Mesa hispana de Danza Conchera*); members of the Clans of Quetzalcóatl; Shamanic practitioners of the magic of the four elements; Instructors at the Chrisgaia School; and other Pilgrims on the sacred paths of the Goddess (...). Just as it has been promised, and as I

41 Retrieved from http://www.elblogdemiyo.com/?p=4286 consulted 18 March 2012; this blog was later erased and Mayo also wrote about that in http://www.emiliofiel.com/2011/10/21/consenso-e-indignados/.

> have been saying for four decades, nothing of the old will remain standing, especially the four worn out pillars of money, science, governments and religions. These make up the essence of the conditioning power of the Matrix. We are elaborating a programme related to the Council of 2013 itself to which several individuals will come, especially the Mexicans Antonio Velasco Piña and Alberto Ruz, as well as some thirty Hispanic leaders and co-ordinators of different new energy movements (…) and every one of you who feels this call close by, and in the heart.[42]

So The Matrix is now the enemy to be overcome, and is the point around which he makes a new call to congregate different actors from the network of alternative spirituality to create an encounter that goes beyond the screens, in the hopes of a struggle beyond the real and the virtual.

Conclusions

In this chapter we have addressed the transformations that the translocalizing of the Conchero dance has had in relation to two worlds of meaning that resignify it and give it new ritual meanings.

First we referred to the narrative matrix of New Age spirituality, that contributed to creating a hybrid identity recognized as Neo-Mexicanism, and took up again the sense of 'cultural conquest' proper to the Conchero tradition, only to implement it in an ingenious and original manner for the conquest of the spirit of nature, interpreting the routes of Catholic pilgrimages as though they were a system of Gaia's chakras, and impressing on their ritual a therapeutic action able to unblock and activate the energy of the planet, or Mother Earth.

Secondly, the dance has been taken up by the Hispanekas, and Hispanic networks of alternative spirituality, as a ceremony that allows the network and practice on the internet to be symbolized. In spite of modifications to its contents and spaces of action, the Conchero dance has kept a shared meaning, which is the meaning of the cultural act of a 'conquest'. This conquest is like 'the ornamental wars', a ceremonial act, that is to say, a symbolic act of conquering and thereby transforming the uses and cultural

---

42 Retrieved from https://loquepodemoshacer.wordpress.com/2012/05/22/llamado-al-100-consejo-de-visiones-de-los-guardianes-de-la-tierra/.

meanings of the spaces where it is practiced. For this reason we sustain that the dance (practiced narratively) is a practice whose symbolic efficacy is performative, and say it is applied to generate sacred geographies, even though these may be ephemeral. This is based on the fact that through the dance there is a search for reconquering the Indian meaning of the ancestral sacred spaces.

The dance was used as the matrix that metaphorizes the action of navigating through the internet, as though it were a ritual act sacralizing the technology, equating technology with the noosphere, the network of light, with cosmic energy, or with Planet Gaia, the field where flowers and songs are sown, the Four Winds or four directions, etc. This notion, in the light of the holistic conception of a New Age, has contributed to the development and the evolution of consciousness, both inner and cosmic.

Thirdly, the notion of the network, of virtualized reality, and the overlapping of the borders dividing science fiction from offline reality, have contributed to creating narrative matrices that are in turn resemanticizing, and creating new horizons for, the traditional rituals. Internet not only supplies a platform for putting out one's beliefs or rites, it also gradually becomes a practiced space that generates certain dynamics of exchange, and specific narratives, strategies for communication, or graphic representations, which are transformed in order to adapt to this medium. However, internet is also offering more conceptual elements all the time to structure reality according to specific beliefs, as in the example of The Matrix.

Finally, it is worth starting a reflection on the role that the New Age interpretive frame has had on the Conchero practice itself, continually translocalizing it, and on contributing to a permanent resignifying of its ceremony and its sense of identity. But it is also worth highlighting the role that a ritual, such as the Conchero dance, valued by Mexicans as ancestral heritage from the Pre-Hispanic peoples, when taken up by networks of New Age spirituality, has had on enrooting both New Age narratives and the 'virtual' practices of cyberspace. And as well as this, its own condition being one of spiritual conquest is what has allowed it to move from Mexico to Spain, from the forecourts to the ashrams, and from pilgrimage routes to internet links, widening its capacity for ritual performance as it has gone from the local to the national, from the national to transnationalization, and from space to cyberspace, sacralizing and reconverting the spaces it passes through, into traditionalized and ethnicized territories. With which we wish to demonstrate that most of the time emphasis has been placed on the effects that the New Age has had on the contents and aesthetic manifestations of the traditions; however, in this work we wanted to ponder the role played by the Conchero dance, though made 'Hispaneka', in getting the virtual—as in the belief in a Matrix—projected with a halo of reality, through its being practiced in traditional rituals, which create continuity with the new ways of being and of passing through the world (such as cyberspace), and contribute to anchoring recently invented lineages, to ancestral traditions.

Final Notes

Cristina Gutiérrez Zúñiga and Renée de la Torre

As the contributions to this book are the fruit of the work and reflections developed by the authors in the course of their own research careers, tracing out general conclusions will be complicated. In some cases the careers are those of individuals, in others they are the collective result of specific research projects on the transnationalization of religious practices; some chapters report on initial research findings, others re-examine, from the point of view of ethnic and popular New Age appropriations in Latin America, long term research experiences originally conducted with other interests in mind. However, convergence around this particular research interest, through discussions and reading each other's work, was achieved mainly in the context of the conference *Reinterpretaciones New Age de las tradiciones sincréticas latinoamericanas* (New Age Reinterpretations of Latin American Syncretic Traditions), where we came up with the questions, concepts and proposals we will review in this section.

The question we originally set out to answer was: What impact has the frame of interpretation proper to the New Age had on the contents, styles and practical uses of Latin American popular and ancestral traditions? But as time went on, the various cases studied led us to broaden our initial question, and ask also: In what way did the phagoticyzing syncretic germ-cell of Latin American popular religiosity appropriate to itself and transform the meanings of the New Age in traditionalized versions of cultural resistance? In what way do the mercantile intermediaries apply it? How do institutions respond and incorporate it into themselves?

Contact with the New Age matrix has created a series of expressions that are described and analyzed in the course of the chapters included in this book. The chapters show that far from remaining intact, these expressions are the result of an apparent fusion and hybridizing between New Age and the cultural and religious traditions of Latin America, which we have had to distinguish by using the prefixes '*neo*', '*new*' or '*exo*', imposed over the traditional or ethnic ancestral substratum on which they have been created. However, the impact on this substratum could not be more paradoxical: although incorporation of the New Age matrix de-traditionalizes and de-contextualizes the ethnic (as Galinier notes), at the same time it renews and resignifies the deterritorialized cultures and keeps them relevant (Argyriadis and De la Torre, 2008). The resignifying in turn contributes to the revaluing, rescue and reinvention of memory, as well as the retraditionalizing and the safeguarding of

 | DOI 10.1163/9789004316485_021

the cultural patrimony of the Pre-Hispanic peoples or Afro-descendants of America. So we were able to see in the works presented on the *Wixarika* (Huichol) ethnic group, historically based in the mountain chains of Jalisco and Nayarit, in Mexico; the Otomi ethnicities of the state of Querétaro and of the state of Mexico; the Mazatecs of Veracruz; the Amazonian Indians of Brazil; the Mayans of Santiago Atitlán and the Guatemalans who take San Simón with them on their migrations to Los Angeles, where he is incorporated into the esoteric merchandise on offer in the Hispanic spiritual market and becomes a part of the folksifying of the 'Latin' identity; Santeria which was practiced until a few decades ago by descendants of Africans living in Cuba, but has now been exported to countries such as Mexico and the U.S.A.; and Umbanda, originally from Brazil but also present in France. What we said about ethnic groups could also be seen in the popular traditions studied: the 'New Aged' Catholicism of Brazil; therapeutic Neo-Mexicanism; Hispanekas conquering the Matrix in cyberspace; and the eclectic, popular and kitsch Neo-spiritism of the Valley of the Dawn in the city of Brasilia. In a category of its own is the phenomenon of the ceremonial consumption of power plants that accompanied the sacred rituals of ethnic groups, and has now been incorporated by New Agers either as rites of initiation to 'Neo-Indianism', or as an experience in their quest for the inner self, as in the case, for example, of the exporting of the taking of Santo Daime, ayahuasca or the yajé (from Colombian and Brazilian Amazonia), or the spiritual tourism route taken in order to have an experience of Mazatec sacred mushrooms, and the pilgrimage of Wirikuta during which peyote is searched for, formerly only by the *Wixarika* but today in the company of tourists and spiritual seekers. Not all cultures are adopted by the New Age, as those that are chosen have to be in tune with the exotericizing eyes that would like them to be refuges for magic, shamanism, esotericism, ancient wisdoms, harmonious relations with nature, or holistic therapies; so, generally, Afro-American traditions are not the most popular, although there are also cases in this book like that of Cuban Santeria in Mexico which has reallocated the *Orisha* into the Neo-esoteric circuits of Mexico City (Juárez Huet). These expressions show us the possibility that Afro-American religions are New Ageing not only in France (Guerriero).

The reinterpretation of traditional and popular elements from local environments in Latin America under a global matrix, occurs in an asymmetircal situation, both in terms of scale, and with regard to the social, ethnic and economic position of the actors; and also in terms of access to the global spiritual market, which has made us resort to the metaphors of 'absorption' and 'omnivorousness' to represent this phenomenon of cultural contact. However, the cases studied require us to analyze the transformation that the traditionalizing, which is characteristic of the syncretism of popular Latin American religiosity, has exercised on the New Age itself, as a consequence of this cultural exchange. The conjunction of New Age cosmopolitan spirituality and ethnic and popular Latin American traditions has created in the last twenty-five years a variety of spiritual and religious expressions and options that appear today to the spiritual seeker as, at the very least, an enlarging of the menu available, say, in the eighties, making it more complicated than ever. A clear example of this fact in the book is the case of the Valley of the Dawn, which has traditionalized a number of the concepts and symbols of the New Age. Is this only a case of incorporating new exotic elements into the same matrix of global spirituality? Or are we speaking here of a transformation of the New Age itself as the result of this conjunction? Can we still speak of just one New Age? Or are we seeing a diversification of the phenomenon, which suggests the creation of a Latin American version of the New Age?

The book has responded to these concerns by showing a variety of cases that allow us to conclude that there is no longer just one New Age—the one first described by English speaking sociologists—there are different New Age modalities. It is not only a New Age that has turned its gaze from Oriental spiritual disciplines and the vestigial traces of pre-Christian Europe to look at the indigenous groups alive on the reservations of North America described by Lewis and Melton, helping, with the hippie movement, to create the great cultural matrix of Native Spirituality. Neither is it only the New Age whose therapeutic ritual services have stocked the global supermarket of spiritual development conceptualized by Van Hoove. We believe there are some traits that mark the differences between the 'classical', or 'original', New Age with an emphasis on the sacralization of the self (first described in the English literature by early Melton (1990) and Heelas (1996), amongst others), and its subsequent psychologizing which took place in the nineties and was alluded to by Heelas. It was even taken up in motivation courses aiming for success and material prosperity (Heelas 2008); it also became a supermarket spirituality (Hanegraaf 1999b), and New Age qualities were hyper-commercialized as they were applied to the sale of light, healthy, relaxing and energizing products (Ferraux, 2000). Another difference between then and now is the Pan-Indianizing of New Age and the emphasis on Neo-paganism that it acquired across continental America. We may conclude that its passage through the knowledge and ethnic rituals of native American peoples, and the exchanges it made with them, helped to create a Neo-pagan and Pan-Indian current, whose sensibility would tend to be less centered on the Self and more propelled towards a holistic and cosmic action-thought, in the sense of connecting itself proactively to intitiatives for revaluing various ecological and cultural ethnic worlds, and promoting a commitment to environmental and cultural transformation.

The holistic syncretic frame of meaning of popular religion, in turn, has also appropriated signifiers that were originally spread by the New Age, and have been resignified, thus contributing to a transformation of their meanings. For example, New Age notions that were linked to experience of the self have been changed into elements that have magical and miraculous properties (belonging to practices of witchdoctor healing, reading the cards, or cleansings). Some New Age signifiers are also present in Neo-esoteric circuits, such as popular markets, Santeros folk remedy shops, or in popular expressions of spiritism (as in the case of Vale do Amanhecer), at Neo-esoteric fairs, and even in rituals honoring popular or secular Saints and Virgins (as seen in the case of devotions to San Simón and in the case of the Conchero ceremonial dances in Mexico). This marks the New Age with a new seal, traditionalizing it and inserting it into popular collective ritual forms.

Finally it is important to keep in mind the appropriation made by native agents (who vindicate indigenous ancestral traditions) of the exoticizing New Age narratives, to recover, purify and reinvent their own memories of ancestral history and ethnicity. This has contributed to a legitimizing by the New Age of the re-creation of ethnic origins, of proto-nations or spiritual nations, whose values vindicate the ancestral, a relationship of harmony with nature, the idea of first nations, and the shared idea of appearing in places considered strategic points in a sacred geography of the world. This has been documented in cases where the new Mayan, Inca and Aztec movements are addressed.

These differences may be thought of as a Latin American revival of the countercultural and utopian stereotype originally present when the movement started in Europe and North America in the nineteen sixties. However, we also find that its transversalizing character makes it into a continually transversalized movement: which ranges from ethnic claims for the right of peoples to have their ancestry recognized, to its metaphorization in the light of narratives belonging to the information age and its condition of virtual reality.

In short, we have been able to recognize the following modalities that the New Age has acquired in Latin American uses and significations: (1) New Age sensibility and contents have generated new resemanticizings of Latin American popular traditions, creating hybrids of Neo-shamanism (Guerriero, Aguilar Ros, Rodríguez, Galinier and Magnani), Neo-Indianism, Neo-magic (Juárez Huet), Neo-Mayanism (Batos, Telly and Zamora), Neo-Mexicanism (Gutiérrez Zúñiga and De la Torre and Campechano) and Neo-Incaism (Molinié); (2) the popularization and traditionalizing that practices of popular religiosity have made of the New Age (for example, in the creation of the Valley of the Dawn and the case of Max Simón); and (3) the transversalizing by the New Age of institutions, such as the Catholic church or ethnic communities, which while being permeated by this new way of resemanticizing the symbols brought in by the New Age matrices and by rituals, are at the same time reincorporated into strategies seeking to combat them (for example the movement of Charismatic Renewal described by Carlos Steil), and (4) the metaphorical and ritual metaphorization to colonize technology, as is shown by the case of Neo-Mexicanism appropriating the web as an extension of nature and the forces of the cosmos (De la Torre and Campechano).

In its interaction with the syncretism of Latin American popular religiosity the New Age has generated relations and meanings that are ambivalent in different worlds.

In the political realm, although there are some who give it the value of a 'light' ideology appropriate to contemporary neoliberalism, which decontextualizes traditions from the conflicts and power relations that they are involved in (Galinier); it has also become a source of inspiration for social conscience and utopian activism, especially in matters related to defense of the environment (Pachamama-ization and sacralizing of territory valued as Mother Earth); for cosmologicalizing Indian tribes considered today to be guardians of the wisdoms of ancient civilizations; for the awakening of feminine consciousness, and for alternative health care with a holistic view of the body and the spirit (Gutiérrez Zúñiga). It should be stressed that one of the principal problems faced by indigenous peoples and communities in the context of neoliberalism and global imperialism, is that of the brutal extraction of their natural resources. Oil companies, miners, thermoelectric and tourist businesses are causing the displacement of entire peoples, who have found in the cosmologicalizing of Mother Earth and the Pachamama a fertile narrative for defending their sacred territories and the relation of their ethnic groups with the earth.

The cultural realm in turn, is the source of hybridations that decontextualize the cultures; but at the same time, the hybrids provide a ferment for the reinvention and rescue of essentializing projects of the autochthonous.

In the social realm of the New Age, as it is a transversal and fluid ideology, it becomes a vector of cultural translocalization that at the same time, while it borrows cultural fragments and displaces them onto networks and global narratives, manages to be a ferment for the relocalizing and enrooting of innovative communities, who are local but interact with global networks.

In the religious realm, although it is the ferment for a new way of living the spirituality of the Self (a self-spirituality)—seeking personal improvement—it is also the engine for new ways of creating translocal and even transnational communities. Its non-institutional character, reconverts it into a movement transversalizing the churches, their structures, their practices and their dogmas.

Interpreting these new forms of religiosity and spirituality will probably turn out to have been one of the greatest challenges for the sociology and the anthropology of religion in Europe and North America since the middle of the twentieth century, as the contributions by Frigerio and Guerriero clearly demonstrate. Starting from this important theoretical baggage, the works presented here perform an exercise, in some cases implictly and in others explicitly, of making critical use of the existing theory to work on the meeting points of Latin American religions with the New Age. The logical direction of the exercise is not simply confirmation. On the contrary, the delimitation of the specific characteristics of these religiosities and of the processes of exchange, with all due historical and ethnographic rigor, is presented as a fundamental challenge, as is the coining of analytical categories that will allow it to be properly conceptualized. From this approach arises the possibility of formulating questions not limited just to the area of study, but of general theoretical relevance, about a global and globalizing phenomenon. For example, it is necessary to revise critically the mystifying images of globalization that make it impossible to analyze the differences and asymmetries that continue to exist and are even recreated in the processes of transnationalization. To do so one has to ask about the problems of incorporating certain practices and traditions; about the geopolitical location from which the various appropriations of ancestral traditions in the post-colonial era are made; or about the limits of the hybridizing of this movement and its particularity faced by long term syncretic processes in ex-colonial countries. This is achieved through the chapters that highlight the fact that not everything is 'attractive' to incorporation by the New Agers, but only those aspects which match certain characteristics that are sought: the virgin, the natural, the spiritual, the ancestral, the magical, the intuitive, etc. However, these qualities are appreciated in different ways depending on where the exoticizing directs its attention (both from inside and from the outside) to indicate what is worth guarding, seeking or perpetuating. As though in a kaleidescope, the exoticizing scrutinies of the Western world (which have focused on 'others' like the East, Nature and the Indian) interact with the very 'regimes of difference' of the nation and the region, that is, with the matrix producing differences which is brought to life in the particular historical processes of each nation and/or region.[1]It is from here that the unequal valuing of cultural differences in each nation and each region is traced, and

1 Formations of otherness refers to 'the production and tracing of lines of fracture belonging to particular historical processes that go to make up the matrix for producing differences' (Segato, 2007: 28).

this has an influence on the way in which ethnicity or blackness vary according to the historical logic of each (Segato, 2007: 20).

Frigerio also proposes that it is necessary to look for the limits of what can be hybridized both with respect to the limits of the seducer, and in terms of how much of what is theirs the traditional cultures are willing to exchange. In this context, several articles such as those by Aguilar Ros, Rodríguez, Galinier and Magnani provide ethnographic and theoretical elements to discuss the rise of a new form of shamanism outside the traditional territorial communities, which interacts with New Age circuits, evidently creating a wider circulation of indigenous traditions resignified in the new urban context, at the same time as new tensions, negotiations and uses within the traditional ethnic community.

Appropriations of the New Age in the context of Latin America also offer, taken as a whole, an opportunity to discuss the rise of new modalities of institutionalization within the movement, which has always been characterized as being the antipode of the ecclesiastical model. Several chapters suggest to the reader how, beyond these dichotomous forms of classification, the ethnic and popular expressions studied show that the New Age is creating its own relatively stable, continuous and characterizable forms of interaction through circuits (as proposed by Magnani), and even crosses over religious traditions and churches, creating original New Age types of religiosity joined to ecclesiastical forms, as explained by Steil and Guerriero.

We are confident that this book will contribute to broadening international scholarly debate on New Age, new religious movements, and the contemporary transformation of religion. This debate may also attract scholars interested in other phenomena of identity, ethnicity, politics and the environment in Latin America, as we hope we have shown how the cultural process of reinterpreting the New Age in Latin America has turned out to be a privileged area for addressing contemporary reconfigurations of a world that is constantly more interrelated.

Bibliography

Adame, Miguel Ángel. 2005. "Contribución conceptual y metodológica en torno al chamán/chamanismo". *Boletin de Antropología Americana* 41 (January–December): 65–88.

Aguilar Ros, Alejandra. 2008. "Danzando a Apaxuki: La Semana Santa en San Andrés Cohamiata desde los mestizos visitantes", pp. 159–192 in *Raíces en movimiento. Prácticas religiosas tradicionales en contextos translocales* edited by Kali Argyriadis, Renée De la Torre, Cristina Gutiérrez Zúñiga and Alejandra Aguilar Ros. Guadalajara: El Colegio de Jalisco/CEMCA/CIESAS/IRD/ITESO.

Aguirre Beltrán, Gonzalo. 1980. *Medicina y Magia. El proceso de aculturación en la estructura colonial.* Mexico: INI/SEP.

Albanese, Catherine. 1992. "The Magical Staff: Quantum Healing in the New Age", pp. 68–86 in *Perspectives on the New Age* edited by James Lewis and J. Gordon Melton. Albany: State University of New York Press.

Alexander, Kay. 1992. "Roots of the New Age", pp. 30–47 in *Perspectives on the New Age* coordinated by J. Lewis and J. Melton. Albany: State University of New York Press.

Altamirano, José. 1993. *Saqsaywaman: Síntesis de la cultura andina (interpretación mística)*. Cusco (Qosqo) Región Inka: Proyecto Especial Regional Parque Arqueológico Saqsaywan.

Amaral, Leila. 1999. "Sincretismo em movimento: o estilo Nova Era de lidar com o sagrado", pp. 47–80 in *A Nova Era no Mercosul* edited by María Julia Carozzi. Petrópolis: Editora Vozes.

———. 2000. *Carnaval da alma. Comunidade, essência e sincretismo na Nova Era.* Petrópolis: Vozes.

———. 2003. "O comando da felicidade: sobre a dimensão trágica dos rituais de cura *new age". Ciencias Sociales y Religión/Ciências Sociais e Religião*, v. 5, n. 5: 99–122.

Andrade, Maristela De Oliveira. 2002. *500 anos de catolicismos & sincretismos no Brasil.* Rio de Janeiro/João Pessoa: Editora Universitária/UFPB.

Appadurai, Arjun. 1996. *Modernity at large. Cultural Dimension of Globalization.* Minneapolis/London: University of Minnesota Press.

———. 2001. *La modernidad desbordada. Dimensiones culturales de la globalización.* Mexico: Fondo de Cultura Económica.

Arguedas, José María. 1968. *Los mitos quechuas posthispániscos.* Havana: Casa de Las Américas.

Argüelles, José. 1987. *The Mayan Factor. Path Beyond Technology,* Rochester: Bear & Co.

Argyriadis, Kali. 1999. *La religión à la Havane. Actualité des répresentations et despratiques culturelles havanaises.* Paris: Éditions des archives contemporaines/Centre d'antropologie des mondes contemporains/EHESS.

———. 2006. "Les bata deux fois sacres: la construction de la tradition musicale et chorégraphique afro-cubaine". *Civilisations*, v. LII, n. 1–2: 45–74.

Argyriadis, Kali and Juárez Huet, Nahayeilli. 2007. "Las redes transnacionales de la santería cubana: una construcción etnográfica a partir del caso La Habana-Ciudad de México", pp. 329–356 in *Redes Transnacionales en la Cuenca de los Huracanes. Un aporte a los estudios interamericanos* edited by Francis Pisani, Natalia Saltalamacchia, Arlene Tickner and Nielan Barnes. Mexico: Miguel Ángel Porrúa-ITAM.

———. 2008. "Sobre algunas estrategias de legitimación de los practicantes de la santería en el contexto mexicano", pp. 344–383 in *Raíces en Movimiento, Prácticas religiosas tradicionales en contextos translocales* coordinated by Kali Argyriadis, Renée de la Torre, Cristina Gutiérrez Zúñiga and Alejandra Aguilar Ros. Guadalajara: COLJAL/CEMCA/IRD/CIESAS/ITESO.

Argyriadis, Kali and Renée De la Torre. 2008. "Introducción", pp. 11–42 in *Raíces en movimiento. Prácticas religiosas tradicionales en contextos translocales* edited by Kali Argyriadis, Renée de la Torre, Cristina Gutiérrez Zúñiga and Alejandra Aguilar Ros. Guadalajara: El Colegio de Jalisco/CEMCA/CIESAS/IRD/ITESO.

Argyriadis, Kali, Renée De la Torre, Cristina Gutiérrez Zúñiga and Alejandra Aguilar Ros (eds.). 2008. *Raíces en movimiento. Prácticas religiosas tradicionales en contextos translocales.* Guadalajara: El Colegio de Jalisco/CEMCA/CIESAS/IRD.

Argyriadis, Kali, Stefania Capone, Renée De la Torre and André Mary (eds.). 2012. *En sentido contrario: transnacionalización de religiones africanas y americanas.* Mexico: CIESAS.

Arias Yerena, Aldo Daniel. 2011. "La Danza del Sol de Ajijic: un ritual nodo en la red de espiritualidad alternativa". Masters thesis, CIESAS Occidente presented in 2011.

Asturias, Miguel Ángel. 1946. "Maximón, divinidad de agua dulce", *Revista de Guatemala*, n. 4 (April–June): 55–61.

Ba Tiul. 2011. *Siwan Tinamit: Mayas y Participación Política.* (*Hacia el Oxlajuj B'aqtun*). Guatemala: manuscript.

Báez Cubero, Lourdes and Rodríguez Lazcano Catalina (eds.). 2008. *Morir para vivir en Mesoamérica.* Veracruz: Consejo Veracruzano de Arte Popular/Instituto Nacional de Antropología e Historia.Báez-Jorge, Félix and Lupo, Alessandro (eds.). 2010. *San Juan Diego y la Pachamama, Nuevas vías del catolisicmo y de la religosidad indígena en América Latina.* Veracruz: Sapienza Univesitá de Roma/Editora de Gobierno del Estado de Veracruz.

Bainbridge, William. 1997. *The sociology of religious movements.* New York: Routledge.

Bakhtin, Mikhail. 1987. *A cultura popular na Idade Média.* São Paulo: Hucitec.

Barker, Eileen. 1989. *New Religious Movements. A Practical Introduction.* London: Her Majesty's Stationery Office.

Bartra, Roger. 2011. *El mito del salvaje.* Mexico: Fondo de Cultura Económica.

Basch, L., N. Glick Schiller and C. Blanc-Szanton. 1994. *Nations Unbound: Transnational Projects, Postcolonial Predicaments and Deterritorialized Nation-States.* Amsterdam: Gordon and Breach Publishers.

Bastide, Roger. 1971. *African Civilizations in the New World.* New York: Harper and Row Publishers.

Bastos, Santiago. 1998. "Los indios, la nación y el nacionalismo", pp. 87–157 in *La construcción de la nación y la representación ciudadana en México, Guatemala, Ecuador y Bolivia,* edited by Claudia Dary and Guillermo de la Peña. Guatemala: FLACSO Guatemala.

———. 2007. "La ideología multicultural en la Guatemala del cambio de milenio". In *Mayanización y vida cotidiana. La ideología multicultural en la sociedad guatemalteca,* v.1, edited by Santiago Bastos and Aura Cumes. Guatemala: FLACSO/CIRMA Cholsamaj.

Bastos, Santiago and Manuela Camus. 2003. *Entre el mecapal y el cielo. Desarrollo del movimiento maya en Guatemala.* Guatemala: FLACSO/Cholsamaj.

Bauer, Brian. 2000. *El Espacio Sagrado de los Incas. El Sistema de Ceques del Cuzco.* Cusco: Centro de Estudios Regionales Andinos Bartolomé de Las Casas.

Bauman, Zygmunt. 1999. *La globalización. Consecuencias humanas.* Mexico: Fondo de Cultura Económica.

Bayardo Casillas, María Guadalupe Xochitexcatl. 2007. *Terapia para el cuerpo y el alma. Danza mexicana prehispánica.* Guadalajara: published by the author.

Beck, Ulrich. 2008. *La sociedad del riesgo mundial. En busca de la seguridad perdida.* Barcelona: Ed. Paidós.

———. 2009. *El Dios Personal. La individualización de la religión y el "espíritu" del cosmopolitismo.* Barcelona: Ed. Paidós.

Bengoa, José. 2000. *La emergencia indígena en América Latina.* Mexico: FCE.

Bertonio, Ludovico. [1612] 1984. *Vocabulario de la langue aymara.* Cochabamba: CERES/IFEA/MUSEF.

Beyer, Peter. 1994. *Religion and Globalization.* London: Sage Publications Limited.

Bhabha, Homi K. 1998. *O local da cultura.* Translation by Myriam Ávila, Eliana Lourenço and Lima Reis. Belo Horizonte: Gláucia Renate Gonçalves/UFMG.

Birman, Patricia. 2000. "Multiculturalité religieuse en France: vers un nouvel Orient?" *Ethnologie Française,* v. 30, n.4: 565–574.

Bittencourt Filho, José. 2003. *Matriz Religiosa Brasileira: Religiosidade e Mudança Socia.* Petrópolis and Rio de Janeiro: KOINONIA/Vozes.

Bloom, Herbert. 1996. *Omens of Millennium.* New York: Putnam's.

Boege, Eckart. 1988. *Los mazatecos ante la nación. Contradicciones de la identidad étnica en el México actual.* Mexico: Ed. Siglo XXI.

Bonfil Batalla, Guillermo (comp.). 1981. *Utopía y revolución. El pensamiento político contemporáneo de los indios de América Latina.* Mexico: Nueva Imagen.

———. 1995. *Obras Escogidas.* Mexico: INI.

Bourdieu, Pierre. 1977. *Outline of a theory of practice*. Cambridge: Cambridge University Press.

Bouysse-Cassagne, Thérèse. 1987. *La identidad aymara. Aproximación histórica (Siglo XV, Siglo XVI)*. La Paz: HISBOL/IFEA.

Bove, Frederick. 2002. "The People With No Name: Rulership, Ethnic Identity, and the Transformation of Late-Terminal Formative Societies in Pacific Guatemala", conference paper from *The Southern Maya in the Late Preclassic: Urbanism, Rulership, and Ethnic Interaction*. American Anthropological Association, New Orleans.

Braga, Antônio Mendes da Costa. 2004. "TV Católica Canção Nova: providência e compromisso x mercado e consumismo" *Religião e Sociedade*, v. 24, n. 1: 113–123.

Brandon, George. 1993. *Santería from Africa to the New World: the Dead Sell Memories*. Bloomington: Indiana University Press.

Burga, Manuel. 1988. *Nacimiento de una utopía: muerte y resurección de los Incas*. Lima: Instituto de Apoyo Agrario.

Burguete, Araceli. 2010. Autonomía: la emergencia de un nuevo paradigma en las luchas por la descolonización en América Latina, pp. 63–94 in *La autonomía a debate. Autogobierno indígena y Estado plurinacional en América Latina*, edited by Miguel González, Araceli Burguete and Pablo Ortiz. Quito: FLACSO/GTZ/IWGIA/CIESAS/UNICH/Cayzac.

Calil Júnior, Alberto. 2008. "Uma etnografia do mundo espirita virtual: algumas aproximacoes metodológicas". *Ciencias Sociales y Religión*, 10 (10): 117–136.

Campbell, Colin. 1972. "The Cult, the Cultic Milieu and Secularitazion", pp. 119–136 in *A Sociological Yearbook of Religion in Britain,* edited by Michael Hill, v. I. London: SCM Press.

———. 1978. "The secret religion of the educated classes". *Sociological Analysis* 2, v.39: 146–156.

———. 1997. "A orientalização do Ocidente: reflexões sobre uma nova teodicéia para um novo milênio". *Religião e Sociedade*, 18/1: 5–22.

———. 2001. *A ética romântica e o espírito do consumismo moderno*. Rio de Janeiro: Rocco.

Campechano, Lizette. 2010. "Netnografía del circuito de la mexicanidad y neomexicanidad en el ciberespacio". First Degree Thesis for the Departmeent of Philosophy and Humanities of the Instituto Tecnológico y de Estudios Superiores de Occidente (ITESO), Guadalajara.

———. 2012. "El retorno virtual de Quetzalcóatl: una netnografía de la mexicanidad y neomexicanidad". *Cuicuilco,* v. 19, n. 55 (September–December): 171–194.

Capone, Stefania. 1999. *La quête de l'Afrique dans le candomblé: pouvoir et tradition au Brésil*. Paris: Karthala.

———. 2001–2002. "La difusion des religions afro-américaines en Europe". *Psychopathologie africaine*, v. XXXI, n. 1: 3–16.

Carneiro De La Cunha, Manuela. 1999. "Xamanismo e tradução". In *A outra margem do Ocidente* edited by Adauto Novaes. São Paulo: Companhia das Letras.

Carozzi, María Julia. 1995. "Definiciones de la New Age desde las Ciencias Sociales". *Lecturas Sociales y Económicas*, v. 2, n. 5: 19–24.

——— (ed.). 1999a. *A Nova Era no Mercosul*, Petrópolis: Editora Vozes.

———. 1999b. "Introduçao", pp. 8–26 in *A nova Era no mercosul* edited by María Julia Carozzi. Petrópolis: Editora Vozes.

———. 1999c. "La autonomía como religión: la Nueva Era". *Alteridades. Antropología de los movimientos religiosos*, y. 9, n. 18: 19–38.

———. 1999d. "Nova Era: a autonomia como religião", pp. 47–80, in *A nova Era no mercosul* edited by María Julia Carozzi. Petrópolis: Editora Vozes.

———. 2000. *Nueva Era y terapias alternativas*. Buenos Aires: EDUCA.

———. 2004. "Ready to Move Along: The Sacralization of Disembedding in the New Age Movement and the Alternative Circuit in Buenos Aires". *Civilisations*, v. 51, n. 1–2: 139–154.

———. 2007. "A Latin American New Age?" pp. 341–357 in *Handbook of New Age* edited by Daren Kemp and James Lewis. Boston: Brill.

Carrera, Juan. 2000. *La otra vida de María Sabina.* Toluca: UAEM.

Carrillo, Hugo. 1992. "Las orgías sagradas de Maximón. Obra en diez y siete cuadros rituales". Guatemala: April (unpublished text).

Carvalho, José Jorge De. 1994. "Idéias e Imagens no Mundo Clássico e Tradição Afro-Brasileira". *Revista Humanidades*, v. 10: 77–86.

———. 1999. "Uma querela dos espíritos: para uma crítica brasileira do suposto desencantamento do mundo moderno". *Sociedade e Estado*, v. 14, n. 01:175–186.

Castells, Manuel. 2000. Materials for an Exploratory Theory of the Network Society. *British Journal of Sociology* 51 (1): 5–24.

———. 2006. *Sociedad Red.* Madrid: Alianza Editorial.

Catroga, Fernando. 2001. "Memória e história", in *Fronteiras do milênio* edited by S.J. Pesavento. Porto Alegre: Editora da UFRGS.

Cavalcante, Carmen Luisa. 2005. "*Dialogias no Vale do Amanhecer: os Signos de um Imaginário Religioso Antropofágico*". Ph.D. thesis, Pontifícia Universidade Católica de São Paulo/PUC, São Paulo.

CEH. 1999. *Guatemala, Memoria del Silencio*. Guatemala: Report presented by the Historical Clarification Commission.

Ceto, Pablo. 2010. "Un nuevo amanecer. La Guatemala plural de los Acuerdos de Paz frente al racismo y la debilidad del Estado actual". In *Plan de Operaciones Sofía.* Madrid: CCOO.

Champion, Françoise. 1989a. "Les sociologues de la post-modernité religieuse et la nébuleuse mystique-ésotérique". *Archives de sciences sociales de religions*, 67(1): 155–169.

———. 1989b. "D'une alliance entre religion et utopie post 68: le rapport à La société Du groupe 'Eveil à la conscience planétaire' ". *Social Compass*, v. 36, n. 1: 61–69.

———. 1993. "Nouvel-Age Et Nebuleuse Mystique – Esotérique Mise En Perspective Historique". *Cahiers Rationalistes*, n. 475: 167–177.

———. 1995. "Persona religiosa fluctuante, eclecticismos y sincretismos", pp. 705–737 in *El hecho religioso. Enciclopedia de las grandes religiones* edited by Jean Delumeau. Madrid: Alianza Editorial.

Champion, Françoise and Danièle Hervieu-Léger. 1990. *De l'émotion en religion. Renoveaux et traditions.* Paris: Centurion.

Chartier, Roger. 1991. "O mundo como representação". *Estudos Avançados,* v. 5, n. 11: 3–11.

Chauí, Marilena. 2000. *Convite à Filosofia*, 12ª ed. São Paulo: Ática.

Chief Fama. 1996. Diccionario yoruba *orisa*, Ilé Orúnmila Communicatios.

Clark, Paul. 2006. *New Religions in Global Perspective*. Oxon: Routledge.

Clifford, James. 1999. *Itinerarios transculturales*. Barcelona: Gedisa Editores.

Cobo, Bernabé. 1964. "Historia del Nuevo Mundo" (Lib. XI–XIV), pp. 8–275 In *Obras del P. Bernabé Cobo*, t. 2. Madrid: Ediciones Atlas (Biblioteca de Autores Españoles 92).

Cojtí, Demetrio Waqi' Q'anil. 1997. *Ri Maya' Moloj pa Iximulew. el Movimiento Maya (en Guatemala)*. Guatemala: Cholsamaj.

Concone, Maria Helena Vilas Boas. 1987. *Umbanda: uma religião brasileira*. São Paulo: FFLCH/USP – CER.

Consejo Político 13 Baktun. 2010. "Declaración política a los 14 años de la Firma del Acuerdo de Paz Firme y Duradera", 29 December 2010.

Cowan, Douglas E. and Jeffrey K. Hadde. 2004. "Virtually Religious: New Religious Movements and the World Wide Web", pp. 119–142 in *The Oxford Hadbook of New Religious Movements* edited by James R, Lewis. New York: Oxford University Press.

Csordas, Thomas. 1994. *Embodiment and Experience. The Existential Ground of Culture and Self.* Cambridge: University of California Press.

———. 1996. *Language, Charisma and Creativity: the Ritual Life of a Religious Movement.* Cambridge: University of California Press.

———. 2002. *Body/Meaning/Healing*. New York: Palgrave Macmillan.

———. 2009a. "Introduction", pp. 1–29 in *Transnational Transcendence* edited by Thomas J. Csordas. Berkeley/Los Ángeles/London: University of California Press.

———. 2009b. "Modalities of Transnational Transcendence", pp. 1–29 in *Transnational Transcendence. Essays on Religion and Globalization* edited by Thomas Csordas. San Diego: University of California Press.

Cumes, Carol and Lizárraga Valencia, Rómulo. 1999. *Pachamama's Children*. St Paul, Minneapolis: Llewellyn Publications.

D'andrea, Anthony. 1998. "Self and Reflexivity in Post-traditional Religiosities: the Case of the New Age Movement". *Chicago Anthropology Exchange*, v. XXVII: 5–24.

———. 2000. *O Self Perfeito e a Nova Era: Individualismo e Reflexividade em Religiosidades Pós-Tradicionais*. São Paulo: Loyola.

———. 2006. "Neo-Nomadism: A Theory of Post Identitarian Mobility". *Global Age Mobilities,* v. 1, n. 1: 95–119.

Dantas, Beatriz Góis. 1988. *Vovó nagô e papai branco: usos e abusos da África no Brasil.* Rio de Janeiro: Graal.

Davie, Grace. 1994. *Religion in Britain Since 1945: Believing Without Belonging,* Blackwell, Oxford.

———. 1996. "Croire sans appartenir: le cas britannique", pp. 175–194 in *Identités religieuses en Europe* edited by Grace Davie y Danièle Hervieu-Léger. Paris: La découverte.

De Certeau, Michel. 1996. La *invención de lo cotidiano. 1 Las artes de hacer.* Mexico: Universidad Iberoamericana/ITESO/CEMCA.

Defesche, Sasha. 2007. "The 2012 Phenomenon: a historical and typological approach to a modern apocalyptic mythology", Department of Religious Studies (Subdepartment History of Hermetic Philosophy and Related Currents) M.A. Program Mysticism and Western Esotericism, University of Amsterdam.

De La Cadena, Marisol. 2000. *Indigenous mestizos: The Politics of Race and Culture in Cuzco, Peru, 1919–1991.* Durham/London: Duke University Press.

De la Peña, Francisco. 2001. "Milenarismo, nativismo y neotradicionalismo en el México actual". *Ciencias Sociales y Religión,* year 3, n. 3: 95–113.

———. 2002. *Los hijos del sexto sol.* Mexico: INAH.

De la Torre, Renée. 2000. "Los nuevos milenarismos de fin de milenio". *Revista Estudios del Hombre* n. 11: 57–78.

———. 2002. "Dilemas y retos metodológicos para dar cuenta de la diversidad religiosa en México". *Revista Imaginário* n. 8 (November): 351–372.

———. 2005. "Las danzas aztecas en la Nueva Era", presented at the *VII Encuentro de la Red de Investigadores del Fenómeno Religioso,* Lagos de Moreno, Jalisco, CUAltos – University of Guadalajara, 24 April.

———. 2006. "Circuitos mass mediáticos de la oferta neoesotérica: new age y neomagia popular en Guadalajara". *Alteridades,* year 16, n. 32 (July–December): 29–41.

———. 2007. "Alcances translocales de cultos ancestrales: el caso de las danzas rituales aztecas". *Revista Cultura y Religión* n. 1, v. I. Available at: http:www.culturayreligion.cl/normas.htm.

———. 2008a. "Tensiones entre el esencialismo azteca y el universalismo *New age* a partir del estudio de las danzas 'conchero-aztecas'". *Trace* 54: 61–76.

———. 2008b. "La estetización y los usos culturales de la Danza Conchera-Azteca", pp. 73–110 in *Raíces en movimiento. Prácticas religiosas tradicionales en contextos translocales* edited by Kali Argyriadis, Renée de la Torre, Cristina Gutiérrez Zúñiga and Alejandra Aguilar Ros. Guadalajara: COLJAL/CEMCA/CIESAS/IRD/ITESO.

———. 2011a. "Les rendez-vous manqués de l'anthropologie et du chamanisme" (Introduction to the dossier *Religions Amérindiennes et New Age*). *Archives de Sciences Sociales des Religions* n. 153, 56 (January–March): 145–158.

———. 2011b. “Religiones amerindias y circuitos de espiritualidad New age”, manuscript.

———. 2012a. “La danza conchero-azteca cosmovisión indígena oculta tras el catolicismo popular”, pp. 34–53 in *El don de la ubicuidad. Rituales étnicos multisituados* edited by Renée de la Torre. Mexico: CIESAS.

———(ed.). 2012b. *El don de la ubicuidad: Rituales étnicos multisituados.* Mexico: CIESAS.

———. 2012c. *Religiosidades nómadas. Creencias y prácticas heterodoxas en Guadalajara.* Mexico: CIESAS.

———. 2014. “Los newagers: el efecto colibrí. Artífices de menús especializados, tejedores de circuitos en la red, y polinizadores de culturas híbridas”. *Religião e Sociedade*, v. 34, n.2: 36–64.

De La Torre Renée; Alma Dorantes; Patricia Fortuny and Cristina Gutiérrez Zúñiga. 1999. “El campo religioso de Guadalajara: tendencias y permanencias”, pp. 33–72 in *Creyentes y creencias en Guadalajara* edited by Patricia Fortuny Loret de Mola. Mexico: CONACULTA/INAH/CIESAS.

De la Torre, Renée and Cristina Gutiérrez Zúñiga. 2005. “La lógica del mercado y la lógica de la creencia en la creación de mercancías simbólicas”. *Desacatos* n. 18: 53–70.

———. 2011a. “La neomexicanidad y los circuitos *new age*: ¿un hibridismo sin fronteras o múltiples estrategias de síntesis espiritual?” *Archives de Sciences Sociales des Religions*, in dossier *Religions amérindiennes et circuits de spiritualité new age* n. 153, 56: 183–206.

———. 2011b. “Los hispanekas: concheros con aires de nueva era”, pp. 395–426 in *Nuevos caminos de la fe. Prácticas y creencias al margen institucional*, edited by Alberto Hernández. Mexico: North Border College/Michoacán College/Autonomous University of Nuevo León.

———. 2012a. “Atravesados por la frontera. Anáhuac-Aztlán: Danza y construcción de una nación imaginada”, pp. 145–173 in *En sentido contrario Transnacionalización de religiones africanas, latinoamericanas* edited by Kali Argyriadis, Stefania Capone, Renée de la Torre and André Mary. Mexico: CIESAS-IRD-Academia L’Harmattan.

———. 2012b. “¿Cómo creen y practican los jaliscienses su religiosidad hoy?” pp. 67–103 in *Jalisco Hoy. Miradas antropológicas* edited by Renée de la Torre and Santiago Bastos. Mexico: CIESAS.

De la Torre, Renée and José Manuel Mora. 2001. “Itinerarios creyentes del consumo esotérico”. *Imaginário*, n. 7: 211–240.

De la Torre, Renée *et al.* 2014. *Creer y practicar en México: comparación de tres encuestas sobre religiosidad.* Aguascalientes: Autonomous University of Aguascalientes/ CIESAS/COLJAL.

Demanget, Magali. 2000. “El precio de la tradición. En torno a los intercambios entre riqueza económica y espiritual en la comunidad mazateca de Huautla de Jiménez, Oaxaca”. *Cuadernos de Trabajo, Universidad Veracruzana*, n. 6: 7–59.

De Moura, Isabel and Carlos Steil. 2013. "The Experience of Contemporary Ecological Subjects Seems to Point to a Type of Transcendence Within Immanence Closer to the World of New Age Type Spiritualities". *Ambiente e Sociedade* v. XVI, n. 4: 103–120.

De Paz, Marco Antonio. 2010. *2012 Del baktun 13.0.0.0.0 4 ahaw 8 k'umk'u al baktun 13.0.0.0.0 4 ahaw 3 kankin. La Quinta Era en la historia del Pueblo Maya*. Guatemala: Fundación CEDIM.

De Rose, Isabel and Esther J. Langdon. 2006. "La chair des dieux est-elle à vendre? Chamanisme, tourisme et ethnicité en terre mazatèque (Mexique)". Ph.D. thesis, Université de Paris X, Paris.

———. 2010. "Diálogos (neo)xamânicos: encontros entre os Guarani e a ayahuasca". *Tellus*, year 10, n. 18 (January–June): 83–114.

De Sousa Santos, Boaventura. 2005. *El milenio huérfano. Ensayos para una nueva cultura política*. Madrid/Bogotá: Trotta/Isla.

———. 2009. *Una Epistemología del Sur. La reinvención del Conocimiento y la Emancipación Social*. Buenos Aires: Siglo XXI Editores/CLACSO.

Dictionnaire alphabétique et analogique de la langue française (*Le nouveau Petit Robert*), Dictionnaires Le Robert, 2002, Paris.

Diem, Andrea Grace and James R. Lewis. 1992. "Imagining India: The Influence of Hinduism on the New Age Movement", pp. 48–58 in *Perspectives on the New Age* edited by Lewis and Melton. New York: State University of New York Press.

Donard, Véronique. 2009. *Du meutre au sacrifice – Psychanalyse et dynamique spirituelle*. Paris: Cerf.

Dos Reis Rodrigues, Marcelo. 2001. "A apropriação do tempo na construção do imaginário e da identidade no Vale do Amanhecer". Monograph for bachelor degree in Sociology, Brasilia University, Human Science Institute, History Department, Brasilia.

———. 2004. "Discurso e Temporalidades, A Construção da memória e da identidade no Vale do Amanhecer (1957–2004)". Masters thesis, Brasilia University, Human Science Institute, History Department, Brasilia.

Duarte, Luiz Fernando Dias. 2006. *Família e Religião*. Rio de Janeiro: Contra Capa.

Dumont, Louis. 1992. *Homo hierarchicus: o sistema de castas e suas implicações*. São Paulo: EdUSP.

Durín, Severine. 2003. "Sur les routes de la fortune. Commerce à longue distance, endettement et solidarité chez les Wixaritari (huichol), Mexique". PhD Thesis, Paris University 3/Sorbonne Nouvelle, Paris.

Durín, Severine and Alejandra Aguilar Ros. 2008. "Regios en busca de raíces prehispánicas y wixaritari eculturísticos", pp. 255–292 in *Entre luces y sombras: Miradas sobre los indígenas en el área metropolitana de Monterrey* edited by Séverine Durin. Mexico: CIESAS-CDI.

Durkheim, Émile. 2000. *As formas elementares da vida religiosa*. São Paulo: Martins Fontes.

Eliade, Mircea. 1986. *El chamanismo y las técnicas arcaicas del éxtasis.* Mexico: Fondo de Cultura Económica.

———. 1998. *Tratado de História das Religiões*. Translated by Fernando Tomaz and Natália Nunes, 2nd edn. São Paulo: Martins Fontes.

Ellwood, Robert. 1992. "How New is the *New Age*", pp. 59–67 in *Perspectives on the New Age* edited by James R. Lewis and J. Gordon Melton. New York: State University of New York Press.

Eroza Solana, Enrique. 1996. "Tres procedimientos diagnósticos de la medicina tradicional indígena". *Alteridades*, year 6, n. 12: 19–26.

Escobar, Arturo. 2005. "Bienvenidos a Cyberia. Notas para una antropología de la cibercultura". *Revista de Estudios Sociales* (22): 15–35.

———. 2008. *Territories of Difference. Place, Movement, Life, Redes.* Durham: Duke University Press.

Esparza, Juan Carlos. 2002. "El sistema Ocha-Ifá, producto de importación garantizado", pp. 41–75 in *Cambios religiosos globales y reacomodos locales* edited by Karla Y. Covarrubias and Rogelio de la Mora. Colima: Altexto.

———. 2003. "Una fiesta de cumpleaños de santo en Guadalajara. La catolización de una ceremonia sincrética", pp. 143–163 in *Religión y Cultura* edited by Miguel Hernández Madrid and Elizabeth Juárez Cerdi. Mexico: COLMICH/CONACYT.

Espinosa, Eduardo. 1996. "En compañía de los espíritus". *Alteridades*, year 6, n. 12: 77–97.

Esquit, Edgar. 2003. *Caminando hacia la utopía. La lucha política de las organizaciones mayas y el Estado en Guatemala.* Guatemala: Universidad de San Carlos de Guatemala. Instituto de Estudios Interétnicos. Reflexiones.

Estenssoro, Juan-Carlos. 1992. "Modernismo, estética, música y fiesta : élites y cambio de actitud frente a la cultura popular. Perú, 1750–1850" pp. 181–195 in *Tradición y modernidad en los Andes* edited by Hernrique Urbano. Cuzco: Centro de Estudios Regionales Andinos "Bartolomé de las Casas".

Estrada, Álvaro. 1977. *Vida de María Sabina. La sabia de los hongos*. Mexico: Ed. Siglo XXI.

Fabian, Johanes. 1983. *Time and the Other. How Anthropology Makes its Object.* New York: Columbia University Press.

Fagetti, Antonella. 2010. "Iniciaciones, trances, sueños. Una propuesta teórico-metodológica para el estudio del chamanismo en México", pp. 11–40 in *Iniciaciones, transes, sueños, Investigaciones sobre el chamanismo en México.* Mexico: Plaza y Valdés.

Farfán, Olimpia, Jorge Castillo and Ismael Fernández. 2005. "Los otomíes: identidad y relaciones interétnicas en la ciudad de Monterrey" v.I, pp. 313–358 in *Visiones de la diversidad, relaciones interétnicas e identidades indígenas* edited by Miguel Bartolomé. Mexico: INAH.

Ferguson, Marilyn. 1981. *The Aquarian Conspiracy: Personal and Social Transformation in the 1980s*. London: Routledge & Kegan.

Ferreux, Marie-Jeanne. 2000. *Le New Age. Ritualités et mythologies contemporaines*. Paris: L'Harmattan.

Fikes, Jay. 2009. *Carlos Castaneda oportunismo académico y los psiquedélicos años sesenta*. Mexico: Xlibris.

Fisher, Edward F. 2001. *Cultural Logics & Global Economics. Maya Identity in Thought and Practice*. Austin: University of Texas Press.

Flanagan, Kieran. 2011. "Introduction", pp. 1–22 in *A Sociology of Spirituality* edited by Kieran Flanagan and Per Jupp. Farnham: Ashgate.

Flores Galindo, Alberto. 1986. *Buscando un Inca. Identidad y Utopía en los Andes*. Cuba: Casa de América.

Flores Ochoa, Jorge. 1996. "Buscando los Espíritus de los Andes: Turismo Místico en el Qosqo,", pp. 9–29 in *La Tradición Andina en Tiempos Modernos* estited by Hiroyasu Tomoeda and Luis Millones. National Museum of Ethnology (Senri Ethnological Reports 5).

Flores Ochoa, Jorge and Juan Víctor Nuñez del Prado (eds.). 1984. *Q'ero, el último ayllu inka. Homenaje a Oscar Nuñez del Prado*. Cuzco: Qosqo, Centro de Estudios Andinos.

Fonseca, Alexandre B. 1998. "Nova Era evangélica, Confissão Positiva e o crescimento dos sem religião", paper presented at the VIII Jornadas sobre Alternativas Religiosas na América Latina, São Paulo.

Frigerio, Alejandro. 1993. "La invasión de las sectas: el debate sobre nuevos movimientos religiosos en los medios de comunicación en Argentina". *Sociedad y Religión* n.10: 24–51.

———. 1995. "Secularización y Nuevos Movimientos Religiosos". *Boletín de lecturas sociales y económicas*, year 2, n. 7: 43–48.

———. 1999. "Estableciendo puentes: articulación de significados y acomodación social en movimientos religiosos en el Cono Sur". *Alteridades*, year 9, n. 18 (July–December): 5–17.

———. 2002. "Outside the Nation, Outside the Diaspora: Accommodating Race and Religion in Argentina". *Sociology of Religion* v. 63, n. 3: 291–315.

———. 2004. "Re-Africanization in Secondary Religious Diasporas: Constructing a World Religion". *Civilisations*, v. (1–2): 39–60.

———. 2005. "Identidades porosas, estructuras sincréticas y narrativas dominantes: Miradas cruzadas entre Pierre Sanchis y la Argentina". *Ciencias Sociales y Religión/ Ciências Sociais e Religião*, n. 7: 223–237.

———. 2007. "Repensando el monopolio religioso del catolicismo en la Argentina", pp. 87–118 in *Ciencias sociales y religión en América Latina* edited by María Julia Carozzi y César Ceriani. Buenos Aires: Biblos/ACSRM.

Galavis, Edgar. 2003. "Ciberreligiones: aproximación al discurso religioso católico y afro americano en Internet". *Opción*, 19 (41): 85–106.

Galinier, Jacques. 2005. "Malestar en el culturalismo. La transnacionalización de mesoamérica como capital simbólico", memorias de la reunión anual de *IDIMOY*, Xalapa Veracruz, November 2005 (mimeograph).

———. 2008. "Indio de estado *versus* indio nacional en la Mesoamérica moderna", pp. 45–72 in *Raíces en movimiento. Prácticas religiosas tradicionales en contextos translocales* edited by Kali Argyriadis, Renée de la Torre, Cristina Gutiérrez Zúñiga and Alejandra Aguilar Ros. Guadalajara: COLJAL/CEMCA/CIESAS/IRD/ITESO.

———. 2010. "Dentro y fuera: la comunidad indígena y el reto del New Age mexicano", pp. 345–369 in *San Juan Diego y la Pachamama. Nuevas vías del catolicismo y de la religiosidad indígena en América Latina* edited by Félix Báez-Jorge and Alessandro Lupo. Veracruz: Editora del Gobierno del Estado de Veracruz/Universitá di Roma Sapienza.

Galinier, Jacques and Antoinette Molinie. 2006. *Les néo-Indiens. Une religion du IIIè millénaire*. Paris : Odile Jacob.

———. 2011a. "Le montage des autochtonies – Translocalisation de la Terre Mère dans le New Age amérindien". *Topique*, n.114: 23–34.

———. 2011b. *The Neo-Indians. A Religion for the Third Millennium*. Boulder: University Press of Colorado & Utah State Univesity Press.

Gallardo Ruiz, Juan. 2002. *Medicina tradicional p'urhépecha*. Mexico: COLMICH/ Instituto Michoacano de Cultura.

Galovic, Jelena. 2002. *Los grupos místico-espirituales de la actualidad*. Mexico: Plaza y Valdés editores.

García Canclini, Nestor. 1989. *Culturas híbridas. Estrategias para entrar y salir de la modernidad*. Mexico: Grijalbo.

———. 1995. *Consumidores y ciudadanos. Conflictos multiculturales de la globalización*. Mexico: Grijalbo.

———. 1997. *Culturas híbridas. Estratégias para entrar e sair da modernidade*. São Paulo: Edusp.

———. 2000. "La globalización: ¿productora de culturas híbridas?" In Actas del III Congreso Latinoamericano de la Asociación Internacional para el Estudio de la Música Popular, Bogotá. Available at: http://www.hist.puc.cl/historia/iaspmla.html.

———. 2004. *Diferentes, desiguales y desconectados. Mapas de la interculturalidad*. Barcelona: Editorial Gedisa.

García Medina, Jesús. 2010. "La Recuperación de la Sabiduría Ancestral Indígena y a Nueva era en Guadalajara, 1967–2002", Masters Thesis, Division of Human and Historical Studies, University of Guadalajara.

García Medina, Jesús and Cristina Gutiérrez Zúñiga. 2012. "La indianización de la nueva era en Guadalajara". *Cuicuilco. La mexicanidad y el neo-indianismo hoy*, v. 19 n. 55 (September–December): 219–244.

Garcilaso De La Vega, Inca. 1960. *Obras completas*, 4 vols. Madrid: Biblioteca de Autores Españoles.

Geertz, Clifford. 1977. *La interpretación de las culturas*. Barcelona: Gedisa Editorial.

———. 1978. *A interpretação das culturas*. Rio de Janeiro: Jorge Zahar.

———. 2001. *O beliscão do destino: a religião como experiência, sentido, identidade e poder. Nova luz sobre a Antropologia*. Rio de Janeiro: Jorge Zahar.

Giddens, Anthony. 1995. *Modernidad e identidad del yo*. Barcelona: Península/ideas.

———. 1997. "A Vida em uma Sociedade Pós-Tradicional". in *Modernização Reflexiva* edited by Anthony Giddens, Ulrich Beck and Scott Lash. São Paulo: UNESP.

Glick-Schiller, N. and G.E. Fouron. 1999. "Terrains of Blood and Nation: Haitian Transnational Social Fields". *Ethnic and Racial Studies*, v. 22: 341–366.

Gobin, Emma. 2003. "Les religions d'origine africaine à La Havane. Ethnologie d'une harmonie rêvée". Thesis for Master, Paris-X Nanterre University.

———. 2014. "Un 'New Age' afro-cubain? Créativité rituelle, diffusion et processus d'appropriation de nouvelles spiritualités à La Havane". Paper presented in Journée d'étude: Religions, transnationalisation et nouvelles médiations, Nice University, April 4.

González Torres, Yólotl. 1997. "El movimiento de la mexicanidad". *Religiones y sociedad, expédiente nuevo milenio y nuevas identidades*, n. 8 (January–April): 9–35.

———. 2006. *Danza tu palabra. La danza de los concheros*. Mexico: CONACULTA/INAH/Plaza y Valdés.

———. 2008. "Las religiones afrocubanas en México". In *América Latina y el Caribe. Territorios religiosos y desafíos para el diálogo* edited by Aurelio Alonso. Buenos Aires: CLACSO/Consejo Latinoamericano de Ciencias Sociales.

———. 2010. "Libros de la Mexicanidad", pp. 457–522 in *San Juan Diego y la Pachamama. Nuevas vías del catolicismo y de la religiosidad indígena en América Latina* edited by Felix Báez-Jorge and Alessandro Lupo. Veracruz: Editora del Gobierno del Estado de Veracruz/Universitá di Roma Sapienza.

Gonzalez-Wippler, Migene. 1994. *Santería: The religion*. Minnesota: Llewellyn Publications.

Greimás, Algirdas Julien, and Joseph Courtés. 1990. *Semiótica. Diccionario razonado de la teoría del Lenguaje*. Madrid: Ed. Gredos.

Groisman, Alberto. 2009. "Trajectories, Frontiers, and Reparations in the Expansion of Santo Daime to Europe", pp. 185–204 in *Transnational Transcendence* edited by Thomas J. Csordas. Berkeley/Los Angeles/London: University of California Press.

Grossberg, Lawrence. 1996. "On Postmodernism and articulation. An interview with Stuart Hall", pp. 131–150 in *Stuart Hall: Critical Dialogues in Cultural Studies* edited by David Morley and Chen Kuan-Hising. New York and London: Routledge.

Guerriero, Silas. 2003. *A magia existe?* São Paulo: Paulus.

Guillot, Maia. 2009. "Du mythe de l'unité luso-afro-brésilienne: Le candomblé et l'umbanda au Portugal". *Lusotopie*, v. 16, n. 2: 205–219.

Guillot Maia and Juárez Huet Nahayeilli. 2012. "Dynamiques religieuses et logique marchande des religions afro-américaines au Mexique et au Portugal", pp. 63–84 in *Transnationalisation des religions africaines, Afrique, Europe, Amérique* edited by Kali Argyriadis, Stefania Capone, Renée de la Torre and André Mary. Paris: Academia l'Harmattan/IRD/CIESAS.

Gutiérrez, Cristina and Alejandra Aguilar Ros. 2008. "Conclusiones", pp. 393–411 in *Raíces en movimiento. Prácticas religiosas tradicionales en contextos translocales* edited by Kali Argyriadis, Renée de la Torre, Cristina Gutiérrez Zúñiga and Alejandra Aguilar Ros. Guadalajara: COLJAL/CEMCA/CIESAS/IRD/ITESO.

Gutiérrez Martínez, Daniel. 2005. "Multirreligiosidad en la Ciudad de México". *Economía, Sociedad y Territorio*, v. 5, n. 19: 617–657.

Gutiérrez Nájera, Raquel and Marina Villalobos Díaz (eds.). 2000. *Espiritualidad de los Pueblos Indígenas de América, Memoria del Primer Foro Internacional.* Morelia: Secretaría de Difusión Cultural.

Gutiérrez Zúñiga, Cristina. 1996a. *Nuevos movimientos religiosos. La Nueva Era en Guadalajara*. Guadalajara: COLJAL.

———. 1996b. "Procesos de globalización cultural: El New Age en Guadalajara". *Este País* n. 61, April, Mexico.

———. 2008. "La danza neotradicional como oferta en la estantería exotérica new age", pp. 363–392 in *Raíces en movimiento. Prácticas religiosas tradicionales en contextos translocales*, edited by Kali Argyaridis, Renée de la Torre, Cristina Gutiérrez Zúñiga, and Alejandra Aguilar Ros. Guadalajara: COLJAL/CIESAS/IRD/CEMCA/ITESO.

Gruzsinki, Serge. 1990. *La guerra de las imágenes. De Cristóbal Colón a "Blade Runner" (1492–2019)*. Mexico: Fondo de Cultura Económica.

Hagedorn, Katherine. 2001. Divine Utterances: *The Performance of Afro-Cuban Santeria.* Washington: Smithsonian Books.

Hall, Stuart. 1993. "Encoding, Decoding", pp. 507–517 in *The Cultural Studies Reader* edited by Simon During. London: Routledge.

Hanegraaff, Wouter. 1999a. "Defining Religion in Spite of History", pp. 337–378 in *The Pragmatics of Defining Religions: Concepts, Contexts and Contests* edited by J.G. Platvoet and A.L. Molendijk. Leiden/New York/Köln: Brill.

———. 1999b. "New Age Spiritualities as Secular Religion: a Historian's Perspective". *Social Compass*, 46(2): 145–160.

———. 2001. "Prospects for the Globalisation of New Age: Spiritual Imperialism Versus Cultural Diversity", pp. 15–30 in *New Age Religion and Globalization* edited by M. Rothstein. Aarhus: Aarhus University Press.

Hannerz, Ulf. 1992. "Cosmopolitas y locales en la cultura global". *Revista Alteridades. Ideología, simbolismo y vida urbana*, year 2, n. 3: 107–115.

Haraway, Donna J. 1991. "A Cyborg Manifesto: Science, Technology, and Socialist-Feminism in the Late Twentieth Century", pp. 149–181 in *Simians, Cyborgs and Women: The Reinvention of Nature*, New York: Routledge.

———. 1999. "Las promesas de los monstruos: Una política regeneradora para otros inapropiados/bles". *Política y Sociedad*, n. 30: 121–163.

Heelas, Paul. 1996. *The New Age Movement. The Celebration of the Self and the Sacralization of Modernity*. Oxford: Blackwell Publishers.

———. 2008. *Spiritualities of Life: New Age Romanticism and Consumptive Capitalism*. Oxford: Blackwell Publishers.

Heelas, Paul and Woodhead, Linda. 2005. *The Spiritual Revolution. Why Religion is Giving Way to Spirituality*. Oxford: Blackwell.

Herin, Robert. 2006. "Por Una Geografía Social, Critica y Comprometida". *Scripta Nova Revista Electrónica De Geografía Y Ciencias Sociales*, v. X, n. 218 (93), 1 August. Available at: http://www.ub.es/geocrit/sn/sn-218-93.htm#_ftn1 Consulted: 6 October 2009.

Hernández-Avila, Ines. 2000. "Mediations of the Spirit. Native American Religious Traditions and the Ethics of Representation", pp. 11–60 in *Native American Spirituality. A Critical Reader* edited by Lee Irwin. Lincoln: University of Nebraska Press.

Hernández Madrid, Miguel J. 2005. "Entre las emergencias espirituales en una época axial y la mercantilización contemporánea de los bienes de sanación". *Desacatos*, n. 18 (May–August): 15–28.

Hervieu-Léger, Daniéle. 1993. *La religion pour mémoire*. Paris: Les éditions du Cerf.

———. 2004. *El peregrino y el convertido. La religión en movimiento.* Mexico: Ediciones del Helénico.

Hess, David J. 1989. "Disobsessing Disobsession: Religion, Ritual, and Social Science in Brazil." *Cultural Anthropology* 4(2): 182–193.

Hobsbawm, Eric and Terence Ranger (eds.). 1983. *The Invention of Tradition*. Cambridge: Cambridge University Press.

Holmes, Peter. 2011. "Spirituality. Some disciplinary perspectives", pp. 23–42 in *A Sociology of Spirituality* edited by Kieran Flanagan and Per Jupp. Farnham: Ashgate.

Hoover, Stewart and Lynn S. Clark. 2002. *Practicing Religion in the Age of the Media: Explorations in Media, Religion, and Culture*. New York: Columbia University Press.

Icke, David. 2010. *Hijos de Matrix. Cómo una raza interdimensional controla el mundo desde hace miles de años*. Barcelona: Ediciones Obelisco.

Iglesias Prieto, Norma. 2008. *Emergencias: Las Artes Visuales en Tijuana. Los Contextos Urbanos Glo-cales y la Creatividad v.* I. Tijuana: Conaculta Centro Cultural Tijuana/ Universidad Autónoma de Baja California.

Instituto Nacional de Estadistica y Geografía (INEGI). 2010. Censo de Población y Vivienda 2012. Main results by locality (ITER).

Inomata, Takeshi. 2006. "Plazas, Performers, and Spectators: Political Theaters of the Classic Maya". *Current Anthropology* 47 (5): 805–842.

Irwin, Lee. (ed.) 2000. *Native American Spirituality. A Critical Reader*. Lincoln: University of Nebraska Press.

Itier, César. 1997. *Parlons quechua. La langue du Cuzco*. Paris: L'Harmattan.

———. 2009. "Una percepción folclorizada y arcaizante del quechua: el Diccionario quechua-español-quecha de la Academia Mayor de la Lengua Quechua", pp. 265–285 in *El regreso de lo indígena. Retos, problemas y perspectivas,* edited by Valérie Robin Azevedo & Carmen Salazar-Soler. Lima: Institut Français d'Etudes Andines/ Centro de Estudios Regionales Andinos Bartolomé de Las Casas.

Jáuregui, Jesús and Carlo Bonfiglioli (coords.). 1996. *Las danzas de conquista I. México contemporáneo*. Mexico: Conaculta/FCE.

Jenkins, Elizabeth B. 1997. *Il ritorno dell'Inka*. Milan: Sonzogno.

Jenkins, Henry. 2008. *Convergence Culture*. Barcelona: Paidós.

Jenkins, John Major. 2009. *The 2012 Story. The Myths, Fallacies and Truth Behind the Most Intriguing Date in History.* Santa Fe: Bear & Company.

Jovchelovitch, Sandra. 1998. "Re(des)cobrindo o outro: para um entendimento da alteridade na Teoria das representações sociais", pp. 69–82 in *Representando a alteridade* edited by A. Arruda. Petrópolis: Vozes.

Juárez-Huet, Nahayeilli B. 2007. *Un pedacito de Dios en casa: transnacionalización, relocalización y práctica de la santería en la ciudad de México*. Ph.D. thesis. El Colegio de Michoacán.

———. 2009. "Transnacionalización y relocalización de la santería cubana: el caso de la ciudad de México", *Stockholm Review of Latin American Studies*, n. 4 (March): 85–94. Available at: http://www.lai.su.se/gallery/bilagor/SRoLas_No4_2009_web.pdf.

Jungblut, Airton. 2006. "O Evangelho New Age: Sobre a gnose evangélica no Brasil na visao dos seus detratores". *Civitas*, v.6, n. 2: 101–121.

Karnoouh, Lorraine. 2011. "Processus de recomposition religieuse à La Havane: la religión et le New Age", pp. 211–242 in *La religion des orisha. Un champ social transnational en pleine recomposition* edited by Kali Argyriadis and Stefania Capone. Paris: Hermann.

Knauer, Lisa Maya. 2001. "Afrocubanidad translocal: la rumba y la santería en Nueva York y La Habana", pp. 11–31 in *Culturas encontradas: Cuba y los Estados Unidos* edited by Rafeal Hernández and John H. Coastworth. Havana: CIDCC Juan Marinelo/ Universidad de Harvard (DRCLAS).

Labate, Beatriz. 2004. *A reinvenção douso ritual da ayahuasca nos centros urbanos*. Campinas: Mercado das Letras.

Laclau, Ernesto and Chantal Mouffe. 1987. *Hegemonía y Estrategia Socialista, Hacia una radicalización de la Democracia*. Madrid: Siglo XXI.

Lagarriga Attias, Isabel. 1991. *Espiritualismo Trinitario Mariano, Nuevas Perspectivas de Análisis.* Xalapa: Colección SEP/SETENTAS/Universidad Veracruzana.

———. 2004. [Book review] "Silvia Ortiz Echániz, Una religiosidad popular: el espiritualismo trinitario mariano, Mexico, INAH (Científica, 220), 2003". *Dimensión Antropológica*, Online journal, v.31 (May–August): 171–176. Available at: http://www.dimensionantropologica.inah.gob.mx/?p=771.

Lagarriga Attias, Isabel and Silvia Ortíz Echaniz. 2007. "Santería y espiritualismo trinitario mariano. Interrelación e imaginario ideológico en la ciudad de México", pp. 211–226 in *Enfermedad y religión: un juego de miradas sobre el vínculo de la metáfora entre lo mórbido y lo religioso* edited by Juan Luis Ramírez Torres. Toluca: UAEM.

Lagarriga, Isabel, Jacques Galinier, and Michel Perrin (eds.). 1995. Chamanismo en Latinoamérica. México: Plaza y Valdés/Universidad Iberoamericana/CEMCA.

Lambert, Renaud. 2011. "Le spectre du pachamamisme". *Le Monde diplomatique*, February. Available at: http://www.monde-diplomatique.fr/2011/02/LAMBERT/20148.

Lambert, Yves. 1991. "La 'tour de Babel' dês définition de la religion". *Social Compass*, v. 38, n. 1: 73–85.

———. 1995. "Une definition plurielle pour une realité em mutation". *Cahiers Français* n. 273: 3–12.

Laplantine, Francois and Alexis Nouss. 1997. *Le Métissage: un exposé pour comprendre, un essai pour réfléchir*. Coll. «Domino» no. 145. Paris: Éditions Flammarion.

Latour, Bruno. 2008. *Reensamblar lo social. Una introducción a la teoría del actor-red.* Buenos Aires: Manantial.

Le Borgne, Yann. 2005. "Evolución del indigenismo en la sociedad peruana. El tratamiento al grupo étnico q'ero", pp. 159–179 in *Etnografías de Cuzco*, edited by Antoinette Molinié. Cuzco: Centro de Estudios Regionales Andinos Bartolomé de las Casas.

Lemieux, Raymond, Jean Paul Montminy, Alain Bouchard and Martin Meunier. 1993. "De la modernité des croyances. Continuités et ruptures dans l'imaginaire religieux". *Archives de Sciences Sociales des Religions* 38, n. 81: 91–106.

León Portilla, Miguel. 2002. "Prólogo", in Jelena Galovic, *Los grupos místico-espirituales de la actualidad.* Mexico: Plaza y Valdés editores.

Leopold Anita M., and Jeppe S. Jensen. 2005. *Syncretism in religion. A Reader*. NewYork: Routledge.

Levy, Carminha. 1996. "*Encontro de Tradições: Budismo Tibetano, Candomblé, Povos Indígenas, Xamanismo Urbano*", took place on 9 October 1996, at the Social Science Department of PUC/São Paulo.

Levy, Carminha and Machado, Álvaro. 1995. *A sabedoria dos animais: viagens xamânicas e mitológicas*. São Paulo: Opera Prima Editorial.

Liffman, Paul. 2005. “Fuegos, Guías y Raíces: estructuras cosmológicas y procesos históricos en la territorialidad huichol”. *Relaciones, XXVI* (101): 53–79.

———. 2012. *La territorialidad wixarika y el espacio nacional. Reivindicación indígena en el occidente de México.* Zamora and Mexico City: COLMICH and CIESAS.

Lofland, John and Richarson, James. 1984. “Religious Movement Organizations: Elemental Forms and Dynamics”. *Research in Social Movements, Conflict and Change*, vol. 7: 29–51.

Lombardi, Denise. 2010. “Neo chamanismo. El ritual transferido”, *Coloquio Internacional de Otopames*, Tlaxcala, m.s.

———. 2012. *Les Français et le néochamanisme*, CNRS, unpublished.

Longato, Renato. 1991. “Perú centro magnético”. *Gnosis. Revista de esoterismo iniciático*, n. 5.

López Molina, Ana. 2007. “La Asociación de Sacerdotes Mayas de Guatemala”, pp. 413–443 in *Mayanización y vida cotidiana. La ideología multicultural en la sociedad guatemalteca.* v. 2. edited by Santiago Bastos and Aura Cumes. Guatemala: FLACSO/CIRMA Cholsamaj.

Lothrop, Samuel Kirkland. 1929. “Further notes on Indian Ceremonies in Guatemala”, *Indian Notes*, vol. VI, n. 1.

Luckmann, Thomas. 1967. *The Invisible Religion: The Transformation of Symbols in Industrial Society*. New York: Macmillan edition.

Maffesoli, Michel. 1990. *El tiempo de las tribus.* Barcelona: Icaria.

Magnani, José Guilherme Cantor M. 1991. *Umbanda.* São Paulo: Editorial Ática.

———. 1999a. *Mystica Urbe: um estudo antropológico do circuito neo-esotérico na cidade*. São Paulo: Studio Nobel Editora.

———. 1999b. “O circuito neo-esotérico na cidade de São Paulo”, pp. 27–47 in *A Nova Era no Mercosul* edited by María Julia Carozzi. Petrópolis: Editora Vozes.

———. 1999c. “O xamanismo urbano e a religiosidade contemporânea”. *Religião e Sociedade*, v. 20, n. 2.

———. 2000. *O Brasil da Nova Era.* Rio de Janeiro: Jorge Zahar Editor.

———. 2002. “De perto e de dentro: notas para uma etnografia urbana”. *Revista Brasileira de Ciências Sociais*, ANPOCS, v. 17, n. 49.

Malimacci, Fortunato. 2011. “De la Argentina católica a la Argentina diversa. De los catolicismos a la diversidad religiosa”, pp. 75–130 in *Pluralización religiosa de América Latina* edited by Olga Odgers. Tijuana: El Colegio de la Frontera Norte/ CIESAS.

Mardones, José María. 1994. *Para comprender las nuevas formas de la religión. La reconfiguración postcristiana de la religión.* Navarra: Verbo Divino.

———. 1996. *¿Hacia dónde va la religión? Postmodernidad y Postesecularización.* Cuadernos de Fe y Cultura n. 1. Mexico City: Ibero/Iteso.

———. 2005. *La transformación de la religión. Cambio en lo sagrado y cristianismo.* Madrid: PPC.

Mariátegui, José Carlos. 1928. *Siete ensayos de interpretación de la realidad peruana.* Lima: Amauta.

Marín, Mónica. 2010. "'La fuerza ha disminuido'. Cambios relacionados con el uso del hongo en Huautla de María Sabina". First degree thesis, Universidad Veracruzana, Xalapa, Mexico.

Martín Barbero, Jesús. 1987. *De los medios a las mediaciones.Comunicación, cultura y hegemonía.* Mexico City: Editorial Gustavo Gili S.A.

Martínez González, Roberto. 2007. "Lo que el chamanismo dejó: cien años de edstudios chamánicos en México u Mesoamérica". Anuario Antropológico 41-II:113–156.

———. 2009. "El chamanismo y la corporalizacion del chamán: argumentos para la deconstrucción de una falsa categoría antropológica". Cuicuilado, n. 46 (May–August): 197–220.

Mary, André. 2003. "Parcours visionnaires et passeurs de frontières". *Anthropologie et Sociétés*, v. 27, n. 1: 111–130.

Maués, Raymundo Heraldo. 2002. "Mudando de vida: a "conversão" ao pentecostalismo católico". *Religião e Sociedade*, v. 22, n. 2: 37–64.

Mc Guire, Meredith. 1987. *Religion: the Social Context.* Belmont: Wadsworth Publishing Company.

Mechú, Rigoberta and Francisco Calí. 2006. "Prólogo". *Raxalaj Mayab' K'aslemalil Cosmovisión Maya, plenitud de la vida.* Guatemala: Programa de Naciones Unidas Para el Desarrollo.

Meintel, Deirdre and Marie Nathalie Leblanc. 2003. "La mobilité du religieux à l'ère de la globalisation". *Antropologie et sociétés*, 27 (1): 5–11.

Melton, Gordon. 1992. "New Thought and the New Age", pp. 15–29 in *Perspectives on the New Age* edited by Lewis and Melton. New York: State University of New York Press.Melton, Gordon J. *et al.* 1990. *New Age Encyclopedia.* Detroit: Gale Research.

Mendelson, Michael. 1965. *Los escándalos de Maximón. Un estudio sobre la religión y la visión del mundo en Santiago Atitlán.* Guatemala: Tipografía Nacional.

Mendizabal, Sergio. 2007. *El encantamiento de la realidad: Conocimientos mayas en prácticas sociales de la vida cotidiana.* Guatemala: Universidad Rafael Landívar.

Menéndez, Lázara. 2002. *Rodar el coco. Proceso de cambio en la santería.* Havana: Editorial de Ciencias Sociales.

Mercante, M.S. 2009. "Ayahuasca, dependência química e alcoolismo". *Ponto Urbe* (*NAU/USP*), v. 5: 01–23. Available at: http://www.pontourbe.net/.

Michalik, Priotr Grzegorz. 2011. "Death with a Bonus Pack: New Age Spirituality, Folk Catholicism, and the Cult of Santa Muerte". *Archives des Sciences Sociales de Religion* n. 153 (January–March): 59–182.

Mier, Raymundo. 2002. "Complejidad: bosquejos para una antropología de la inestabilidad", pp. 77–104 in *Antropología y complejidad* edited by Rafael Pérez Taylor. Barcelona: Gedisa.

Mills, Charles Wright. 1940. "Situated Actions and Vocabularies of Motive". *American Sociological Review* 5(6): 904–913.

Minero, Fabiola. 2012. "Las mujeres sabias y las veladas con "hongos sagrados": el chamanismo mazateco". First degree thesis in Etnology, ENAH. Mexico.

Moedano, Gabriel. 1986. "El tema de la conquista en la tradición literaria-musical de los 'concheros'", paper presented in *Memoria del Primer Congreso de la Sociedad mexicana de Musicología*, Gobierno Constitucional del Estado de Tamaulipas/Dirección General de Asuntos Culturales, Ciudad Victoria, pp. 62–73, Mexico.

Molinié, Antoinette. 1979. "Cure magique dans la Vallée Sacrée du Cuzco". *Journal de la Société des Américanistes* t. LXVI: 85–98.

———. 1996. "Las tres madres del Perú. Cuzco en las representaciones de la identidad nacional peruana". *Crónicas urbanas,* year V, n. 5: 79–84.

———. 2004. "The Resurrection of the Inca: The Role of Indian Representations in the Invention of the Nation". *History and Anthropology* v. 15, n. 3 (September): 233–250.

———. 2009. "Del inca nacional a la Internacional inca", pp. 237–264 in *El regreso de lo indígena. Retos, problemas y perspectivas* edited by Valérie Robin Azevedo and Carmen Salazar-Soler. Lima: Institut Français d'Etudes Andines/Centro de Estudios Regionales Andinos Bartolomé de Las Casas.

Montejo, Víctor. 2005. *Maya Intellectual Renaissance. Identity, Representation and Leadership.* Austin: University of Texas Press.

Montero, Paula. 1999. "Religiões e dilemas da sociedade brasileira". *O que ler na ciência social brasileira* v. 1: 327–367.

Moore, Robin. 2001–2002. "La fiebre de la rumba". *Encuentro de la Cultura Cubana* n. 23: 175–194.

Mora Rosas, José Manuel. 2002a. "Oferta esotérica en Guadalajara: una visión socio semiótica". Thesis for Masters in Communication, DECS, Universidad de Guadalajara, Guadalajara.

———. 2002b. "Nuevas prácticas mágico-religiosas: itinerarios de consumo y construcción de sentido", pp. 105–123 in *Cambios religiosos globales y reacomodos locales* edited by Karla Y. Covarrubias and Rogelio de la Mora. Colima: Altexto.

Moraes, Renate Jost de. 1995. *O inconsciente sem fronteiras.* Aparecida do Norte: Ed. Santuário.

Morales, Mario Roberto, 1998. *La articulación de las diferencias o el sídrome de Maximón: los discursos literarios y políticos del debate interétnico en Guatemala.* Guatemala: FLACSO.

Morales Sic, José Roberto. 2007. *Religión y política. El proceso de institucionalización de la espiritualidad maya en el contexto del Movimiento Maya guatemalteco.* Guatemala: Colección Cuadernos de Maestría. Posgrado Centroamericano en Ciencias Sociales/ Editorial de Ciencias Sociales FLACSO, Guatemala.

Mori, Koichi. 2008. Interview in *Revista Cuadernos de Campo*, n. 17 (January–December).

Mulcock, Jane. 2001. "(Re)-discovering our Indigenous Selves: the Nostalgic Appeal of Native Americans and Other Generic Indigenes". *Australian Religion Studies Review*, 14 (1): 45–65.

Murga, Jorge. 1999. "Sociétés mayas, changement social et processus de recomposition des systèmes de représentations (Santiago Atitlán, Guatemala)". PhD thesis in Entnology. Universités Paris VIII – Paris I, Paris.

Murphy, Joseph. 1988. *Santeria: African Spirits in America*. Boston: Beacon Press.

Murra, John. 1975. "El control vertical de un máximo de pisos ecológicos en la economía de las sociedades andinas", pp. 59–115 in *Formaciones écónómicas y políticas del mundo andino*. Lima: Instituto de Estudios Peruanos.

Negrão, Lísias Nogueira. 1997. "Refazendo antigas e urdindo novas tramas: trajetórias do sagrado". *Religião e Sociedade* 18/2: 63–74.

———. 2008. "Pluralismo e multiplicidades religiosas no Brasil contemporâneo". *Sociedade e Estado*, v. 23, n. 2: 261–279.

Núñez Del Prado, Juan Víctor. 1991. "Opiniones acerca de la reivindicación del nombre Qosqo para nuestra ciudad". *Revista Municipal del Qosqo* I, n. 3. Available at: http://www.ugr.es/~pwlac/G27_13Daniela-di-Salvia.html.

———. 1998. *Camminando nel cosmo vivente. Guide alle tecniche energetiche e spirituali delle Ande*. Cesena: Macro Edizioni.

Nuñez Del Prado, Oscar. 1973. "Versión del mito de Inkarrí en Q'eros", pp. 275–280 in *Ideología mesiánica del Mundo Andino* edited by Juan Ossio. Lima: Ed. Ignacio Prado Pastor.

ODHAG. 1998. *Guatemala. Nunca más. Informe del Proyecto Interdiocesano de Recuperación de la Memoria Histórica (Remhi)* 4 volumes. Guatemala: Oficina de Derechos Humanos del Arzobispado de Guatemala.

Oliveira, Pedro Ribeiro de. 1985. *Religião e dominação de classe: gênese, estrutura e função do catolicismo romanizado no Brasil*. Petrópolis: Vozes.

Olmos Aguilera, Miguel. 2008. "Las creencias indígenas y neo-indias en la frontera México/USA". *Trace*, 54 (December): 45–60.

O'phelan Godoy, Scarlett. 1995. "La gran rebelión de los Andes: de Tupac Amaru a Tupac Catari". *Archivos de Historia Andina* 20. Lima/Cuzco: Centro de Estudios Rurales Andinos Bartolomé de Las Casas.

Oro, Ari Pedro. 1996. *Avanço pentecostal e reação católica*. Petrópolis: Vozes.

Ortiz, Fernando. 2001. *Los Negros Brujos*. Havana: Editorial de Ciencias Sociales.

Ortíz Echaniz, Silvia. 1977. "Espiritualismo en México. ¿Quiénes y cuáles son los espiritualistas?" *Cuadernos de Trabajo* n. 20. Mexico City: INAH.

Ortiz Rescaniere, Alejandro. 1973. *De Adaneva a Inkarrí*. Lima: Ed. Retablo de Papel.

Ossio, Juan. 1973. *Ideología mesiánica del Mundo Andino*. Lima: Ed. Ignacio Prado Pastor.

Parisi Wilcox, Joan and Elizabeth B. Jenkins. 1996. "Journey to Q'ollorit'i: Initiation into the Andean Mysticism". *Shaman's Drum* n. 40: 34–49.

Parker Gumucio, Cristian. 2001. "Las nuevas formas de la religión en la sociedad globalizada: un desafío a la interpretación sociológica", paper presented at the *26th Conference of the International Society for the Sociology of Religión*, Ixtapán de la Sal, Mexico.

———. 2008. "Pluralismo religioso, educación y ciudadanía". *Sociedad e Estado*. Dossié Pluralidade religiosa na América Latina, v. 23, n. 2: 281–354.

Pédron Colombani, Sylvie. 2005. *Maximón, Dieu, Saint ou traître*. London: Periplus.

———. 2006. "Maximón au Guatemala. Entre ambivalence éthique et rites de fertilité", pp. 289–314 in *De l'ethnographie à l'histoire. Paris/Madrid/Buenos-Aires. Les mondes de Carmen Bernand* edited by Jean-Pierre Castellain, Serge Gruzinski and Carmen Salazar-Soler. Paris: L'Harmattan.

Pereira, Karen, Bárbara Arroyo and Margarita Cossich. 2007. "Las estelas lisas de Naranjo. Guatemala", pp. 1054–1080 in *XX Simposio de investigaciones Arqueológicas en Guatemala* edited by J.P. Laporte, B. Arroyo and H. Mejía. Guatemala: Museo Nacional de Arqueología y Etnología.

Pereira, Ronan. 1992. *Possessão por espírito e inovação cultural: a experiência religiosa das japonesas Miki Hakayama e Nao Deguchi*. São Paulo: Massao Ohno/Aliança Cultural Brasil-Japão.

Pesavento, Sandra Jatahy. 2003. *História & História Cultural*. Belo Horizonte: Autêntica.

Piette, Albert. 1993. *Les religiosités Séculières*. Paris: PUF.

Pierucci, Antônio Flávio. 2004. "*Bye bye, Brasil*: o declínio das religiões tradicionais no Censo 2000". *Estudos Avançados* v.18, n. 52 (September–December).

Pilares Villa, Rubén. 1992. *Turismo místico. Parodia o trascendencia*. Qosqo: Ed. Ayar.

Pinkola Estés, Clarissa. 2009. *Mujeres que corren con lo lobos*. Buenos Aires: No ficción ZETA.

Platt, Tristan. 1978. "Symétries en miroir. Le concept de *yanantin* chez les Macha de Bolivia". *Annales ESC* year 33, n. 5–6: 1081–1107

Polk Patrick, Arthur. 2004. "Botánica Los Ángeles. An Introduction", pp. 14–26 in *Botanica Los Angeles. Latino Popular Art in the City of Angels* edited by P.A. Polk. Los Angeles: UCLA Fowler Museum of Cultural History.

Popkin, Eric. 1999. "Guatemalan Mayan Migration to Los Angeles: Constructing Transnational Linkages in the Context of the Settlement Process". *Ethnic and racials studies* v. 22, n. 2 (March): 267–289.

Possamai, Adam. 2001. "Not the New Age. Perennism and Spiritual Knowledges". *Australian Religion Studies Review* 14 (1): 82–97.

Prandi, Reginaldo and Souza, André Ricardo de. 1996. "A carismática despolitização da Igreja Católica", pp. 59–91 in *A realidade social das religiões no Brasil* edited by Antônio Flávio Pierucci and Reginaldo Prandi. São Paulo: Hucitec.

Quezada, Noemí. 1989. *Enfermedad y Maleficio. El curandero en el México Colonial.* Mexico City: UNAM Instituto de Investigaciones Antropológicas.

Reis, Marcelo Rodrigues Dos. 2001. *A apropriação do tempo na construção do imaginário e da identidade no Vale do Amanhecer.* Monograph for degree, Universidade de Brasília, Instituto de Ciências Humanas, Departamento de História, Brasilia.

———. 2004. *Discurso e Temporalidades, A Construção da memória e da identidade no Vale do Amanhecer (1957–2004).* Masters thesis, Universidade de Brasília, Instituto de Ciências Humanas, Departamento de História, Brasilia.

Ricard Lanata, Xavier. 2007. *Ladrones de sombra. El universo religiosos del Ausangate (Andes surperuanos).* Cuzco: Instituto Francés de Estudios Andinos/Centro Bartolomé de Las Casas.

Ríos, Andrés. 2000. "Evangelion: la futurización milenarista en el comic japonés. Una mirada antropológica". Revista. *Estudios del hombre* (11): 127–143.

Rivas Neto, F. 2002. *Umbanda. A proto síntese cósmica.* São Paulo: Melhoramentos.

Robertson, Roland. 1990. "Glocalización: tiempo-espacio y homogeneidad-heterogeneidad", *Zona Abierta,* n. 92–92, translation by Juan Carlos Monedero and Joaquín Rodríguez, published in www.cholonautas.edu.pe/Biblioteca Virtual de Ciencias Sociales.

Robinson, William I. 2003. *Transnational Conflicts. Central America, Social Change and Globalization.* London/New York: Verso.

Rocchi, Valérie. 2003. "Des Nouvelles Formes Du Religieux? Entre Quête De Bien-être Et Logique Protestataire: Le Cas Des Groupes Post-Nouvel-Age En France". *Social Compass* v. 50, n. 2: 175–189.

Rocha, Cristina and Manuel A. Vásquez. 2013. "Introduction: Brazil in the New Global Cartography of Religion", pp. 1–45 in *The Diaspora of Brazilian Religions* edited by Cristina Rocha and Manuel A. Vásquez. Leiden-Boston: Ed. Brill.

Rodrigues, Arackci and Francine Muel-Dreyfus. 1987. "Reencarnações. Notas de pesquisa sobre uma seita espírita em Brasília". *Revista Brasileira de Ciências Sociais* n. 31: 12–28.

Rodríguez, Pepe. 2000. *El poder de las sectas.* Barcelona: Editorial B.

Romero, Sergio. 2000. "Estudio Comparativo de Dos Calendarios Coloniales Mayas del Siglo XVIII". First Degree Thesis, Universidad Valle de Guatemala, Guatemala.

Roskind, Robert. 2008. *2012. The Transformation From the Love of Power to the Power of Love.* Blowing Rock: One Love Press.

Rostas, Susanna. 2008. "Los concheros en un contexto mundial. Mexicanidad, espiritualidad new age y sufismo como influencias en la danza", pp. 193–226 in *Raíces en movimiento. Prácticas religiosas tradicionales en contextos traslocales* edited by Kali Argyridis, Renée de la Torre, Cristina Gutiérrez Zúñiga and Alejandra Aguilar Ros. Guadalajara: COLJAL/CEMCA/IRD/CIESAS/ITESO.

Rueda, Rocío. 2008. "Cibercultura: metáforas, prácticas sociales y colectivos en red". *Nómadas* n. 8 (April): 8–20.

Russo, Jane. 1993. *O corpo contra apalavra*. Rio de Janeiro: Ed. UFRJ.

Ruz Buenfil, Alberto. 1992. *Los guerreros de arcoíris*. Mexico City: Círculo Cuadrado.

———. 2002. "La imaginación al poder: 33 años después", in several editions, *Regina y el Movimiento del 68 treinta y tres años después*. Mexico City: EDAF.

Ruz Mario, Humberto. 2009. "Tres milenios de movilidad maya. A modo de preámbulo", pp. 13–57 in *Diásporas, migraciones y exilios en el mundo maya* edited by Mario Humberto Ruz, Joan García Targa and Andrés Ciudad Ruiz. Mérida: Sociedad Española de Estudios Mayas/Universidad Nacional Autónoma de México.

Sahlins, Marshall. 2002. "Les cosmologies du capitalismo. Le 'système-Monde' vu du Pacifique". *Le Débat* n. 118 (January–February): 166–187.

Salcedo, Rodrigo. 2008. "Reflexiones en torno a los guetos urbanos: Michelle de Certeau y la relación disciplina/anti-disciplina". *Bifurcaciones* [online] n. 7, World Wide Web document (URL www.bifurcaciones.cl/007/DeCerteau.htm) Consulted: 1 September 2009.

Sanchis, Pierre. 1994. "Para nao dizer que nao falei de sincretismo". *Communicaçoes do ISER* n. 45: 5–11.

———. 1995. "As tramas sincréticas da história. Sincretismo e modernidades no espaço luso-brasileiro". *Revista Brasileira de Ciências Sociais* v. 28, n. 10.

———. 2001. *Fiéis & Cidadãos: percursos de sincretismo no Brasil*. Rio de Janeiro: Eduerj.

———. 2004. "Para nao dizer que nao falei de sincreismo". *Comunicadao do ISER* v. 45: 4–11.

———. 2008. "Cultura brasileira e religi~ao…passado e atualidades…". *Cuadernos CERU* 2, v.19: 71–92.

Sanchiz Ochoa, Pilar. 1993. "Sincretismos de ida y vuelta: el culto de San Simón en Guatemala". *Mesoamérica* 26 (December): 253–266.

Saraiva, Clara. 2011. "Energias e Curas: A Umbanda em Portugal". *Pós Ciências Sociais* v. 8, n. 16: 55–76.

Sarrazin, Jean-Paul. 2008a. "El Chamanismo es un camino. Las culturas indígenas como fuentes de sabiduría espiritual en Bogotá", pp. 329–362 in *Raíces en movimiento. Prácticas religiosas tradicionales en contextos traslocales* edited by Kali Argyridis, Renée de la Torre, Cristina Gutiérrez Zúñiga and Alejandra Aguilar Ros. Guadalajara: COLJAL/CEMCA/IRD/CIESAS/ITESO.

———. 2008b. "La 'espiritualización' de los discursos neoindigenistas en Colombia", pp. 77–91 in *Trace 54 Reacomodos religiosos (neo) indígenas*. Mexico City: Centro de Estudios Mexicanos y Centroamericanos.

Segato, Rita Laura. 2007. *La nación y sus otros. Raza, etnicidad y diversidad religiosa en tiempos de Políticas de la identidad*. Buenos Aires: Prometeo.

Semán, Pablo. 2001. "Cosmológica, holista y relacional: una corriente de la religiosidad popular contemporánea". *Ciencias Sociales y Religión/Ciências Sociais e Religião,* n. 3: 45–74.

———. 2008. "Cosmológica, holista y relacional: una corriente de la religiosidad popular contemporánea". In *Latinidade da América Latina. Enfoques sócio-antropológicos* edited by Ari Pedro Oro. São Paulo: Editora Hucited.

Sena, Luiza M. de Oliveira. 2011. *Dançando para Deus: música e dança a serviço da fé nas cristotecas católicas.* Dissertation Masters in Ciências da Religião, Pontifícia Universidade Católica de São Paulo.

SEPAZ/FONAPAZ/GOODWILL AMBASSADOR. 2005. *Agenda pública hacia los pueblos indígenas en el marco de los acuerdos de paz. 2005–2012.* Guatemala: Working paper.

Sharer, Robert. 1994. *The Ancient Maya.* Stanford: Stanford University Press.

Sharon, Douglas. 1988. *El chamán de los cuatro vientos.* Mexico City: Siglo Veintiuno Editores.

Shepard J.R., Glenn, H. 2004. "Native Central and South American Shamanism" v.1, pp. 365–370 in *Shamanism: An Encyclopedia of World Beliefs, Practices and Culture* edited by M.N. Walter and J.N. Fridman. Santa Barbara: ABC-CLIO.

Silva, José C. Do Nascimento. 1999. *Observações Tumarã.* Brasilia: Ed. Out.

Siqueira, Deis. 2002. "Novas Religiosidades na Capital do Brasil". *Tempo Social* v. 14, n. 01, 35–48.

———. 2003. "A labiríntica busca religiosa na atualidade: crenças e práticas místico-esotéricas na capital do Brasil", pp. 25–64 in *Sociologia das Adesões: novas religiosidades e a busca místico-esotérica na capital do Brasil* edited by Deis Siqueira and Ricardo Barbosa de Lima. Rio de Janeiro: Garamond/Vieira.

Siqueira, Deis and Ricardo Barbosa Lima. 2003. *Sociologia das Adesões: novas religiosidades e a busca místico-esotérica na capital do Brasil.* Rio de Janeiro: Garamond/Vieira.

Siqueira, Deis and Lourdes Bandeira. 1997. "O profano e o sagrado na construção da 'Terra Prometida'." Pp. 229 in *Brasília a construção do cotidiano* edited by Brasilmar Ferreira Nunes. Brasília: Paralelo 15.

Siqueira, Deis, L. Bandeira, A. Valle-Hollinger, F. Hollinger. 2002. "Religião e esoterismo entre estudantes: um estudo comparado internacional". *Religião e Sociedade* v. 22: 56–69.

Sivirichi, Atilio. 1946. *Derecho indígena peruano.* Lima: Ed. Kuntur.

Sloterdijk, Peter. 2003. *Esferas I. Burbujas. Microsferología.* Madrid: Ediciones Siruela.

Smith, E.R. and D.M. Mackie. 1995. *Social Psychology.* New York: Worth Publishers.

Snow, David. 1986. "Frame alignment processes, micromobilization, and movement participation". *American Sociological Review* v. 51, n. 4: 464–481.

Soares, Edio. 2009. *Le butinage religieux. Practiques et pratiquants au Brésil.* Paris: Karthala.

Soares, Luiz Eduardo. 1990. "O Santo Daime no Contexto da Nova Consciência Religiosa". *Sinais dos Tempos. Diversidade religiosa no Brasil,* Cadernos do ISER n. 23.

Solís Robledo, Gabriela. 2005. *Entre la tierra y el cielo. Religión y sociedad en los pueblos mayas del Yucatán colonial.* Colección Peninsular. Mexico City: CIESAS/ICY/Porrúa.

Stark, Rodney. 1985. *The future of religion: secularization, revival and cult formation.* Berkeley: University of California Press.

Stark, Rodney and William Sims Bainbridge. 1979. "Of Churches, Sects and Cults: Preliminary Concepts for a Theory of Religious Movements". *Journal for the Scientific Study of Religion* v. 18, n. 2: 117–133.

Steil, Carlos and Sandra de Sá Carneiro. 2008. "Peregrinação, turismo e nova era: caminhos de Santiago de Compostela no Brasil". *Religião e Sociedade* 28(1): 105–124.

Steil, Carlos Alberto. 1999. "A igreja dos pobres: da secularização à mística". *Religião e Sociedade* v. 19, n. 2: 61–76.

———. 2001. "Aparições marianas contemporâneas e carismatismo católico", pp. 117–146 in *Fiéis & cidadãos: percursos de sincretismo no Brasil* edited by Pierre Sanchis. Rio de Janeiro: EDUERJ.

———. 2004. "Renovação Carismática Católica: porta de entrada ou de saída do catolicismo? Uma etnografia do Grupo São José, em Porto Alegre". *Religião e Sociedade.* v. 24, n. 1: 11–36.

———. 2006. "Os demônios geracionais. A herança dos antepassados na determinação das escolhas e das trajetórias pessoais", pp. 219–239 in *Família e religião* edited by Luiz Fernando Dias Duarte, Myriam Lins de Barros and Clarice Peixoto. Rio de Janeiro: Contra Capa.

Sten, María. 1990. *Ponte a bailar, tú que reinas. Antropología de la danza prehispánica.* Mexico City: Joaquín Mortiz.

Stoll, Sandra. 2002. "Religião, ciência ou auto-ajuda? Trajetos do Espiritismo no Brasil". *Revista de Antropologia,* 45–2: 361–402.

Stolow, Jeremy. 2014. "Religião e Mídia: notas sobre pesquisas e direções futuras para um estudo interdisciplinar". *Religião e Sociedade* 34(2): 146–160.

Stone, Donald. 1976. "The Human Potential Movement", pp. 93–115 in *The New Religious Consciousness* edited by Glock and Bellah. Berkeley and Los Angeles: University of California Press.

Stone, Martha. 1975. *At The Sign of Midnight: the Concheros Dance Cult of Mexico.* Tucson: University of Arizona Press.

Sullivan, William. 1999. *El secreto de los Incas.* Barcelona: Ed. Grijalbo.

Tally, Engel. 2006. "Turismo espiritual en tiempos posmodernos. El estudio del caso de San Marcos de la Laguna, Sololá, Guatemala". First degree thesis at the Social Science Faculty, Anthropology Department, Universidad del Valle de Guatemala, Guatemala.

Tally, Englebert and Josué Chavajay. 2007. "Multiplicidad y antagonismo en torno a la mayanización en San Pedro la Laguna", pp. 495–532 in *Mayanización y vida cotidiana* volume 2, edited by Santiago Bastos and Aura Cumes. Guatemala: CLACSO/CIRMA/CHOLSAMAJ.

Tamayo Herrera, José. 1980. *Historia del indigenismo cuzqueño, siglo XVI–XX*. Lima: Instituto Nacional de la Cultura.

Tarn, Nathaniel and Martin Prechtel. 1997. *Scandals in the House of Birds. Shamans and Priests on Lake Atitlan*. New York: Marsilio.

Taussig, Michael. 1993. *Xamanismo, Colonialismo e o Homem Selvagem*. São Paulo: Paz e Terra.

Tedlock, Barbara. 1982. *Time and the Highland Maya*. New Mexico: University of New Mexico Press.

Teisenhoffer, Viola. 2007. "Umbanda, New Age et psychothérapie. Aspects de l'implantation de l'umbanda à Paris". *Ateliers du LESC*, 31, http://ateliers.revues.org/document872.html.

———. 2008. "De la "nebulosa místico-esotérica" al circuito alternativo. Miradas cruzadas sobre el new age y los nuevos movimientos religiosos", pp. 45–72 in *Raíces en movimiento. Prácticas religiosas tradicionales en contextos translocales* edited by Kali Argyriadis, Renée de la Torre, Cristina Gutiérrez Zúñiga and Alejandra Aguilar Ros. Guadalajara: COLJAL/CEMCA/CIESAS/IRD/ITESO.

Thompson, J., Eric S. 1987. *Historia y religión de los mayas*. Mexico City: Siglo Veintiuno.

Thompson, John B. 1998. *Ideología y cultura moderna*. Mexico City: UAM.

Touraine, Alain. 2002. *Crítica da Modernidade*. Petrópolis: Vozes.

Towsend, Joan B. 1993. "Neochamanismo y el movimiento místico moderno", in *El Viaje del Chamán: curación, poder y crecimiento personal* edited by Michael Harner (*et al.*). Barcelona: Kairós.

Troeltsch, Ernst. 1931. *The social teaching of the Christian Churches*. London: George Allen and Unwin.

Tufte, Thomas. 1997. "Televisión, modernidad y vida cotidiana. Un análisis sobre la obra de Robert Silverston desde contextos culturales diferentes". *Comunicación y Sociedad* n. 31: 65–96.

Turkle, Sherry. 1997. *La vida en la pantalla. La construcción de la identidad en la era de Internet.* Madrid: Paidós Transiciones.

Turner, Víctor. 1974. *Dramas, Fields, and Metaphors: Symbolic Action in Human Society*. Cornell: University Press.

———. 1989. *La selva de los símbolos*. Madrid: Ed. Siglo XXI.

Uk'ux B'e. 2009. *Cosmovisión Mayab'. Dos tres palabras sobre sus principios.* Guatemala: Serie Oxlajuj Baqtun, Asociación Maya Uk´ux B´e.

Uriel García, José. 1973. *El Nuevo Indio*. Lima: Ed. Universo.

Valcárcel, Luis. 1927. *Tempestad en los Andes*. Lima: Biblioteca Amauta.

Valderrama, Ricardo and Carmen Escalante. 1995. "El inka vive". *Revista del Museo e Instituto de Arqueología* n. 25: 241–270.

Valencia Espinoza, Abraham. 1991. *Taytacha Temblores, patrón jurado del Cuzco*. Cuzco: Centro de Estudios Andinos.

Van der Veer, Peter. 2009. "Global Breathing. Religious Utopias in India and China", pp. 263–278 in *Transnational Transcendence. Essays on Religion and Globalization* edited by Thomas Csordas. Oakland: University of California Press.

Van Hove, Hildegard. 1999. "L'émergence d'un 'marché spirituel'". *Social Compass* v. 46, n. 2: 161–172.

Vásquez, Diego. 2011. "¿Permanencia de la Tradición o restauración acrítica del pasado?" Presented at *Congreso de Estudios Mayas*, Universidad Rafael Landívar, Guatemala.

Vásquez, Juana. 2001. *Mujer y Cosmovisión Maya*. Guatemala: Moloj Kino'bij'al mayib'ixoqij'/Asociación Política de Mujeres Mayas.

Velasco Piña, Antonio. 1987. *Regina. 68 no se olvida*. Mexico City: Jus.

Velho, Otávio. 1997. "Globalização: antropologia e religião", pp. 43–62 in *Globalização e religião* edited by Ari Pedro de Oro and Carlos Steil. Petrópolis: Vozes.

———. 1998. "Ensaio herético sobre a atualidade da gnose". *Horizontes Antropológicos* v. 8: 34–52.

———. 2000. "Globalization: object—perspective—horizon". *Journal of Latin American* 4(2)–5(1): 320–339.

Vernette, Jean. 1993. *Le New Age*. Paris: Presses Universitaires de France (coll. Que sais-je?).

Villa Rojas, Alfonso. 1955. *Los mazatecos y el problema indígena de la Cuenca del Papaloapan*. Mexico City: INI.

Viotti, Nicolás. 2011. "La literatura sobre las nuevas religiosidades en las clases medias urbanas. Una mirada desde Argentina". *Cultura y Religión* v. 5, n. 1: 4–17.

Warman, Arturo. 1972. *La danza de Moros y Cristianos*. Mexico City: Sepsetentas.

Warren, Kay. 1993. "Interpreting *La Violencia* in Guatemala: shapes of Mayan silence and resistance", in *The violence within. Cultural and political opposition in divided nations*, edited by Kay Warren. Boulder: Westview Press.

———. 1998. *Indigenous Movements and their Critics. Pan-Maya Activism in Guatemala*. Princeton: Princeton University Press.

Weeks, John, Franke Sachse and Christian Prager. 2009. *Maya daykeeping. Three calendars from Highland Guatemala*. Colorado: University Press of Colorado.

Weigand, Phil and Jay Fikes. 2004. "Sensacionalismo y Etnografía. El Caso de los Huicholes de Jalisco". *Relaciones* 98, Spring, v. XXV: 50–68.

Wood, Matthew. 2010. "The Sociology of Spirituality: Reflections on a Problematic Endeavor", pp. 267–287 in *The New Blackwell Companion to the Sociology of Religion* edited by Bryan S. Turner. Oxford: Wiley-Blackwell.

Woodward, Kathryn. 2000. "Identidade e Diferença: uma Introdução Teórica e Conceitual". In *Identidade e Diferença: a Perspectiva dos Estudos Culturais* edited by Tadeu da Silva. Rio de Janeiro: Vozes.

Wuthnow, Robert. 1998. *Alter Heaven, Spirituality in America since the 1950s*. Berkeley and Los Angeles: University of California Press.

York, Michael. 1995. *The Emerging Network: A Sociology of the New Age and Neo-Pagan Movements*. Lanham: Rowman and Littlefield Publishers.

———. 1999. "Le supermarché religieux: ancrages locaux du Nouvel Age au sein du réseau mondial". *Social Compass* v. 46, n. 2: 173–179.

———. 2001. "New Age commodification and appropriation of spirituality". *Journal of Contemporary Religion* v. 16, n. 3: 361–372.

Zuidema, R. Tom. 1964. *The Ceque System of Cuzco. The Social Organisation of the Capital of the Inca*. Brill: Leiden.

———. 1986. *La civilisation inca de Cuzco*. Paris: Presses Universitaires de France.

———. 2010. *El calendario inca. Tiempo y espacio en la organización ritual del Cuzco. La idea del pasado*. Lima: Fondo Editorial del Congreso del Perú/Fondo Editorial de la Pontificia Universidad Católica del Perú.

Digital References

Albarrán, Rosalío "Olpamitzin". 2012. "Palabra del abuelo Olpamitzin". In *Nikan Axkan* (http://nikanaxkanrevista.blogspot.mx/2010/10/abuelo-ollpamitzin-xiuhtlahtolli.html) Consulted: 25 April 2012.

Argyriadis Kali, Juárez Nahayeilli, http://www.ird.fr/relitrans/?Santeria,304 Consulted: 1 May 2012.

Argyriadis, Kali, Juárez Nahayeilli and Capone Stefania, http://www.ird.fr/relitrans/?Ifa,309 Consulted: 15 October 2012.

Bordes, Mariana. 2006. "El fluir de la energía en las teorías etiológicas de la enfermedad, el caso de la reflexología". *Mitológicas* (online), v. XXI: 69–91, available at: http://redalyc.uaemex.mx/src/inicio/ArtPdfRed.jsp?iCve=14617733005.

Brostom, Nick. 2003. "El argumento de la simulación: por qué la probabilidad de que usted viva en una Matrix es bastante alta", *Times Higher Education Supplement, May 16,* available at http://www.simulation-argument.com/matrix-spanish.html.

Llamado del Corazón de la Tierra. 2014., at: http://www.llamadodelcorazondelatierra.com/nosotros/historia.html Consulted: May 2, 2015.

Montaner, Eduardo. 2012. "Más línea que linaje", www.scribd.com/doc/12340024/Mas-linea-que-linaje Consulted: 25 April 2012.

Negrín, Juan. 2008. *Yauxali. Pablo Taizán de la Cruz*. Document available at: http://wixarika.mediapark.net/sp/documents/YAUXALI.pdf.

Paz, Octavio, "Prólogo al libro de Carlos Castaneda", *Las enseñanzas de don Juan*, quoted from http://www.mercurialis.com/EMC/Octavio%20Paz%20-%20La%20Mirada%20 Anterior%201.htm.

Relitrans. *Transnationalisation religieuse des Suds: entre ethnicisation et universalisation. "Réflexion comparative"*: Available at: http://www.ird.fr/relitrans/?Reflexion -comparative&var_recherche=noeuds.

Ríos, Levi, n/d *Arquitectura Natal: la tierra es nuestra casa.* Available at: http://www2 .ine.gob.mx/publicaciones/libros/515/cap2.pdf.

Red cultural para la Fraternidad Humana (GFU)., Web Page of the GFU. Available at: http://www.gfu.org/2012/index.php.

Sarrazin, Jean Paul. 2008. «La "espiritualización" de los discursos neoindigenistas en Colombia », *Trace* [online], 54, Uploaded 24 July 2009 Consulted 27 March 2012. URL: http://trace.revues.org/index470.html.

Volcoc, K.; Antunes, H.; Roberta and Mercante, M. 2011. "Observações do não observável: breve relato sobre o I Encontro 'Ayahuasca e o tratamento da Dependência'". Revista Ponto Urbe [online], year 5 (December). Uploaded 14 August 2014 Consulted 23 July 2015. URL : http://pontourbe.revues.org/1948.

Digital Resources

http://raicesdelatierracolombia.com/raices-de-la-tierra/historia/ Consulted: May 2, 2015.

http://www.pewresearch.org/topics/latin-america/ Consulted: May 2, 2015.

http://fairbanks-alaska.com/alaska-native-corporations.htm/ Consulted: 8 February 2012.

http://forum.davidicke.com Consulted: 12 April 2015.

http://redesdeluz.blogspot.com Consulted: 12 April 2015.

http://redesdeluz.blogspot.mx/2007/12/los-nuevos-entramados-mal-llamados.html Consulted: 12 April 2015.

http://redesdeluz.blogspot.mx/2008/12/el-desafo-de-las-redes.html Consulted: 12 April 2015.

http://resistenciaespiritual.blogspot.com/2008/03/espiritualidad-azteca-parte-3.html Consulted: 15 July 2011.

http://tonebytone.com/hatunkarpay/0 Consulted: 24 October 2012.

http://web.jet.es/planetagaia/mesa.htm Consulted: 12 April 2015.

http://www.alaskanative.net/en/paranav/resources/corporations/ Consulted: 19 December 2011.

http://www.ciri.com/content/history/regional.aspx/ Consulted: 28 January 2012.

http://www.earthandspirit.org/ Consulted: 7 September 2011.
http://www.elblogdemiyo.com/?p=2213 Consulted: 10 March 2012 and, changed to http://www.emiliofiel.com/2012/03/10/10-de-marzo-la-maestria-de-la-red/ Consulted: 12 April 2015.
http://www.emiliofiel.com/2011/10/21/consenso-e-indignados Consulted: 12 April 2015.
https://loquepodemoshacer.wordpress.com/2012/05/22/llamado-al-100-consejo-de-visiones-de-los-guardianes-de-la-tierra Consulted: 12 April 2015.
http://www.globalcommunity.org/ Consulted: 4 February 2012.
http://www.grandmotherscouncil.org/ Consulted: 10 September 2011.
http://www.intk.org/ Consulted: 11 February 2012.
http://www.lbblawyers.com/ancsa.htm/ Consulted: 10 January 2012.
http://www.mothersgrace.com/ Consulted: 2 February 2012.
http://www.nativeco.com/ Consulted: 16 January 2012.
http://www.paraisomexico.org/?p=30 Consulted: 15 July 2011.
http://www.redindigena.net/conao/universidad.html Consulted: 15 July2011.
http://www.redplanetaria.com Consulted: 12 April 2015.
http://www.sacredstudies.org/ Consulted: 8 September 2011.
http://www.shamanism.org Consulted: 24 October 2012.
http://www.stillpointfarmsfestival.com/ Consulted: 22 January 2012.
http://www.thefourwinds.com/ Consulted: 24 October 2012.
www.casadelared.org Consulted: 26 March 2012 and, moved to http://lacasadelared.blogspot.mx/ Consulted: 12 April 2015.
www.iluminado-tours.com Consulted: 26 March 2012.
www.xamanismo.com.br Consulted: 24 October 2012.

Interviews

Alejandra. 2010. Member and leader of the Chicáhuac group. Interviewed by Alejandra Aguilar, April, Tijuana, Baja California, Mexico.
Caballero, Carlos. 2009. Interviewed by Cristina Gutiérrez Zúñiga, 18 July, Santiago de Compostela, Spain.
Claudia. 2010. Member of the Chicáhuac group. Interviewed by Alejandra Aguilar, April, Tijuana, Baja California, Mexico.
Claudio. 2009. Interviewed by Cristina Gutiérrez Zúñiga, 19 July, Santiago de Compostela, Spain.
Fiel, Emilio. 2009. Interviewed by Renée de la Torre and Cristina Gutiérrez, 10 June, in "Torre Nanita-Chrisgaia", Zaragoza, Spain.

Jiménez, Francisco "Tlacaélel". 2009. Interviewed by Aldo Daniel Arias Yerena, 26 December, San Martín de las Pirámides, Mexico.

Mizcoatzin. 2005. Interviewed by Cristina Gutiérrez Zúñiga, 22 September, Zapopan, Jalisco, Mexico.

———. 2005. Interviewed by Cristina Gutiérrez Zúñiga, 20 October, Zapopan, Jalisco, Mexico.

Mendoza, Raymundo. 2005. Interviewed by Renée de la Torre and Cristina Gutiérrez Zúñiga, Casa Mexhico, Lagos de Moreno, Jalisco, 27 May 2005.

Ramiro O. 2008. Interviewed by Juárez Huet, 23 March, Chetumal, Quintana Roo, Mexico.

Rubí Alba. 2006. Interviewed by Juárez Huet, 16 June, Cancún, Quintana Roo, Mexico.

Index